THE DIARIES OF
WILLIAM CHARLES MACREADY

WILLIAM CHARLES MACREADY

(1850)

From the bust by William Behnes, in the collection of Major-General C. F. N. Macready, C.B.

THE DIARIES

OF

WILLIAM CHARLES MACREADY

1833—1851

EDITED BY

WILLIAM TOYNBEE

WITH FORTY-NINE PORTRAITS

IN TWO VOLUMES

VOL. II.

BENJAMIN BLOM  New York / London

First Published 1912
Reissued 1969 by
Benjamin Blom, Inc., Bronx, New York 10452
and 56 Doughty Street, London, W.C. 1

Library of Congress Catalog Card Number 78-84519

Printed in U.S.A. by
NOBLE OFFSET PRINTERS, INC.
NEW YORK 3, N. Y.

LIST OF PORTRAITS

LIST OF PORTRAITS

THE DIARIES OF
WILLIAM CHARLES MACREADY

1839 (*continued*)

May 6th.—Looked at the newspaper. Went to Covent Garden theatre, looking over *Coriolanus* by the way. Rehearsed *Coriolanus*, which gave me much uneasiness, for it ought to have been prepared on Saturday. I was much fatigued by the rehearsal. Was in a state of extreme nervousness—dispirited and unwell. Note from Miss Burdett, enclosing £5 for tickets. Rose in a very nervous state. Acted Coriolanus. Was quite struck, as by a shock, on seeing the pit *not full* at my entrance. I instantly, whilst I bowed to the audience, rallied and resolved to do my best. It is a useful lesson to teach me how I ought to estimate my own exertion. The public is, *of course*, the most selfish of human bodies, and a sensible man ought to act upon it accordingly. Acted the part moderately, not very satisfactorily; was called for at the end, and on my appearance a great number of bouquets and wreaths were thrown upon the stage. I was not the less low-spirited, and still " gather from the *few* my coronal "—that *was a prophecy*.

May 7th.—Arose in somewhat better spirits than I lay down; consoled by the reflection that the disappointment in the amount of the house last night was a *salutary check* to the growth of my self-estimation. We are naturally led to expect that the exertions and sacrifices which are the utmost we can make, and therefore are great to us, should be esteemed so by the public, and that our own ideas of our own importance should be echoed or reflected by the enthusiasm of the public. Whoever thinks thus is *sure* of disappointment. Went to Covent Garden theatre; found the receipt *awful !* Spoke to Serle and Willmott. Saw Talfourd, who was very tipsy and told me of Lord John Russell's speech in the House, announcing the resignation of

Ministers and his proposal to the House to adjourn to Monday.[1]
Talfourd was very tipsy, and talked very loud as we passed through the
hall of Peel, Inglis, Warburton, etc., not caring who was in, so long
as he passed his Copyright and Infants' Bills!! Patriotism!

May 8th.—Heard that Sir R. Peel had received the Queen's orders
to form a Ministry; was deeply distressed to hear it, feeling that the
hopes of those who looked forward to a Government as an instrument
to effect the moral and intellectual improvement, and the amelioration
of the condition, of the people are now crushed. I suffered much from
low spirits. Acted Cardinal Richelieu pretty well; was called for by
the audience and well received.

May 9th.—Read the paper, in which was O'Connell's letter—a
very good one—to the people of Ireland, urging them to rise against
Tory oppression; a very good leading article upon the suicidal conduct
of the Whigs, more particularly of Lord John Russell; a letter from
Sir W. Molesworth to his constituents, and offering, if his conduct be
disapproved, to resign his seat. In the paper to-day—the *Times*—I
read an advertisement of the closing of Drury Lane, " the Promenade
Concerts having terminated," etc. Here, then, it is to be hoped, is
the end of this wretched villain! Here is an end of the " honourable
and eminent " subject of Mr. Thesiger's and Lord Hertford's praise!

May 12th.—Forster called, evidently to make himself my companion
to our dinner-party; this was not quite right, but we went together,
and found at Sir Edward Bulwer's—Lords Lansdowne, Normanby,
Durham, Comte D'Orsay, Colonel Maberley,[2] Macaulay, Lady Cork,
Mrs. Maberley, and a young man unknown. It was a cheerful day.
I was amused and interested to see the anxiety—betraying itself—of
Bulwer as to the success of his dinner. He *could not be at his ease.*
What a picture he would have made of himself if he could have trans-
ferred it to a novel. In the evening Sir de Lacy Evans,[3] D'Eyncourt,

---

[1] The Government had brought in a Bill to suspend the constitution of Jamaica, and in
the course of the debate upon it were only able to carry the motion that the Speaker should
leave the Chair by a majority of five. This they treated as a vote of non-confidence, and
tendered their resignations. The Queen then sent for the Duke of Wellington, who recommended that Sir Robert Peel should be commissioned to form a Government. Peel
consented, but stipulated that Whig ladies holding Bedchamber and other prominent
appointments in the Household should relinquish them. To this the Queen objected, and
Peel, in consequence, declined to proceed with the formation of the Ministry. The
Melbourne Government was accordingly reinstated. The incident became known as the
" Bedchamber Plot."

[2] Lieutenant-Colonel William Leader Maberley (1798–1885), then joint-secretary of the
Post Office; he was a vigorous opponent of Sir Rowland Hill's reforms.

[3] Sir George de Lacy Evans (1787–1870); General, G.C.B.; served in the Peninsula,
present at Waterloo, and engaged in the Crimean War.

2

SIR EDWARD BULWER LYTTON

From an engraving

Fonblanque, Lord Nugent, Sir C. and Lady Morgan, Jerome Bonaparte and some few more came. Lord Lansdowne is pleasant, but, I thought, aristocratic. I did not *quite* feel satisfied with him. Lord Durham is quiet and gentlemanly; but I saw both him and Bulwer do things—in fact, betray a *gaucherie* of manner (!) that I dare not for my life have done. What a farce is rank! The *man's* the gowd for a' that!

May 14th.—Read the paper, in which were the explanations of Sir R. Peel and Lord John Russell. I thought that Peel looked little, very unlike a great man, relying on his purity of purpose and on his claims to confidence; but his party cheered him, and he is, to his party, a great man! Went to Covent Garden theatre; gave long audience to Miss H. Faucit, who wished to consult me on a proposal made to her to engage with Madame Vestris, the expected lessee of Covent Garden theatre.

May 15th.—Read the paper, in which was Lord Melbourne's explanation. In the evening went to Lord Nugent's, where I met Mrs. Norton, Sir F. Chantrey, Lover, Sir R. Westmacott, Westmacott, jun. Heard Mrs. Norton sing a song of her own, most touching, most charming. Found Forster at home; Dickens had been there, much pleased with Virginius.

May 20th.—Rehearsed *Ion*, in which I did not find myself at all prepared—this could not be if I had only my own reputation to be careful of. All things tend to show me that all is for the best, and that my happiness and well-being is more likely to be ensured by a good income as an actor than as a manager. Spoke to Miss Faucit about her engagement. Mr. Farren *now* wishes her to go to Madame Vestris. She does not. Talfourd, Forster and Brydone came into my room.

May 24th.—Went to my appointment with Lord Uxbridge,[1] of whom I do not entertain a very high opinion. His manners are merely average; his understanding seems far below average; I fancy him a very proud man, which the deficiency of intellect, if I am right in that judgment, accounts for. I asked him if he would be disposed to exercise the power he possesses as Lord Chamberlain to give a licence to the *artists* (a term he did not seem to understand) who might be deprived of the means of employment by the abuse of the patents by the present patentees of the two large theatres. He promised to take the matter into consideration and give me an answer. I told him I should apply to Parliament if he declined, but that I applied, in courtesy, to him

---

[1] Afterwards second Marquis of Anglesey.

first. I then asked him to request the Queen to visit us in state before I closed the theatre, which he promised he would do. Miss Faucit came in. I wished to speak with her on her Covent Garden engagement, and *I am very sorry I did.*

May 25th.—Letter from White and Whitmore with the version of the proprietors' agreement—a *string of falsehoods.* It made me very angry, and I went *very imprudently* to speak to Bartley about his friend Robertson. I could see that the wretched fellow *enjoyed* my anger. I soon cooled, but was ill through it. Acted ill—called for. Forster came—*ill—ill.*

May 26th.—What a dreadful calamity to me—what a source of continued suffering is this excitability of temper to me. Impatience of practices upon me, whether fraudulent or violent, gives my enemies a power over me that my own right intentions and virtuous purposes are weak before. I lose all power of self-examination in the fever of the mind, and my previous discipline—through religious and philosophical meditation—has lost all its effect upon me. I have scarcely slept the whole night, the pressure on my head made me at one time alarmed for my clearness of reason. I got up and took medicine, and tried to think (though vainly for a long time) on other subjects than this detested theatre. God forgive, protect, and assist me. Unwell, but better than in the night. Looked at the newspaper. Browning called, told me *Sordello* was finished.

May 27th.—Phelps came in and asked for leave to quit the theatre; he had become security for a relation who had embezzled money, and was in dread of the consequences. I asked him of the particulars, and, on his acquainting me with them, recommended him not to think of going, but that I would endeavour to advance him the money, and he should repay me upon his salary. Miss Faucit came in to speak to me about stuffed stockings. Serle and Willmott spoke about the closing three nights next week. Brydone came in on business—spoke with Stanfield. Read *Foscari*, which I acted very indifferently; was called for and well received. Bulwer and Forster came into my room. Bulwer told me that Lord John Russell had postponed his Education Bill!

May 31st.—It was for Mr. Sheridan Knowles that Forster asked me for a private box! This man, on whom I have *heaped* benefits, unrequited, many unacknowledged, all forgotten, now, because he is envious of Bulwer's success and angry at his own idleness, descends to the baseness of requiring a favour from me through another to save himself the duty of acknowledging it. Poor creature!

4

June 1st.—Saw in the *Gazette* the name of that bad man, Bunn, as having sold the commission of Gentleman Pensioner,[1] purchased out of the pillage of the actors' salaries. I could not see without some satisfaction that retribution has been at last awarded to him. I questioned myself upon the subject of revenge. I have many misgivings on it. If interrogated on my feelings when thinking on this vile creature, I must admit that I have very much wished his downfall. Did this arise solely from the injury to my art and my own advancement that his continuance in power occasioned? Was it on grounds of sympathy with other sufferers and on abstract points, or was it from personal detestation that I desired his degradation? When put out of the theatres, shall I feel indifference towards him? Shall I forget to think with bitterness on the injury he did me? I think—I hope I shall. But, alas! I *ought* to have felt thus long since. Passion, the want of due control on the violent impulses of an ill-educated disposition has been the cause of much, much misery to me. God Almighty grant that my blessed children may avoid my errors, and escape my bitter hours of internal struggling, and severe compunction, and depressing shame! Forster called. George Robins came and offered me Drury Lane theatre on the lowest possible rent—on one that I must gain. I said I could not risk—could not undertake the labour except for certain payment. Went to Elstree with Letitia. Delighted and elevated to a lighter-hearted feeling than I have known for many, many days, in looking again at the well-remembered spot, endeared to me by happy hours and years of enjoyment, and also by moments of sadness and reflection.

London, June 3rd.—Business with Stanfield, who came to consult me on the subject of the painting of the *Conspiracy*, in which he had sketched a thought that I had before entertained, but I do not, on reflection, feel quite sure about. The last night, the fifty-fifth, of the *Tempest* was crowded. I felt quite melancholy as we approached the end of the play; it had become endeared to me from success and the benefit it had conferred upon my undertaking. I acted Prospero as well as I could, and was called for and well received. I look back upon its production with satisfaction, for it has given to the public a play of Shakspeare which had never been seen before, and it has proved the charm of simplicity and poetry.

June 5th.—Went to Covent Garden theatre, where I had a long

---

[1] The possibility of such a transaction during the reign of Queen Victoria is astonishing but not more so than that such a person as Mr. Bunn should have been eligible to the Honourable Corps of Gentlemen-at-Arms.

5

rehearsal of four acts of *King Henry V*. Tried on the armour of Henry and dined in it. Sent for Stanfield and laid before him my objection to the trick-ship in the diorama, as giving a character of pageant and pantomime to the whole production; he agreed with me, and arranged differently on my suggestion. Lay down and slept for about an hour, which was a great relief to me. Note from Bulwer addressing me " My dear Sir," and asking for a box and admission for persons behind the scenes. I had a very *satisfactory* conversation with Miss H. Faucit, to whom I communicated Mr. Webster's message, and who was very open with me as to her objects; she was to write to him. Talked afterwards with Serle on the advantage that might accrue to his play if she were to play the serious part and Miss Taylor the comic, provided he could induce Miss Taylor to relinquish the serious one, all rights to be, of course, respected.

June 7th.—Rehearsed the play of *King Henry V*, trying to make the most of the opportunity in all ways; but I was sadly tired—indeed exhausted. Amused with Mr. Healey's excessive apprehension about receiving an accidental blow or two in Pistol, and his anger at Mr. Baker's laughter when he *did* receive one—he is a great ass!

June 8th.—Tried on my armour, which I wore through the afternoon, and was obliged at last to put off for its weight. Lay down to rest. Brydone came in. Forster, Mr. Kenyon, Dickens and his friend Maclise, came to the night rehearsal of *King Henry V*, which went off tolerably smoothly. Forster walked home with me.

June 9th.—Put on my armour for *King Henry V*, and moved and sat in it until half-past three o'clock. Sent a note to Forster, from whom I received an answer, and who shortly afterwards called. Endeavoured to master some difficulties in the acting of *King Henry V*, rehearsing in my armour.

June 10th.—Went to Covent Garden theatre, where I saw Stanfield, Bradwell, Head, etc. Sent out the notes due. Had a very fatiguing rehearsal of the play, with which I was much annoyed. Lay down on the bed for about three-quarters of an hour, and rose unrefreshed and very nervous. Strove to reason myself into a state of self-possession and collectedness, but felt that I had bestowed so much time and thought on others' characters and on the *ensemble* of the play that I was not in perfect command of what I had to do for my individual part. Began the play of *King Henry V* [1] in a very nervous state, but en-

---

[1] The Covent Garden playbill of June 10, 1839, contains the following notice: " In announcing this last Shakspearian revival it may be advisable, if not necessary, to depart so

6

deavouring to keep my mind clear. Acted sensibly at first, and very spiritedly at last; was very greatly received, and when called on at last, the whole house stood up and cheered me in a most fervent manner. I gave out the repetition of the play for four nights a week till the close of the season. Lord Nugent, Jerdan, Forster, Browning, Serle, etc., came into my room. Catherine and Letitia were there, and I accompanied them back to Elstree in a state of the greatest excitement. It is the last of my attempts to present to the audience Shakspeare's own meaning.

Elstree, June 11th.—I slept very little, woke early, unrefreshed and unequal to a day of labour. Rose very late, saw my darling children and dined with them; walked in the garden and at three o'clock returned in the carriage to town, Catherine and Letitia accompanying me. Stopped Billings's coach, and got from it a parcel containing the newspapers which Forster had sent. They were all favourable. Was quite beaten to the ground by fatigue, I may say exhaustion of mind and body. Attended to business afterwards. Forster called, and I came to my lodgings, scarcely able to crawl. I have never felt a heavier weight than this play has been. Thank God that it is over, and so well over.

London, June 12th.—Serle read me a letter from myself to the Lord Chamberlain, asking for a personal licence, which I approved. I lay down and tried to compose myself to read or think of *King Henry V;* it was utterly impossible. I acted the part. My God, what a state to be in to act! I got through it, was called for and well received. After the play had a long conference with Serle, Brydone, Forster and Willmott, on what was to be done. Brydone had appointed White and

---

far from the usual practice of this management as to offer a few words in explanation or apology for what may seem an innovation.

"The play of *King Henry V* is a *dramatic history*, and the poet, to preserve the continuity of the action, and connect what would otherwise be detached scenes, has adopted from the Greek Drama the expedient of a Chorus to narrate and describe intervening incidents and events.

"To impress more strongly on the auditor, and render more palpable those portions or the story which have not the advantage of action, and still are requisite to the drama's completeness, the narrative and descriptive poetry spoken by the Chorus is accompanied with pictorial illustrations from the pencil of Mr. Stanfield."

The cast of the play included Mr. Vandenhoff as the Chorus, Mr. Elton as the Duke ot Exeter, Mr. Bartley as Erpingham, Mr. Anderson as Captain Gower, Mr. Meadows as Fluellen, Mr. Warde as Williams, Mr. Bedford and Mr. Harley as Bardolph and Pistol, Miss P. Horton as their Boy, Mrs. C. Jones as Mrs. Quickly, Mr. G. Bennett as the King of France, Mr. Vining as the Dauphin, Mr. Howe as the Duke of Orleans, Mr. Phelps as Charles d'Albert, and Miss Vandenhoff as Katherine—(*note by Sir F. Pollock*).

7

Whitmore to come at twelve to-morrow. I left at twelve. Wallace accompanied me to ask me to lend him £12—this is not right; he has had enough from me. He told me he never went to bed till two or three, so kept me up *lathering* me with this business till two!

June 13th.—Looked at newspaper; saw a letter calling on certain *distingués* to form themselves into a committee to make a public testimonial to me—which was suggested last year and will be carried into effect.

June 16th.—Came to town with Catherine and Letitia, reading Bulwer's play of *Norman* by the way. *I do not like it.* Dressed in great haste, and went with Catherine to Horace Twiss's to dinner. Met there Sir George Grey, T. Hope, Pemberton, Herries, B. Disraeli, Miss Herries, Mrs. Blackburn, Mrs. Wyndham Lewis,[1] Bonham-Carter, etc. Rather an agreeable day, though we arrived after all had sat down. Disraeli made acquaintance with me, and told me a good story of Hume. Pemberton renewed our acquaintance formed at Rome in 1822. I found that Daniel Webster[2] had called upon my return home.

June 17th.—Daniel Webster called and sat a short time. He seemed greatly pleased with England. Settled on closing the theatre, July 16th, with Willmott. I am anxious to feel free of it.

June 18th.—Went out to breakfast with Harness. Met there, besides his sister, Mrs. Opie, Miss Rogers, Dyce,[3] whom I like very much, and Sir W. and Lady Chatterton.[4] Mr. Kenyon came later. I passed an agreeable morning. I was very glad to hear that Dyce had seen all the Shakspearian revivals, and been greatly pleased with them. I was also glad to find (in confirmation of his judgment) that he did not at all coincide with Harness in his opinion of Mrs. Butler as an actress; Harness, who some time ago could see nothing to like in me, was obliged to be restrained by Dyce last night in the vehement expression of his enthusiasm! How we are the creatures of prejudice! How little truth is in us! Sent for the *Sunday Times*, with the notice of *King Henry* in it. I was disgusted—these *ignorant* coxcombs are our *critics!* What wonder if our art is low, when such are the distributors of its rewards!

June 19th.—Read the papers, the debate on the Ballot, which, I rejoice to see, gains advocates. Read *Henry V* and rested, having

---

[1] Afterwards Mrs. Disraeli.   [2] The American orator and statesman.
[3] William Dyce, R.A. (1806–1864); chiefly known as a painter of frescoes.
[4] Henrietta Georgiana Marcia Lascelles Chatterton (1806–1876); an authoress of some note in her day.

again tried on my armour. Acted King Henry V (I think) better than on any previous occasion, but was not called for, which shows the actual value of this idle compliment.

June 20th.—Began the sketch of my last speech. Read *Norman* again; was much struck with the *effect* of the two last acts, though I do not altogether like the play, it is far too melodramatic. Wrote to Bulwer upon it. Mr. Phelps called, and spoke to me about his engagement at Haymarket; seemed to entertain very sensible views. Read the newspapers—the debate on education, in which Charles Buller made a very good speech. Saw in the Court news that the Websters[1] were at the Queen's ball, which I was glad to know. Bulwer, C. Buller, and Talfourd were also there. It is not a pleasing reflection, without caring for the thing itself, that my pariah profession should entitle me to the lavish expression of public praise, and exclude me from distinctions which all my compeers enjoy. *Mais*, Monsieur, "il faut cultiver notre jardin." Brydone came in and spoke about accounts. It appears that we have acted the *Tempest* fifty-five nights to an average exceeding £230. This is not a common event. Forster came, and hearing that I had hashed venison, consented to have a dish sent for.

June 21st.—Tried to make way with my speech, but found it very difficult. I wish to say *much*, and if I do not say it very briefly, I had better say nothing. Came to town in a chaise that seemed to have hatched all the poultry in the village for half a century back. I was ashamed to be seen in such a thing, and slept my journey to town away in it. The driver took me all down Regent Street to Carlton Place, Pall Mall, then round the National Gallery, up St. Martin's Lane, through Long Acre, down Bow Street to the stage-door, Covent Garden theatre. My patience was quite exhausted. Miss H. Faucit had sent me a note asking me for a box for Monday. She came to me for it, and I took the opportunity of delivering Webster's message to her, and of feeling how far she was disposed to receive the proposition. She was open to reason, but her advisers at home are her objection to a short engagement. I do not think anything will result from it.

June 22nd.—I was speaking with Willmott, who "did not think Mr. Bunn an honest man"—mighty God!—whilst he described him as afraid to take the benefit of the Insolvent Act, as being liable to be remanded for three years, and unable to become a bankrupt, when Brydone and Lardner entered, Brydone's face full of gloom; he began to say he had sad news. I, of course, only thought of Covent Garden

---

[1] Daniel Webster and his wife.

with his news.   But Lardner abruptly interrupted him and said, " It's best to speak out—poor Wallace is dead! "   I really did not clearly understand at the first moment what the words meant.   Brydone repeated the news, and I became too well assured that another friend— a faithful and affectionate one, as far as his nature could form attach- ment—had gone from me; it gave me a shock that I could not get over.   I shall never see him, never hear again what I would now give so much to endure—his prolixities, his important nothings, but above all his shrewd and sensible observations where action and conduct were needed.   My poor, poor friend; God receive and bless him!   Amen! He was utterly unaware of his approaching death, and thought to nearly the last moment that he should be well.   He died quite tranquilly. Farewell! farewell!   Desired Lardner to consider that I would willingly do whatever might be required in his funeral, etc.

Elstree, June 24th.—Called on Mr. D. Webster, whom I found at home, some gentleman calling on him.   I did not think he seemed quite easy at my call.   Is it that he has been much caressed, and not met me in the *high regions*, where he has been spending his days in England, or to what am I to attribute what, without anything like jealousy or even uncomfortableness of feeling, I cannot help perceiving to be a changed and, I should say, an awkward demeanour?   It does not distress me at all.   I have a consciousness, at least, of equal worth with all these men in the intentions of my heart towards my fellow-men, and much more honesty than nine-tenths of them.   I talked with him and his other visitor for a little while, and then left him on the under- standing that he would not make his intended visit to Greenwich but with me.   I am now so indifferent about it that I hope he will not remind me of it.   Very civil note from Mr. Holt of the *Age*, which I answered.

June 25th.—Catherine and Letitia wished to dissuade me from my intention of going to the funeral of my poor friend, Wallace.   I felt that any neglect, or slight, or selfish excuse I could, were he alive, atone for or justify; this is the last tribute of respect and attachment I can show to him, and I should think with painful regret, indeed, with compunction on my dereliction of this last duty if I am able to discharge it.   I was much better; dressed and set off in the carriage, reading Serle's play upon the road.   I fear it is heavy and *slow*—a grievous fault; but this might be concealed if the heroine, upon whom the play rests, were a first-rate actress.   On reaching poor Wallace's, I looked at the coffin, containing all that remained of my poor friend.   His age was stated fifty-three; I think he was older. How difficult to believe that what only three days since had life, affections, strong intellectual faculties—what five days ago I parted with in the cordial hope of meeting again, lies, a mass of corruption, encased in that mournful narrow piece of *furniture !* It is not easy to persuade oneself of all the reality before us. Lardner, Brydone, Dr. Burke arrived. We talked much of poor Wallace. Dr. Burke observed that no one would have done for Wallace what Lardner did, and that he always spoke of Lardner in most grateful terms. How strange this is! He did not. He thought Lardner acted too much *en marchand* with him; and certainly, though Lardner's connection was of service to Wallace, he gave it on terms, not only safe, but really advantageous to himself. Lardner, however, took the compliment, and in my hearing, though he knew I had assisted the poor fellow to an amount that *shocked* him when mentioned to him! His poor little dog remained in his corner by his dead master's empty chair, never leaving it but at the sound of the gate-bell, when he would rush to see if it was Wallace, and then return to his fireside corner! Sheil arrived, and we set out to the church. The poor servant girl, who had lived with Wallace some years, had been in a state of dreadful anguish ever since his death. It was a relief to lose the sound of her moans and sobs. Sheil observed that it was " very extraordinary to see so much feeling in those kind of people." I did " not see that." He said, " There's nothing of the sort among people in high society." I answered, " Then, thank God, it exists somewhere." I followed his body and saw it laid in its last resting-place. The earth was thrown upon him, and my heart uttered a prayer for him. God bless him, and farewell!

June 30th.—Came to the conclusion that if it were ever proposed to me to undertake the management of a theatre again, I should give no answer *until I had read carefully over the diaries of the two years now past.*

London, July 2nd.—Miss H. Faucit asked to speak with me—I expected she would; it was to tell me, what I knew, that she was engaged at the Haymarket. Bulwer called, and told me that Lord Lansdowne was very friendly to my cause, and thought my request would be granted for a licence. He advised me to apply directly to Lord Melbourne, and that he would also move Lord Holland and Lord John Russell.

July 3rd.—Finished Serle's play, of which I hold a very good opinion, regretting that the entire strength and weight of the play is thrown upon the woman's character, which has been assigned to Miss Taylor. Renewed my attempts at my closing speech, and with much better promise of successful completion. I think I see my way into all that I need say. Sent, in answer to his request, six places to *Mr. Delane* [1] of the *Times*! Forster mentioned to me that Talfourd had Mr. C. Kean at his dinner-party on Sunday, and actually finessed to get him as his companion in his carriage to Lord Morpeth's fête! He said that he was " glad " poor Wallace " was dead." The pen stops in noticing the behaviour of this weak and foolish man. I have been reluctant long to see what I cannot close my eyes to. Lord Nugent came into my room and told me that the Duke of Sussex had very readily agreed to take the chair at the dinner to be given to me, which he proposed for the 20th, to which I assented.

Elstree, July 7th.—Walked in the garden, enjoying this delicious air and the sight and smell of the beautiful flowers, and listening to the happy songs of the birds. Went to afternoon church with Nina and Catherine. What a waste of time to hear such unintelligible stuff forced upon the patience, and perplexing the bewildered intellects of the poor labouring people! What a benevolent and rational man might do with the high resolve of devoting himself to the improvement of the condition, moral and intellectual, of his fellow-men! Read a little in the Greek Testament.

London, July 8th.—Read the newspapers. Was in very low spirits at the prospect in the box-office, and the complete silence in the papers upon the dinner. This is my own fault. I suffer myself to be so elated by the mere prospect of any good that I exhaust my enjoyment of it before it arrives. This is my unhappy want of mental discipline; to live for the present, and to do one's duty in that little point of time, enjoying all it brings, is the best wisdom. Sent to Head about my clothes, which he brought; but he informed me that he had received an order from Mr. Robertson, that by order of the proprietors he was not to allow me to take away any of the clothes which I had had made for myself! I really did not well know what to say to him; he was very civil; I told him he was quite right, but to bring the clothes—he was my servant, and if he did not obey my orders I should discharge him. He brought them immediately, and I locked them in my imperials. Serle came in, and we held a long consultation upon what was to be done with these *blackguards*. I observed that the high

---

[1] Probably J. T. Delane's father ; the future editor was then not more than twenty-two, and did not enter upon his office till two years later.

position—regarded at the present moment so widely and so respectfully —in which I stood, set a direct bar against the *thought* of any squabble, row, or vulgar imbroglio—a loud dispute, personal resistance, or the interference of a police officer would ruin all that had been done and was doing. People would *shrink away* from what at present engaged so much of their interest. I must *bear* still every accumulation of indignity and insult that, in their way, they dare offer me. *I saw it clearly,* and resolved not to *attempt to remove anything,* but to lock my boxes, and prosecute them if they detained my property. I *suffered very much* from the state of mind into which this threw me, but reasoned myself into something like calmness. I felt as if a gnat or bug had stung me, and as if I had thrown away my temper on it. Wrote to Mrs. Buller a doubtful answer, but I could not—I had not the heart to think of going out. Acted tolerably well, my voice occasionally failing me and keeping me in fear. Was called for and well received. Brydone brought me an account (counted) of the Haymarket house—£104—*including the Free List.* These are their great houses! Note from Mr. Skerrett. The Queen Dowager was in the Warwick box to-night. Browning came and talked with me.

July 9th.—Tried to confirm my resolution to preserve a dignified bearing through the attempts to insult and cheat me which these knaves and their agent are making; it is only the bite or sting of some disgusting insect or reptile—it is nothing more! Pray God, I may continue to reason thus! Copied out the materials for my dinner speech—a ceremony I could well dispense with. Walked to Covent Garden theatre, Willmott came in, and showed me the Haymarket Bill, in which Mr. Webster has announced Mr. C. Kean for Shylock, as well as Sir E. Mortimer; the man is a fool, there is no hope from him. *The art is all at sea again.*

July 11th.—Was in a tumult of excitement which, after some time, I perceived and endeavoured to subdue. The freedom from further responsibility and care, the honourable mode of terminating my engagement with the performers, the flattering testimonials in the public reception of me, and in the compliment offered, are altogether enough to interfere with the sober and steady course of any man. Prosperity is most intoxicating, but adversity is the real benefactor of mankind.

July 13th.—Darling little Joan's birthday. God Almighty bless and watch over and make her grow in goodness and in happiness. Went to town in the carriage with Letitia. The weather was most delightful, and I enjoyed it very, very much. Thinking of the estimation in which I seemed to be held, which, when I reflect, extends throughout so very small a circle! Each man's "world" is, in truth, a very, very little globe, while to himself it is a universe; we indulge great hopes, form great plans, bustle about, and die! What was of value amidst all the tumult? The little virtue and the little love that made its intervals.

July 15th.—Addressed the performers assembled in the green-room. Told them that to-morrow would have its own business, and I did not wish to extend my stay in this theatre; that I wished to see them merely to say that at our last meeting I had pledged myself to keep the theatre open to the latest possible period, without requiring any condition from them. I had done so under every species of outrage and petty insult that these persons, the proprietors, could put upon me through my own servants; that I had laid a moral obligation on myself, and as what I had said to them on the subject of my undertaking not being a mercenary one, I was here to-day to discharge it. At the same time, in the kindest spirit, as my connection with them must end here, I felt that they had not done me justice in evading the direct statement of the proprietors' conduct, which they *admitted* to be false and treacherous. I hoped if another person, equally disposed to befriend their art and them, should ever step forward again, that they would be truer to themselves in being truer to him. Vining and Bennett said something in exculpation, but it went to nothing. I imputed blame to them only for yielding to the advice of a person who had misled them. They would know who had done so. Colonel Cavendish came from the Queen to say she would come to-night. Acted King Henry V very well; was called for and well received.

July 16th.—Tried to sleep on the sofa for a short half-hour. Rose and prepared to play in a very depressed condition. My reception was so great, from a house crowded in every part, that I was shaken by it. I acted King Henry V better than I had yet done, and the house responded to the spirit in which I played. The curtain fell amidst the loudest applause, and when I had changed my dress I went before the curtain, and, amidst shoutings and wavings of hats and handkerchiefs by the whole audience standing up, the stage was literally covered with wreaths, bouquets, and branches of laurel. When at last the dense mass resumed their seats, and the tumult subsided to the stillest silence, I began my address. The cheering was renewed as I bowed and left the stage, and as I passed through the lane which the actors and people, crowding behind, made for me, they cheered me also. Forster

14

came into my room, and was much affected; Fox was quite shaken; Dickens, Maclise, Stanfield, T. Cooke, Blanchard, Lord Nugent (who had not been in the theatre), Bulwer, Hockley of Guildford, Browning, Serle, Brydone, Willmott, came into my room ; most of them asked for memorials from the baskets and heaps of flowers, chaplets, and laurels that were strewn upon the floor. Went home with Catherine and Letitia, carrying the wreaths, etc.

Elstree, July 17th.—Late up, and when up only feeling the freedom from heavy duties, and enjoying the air and trees and flowers. Received the newspapers. The *Morning Herald* I presume to have been done by Mr. Honan ; whoever is the writer, he is a vile and wretchedly low-minded creature. The *Times* was consistent in its open knavery— not one word in report or comment upon the speech or the evening. It acted well upon my inflated state of mind, and brought it down again to its poor level. " Quite, quite down." My spirits sunk. I look at myself and think that many think me in a *state* of *glory !* Ah me !

London, July 20th.—Thought, and recited during the greater part of the morning my speech for the dinner, which makes me very nervous. Went to town in the carriage with Catherine and Letitia—recurring constantly to the important subject of " the speech," which gave me continued uneasiness. This honour is a business of much, very much solicitude and, like most honours, carries with it its full share of trouble. Catherine and Letitia went to dine with Mrs. Rolls; I remained, read over my speech, with an occasional sensation of apprehension, approaching to despair, of my ability to master it; I suffered very much. The carriage at last arrived, and I drove, with the resolution of doing my best, to the Freemason's Tavern. I caught a glimpse of a horrible picture of myself in King Henry V at the corner of the street, and thought it looked like a good omen : on passing from my carriage through the crowd, which was considerable on and about the steps, they cheered me lustily, and I bowed as I passed through them. In the reception-room, I found Mr. Pope, Sir M. A. Shee,[1] Mr. Milnes,[2] who was introduced to me, but I did not catch his name.

---

[1] Sir Martin Archer Shee (1769–1850); President of the Royal Academy from 1830 to 1850.

[2] Richard Monckton Milnes (1809–1885); the well-known litterateur and conversationalist, at that time Conservative M.P. for Pontefract ; he afterwards joined the Whigs, and received a peerage from Lord Palmerston, when he became Lord Houghton. His only son is the Marquis of Crewe, K.G., Secretary of State for India. It was said that Lord Houghton was indebted for his peerage in large measure to the circumstance that his father (Robert Pemberton Milnes) and Lord Palmerston had been parliamentary associates early in the century, when both were regarded as young Tories of high promise. On the strength

Others came in; to some I was introduced, others I knew. Lover, Jerdan, Captain Tyndale, two foreign noblemen, Lord Nugent, Young, Dickens, Robertson (Westminster), Scholefield (M.P. Birmingham), General Alexander, O'Hanlon, Byng, Bulwer, Lord Conyngham. The Duke of Sussex at last arrived; I was introduced to him; he told me that he had " seen a cottage that I had lived at, near Denbigh; how beautiful the country was! " etc. We went into the room, I hanging back, Lord Conyngham placing me forward, and chatting with me as we entered : the room was very full (who could have expected such an occurrence?). The Duke was well applauded as he passed; and, as I followed the plaudits, were very loud. I was at a loss what to do. What were my feelings it is difficult to recollect, as the various persons in different parts of the room stood up to look at me. I felt that I was the object of the regard of that large assembly, and that all that was done was in my honour. I looked up at the gallery on the left, where Catherine was, and the tears rushed to my eyes as mine met hers; that was perhaps the sweetest moment of the night to me. I sat on the right of the Duke of Sussex, Lord Nugent on my right, Sheil, Dickens, Monckton Milnes, Fonblanque, etc., on the left; Lord Conyngham, Sir M. A. Shee, Tennyson D'Eyncourt, Sir E. L. Bulwer, Forster, Bernal, the Hon. W. Cowper, Savory, Colonel Fox, Babbage, C. Buller, Robertson, and many others in front of us. I shook hands with Jonathan Birch as I passed up the room—the eternal and dis-agreeable *one finger* of that excellent and warm-hearted man. The Duke talked much to me, more than I wished; but a full glass of sherry seemed to steady my nerves a little, though I looked very grave and pale, as I was afterwards told, and Bulwer said I looked like a " baffled tyrant." C. Buller was making me something worse, by laughing and observing across the table, that " Macready was thinking of his speech." The music was beautifully performed, and when, after the Duke's panegyrical proposal of my health, in which he was very cordially greeted, I arose, the whole room stood up, shouting and waving their handkerchiefs, as did the ladies in the gallery. I never witnessed such a scene, such wild enthusiasm, on any former occasion. It was not like an English asembly. When they had resumed their seats and

---

of a single speech of great ability, Pemberton Milnes at the age of twenty-five was offered by Perceval, then Prime Minister, the Chancellorship of the Exchequer, which, on his refus-ing it, was offered to Palmerston, also only twenty-five, who, with equal prudence, followed Milnes's example. Milnes, then considered the abler of the two, sank into obscurity, while Palmerston crowned a long series of political successes by becoming the most popular Prime Minister of the nineteenth century.

silence was obtained, I spoke nearly *verbatim* as follows : " May it please Your Royal Highness, my Lords, and Gentlemen,—I really know not how to reply to your kindness, to the too indulgent, too flattering terms, in which His Royal Highness has proposed my health, and the very complimentary manner in which you have received it. I beg to thank you for the great honour you have done me. I must at the same time regret my inability to do justice to your kindness, or my own estimation of it. In any labour I may have chosen to encounter, in any sacrifice of personal ease or pleasure my late undertaking may have cost me, I could never calculate on, I could never contemplate, such a recompense, and am utterly at a loss to satisfy myself with any terms of acknowledgment. I must therefore request His Royal Highness, and you, Gentlemen, to supply, in the indulgent spirit that has made me your guest to-day any deficiency in my expressions, and in the same spirit to believe me deeply sensible of the flattering distinction conferred on me by your invitation and by the obliging condescension of our illustrious Chairman. Indeed I am fully conscious how much my humble services are overrated, and, in reference to the allusion so kindly made by His Royal Highness of any further requital, must declare that, in the honours already conferred on me, I am greatly overpaid. My office has been a simple one ; I can claim credit for little more than devotion, zeal, and intention ; for little beyond an earnest faith in the power and ultimate triumph of truth, and in its elevating influence, however humble the sphere of its exercise. In that faith I have only endeavoured to ' piece out some of the imperfections,' as they appeared to me, of our theatrical system. It had struck me, among the many causes adduced for the drama's decline, that, whilst every other branch of art or pursuit of science was in a course of rapid advance, the drama—except in regard to a valuable change in its costume by that great artist whose name I can never mention without admiration and respect, John Kemble—the drama was stationary, its stage arrangements remained traditional, defended from innovation in each succeeding age by the name and authority of the leading actor who had gone before. This is so, whether we recall the witches of *Macbeth*, the Roman Senate and people—the *Senatus populusque Romanus*—the Venetian Councils, Banquo's Ghost, or the moving wood of Birnam, which, if presented, should at least explain themselves. All were little more than barbarous burlesques of the great poet's conceptions. It had long been my ambition, and has been my endeavour to ' reform this indifferently,' if not ' altogether,' and to present the works of our

dramatic poets, and chiefly Shakspeare's, with the truth of illustration
they merit, and that a public, possessing a dramatic literature like ours,
has a right to demand.   Some exceptions have been taken to the
amount, the extent of decoration lavished on our plays; but I would
beg, with deference, to inquire the particular instance (for I do not
know it) where the embellishment has exceeded propriety and the
demand of the situation.   In all that has been attempted, the object
has been simply truth.   What my own imagination has presented to
me, in turning over the pages of our great poet, I have endeavoured to
make palpable to the senses of my audience, and I would beg distinctly
to repudiate the idea that has been entertained by some persons, that it
is to the care bestowed on our wardrobe and scene-room that we are
alone indebted for our successes; the plays of Shakspeare have been
produced of late years in the same theatre with far more lavish expendi-
tures, but the results have not been equally fortunate.   Indeed, the
tragedies of *Coriolanus* and *King Lear*, so far from being overloaded
with ornament, have, in their recent revivals, been actually stripped
of the ' barbaric pearl and gold ' with which they were before invested,
and are now represented in the rude simplicity of their respective
periods.   Our aim has been fidelity of illustration.   The ' delicate
Ariel ' is now no longer in representation a thing of earth, but either
' a wandering voice ' or a visible spirit of air, flitting in his own element
amid the strange and sweet noises of the enchanted island.   With the
restoration of the text, our object has been to make palpable the
meaning of Shakspeare, and to this is to be attributed mainly, if not
entirely, the popularity of our theatre.   In following out an observation of Sir Thomas Lawrence, that ' every part of a picture required
equal care and pains,' we have sought, by giving purpose and passion
to the various figures of our groups, to spread over the entire scene
some portion of that energy and interest which, heretofore, the leading
actor exclusively and jealously appropriated.   In this endeavour to
transfer his picture from the poet's mind to the stage, complete in its
parts and harmoniously arranged as to figure, scene, and action, we
have the satisfaction of recording the success of a season unequalled,
I believe, by any not having the attraction of a new performer, for the
last sixteen years.   This at least furnishes a proof not to be mistaken,
that there is no lack either of intelligence or taste in our audiences
to appreciate and support our noble drama, if properly presented.
My hope and my intention was, if my abilities had kept pace with
them, to have left in our theatre the complete series of Shakspeare's

acting plays, his text purified from the gross interpolations that dis-figure it and distort his characters, and the system of re-arrangement so perfected throughout them that our stage would have presented as it ought, one of the best illustrated editions of the poet's works. But ' my poverty, and not my will,' has compelled me to desist from the attempt. Yet, though I may not again be called to ' bear my part, or show the glory of our art,' let me indulge the hope that the path which has been so successfully and auspiciously opened under your encouragement may be steadily and perseveringly pursued by others; that our theatre will remain, as Shakspeare's temple, con-secrated to its loftiest purposes, dedicated to the highest intellectual amusements, and no longer, as a mere place of demoralizing and licentious resort, degrade our character for refinement among the other European nations. I would beg to trespass one short minute further on your attention, and avail myself of this occasion to express thus publicly my thanks to those friends whose ardour and zeal in my cause have loaded me with benefits that I never can repay. Amongst them I must beg to particularize Sir Edward Lytton Bulwer, who wrote his delightful play of *The Lady of Lyons* expressly to serve my interests, and, after public opinion had stamped it as the most attractive pro-duction of many years, obstinately—I must use the word, obstinately—refused to consider it in any other light than as a gift to me. To my esteemed friends Mr. Stanfield, Mr. Dickens, Serjeant Talfourd, and Mr. Serle I am also proud to be indebted, and, uniting my thanks to them with those I owe to you, I beg once more to repeat the assur-ances of my lasting gratitude and my deep sense of your great kindness, which, whilst I can remember, I never can forget." [1]

Elstree, July 21st.—Dearest Katy's birthday. God bless her! . . . Rose very late; could only talk—only think over the exciting circumstances of yesterday and last night. My head ached much; breakfasted, and glanced at the paper. Walked in the garden and entered a few lines, but could not apply to business. Went to after-noon church; overcome by fatigue and drowsiness. In the garden afterwards. Read prayers to the family.

[1] The other chief toasts of the evening were those of Lord Conyngham (then Lord Chamberlain) and of Charles Young; the Memory of Shakspeare, proposed by Milnes; Sir E. L. Bulwer; the Senate and the Bar, proposed by Lord Nugent, coupled with the names of Talfourd and Sheil, and to which Sheil responded. Sir Martin Archer Shee returned thanks for the Royal Academy, as its President; Dickens proposed the health of the late Company of Covent Garden theatre, which was acknowledged by Mr. Serle; and the Hon. W. Cowper, M.P., returned thanks for the stewards—(*note by Sir F. Pollock*).

London, July 22nd.—Went to town in the carriage with Forster, Catherine, and Letitia. On our way we met the postman, who gave many papers to Forster; the greater part were in a kind, or fair, spirit, but in *John Bull* was a rabid attack, full of falsehoods upon me and my management, and my conduct to the actors. Forster was at first reluctant to let me see it, but after a little hesitation he gave it to me. It did not make me angry—the falsehoods were so palpable, the malignity and the purpose so apparent, that I felt myself secure against its evil effect. Talked with Forster on the steps to be taken to procure a contradiction of the misstatements. Having finished all my business, I went with Catherine, Letitia and Forster to dinner at Mrs. Rolls's. Met there Dr. Elliotson, Mr. Herving, Mr. and Mrs. Williams, our bankers, Etty, etc.—an agreeable day. Went on to Fonblanque's, where I saw C. Buller, Lover, Young, Sheil, Bulwer, Lord Lansdowne, who was civil, but who is too aristocratic in his *manners*—too economical of that endearing quality, *bonhomie,* for me to like him much. Fonblanque told me that my speech at the dinner was "beautiful." I was happy to hear *him* say so. We did not remain long, but reached home at a late hour. The ride in the cool night, ruminating on the past, was *delightful.*

Elstree, July 24th.—Fox, Miss Fox and Mrs. Adams arrived with Forster, who showed me Stanfield's letter and the newspaper (*Morning Chronicle*) contradicting the assertion of *John Bull* as to his non-payment; amused himself with letting off some balloons. Leigh Hunt arrived, and after dinner he read an act of his tragedy. I saw at once that it would not do, and showed him that it would not. He consented to leave it with me, to receive my digested opinion upon it with any recommendations I could suggest for its improvement.

London, July 27th.—Met Collier, and had some conversation with him, telling him that I had never directly or indirectly puffed, but in all things had dealt as between gentleman and gentleman. Met Blanchard, who spoke of Forster's unpopularity and meddling.

July 29th.—Went with Catherine in the carriage to Bulwer's.[1] The day was very cold—and began soon to rain. There was a rowing match on the river upon which the lawn opens, which would have been very interesting if the rain, which began to fall heavily and continued the whole day in torrents, had permitted us to see it. We saw only two heats, the last Catherine and myself from underneath a marquee. The grounds are very beautifully laid out, and, though

[1] At Fulham, where Bulwer had a villa.

20

fantastic, it is a very nice house.   There were Colonel and Mrs.
Webster and their two sons; the Colonel Webster, Lady Holland's
son, who wrote the silly letter about his mother's *faux pas* [1]; Lady
Jenkins, between whom and the Colonel was a most determined understanding; Mrs. Gurwood and her daughter, both very beautiful, and
an old gentleman, a Mr. Boddington; Colonel Gurwood and Sir R.
Jenkins joined us at dinner with Dr. Quin.   We had a very cheerful
day.   Received a play from Dickens.   Bulwer engaged to be godfather
to dearest Henry, and to be present on Wednesday week.

Elstree, August 6th.—An acknowledgment of his box from my
dear friend, Fox, which makes me weep and shrink into myself when
I feel how imperfectly he knows my real value, and how much, how
very much above my real work he estimates me.   Would to God I
could be conscious of at all approaching the high standard to which
he raises my supposed deservings!   My God, strengthen me in purpose
and in power to enter on and pursue a course of energetic industry and
consistent good.   Drove out to Watford.   Mr. Sheridan Knowles
and Miss Elphinstone passed by the carriage; I was astonished.   He
saw me, but as he passed, *would not* see us.   Forster and Catherine
with Joan were in the garden grounds; when they returned we continued our drive and passed Mr. K—— and Miss E—— beyond the
turnpike.   He was instantly (!) reading his MS. tablets to her.
Forster called to him by name, but he only read the harder!   Dickens
and Maclise had arrived when we reached home.

August 7th.—Went to church with Dickens, Forster, Maclise—to
meet Catherine and her party with darling little Henry, who was
christened by Dr. Morris.   Dickens gave him a silver cup—as his
godfather.   He is one to be proud of.   After the children's dinner
went to the reservoir, where Dickens, Maclise and Forster joined us;
pulled on the water with Dickens.   Welsh came to the bank to tell
me I was wanted; saw Bulwer and Willie as I went up the field.   They
returned with me, and Forster landed and joined us.   I talked much
with Bulwer about a play.   Forster, Bulwer, and myself went into the
field and shot with the bow for some time.   A pleasant day.   Dr. Quin
arrived to dinner.   Looked over Flaxman's illustrations of Dante and
Homer.

August 8th.—Talked much with Bulwer about a new play.   He

---

[1] Lady Holland, *née* Vassall, married first Sir Godfrey Webster, Bart., who divorced
her on account of her relations with Lord Holland, whom she afterwards married.   There is
an interesting account of her, as Lady Webster, in Lady Maria Holroyd's Journal.

made Catherine a present of a bracelet, and left us. Was not pleased with Forster's behaviour, but soon reflected myself into forgetfulness of it. Dickens and Maclise left us.

August 9th.—Talked after dinner with Forster about the opening play of the Haymarket; read some scenes in *The Fatal Dowry*, which he thought excellent. Early to bed.

August 13th.—Sent a note to Mr. Willmott, who soon after called with Mr. Webster, and we made every effort to fix upon the opening play. Deciding at last on *Othello* as the first.

London, August 19th.—Looked out my clothes at my lodgings; went to rehearsal at the Haymarket.[1] Acted Othello, in part well, in part languidly. The audience did not seem to be of the same quality of intellect as I had been used to at Covent Garden. But let us hope.

August 21st.—Went to theatre for rehearsal. I sensibly feel the descent from Covent Garden into this dog-hole of a theatre—dirt, slovenliness, and puffery make up the sum of its character. Found Browning at my lodgings on my return, and was kept by him long; but he left me where he found me. His object, if he exactly knew it, was to learn from me whether, if he wrote a really good play, it would have a secure chance of acceptance. I told him certainly, and after much vague conversation, he left me to read and rest as I could. Acted Claude Melnotte fairly, but I can scarcely now judge of myself; the audience is so close upon me, and yet I cannot feel their sympathy, if they have any. Was called for and well received.

Elstree, August 25th.—Finished *Deerbrook*[2] before I could rise this morning. I close this book with feelings of gratitude and veneration to the author, for I have been much benefited by the confirmation of good aspiration and intention that has existed feebly within me. Rose and heard the dear children their hymns, and afterwards examined them in their multiplication and the French verbs. Arranged my accounts, etc., and afterwards read in *Othello*.

London, August 26th.—Felt very unwell. Went to the theatre, anxious to do my best, but with little hope of doing much. Acted Othello with as much energy as I could—and in some instances well; but the audience did not seem to sympathize with me; at least I did not feel their sympathy; was called for and well received.

Elstree, August 27th.—Continued Leigh Hunt's play, of which I read four acts; they are hopeless; he *cannot* write a dramatic work.

[1] The engagement at the Haymarket, now commenced, continued to the end of the year, and up to January 15 of the following year (1840)—(*note by Sir F. Pollock*).

[2] By Harriet Martineau.

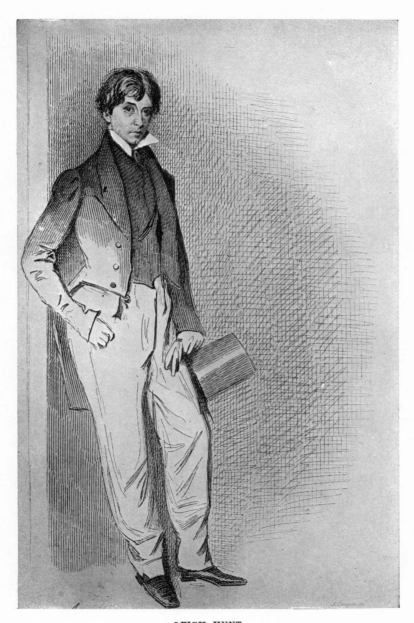

LEIGH HUNT

From a drawing by Daniel Maclise, R.A.

London, September 2nd.—Read Iago—lying down. Acted Iago very unsatisfactorily, and *quite lost my temper—an inexcusable fault.* The audience applauded Othello, Mr. Phelps, who got through the part very respectably, but seemed not to understand me. They called for me after Mr. Phelps, but I was undressed and did not go. Fox, De Fresne, and Edward came into my room. Fox was annoyed with the audience, and De Fresne said *" Il faut venir à Paris, là on peut vous apprécier."*

Elstree, September 3rd.—Rose rather late, not comfortable from my failure of duty, in giving way to passion, and, as I apprehend, in avoiding the needful labour in my profession yesterday. Entered arrears of record and gave some attention to my accounts. Attended to my children's lessons in arithmetic. Read over with attention Shylock and afterwards Sir Oswin Mortland; feel that I *must make a rally* and return to earnest labour in my art, if I desire to maintain my standing.

London, September 4th.—After dinner took up Mrs. Inchbald's [1] *Nature and Art,* which I could not lay down again. Read the newspaper, in which I saw the tumultuous reception and crowded house to Miss E. Tree—who left us a mediocre actress, and having been puffed in her absence returns to be an attraction, reversing the case of Madame Vestris. What a mass of sottish stupidity the *public,* quasi public, is! Acted Claude Melnotte in a middling manner; was called for, and despite resistance was obliged to go forward. Well received. Mr. Webster is playing his game of tradesman with me. Edward, Browning and Brydone came into my room. Webster showed me Bulwer and Forster's letters. Forster is very *unsafe.* Came home with Browning.

September 5th.—Read Browning's play on Victor, King of Sardinia—it turned out to be a *great mistake.* I called Browning into my room and most explicitly told him so, and gave him my reasons for coming to such a conclusion.

September 6th.—Bulwer called in the afternoon, and talked a good deal about his projected play. Read a little of Shylock in the course of the morning, and got a glimpse or two of light upon it. Acted Claude Melnotte very indifferently—worse than, I think, I have ever before done. I was not well prepared. Forster called and spoke of Knowles's play as good, but not overwhelming. Miss Faucit was very unhappy about something. It was Miss E. Tree's position,

---

[1] Elizabeth Inchbald (1753-1821); the well-known authoress and actress.

23

I do not doubt, and her annoyance was aggravated by not having Hester in *To Marry* to act. I consoled her as I best could by showing her that her griefs were unreasonable discontents.

Elstree, September 7th.—Read Shylock, which does not approach me as it should. I know how it should be done, but have not yet acquired the method—the key-note of the character.

September 17th.—Letitia mentioned to-night that Forster had told them that Dickens intended to dedicate *Nickleby* to me. I was sorry he had mentioned it, for such an honour—as great a one as a man can receive—should not be divulged, for fear of accident.

September 20th.—Received a note from Forster, which induced me to write one to him, wishing him not to be severe on Ellen Tree. Forster called and told me of Browning's intemperance about his play which he read to Fox, Forster, etc. He showed me his notice of *Twelfth Night*, in which he has *over-praised* Miss Tree.

September 22nd.—Received a most kind letter from Dickens with the proof sheet of the dedication of *Nickleby* to me. Surely this is something to gratify me. Looked at the newspaper, and saw an announcement of the Haymarket performances, which irritated me considerably, but upon reflection it is to *ourselves,* singly almost, that these fine *shades* of distinction are of importance. I wonder at others, and yet suffer myself to be annoyed by the very weakness I reprove in them. Let me keep on my course—" onward, right on "—undisturbed by these pettinesses, unworthy of me, and so deserve the blessing of God, which I invoke on my efforts. Answered Dickens's letter, thanking him, as well as I could, for the high compliment conferred on me.

London, September 25th.—Read Bulwer's play, which I did not like so well as the original *Norman.* Acted Claude Melnotte tolerably well; was called for and well received. Miss Faucit wished to speak to me after the play; she was very open in her disclosures. Webster came to speak to me about Mrs. Warner, who is not so.

September 30th.—Rose in a very nervous and wandering state of mind; very much magnifying to myself the possibilities attendant on my experiment of Shylock this evening, and suffering under imaginations and apprehensions that appear absurd upon the occasion. The unpleasant position of this character is that its success would not be any great accession to my reputation, and failure must do some harm in any undertaking. My mind, however, is made up to do my best, and what more can any man do? Or what more does a reasonable and conscientious man require than such a consciousness to place his mind at ease? Acted Shylock, and tried to do my best; but how unavailing is all reasoning against painful facts—the performance was an utter failure. I felt it, and suffered very much for it. Browning came into my room and said all that sympathy and friendly feeling could suggest.

Elstree, October 1st.—My spirits had very much rallied, and I was much more reconciled to the result of last night, I suppose because I have still a hope that the papers may not be harsh with me; but I am "in Heaven's hand."

London, October 4th.—I lay down on the bed to rest, and think over Shylock. I was very nervous again, but on going upon the stage I regained much self-possession; identified myself more with the scene, and was able to give more decision and clear effect to what I said than on Monday night. I acted Shylock in many instances very fairly.

Elstree, October 5th.—My whole morning was occupied in endeavouring to think of something to say in the speech for which I am engaged —to propose Dickens's health. I went to town with Edward. Dressed, went with Edward to the Albion, Aldersgate Street, where we met Dickens, Maclise, Forster, Stanfield, Sir D. Wilkie, Cattermole, Tom Hill, Harley, Jerdan, Browne [1] (artist), Chapman & Hall, the publishers—Bradbury & Evans, etc., the printers of *Nickleby*. We sat down to a *too* splendid dinner—the portrait of Dickens by Maclise was in the room. I had to begin what the Duke of Sussex terms "the business" of the day, by proposing Dickens's health. I spoke of him as one who made the amelioration of his fellow-men the object of all his labours—and whose characteristic was philanthropy. I did not get through well. Dickens was not so good as he usually is. He stated that the *Nickleby* had been to him a diary of the last two years: the various papers preserving to him the recollection of the events and feelings connected with their production. The response of Hall, the publisher, to Dickens's eulogium on them was very sensible and genuine. I was quite touched with it. Sir D. Wilkie spoke of Richardson having produced *Clarissa Harlowe* in single volumes, and of persons, ladies, having written to him to beg of him to save Lovelace—at least his *soul*. I replied to my health, that the declaration of Dickens in his dedication was a tangible manifestation to me that I was not wholly

---

[1] Hablot Knight Browne (1815-1882); the well-known "Phiz," Dickens's chief illustrator.

valueless, and that the friendship of such a man increased my self-respect. We returned home very late.

London, October 7th.—Acted Shylock not so well as on the two previous nights. *I must take care.* Spoke to Miss H. Faucit, appointing to see her at my lodgings on Wednesday to give her some instructions in Portia.

Elstree, October 8th.—Walked with Edward to Edgware to meet Dickens, who was waiting for us with Maclise, Jerdan, Forster. Forster displayed his unfortunate humour at dinner; first very indelicately objecting to my participation in the use of Bulwer's assumed name of Calvert—suggested by myself in the play of the *Lady of Lyons* —and then behaving very grossly on a question which arose about a bet, in which I was deputed one of the arbiters. The harmony of our evening was quite destroyed, and I was made very uncomfortable by Forster's ill humour, and rude language.

London, October 9th.—Arriving, waited for Miss H. Faucit, to whom I gave some very excellent advice upon the part of Portia, and other things, for which she was very much obliged. I dismissed her very kindly and properly. Webster and Willmott called, and I read to them the three acts of Bulwer's play. Bulwer came in while we were thus engaged, and was gratified in hearing that the acts had made so favourable an impression. He left with me the other two acts, which I read to them. They approved, and I observed that my hands were now washed of the business; if Webster chose to accept it he had only to signify as much to Sir Edward Bulwer and arrange all the rest with him. They left me. A letter from Mr. ——, pestering me with his disgusting play of *Catiline*, wishing me to give it with a note from him to Mr. Webster—which I did. Bulwer called, and I went over the play with him, he taking notes of alterations. I told him the half-quire of paper, which he had before him, was that which he had sent me by mistake. When he had done his notes he went on talking, evidently to divert my attention, as he folded up the half-quire and put it in his pocket! How very whimsical! When at the theatre I received a note from Forster, apologizing for his behaviour, and requesting me to forget it. I answered in a very kind and cordial spirit.

October 12th.—Spoke to Mrs. Warner about her very ill-judged and unseemly conduct. Miss H. Faucit is ill, and makes me quite uncomfortable in playing. Jerdan came in. Webster spoke to me about Mrs. Warner. I advised him to promise her to give her in every respect fair play with *every other* actress, as to announcement, etc., but to do no more.   Came home to our newly-taken house, York Gate, Regent's Park.

October 15th.—I read some part of Bulwer's play, *The Sea Captain*.[1]   Webster called; I spoke with him about the dresses and scenery, and we then settled the terms of an engagement for next season at £100 per week, play or no play, with the choice of a month's vacation on my part.   Devoted the whole day, without intermission, to Bulwer's play.   Forster came to dinner; afterwards I read the play, which seemed to interest, but the employment of the pirates, and the violence in the fifth act was unanimously disapproved.   Forster took the book home to consider it.

October 17th.—On my return found a letter from the Lord Chamberlain, in reply to mine, "regretting that he was obliged to refuse my request."[2]   I expected this, and it only adds to the strength of my case, whenever I wish to put it forward.

October 20th.—Bulwer called, as I was beginning to read his play, and talked over the required alterations with me.   What he had done in them was very bad.   George Bucknill called, and I asked him to dine.   Returned to the new play, when Forster called and interrupted me—annoyed me with a paragraph stating that I was performing to bad houses at the Haymarket.

Octobed 21st.—Bulwer called with his alterations; in good spirits, thinking he had done them well, in which opinion I agreed.   He gave them to me; we looked over the play together, and then I transmitted them to the performers, who altered their parts.   Went to the theatre, and acted Shylock very well, except the first scene, which was not so collected and fresh as the remainder.   Head informed me that there was a report of Lord Brougham's death in Covent Garden theatre.[3]   Will there be any lamentation upon the absence of this highly-gifted but ill-conditioned man?

October 22nd.—Read in the paper an account of Lord Brougham's death.   I was not able to sympathize with the expressions of respect

---

[1] The play so mercilessly parodied by Thackeray.

[2] For a personal licence to perform the legitimate drama.—(*note by Sir F. Pollock.*)

[3] A hoax, said to have been inspired by Brougham himself.   The report originated in a letter received by the late Mr. Alfred Montgomery, stated to have been written by a guest at Brougham Hall (a Mr. Shafto), who professed to have been an eyewitness to a carriage accident in which Brougham was killed on the spot.   Most of the morning papers published memoirs which must have been interesting reading to the supposed victim.   The *Times* however, was sceptical as to the occurrence.

and regret that the writer in the paper appended to his narration. He was a man who betrayed and deserted every great cause, even to the last and greatest, that of education, that he advocated. His abilities, to my poor thinking, only heaped damnation upon such apostasy. I cannot see that any feeling of benevolence is due to his particular errors. For sin and moral degradation a truly religious and philosophic mind should always cherish pity, while it condemns, and in the abstract Lord Brougham's character must in a tenfold degree excite our regret; but I do not see any redeeming traits in it that should qualify our judgment.[1] Rehearsed the new play of *The Sea Captain*. Bulwer came in to ask me for his MS. alterations. A letter came from Lord Fitz. Somerset[2] to Edward, giving him the liberty—after twenty-six years' *creditable* service—of purchasing for £1400 a half-pay majority, and informing him in the same letter that such purchase would cut off his wife and children—if he had any—from all title to pension or claim on the compassionate fund! This is our glorious institution of this *free country*. One lifts one's eyes above, and asks if such systems of the many trampled on by the few ought to exist. Has patriotism any meaning—beyond attachment to habits and conveniences? I am *sick* of the whole business.

October 23rd.—Lord Brougham's death is contradicted.

October 25th.—Was informed by Lunn that Mr. Hammond had announced me in the Drury Lane playbills. I was shocked and indignant at appearing thus compromised with Mr. Webster, and instantly wrote down to Mr. Hammond to protest against the violation of good faith in the measure. Webster came in and expressed his conviction of my ignorance of Mr. Hammond's intentions. Acted Shylock very fairly, better, I think, than on any previous occasion. Head came with part of my dress. Returning home, found a parcel with a note from Dickens, and a presentation copy of *Nickleby*. What a dear fellow he is!

October 27th.—Forster came to dinner, and brought with him an *Observer*, in which that very absurd, mischievous and contemptible person, Collier, continues his false assertions respecting me.

---

[1] Macready's comment on Brougham was, on the whole, merited. With great abilities he had very little principle, as was evidenced by his conduct when negotiating with Queen Caroline, and to his colleagues during his tenure of the Great Seal. It was this grave deficiency that was responsible for his political ostracism from 1834 till his death in 1868. That he well deserved his nickname of "Wickedshifts" (conferred by his own party) there can be no question, if the leading diaries and memoirs of the day are to be credited.

[2] Afterwards the first Lord Raglan, Commander-in-Chief in the Crimea.

28

October 28th.—Attended to the new play. Found Bulwer and Forster at the theatre. Rehearsed the new play. Bulwer was very doubtful about its success, Forster and Willmott equally confident. There was a long debate upon the question of withdrawing it, to which Bulwer seemed inclined. I could not give any opinion, for I have not had time to form one. It was at last decided to trust to Cæsar and his fortune. Webster came into my room and told me that the proprietors of Covent Garden theatre had let it to Vestris for £5000! They have made a good bargain.

October 29th.—Rehearsed with much care four acts of the play. I see clearly that Mrs. Warner and Strickland are both far below their parts. Bulwer came to give me the lines for the third act. He wished me to give an opinion. I really *could not.* I could not see the play's chances, having so little to *do* myself, and not knowing—as no one ever can, *without action* or rather *agency*—the value of what I have to say. I would speak out at once if I knew which course to take for his interest —his interest is mine and that of the theatre. Forster might have relieved us from our embarrassing position. He left it, however, to the " fortune of Cæsar " ! Came home, reading his new lines; ate as little dinner as I could, that I might return to work; wrote out and tried to master the new lines; at last was obliged by unconquerable drowsiness to lie down on the sofa and get a few minutes' sleep.

October 30th.—Walked down to the theatre. Rehearsed the new play. Bulwer and Blanchard came to the rehearsal. Bulwer became more confident as the rehearsal proceeded, and seemed at ease in his mind when it had concluded. I am not. I want time for myself and much more for other persons and things. Answered Dickens's news, congratulating him on the birth of his baby, my little god-daughter. Gave the whole evening, to a late hour, to the consideration of the new play.

October 31st.—Went in great anxiety, and uncomfortably to the theatre. Rehearsed the new play. Blanchard and Mr. Tyas came in. Returned home very, very uncomfortably. My mind depressed, and my spirits suffering much from misgiving and apprehension. Read the play over. Went to the theatre. Acted Norman in Bulwer's new play with some energy and occasional inspiration. Was received very warmly, and called for at the end, greeted with much enthusiasm.[1] Jerdan came into my room—Forster, Webster, who thanked me very

---

[1] The *Sea Captain* was played frequently at the Haymarket to the end of Macready's engagement of this date.—(*note by Sir F. Pollock.*)

earnestly—Willmott, Bulwer. There were wreaths thrown upon the stage. I am most thankful to God for what I feel a great escape. Sat up late, talking over the occurrences of the night.

November 1st.—Very much fatigued and overcome; did not rise early. Gave the children their lessons; looked at the newspaper. Went to the theatre, and waited some time with the performers for Bulwer's arrival; we proceeded with the alterations, and continued them upon his coming. After the play had been altered, Bulwer wished to speak with me. We went up to my dressing-room, where Bulwer showed me in the *Times* newspaper a letter from his wife, insinuating unworthy conduct on his part. He read me a letter he had written to the newspaper, and asked my counsel upon the policy of sending it. I most earnestly dissuaded him from any step of the kind, explaining to him the necessity of maintaining the dignified posture, which his silence gives him, and of disproving by his life the calumnies of this bad woman. I told him of my full consciousness of the difficulty of following the advice I gave, and of my perfect sympathy with his impatience of the libellous attacks he had to endure, but at the same time asserted my strong confidence in the propriety of my advice. He thanked me, and decided on abiding by my opinion. Webster spoke to me about the papers, complaining of the *Morning Herald*. Schloss called, and I spoke to him about altering the word in his prospectus— that I had *condescended* to sit for my picture. Went to the theatre. Acted Norman. I scarcely know how; my spirits sink in thinking of the play; I fear it has not *substance* to sustain it. I have nothing *to do* in it, as I have always said. Was called for and well received. Spoke to Miss Faucit about giving up her part and dissuaded her from it. Spoke with Willmott and Webster, who told me that Mr. Jerrold had said, if he had been a baronet his play would have been accepted at Covent Garden! I gave him £50 for his bad play, which I did not accept!!!

November 2nd.—Bulwer came into my room, and spoke about further curtailments in the play; he also expressed his satisfaction that he had not published his answers to Lady Bulwer.

November 10th.—Looked at the newspaper; had been excited by the complaints of my family against Forster's partisanship (which as far as Bulwer is concerned is " not fidelity "), and was obliged to reason with myself as I read his somewhat exaggerated praise of Knowles's play; still, there is much to praise in it, and I doubt not there seems to him more than to me.

November 11th.—I looked at the newspapers and wrote to Bulwer, giving him a satisfactory account—I fear too soon reported—of the success of *The Sea Captain.* Acted Norman indifferently; was sorry to see the house not so good as I could have wished. I tremble for this play. Was called for and well received. Mr. A. Watts sent me a *United Service Gazette,* reflecting on Bulwer and lauding Knowles—why, I do not know.

November 18th.—Went to breakfast with Mrs. Reid to meet the Princess Belgiojoso. She did not arrive till past twelve o'clock. Dr. Roget [1] called in afterwards. I passed an agreeable morning with this charming woman. Called on Maclise and saw a splendid beginning of a picture on the subject of Macbeth seeing the ghost of Banquo at the banquet. It appeared to me a sublime conception. Went to the theatre and acted Norman fairly. Spoke with Miss Faucit about continuing in the part. She readily yielded to my representations. Bulwer came in and reported a fine house at Covent Garden theatre. Our house was indifferent, and I fear and feel that we are sunk beyond rising in this play.

November 20th.—Called on Mr. T. Landseer [2] to thank him for his beautiful engraving; he was very much pleased with my visit; showed me some beautiful engravings and some beautiful pictures by Edwin Landseer. I was much moved by the pleasure he expressed at seeing me, and the delight he testified at my performances. I promised to write to Miss Martineau about an ear-trumpet. [3] Spoke with Miss Faucit about an engagement at Drury Lane, to which she assented thankfully. Webster and Willmott came into my room, and reported that there was an excellent house at Covent Garden—*tant pis pour nous !*

November 21st.—Went to theatre; acted fairly. Spoke to Miss Faucit on the stage. She seemed low-spirited and unwell. On coming off, I asked her what was the matter. She said she had been very much shaken by some ill-natured thing—that she did not like to speak of it then, as it would upset her. She was passing my room, and I said, " You had better come in and sit down." She did, and to my request explained to me that she had been greatly distressed by informa-

---

[1] Peter Mark Roget (1779–1869); nephew of Sir Samuel Romilly; a well-known physician and scientist. His *Thesaurus of English Words and Phrases* became a standard work.

[2] Thomas Landseer (1795–1880); A.R.A.; elder brother of Charles and Edwin Landseer; an eminent engraver; he etched and engraved Sir E. Landseer's principal pictures.

[3] Both T. Landseer and Miss Martineau were extremely deaf.

tion that Mesdames Warner, Ellen Tree, and Lacy had been talking in a very malignant manner about her coming into my room to speak with me after the play, as they said, "every night"—Mrs. Warner observing it was a great pity, it being the talk of the Haymarket and Covent Garden theatres; Miss E. Tree adding her charitable compassion to the stock, and thinking it a pity that some one did not speak to Miss Faucit; Mrs. Lacy in a similar strain, saying also that there had been a paragraph in the *Satirist* to a like effect. I told her not to disturb herself about the matter; that my door had always been opened to every one who came; that my brother had come in without knocking; that Messrs. Webster and Willmott were informed of the subject of every conversation we had had, and that on no one occasion of her speaking to me in my room had I omitted to mention it, and the matter spoken of on going home at night. I told her not to distress herself, painful as it was, for that I was quite sure Mrs. Macready would show her sense of it by making a party on purpose to invite her. She was very thankful. This occurred in two conversations, during and after the play. Webster and Willmott came in and spoke, but to little purpose. On going home I mentioned all that had occurred, and my wish that Catherine should invite Miss Faucit, to which she instantly assented.

November 22nd.—Catherine sent a note with a card of invitation to Miss Faucit. At Mr. Webster's request, spoke with Miss Faucit about playing Lydia Languish, which she said she would give an answer to to-morrow. Spoke with Willmott and Webster about Knowles, who, it seems, said to Webster, "I will not write for Macready."

November 23rd.—Went to theatre. Spoke with Webster and Willmott. I took the opportunity of alluding to the conversation of last night, in which I had designated Mr. Knowles as a *blackguard*, and I observed that it was under strong excitement I used so coarse a term, which, however bad a person might be, was only applicable to such persons as Mr. Bunn, Mr. ——, Captain ——, etc.; that I distinctly and unequivocally *unsaid* and *retracted* the term, as unfit to use to a man of Mr. K.'s talent and standing, and that I thought it right to say so, as I would not say that *of* a man which I would not say *to* him. At the same time I did not qualify my assertion that he is a very ungrateful man. They told me—both—that he had said *I had used him ill.* Miss Faucit wished to speak to me in my room, but I told her on her account I had thought it better not; the few things I had to say I said to her behind the scenes.

32

November 29th.—Forster called, and spoke in terms of violent reprehension of Bulwer's preface. He said that he had taken Mr. Knowles to task for the tone in which he spoke of me, who, after some conversation, proposed to the assembled party—Hunt, Procter, etc.— "my health." Forster, after much circumlocution, stated directly that Mr. Knowles could say nothing in any degree impugning my behaviour to him, to the latest period of my dealing with him, without subjecting himself to the charge of gross ingratitude. Unluckily, poor Forster is *not direct. Eheu !* Wrote a note to Warren on learning that Lardner had sent an excuse for Sunday.

November 30th.—Forster called, and only further confirmed me in the persuasion that he is a mere hooter-on of any successful person ; as readily the toady of such a wretched, unprincipled fellow as Mr. Knowles as the staunch friend of a manly and gentlemanly person. He is a poor-talking, low-minded man. "Never more be *friend* of mine." Keep his acquaintance I may, but I strike him out of the list—the very little list of *friends.*[1] Rested ; went to the theatre ; found an invitation from the Fishmongers' Society ! Acted Norman fairly. O'Hanlon called ; annoyed me very much by saying, *par parenthèse*, that I had behaved *ill* in the affair of Mr. Bunn. Passion and revenge are always to be reprehended, but I simply took that vengeance and inflicted that just punishment which the law would not.

December 1st.—Dickens and T. Landseer called. I was about to write to Landseer, as I told him, but was delighted to produce the trumpet to him ; gave him Miss Martineau's letter to read ; his experiment of the trumpet was very successful ; he heard at the distance of a yard from the speaker, but complained of the vibration of the instrument. He was much obliged, and I am very pleased. Stanfield, Lovers, Procters, Rollses, Mrs. Reid, Elliotson, O'Hanlon, Warren, Herring, Misses Faucit, and P. Horton came to dinner. The Loughs, T. Cookes, Lane, Egbert Webbe, Z. Troughton, Quin, Ainsworth, Edwin Landseer, Bennett, Mrs. Kitchener, came in the evening. The day was cheerful, the music very good, and all passed off very pleasantly.

December 6th.—Dickens gave me a play to read, called *Glencoe.*

December 7th.—Finished the play of *Glencoe*, which has so much to praise in it. This night's labour paid off the £600 advanced by Webster.

December 8th.—Arranged my accounts, and found myself possessed

[1] In spite of many such ebullitions, the friendship continued till Macready's death.

of £10,000, a small realization out of such a receipt as mine has been the last twenty years. But I have lost much, given away much, and, I fear, spent much; but what I have lost, and what given, would leave me with all my spendings a rich man. Forster came in the evening, and we learnt from him part of an account of his having made an outbreak at the Shakspeare Club last night, which ended in the breaking up of the Club! An additional evidence of his want of self-government, tact, and good breeding. His own relation states that some indecorous proceeding on the part of three or four persons during Mr. Bell's speech was not noticed either by Bell or Dickens, the chairman; upon his, Forster's, rising to make a speech, he made a "slashing" attack on these persons. After his speech, three or four rose to question *his* right to rebuke them, avowing their willingness to submit to the reproof of the chair, but disputing Mr. Forster's right to take such a duty on himself. Forster says he disclaimed anything personal (!) and left the room. Dickens, after returning thanks for his health being drunk, requested those who sympathized with him to leave the room. Forster says thirty went out; Miss Flower said twenty. It is evidently a bad business. Came home and went to bed, reading Carlyle's *Revolution*.

December 12th.—Thought much about Miss Faucit. Let me hope that I may yet be able to advance her in her profession, and to see her happy and respected. Went to dine with Talfourd, calling on Dickens, who said he was too ill to accompany me. Dined. Talfourd, Forster, and self. After dinner the conversation turned on plays. I mentioned one I had of a striking character upon a popular subject; Talfourd asked me the title. I told him *Glencoe*. He questioned me about its possible melodramatic tendency. I told him that the treatment avoided the melodrama of the stage; that the style was an imitation of his writing, but without the point that terminated his speeches; that the story was well managed and dramatic; and that I intended to act it. At last, to my utter astonishment, he pulled out two books from his pocket and said, " Well, I will no longer conceal it—it is my play; " and he gave each of us a copy! I never in my life experienced a greater surprise. This play had been represented to me as Mr. Collinson's. Forster affected great indignation, and really stormed; I laughed, loud and long, and put down his *affected* feeling; it was really a romance to me. Talfourd told us that he had written this to preserve his recollections of Glencoe. I strongly advised him to take one of two courses, either to flood the town with the edition, published anonymously, and to engage the suffrages of the Press, and leave it to be acted with his name, as it might escape; or to preserve it a profound secret, giving him at the same time a right to call upon me if he heard it anywhere through me. *Forster showed a character of sycophancy*—affected friendship where he felt it not—*bad acting*—super-enthusiastic. We went in a coach to Dickens, whom we found at home, and Talfourd dismissed the coach, expecting to " be kept late." Forster and self went with Dickens into another room, and we there discussed the business, Forster again *affecting the right to dance on the high ropes ! Foolish man !* I put him down again, and spoke coolly to Dickens, urging him strongly to go *with* Talfourd to Moxon, and impress upon him the necessity of enforcing him to silence. I invited him to dinner on Sunday, and Talfourd, who could not answer for the power to " get away." Came home.

December 13th.—Read through the play of *Glencoe,* which I trust is destined to be a great success, but my opinion of its poetical merits is still unchanged : it is superior to, in dramatic construction, and very much below in poetry, the play of *Ion.*

December 15th.—Looked over my accounts, and examined what had been my expenses this year. I found upwards of £400 for theatre expenses, and £200 given away in small donations to poor or importunate people. The Dickenses, Forster, and Maclise dined with us—not a pleasant day. Forster made it especially disagreeable by his rude style of argument. He afterwards detained me, and very nearly quarrelled with me, giving me what I first understood a message from Talfourd, wishing me to act either *Ion* or the *Athenian Captive.* I said I would write to Talfourd on the subject. He took fire at this and affected to be annoyed—he was alarmed. He detained me in a very *disagreeable discussion,* which ended by my permission to Talfourd to ask Mr. Webster, if he chose, to act *Ion.*

December 18th.—Read an account of that wretched fellow Bunn's examination in the bankruptcy court. No one appeared to make any complaint, and though there is no doubt the swindler has secreted at least £700, to say nothing of goods, yet the Commission actually dismissed him with praise ! ! ! My God ! What is the value of character or fair dealing in this world? A letter from Miss Martineau, wishing to interest me about a play, translated from the German by a son of Godwin, now in the possession of Mrs. Godwin, for the purpose of adding to the means of supporting her in her aged widowhood. I directly wrote a note to Mrs. Godwin, and afterwards answered Miss Martineau.

35

December 20th.—A note from Bulwer, a most kind one, inquiring of me if I had any wish to accept the place of Dramatic Censor; that applications were being made for the office in the expectation of Charles Kemble's death, and that he had heard to-day that they would give the preference to me. A note from Mrs. Godwin, thanking me, etc. Answered Bulwer, expressing my anxiety to obtain the office if I could have it with my profession for four years, or even for one year; thanking him very cordially. In talking with Miss —— I learned what seemed tantamount to an assurance that she thought partially of me. If it be so, how are persons in our profession to guide themselves? Is it surprising that a person regarding one elevated in their own course of life should magnify all his merits and see him through a false medium? We have much to resist, if we *can* resist it.

December 21st.—Received a note from Bulwer, urging me to write directly to Lord Uxbridge and ask for the appointment of Deputy Licenser, expressing his delight at the opportunity of serving me, and recommending me to state to Lord Uxbridge my readiness to leave the stage if that were made the condition of my nomination. Consulted, after writing a letter, with Catherine, Edward, and Letitia, who thought it fitting, but objected to the proffer of the resignation of the stage; I agreed with them, and erased the passage containing the offer. Wrote it out and sent it to Lord Uxbridge; copied it, and sent it with a note to Bulwer. But what a contrast does Bulwer offer to my other friends! How kind! how grateful in act! how thoroughly a gentleman!

December 22nd.—Bulwer called and recommended me to write and ask the interest of Lord Normanby with Uxbridge, which shows me my chance is very bad; natheless, I will do my utmost.

December 23rd.—I wrote a letter to Lord Normanby, asking his interest with the Chamberlain for the office of Licenser, and enclosed with it a copy of my letter to the Lord Chamberlain. Received a perfumed rose with a note requesting me to wear it to-night. Miss Faucit wished to speak to me about the Drury Lane engagement. Mr. Copeland came and had a long interview with her first, then he came down to me, and stayed some time, wishing me to combat a clause on which Miss Faucit insisted, *viz.* the insertion of *her name in large letters in the bills!* I spoke to him about Phelps, of whom Willmott had told me as being at liberty; he was rejoiced to catch at him, Warde being too embarrassed to depend on. When he was gone, Miss Faucit came, and I had a long conference with her. I could make little impression with regard to the *large letters*, though I urged *strongly* the absurdity of it.

December 24th.—A card from Mr. Martin, who had called with a "private message from Lord Uxbridge," and wished me to call on him. I set off to St. James's and found him. His errand was to express to me, in honied phrase, that Lord Uxbridge had given to Mr. J. Kemble [1] the appointment of Deputy Licenser. I heard the news as indifferently as I could endeavour to seem to do, and after some conversation left him. He said, among other things, that Lord Uxbridge desired him to say, "*If there was anything else that I could point out which he could serve me in, he should be happy,*" etc. Knowing well *that there was nothing*—he refused me a licence—and admitting, as he did, through Mr. Martin that no one could be better qualified for the office, or have better pretension or title to ask for it, he has given it to a person without the slightest grounds for expecting notice or recompense from a Government. My heart turned very sick within me as my steps bent homeward. We all indulge in hope that, spite of our efforts, grows into expectation, and I had resolved on leaving the stage at once, and quitting scenes where my mind is in a whirl of passion, intrigue, and tumult, where temptations to error are constantly before me and provocations beset me on every side. I had hoped to retire from this to the serenity of a country life, to a slender establishment and the society of my children. I have now no hope of any assistance in life, but must finish it and play out the game myself. God assist me. Amen.

December 26th.—Gave the entire morning to Miss F——, [2] entering into the subject, generally and in detail, of the study of the art of acting, cautioning her not to entertain the subject unless resolved to give herself up to it. Told her of all the faults I could recollect in her style, and showed her how to remove them. She was most grateful, and seemed sensible that what I said was true. I was very glad indeed to have her here. Catherine received her very kindly, and saw her two or three times.

December 28th.—Spoke to Miss Faucit for two or three minutes about the effect of her subdued acting, and explained to her how much might be done. Recommended her to ask Dr. Babington [3] if change

[1] John Mitchell Kemble, of Trinity College, Cambridge, the distinguished Anglo-Saxon scholar, son of Charles Kemble, who had been for some time in the actual performance of the duties of the office—(*note by Sir F. Pollock*).

[2] Miss Faucit.

[3] Benjamin Guy Babington (1794-1866); an eminent physician of the day, also an accomplished linguist.

of climate was not necessary for her, and, if so, to avail herself of it.

December 30th.—Went to the theatre. Miss Faucit sent me a note enclosing a certificate from Dr. Babington, stating her inability to continue her professional exertions; it threw me quite into low spirits. I rallied, and played Othello very fairly. Was called for, and well received. Spoke after the play to poor dear Miss Faucit, who was in very low spirits. I urged her strongly not to go to Hastings, but, if not abroad, at least to go to Devonshire. Mr. Copeland came in and I told him the news; read him the certificate—we were all in despair.

1840

London, January 1st.—Willmott informed me as we went to Drury Lane that the women in the dressing-rooms had been saying that —— left the theatre from "being in the family way." It is monstrous and terrible to live and carry on one's daily occupations among such a set of ——s and bl—g—ds as this profession (!) is composed of! Scarcely one among them that would not think it a *gain* to obtain a profitable paramour, and all ready to fabricate the grossest and most unfounded calumnies to justify their own profligacy.

January 2nd.—Gave the children their lessons in arithmetic, and looked at the paper when I came down, which was filled with the trial of the prisoners at Monmouth, Frost being the first. What can we learn from our experience, but that nothing can be known? Is it not to be supposed that this Frost [1] believed himself right? Are those, who are pampered by the laws, which the profligate and purse-proud have made, fit judges of the sufferings or patience of the poor, who are starving by them? Are the Attorney-General and his fellow prosecutors quite innocent in stretching their little wits, to put these men to death? Are the defending counsel justified in seeking to procure them exemption from punishment by legal quibbles? What a shuffling miserable scene it is of chicanery and grave pettifogging among these torturers of phrase and word—the lives of several, and the anguish or relief of many more, depending on the success of a quibble or a declamation.

January 5th.—Heard the children their hymns, and arranged my

[1] A Chartist leader and ex-magistrate for the borough of Monmouth. He had been removed from the magistracy early in the previous year in consequence of his revolutionary utterances. In the following November he was the ringleader of an immense body of rioters at Newport, which led to serious disturbances and loss of life, necessitating the intervention of the soldiery. On the suppression of the riots Frost was arrested and, with others, was tried for high treason on December 31. Three of the prisoners, among them Frost, were on conviction sentenced to death; but a majority of the judges having reported to the Home Secretary that, in their opinion, there had been a defective delivery of the list of witnesses at the trial, the death sentence was commuted to one of transportation for life. Frost, some years afterwards, was pardoned.

accounts. In thinking over and speaking of my expenses, I came to the conclusion that it was absolutely indispensable that I should give up Elstree and take a house in town. The T. Twisses, Browning, and Miss Faucit came to dinner. We passed a cheerful day. I gave Miss Faucit de Staël's *Germany*, and Schlegel's *Dramatic Literature*. I asked her, as I took her to her carriage, if I should not see her again. She said no—she thought not. I felt very low at parting with her, and did not know before how deep and tender an interest I felt for her. I do entertain a most sincere and affectionate regard for her. God bless her! dear girl! I go to bed in very low spirits—I feel great apprehension for her. God bless and assist her! Amen!

January 9th.—Wrote out after tea the memoranda of rules and hints on acting for Miss Faucit, read them to Catherine, and enclosed them with a note to Miss Faucit, but before the servant had taken it a note arrived from her, not wishing to receive it until she reached Hastings, where she is going. From my inmost heart I pray to God that she may derive benefit from it.

January 12th.—Read Mr. ——'s trash—which I still believe to be more malignant than silly—he mentions my name with Miss Faucit in a way that I think is intended to convey gross insinuations. I care more for her sake, if such innuendoes should reach her, than for anything else—these are your *gentlemen of the Press!*

January 13th.—Gave the children their lessons; cast a glimpse over the paper, and walked down to Drury Lane [1]; the exercise is quite renovating to me. Rehearsed *Macbeth*, from which several of the performers were absent. My mind had been made very uneasy by the innuendoes of yesterday's paper, and my deep concern for my poor young friend, in whom I feel so very strong an interest. The thought that the success of the *débutant* at Covent Garden this evening might prostrate my future attempts did not add to my serenity; but I grew placid from the exercise of the morning and feeling my power at rehearsal. I was struck with the contrast of my situation at the present moment with what it was at Drury Lane when I last left it— driven out by the repeated insults and outrages of that wretched creature Bunn, and quelling my nature to the utmost task of endurance, I return to a splendid salary and with homage universally rendered to me from the people around me. I am deeply grateful, and I pray God's blessing on my endeavours, and that avoiding all tempta-

---

[1] Macready was now engaged there as leading tragedian under the management of a Mr. Hammond.

tion to evil, I may use the advantages of my position for the benefit of my blessed children.

January 14th.—Gave the children their lessons in arithmetic. Looked at the paper, and perceived that no impression was made by the *débutant* in Hamlet last night. It seems envious and ungenerous to watch thus circumstances out of one's individual concerns; but unhappily for me my destiny is very much influenced by that of others. If a very successful appearance were to carry with it the fashion of the town, my value, from its present estimate of £100 per week, which is *offered* me, would sink down to £30 or something of that sort, and all my hopes of independence and retirement, still more the prospects of my blessed children's education, would be painfully jeopardized. I hang on a thread—or rather there is Damocles' sword over my fortunes perpetually. It is sad, but I cannot help it, although I strive to think as little of it as possible. I thank God for my present benefits.

January 15th.—Webster came into my room with Willmott; thanked me for the service I had rendered him; he told me that Mr. Knowles had exultingly said to him that the success of Mr. Moore (Hamlet) would put down the pretension of the actors (meaning myself) and that he (W——) would not have to give £100 per week to his tragedians again!

January 18th.—Glanced at the newspaper—sickened with politics and the whole system of *shams* that politicians and newspaper writers endeavour to support. Oh, for one strong word of truth to smash it all! Went to Drury Lane theatre; began to rehearse *Macbeth;* thought Mr. Archer drunk from his rude and insolent manner; in the banquet scene he became so wantonly rude that at length I took up my umbrella and left the stage. Mr. Copeland wished to speak to me—I very readily assented, but he could not find the key of Mr. Hammond's room. I left him and the stage at the beginning of the banquet-scene. Came home; dined. Lunn called to tell me that Mr. Archer was discharged; Mr. Lee put into his part in *Macbeth,* King into that of Chalmers. Willmott wished me to write a line. I wrote to Hammond and Willmott, to say that it was not my *wish* Mr. Archer should be discharged, that I should discharge my obligations with *whatever performers,* claiming the right of absenting myself from disagreeable rehearsals. Went with Catherine to look at a house —Clarence Terrace—which I liked. At a quarter-past eleven Willmott called to tell me that Mr. Elton would *not* act Banquo, and that the

Licenser had cut out some most important passages in the play of *Mary Stuart*,[1] passages that destroy its power and interest! I was very angry. What must I now do? The bread of hundreds jeopardized, my own interests ruined, and the long cherished hopes and labours of a man of genius crushed! I advised Hammond, through Willmott, to shut the theatre and advertise it as by the interference of the Chamberlain with the play. I am *very angry*, but I think, at present, that this is the best advice. I must, however, keep the fact before me that though I am made very important among the persons with whom my business lies, I am *very insignificant* in the sight of men, who have power. I should therefore act with deliberation—or rather counsel so. *In nocte consilium.*

January 19*th.*—Much excited and irritated by this matter of the Licenser; but after some nervous misgivings upon the effect on my estimation and my income which the failure of this Drury Lane engagement might occasion, and some doubts as to the prudence of entering on a new house, I subsided into the calm resolution to let things pass, and make the best of them—in fact, I went to the sum total of good and ill, and put aside the vexatious question of items. I considered the good I possessed in my beloved family, and the means, though small, of preserving them and myself from destitution. I determined *to do my utmost* for success as far as I was individually concerned, and to leave results to higher powers. It is certain that this interference with the play has been either the act of an unwise man, or a dishonest one, for the sake of the interests of Covent Garden theatre. It looks very ugly, but my province is endurance, and to " do nothing," or say nothing, " from *strife*."

January 20*th.*—Went to Drury Lane theatre. Acted Macbeth tolerably fairly, was called for, and well received. Was very grateful to see so excellent a house. How different my return to this theatre to my departure from it! How grateful I ought to be!

January 21*st.*—Went to Drury Lane theatre; rehearsed very particularly the play of *Mary Stuart*. A letter from Mr. John Kemble, the Licenser, came with the command of the Lord Chamberlain to omit certain other passages, which had not been erased in the copy which Mr. Hammond had returned to his office.

January 22*nd.*—Went to Drury Lane theatre with hopes and prayers in my heart for the successful result of the undertaking I had in hand. Rehearsed the play of *Mary Stuart*. Returned home and

[1] By James Haynes.

42

assisted Willie in his exercise—*instead of attending to my own business,* and *reading my part.* I did it most reluctantly, but could not bear to leave him to his own apprehensions. Rested for about half-an-hour. Went to Drury Lane theatre, and acted Ruthven; was nervous, and, to my own surprise—in fact, I cannot now understand the cause—I lost the words in my great effect of the fourth act. I came off the stage in a state of desperate fury, rushed to my book, and, when I looked at the words in which I had been perfect six weeks ago, I saw that if my life depended on it I could not have spoken them—they had gone out of my head! Was called on after the play, and very well received.[1]

January 23rd.—Saw the newspapers, which were tolerably favourable in their report of last night's play. Mr. Jerrold, the writer in the *Herald,* wrote a long tirade of false accusation against me—to the effect that I had made Mr. Haynes cut and alter and spoil his play to elevate my own character of Ruthven! John Twiss called. Went to dine with Dickens. Met Rogers,[2] Cattermoles, Maclise, Forster. Was much pleased in meeting Rogers, who was very amusing in his anecdotes and humorous manner; he expressed a hope to see me at his house.

January 28th.—Was very much pleased to learn that the House of Commons had reduced Prince Albert's grant to £30,000.[3] Found Forster at home, who dined with us. The conversation, in turning on the twaddle of the *Observer,* led us to speak of the reflection upon Miss Faucit—of which Forster had also heard, and our conversation turned very much upon it. As I told him, the ill-treatment which this poor girl has received only binds me more strongly to her. I will not desert her.

January 29th.—Dickens sent me a parcel—the pamphlet relating to *Glencoe,* and the proof sheets of his first number of his new work —*Master Humphrey's Clock.* I read it first myself, and then read it to Catherine and Letitia, who, as well as myself, were much affected and amused by it. Mrs. Dickens called whilst we were at luncheon.

---

[1] The piece was acted twenty times, but with little benefit to the treasury.

[2] The famous banker-poet.

[3] Lord John Russell, representing the Government in the House of Commons, had moved that £50,000 per annum should be settled on Prince Albert. Joseph Hume moved that the amount should be reduced to £21,000, but the motion was negatived by 305 to 38 votes. Colonel Sibthorp, the Tory M.P. for Lincoln, then moved a reduction to £30,000, and with the support of Sir Robert Peel and the Opposition the motion was carried by 262 to 158 votes.

January 31st.—Looked at the *Morning Herald,* which had an article on the new tragedy by Jerrold abusive of Bulwer. Went to Drury Lane theatre; acted Ruthven fairly. Forster and Bulwer came into my room. The latter seemed very urgent that I should take Drury Lane theatre. Sent for Hammond, and spoke to him on the subject of backing up the tragedy.

February 2nd.—The *Observer* talked some nonsense about having set me " right with the public." What the ass means I cannot guess.

February 4th.—Mrs. Braysher called with a note from dear Miss Faucit, and a note and some shells from her to Catherine. I had a very long conversation with Mrs. Braysher, and recommended her calling on Mr. Collier and informing him where Miss Faucit was, why she was there, and at whose instance, and to say that any information about her might be had for the inquiry.

February 7th.—Forster came into my room bringing the news of Leigh Hunt's play having been successful at Covent Garden, although he could not define exactly the nature of its success.

February 8th.—Looked at the paper, and read hastily the criticism on Leigh Hunt's play—which I cannot think genuinely successful. I can scarcely believe that it will attract.

February 9th.—Looked over the newspaper, and was sorry to see Fonblanque [1] so entirely surrendering his sturdy opinions upon social and human rights to the maintenance of a miserable, miserable party. Arranged my weekly accounts. Forster called, and I gave him my opinion, when asked, of his violent praise of Miss E. Tree's performance, which being, as I can suppose, good in little, he praised as great in great.

February 10th.—Went to the Piazza Coffee House to congratulate and sup with Maclise on the occasion of his election as a Royal Academician. Poor Maclise was very tipsy with the wine and the event. Stanfield was there with others. Walked home with Edward and Dickens.

February 11th.—Went to Drury Lane theatre. Acted Macbeth as well as I could, but distressed by weakness and by the disgusting rudeness and inattention of the people behind the scenes. Was called for and well received. Miss Horton sent me in a note waiting for an answer. I saw her and advised her not to accept an engagement at the Surrey theatre. Heard to-night that a message had been sent from the Lord Chamberlain yesterday to the theatres, informing the managers that they might in future act on the Wednesday and Fridays

---

[1] Fonblanque was then editor of the *Examiner.*

in Lent excepting Ash Wednesday and Passion Week. This *boon* from the persons in brief authority is something like the gifts of Ajax and Hector.

February 13th.—Went to dine with Mrs. Rolls and passed an agreeable day. Met Dottin, M.P. for Southampton, Walpole, Boxall, Whately and Lady Henrietta Churchill, Dickens and Mrs. Dickens, Miss Morice, etc.

February 15th.—Looked at the papers. In one of them I read the account of Mr. Stephen Price's death. The announcement was accompanied with some praises of his qualities of head and heart. All that I knew of him, which was not little, tended to prove him an arrogant, bullying, envious, false, and dishonest man; he tried in life to bully me, he cheated me, and cowered from the responsibility when charged with it; he abused and depreciated me behind my back, and curried favour to my face; he had done his best to injure me by defamation, and then was obliged to sue to me for the assistance of my talent. He is gone—unpitied, unlamented; he had no friend.

February 16th.—Forster told me of Leigh Hunt's ingratitude to him, who has done everything for him for years; he is not a good man, nor a good-*natured* man.

February 19th.—Went to Drury Lane theatre. Acted Ruthven fairly; was called for and well received by the audience. Very much disgusted and irritated by Mr. Elton *walking out* in the last scene, and converting what was arranged as a most terrible and picturesque murder into a miserable hustle! I was excessively annoyed, but on reflection thought it wiser to leave him to a beggar's consolation—of having had his own way, and paying for it; he is a most wretched specimen of imbecile vanity.

February 21st.—A Mr. Esdaile called, wishing for instruction to aid him in going on the stage; I with kindness and earnestness dissuaded him from following so unprofitable and demoralizing a calling, and told him I had rather see one of my children dead than on the stage. He left me very grateful for my advice.

February 23rd.—Walked out with Edward and called on Dickens, having seen his solicitor's advertisement versus Bartley in the *Examiner*. Urged on him the necessity of arranging the quarrel with Bartley, and dissuaded him from answering any attack that B—— might make upon him next week. He showed me a letter he had prepared, but I requested him not to send it. He is quite in the wrong. He makes a contract, which he considers advantageous at the time, but subsequently finding his talent more lucrative than he had supposed, he

45

refused to fulfil the contract. Talfourd came in in the evening and gave us an amusing account of a correspondence between Lady Seymour and Lady Shuckburgh.[1] Madame Vestris, it appears, has issued a rescript in her *affiches* to the effect that all places reserved are to be charged one guinea each. No newspaper takes notice of this ; no newspaper noticed the difference of my arrangements. Had I done half as much, how they would have swooped upon me. What is there more vile and worthless than a newspaper writer ?—perhaps a lawyer.

February 24th.—Spoke to Mrs. Warner, requesting her to be more careful, as she struck the dagger in my face. She said, " I beg your pardon, sir, etc." It was most painful to me to think that a woman, for whom I had entertained an affection, and who had once loved me, could be so estranged from me. Such is the world !

February 28th.—Went to Drury Lane theatre and acted there Ruthven very fairly ; was called for and well received by the audience. Willmott had mentioned to me a rumour that Mr. Hammond had not been seen for two days, and the general belief was that he had decamped with the receipts of the Command night ; but this we both thought unlikely. After the play Lunn informed me that the report through the theatre was that Mr. Hammond had been captured and was in prison. I sent for Mr. Copeland, who was not to be found. Willmott came, and told me his belief was that the worst reports were true, that it was quite certain there were sheriff's officers in the theatre. I sent for Mr. C. Jones, treasurer, and for Mr. Copeland ; messengers searched for them all through the theatre. They were not to be, or would not be, found. Not a person in the theatre to speak with on business ! ! I talked with Willmott, and our confident apprehension was that the worst was true. He promised to send or let me know in the morning. A note, asking my autograph, and one from Bulwer, asking me to subscribe to an annuity for the destitute mother of L. E. L. Came home and told the sad news.

February 29th.—Willmott came and informed me that a fiat of

[1] Lady Seymour, afterwards Duchess of Somerset, who had recently enacted the " Queen of Beauty " in the Eglinton tournament, wrote to Lady Shuckburgh for the character of a servant named Stedman, inquiring whether she was a good plain cook. Lady Shuckburgh, a baronet's "lady" who would have made a suitable consort to Sir Vavasour Firebrace, replied that having a professed cook and housekeeper she knew nothing about the under-servants. Lady Seymour retorted that she understood Stedman had some practice in cooking for the little Shuckburghs. The baronet's " lady " retaliated by directing a housemaid to reply in the following terms : " Stedman informs me that your ladyship does not keep either a cook or a housekeeper, and that you only require a girl who can cook a mutton chop ; if so, Stedman or any other scullion will be found fully equal to cook for or manage the establishment of the Queen of Beauty."

46

bankruptcy had been issued against Hammond, which sequestered his effects and monies up to Friday; that the proprietors had seized on the receipts of last night, and that the agreements with the actors, etc., were at an end.   He spoke of several plans suggested; I would hear of none involving myself, but expressed myself willing to act gratuitously on Monday for the poorer performers.   Phelps, Bennett and Yarnold called to tell me they would not act and to ask, I suppose, my opinion.   I told them, the best thing was to take the best situations that offered, and wait for better times, which could not come until worse had passed away.   Willmott came with a deputation from the Drury Lane Company—Messrs. Vining, W. Bennett, and A. Lee—to say that the Sub-Committee had agreed to let them the theatre for £25 per night—which was not to be exacted if not received—and that they would guarantee my full salary if I would play next week for them.   I expressed myself willing and happy to see the gentlemen on any other business, or in any other capacity than as deputies from the Drury Lane Company, to which I did not belong; but if there was any business Mr. Willmott could acquaint me with it.   Willmott, therefore, came, and the others were left in the coach (which was an oversight on my part, I ought to have asked them into another room whilst I spoke with Willmott).   I told him, as to receiving the whole of my salary, whilst any one else received only a part of his or hers, *he knew* I would not hear of such a thing: he said he had told them so.   I added that I would not be concerned in any sharing plan, nor be mixed in any way with them; that I would play gratuitously on Monday, but could not do more.   He had scarcely left me when I felt so uncomfortable and agitated that I was conscious I had done wrong.   I came into the drawing-room, wishing to vent my confused and tumultuous thoughts for mere relief.   I sent the children, rather abruptly and pettishly, to bed, which I should not have done, but I was suffering very much, and had lost command of myself.   When they were gone I said I had placed myself in an assailable position—I had not done right, I must instantly correct the fault I had committed, I must write to Willmott and say I would play gratuitously the whole week.   Edward was against it, but Catherine and Letty were instantly and strongly in favour of it.   I went down-stairs, wrote the note, persisting in refusing the actors' offer, but agreeing to play for them through the week, on condition that Haynes's three nights' pay was secured to him.   Sent it and received Willmott's acknowledgment.   Went to Lord Northampton's, P.R.S.   Met Sir H. Ellis, Dr. Lardner, Elliotson, Jerdan, Stanfield, Sir M. Shee, Irwins, Pickersgill, G. Byng, Brockedon,

Babbage, Lord Lansdowne, Dr. Williamson, Bishop, Emerson Tennant, T. Moore, etc., Passed a pleasant evening.

March 1st.—Called on Bulwer, whom we found before his breakfast-table, apparently jaded and worn out with last night's debauch; he told us he had only got to bed by half-past seven. I asked him if he was at Lord Northampton's; he said no, but had heard from Lord Lansdowne that I was there—that Lord L—— spoke very pleasantly of me. We talked of the Drury Lane paralysis, and of the prospect of the Haymarket, etc., of the vote on Sir John Newport's job [1]; he said the Ministers were too strong to care for anything, having a vote of confidence. I was sorry to hear this. Edward left us, and Willie and I went on to Lady Blessington's. I met Fonblanque by the door and was very glad to see him. Sir Andrew Barnard [2] was with Lady Blessington and a very pretty girl, a Miss Power. Lady Blessington talked almost to fatigue me, and chiefly in abuse of the Queen.

March 3rd.—Mr. W. Farren called, and detained me the whole afternoon, informing me of a libellous paragraph in the *Satirist* about Miss H. Faucit and of his hope of discovering the propagator of the scandalous rumours against her; mentioned his desire that she should come up, and attend the meeting of the Haymarket performers and that Webster should publish her physician's certificates. I had spoken to Lunn in the early part of the evening, and asked him very *searchingly* if he had ever said anything light, or disrespectful of, or in any way reflecting on, Miss Faucit. He very solemnly denied any such charge—repeatedly to my various interrogatories; he said he had heard persons speak lightly and jestingly of her at Covent Garden and at Drury Lane, that he had always asserted she only saw me on business, etc. I asked him if any other lady's name had been mentioned with mine. He said "Yes: Miss Montague's" (!!!). I asked if any other; he said "Yes: Miss Horton's!" This almost assumes a ridiculous appearance, if it does not involve the reputation—in some *degree*—and perhaps the peace of mind of an amiable girl.

March 4th.—I went with Nina and Letitia to Elstree. My journey was a melancholy one; every familiar object on the road, the road itself, leading over Brockley Hill, as I caught it in the distance, looked as if

---

[1] Sir John Newport was Comptroller of the Exchequer, a post which the Government induced him to resign in favour of Mr. Spring Rice, who was retiring from the Ministry with a peerage. A vote of censure on the conduct of the Government was carried by 240 to 212 votes, but they refused to resign, relying on a vote of confidence carried by a majority of a few weeks before.

[2] Sir Andrew Francis Barnard (1773–1855); a distinguished general.

part of the happy thoughts that were associated with what I think of as my home of many happy years. How often in coming here have I left care, and evil passion, and degrading thoughts behind me, and felt, as the beauty of the landscape opened and the inspiring freshness of the air breathed on me, my heart spring up and burn within me in gratitude to God and love of His works seen, heard, and felt around me. I must leave it—my home, my home! Farewell, dear, dear Elstree! I leave the fields, the trees, and flowers, among which my heart has pondered on the infinite benevolence of God, and worshipped Him in wonder and fulness of delight. Saw old Norma, who bounded about with delight, dear old dog. The tears were on the cheeks of Nina and Letitia more than once, and filled my eyes. Farewell. Note from Mr. Farren about Lunn and Miss Faucit. Miss Horton came, with Serle, to dine; I spoke to her about Ophelia. We had a very cheerful and pleasant day.

March 5th.—I subjected Lunn again to a very stern questioning in the presence of Catherine on the subject of the calumnies spread abroad about dear Miss Faucit. He steadfastly denied ever having encouraged a thought against her. Browning called. Wrote to Mrs. Braysher,[1] telling her of the evidence we had obtained. Wrote note to Pratt. Mr. Braysher called and talked very long about this unhappy affair of Miss Faucit. He gave me Mrs. Braysher's letter. I objected, as he did, to notice the *Satirist*.

March 7th.—A letter from Mr. Braysher expressing his apprehensions of the injury done to Miss Helen Faucit being beyond the reach of law; it staggered me very much at first, but on reflection I could not believe it. Miss P. Horton called, and I went over the part of Ophelia with her. Mr. Farren called—to meet Mr. Braysher, who came at his appointed hour—half-past four. I strongly urged, against all lawyers, the necessity of commencing an action against Miss Faucit's defamers and of putting up the notice in the green-room.

March 8th.—Went with Edward to the railway station. Took my seat, and reached Twyford in an hour and five minutes. Continued my journey by coach, and read through the first volume of *Wilhelm Meister*, with which I was so charmed that I could not discontinue it. There were many passages on it, which forced upon me sad reflections on my own position, and the recurrence of these painful thoughts made my journey one of the most melancholy I have taken for some time. Where there is sorrow in this world, except for a bereavement under

---

[1] A friend of Miss Faucit, who was for some time a resident in her house.

the dispensation of God, there is certainly error, and I cannot conceal from myself that I have erred, though not, I think (and I hope I do not deceive myself) as from a superficial glance it might appear. There is no doubt —— had felt an admiration for me, which amounted to love. Her manner in parting with me was manifest proof of it. Her subsequent meeting with me strengthened this feeling in her and made her an object of interest to me. I could not—at least I did not feel that I could—show coldness to her, though I really wished her good angel had removed her from me. Time has made her partiality a passion and her injuries and sufferings have deepened my interest for her into a sincere affection, but one which I can avow without any self-reproach for the feeling. My anxiety for her is quite a painful sensation.

Bristol, March 9th.—Rehearsed Macbeth, and tried to profit by the suggestions I had caught from Goethe yesterday, in *making* myself my character independently of the persons around me ; hoped to be able to carry my purpose into effect at night, but shuddered at the styles and language of those who environed me. Dined frugally and rested— looking at *Wilhelm Meister*, and then tried to get my mind filled with Macbeth. Went to the theatre and tried to act Macbeth ; but, the witches first—ducking or burning could only have properly rewarded them ; then Banquo, shutting his eyes, and making himself amiable and heroic in turns ; then Duncan, an out-and-out-wretch ; but it was all so bad—Banquo coming on as the ghost with his face painted exactly like the clown in a pantomime ! It was so bad that I felt and said, "money could not pay for the sense of degradation endured in such a set of persons." Nor can it—it is impossible to preserve one's self-respect. I laboured—I thought of Goethe, I thought of using the occasion as a study—it would not do, *it was too bad.* I was "hewed like a carcase fit for hounds." Was called for, and well received.

March 10th.—What a mere dream my life appears as I look back upon it ! This most unfortunate calling of a player—which never permits a man to feel that he is growing old, but lets him start out of a sort of opium-sleep of fantasies, air-built castles, flatteries and frettings, sensual dreams, and ill-kept resolutions, to find himself on the very verge of age—has been to me a greater misfortune than to most of those who have embarked on it. I am not philosophic enough to be patient under wrong or misconstruction, or misrepresentation, and in losing the sedative of "the country" I lose my hold on hope of self-amendment. I am the victim of an ill-regulated, and morbid imagination, and to what its agency may lead me I cannot see. For my dearest children's sake God grant it may be to good. Amen! I thought, and resolved much—but with what result!

March 11th.—A morning of angry and painful thought follows a restless night. But in *any situation of life of what use is anger?* It occupies and weakens in its after-effects the mind, and incapacitates the judgment. Vindictive measures, personal retaliation—recrimination on the circulators of these falsehoods about Miss Faucit, have alternately held fierce possession of my mind; but it is only from calm reflection we can act with propriety and dignity, and I am persuaded that an inflexible adherence to principle is the only sure, at least the surest, plan of human happiness. A letter from my beloved Catherine, in the sweetest tone of mind, comes like a sunny omen of good from heaven to cheer and confirm me. It expresses fears for her mother's declining health, which I think is breaking—and gives me a detailed account of home; encloses cards for dinner on Sunday next from Lord Lansdowne and Lady Blessington. Answered her, and the invitations, accepting Lord Lansdowne's, which was the first, and declining Lady Blessington's. I learned to-day that the Chancery suit on my grandfather's will, begun about the year 1811—or 12, was terminated a short time since; the amount contested was about £20,000, and a few weeks, or months ago, Mrs. McC—— received as my father's share £37 11s.!!! The family of my Uncle Tom are left in actual indigence, and all the other members of the family have spent considerable sums; my father £200 or £300—to get this £37, etc. It is one of many lessons on *accursed Law*—not to be lost.

March 12th.—Began the day with reflections on my expenses, my slanderous assailants, and turned to the personation of Hamlet, which I continued till I rose. Computed the expense of my new furniture with the omission of several intended things, and *decided.* Began working on *Richelieu,* which I have forgotten. Received letters from dearest Catherine; very comfortable and comforting, except in the account of her mother's health; and one from ——; the latter is very nicely written, but she signs it ——. Is this in her fond gratitude, or is it that she does not see, that she has not learned the necessity of wrestling with a passion, and moderating it to a deep and tender friendship? Such is the feeling, before God, that I desire to preserve and prove to her. God assist and carry into purpose and act, even to the end, my proper and honourable intentions. Went to the theatre to play; but all the day, and all the night, through the whole play, I was *haunted* by one word—it was in my brain as I walked behind the scenes, and seemed written down before me as I sat at my toilet, each time that I returned to my room. This word was ——. Does it mean anything? *Does it not?* Does she examine her own heart? I fear not. She really is amiable, but I believe she is *blind* to her own position. She would seem to intimate to me that she loves me with a love beyond what friends indulge in, or why ——? Here is an evidence of the ill-effect of the absence of a *principle*. She may very naturally love me more than she has ever done. She may think or feel she has more reason. But she has noble and solacing motives to sustain her in at least *the struggle* with her emotion. It is a subject on which I cannot write to her, lest her letters be seen, but I pray to God that I may act rightly towards her, and make her *my friend* by deserving still more her gratitude and friendship. I will hope so and strive so. God strengthen and assist me. Acted Ruthven as well as I could, but with such a set—oh! it was too bad. This *word* still pursues me. And it is addressed to an ill-regulated, an over-excited, a morbid imagination —one that I have difficulty in controlling even without suggestion to unhealthy action. But I will do what is right. I will believe all that is good of her, and think, as is probable, it is the mere want of the strong terms, "affectionate, etc.," which her feelings *need* to express themselves, that she has recourse to this most familiar method. God bless her, and make her, and keep her a good girl.

London, March 15th.—Went to dinner at Lord Lansdowne's. Met some agreeable persons, with Fonblanque, Bulwer, Pigott, the Solicitor-General for Ireland, and Lord Normanby. Liked Lady Lansdowne, though she impressed me with the idea of a proud person at first. The day was pleasant to me, and I was much struck with the beautiful works of art I saw there. *Fortunati nimium,* who are born to such possessions.

March 16th.—Was nervous and uncertain about the performance of Hamlet to-night—regretting that I had not made myself secure of my feeling through the part. Went to the theatre and rehearsed Hamlet; took pains with Miss Horton also. First night of engagement at Haymarket.[1] Went to theatre and acted Hamlet very carefully and very well. The new effect of the pictures on the wall of the apartment was a very great improvement on the old stupid custom. Was called for and very well received by the audience. Miss Horton

---

[1] This engagement at the Haymarket continued to the end of this year and up to March 13 in the following year (1841)—(*note by Sir F. Pollock*).

52

made quite a success in Ophelia, and was very warmly received indeed. Bulwer, Jerdan, Forster, Maclise came into my room. All were much pleased, but Bulwer was quite delighted; I never saw him so enthusiastic. I was very much pleased. Thank God, all went so well.

March 17th.—Went to Forster, and did not spend a pleasant evening with him and Mr. R. Cattermole over disputation. Dickens came in in the evening—Procter had previously gone. Upon reflection I cannot too heavily blame myself for permitting my feelings so to overmaster me as to enter into a discussion with Mr. Cattermole on religion and policy. I was shocked at the narrow and uncharitable views he took of the rights of his fellow-men. God help them, these are their souls' curators!!

March 19th.—Went with dear little Edward to Elstree, reading *Wilhelm Meister* by the way. My heart yearned within me as I again approached the village and the home endeared to me by so long a residence, by so much enjoyed, so much endured, by my blessed children's births and by my own meditations amid the fields and flowers —among the birds and beneath the naked cope of heaven. And to leave it—to leave so much that is so dear! It is consecrated in my memory by all that makes life dear. Beloved home—farewell—farewell—my heart is torn in departing from you! All was in the confusion of packing and removal. The once cheerful little rooms looked desolate, sad, and dreary, and poor Mrs. East looked the picture of melancholy. I looked at all around me perhaps for the last time.

March 20th.—Went to theatre, and rehearsed Shylock. Heard of the return of Mr. C. Kemble to the stage being announced for Tuesday next by special Command! It is only what might be expected from him—what else has he?—he can neither think, nor read!

March 21st.—Called on Maclise, and saw again his grand picture of Macbeth. The figure of Lady Macbeth, which I had not seen before, I thought the ideal of the character: it is a noble conception. His picture of Olivia I can look at for ever; it is beauty, moral and physical, personified. Forster told me some news that shocked us all —that Dr. Lardner had eloped with a married woman, the wife of a magistrate at Brighton, who had left a husband and three children to accompany him; they were said to have gone to France. I am truly sorry for this wretched act of folly and crime, which I believe to have originated in *vanity*.[1]

[1] See note, p. 6, Vol. I.

March 22nd.—Mr. T. Landseer called, the amiable, kind-hearted creature! Maclise called, the poet-painter! Looked at the papers. Spent the evening with my blessed, blessed children and family, talking afterwards with dearest Catherine and Letitia.

March 24th.—Dickens called, and we walked together, calling on Maclise, to Forster's, where we met at dinner Raymond, Chitty,[1] T. Hill, Jerdan, Stanfield, R. Price, Procter and Fox. Blanchard came in the evening. A cheerful day.

March 25th.—Gave the children their lessons and hurried to the theatre, where I rehearsed Richelieu. Heard that Mr. C. Kemble, who played to an overflowing house last night, is announced for Mercutio to-morrow. Here is one of the most striking instances of charlatanry that ever was exhibited. A man, only a second-rate performer, and never in any esteem beyond that grade in his best day, on breaking the pledge he had given not to appear again, *attire la foule*, and is spoken of by the papers (the papers—the moral filth of humanity!) as something wonderful! It is a waste of indignation and contempt to give a thought to such quackery.

March 27th.—Read an account of Mr. C. Kemble in the *Times*, which seemed really ironical, so hyperbolical in its overlaid fulsomeness. These are your critics!

March 28th.—Read the newspapers; lifted my eyes in astonishment at Jerdan's *ecstatic* notice of C. Kemble's performance of Don Felix, which he began with the observation that " no one who had not seen it could form an idea of it "; and as he *had not seen it himself*, being at dinner with me in Forster's chambers, I wasted no thought of indignation on a thing so ridiculously profligate.

March 29th.—Browning called, and presented me with his book of *Sordello;* he sat some time, and the Procters called. When they had gone I asked Browning to stay dinner, which he did. He gave his account of his quarrel with Forster, in which certainly Forster appears the blamable party.

March 30th.—Saw with pain and sorrow Bulwer's name and his domestic troubles vulgarized by the report of the trials in France. It is a sad instance of the dreadful penalties attending an *indiscretion !!!* or rather, in his case, indiscretions; for though the first includes all, his ill-advised, ill-assorted *marriage—the great cast in every man's life for good or ill*—yet still his infidelities since to his detestable wife,

---

[1] Probably Thomas Chitty (1802–1878), the eminent special pleader; father of Lord Justice Chitty.

however provoked or excusable to some persons they may appear, now bitterly revenge themselves on him, in preventing him from gaining the redress he might seek, and in many instances excluding him from sympathy.   A high-hearted, honourable man, condemned for life to misery !   *What an example !*

April 1st.—A letter from Miss Helen Faucit, informing me that she had fallen back in health, and was now going for change to Brighton. I do not think she will recover ; she has been cared for too late.   How very, very much we miss her now, with these Mrs. Warners and Yarnolds !   Copy of *Lear* from C. Knight, who gives a long disquisition upon the bad taste of N. Tate and those who acted his version of *King Lear,* but cannot spare one word for the successful attempt to place Shakspeare in his own form again upon the stage.

April 3rd.—Went to the theatre, and acted Shylock very well. Was in low spirits, hearing of the houses at Covent Garden—to see that which when at its best was merely second-rate, and now that it is incapable, *attire la foule*—of fools.   Our houses are falling, and the want of something to draw attention to our theatre makes me, apprehensive as I always am, nervous and uneasy.

April 4th.—Read the newspapers ; was really sickened by Jerdan's absurd notice of C. Kemble.   Forster called, and told me that I had been abused in the *Sunday Times !*   Received a pamphlet in verse called *The Lament,* on the closing of Drury Lane.   Found first number of *Master Humphrey's Clock,* which I pray may have great success.

April 5th.—Read over Haynes's three acts, which he left with me yesterday, and found them *hopeless.*   His indolence gives him much more trouble and labour than a more daring and enterprising man would have to undergo.   *Because* he had written part of this play before, he did not like to lose it, and so has expended these two months on utter trash, as far as the subject is concerned, instead of rushing at some bold and stirring plot.   Poor Haynes ! he has too little of the Promethean quality ever to do anything great.   Went out with Willie, and called to see Maclise's pictures ; was greatly pleased with all he had done to the picture of Macbeth, which I think is a grand and wild treatment of a finely imagined and most poetically conceived subject. We continued our walk to Stanfield, and saw his beautiful pictures of Sorrento, Salerno, Avignon, St. Malo, etc.   Went on with Willie to Mr. T. Landseer's ; saw Mrs. Landseer and her little boy.   Mr. T. L—— went with us to Edwin Landseer's ; we had to wait some time. I saw his father—an old, deaf man ; [1] in his large painting-room were Count D'Orsay, Lord Normanby, and some others whose faces I knew, but could not recollect. E. Landseer had his hat off, and D'Orsay took off his, as I did mine. Seeing Normanby and the others *covered*, I put on mine, but in a moment reflected that it was to Landseer I owed the courtesy of a gentleman, if the others chose to forget it, and I directly uncovered. I saw at once the superiority of E. Landseer's pencil—his sure expression and absence of all hardness. Mrs. Norton, Duke of Beaufort, Mrs. Jameson, Miss Rogers and others came in. I was very much delighted.

April 9th.—Letter from Miss Faucit, informing me of the improvement in her health, which I was truly grateful to learn. Looked at the paper, in which was the maiden speech of Mr. Thesiger—bullying and foul-mouthed according to custom.[2] Going out, called on Dickens, who told me that if the demand for *Humphrey's Clock* was sustained to its present pitch, it would be £10,000 per annum to him, at which I heartily rejoice. Walked to Regent Street with Dickens, and took a cab home. Rested after dinner. The servant brought me in a card, Mr. Thomas Moore, and told me the gentleman would take no denial. I could not imagine it to be Tom Moore, and went out in a very ill humour ; to my surprise, it was the bright little man himself. We went up-stairs, and he wanted to visit the Haymarket with Mrs. Moore and his son, who is going out to India. I told him to ask for his own private box, which I procured for him when I went to the theatre.

April 10th.—Returning, read over *Master Humphrey*—No. 1 again —on which I had a questioning feeling of whether or no it was too good for so wide a circulation. I trust not. Mrs. Talfourd called in a new equipage.

April 11th.—Webster called after dinner, and asked me about Miss Faucit's first appearance, having received a letter from her. She wished to open in the *Lady of Lyons*. I think it would have been as well *not*.

---

[1] John Landseer (1769–1852) ; a well-known engraver.

[2] Poor Mr. Thesiger *avait toujours tort !* It would be difficult to cite a single instance, in the nineteenth century at all events, of a "bullying and foul-mouthed" maiden speech in the House of Commons. If Macready is to be credited, Thesiger was a liberal blend of Lord Thurlow and Sir Fletcher Norton, whereas in reality he was the essence of courtliness and good manners, but he had committed the unpardonable crime of holding a brief for Alfred Bunn and of commenting with a certain amount of freedom on the manager's assailant. Talfourd, however, Macready's own counsel, came off very little better, having, in his client's estimation, sold the case.

Dickens called for me, and we went together to Lord Northampton's.[1] Saw there Babbage, Maclise, Etty, Pickersgill, Horner, Jerdan, Stanfield, Lord Aberdeen, Archbishop of Canterbury, Cartwright, Sir H. Ellis, Sir Richard Jenkins, T. Hook, Dr. Dibdin, Sir D. Wilkie. Walked home with Dickens.

April 12th.—Mrs. Carlyle and a Mrs. Stirling[2] called and sat some time. Mr. Howe then came, and I read over to him the part of Henry in *Glencoe*, observing to him that in giving him the opportunity of playing the part, I did not pledge myself that he should do it, unless he proved himself qualified for it. He took the book to write out his part, promising to return it to-morrow afternoon. Etty, Forster, Maclise and Mrs. Dickens came to dine with us.

April 14th.—Looked at the paper, and read with grief, and really with horror, the account of the husband and father of Mrs. Heaviside entering the apartments occupied by Dr. Lardner and herself at an hotel in Paris—the Hôtel Tronchet—and forcibly removing her, and inflicting dreadful punishment on that wretched man, Lardner. The very hopelessness of his condition—the fact, as I perceive it, of his being out of the pale of sympathy, makes the consequence of his guilt and folly so terrible, so utterly miserable, that whilst I condemn him to the utmost extent of his fault, whilst I admit that I would have shot him as a *dog* for the same outrage on my peace, still, I cannot help pitying the wretched, the deplorably wretched man. He has shown real interest in me ; he has sat often and often at my table—I had a sincere regard for him, and I cannot see him sink thus into hopeless misery and infamy without compassion. God help us all. I cannot help mingling sorrow and pity with the angry censure I pronounce upon him.

April 17th.—Mr. Boyle called, and we went to Elstree, taking dear Katy with us. I was again quite sad to think of leaving it. I walked again and again in the garden and through the various rooms, imagining hours and faces and voices that have, as it were, furnished them to me with sweet and sad recollections. Saw our dear old dog Norma, who leapt about me with so much joy that my reluctance to part with her is greater than ever. Left the dear old house and returned to London, setting down Mr. Boyle in Edgware Road, and driving to Clarence Terrace, where I found the greater part of the family and Mrs. Dickens,

---

[1] The Marquis of Northampton was then President of the Royal Society, and gave soirées at his house in Piccadilly—(*note by Sir F. Pollock*).

[2] Probably Mrs. Sterling, the mother of Carlyle's friend, John Sterling.

who came to ask us to dine with them on Sunday. I demurred, for I did not wish it, but at length assented. Took Mrs. Dickens home and saw Dickens, who gave me No. 3 of *Humphrey*. Saw my little god-daughter; God bless her! Came to York Gate; found a note from Forster. Read No. 3; the first part very pleasing, the latter portion of extraordinary power.

April 25th.—Rehearsed the *Lady of Lyons*; saw Miss Helen Faucit. I was quite pleased to see her so well and apparently so strong; she was very glad to see me. Acted Claude Melnotte partially well; was called for, but hearing Miss Faucit's name, thought it right she should have her undivided applause, and desired that some one else should lead her on, which was done. Went on afterwards, to the continued call, and was well received. David Colden came into my room and accompanied me to Babbage's, where I saw Sidney Smith, Professor Wheatstone, the Brockedons, two or three whom I knew, but not by name, Harness, Travers, Hawes, Lady Stepney, Dr. Arnott, Milman, the Bishop of Norwich (Stanley),[1] who wished to be known to me. I had a very interesting conversation with him, a man I admire and reverence so much, speaking with great warmth of the effort I had made and the probable effect if carried out. I was very much pleased with him.

April 29th.—Looked over the paper, which affords me very little satisfaction. I see human nature degrading itself to a state of mental subjection that makes the heart sick with despondency of good. Went out, and hastened down to King's College, where I saw Professor Wheatstone, who showed the persons present his electric telegraph, and his speaking machine, which uttered clearly the words " Mamma, papa, mother, thumb, summer." I was amply recompensed for the visit I paid him. I saw Milman there, who was very courteous. Called at several shops and priced various articles of furniture. Looked in at the Water-colour Exhibition, and saw some very beautiful things by Copley Fielding and Prout. Called at the Haymarket, and spoke to Webster on business. Called at Holloway's and paid for my prints.

May 1st.—Looked at the newspaper, and was amused with the staunch and vigorous inveteracy of O'Connell. Went to the private view of the Royal Academy, and was much gratified with what I saw; I think it is one of the best exhibitions I have seen; all the distinguished artists are up to a high mark, except Turner, who is lamentable. Saw

---

[1] Edward Stanley (1779–1849); Bishop of Norwich from 1837 to 1849. A church reformer, and advanced Liberal; father of Dean Stanley.

D'Orsay, Etty, C. Landseer, Edwin Landseer, Maclise, Mrs. Dickens, Stanfield, T. Hill, Mr. W. Russell.

May 5th.—Went to Carlyle's lecture, which I cannot recollect although I listened with the utmost attention to it, and was greatly pleased with it. Saw, among others, Mrs. Jameson and Browning. Went to the theatre. Thought on Hamlet. Acted Hamlet, as I thought, in a most real and effective manner. Was well satisfied with myself. Alexander Dumas, with two friends, came into my room after the play. Very much pleased. Dumas told me he had undertaken to translate Macbeth, and that Ligier [1] would come over to consult me about its performance. Talfourd came—Browning to speak about his play.

May 8th.—Attended Carlyle's lecture, " The Hero as a Prophet : Mahomet " ; on which he descanted with a fervour and eloquence that only a conviction of truth could give. I was charmed, carried away by him. Met Browning there. The only point on which I did not assent to the doctrines of Carlyle—for in some instances he uttered thoughts that had been brooding in my own heart, and even found a voice, particularly that of Mahomet's instancing man himself as the greatest miracle—the point of exception was in his attributing sincerity to David. David might have been sincere through all his errors of passion and the infirmity of a resisting power to sensual temptation, but on his death-bed recommended the cold-blooded slaughter, or assassination, of Joab—his faithful soldier—to Solomon. What can excuse the dastardly hypocrisy of such an act, and at such a time?

May 9th.—Talfourd came into my room. He mentioned the report that the valet of Lord William Russell had confessed the murder. [2] The *bruit* which is made about this poor old man's death makes one ask why was poor Mr. Templeman permitted to die without any anxiety on the part of Prince Albert and Lord Normanby? When will the day of humanity's vindication arrive? Dickens came, and we went in his carriage, all three, to Babbage's. The room was very much crowded, but I saw few that I knew there—Wheatstone, Edward Kater, Lady Stepney, and Rogers, who invited Dickens and myself to dine with him on Sunday fortnight. Talfourd left us soon ; Dickens set me down.

[1] The distinguished tragedian of the Théâtre François—(*note by Sir F. Pollock*).

[2] Benjamin Courvoisier, a Swiss ; the trial as well as the murder created a great sensation, the conduct of Courvoisier's counsel, Mr. Charles Phillips, who continued his efforts to obtain acquittal although aware of the prisoner's confession, being much censured.

May 10th.—Forster came in as we sat down to dinner. He talked very much of my abjuration of the Whigs. I abjure them as a set of heartless, empirical, political scoundrels—in a Pickwickian sense; nothing personal, of course.

May 11th.—Went to theatre. Rehearsed *Glencoe*, which wears an appearance of much promise. Acted Claude Melnotte fairly; was called for. Miss —— said something about striving to overcome her fondness for me, and that she thought I wished it. I do wish it. For I have a sincere and strong regard—an affectionate one for her, and do not wish it to be endangered or interrupted.

May 12th.—Went to Carlyle's lecture on Dante and Shakspeare. Saw Browning and Mrs. Jameson there; was disappointed in his treatment of the subject; his comments were not up to the height of his great argument. He said little that was impressive; he quoted a passage about "histriones et nebulones," and spoke of managers of playhouses being the most insignificant of human beings, which made me smile, but sent the blood into my face, as I fancied the thoughts of many present would revert to myself—but possibly they never descended from the subject to me.

May 17th.—Forster came to dinner; passed a cheerful day, but Forster annoyed me by his absurd controversial spirit, which he never indulges without displaying the most vexatious casuistry.

May 18th.—Went to the theatre, reading *Glencoe*. Began the rehearsal, but only proceeded in it for two scenes, Messrs. Warde, Phelps, and J. Webster being absent. McIan called to speak to me about the dress. Miss P. Horton told me that I was the subject of general abuse in the green-room, which I can easily believe. I have had experience enough of players to know that their ignorance and their vanity combine to make them a most ungrateful set of persons.

May 19th.—Went to the theatre, where I found confusion and uncertainty. After some time rehearsed the fifth and first acts. McIan was there, and one would suppose the being of his clan depended on the issue of this play. Dickens and Forster came, and thought Mr. Webster the best available representative for McIan; but the play is not cast to its demand, and is *hurried* forward. God prosper it! Went with Maclise and Forster to Carlyle's lecture on the man of letters as the great man; was very interested and edified. Read three acts of *Glencoe*.

May 21st.—Went to the theatre and remained there the whole day, Dickens and Forster were at the rehearsal, and Forster prompted

me on one occasion, with which I could have well dispensed.   Dined
at the theatre, and was quite overcome with fatigue.   Read over my
part of Halbert Macdonald.   Webster came in, and informed me that
Mr. S. Knowles had been to the box-office, booked himself at *full length*
for a place, and told the box-keeper that he must come and see his
friend Talfourd's play; that he knew it was Talfourd's; that it was
printed, and that Moxon, who was Talfourd's publisher, was his also!
This man calls Talfourd his friend, and a good friend Talfourd has
been *to him*.   He *knows* that Talfourd wishes to conceal the authorship, but he does not know how strong may be his motives, nor
whether he may wish it *ever to be known* that he has written it, and yet
he is the man who goes about to publish this important secret of his
friend.   Qu. : Was it not confided to him under a promise of secrecy?
Such is Mr. James Sheridan Knowles.

May 22nd.—Called on Dickens; told him of this Mr. Knowles, etc.
He determined to go to Talfourd at once and tell him.   Went to the
theatre and carefully rehearsed the play of *Glencoe*.   Dickens called to
tell me that Talfourd would write to Moxon immediately about the
breach of confidence in regard to his play.   Received a note from
Talfourd, evidently much annoyed by the treachery of Moxon and
Knowles.   Answered it, stating what I wished to be in his preface.
Read over my part of Halbert Macdonald.

May 23rd.—Thought over the possible issue of to-night and what
I resolved to do, and drew omens of good from many incidents about
me.   Looked at the newspaper and went to the Haymarket theatre.
Rehearsed the play and returned home.   Lay down to rest afterwards.
Went to the theatre, and, in the character of Halbert Macdonald
in Talfourd's play of *Glencoe*, I did all I could do—all that the
very short period allowed for preparation allowed me to do.   The
audience became very fervent, although I felt, in the second act, that
the persons in the front were disposed to be ill-natured.   Was called
for by the house, and, when silence was obtained, I informed them that
I had a little history to relate concerning the play; that it had been
placed in my hands by a friend, as the work of a gentleman named
Collinson, who had written to me once, but that, in entering on the
work, I felt no more interest in it than the general anxiety I feel on
subjects appertaining to dramatic literature.   I felt deeply as I read
it, and I argued that what had touched me so nearly could not be
without effect more generally.   Mr. Webster accepted it unhesitatingly,
and it was some time after that I was made acquainted with the real

author, a name which I had pleasure in communicating as they would have in hearing, being that of one whose pen had been invariably exercised in asserting the benefit and beauty and blessing of an earnest faith in good—it was Mr. Serjeant Talfourd's. This was greatly applauded, and I gave out the play for three nights' representations per week till further notice. Talfourd rushed into my room to thank me, and Dickens, Maclise, etc., also came. Went to sup with Talfourd —a heavy supper—taking David Colden with me. Speech-making was the order of a dull evening.[1]

May 24th.—Talfourd and Dickens called for me and we went together to Rogers's, where we dined. Lord and Lady Seymour, Mrs. Norton, Lady Dufferin, Lord Denman, Luttrell, and Poole, with Miss Rogers, were our party. I was pleased with the day, liking Mrs. Norton very much, and being much amused with some anecdotes of Rogers. His collection of pictures is admirable, and the spirit of good taste seems to pervade every nook of his house.[2]

May 25th.—Went to the theatre, and found a card of admission from Miss Kelly for her " Little Theatre," and a note from Mr. Archer, asking me not to exert my influence to prevent his engagement at the Haymarket. Acted Halbert Macdonald better, I think, than on Saturday. The performers in general were languid and careless; the play went very well; I was called for and well received.

May 26th.—Head called about the alteration of my dress. He told

---

[1] The next morning Macready received the following note from Dickens—

> " *Devonshire Terrace,*
> " *Sunday Morning, May 24th.*

" MY DEAR MACREADY,

"Talfourd armed with his proposed preface will call with his carriage first for me to-day and then for you. I arranged on our joint behalf that we would be ready for him at half-past six. I enclose you the letter he received from Knowles and Moxon. Will you put them in your pocket so that he may have them back. The messenger waits to know how Mrs. Macready is after the anxieties and delights of last night. I should think you must be rather the worse to-day. I have seen you play ever since I was that | high, but I never saw you make such a gallant stand as you did last night, or carry anything through so triumphantly and manfully by the force of your own great gifts. If I felt the agitation of an anxious author yesterday, I assure you that I feel the gratitude and admiration of a successful one this morning.

> " Always, dear Macready,
> " Faithfully yours,
> " CHARLES DICKENS.

" W. C. Macready, Esq."

[2] A dinner-party that included the three Sheridan sisters, Dickens, and Luttrell, was exceptional even at Rogers's table.

me that Madame Vestris had got a letter of licence from her creditors for two years! A prosperous mode of managing a national theatre. Acted Halbert Macdonald as well as I could, but the play is borne down by the bad acting—Howe, Phelps, and Mrs. Warner—Mr. Webster also. Talked after the play with Helen Faucit about the languid manner in which she has acted the last two nights.

May 27th.—Looked at the paper, in which I saw that the bishops— those good, religious, charitable, meek and Christian men, those patterns of humanity, those apostles of truth, who make men almost feel assured there *must be hell*—had, with the exception of one qualify- ing voice, the Bishop of Norwich, risen up against the idea of any modification of the *Christian* expressions and simple piety—the clear and intelligible profession of faith—contained in the Prayer Book of the Church of England! The Commons have on the same night refused to entertain the question of modifying the Corn Laws. It is all right, according to the Duke of Buckingham, who thinks nine shillings per week enough for a labourer and his family, and the Arch- bishop of Canterbury, who thinks that *actually* a king—George IV, for instance—*can do no wrong!* Spoke to Helen Faucit, and assured her on the subject of her improvement.

May 28th.—Read *Glencoe* in the afternoon, and went to the theatre. Acted Halbert Macdonald, I think, better than I had before done; was called for, and well received. Forster came into my room and told me that Bulwer was unwell, which I was very sorry to hear. Found Mrs. Reynolds at home; heard that my statement about the play of *Glencoe* was doubted, as I must have known Talfourd's writing : gave her the *original printed copy* I had received. Heard of Leigh Hunt's distress, and of his consequently seeking neglected friends.

May 30th.—Acted Halbert Macdonald with much feeling and pre- cision. I heard Vestris was in the theatre, and saw her applauding vehemently. Has she discovered that a theatre cannot be conducted without actors? or does this mean anything? Was called for by the audience and very warmly received. A note from Talfourd. Forster and Maclise came again to my room.

May 31st.—I called on Lady Blessington, and chatted some time with her and D'Orsay; they wished me to go in the evening. We went on to the Carlyles' and sat half-an-hour with Mrs. Carlyle. I was late home, and late at Talfourd's, where I dined, meeting Serjeant Goul- burn, John M. O'Connell, Serle and Forster. A very bad dinner, and very uninteresting day. Went to Lady Blessington's, where I saw the

Fonblanques, Lords Normanby and Canterbury, Milnes, Chorley, Standish, Rubini, Stuart Wortley, an Italian—Count something, Mr. Palgrave Simpson,[1] and Liszt, the most marvellous pianist I ever heard. I do not know when I have been so excited.

June 2nd.—Acted Halbert Macdonald indifferently; was called for and well received. Spoke to dear Helen Faucit about her languor in acting; she did not seem to meet my objections with the strength of mind and good sense that I had anticipated. She was much depressed. I am much concerned about her. Miss Horton had told me, in reference to Mr. C. Kean, that she thought there was none like myself. I wish the public would think so; but it is pleasant to see oneself loved, if only by a few individuals.

June 6th.—Saw dear, dear old Elstree; looked over with the clerk the fixtures, etc. Spoke to Mr. Wilson on business; left directions with Mrs. East; saw dear old Norma, and, under the faint silver of the afternoon's moon, bade my last adieu to the scene of many, many joys, of many tender and fond associations. May God bless me where I now live or may hereafter live or die! Found Forster at home, who dined with us. Attended to the hanging of the pictures in dining-room. Read "Hope on, hope ever," which wrung my very heart. God bless the writer! Mr. Stuart Wortley called, and I gave him to understand that it was hopeless to think of getting Mr. Webster to produce Lady E.'s play.

June 13th.—Saw in the *Literary Gazette* extracts from that wretched and base fellow's book—Mr. Bunn, which is reported to be full of personalities, but the specimens quoted are very dull and, as might be expected, written very ambitiously in very bad English. Rested and went to the theatre, where I heard that Madame Vestris's liabilities were for £14,000!

June 17th.—After dinner tried—another attempt—utterly desperate—on *Sordello;* it is *not* readable.

June 21st.—Looked at paper; grieved and ashamed to see the courtly—I must say drivelling tone of subserviency that the once proud defender of humanity's rights now takes upon all that is courtly. Is this Fonblanque?

June 23rd.—Wrote to Bessy Robinson, the poor woman with whom I had lodged at Newcastle when I was sixteen years old, thirty-one years ago. What ages of suffering, of passion, of doubt and fear have I since then endured! Would I live it over again? *No.* How truly

[1] John Palgrave Simpson (1807–1857); the well-known dramatist and amateur actor.

do I feel in answering that question what I have often disputed before, that "Joy's recollection is no longer joy, But sorrow's memory is a sorrow still." I sent her £3, for auld lang syne; poor thing, she was always needy. Looked at *Timon of Athens*, but it is (for the stage) only an incident with comments on it. The story is not complete enough—not furnished, I ought to say—with the requisite varieties of passion for a play; it is heavy and monotonous. Received a note and presentation copy of *Glencoe* from Talfourd.

June 24th.—Met Charles Phillips, who talked about Courvoisier, and seemed painfully anxious *to make out his own case* to Edward and myself. He said that the statements of Courvoisier's confession were true; that when he heard of Madame Piolaine he said, "It's all up; I did the deed"; that he, Phillips, upbraided him for telling him so much, and that Courvoisier said his life was in his hands, and he trusted to him to do his best for him; that he, C. Phillips,[1] asked the opinion of an eminent person in Court, who said he ought to go on. That the judges said he did only what was right. He said that Courvoisier admitted the perfect truth of the woman's evidence, but that the police were perjured; that they did not search him on the Wednesday as they said, for he had then about him the gold watch of Lord W. Russell! He said he was snoring when he killed him, that he was dead in a minute, merely making a slight movement of his hand.

June 25th.—Read the paper. Holloway called with some most beautiful engravings, which I could scarcely resist at the enormous

---

[1] Phillips was in an extremely difficult position, but he evidently acted with a great want of judgment. Serjeant Ballantine in his *Experiences*, gives the following view of the situation: "He was bound to continue the defence; although, no doubt, his mode of conducting it could not but be materially affected by the new circumstances. Mr. Phillips, however, adopted a line that was wholly inexcusable. He sought an interview with Mr. Baron Parke—who, it must be remembered, although not the presiding judge, was assisting at the trial—communicated to him the confession of his client, and asked his advice. It is probable that if Baron Parke had not been taken by surprise he would have declined to express any opinion. I happen, however, to know that having learnt that the prisoner did not intend to relieve his counsel from the defence, the learned Baron said that, of course, he must go on with it. And if he gave any advice at all this was the only advice he could give, and it ought to have been patent to the inquirer; certainly no censure can be too severe upon the conduct of Phillips, who, when assailed for the management of his case, violated the confidence that his interview with Baron Parke demanded, and endeavoured to excuse himself by saying he had acted under that learned judge's advice." The Serjeant further remarks that such expressions as "Supposing him to be guilty of the murder, which is known to Almighty God alone," and "I hope for the sake of his eternal soul that he is innocent," proceeding "from the mouth of an advocate possessing the knowledge that Phillips did at the time he used them, were not only offensive to good taste, but scarcely escaped conveying a positive falsehood."

65

prices they were charged. I bought some of the lower-priced ones. I *must* put a stop to any further purchases if I wish to secure my independence and my children's comfort. *I will stop here with the order I have given.* A note, with a small bouquet for my character, from ———. It was short, but it read as if the words in it could not be repressed. It is well for the censorious to exclaim and declaim against the profligacy of persons on the stage, but I am sure no persons are exposed to such temptation, and the wonder is that, with the provocation of so much excitement and so much opportunity, the tendency of our nature is repressed even as it is.

June 26th.—Thought much on the subject of ———. Concluded that I must explain to her the dangers that beset her in cherishing feelings which cannot be indulged without all the pain of apprehension, of consciousness, of self-reproach. There is certainly no blessing in this world equal to a *pure conscience.* How strange it is, after the dreadful danger she has so narrowly, it may almost be said, so miraculously escaped, that she should not see the necessity, the vital need there is for the extinction of every thought of fondness, and a rigid self-questioning upon every emotion that she is conscious of! I must prevent her lapsing into danger, but I fear—and I shall grieve if it be so—that I cannot hold possession of her friendship if I discourage her love.

June 27th.—A son born.[1]

June 29th.—Looked at the paper. I am glad that this trial of Courvoisier has brought the question of the licence assumed by counsel into public notice. Continued the reading of *Marino Faliero.* Saw Danby's picture of The Deluge. It almost made me weep, and made one say to the statement that *God destroyed the world and mankind for its sins—He did not.* Who shall dare to ascribe motives to the effect of general laws, acting through means of partial ill to universal good? The *Bishops, Priests and Deacons.* But not the mind of man, nor the heart of man, that adores the Creator of itself and all its blessings. The picture, which is grandly conceived and executed in the completeness of its details with wonderful felicity, is unfortunate in a too strong light, the cause of which is not clearly made out. It wants Poussin's tone!

June 30th.—Acted Halbert Macdonald fairly; was called for and well received by the audience. Spoke to Miss P. Horton about her engagement; whilst she was with me, Talfourd and a friend came in.

[1] Walter Francis Sheil, died February 8, 1853—(*note by Sir F. Pollock*).

He was going down to the House of Commons, but had been to see the play with Mr. Justice Maule,[1] who sent word that he had been delighted. A very humorous card of *inquiry* from Dickens, Maclise and Forster.

July 2nd.—Spoke with —— on the subject of her attachment to me. She is truly amiable. In explaining to her that my motive in seeking to occupy and engross her mind was to weaken the strength of that affection which had excited so much apprehension in my breast for her happiness and health and divert her thoughts, I went fully into the description of the course of study and artistical discipline which she should undertake, and particularly urged upon her the distress it occasioned me to think that she was, as it were, widowing her heart, in its youth and freshness and fulness of feeling, by allowing it to dwell upon one object, whose rare opportunities of enjoying her society afforded him no power of recompensing her tenderness; at the same time assuring her how truly and devotedly I was her friend, how firmly I was bound to her interests and the care for her happiness by the very persons whose persecutions had sought to make my regard destructive to her. She said she could not, as I wished, and as her friends wished, think of any person as a husband (on which I remonstrated), that she feared I blamed her, and that she would try to do what was right. She told me of her family—so wearing, so sordid, so vulgar, so cruel as they are. I hope she may leave them. She was to tell me hereafter what conclusion she would come to. Spoke again with ——, who could *not* bring herself at present to entertain the thought of any connection, as unjust to some one who might trust her, and distressingly painful to herself. But she would try to do all I wished. She feared I might not respect her, and could not bear the idea of altering my present demeanour or feeling towards her. I assured her, if that would tend to give peace to her heart, that whilst I had life, she might regard my devoted friendship and affectionate care for her as unalterable. She left me in a more cheerful state of mind, and I trust in God will be happy. Amen! . . . In my conversation with ——, expatiating upon the hopelessness of her affections so bestowed, I observed that I was now advancing into age, to which she answered : " Ah! your mind must always be young."

July 3rd.—After dinner read the number of *Master Humphrey's*

---

[1] William Henry Maule (1788–1858) ; Senior Wrangler. Justice of the Court of Common Pleas. One of the ablest judges of the nineteenth century ; noted for his sardonic humour, to which he frequently gave expression on the Bench.

Clock—very humorous—wonderful Dickens! He had told me, as I left his house, that he should now stick to the single story.

July 4th.—Gave lessons to Willie and Katy; looked at the paper, in which was a review of Mr. Bunn's book. There is nothing, it appears, so low, so vile, so degraded—regarding it either as respects honour or common morality—that reaches a level which the sympathies of the gentlemen of the Press cannot descend to. I certainly agree with Edward in his opinion that the extremity of blackguardism is kept possession of in the most intrepid manner by the gentlemen of the Press; it is their stronghold, and certainly impregnable to every remonstrance of decency or prayer of virtue and honour. What especial nook of filth and torment would Dante have assigned these vermin if a journal had been contemporary with the *Inferno?* Looked at *Godolphin*, and thought the pages I read very powerful and beautiful. Bulwer, its author, is, of course, vilified by the Press.

July 5th.—Saw the *Athenæum's* review of that bad man's book; it is treated according to its desert, though no justice is done to the character of the man, for it is only *from his own* account of himself that he is condemned. Miss P. Horton came to dinner. Miss Horton sang several airs, but wants cultivation. She told me some stories of the impertinence of some of the actors in the green-room; among the rest, of Mr. Kean, which I have no wish to hear, and which I had rather she kept to herself.

July 6th.—The uncertainty of my condition, my limited means, and the large outgoings for the furnishing of this house pressed on me like a nightmare. I could not sleep—all attempts were vain; I was fevered, and in the most wretched and gloomy state of mind. It seemed to me presumptuous to furnish my house as I had done, and it occurred to me that I had only incurred the ridicule and sarcasm of my acquaintance. The thought of the effect of an *illness* upon my resources and the condition of my seven beloved children excited me in a most miserable way. I had resolved in my mind not to send any cards for dinners. I thought of how I could save more money. I rose and looked out upon the clear grey morning, the moon just extinguishing the useless lamps. I made a vow to Heaven, as I said my prayers, to do nothing hereafter from vainglory, but to live for my blessed children only.

July 9th.—Saw ——. Her spirits were very much depressed; it seemed to have been the effect of the struggle she is making (*in the sweetest and noblest spirit of self-denial and infliction*) to overmaster the tenderness and absorbing passion which swells her too susceptible

68

heart almost to bursting. I could offer only the comfort of that promise of content and peace, which the consciousness of having done what we think right is sure to realize. *It was a most distressing interview.* She told me she wished to do what she ought at the sacrifice of feeling and at any cost. I assured her that I could not, and would not for the world, for any consideration, seek to alter such a resolution; that it was right, and was in her most sweet and amiable and honourable to think so. *It was a bitter, a most afflicting scene.* She felt as if she was parting for ever from me, and seemed as if she could not tear herself away. I behaved *well;* I felt for her; I felt myself that she was really dear to me—she is so, and I never will forgo the affectionate interest I take in her welfare; dear, dear, good girl. Her whole heart in all its freshness had been given up to me, and it was a cruel necessity that thus had made her strive to tear it away. I *could not,* as I told her—I *dared not,* interpose the hint of a wish, or a thought, between herself and the course she saw herself obliged to take; but it wrung my very soul to witness the agony it cost her. She is indeed a *good*—a *good* and most amiable girl. She had not known how deeply her affections were engaged until her illness, when she felt that her love was all she had to live for. May God Almighty restore her dear heart to tranquillity, and bless it with one that can recompense her as she merits. God Almighty bless her! I took one little remembrance from her, which will be always precious to me. I kissed her forehead—and no more. Our parting was really terrible. She takes with her my affectionate respect, and all the love that with due regard to her honour I can bear her she shall have, while I can feel or think. Again and again God bless her! Amen! My spirits were and are wretchedly low. I do not think with the world, though I conform to its requisitions. I suppose they are, in the main, right. I will not reason it.

July 10th.—Felt so utterly weighed down in spirit—so dejected—so prostrated by the painful thoughts which had disturbed me in the night, upon the interview of the foregone evening—poor dear ——. It is very sad to think of her, and her sweet mode of binding up her resolution to do right. God bless her! Wrote a note to dear ——, to sustain and comfort her. Mr. Fox, Miss Flower, Mr. and Mrs. Adams, Greaves, and Forster came to dine with us—a pleasant day. Mrs. Adams sang her scenas in the evening—in a style as regards expression, pathos, and power unsurpassed (I question if equalled) by any singer I ever heard. Went in the evening to Fonblanque's. Saw the Jenkins, Gurwoods, Fitzgeralds, Chorley, Chitty, Lovers, Lord Segrave, Wombwell, Lords Lansdowne and Normanby, Lady Morgan, Ayrton, Poole—several others unknown to me, but knowing me.

July 11th.—Looked at the paper, and was pleased to see the good sense of the jury who tried Oxford.[1] Read the paper of *Humphrey's Clock*, which was most beautiful. Received an answer, a most touching one, from my dear friend; it cuts my heart to think of her unmerited sufferings, and to see how she bears them. God bless her. Acted Halbert Macdonald very fairly; was called for and well received.

July 13th.—My darling little Joan came among my other blessed children to announce her birthday, and received my congratulatory kiss and blessing. The dear child! May the Good and Almighty God shower down his choicest blessings upon her, causing her mind to grow in wisdom and in virtue, and strengthening her body in the beauty of health. Finished my note—or lecture on acting—to Helen Faucit. Wrote to Etty. Gave the dear children their *Birthday* dinner: little Joan receiving her toys. Forster called; Mrs. Dickens had been here. I walked in the Park with Forster; he told me of the plot of Bulwer's projected comedy,[2] which pleased me. He dined with us.

July 14th.—Browning called, and Mrs. Dickens. Sat talking with Edward, who had seen the book of that bad man, Bunn. A note from dear —— in very low spirits. Acted Jaques moderately. Talfourd came in and spoke about *Glencoe*, also about Mr. C. Kean's Macbeth, which he declared to be irredeemably bad.

July 15th.—Was detained a very long time in endeavouring to tinker together a few lines in verse for dear ——'s album. My muse is cold—she never had much vitality.

July 16th.—Remonstrated with —— upon the unreasonable course she had adopted of subduing her attachment by goading, and racking and prostrating herself mentally and physically with incessant self-accusations; that so long as she had confidence and security in me (knowing that I would not take advantage of her for the world), and had reliance on the strength and purity of her own intentions, that it was unreasonable to waste her heart and health in frettings and self-reproach; that she should preserve her resolutions, and use her reason calmly and clearly, and with time might change her affection to an ardent friendship which I hoped would never diminish; that she

---

[1] The pot-boy who fired at Queen Victoria. He was found not guilty on the ground of insanity.

[2] *Money.*

should give her mind a pursuit, as the best way to achieve the object in view, and the best was her *art*. I parted from her (thank God) cheerfully. Saw Willmott and Forster. Willmott said they hissed Mr. C. Kean frequently—that his performance was *execrable*.

July 17th.—Went down to the Haymarket to see *Macbeth*. Mr. C. Kean was really so bad—so idealless, made up of long pause, whimpering, rant, and the falsest system of intonation, all built up on the most offensive imitation of his father's worst habits and tricks, that I could not stay beyond the second act. Mrs. Warner seemed noble and Mr. Phelps fresh and vigorous beside such acting.

July 21st.—Noticed the increase of crime in the indifference to human life, which seems to have prevailed more as pugilism has fallen into disuse. Went to theatre. Began to act Jaques very fairly, but was thrown off my balance by a man in the gallery vociferating : " What do you go on for, spoiling Shakspeare," etc. I caught no more, for the audience were roused and he was turned out. But he was right in judgment, however barbarous and ungentlemanly his method of giving publicity to it. I ought not to have resumed those speeches, which I always censured as so misappropriated, and which I restored to the First Lord when I was in Covent Garden. It made me low-spirited and ill-humoured for a time.

July 27th.—I made the best of my way to Brompton and called on Mrs. Braysher to meet Miss Helen Faucit there by appointment. Mrs. Braysher sat some little time with us and left us, observing that she understood my call was one of business. I entered unreservedly into the examination of H. Faucit's defects in acting, and pointed out to her the remedies. I gave her a lecture of more than two hours, chiefly on the characters of Rosalind and Lady Townley. She seemed very sensible of the truth of what I urged, and appeared very grateful.

July 29th.—Saw in the paper the announcement of Lord Durham's death.[1] It was no surprise to me. A striking instance he was of opportunity not being all in all for a man. How many men would

---

[1] At the age of forty-eight. Arrogance and egotism, coupled with a lack of sound judgment, had much impaired the usefulness of Lord Durham's undoubted abilities. His pretensions were quite disproportionate to his political status, and they rendered him as a colleague only one degree less intolerable than Brougham. A professed democrat, he never rested till he had secured ennoblement first as a baron, then as an earl, an example by which modern politicians of his school have not failed to profit. His friends predicted for him a brilliant future, but he was too much bent on aggrandisement to achieve greatness. If he had lived he would probably have shared the fate of Brougham, though not without the solatium of an additional step in the peerage.

have made themselves great through all time by such an opportunity as that man enjoyed. But he had not the qualities of a *great man;* he had a little splenetic soul. His views were not large—his soul was not great—he looked too much on that "least of nature's works," himself; his eye was not filled with the work he had to do and with the splendour of the *distant reward.*

July 31st.—Browning called and gave me his play, which *does not look well.*

August 2nd.—Read the *Examiner*, which now openly abandons its republican predilections, and is avowedly a Ministerial—*i. e.* uncharactered—paper. Forster called to take me with him to Bulwer's. Saw the Duke of Wellington, looking very well. Heard from Forster the news of Dr. Lardner's trial for crim. con. and that he was cast in £8000 damages. In the disgusting state of the administration of justice in this country, it is another instance to make one ask where is the standard by which the crimes and qualities of men are measured? He may say of those who tried him: "I am not innocent, but are these guiltless?" Found Bulwer not well—looking weak and shaken; he was cheerful, and the place, Craven Cottage,[1] with its beautiful rooms, its well-arranged grounds, and the animating view of the Thames, was enough to soothe the lowest spirits. We talked about his comedy, of which he read some scenes, and I agreed to think them over. He also spoke of a novel on which he was employed. I passed a very agreeable day with him, and returned with Forster.

August 3rd.—A young man, a Mr. ——, called, and, explaining to him the distress and difficulty and disrepute attending a life spent on the stage, I induced him to promise me that he would abandon the idea, and, returning to his fealty to his father, would resume the occupation of a merchant, as he wished. Read Browning's play,[2] and with the deepest concern I yield to the belief that he will *never write again*—to any purpose. I fear his intellect is not quite clear. I do not know how to write to Browning.

August 6th.—Want of good arrangement occasioned an *embarras* with the *voituriers,* and the whole party, destined for Broadstairs, after being packed in the carriages, turned out, and rather than submit to imposition deferred their journey till to-morrow. Looked at the newspaper. Saw in it a special advertisement from the box-keeper of the "popular character of Mr. C. Kean" Macbeth. I was annoyed in some measure by this impertinence; but quackery is this person's trade.

---

[1] At Fulham.   [2] The *Return of the Druses.*

72

August 7th.—Looked at the paper, and then sat down to read for a subject to suggest to Bulwer. Read very carefully through Voltaire's *Nanine*, which I like very much; and afterwards Goldoni's *Pamela*. Deliberated long and made notes upon a subject for Bulwer to write upon. Had to attend to some business of the house. Bulwer and Forster came to dinner. After dinner we discussed at great length the subject I had thought upon; indeed, we gave the whole evening to it.

August 8th.—Read the account of that most silly but serious piece of vanity—the expedition of Louis Napoleon to Boulogne [1]—the fool! Acted Oakley miserably. I was quite knocked down by the house—I never saw so bad a one in London—*I was not received!* I could not bear up against it.

August 9th.—My thoughts have been uneasy and I have suffered much from them. The position in which I find myself professionally has much distressed me. The house last night was humiliating—the charm of my name, as an attraction, seems broken up; my Haymarket income is trembling. This, I perceive (my vexation being now subdued and my cool insight into things having become more clear), results from the want of nice calculation in myself as much as in the inertness and incapacity of the manager. To waste time and mind in anger is absurd. Being more cheerful from the view I take of the state of affairs (which is very bad) I will do my best to repair them, and if I am successful, I shall profit by the lesson; if not so, I have at least done my best under the circumstances.

August 12th.—Browning called, and walked out with me on my way to the theatre. As he accompanied me he talked of his play and of *Sordello*, and I most honestly told him my opinion on both, expressing myself most anxious, as I am, that he should justify the expectations formed of him, but that he could not do so by placing himself in opposition to the world. He wished me to have his play done for nothing. I explained to him that Mr. Webster *would not* do it; we talked to the Haymarket, and in parting I promised to read it again. Forster called and read me a letter from Bulwer, who has already written one-third of the comedy. His expedition is wonderful! Went to theatre. Acted Jaques fairly. Watched one scene of Miss Faucit's Rosalind, which is not humorous and joyous enough.

August 13th.—Went to theatre. Acted Claude Melnotte tolerably well; began with great spirit, but had a dull, ignorant, and apathetic

[1] The historic "tame eagle" expedition.

audience. Oh! that *Haymarket audience!!!* Was called and pretty well received.

August 16th.—Went to dine with Dickens, and was witness to a most painful scene after dinner. Forster, Maclise and myself were the guests. Forster got on to one of his headlong streams of talk (which he thinks argument) and waxed warm, and at last some sharp observations led to personal retorts between him and Dickens. He displayed his usual want of tact, and Dickens flew into so violent a passion as quite to forget himself and give Forster to understand that he was in his house, which he should be glad if he would leave. Forster behaved very foolishly. I stopped him; spoke to both of them and observed that for an angry instant they were about to destroy a friendship valuable to both. I drew from Dickens the admission that he had spoken in passion and would not have said what he said, could he have reflected; but he added he could not answer for his temper under Forster's provocations, and that he should do just the same again. Forster behaved very *weakly*; would not accept the repeated acknowledgment communicated to him that Dickens regretted the passion, etc., but stayed, skimbling-skambling a parcel of unmeaning words, and at last finding he could obtain no more, made a sort of speech, accepting what he had before declined. He was silent and not recovered—no wonder!—during the whole evening. Mrs. Dickens had gone out in tears. It was a very painful scene.

August 19th.—My temper is falling—or, rather, has fallen—back into its most vicious state! I am miserable, morose. My God! what can I do—with nothing but suggestions to impatience and anger about me—with nothing to ease and soothe my mind? I know not what to do. I sometimes think that I could be content to relinquish life. Certainly life is not happiness to me. I am fretted with fears for the future and irritated by present occurrences. Acted Richelieu as well as I could with such actors! But was not good—and dreadfully passionate. Oh God, oh God! Was called for and well received.

August 20th.—Rose with very unhappy reflections upon my wretched temper, which makes so much of what is unhappy in my life. I know its sin, its folly, its unamiable effect, its terrible punishment, and yet I cannot—exposed as I am to these excitements—I cannot subdue it to my will. I am constantly in apprehension of some indignant remark upon it. I strive and strive, but I fear hopelessly. Called on Dickens, and walked with him to the sale of Louis Napoleon's effects, where truly enough we saw manifest indications of the *one idea* being all his intellectual stock.   Talked much with Dickens, whose views on politics and religion seem very much to square with mine. We talked about Forster, and he made the same remark on him that Edward had done : that he assumed a supercilious tone before people to give the idea that he was the patron, or *padrone*.   How little and how silly !   Disgusted with the vulgar buffoonery of Mrs. Glover, and the inaccuracy of Mr. Strickland—these wretched Haymarket actors ! Was called for and well received.

August 23rd.—Gave the entire day to the cutting and arrangement of Serle's play of *Master Clarke*, and found I had only completed four acts when obliged to go and dress for dinner.   Dined with Dickens and met Mrs. Burnett, Maclise, Fletcher the sculptor, Mr. Collinson—whose name was taken in vain upon the subject of Talfourd's *Glencoe*—and Forster, who was there just the same as ever. Poor Forster !   A little more strength of mind, and a little more judgment to bring his vanity under control, would greatly enhance his valuable qualities to himself and his friends.

August 24th.—As I sat at dinner I looked around me—at the handsome room in which I sat, the table with all I could wish before me or at my command, the servant in livery attending on me alone, and I thought how difficult it must be, and it is, for men to draw back their *naked selves*—their ideas of man, as God made him—from the disguise of pomp and circumstance with which they have invested him. Oh God ! in the gratitude I ought to feel for the blessings Thou hast bestowed on me, teach me the duties of charity, of kind consideration, of compassionate allowance towards those who have been less favoured. In the accident of that destiny which gave me sufficient intellect to attain a certain degree of general respect, and to surround myself with objects of taste that gratify my eye and feed my mind, and with luxuries which so much increase the enjoyments of my physical existence, let me ever acknowledge Thy bounty and be still happier in blessing Thy name as the source of all that I have or may enjoy.

August 25th.—Went to Dickens's, presented my sponsorial offering of a watch and chain, which I was pleased to see very much admired.   Went to church, and observed the impatient and clergyman-like temper of the *parson* at the non-arrival of another expected party. After the entry had been made of the names in the vestry, we proceeded to the font, and when about *one* third of the service was read the other party appeared ; the parson had them forward, and christened the two children together, the little late-comer having lost all the

Christianity contained in that part of the ceremony which the parson could not afford a repetition of! And these are Christians ministers —the apostles of a religion of Charity and Love. The hypocrites! The villains! The liars to God, the cheats to human nature! Gave the nurse a sovereign and returned—after hearing the clergyman's compliments on the *distinction* of the party—with Mr. and Mrs. Dickens, Mr. Fletcher, and the two godmothers. Lunched, and then walked out with Dickens and Fletcher; purchased the *Æschylus*, *Odyssey*, and *Hesiod* of Flaxman, and wended on to Cold Bath Fields Prison. Captain Chesterton, the Governor, accompanied us over the whole prison. Went to dine with Dickens. Met some relations of his, uncles; Miss Ayrton, Mrs. Burnett, Maclise, Jerdan, Forster, Mr. Charlton, etc. Rather a noisy and uproarious day—not so much *comme il faut* as I could have wished.

August 26th.—Received a note from Forster asking for orders, and informing me of a letter he had received from Bulwer that made him fear for his health. *I fear very much for it!* Went to the theatre. Forster came into my room and Browning, who did not stay long. They did not speak to one another—how bad this is! How little wisdom or generosity it shows! Forster told me that Bulwer was in very low spirits about his health, being in fear of *decline*, which I fear too. *I shall be grieved to lose him.* Forster told me that Collier had been again attacking me in the *Observer*, and that a portrait of Mr. Bunn was announced by R. J. Lane, A.R.A.!!! This is really amusing.

August 27th.—Browning came before I had finished my bath, and really *wearied* me with his obstinate faith in his poem of *Sordello*, and of his eventual celebrity, and also with his self-opinionated persuasions upon his *Return of the Druses*. I fear he is for ever gone. He speaks of Mr. Fox (who would have been *delighted* and proud in the ability to praise him) in a very unkind manner, and imputes motives to him which on the mere surface seem absurd. Looked at the paper. Browning accompanied me to the theatre, at last consenting to leave the MS. with me for a second perusal. Rehearsed *Master Clarke*, which appeared so dull in the rehearsal that Serle, Webster, and Willmott held a council with me upon the expediency of substituting the *Spanish Maid* for it. I went home to read the *Spanish Maid*, which was not there.

August 28th.—Began the day with packing for my brief holiday, which has been " haunting me like a passion " for these three weeks past. My dear wife ought to be satisfied with my love to her, for I rejoin her more with the fondness and ardour of a bridegroom than with the sedater feelings of an old married man. Heard the voice of my dear old dog Norma in the yard, and went down from my bathroom to see her, and took my farewell to her. Dear old dog—many have been the happy moments that I have seen thee bounding and wantoning in thy strength, great and beautiful brute! Farewell! I shall never see thee again! Farewell! Left London at half-past eleven and reached Canterbury at half-past six.

Broadstairs, August 29th.—Left Canterbury in a chaise, and came very slowly along to Broadstairs; was pleased to look again upon the fields and trees, though it seemed like a surprise to me to see the stubble fields and the harvest gathered. The beauty of the wild flowers by the roadside, few as they were, was sweet and pleasing to my sight. I found my wife and dear family all well, thank God, and after breakfast lay down for two of three hours. I arranged my accounts and surrendered all the rest of my day to idleness and the enjoyment of the society of my dear children. Was much irritated and annoyed by the report of fresh instances of impertinence and falsehood in the *Observer* newspaper. My anger was greatly excited, but reflection shows me that the baseness is only elevated by taking notice of it.

August 30th.—Read—indeed almost spelled—the newspaper. Listened to my children's repetition of French fables and verses. After their dinner walked out to call on Dickens—who had not arrived—then on the cliffs and on the sands. Spent an idle evening with my family.

August 31st.—Left Margate in the iron steamboat, which I did not like at all in the heavy swell that we had to ride through nearly to Gravesend. The boat was so light, being of metal, that her motion made me very uncomfortable. There was abundance of sickness and altogether a disagreeable passage. As it grew dark the effect of the various and many boats with their lights on their prows and mastheads gliding through the water had a very beautiful effect. Came by the Blackwall Railway to London.

September 2nd.—Webster came into my room, and we had a long talk on various matters. He told me he had given Knowles (on *his own writing down* the terms) £200 cash for a play in March next—that now Mr. Knowles wanted to be off the bargain, or if he wrote the play to receive £800 instead of £600—*the sum proposed by himself!* Talked about Helen Faucit's fitness for Beatrice, of which I begin to entertain doubts.

77

September 3rd.—Went to theatre and rehearsed three acts of *Master Clarke*, which has no strong salient point, no great scene in it, and is *not worth doing*, which I lament for Serle's sake. Talked very needlessly to Webster; met and passed Mr. Knowles in the lobby as I left the theatre—he, of course, not offering to speak to me—a fitting return for the benefits I have heaped upon him. Received a very pretty flower and note, affectionately written, from ——.

September 4th.—Read great part of a paper in *Foreign Quarterly* on Bernadotte, a man who does not much interest me. But what is the end and object of this world? Reading, as we do daily, the drunken ravings of a large body of rational creatures—creatures at least gifted with the power of reason, calling out for *war*—for *war!* Mighty God! if human passion and vanity is so strong, and reason so weak to subdue it, what hope is there for our improvement as really intellectual beings? Note from Mr. ——, asking for assistance in clothes, etc., being in great indigence—poor man! God help him, and all that suffer, and blest be His name that has given me some means to alleviate the woes of those less happily destined. Forster and Blanchard came to dine with me, and my bachelor fare was a most complete success. We spent a very pleasant evening.

September 5th.—Not quite so well as I should have been, but cheerful, indeed light-hearted, in the thought of doing something for this poor fellow who wrote to me last night. Made up a parcel of clothes, etc., for him. Answered poor ——'s note, enclosing him a cheque for £2. Acted Sir Oswin Mortland very unequally—was prepared to act well, but the vulgar exaggeration of Mrs. Glover, who acts the sister of Sir Oswin in the style of a very impudent housekeeper of the baronet, quite unsettled and threw me out of my self-possession. She was acting to Madame Vestris and Mr. Mathews, who were in the theatre! Godlike ambition! what various forms thou takest!

September 7th.—Notes from Ransom, from Mr. French, from Miss E. Spicer wishing the autographs of Bulwer, Dickens, Landor, Mrs. Butler and—Mr. C. Kean! I fear it is quantity, not quality for her!

September 8th.—Walked down to the theatre. On going into a private box I started back and called to the box-keeper on seeing Mrs. Glover satined-out and acting Violante. He told me that Miss Faucit was indisposed and that an apology had been made. Sat through part of the second, the third, fourth and part of the fifth acts—it was very, very badly acted. It does not surprise me that the

78

MRS. GLOVER

From an engraving by Carden

taste for the drama—as acted—should wax feeble. Who would go to see such a performance? I did not hear one line given with propriety—not to say with an artist's discrimination. The play,[1] too, was bunglingly arranged. Mr. Wallack was quite out of place in Don Felix—quite below the part, but it was throughout a very indifferent provincial representation.

September 10th.—Called, paid for and obtained the key of the Park Square Gardens at North Lodge; on my way there met Mrs. Procter, and talked long with her about Browning, of whom she and all think as I do. She told me Milnes was writing a play. After dinner read *Gisippus*, received yesterday from Mr. Griffin. Went to theatre. Acted Claude Melnotte well; called for and well received. Talfourd, Forster and Maclise came in.

September 11th.—Maclise, Forster and Talfourd came to dine, our dinner was very cheerful. Talfourd grew so tipsy that he quite impeded conversation. I was sorry to see him; otherwise it would have been very pleasant. It was curious, and a sad demission of character to hear the violent manner in which he attacked Bulwer; siding with his beastly wife—abusing the *Lady of Lyons*—in short, showing a spirit of littleness and envy that was most unworthy. In him and in Knowles we see how this base quality prevails. They both hate Bulwer, and his demerit is success. But he is a gentleman and a high-minded man—worth both of them and twenty more such, to boot, squeezed up into one.

September 12th.—Dr. Griffin called on the subject of the play of *Gisippus*. I questioned him about his brother,[2] who had written the novel of the *Collegians*, a piece called *The Noyade*, acted at the English Opera House fifteen years ago, and other things. Latterly he had, since an attack of illness, become devout and enthusiastic; lived with his brother for some time, and only wrote upon the spur of occasion —wanting money. He wished to go into the monastery of La Trappe, and finally retired into some other monastery, where he died about three months since. I told Dr. Griffin that I had a great opinion of the play, and if I saw no reason to change it that I would, with his concurrence, prepare it and present it to Mr. Webster. He gave me carte-blanche regarding it, and left me. Priscilla Horton came to my room and asked me to advise about a note she received with a present

[1] The *Wonder*.
[2] Gerald Griffin (1803–1840); novelist and playwright. *Gisippus* was produced by Macready at Drury Lane in 1842.

79

of jewellery from an admirer of her acting.   I wrote an answer for her.

September 13th.—Brydone called, and gave me a picture of Covent Garden and its management, that tends to confirm my belief of its rottenness.   Luck alone can sustain it, and chance acts two ways.   It is not a fitting spectacle—the national drama in the hands of Mrs. Vestris and Mr. Charles Mathews!   Began to read *Hamlet*.   Forster called to consult me on Dickens's preface, to which I made objections.   His dedication to Rogers I thought very well done.   Forster remained, inviting himself to dine.   I read the greater part of *Gisippus* to him—by which he was astonished; he was delighted with it, and thought it better than Knowles's.

September 14th.—Lay down and thought of *Hamlet*.   Received a note from Forster about Dickens's preface, which I answered, though in great haste.   Went to theatre.   Acted Hamlet—in bad spirits— *against the grain—no flow*.   The soliloquy on death I never spoke so well, but altogether I did not satisfy myself.   Was depressed by the bad house, and became very much irritated in thinking of that blackguard ——— ; was quite out of temper, and lost the keynote of the character.   Was called for and well received.   Forster came into my room, and we sent for Webster; advised him to defer Serle's play on account of Knowles's.   Asked him to act *Glencoe* for Talfourd.

September 15th.—Read the paper, my disgust and impatience at the conduct of mankind increasing, as I see them rushing into deeds of murder and plunder which they dignify with the term of heroism, because done upon a large scale and upon system!   Is this Christianity? Received letter from Mrs. ———, who writes very much as if she used her fingers over the paper for want of a power of exercising her brains. Read for five hours my part in *Master Clarke*, which is difficult to retain, there being nothing in it to excite me.   At dinner read a pamphlet on education, which has made me think on the course pursued with my children, and resolve not to goad them too early to learn—let me teach them to *know*.   Again read what I could of Browning's mystical, strange and heavy play of the *Return of the Druses*.   It is not good.   Wrote to him, and, offering to do all in my power, gave him my reconsidered opinion.   Was captivated by the plates and songs of Béranger, and spent too much time in looking them over.

September 16th.—Received letter from ———, written to write— *poverina!*   Received a note from Mr. Spencer Plumer, inviting me to join in a new dramatic company—subscribed to in shares, to take all the unlet principal theatres, to form a school for actors, to remunerate in a better way the actors, etc.—too wild and visionary to think of for an instant. Answered it courteously. Wrote to the secretaries of London Library for prospectuses, etc. Went to the theatre; the house was very bad. Acted Sir Oswin Mortland very well. Procter and Forster came into my room and chatted. My spirits are low, our houses are bad, and there seems nothing in this manner of doing business to give us a hope of rallying —it all rests with me, and I am worn out.

September 17th.—Looked at the paper, was disgusted and irritated by the narration of the circumstances of Lord Cardigan's conduct to an officer—Captain Reynolds—and Lord Hill's behaviour, which seems quite as bad as that ruffian Cardigan's. When will the soul of man walk abroad in its own majesty—oh God! The slaves that we are— to read the tone which an injured and insulted man, Captain Reynolds, is obliged to use to two aristocratic miscreants like these Lords Hill and Cardigan! It is monstrous.[1] Read in *Master Clarke*, and was interrupted in my business by the arrival of Browning, who took his MS. and walked with me to the theatre. Went to the theatre; spoke to Willmott about the plays—he is quite desperate about the fate of the theatre. Acted Claude Melnotte tolerably—was called for and well received.

September 18th.—Concluded the letters to Lord Hill, etc., in the newspaper upon the dispute between this Lord Cardigan and Captain Reynolds. Here is a simple question: Would any man—*not of wealth and rank*—who had so infamized himself as this lord has done, and suffered degradation, have been restored to a power and rank he had abused? *He would not.* It is alone enough to damn Lord Hill,

---

[1] This was the notorious "black bottle" incident which led to a court-martial on Captain J. W. Reynolds of the 11th Hussars and his dismissal from the service, a circumstance that excited a good deal of indignation against Lord Cardigan, who had only a few days before fought a duel with another officer for which he was later on tried by the House of Lords and acquitted. Captain Reynolds's original offence consisted in his having allowed a bottle of Moselle, which he had ordered after a "guest-night" mess-dinner, to be placed on the table in a black bottle. In consequence Lord Cardigan, who was in command of the regiment, caused the following message to be delivered to Captain Reynolds by the president of the mess committee: "The Colonel has desired me, as president of the mess committee, to tell you that you were wrong in having a black bottle placed on the table at a great dinner like last night's, as the mess should be conducted like a gentleman's table and not like a tavern or pot-house." A correspondence ensued, in which Captain Reynolds wrote to Lord Cardigan in terms that were held to be a breach of discipline as addressed by a subordinate officer to his colonel. Lord Hill was then Commander-in-Chief.

whom I look upon as a most unjust and base man.[1] Received by post a letter and two acts, fourth and fifth, of a comedy from Bulwer; the others are sent by the Ambassador's bag—it is completed!

September 19th.—Spoke to Webster in consequence of what Willmott had said to me, that he had expected *me* to bring plays, etc., to him. The mere excuse of his own indolence and neglect of his business. Received the other three acts of Bulwer's comedy. Began the play as I came home in a cab. Proceeded with Bulwer's comedy. Went to the theatre. Acted Sir Oswin Mortland feebly, being overwhelmed and put quite *hors de la scène* by the vulgarity and provincial mummery of Mrs. Glover. Continued the comedy—deeply interested —at the theatre, where I was waiting for Forster, who had gone to Covent Garden to see Knowles's play. Came home, and continued to completion Bulwer's comedy of *Money.* Forster came, and had tea —reported Knowles's play of the *Bride of Messina* as very partially applauded, very indifferently acted, with the exception of Mr. Anderson's part. I began to read the comedy to Forster, and was led on to read it through, to our mutual amusement. Went to bed at half-past three o'clock.

September 20th.—Rose late, suffering from headache, proceeding from my late hours last night, or rather this morning. Arranged my accounts. Made calculations on what *ought* to be our expenses, which, being very liberal, would still allow me a very handsome profit. Gave the whole afternoon, after looking at the newspaper, to the words of *Master Clarke.* Dined with Talfourd, and had a very cheerful day. Serle, T. Hill, Forster, Maclise were present. I was amused with the frank declaration of Mrs. Talfourd, that she could not wish any play to succeed now. So Talfourd is to supply and occupy the stage! Talfourd again began to gird at and depreciate

[1] Lord Cardigan did not escape scot-free, Lord Hill having administered to him the ollowing rebuke in a memorandum which the Adjutant-General was ordered to read to the regiment : "Lord Cardigan must recollect that it is expected of him not only to exercise the military command over the regiment, but to give an example of moderation, temper and discretion. Such a course of conduct would lead to far less frequent reference to his lordship from the 11th Hussars than has been the case in the last few months." This admonition had, however, very little effect, for a few months later Lord Cardigan ordered a trooper of the regiment to undergo one hundred lashes on a Sunday directly after service and before the men could return to barracks. For this outrage he was merely transferred to the command of another cavalry regiment. A remorseless martinet, and of inordinate arrogance (at Harrow his absurd *hauteur* earned him the nickname of the "star-gazer"), he was wholly unfitted for a military command, though in point of courage, "dash" and good looks he was probably unsurpassed in the service.

Bulwer, of whom I spoke out, eulogizing his excellent qualities, and insisting on my belief in him as a high-minded and a high-hearted man. Talfourd, whose envy, poor fellow, quite makes him commit himself, again acknowledged the unworthiness of his conduct in so ungenerously speaking of him, and expressed his great regret.

September 21st.—A very entertaining letter from Bulwer at Donneworth, or some such place, suggesting alteration in his comedy. Answered Bulwer briefly. Went to the theatre very tired. Acted Richelieu fairly. Saw Daniel, and very foolishly, very improperly, expressed my opinion of Miss Ellen Tree's talent—or rather of the very little share she has of it.

September 22nd.—Looked at a drawing by John Lewis,[1] a charming piece of art—the procession of some priests and monks under a window in a town in Spain—beautiful. Marked to read part of Bulwer's comedy. Received a note from Forster, expressing his opinion of *Gisippus*—that it is above any play since Shakspeare. I think that a hasty judgment.[2] Read in Voltaire, who certainly does take exceptions which reason cannot refuse assent to. He says as the Germans do, that the religion of Christians (so calling themselves) is not the religion of Christ—nor is it. Christ worshipped one God, and never uttered one word about three Gods in one—or any such incomprehensibility. Continued Bulwer's comedy of *Money*. Read the first act of *Gisippus*.

September 23rd.—Read the paper, in which I was glad to see the acquittal of Madame Laffarge upon the charge of poisoning her husband.[3] Head called and took directions about my dress for Richard Cromwell. Went to the theatre; rehearsed the new play. Heard that the Lord Chamberlain had sent a message to the theatres, closing them on account of the decease of the Princess Augusta. I would not speak, nor wish to think, irreverently of dead or living—but why are many poor people to be deprived of their daily bread, and many more of an innocent and profitable amusement, because among the number of human beings that departed life yesterday she happened to be numbered? Went into the Oxford Street theatre; was denied, but on giving my name, was conducted over it by a sort of superintendent.

[1] John Frederick Lewis, R.A. (1805–1876); the distinguished painter of Spanish and Oriental subjects.

[2] It was a powerful play, and captured the critics but not the public.

[3] She was not acquitted, but found guilty with extenuating circumstances, and sentenced to hard labour for life with exposure in the pillory.

It is really beautiful: well placed, it would be a fortune; but, where it is, I have no faith in its success.[1]

September 24th.—Looked at the newspaper at breakfast; and saw my sweet children. Rehearsed the play of *Master Clarke.* An incident occurred which was very unpleasant. Mr. Phelps had come, a habit with him, too late. Mr. Webster was not very courteous in his style of address, and Mr. Phelps walked out of the theatre—taking Mr. Webster at his word and dismissing himself. I suggested Serle to take the part of Disbrowe, which, on being sent for, he consented to do, and we finished the rehearsal. The latter part of the play is weak, and unluckily very badly acted. After dinner looked over some lithographic prints of the collection in the Munich Gallery—which must be worth the journey to see. Rested. I must separate myself from the enjoyment of my family's society if I wish to get forward with my work. *I must do it. I will do it.* Went to the theatre, where I found a note from Kenney, who, it appears, has been, judging from his note, informing his friends that I have been ill-using him; he is too bad. Acted Claude Melnotte fairly, was called for and well received.

September 26th.—Went into the yard with the children, and showed them the gymnastic amusements. Looked at the paper, and felt great indignation at the conduct of this bad and tyrannical man, this Lord Cardigan, and the base weakness of that wretched Lord Hill; and these are soldiers—children of chivalry!—a set of mercenaries selling every noble and independent feeling for pay and partial power. Went to the theatre and rehearsed the play of *Richard Cromwell.* Returning home, read over the part, and going again to the theatre, acted it (Richard Cromwell) very fairly, bringing out some parts of the character with truth and force. I was called for and very well received by the audience. Serle, on leaving the stage at rehearsal, had thanked me very earnestly for my assistance. Talfourd and Forster came into my room, and I collected from their opinions their distrust of the play's attraction; they seemed to feel it weak. Forster told me that Mr. Knowles had at length resigned himself to the belief that Mr. Moore had not acted Procida well, and that "he ought to have played it himself." Here is a key to much of his animosity against me! Webster and Willmott came in. I had a very long conversation with the former, who expressed his opinion that the play would not attract—*this is rather premature judgment*—

---

[1] The Princess's Theatre; of late years it has certainly justified Macready's misgivings.

and wishing me immediately to get *Much Ado* in hand. This led to other things. I told him *gently but fully* of his behaviour yesterday morning, and of the bad example he set—in that and his slovenly performance of the part in the play of to-night. Willmott hinted at the new material in plays that I had, and I told Webster (he having expressed his opinion of *Richard Cromwell*) of Bulwer's comedy, and the tragedy, which it appeared Mr. C. Kean had in his possession, and, "distrusting his own judgment," had given to Webster to read.

September 27th.—Heard the dear children their hymns. Looked at the newspaper, in which I was glad to see the strongest reprobation of Lords Cardigan and Hill. My darling boy, Henry, very unwell; he seems wasting and sinking away—my heart fell down within me as I looked at the thin face of the dear, dear child. May God bless, protect and restore him. Mr. Pope called, and rather confirmed than removed my apprehensions for him. Began reading and making legible Bulwer's comedy of *Money*. Forster dined with us. Read the whole of it to Catherine, etc., with Forster, with which all were delighted. *Floreat.*

September 28th.—Mr. Pope called and saw dear little Henry, who, I fear, is very, very ill. My hopes are wretchedly low about him. God bless him! Spoke to Webster on the subject of next year's engagement. He said that he understood I had said that, while I was comfortable at the Haymarket, I would stay. I mentioned the position of my name on the playbills, that it should not on any occasion be put under any other person's, as it had been; that I should have the right to a private box when they were not let. He wished me to take the month's leave which I had at my option; tried it on for "seven weeks," to which I would not agree. He also wished to alter the mode of play and pay; this I would only hear of so far, that I should be paid weekly £100 for the same number of nights (excepting the month's leave), but he might put the nights in what order he chose through the whole term of engagement. Appointed the reading of the comedy for to-morrow. Read over *Richard Cromwell*. Went to theatre; acted Richard Cromwell tolerably. Called for and well received.

September 30th.—Gave my whole morning to the consideration, revision and arrangement for the stage of *Money*, the comedy of Sir E. Bulwer. Wrote my remarks and suggestions to Bulwer. Mr. and Mrs. Carlyle called. Forster called and accompanied me to the theatre.

Dearest Henry still better, thank God! Spoke to Willmott, telling him that I had thought of Webster for Lord Glossmore—he told me that Mr. Webster himself wished to act Doleful! [1] I acted Richard Cromwell, but indifferently! During the play mentioned to Webster that I thought he would be the best we could have for Lord Glossmore. He began a long desultory harangue about his talent, and what he had been and what done, of which I have lived in total ignorance; and though I told him I had nothing to do with this, that Glossmore was a very good part, and was particularized by Sir E. Bulwer as requiring a good actor, he ran on wearying me—quoting his performance of Louis XIII, which I was much averse to. I hear a storm ringing! God direct and speed me right.

October 1st.—Dearest Henry better, for which I earnestly thank God. Unwell and nervous myself from his fretting. Received a long and interesting letter from Bulwer. Talked with Brydone long about the state of Covent Garden, and learned that all were wishing me to be there, except Vestris. Called on Forster, and had a long conversation with him on the subject of the cast, etc., of the play, and the possibility of transferring it to Covent Garden theatre in case Webster refused to do justice to it. I observed that as Bulwer's nomination of Webster to Doleful took from me the responsibility of its cast, I had no further objection to make; adding that in case Mr. Wallack should not wish to take Smooth, that I would give five extra nights to Mr. Webster to make up a salary to Vining, if he would engage him. Coming home, received a long letter from Mr. Webster, laying many things to my charge, such as "threatening to send Sir E. Bulwer's play to Covent Garden theatre—having accumulated expense on him—spoken contemptuously of him, etc." I answered him very mildly, denying, and, I think, briefly disproving his assertions, and stating my belief that he wished to retract the engagement he had made with me; I gave him full leave to do so, if too onerous for his establishment. I went over *Richard Cromwell*, and went to the theatre, where I acted Richard Cromwell pretty well. Forster called, and had some conversation with Webster, who denied that my engagement would be cancelled. I received, whilst undressing, a rude note from him—ending in his "considering my engagement conclusive." I answered it very mildly, very briefly and very distantly, renewing my offer of releasing him from the engagement. I could do no less, I think.

[1] Afterwards Graves.

86

October 3rd.—Looked at the newspapers. Mr. Pope called, and most grateful to God am I to know that my dear Henry is better. Read with great attention the play of *Gisippus*, which is certainly most powerful in passion, interest, character and situation. I wrote to Dr. Griffin of Limerick to inquire the price at which he would sell the work, and took a copy of the letter. Began a careful investigation of *Money*. Left the theatre without receiving any answer or notice from Mr. Webster. I do not understand him. His business is stopped by his own conduct when least he can afford it. Found Forster at home playing cards with my family.

October 4th.—Read, cut, and remarked on Bulwer's comedy of *Money*. Helped Willie in his lessons. Forster came to dinner. Afterwards read the play of *Gisippus*. It is a wonderful play. All were charmed with it.

October 5th.—Wrote a note to Bulwer with the remarks upon *Money*. Marked two acts and a half of *Nina Sforza*. Went to theatre. Heard there most extraordinary news that Braham—whom I recollect worth £90,000—was obliged to be out of the way and leave the country—that the Covent Garden actors had signed a declaration of allegiance and support to Madame Vestris.

October 6th.—Went to Covent Garden theatre to see Knowles's play of *John of Procida*. I paid for entrance—a slight reproach, I think, to the manners, taste, and feeling of the present management. The play was not interesting; there were good scenes, or rather parts of good scenes, in it. Mr. Anderson was by far the best actor in the play; he is much improved. I saw an interlude after it, full of practical jokes, which was very fairly acted by Messrs. Keeley and Mathews, but it was poor stuff. I was, or seemed to be, quite unknown in the theatre, where not a year and a half ago I was the observed of all observers. Such is the world! Walked home thinking on my art, and meditating on Othello.

October 7th.—Wrote a note, which I meant to be kind and pleasant, to Mr. Anderson on his performance of last night. Read over as much as I could Mr. F. Barham's play of *Socrates*, in which Socrates calls his wife, Xantippe—Tippet. Wrote a note to the author upon it. Marked three acts of the comedy of *Money*. Zouch Troughton called; went over with him the alterations of the tragedy of *Nina Sforza*, with which he was satisfied; he took the book with him for insertions. Went to the theatre. Acted Richard Cromwell well. Spoke to Mr. Willmott before the play, who seemed, I thought, to lack towards me the "alacrity and cheer of mind that he was wont to have." All does not seem right to me. My name is not in the posting-bills of this week—the first time I have noted its absence. Mr. Webster has offered no explanation of the rude and intemperate letters addressed to me last week—which makes it seem to me *impossible* that he can have the purpose or the *power* of working out any further engagement with me; this makes me uneasy, and I do not clearly see what I ought to do. God direct and guide me for the good of my blessed family. Miss H. Faucit spoke with me about her acting. She also mentioned things of Mr. Webster that strengthened my apprehensions. Found Forster at home; talked of the Haymarket engagement; he is a person of temper, therefore a bad counsellor. We talked much of these disagreeable circumstances.

October 8th.—Gave lessons to some of the children, and revolved much the decisive step I was about to take in relinquishing my engagement for next season at the Haymarket; but reflection showed me its necessity. Looked over the newspaper. Wrote notes to Forster, entreating him not to mix me up with the question of producing Bulwer's play at the Haymarket, and not to withdraw it on account of the step I was about to take—viz. of withdrawing from the theatre after the present season. Wrote to Brydone, asking him to call and speak to me. Wrote out the copy of my letter to Mr. Webster. Brydone called, and in a conversation, strictly confidential, acquainted me with the present state of the finances, etc., of Covent Garden theatre. They are not such as would justify my acting upon the speculation of the management seeking me, the only way in which it shall ever come to me—for I will not *seek* it. I told him what had passed at the Haymarket, and he was rejoiced at the prospect of my departure from it. Went to theatre. Mr. Webster, it seems, only received my letter, declining any engagement beyond the present season, as he came to dress. Before the play began, he came into my room in great tribulation and humiliation; he began to talk and say he had instructed Mr. Willmott to carry me an official message, which I told him Mr. Willmott had not done (nor do I believe he was so instructed); he almost wept. I listened, and quietly observed upon his conduct, but he was obliged to go on the stage.

October 9th.—Was very glad to receive a note of grateful acknowledgment from Mr. Anderson. Marked and punctuated two acts of the comedy of *Money*. Played at piquet in order to learn the game for the new play, *Money*. Forster called. I had

88

previously read *Humphrey*, which amuses me, but it does not rise in strength.

October 10*th*.—Looked at the newspaper. Received an additional packet of lines in verse to be added to Mr. Adair's play, which now exceeds 7,700 lines! Helen Faucit wished to speak with me about her engagement. I gave her the book of *Nina Sforza* to mark her part by. Willmott came and talked long about the new comedy—the business of the theatre, etc. I suggested Othello; Mr. Webster was down-stairs as I went to speak to Willmott, and kept me talking very long, convincing me that he is a *man without sense*.

October 12*th*.—Was occupied the whole of the morning with the completion of the MS. of *Money*. Received a letter from Dr. Griffin, declining to sell the play of *Gisippus*.

October 13*th*.—Looked at the newspaper, in which I read the notice of the opening of Drury Lane theatre with *Concerts d'Hiver*. Not one word of regret, remonstrance, or concern at this perversion of the edifice from its purposes; not a whisper of complaint against the tyranny that gives to it the power of preventing other theatres from acting Shakspeare, whilst it cannot or will not represent the drama itself! Went to the theatre to rehearse *The Stranger*. Returning, called on Dickens and appointed to go with him to the theatre. Gave the afternoon to make Willie do and understand his lesson, in which I hope and think I succeeded. Called for Dickens, and went to see *The Spanish Curate* at Covent Garden; with the exception of Messrs. Anderson and Keeley the play was very, very badly acted, dressed with no regard to costume, and, upholstered for all times, the characters were not understood. I expected and sat shrinking to hear the hiss, which did not come; the audience applauded, though coldly and flatly. I cannot but see the vast difference between what Covent Garden was, and what it has descended to, but the public are indifferent to it, and the Government —the Queen—support it! Met Leigh Hunt, Blanchard and Forster going out. Forster walked home with us. Acquainted me with Bulwer's arrival, etc. I wrote a note to Bulwer, with suggestions, and made a parcel of his MS. to him.

October 15*th*.—Read the newspaper and looked over the MS. of *Money;* to my surprise, found that the part of Smooth had only three lines in the first scene and not more than seven in the second, and that I could not, with any respect to his pretensions, propose such a part to Mr. Wallack. He called, and I represented to him what the part was, which he did not then wish to hear. I read him one scene, of which he did not appear to think much. He talked about America, his theatre there, management, etc., Mr. C. Kean and other topics, during a visit of about two hours. Looked over *Gisippus*. Went to the theatre; acted Claude Melnotte very fairly; was called for and very well received. Bulwer and Forster came into my room and had a very long discussion on the cast of *Money*. I at length, on Bulwer's account, authorized Forster to offer Mr. Webster four extra nights towards the engagement of Mr. Vining for the part of Smooth. Webster chose, however, to offer Smooth to Mr. Wallack first—and then, if he declined, he agreed to engage Vining.

October 17th.—Dickens, Mrs. Dickens and friend with Maclise and Forster came to dinner. Read the play of *Gisippus* to the party after dinner. All were delighted with it. Dickens told me of the heavy expenses of *Humphrey's Clock* eating up so very much of the profits. I was grieved to hear of it.

October 18th.—Bulwer called and read to us the alterations, which I thought very good. I then read to him three acts of the comedy, with which he seemed greatly delighted. Corrected and cut the two first acts of the comedy of *Money*.

October 19th.—Went to rehearsal—took pains, not pleased with the self-sufficiency of Mr. Wallack, whom I thought very indifferent as an actor. Forster gave me a mem. of the toasts to be drunk at Dickens's dinner to-morrow. What would I not do for dear Dickens? —but I had rather take so many doses of physic than drink my own toasts; "the misérable!" Webster came into the room, and Forster gave him a letter from Sir E. Bulwer to which he readily agreed.

October 20th.—Dined with Dickens. Met his artists, Cattermole and Browne; publishers, Chapman & Hall; printers, Bradbury & Evans; also Egan, Harley, Talfourd, Forster, T. Hill, Maclise. A very cheerful day.

October 22nd.—Read in the newspaper the sentence of the court martial on Captain Reynolds—a sentence that in my mind stamps the profession of the Army with the brand of slavery—as the vilest and most contemptible of all the means that men have invented in this world of deceit and falsehood to get bread or notoriety by. Bulwer came round with Forster, and talked long about the play and other matters. Webster I sent for when they were gone, and explained to him that it was needful to come to an understanding, if I remained with him—or that we should part. He would not hear of this, and after much idle palaver promised to agree to anything that I might write down in my agreement. News of Lord Holland's [1] death was brought to the theatre by Lunn. I felt extremely concerned at the intelligence, for though I did not know him, I always regarded him as a most kind and liberal man. As we observe the contemporaries dropping away thus rapidly amid all the passion and strife upon petty and worldly things, we ought to learn—what we scarcely ever do—the folly of fretting or concerning ourselves about anything beyond the *real duty* of the present hour, that if the next be that of death, we may meet it well, and ending well, do all well.

October 23rd.—Looked at the newspaper; disgusted and indignant with the officers of the court martial. Gave the whole day till half-past twelve o'clock to the comedy of *Money*. Forster came to dinner. Again returned to *Money*.

October 24th.—Looked at the newspaper, and again *suffered*—really suffered—from the violent feelings of indignation and disgust with which I laboured under the injustice of these military authorities, and the cowardly dereliction of all manly principle evinced by the court martial on Captain Reynolds. Looked over what I could of the comedy of *Money*. Went to the theatre and read it to the company, who were very much excited by it. It was quite successful with them. Willmott told me of Mr. Wallack—that he had stated in the green-room he had refused the part of Smooth. I know this man well, and will have as little as possible to do with him.

October 25th.—After dinner continued my work on *Money*, about which I begin to have my usual apprehensions.

October 26th.—Looked at the paper, sympathizing with every sentiment of indignation against Cardigan, Horse Guards, Ministers, court martial and Court.

October 27th.—Attended to the new comedy of *Money*, giving my afternoon to it. Forster called—as I supposed—to dine, but perceived there was a party, and took his leave. Attended to house affairs. Mr. and Mrs. Braysher, Miss Faucit, Mr. and Mrs. Hall, Blanchard, W. Boxall, and Stone dined with us, and we passed a very quiet cheerful day. Received a note from Bulwer.

October 28th.—Wrote a hasty note of appointment to Bulwer. Went to the rehearsal of *Money*, at the end of which Bulwer came

[1] Henry Richard Vassall, third Lord Holland (1773–1840), at the time of his death Chancellor of the Duchy of Lancaster in Lord Melbourne's Cabinet. Though not prominent as a statesman, he was a cultured Whig of enlightened views who is chiefly memorable as the courtly and genial Mæcenas of Holland House.

91

with a note of the dresses of the various characters. Came home extremely tired, and slept, or tried to sleep, the whole afternoon—at least, as much as I had of afternoon. Acted Claude Melnotte very fairly; was called for and well received. Spoke again to H. Faucit about going to Paris. Came home so very tired that I went up-stairs directly to bed.

October 29th.—Went to the theatre where I rehearsed three acts of *Money*. Spoke to Mr. Webster about the scenery and dresses of the play of *Money*, observing to him most emphatically that I did not wish to have anything whatever to do with them—that I would aid the acting as much as I could, but that I had rather he arranged the other matters in his own way. But that was not his wish. Found Forster at home, who had convoyed the family and Mrs. Carlyle to see Madame Laffarge at the Adelphi ! ! !

October 31st.—Acted *The Stranger* feebly. Spoke with Helen Faucit after the play. She told me that Mr. Farren had said, on the faith of Mr. Robertson, that on one occasion *1000* persons went in free during my management ! ! !

November 3rd.—Indignant and disgusted with a letter written by Captain Reynolds, in the most abject phrase and tone receding from the line of defence he had taken up, and throwing himself on the mercy of his Gracious Mistress. Is there a more contemptible person than an English soldier, if the principles broached by the senior officers of this court martial, and acquiesced in by the Army, are to be received as their rules of guidance? Rehearsed with care two acts of *Money*. Spoke to Mr. Strickland, who (from himself) expressed himself obliged if I would assist him with his part of Sir John Vesey —upon which I appointed to-morrow for our meeting.

November 4th.—Mr. Strickland called, and I gave the whole morning to him, explaining and acting to him the part of Sir John Vesey in Bulwer's comedy—from half-past ten to three o'clock. He seemed much obliged, and expressed himself most anxious to do what I had shown him, *if he could*. Acted Claude Melnotte very well—with great spirit, but with very little applause—to a wretched Haymarket audience. Was called for and well received.

November 5th.—Went to the theatre, where I spent two hours in the rehearsal of one page of the club scene in the new comedy. As I write, doubt and misgivings arise in my mind. I have nothing great or striking in situation, character, humour, or passion to develop. The power of all this is thrown on Mr. Strickland and partially on

Mr. Webster. Went to the theatre, and acted Werner fairly. I am playing with two persons—Messrs. Wallack and Phelps—who both think themselves great actors, and imagine one great evidence of their own talent is to frustrate or weaken the effects of their superiors.

November 7th.—Gave the children their lessons. Looked at the newspapers, and was especially disgusted to see Jerdan yielding a sort of assent to the pretension of character on the part of that wretched fellow Bunn—actually recommending him to make another essay ! ! ! What a thing this Press is—all that is brutal, base, and blackguard is concentrated in its trade, and with the rare exceptions of Fonblanque and a few others, there is not a gentleman to be found throughout the mass of them. Letter from Mr. George Stephens, informing me his play is rejected, evidently very sore upon it—as all authors are ; I am very sorry for him. Went to the theatre under convoy of a rude cabman, whom I parted company with very quietly under a threat of summons—nothing like temper. The time has been that I might have been angry, and have been embroiled. I knew myself right and *was satisfied to be so.* If we could in every affair of life be the same, i. e. *satisfied with knowing ourselves right,* how much wiser and happier we should be ! Rehearsed the club scene in the new comedy.

November 9th.—Read the play of *Money,* and received a letter from Bulwer with alterations in it. Went to the Hopes' house, and was greatly pleased in the hasty saunter we made through the gallery with the wealth of art it contains—his Etruscan vases and antiquities, his sculpture gallery, and the various specimens of the great masters of the Italian, but particularly of the Dutch and Flemish schools, are, I think, as an ensemble, unique in England. They are very fittingly and tastefully arranged.[1] Wrote a note of acknowledgment to Mr. Hope. Acted Werner unequally—being much fatigued, and made very nervous by the shocking state of intoxication in which Mr. —— was ; not assisted by the acting of Mr. Wallack. Was called for and well received. Mrs. Carlyle had accompanied our family to the theatre. Forster came round and spoke with Mr. Webster about Mr. ——.

November 10th.—Mr. and Mrs. Bishop, Mr. and Mrs. Brockedon, Mr. and Mrs. Dickens, Mr. and Mrs. Warren, Beazley, Cartwright, and Price came to dinner.

November 11th.—Went to the theatre, and heard that Mr. —— had been again intoxicated last night, and found that Mr. Strickland

---

[1] The collections were formed by Thomas Hope (1770–1831), the author of *Anastasius,* and owner of Deepdene, which also contained many priceless works of art.

was too ill to attend rehearsal. It was useless to make any attempt
to rehearse, Mrs. Glover being also absent. We talked what was best
to be done. Agreed to go to the Olympic and see an actor called
Roxby. I went to Forster's chambers and requested him to go. I
found him angry about an impertinence of Messrs. Meadows and C.
Mathews regarding myself. I begged him not to think of anything
so miserably mean. Went to theatre, acted Claude Melnotte—
unequally in some parts, the third act excellently, with great spirit
and feeling. Was called for and well received. Spoke to Mr.
Webster, who still clings to Mr. ——.

November 12th.—Gave the morning, not very sternly or diligently,
to the reading of *Money*. A boy called for an order for Mr. Barnes [1]
of the *Times* office! I told him he was fortunate that I did not give
him in custody to a police officer. Went to theatre. Willmott came
into my room, and gave his opinion in favour of engaging Mr. Roxby.
Acted Werner—in parts very well, seeing some persons in the house
whom I fancied I should like to please. Was called for and well
received. Mr. Webster spoke to me in favour of Mr. ——, and told
me he had made an agreement with Mr. Forster; showed me a letter
of protestation from Mr. ——; but a drunkard's vow of sobriety!

November 13th.—Received a most kind and candid exposition of
the state of the public theatrical feeling at Plymouth from Wightwick,
giving it as his opinion that the town would be more likely to make
greater houses to Mr. C. Kean than to me—a piece of information
which I received with the most placid philosophy. Went to the
theatre, where I rehearsed three acts, or the better part of three acts,
of the new comedy. Forster called in and spoke about my engagement with Mr. Webster. Mr. Wrench [2] came to dine, and after
dinner we gave the whole evening to his learning the game of piquet.
In bed read the two numbers 33 and 34 of *Humphrey's Clock*, and was
deeply touched and delighted by 34.

November 14th.—Received a letter from Bulwer with further
alterations, which I thought improvements. Went to the theatre
and rehearsed with much care two scenes—only two scenes in three
hours—of the play, which really *ought*, well acted, to be a success;
it is most painful to see the desperate hazard it incurs in this theatre.
Forster came in and saw part of the rehearsal, with which he was

---

[1] Mr. Barnes was apparently only one degree less objectionable to Macready than
Mr. Bunn.

[2] Benjamin Wrench (1778–1843), a successful light-comedy actor.

greatly pleased. Mr. Webster came to express his wish to leave the rehearsal, in order to go to a sale and make a bargain of some card-tables! Came home with Forster, and, after dinner, half asleep, wrote a letter to Bulwer. Rested, overcome with fatigue. Read *Sir Oswin Mortland*. Went to the theatre. Acted Sir Oswin very feebly, being completely paralyzed by the vulgarity of Mrs. Glover. Willmott spoke to me after the play about the manner in which the theatre is carried on. The curtain would not descend at the close—the man had gone away! Coming home found a letter from Mrs. ——, whom I think very anxious to dispose of her virtue from the stress she lays upon it. Entered Bulwer's alterations.

November 15th.—Rose rather earlier than usual, but was detained long in my dressing-room by my affairs *de toilette* and the hymns of my little darlings. Read *Money*, and learned it, and practised a little in Werner, enough to show me that I need *much exercise in my art*. Attended to *Money* the whole morning.

November 16th.—At the theatre, rehearsed with much pains and care the first, twice over, and half the second act of *Money*. Forster was there, and nearly becoming disagreeable to the actors. After the play spoke to Strickland about his part in the new play, and gave him all the encouragement I could.

November 17th.—Had a carriage for the day, and went in it to the theatre—reading *Money*, the second and third acts of which I rehearsed there. Bulwer and Forster came in; the play is in a seriously backward and ineffective state. Called on Rogers, and sat some time with him. Proposed to him the plan for the monument to Mrs. Siddons, into which he warmly entered, observing that Mrs. Siddons had said to him, on the occasion of her brother's monument, "I hope, Mr. Rogers, that one day justice will be done to women." He cordially took it up. Proceeded to Lady Blessington, from whom I could not get away for a long time. I staid an hour and a half. My guests, Dickenses, Mr. King, and Forster had arrived. We were very cheerful. After dinner I read to them the comedy of *Money*, with which they all expressed themselves greatly pleased. Dickens said he had not supposed that Bulwer could do anything so good.

November 18th.—Went to the theatre; rehearsed with much care and much exertion the fourth and fifth acts of *Money*, which we got into a rough shape. Was painfully struck to see dearest, dearest Henry. He looked so sad and is so thin. I fear, I fear I shall lose that darling boy. God, oh God! bless him, and spare him to me; but

95

Thou has given, and it is in Thy Divine Wisdom to take away! Thy Will be done, oh, good and blessed God! But while he lives I must implore Thee to spare him—spare him—spare him! Went to the theatre, and acted Claude Melnotte with considerable *spirit*, which is a virtue in my acting that I fear I am losing at the Haymarket theatre. I hope not.

November 19th.—Acted Werner in parts extremely well, but I *cannot* play as I ought with Mr. Wallack. Bulwer came into my room, greatly pleased. Was called for and very well received. Bulwer talked much about the comedy. Webster came in after haggling about his broker's bargains. He will spoil the play yet. *He will!*

November 20th.—Very much fatigued by the wakeful night I had through the dear, dear little Henry, who seems falling back. My heart rises in prayer to God for him—dearest boy! Gave the children their lessons—which I am not, with my own business, equal to. Went to theatre. Rehearsed with much pains the three first acts of *Money*, in which I find I have very little to do, but I must strive to make the most of it. Bulwer came to the rehearsal. D'Orsay called to see what I wanted. I inquired of him his hatter, the mode of keeping accounts at the clubs in play, about servants, etc. It was very kind in him. A long debate about announcing the play, which was fixed for Thursday, etc. Gave the whole evening to the cutting, arranging, and preparing *Money*. Wrote out the whole club scene. Very late.

November 21st.—Went to the theatre. Bulwer was there, and Forster during part of the morning. Much of the play went so heavily and unsatisfactorily that Bulwer became very nervous—quite ill-tempered, and spoke harshly to the actors—haughtily, I should say, certainly unphilosophically; but how much has he to excuse the manifestation of his suffering! I quite feel for him. I did and said all I could. Did not reach home till nearly half-past four o'clock. Spoke to Miss Helen Faucit wishing her to *act* at the rehearsal on Monday morning.

November 22nd.—Dearest Henry not much better, having had a very disturbed night, from which dearest Catherine had suffered also. Darling Joan ill too! God bless and restore them. Gave the entire of the remainder of the day to the reading and study of Evelyn, which is long, and not, I fear, profitable.[1] Forster came to dinner. The evening employed with Evelyn.

---

[1] He denounced the character, and with some justice, as a "damned walkin gentleman."

November 23rd.—Was awoke last night almost, as it seemed, every quarter of an hour, by the cries and fretfulness of my darling little Henry—who was very ill through the whole night. I gave the children their lessons, and when I went into the next room to look at my dear suffering boy I was shocked and cut to the very heart to see the little wasted, emaciated child, lying in a state of exhaustion on the nurse's lap. This is what was once my lovely boy—the dear, dear blessed child! My heart clings to him, and to God Almighty I raise my thoughts in earnest prayers, imploring his restoration. Oh God, in Thee alone is my hope. I beseech Thee to give him back to health and happy life. Went to theatre, and rehearsed the three last acts of *Money*, which certainly appeared to me, through the whole of Mr. Strickland's part and much of Mr. Wrench's, dull and dangerous. Bulwer and Forster were so impressed with this that they decided on withdrawing the play. I pointed out to Bulwer the consideration due to Webster, and suggested its retention till the summer, when Farren might be engaged to act the part—the only chance for it! He entered into the idea, and conferred with Webster and Forster, and, when I went up to ascertain if it was to be withdrawn or not, I found them in debate—Mr. Webster declaring that he should be bankrupted if it was (but it was the *agreement* that Sir E. L. B—— should withdraw it at the last moment if not satisfied with the acting) and Bulwer proposing either to withdraw it till the summer, or postpone its performance a few days till a new scene could be substituted to end the fourth act; Mr. Webster adverse to both, and insisting on his confidence of the play's success!—which he has not *seen rehearsed!!* It was left for a final trial at to-morrow's rehearsal. Went home and, thank God, received better accounts of dear Henry.

November 24th.—Gave the dear children their lessons. Thought darling little Henry better—God bless him! Left home early, went to Jackson's and tried on my pantaloons—amused with the extreme pains taken to avoid a wrinkle. Thomas, the bootmaker, was sent for, and was as much *empressé* to have the *sit* to perfection. Went to the theatre, where Bulwer was; he gave me, reading it to us, the scene he had altered for the fourth act; it was a great improvement. Rehearsed with great care the three first acts of *Money*, which looked with golden promise. Spoke to Bulwer about his mode of speaking to Miss Faucit, etc. He was instantly sensible of it, and anxious to apologize to her—he is a gentlemanly-minded man. He spoke quite affectionately about dear little Henry. Note from Lady Blessington inquiring about the production of the play, which I answered. Called at Ashmead's for a hat, and found D'Orsay had been there to speak about one for me! Gave the afternoon, though much fatigued, to the consideration of the altered scene, Act IV. Went to theatre. Acted Claude Melnotte very well; was called for and well received. Spoke to Strickland about his acting, to Miss H. Faucit about her *low* tones in speaking. Forster was present, who told me Bulwer had dedicated this play to him; he has merited it. Spoke to Webster about the properties, etc., of the play. Gave him my engagement.

November 25th.—Felt satisfied, in having passed much of the night without sleep, that my beloved child was better—was told that he was, and went to the theatre relieved in heart and thankful for his advancement, though little. Had glanced over the paper and seen some verses, which I did not read, from the republican Leigh Hunt to the Queen on her infant! At the theatre rehearsed the fourth and fifth acts of the new play, arranging and repeating frequently the new scene. Bulwer and Forster were there—the latter annoyed me by his assumption. Spoke to Mr. Webster about my engagement, mentioning my wish to arrange the revivals, etc., for the ensuing season, to which he assented, taking no exception to the terms of the engagement. I came home and applied myself, wearied as I was, after I had slept some little while, for I could not hold up my head, to learning the words of the new scene. I was depressed by the news that Henry was not better, which always means in sickness that the sufferer is worse, and that dearest little Joan was very ill indeed—dangerously so. The whole afternoon and evening were spent in misery. Mr. Pope came and went —was sent for again, Joan's symptoms becoming more and more alarming, her insensibility continuing; came, went to seek for Dr. Elliotson, whom he brought to see her. Elliotson ordered more leeches and medicine, and told me that it was very alarming, but not quite desperate, that if there were no hope he would tell me so. I saw Henry two or three times—he let me kiss him once. My forebodings are fast becoming prophetic. I shall not kiss that blessed face in life much oftener. *He is to be taken from me*—I feel that I shall lose that dear, dear, blessed child. Oh God, God! if it may be, restore him to me. If not, Thy will must be done. Oh God! Unable to do anything but think and fear. Oh God! I left my study to go up to bed—as well as I can remember, for my head is not clear upon the exact course of wretched circumstances that seemed in some sort to stupefy me. I went up to the nursery to see how dearest Joan was.

Catherine waved me back with her hand, and begged me not to come—that I could do no good.   I felt—I do not know what I felt—a strange agony, a weight at my heart and head, that made me irresolute and tortured what to do.   I had nowhere to go, no one to go to.   All were around this blessed precious infant making despairing efforts. I threw myself on my bed and, wrapping the coverlid over my head, lay in a state of misery such as I never felt before, till dearest Letty came down to me in tears, wrung my hand, and spoke a few words to me.   I asked her if the blessed creature was dead.   My child, my beautiful, my lovely little Joan was gone; I was in a state of desperate wretchedness.   Oh God, I am a wretched sinner! I know it—I acknowledge it.   Thy will is I am to be stricken—let me hope to turn Thy infliction to a healing purpose.   But I scarcely know what I did, or how I felt, except that it was unutterable and hopeless agony.   I rushed up-stairs and saw my sweet angelic child lifeless on her bed. I kissed her, felt her little heart, which seemed to me to beat, I held her pulse and was assured that there was life.   Dearest Catherine and Letitia caught with myself at the hope, and we remained in that dreadful state of anxious hope, longing for the presence of Mr. Pope, until he came to pronounce the dreadful truth.   My child is dead—my blessed, my beloved, my darling child.   She is, I hope, with God.   I stayed beside her, incapable of shedding a tear—I was tranquil— wished to remain with her.   Mr. Pope requested me to go, but I said that it did not agitate me.   I left the dear body of my infant at last on his representation that it was necessary to attend to it.   I went down into the drawing-room and sat there, whilst Susan,[1] Letitia and Catherine alternately came in and stayed.   About two o'clock, when I heard she was laid out, I went up to see her.   She lay stretched out with a smile on that lovely little face like a spirit of God's in slumber. How beautiful, how like a thing of Heaven the blessed creature looked! I wished to be left alone with her, and offered up my prayers—the prayers of penitence and resolution—for bliss to her departed soul, and for a purification of my own heart, and the manifestation of it in an amended life.   Christ tells the sinner to *Go and sin no more*.   I will *endeavour* to sin no more, for her dear memory's sake and the well-being of those precious ones whom God may spare to me.   Oh God Almighty! I bow before Thy will, I bend down to Thy chastening inflictions; but if it be possible—or, rather, if it may be in accordance with Thy will—oh spare my darling Henry, for whom I fear almost

[1] Miss Susan Atkins, Mrs. Macready's sister.

to utter absence of all hope. Oh God, hear me, and save to lives of virtue and wisdom the remaining children Thou hast given to me. I invoke Thy blessing, oh God, on them, on my beloved wife, and my dear sisters. . . . This dreadful and unexpected blow has made me think much more on some words which the wicked, or, I believe, insane old woman, who kept the house for Mr. Boyle, said to me on one of my visits of inspection—wishing to deter me and every one from disturbing her—by taking it: " *There has been death here!* " It sank on my mind as a half-prophecy—it has been fulfilled entirely. God grant that there may be happy and virtuous *life* for the time to come!

November 26th.—Walked about half-past seven from a short but sound sleep, unconscious of anything having happened. A few minutes, or moments, told me that I was bereaved of my sweet child, whom yesterday morning I had believed to be in perfect safety. I did not know what to do—I felt as if I could do nothing. I got up for the children's sake and gave them their lessons. Dear Willie came weeping into my room, and when I asked him the cause, said: "Papa, I am afraid for Joan." I sent them to have their lessons in the dining-room, and went up to look at my dear dead child. She lay there—quite dead—no hope—gone—and yet I could not but think the bosom moved the sheet over her, I could not satisfy myself that the cold marble figure before me that was my living child had not still consciousness. Tears relieved the blank and heavy feeling at my heart. But I could do nothing—I could only see visions of the little bright-eyed creature, entering, from her walks, sitting at the table, pointing out the pictures, calling the infant figures " Henry," or laughing in her wild way upon the stairs. I could do nothing but think and dream and weep. Dr. Elliotson called to see Henry—my blessed, withering, wasting babe. His coming to *me* was reluctant, and though he tried to shape his words consistently with truth into the phrase and tone of comfort, yet they only spoke—confirmation of despair. My boy, once a wonder of beauty and intelligence, will soon be laid by the side of his sweet sister—my babes will both be lost to me in this life. Forster called, and was much affected on seeing me. He had supposed that it was Henry who was gone, and when he learned that dear Joan had been taken from us, he lost all self-control. He rushed out of the study, and remained away at least half-an-hour. When he returned he could say nothing; he left me greatly agitated. Received a dear and most affectionate note from Dickens, which comforted me as much

as I can be comforted. But I have lost my child. There is no comfort for that sorrow; *there is endurance*—that is all. I will try to
endure with resignation and reverential feelings. Mr. Bradley sent
his card, wishing to speak to me, afterwards a note, explaining that
he had only come to offer his services in making a memorial of my dead
child. I answered him very gratefully, explaining that any other
record than that our hearts carried of her lost beauty would be distressing to us. Called in the dear children and told them of their
loss, exhorting them to bear it as the will of God, and making them
kneel down and repeat a prayer after me for her dear sake, and for
their own goodness. They were very much affected, sweet children!
Went from time to time to look at my dear dead Babe. When she
was laid in her coffin I went up before Catherine to look at her. She
was so lovely, so exquisitely, so heavenly pure and beautiful, that I
dared not trust dearest Catherine to see her. I felt it would be too
much for her, and entreated her not to go. After an effort she consented. The children said their prayers to me at night, and were all
affected as they reminded them of dear Joan's loss! Darling Henry
is very restless and in pain. Mr. Pope has just seen him and administered something, persevering in his tone of encouragement, in which
I cannot trust. Wrote out arrears of record. What a record! Oh
God! I go to bed more tranquil, but what is this tranquillity? What
will heal the wound at my heart? What or who can give me back my
child? Oh God, forgive and pity me. Amen!

November 27th.—I expected to find myself better to-day—I feel
quite broken-hearted. The thought of that blessed cherub haunts me
everywhere—and the moans of this dear, dear, yet living child cut me
to the very heart when I hear them, and ring in my ears, even when
beyond their sound. I want patience and the virtue of tranquil
resignation, for comfort there is none; but I must learn meekly and
calmly to endure. God help me. Went up to visit the dear coffined
remains of my sweet, blessed infant. It is a comfort to me to possess
them; I feel as if part of my own heart was enclosed in the coffin.
Blessed spirit—among those many mansions of our Father let me hope
that in another state of being there may be a consciousness of my love
for thee! Oh God! that it may be! To look upon that leaden case
and think that what is now within it so short a time since was beauty,
health, sweet dawning intelligence, and fondest love! Went into the
children's dinner and sat among them, but darling Joan's place was
there unoccupied! I saw her in all her little pretty ways. Sweet,

blessed Joan! Forster called, but I did not see him; he was violently affected on learning that he could not see her; he would call in the evening. Dearest Henry still in pain, but seeming to suffer less. Mr. Pope called again. Revisited occasionally through the day the room which holds my precious lost treasure—my darling infant. Read after tea, in Milton and Wordsworth, to Nina and Willie. The interest of these occupations tended greatly to compose my spirits, for which I thank God devoutly; but the most of all that has relieved me is the hope held out of darling Henry's restoration. Forster called and sat some time with Letitia and myself. I was quite composed; indeed, I feel now entire composure; though the past is still upon my heart, it does not press with that torturing and deadening weight it has done. Dear Mr. Fox wrote to me a most affectionate and beautiful note, which affected but comforted me. I go to bed much more tranquil than I could have expected, after having paid my last visit to my dear children—the dear creatures, whom God still—blessed be His name!—spares to me, and the beloved remains of that precious one whom His will has taken from me. Let me say—and learn to say with true resignation—His will be done!

November 28th.—Awoke to hear the moans and cries of my dear boy. They tortured me. I could not shut them out. My heart was sick with fear, despair, and utter recklessness. The dear blessed being that lies unconscious, and never to be seen or heard again, in the room above me; her loss lies like her coffin itself upon my heart, the sickening agony of almost hopeless apprehension is distracting me, as I vainly try to shut out the voice of pain from my dearest, and still living infant. What am I to do? I try to reason myself down to business or thought of other things—the thought of my blessed Joan, the sweet heavenly little creature, the sufferings, and dreaded fate of my sick child unfit me instantly for any effort. After giving their lessons to my dearest Nina and Katie (dear Willie was suffering from a headache) I went to see darling Henry. His blessed mother, who has been a pattern of affection, of anxious and indefatigable exertion, of courage, and self-denial—oh God, oh God, I pray Thee bless her for her goodness—comforted me with the assurance that he was better. I scarcely dare trust the hope. Went to look again upon the coffin that contains my beloved child—it still is near me. I still possess it—it is not yet taken from me. My God, my God! I renewed my prayers to God, but I fear my mind loses rather than gains strength. I thought, as I looked on the little form before me, that that little case shut up senses, affections, intellect and passions and imaginations, that had, or would have had, no limit; and I thought, looking at it, " and this is a *life!* " Sweet, sweet creature! My heart is with thee. Dearest, dearest, what would I not give to repossess thee! My God, my God! spare to me my ailing child—oh spare him! . . . Forster called again and sat with me in the evening. I devoutly return thanks to Almighty God for the gleam of hope in darling Henry's recovery. He is thought to be much better. Thank God! thank God! Blessed be His name. I will say from my heart it shall become better, I will grieve but not repine or murmur for my blessed Joan. I will pray to meet her spirit and say *Thy will be done.* Amen! . . . Mr. Pope called, and I spoke to him on matters concerning the interment of my child. I made up my mind to remove the dear remnant of my child into the drawing-room to-morrow, for Willie had met me in a state of much uneasiness. On asking him the cause, he said that he had been frightened by seeing the rocking-horse, which he had thought was the coffin of dear Joan. I cheered him, and taking him into my study, explained to him that there was no reason for alarm, that we must feel sorrow for the death of those we love, but that we should not be *terrified* by anything relating to it, and that it might be needful for him to place in a coffin the body of one dear to him, or if he and I were alone and I to die it would be his duty to put my body in a grave, and not run in terror from it. I convinced and appeased him, dear boy. Looked at the paper, but did not read it. Gave Willie a lesson of about five or six lines in Ovid, which he learned and said remarkably well. I was very much pleased and comforted by him. Visited the coffin of my blessed, blessed child several times in the day—the last time in the evening—the last time I shall look upon it in the room where the spirit left that precious body, the sweet, sweet angel. The rough workman, who came to take the dimensions of the coffin, when he saw her, said : " It is a beautiful child." And she is gone! my darling, blessed one! Oh God! oh God! let good come from this infliction to those who are left, for the chastening is most terrible—terrible! Oh God, receive her, and let me know that sweet soul once more! Dr. Elliotson and Mr. Pope called to see Henry. I met Elliotson and Pope returning, and F—— said that " there was no reason he should not get well," but his tone was not assured and his manner evasive. My heart sunk—sick with despair. In God alone—in God is my hope—fragile, so fragile, that it is there with Him alone ; I have none in earth. Went in to look at my sweet, suffering boy. Saw the sweet innocent, and my heart was riven to think I must lose him too. Forster called after early dinner and sat with me some time, our conversation composed me. I told him, if he could control himself, I should wish him to accompany me to the funeral of my beloved child. He said he would promise and should wish to go with me. Spoke with Mr. Smith about arrangements and gave orders for the removal of the dear body to the drawing-room. Men brought the outer coffin. My child—my child!

November 29th.—Woke again sore in heart and unquiet in mind; the continued presence of my precious darling's image—in every condition in which I had so often seen her living, and the sweet music of that happy voice—haunts me. I had been alarmed and disquieted by the occasional moaning voice of my darling little suffering Henry, and I rose in most unhappy state of mind. My children with their prayers and hymns helped to compose me. Went in to see dearest Catherine, and found her weak and wearied, but thinking Henry better. *Thank God!* Visited the nursery; looked upon the bed, the death-place and the bier of my angel child, and renewed to her sweet spirit my vow of an amended life. Came down to the drawing-room, and upon the coffin of my child repeated my prayer to God for constancy in my purpose and resolve to turn this affliction to good by purifying my heart and devoting my future life to my children's benefit in my own amendment. Almighty God, hear and receive my prayer and assist me in my purpose. Prepared prayers to read to my family. Wished Catherine not to see the coffin, but could not resist her desire to do so. Went with her, and over that dear body heard her blessings and prayers. Took the dear children to see it—they stood round it with their mother, and kissed it when I told them to bid their dear sister farewell! I led them away—the dear, blessed infants and blessed, blessed mother! Read prayers to them all, and with them lifted up my thoughts to God. We were all present; it did me much good. Oh God, I bow down to Thy will, I acknowledge with humble gratitude Thy many mercies, and I *will* endeavour to be worthier in thy sight. Help me, oh God! Dined with my family and resumed my place at the table, stretching my arm across the vacant place of the dear being above us; my heart grew very sad. Received a most kind and tender note from Bulwer. Forster called. After tea I told the children a story, applicable to Willie. Forster called again and sat the evening. Dear Catherine went to bed. Forster went to see my child's coffin. Promised not to give way to his emotions to

JOHN FORSTER

(1840)

From a drawing by Daniel Maclise, R.A.

morrow. The dear remains! It is the last night that the body of my child will be within my house. To-morrow I must part with all that is yet left of her. Blessed being! I trust that thou hast life in some happier world, where physical pain cannot be known, and where the purity of our natures will prevent the possibility of worse ill. May I meet thee there, sweet innocent! May I deserve to meet her there is my prayer to thee, oh God.

November 30th.—Went up to bid farewell to the dear, the precious remains of my blessed, darling child; coming down found Forster here—a little time and the door-bell made me inquire of dearest Letty what her silence imparted to me. Darling Katy came in to say her prayers, but I could not hear her. Being summoned I got into the mourning coach, and had the mournful satisfaction of sitting beside my darling's body for the last time. Our journey to the cemetery was a confused state of pain and agony. Oh God, oh God—spare me such another trial! The service was read, but I did not attend to it—my thoughts were on the coffin before me. When the dust was thrown on her dear, dear body and the Lord's prayer was said, and the object of my doting love gradually disappeared, I could have left my seat and clasped it again to my heart. God bless thee! Bless thee! Bless thee, my beloved innocent! Returned—more composed, went into the drawing-room, where I last saw her here, to dearest Catherine —dear woman!—and to the nursery. Forster remained with me the whole day. Elliotson and Pope called, and having seen darling Henry pronounced him certainly better. Devoutly do I thank God.

December 1st.—Thought on the darling little creature, and saw her—sweet angel. Forster breakfasted with us, and on my dissenting from our proposed plan of yesterday, viz. of going to Newbury, and wishing Forster to accompany me in a walk to Hendon, Catherine and Letitia wished me to ride out of town and walk somewhere in the country, and proposed Belvedere and Erith, which I was glad to visit, as so retired. We set out there, and with some melancholy thoughts I got out of London, and felt refreshed in mind, as I felt the free air and the breath of heaven in walking over the heath. The grass and trees, with which my heart has a sort of relationship, imparted a tranquillizing influence to my mind. I could commune with Nature —I could feel thankful to God—in the face of God and Nature—I was not the same man. The pictures at Belvedere interested me very much, but the sky, the turf, the trees, water, and flowers, all these were so many healing influences upon my heart; I thank God—I thank

God for all His mercies. Returned home, very much renovated and cleared in mind. Found all comfortable at home, thank God! thank God! Saw Mr. Pope, who reported most favourably of darling Henry.

December 2nd.—Gave the dear children their lessons. Thought of my darling Joan—sweet blossom! On this day week she was still alive, and I without one fear for her—sweet little angel! as she is now, I trust in God! Dr. Elliotson and Mr. Pope met and saw dearest little Henry, and very confidently asserted him to be much better, for which I devoutly and gratefully thank God. A kind note from Maclise. Read over part of the character of Evelyn in *Money*. Forster called, and we walked round the Park together; I enjoyed the exercise very much. Forster dined with us. Mr. Webster has provided nothing to *back* his new comedy with, and it will in consequence be ruined—at least such are my apprehensions. Finished reading the part of Evelyn.

December 3rd.—Saw darling Henry as I came down-stairs—he was asleep, and looked so pale, so waxen, so unlike the joyous thing of intellect and life that once he looked, that my heart swelled within me to gaze upon his dear, dear emaciated face. Oh, bless and preserve him, great and good God, and let the trials I have endured be sufficient to work out Thy will. Amen! A note from Forster, informing me that Webster would not listen to the suggestion of deferring Bulwer's play, as I confidently expected. Went to the theatre. Rehearsed the play of *Money*. Found at home an anonymous note, cautioning me against a ruffianly person, a low man, called Dr. ——, who goes behind the scenes of the Haymarket theatre.

December 5th.—Arose in a very distressed state of mind, having heard through the long night the cries of pain of my blessed little suffering child. Found him much worse, as I thought, past earthly hope. My beautiful, my brightly intelligent child! and he must be taken from me at last, after this long struggle against death! Oh God! oh God! help my prayers, and grant that I may receive Thy judgments as I ought. But still I must say—spare my child to me! Oh God Almighty! Dr. Elliotson and Mr. Pope came—the former told me that my child was in considerable danger, but not quite hopeless, if he did not improve before to-morrow morning there would be great cause for apprehension. This was like his language before. They are awful words. The dear boy is suffering under an attack of *thrush*. He seemed to suffer greatly—darling child. In the afternoon Catherine recalled us to hope by her report of him, and I was composed and more comfortable. Mr. Pope called and dashed down all my hopes by his language and its tone. I look upon my child as gone.

December 6th.—Darling, dearest little Henry, thank God! seemed better this morning. May I begin once more to hope, oh God! Heard my dear children their hymns, which they said very well. Mr. Pope called, and thought more favourably of dearest Henry. I spoke to him on the subject of my situation with Sir E. Bulwer and Mr. Webster, and observed to him that I was obliged to regard the matter as one of serious business, which it is, and to ask him what probable hope there might be to warrant Mr. Webster in acting, or trying to act, the new comedy on Tuesday. He said that for Tuesday he might perhaps venture, but that if any accession of indisposition should occur to check the onward course of dearest Henry to health, he could not say what might be the result, and he was sure that Dr. Elliotson would say the same. Wrote a note to Mr. Webster, and to Mr. Forster, wishing to see them. Looked out prayers and read them to my family. Saw darling Henry frequently during the day. Mr. Webster called, and I laid before him the state of darling Henry and my apprehensions. Forster came, and after some conversation, in which Mr. Webster expressed himself as much obliged to me for thinking of him, it was settled to proceed with the comedy and wait till we heard Elliotson's report of him to-morrow. God grant it may be good! Read over part of Evelyn. Forster dined. Mr. Pope called again and spoke much more cheerfully of darling Henry.

December 7th.—Found darling Henry much easier, having passed a more comfortable night, for which unlooked-for blessing my heart thanks God. Gave the dear children their lessons. Went out early, taking Letitia with me to Oxford Street; purchased in Bond Street— Conduit Street—and afterwards in Fleet Street the various articles I require for the part of Evelyn. Took considerable pains with the rehearsal of *Money*, and was rather fatigued with it. Forster was there, but left us to go to our house, and hear Elliotson's report of dearest Henry. I thank God—I thank God, that he gave a very decided opinion of his improved health, and encouraged us again, under God's mercy and blessing, to hope. God Almighty spare him to be a good and happy man! Spoke at the theatre to Mr. Webster about my engagement, which he *said* he *had not read*. I wished him to read it. Acted Werner, as I thought, very well, taking great pains, to a very dull audience. Fox came into my room—and Forster.

Webster afterwards, to whom I spoke of various *Money* matters and my engagement, which he had not *yet* read. He would read it to-night. I recapitulated all the variations from the former article—to none of which did he dissent.

December 8th.—Arose in good time after a night disturbed and made unhappy by dear little Henry's distressing moans. Gave the children their lessons. Went to see dear little Henry. Catherine thought him not worse. Went to the Haymarket and rehearsed the play of *Money*. I was very much depressed and low-spirited. Coming home, read over the part and resolved to do my best with it. Laid out and put up my clothes. Acted the part of Evelyn.[1] Not satisfied. I wanted lightness, self-possession, and, in the serious scenes, truth. I was not good—I feel it. In the last scene Miss Faucit, as I had anticipated, had quite the advantage over me; this was natural. Bulwer came into my room; he was, as usual, obliged by my exertions.[2]

December 9th.—Dearest Henry not advanced in health. I know not what to think, but my fears come rapidly upon every check to hope. Oh God, oh God, protect, preserve and bless him! Went to theatre; saw Bulwer and Forster and arranged with them the omissions for to-night in the play of *Money*. Coming home, saw Elliotson and Pope. I was grieved to hear a change towards apprehension in the tone of Elliotson; this dear boy's life seems hanging by a hair. God preserve him to us! Read over *Money*—very weak, nervous and languid. Forster called. Acted Evelyn with effort, but very feebly and not effectively. Was called for and well received. Spoke with Mr. Webster and settled conclusively with him the terms of my engagement, which he is to have copied out and signed; told me of Miss Faucit's demand for next season of £30 per week.

December 10th.—Rose late, felt most grateful, and received something like a return—a faint return of hope in seeing dearest Henry a little better. But in his wasted, dreadful state, it terrifies me to encourage hope. I pray—I pray to God—let my hope rest in Him! Sent, through Letitia, a note to Forster about further omissions in

---

[1] The cast was as follows—

Evelyn, W. C. Macready; Sir John Vesey, — Strickland; Sir Frederick Blount, Walter Lacy; Smooth, B. Wrench; Stout, David Rees; Lord Glossmore, F. Vining; Graves, B. Webster; Clara Douglas, Miss H. Faucit; Georgina Vesey, Miss P. Horton; Lady Franklin, Mrs. Glover.

[2] *Money* had a long run, and no other play was given at the Haymarket until the end of Macready's engagement there, on March 13, in the following year (1841)—(*note by Sir F. Pollock*).

the play.   Read what I could of Evelyn.   Acted the part pretty well ; was called for and well received.

December 11th.—The report of darling Henry was that he was better when I saw him.   I did not think him so much better as I had hoped.   The string is so fine and fragile by which the blessed little sufferer holds to life that it is seemingly blind rashness to cherish any confident hope.   In God is my hope : I have none elsewhere.   God preserve him !

December 12th.—Dearest Henry not so well.   God restore him ! is all I have left to say.   Wrote an answer to Mr. Barham, who had informed me that the newspapers charged me with making the drama a close borough !   I answered him rather indignantly, though very civilly, refuting the calumny.   Acted Evelyn very fairly.   Mr. Webster came into my room, and we signed and exchanged engagements.

December 13th.—After a sleepless night I lay late ; hearing my dear children their hymns, and hearing something of the newspaper's contents, to which I became very indifferent.   I seem to lose all elasticity, all relish for things once pleasing and exciting to me.   I am truly unhappy ; if I had lived in the country I might have been better. As it is, I am actually good for nothing.   I am wretched—I have no spring, no power of exertion ; I feel that I shall—that I must lose my blessed boy ; I cannot compose my mind to serenity.   I must bear it, but it seems to leave me indifferent to everything.   I know not where to turn my thoughts.   Books have no charm for me ; I really know not where to direct my mind.   I began a letter to the Chamberlain. I arranged my accounts.   Dr. Elliotson and Mr. Pope called and saw my poor withering boy.   Elliotson said that his pulse was better—*i. e.* it was lower—but admitted he was weaker ; ordered him stronger food, and said he would see him *to-morrow* again ; this all looks ill.   In fact, *my hope is gone.*   I walked out with Forster to see Wallace's grave, and round the Park.   He remained to dine with us.   I tried to continue the letter to the Chamberlain.   I can think only of my dear, dear boy. God bless him and forgive me !

December 14th.—Not well, and wearied after a restless night. Dearest Henry a little better.   Thank God—thank God ! is all I dare say, except to pray for the continuance of his amendment.   Elliotson and Pope called, and thought dearest Henry better.   God bless him ! Copied my letter to the Chamberlain and sent it to Forster, who called soon after ; he approved it.   Sent it to Lord Uxbridge's house.   Went to theatre; acted Evelyn very indifferently, being distressed and discomposed by Mrs. Glover. Miss Faucit spoke to me on the subject of her engagement; spoke to Mr. Webster on it, and offered to play two nights—*extra*—gratuitously for her benefit if that would make up their difference.

December 15th.—Dearest Henry was, in Catherine's opinion, a little better; but it is vain to talk of better or worse till some decided manifestation of change appears. He is struggling between life and death. God befriend me in him. Read in the course of the afternoon four acts of Landor's *Fra Rupert*, which I liked very much. Acted Evelyn fairly; there was some friend endeavouring to get up an ironical applause at one of my speeches. How easy to molest one!—how noble!

December 16th.—Darling Henry a little better. In God—in God alone there is hope! Read and tried part of Evelyn, which I am anxious to improve. Pope called, and, after him, dear Elliotson. They thought Henry a little better. Finished Landor's *Fra Rupert*, which I like, as a thing of character and picture without design or construction. Rested. Acted Evelyn better than I had previously done, but it is an ineffective, inferior part. Spoke with Willmott afterwards about the club scene.

December 17th.—Encouraged to something like a hope by dearest Henry's apparent improvement. God preserve him to a life of health of mind and body. Acted Evelyn with care and spirit. Called for and well received. Miss Faucit came into my room to speak to me of her engagement; Bulwer and Forster to talk about the play. Miss Faucit told me she had engaged with Webster; that he had shown her a letter from Mr. C. Kean urging him to engage Miss E. Tree to play the *Lady of Lyons* with him—that it would be a great hit; mentioned his intended performance of Romeo, and adding, "No Helen Faucit for me." Webster and Willmott came and spoke to me about doing *Comus*. I scouted the absurdity, or recommended its production in the old way.

December 18th.—Dearest Henry had suffered from a very, very bad night, and had again, in consequence, fallen back. It is useless to be thus swayed, I should say tortured, by daily change from hope to fear. I fear my philosophy or religion is hardly proof against the impatience of my nature. Oh God! forgive and pity me! Nina had bought birthday presents for the other children to give to dearest Henry. She told Willie of it at dinner, and he was greatly pleased, excited in the anticipation, but presently burst into tears—dear, dear boy ! I fear they are prophetic. I have long dreaded the approach of this birthday, thinking the dear child would never see it. I have little hope beyond it—but all is God's. Acted Evelyn pretty well, annoyed and embarrassed (as I have often been) by poor Miss Faucit's cough.

December 19*th.*—Dearest Henry seemed decidedly better, for which I thank God. Went to theatre, and acted Evelyn pretty fairly, not pleased with some unfair advantages taken by Helen Faucit ; it is not wise. She was very prone to this habit once, but I thought had discarded it. Mr. Webster was laughing during the concluding speech, which checked me twice and very nearly made me lose the word. I spoke (which there was no need to do) to him about it when the curtain fell, and he flatly denied it. I (*indiscreetly*) said it was of little consequence to me what he asserted or what he denied. I was very hasty, *but ..othing can justify anger !* Bulwer came in and spoke about cutting the play, and made with Willmott some short cuts. He is very much dissatisfied with the success, and swears he will never write another play.

December 20*th.*—Heard the dear children their hymns. My poor darling Henry not worse, though suffering from a bad night. God bless and restore him. Mr. Pope called and thought him doing well.

December 21*st.*—The birthday of my dear, dear, blessed, suffering child, on whose dear head I invoke the blessing and merciful protection of Almighty God, beseeching Him to raise the darling boy from his bed of pain and sickness to a life of moral and intellectual strength, of health, of virtue, and of wisdom ! This I pray God. Gave the dear children their lessons. A note was given me, half asleep, and only as I was going to the theatre, from the poor actor, Green, in Whitecross Street prison, and brought by his wife. I apologized to her for the delay, and gave her a cheque for £4 to release him from a debt of £3 10*s.* A human being incarcerated—shut from exercise, industry and his house, his wife, and children for £3 10*s. Happy, aristocratical England !!!*

December 22*nd.*—Dearest Henry continues better, thank God. Acted Evelyn tolerably ; some person had come to the theatre to disturb the play, and tried to create opposition as the passage about " man versus money " began.

December 23*rd.*—My dearest boy better. Sent a cheque for £5 to the Nightly Shelter for the Houseless Poor—" poor, naked wretches, wheresoe'er ye are." I would have sent to other hospitals, but am rather straitened in ready money. Received the Lord Chamberlain's answer, who refers my request to the proprietors of Drury Lane and Covent Garden—the oppressed to the oppressor. I was very angry, and began a letter to him, which I had the discretion not to finish. Made some resolutions about the next year, which I hope will be for good; saw that it began on a *Friday;* looked back and discovered that the year in which I chastised that wretch Bunn *began on a Friday. How difficult it is to avoid superstition. Let me hope that it will in this instance tend to good and make me careful to avoid error.* Elliotson spoke very encouragingly of darling Henry. Acted Evelyn fairly. Bulwer came with alterations. Miss H. Faucit was in my room; he gave them to her. I told him of the Lord Chamberlain's letter and of my intention to call on Lord Lansdowne upon it, which he approved.

December 24th.—Lay late in bed. Looked at the newspaper, and when I rose thought dearest Henry a little better, but still—still a subject of painful anxiety to me. God protect and preserve him and my remaining children, for whom I now tremble if attacked by the least illness. An indolent morning. Called on Lord Lansdowne, who was absent from town.

December 25th.—Gave my attention to the composition of my letter to the Lord Chàmberlain. Sat with the children at their dinner. Had read the number of *Master Humphrey's Clock.* Dickens and Forster called, and we walked round the Park at a posting rate together—a delightful afternoon. Returning, copied out the remainder of Bulwer's alterations, and despatched the original with note to Willmott. Forster dined with us. Dearest Katy was weeping when we drank to each other after dinner the old-fashioned wishes of the day. When I asked what made her cry, she told me it was that Joan was not here with us. I had been thinking of the absence of that sweet, precious creature just before. My blessed, blessed, beloved Joan. How often do I see your sweet, blessed face and image before me. Oh, God! bless her, bless her, bless her!

December 26th.—Darling Henry better. Oh, thank God! Whilst trying to divert the dear boy he smiled twice. No sunshine was ever brighter or more cheering to the earth than those dear smiles to my heart! I thanked God for them. Wrote out the fair copy of my letter to the Lord Chamberlain and sent it to him. Mr. King called and Catherine asked him to dine with us. I went into the drawing-room and employed myself with learning the altered passages in the play this evening. Acted Evelyn very feebly; I dislike it so much! The alterations were omitted *to-night,* as all were unsure.

December 28th.—Dearest Henry proceeding well, thank God. Acted Evelyn tolerably. Was grieved to see Miss H. Faucit ill and low-spirited in her performance. Spoke to her after the play; some wretch had been writing a gross and ribald letter of abuse to her! I requested her not to give any thought to it. She is a very sweet girl. Spoke to Miss Horton, who was also very low; her mother is very ill. I promised to write to-morrow to Elliotson about her.

December 29th.—Gave the dear children their lessons, and thought darling Henry progressing very comfortably, thank God! My prayers, the prayers of my heart, are increasing to God to spare the dear boy to a happy life of wisdom and virtue. Talfourd and his son Frank came in. Talfourd thought the play "the merest trash—nothing in it; that it was a great stretch of friendship in me to play Evelyn." He is very envious. Evelyn is not a good part, but I have played, too, the *Athenian Captive.*[1] Spoke to Miss Horton about a note received from Catherine, and wrote a letter of introduction for her to Elliotson. Spoke again with Willmott. Mrs. Warner is discharged! I am truly sorry for her.

December 30th.—Dearest Henry still progressing, I thank God, towards strength and health; it is so sweet to see the little ray of a smile pass over his dear, dear face. God prosper and restore my blessed boy.

December 31st.—The last day of a year has now become a grave and solemn thing to me; I feel my approach towards a change of being, and I cannot contemplate without sad and serious thoughts the "shadows, clouds, and darkness that rest upon it." My heart lifts up its prayer to God for blessings on my beloved family through time to come. Amen. In this year I have received much worldly benefit, for which I thank the bountiful Disposer of all good. But I have lost from among the dearest to my heart one of its very dearest and nearest. My blessed, my beautiful child, my darling, precious Joan, whose sweet face gladdened my heart whenever it met me, now lies insensible and changing to earth in her coffin, lost to me in this world. Farewell, my blessed child, my dear, dear little intelligent creature; in my heart and to my mind you will be often, often present, and I must hope that in a future state of being our spirits may be conscious of the love that joined us here. Farewell—farewell. To the Eternal and All-good I commend thee. Bless thee and farewell.

[1] In Talfourd's drama of that name Macready played the part of Thoas, which was not a congenial one.

1841

January 3rd.—Forster called, and we walked round the Park together, which I very much enjoyed. Confided to him my notion of engrossing a large share of Drury Lane theatre, which he thought very much of, and which I think may be a great thing if I have energy and constancy to carry it through.

January 4th.—Went to the theatre, and left at the stage door, in the hands of the portress (who is one of my inamorata—God help the mark!) the MS. of Mr. Strange.

January 6th.—Forster read me a sketch of characters, for a comedy by Bulwer, of which I thought very poorly. He talked of Cromwell, but that I think beyond all but Shakspeare.

January 7th.—Read a little of *Nina Sforza.* Went to rehearsal with Mrs. Stirling,[1] who takes the part of Clara in the play to-night. Nina called for me, and I went with her to Sir F. Chantrey's; he was out of town; we looked into the studio. We walked home through Belgrave Square and the Park; the weather made the exercise quite an enjoyment to me. Nina did her sum in the afternoon. Edward sent a note with Napier's last two volumes, and borrowed first. He called, after I had rested. Acted Evelyn tolerably well. Was much pleased with Mrs. Stirling in Clara. She speaks with freshness and truth of tone that *no other* actress in the stage now can do.

January 8th.—Received a letter from Bulwer with his sketch of a play for Cromwell, which I do not approve; it has no entirety, no object, and Bulwer is not the poet for historical scenes. Mrs. Warner was in the theatre, and I sent to say I should be glad to speak with her after the play. She came to my room, and I told her I was sorry she was to leave the theatre, and that, as we might not meet again, I did not wish to part with her on terms of estrangement after the affectionate understanding that had subsisted between us. She went into the scandalous affair of last year, endeavouring to make out her case, but

[1] Mary Ann Stirling (1815–1895); *née* Hehl, eventually Lady Gregory ; the well-known actress and teacher of elocution.

114

making admissions that proved her indiscretion. She wished me to say that I considered her as exculpated, which I would not do. I told her I was willing to believe that she believed herself less in fault, and that there had been exaggeration; that, after the attachment I had felt for her, I did not like to think that she might suppose me in absence thinking unkindly of her, and that she might still consider herself as having the right and power of applying to me if ever I could be of service to her. I shook hands with her. She told me she had passed a *most unhappy* year. I was sorry—very sorry to hear it. God help us all! Amen!

January 9th.—Mrs. Warner sent to ask to speak to me again; it was to express her fear that she must have seemed cold and insensible to the kindness of my address to her last night, and that she, in fact, seemed to herself, on recollecting what passed, stunned or stupefied, and that she was anxious to set herself right with me as to her appreciation of my behaviour to her. She talked long, giving me the history of her transactions with Mr. Webster. She admitted her indiscretion and injustice to me, and I parted with her—*very late*—reassuring her of all the kindness I had proffered her yesterday.

January 10th.—Coming down, I saw dearest Henry, who, thank God, is wonderfully better; wonderfully. It is indeed almost a miracle.[1]

January 11th.—Found dearest Henry still advancing in health and strength. I thank God from my inmost heart—but, oh! how often do I think of the sweet and blessed being that is gone from among us, who seems to me now the dearest and the sweetest of all that God had given me. Oh, bless her! Bless her! Beloved child—darling, darling Joan! My heart yearns to thee, sweetest! dearest! Went up to the drawing-room, after reading a scene of *Nina Sforza*, to see Forster, who was there. He read me a letter from Bulwer, starting the idea of Sir Robert Walpole as a dramatic character. I caught at it.

January 12th.—My dear children not very satisfactory over their early lessons; perhaps my desire of seeing them advance may make me too exacting and impatient, yet I try to check my tendency to haste. Looked through chapters of *History of England* for information on Walpole.

January 13th.—Mr. King called to give Willie a lesson, but we

[1] The recovery was, unfortunately, only partial, the mental powers becoming to some extent impaired, and later on epileptic tendencies developed, resulting in the boy's premature death in 1857, at the age of eighteen.

were coated and hatted to go out and I begged him off. We went to
Sir Francis Chantrey's. I showed Willie his statue of Washington;
we went into his library, and I sat with him an inordinate length of
time. I opened my views, into which he cordially entered; I told him
of Rogers, and he said he would see him. He evidently likes the undertaking, and would wish to make a bust of Mrs. Siddons. He preferred
speaking himself to Milman about the place in the Abbey for it, before
I again addressed the Dean and Chapter. He pressed us to stay
luncheon, which we did, and went with him and Lady Chantrey into
the drawing-room.

January 20th.—Acted Evelyn well; was called for and well received.
Lady Essex,[1] once the fascinating Miss Stephens, for whom I *could*
have felt a desperate regard and did cherish a tender one, sat in the
stage box! Ah—*quam mutata !* And I am just as old, as changed!
Alas! Miss H. Faucit resumed her character; does not seem well.

January 21st.—Called on Dickens and gave him Darley's first copy
of *Ethelstan.* We walked out, called on Rogers; I told him that
Chantrey was to see him, and mentioned my proposal of setting the
subscription on foot : he readily approved all. Asked Dickens to spare
the life of Nell in his story (*Master Humphrey's Clock*), and observed
that he was cruel. He blushed, and men who blush are said to be
either proud or cruel; he is not proud, and therefore—or, as Dickens
added—the axiom is false. He invited us to dine on Sunday sennight.

January 22nd.—Arranged the persons to whom I would apply for
Mrs. Siddons's monument, and wrote notes on the subject to Bulwer,
to Young, to Talfourd; Catherine wrote to Fanny Twiss. Went to
the theatre, and acted Evelyn with much effort; I was quite wearied
down. Found at home notes from Ransom, and one from Dickens
with an onward number of *Master Humphrey's Clock.* I saw one print
in it of the dear dead child that gave a dead chill through my blood.
I dread to read it, but I must get it over. I have read the two numbers ;
I never have read printed words that gave me so much pain. I could
not weep for some time. Sensation, sufferings have returned to me,
that are terrible to awaken; it is real to me; I cannot criticize it.

January 23rd.—Was told by Willmott that a paper of a subscription, which I had seen last night in the green-room, was a subscription
to present a testimonial to Mr. T. Duncombe,[2] for moving that plays

---

[1] Catherine Stephens (1794–1882); the well-known actress and singer; married the fifth
Earl of Essex in 1838.

[2] Thomas Slingsby Duncombe (1796–1861); the "dandy democrat"; began his career

be acted on the off-nights in Lent in the House of Commons. I repro-
bated the whole affair, as most unworthy of any art; the object obtained
was not of sufficient value; the labour and talent used was 0; the
character of the individual for acquirement in art or literature, for
eloquence, statesmanlike qualities, or any great distinguishing property
was again 0. And this man is recompensed by the members of the
dramatic art as its champion, patron, protector, etc. Faugh! I told
Willmott that I should enter my protest against it, if it were a public
measure, but it is a hole-and-corner one. I gave Miss Faucit my
opinion, leaving her to act as she thought best.

January 25th.—Called on Campbell, whom I found at home, and
to whom I mentioned the purpose of placing Mrs. Siddons's bust in
the Abbey; he entered into it as cordially as he could into anything,
for he has not the *œstrum* in his manner. He expressed himself
anxious to improve our acquaintance. Called at Forster's, thence to
Ransom's where I paid in my dividends, onward to find Sheil's dwelling,
which I could not discover, to Sir Francis Chantrey's, with whom I
had again a long talk. He interests me much by his downright manner
and his confidence with regard to his conceptions. He approved the
committee. I saw Allan Cunningham, and expressed myself willing
to receive his play of *Wallace*, about which he had written to me.
Called at Lord Lansdowne's; he was just going to the Council at the
Palace. I merely left my card. To Sir M. A. Shee, whom I found at
home and Gally Knight [1] sitting to him.

January 27th.—Thought a good deal upon my prospects and claims;
calculated for my children's good, and see little to reason me from the
necessity of again entering management, if I can do so without hazard
of what I possess. The stage seems to want me. There is no theatre,
but that to a man with a family is no argument; there is no theatre
for me, and that is an overwhelming plea. Then much may be done
of good in all ways.

January 28th.—A very courteous note from Lord Lansdowne giving
his name and co-operation to the Siddons monument. Looked at the
newspaper. Wrote to Horace Twiss, to Lord Northampton, to Thomas
Moore, to Sheil, to Lord Normanby, to Hallam, to Babbage, to Mr.
Milnes, all on the Siddons monument.

as an ensign in the Coldstream Guards, but soon resigned his commission and entered Parliament as an extreme Radical, in which capacity he presented the Chartist Petition of 1842.
He was also an active member of the " Friends of Italy," and a supporter of Kossuth.

[1] Henry Gally Knight (1786–1846); an authority on architecture; for some time in
Parliament.

January 29th.—Acted Evelyn very well. Bulwer came into my room, and talked long about his own defects in public speaking—the effect of his nervousness, etc.—which I explained to him—about Sir R. Walpole as a subject for a comedy.

January 31st.—Dickens called for me and I accompanied him to Rogers's, where we dined. Met Eastlake, Colonel Fox, Kenney, Maltby, Sir George Talbot, Babbage, and a young man whom I had met at Lord Lansdowne's. A pleasant day. Showed Rogers my committee list, with which he was pleased.

February 1st.—Wrote notes to Lockhart, Procter, Sir A. Calcott, Barry, Cockerell, H. Taylor, inviting them to be on the Siddons committee.

February 2nd.—Beazley called, and I inquired of him the condition, prospects, and probable proceeding of the persons directing Drury Lane theatre, mentioning my own views, my inability to continue at the Haymarket theatre, and the necessity there was for my finding some theatre for the drama. He caught at the idea of my entering upon it, but saw a necessity for taking some person, Lord Glengall or Mr. Dunn (both intimates of Mr. Bunn), into confidence. We talked much of it, and parted, each to think of it, and I to make some digest of my views.

February 3rd.—Rose in good time; gave the children their lessons and went out a few minutes after nine to call on Horace Twiss; talked to him of the Siddons monument. He mentioned, among others, Croker's name, but as he—Croker—thought the "art not sufficiently elevated to merit the election of a leading actor into the Athenæum Club," he does not seem to be a proper person to offer honour to the most eminent of the professors of that art. He was to procure me what names he could. Went on to see Mr. Harness, asked him, as Mrs. Siddons's friend, to procure any names he could, and give them to Milman or myself; he evidently wished to be on the committee, but I do not understand his claim; and, if *his own account be true*, which I doubt, he formed a committee for the same purpose, but *never applied to me*. We talked about Mrs. Butler, and he wished to be very friendly, but he has not the *murus aheneus* of Horace when with me. Called on Dickens and Dr. Spry. Letter from Lord Aberdeen accepting the place on the committee; one from Barry, the architect, declining.

February 4th.—Willie and Eddywaddy conspired to pull me out of bed at an early hour this morning—the dear fellows! and by this stratagem they were got out of their beds earlier than usual.   Gave the children their lessons.

February 5th.—Was guilty of bad taste in telling an unbecoming (for *me*) story in the green-room.   I did not think of it.   News of the Duke of Wellington's sudden illness in the House of Lords.   Miss H. Faucit told me of Mr. Farren's report of a splendid comedy at Covent Garden theatre by a Mr. Lee Morton.   Letter from Sheil, declining (!) to give his name to Mrs. Siddons's monument.   Calculated its value.

February 6th.—Miss Faucit told me on the stage after the play that I had *seen a play* by the Mr. Lee Morton who had read his comedy at Covent Garden theatre; I could not remember it.   She came into my room and gave me a history that was reported of me—" that this Mr. Lee Morton, on the rejection of a play called *Woman* by Madame Vestris, had sent it to me; had had interviews with me; that I had said I would act the play if he would take the good speeches out of the woman's part and put them into mine, particularly a speech in praise of Shakspeare, and the tag; that although his play had been rejected at Covent Garden theatre, he nevertheless would not submit to this. I tried vainly to recollect in years back any circumstances respecting such a play, on which these statements could have been founded.   I could think of none.   I told Miss Faucit that it did not at all disturb me; that the calumny of actors was what I had always had to bear, but that it did not reach me in the opinions of the intelligent and estimable.   Miss Faucit seemed concerned that these things were said of me by everybody; *viz.* that " I was so selfish, and would let no one have a chance." How everybody's " everybody " differs, the one from the other!   I told her I had never seen the man; never seen the play; that it was altogether a falsehood.   I laughed a good deal at it, and told her these things did not reach me.   She could not inform me of Mr. Lee Morton's *real* name, and I said I would ask Willmott of it. Mr. Farren had been her informant, to whom Mr. C. Mathews had related the slander, Mr. Lee Morton standing by!!   Willmott came in; had heard of the Covent Garden comedy, and its author, Mr. Lee Morton; did not know his real name, but John Webster knew everything about him, having lived with him.   I sent for John Webster, who, without any reservation, related to me that he knew the man well; his name was Belvedere Dion Boucicault; that Dr. Lardner was his guardian (Dion! by the gods!); that he had tried the stage at Cheltenham and Brighton; had become acquainted with a Miss Lacy of the

Bristol theatre; through her with a Mr. Parratt; through him with Mr. Bartley, to whom he had shown two acts of a play; that he wrote the play of *Woman* under John Webster's eye, as he lived with him at the time, and John Webster read each scene as it was written; that he took it to Covent Garden theatre, where it was rejected, and it was proposed to him to write a comedy; that John Webster wished him to let him bring it to me, assuring him that if he told me it was the work of a young man I was certain to read it. He did not. If he *had* sent the play to me, it must have been within the last three months. Here was the whole lie exploded. I sent for Miss Faucit, and, in the presence of Willmott, told her what had passed.

February 8th.—Acted Evelyn very feebly. Spoke again with Miss Faucit about the affair of Mr. Lee Morton, etc. She told me that Mr. Farren had spoken with him on Saturday night and questioned him; that he had said he had not had any direct communication with me, but the transaction was through a friend. Mr. Farren thought that the falsehood was chiefly Mr. C. Mathews's, as he now was *made to confess* that Mr. Lee Morton was not "standing by," but only "in the room" when the falsehood was told.

February 9th.—Thought over, dictated, and wrote a letter to Mr. C. Mathews, simply, and I think tranquilly, observing that there was not one word of truth in the statements reported to have been made by him, Mr. C. Mathews, in the Covent Garden green-room. Copies were sent to Mr. Harley and Cooper, the persons present at the narration, and one I kept to give Miss Faucit for Mr. Farren.

February 11th.—At home found a very foolish (I think) and impertinent note from Mr. C. Mathews, which I folded up altogether to return to him; on reflection, however, I did not see that I should be clearly justified in that, and wrote a brief answer to the effect that the note he had termed "anonymous" was in my name. I rested through the afternoon. Forster called. I was not easy at having perhaps having embroiled myself with Mr. C. Mathews; but I reflected that I was not the aggressor—indeed was *seriously injured.* Acted Evelyn very fairly. Spoke to Miss Faucit, asking her what Mr. Farren said to the note to Mr. C. Mathews. He thought it *quite proper.*

February 12th.—Miss Faucit sent to express her wish to speak to me. She told me that Mr. Farren had turned round in his idea of the Lee Morton slander, that Mr. C. Mathews would send me another letter, and if I did not reply to him as he required, the whole matter would appear in the newspapers; that they had proof (!!)—letters, etc., from some intimate connection of mine!! I laughed much; and these are players—my *brother* performers!!! Great God! is there a viler thing, a thing more ridiculously base, than a mere player!

February 13th.—A note was brought to me from Mr. Charles Mathews. I enclosed it in a cover, observing that "having already intimated, upon his admission of facts and his threat of publication, that I should decline further correspondence with him, I begged to be excused opening the enclosed," which I sent directly back to Covent Garden theatre unopened. Saw Miss Chester [1] in a private box. We are growing old; it is visible that we are so in the faces of those around us—the best looking-glass.

February 14th.—Anderson called. I told him that what I wished to speak with him upon was under the condition of the strictest secrecy and in the most perfect confidence. He assured me of my perfect dependence on his faith, and I developed to him my views on Drury Lane, in case the proprietors were willing to entrust the theatre to me; observing to him, that if he were not satisfied with his condition at Covent Garden theatre (which he represented himself not to be), that I should be willing to regard him as one attached to the undertaking, if it reached anything; that I should place him in an official situation, and should look forward to him as my successor in the course of time. He expressed his readiness and happiness to be made a participator in such an undertaking. The conversation led on to other things, and what I wished to avert—my correspondence with Mr. Mathews. I told him of it, and, as I could not recollect it, read the correspondence to him. I told him I would as soon as possible for his own sake apprise him of the chances of proceeding; he left me, gratified, if with no other result, with the conversation he had had.

February 15th.—Found Edward here, who had written a note to me—among other things complaining of Forster's Caliban manners—which I cannot defend.

February 16th.—Acted Evelyn well. Miss Faucit had sent me a note, enclosing a letter from Mr. C. Mathews, which I would not read. Afterwards she told me that his *returned* letter contained a *denial* of "having made the assertions," with certain recriminating charges, showing his consciousness of all that could be urged against him. Farren, it appears, attacked him upon this denial, which resolved itself

---

[1] An actress whose personal attractions had obtained for her the post of "reader" to George IV.

into a "*denial* that he had *asserted*, he had only *repeated*——"!!! I told her Mr. Farren must write his own exculpation.

February 17th.—Wrote a note to my brother Edward to come over, which he did. After very much talk, we agreed that I should wait at home all day for the chance of Mr. Lee Morton's promised call; should make an appointment with O'Hanlon to-morrow, find this L. Morton and obtain some satisfaction respecting these "proofs." Wrote to O'Hanlon for to-morrow; wrote to Farren, demanding his authority for what he had repeated of me. Miss Faucit told me that *they*—the set—insisted they had seen *proofs*. I told her I should search for them. Willmott would tell me that Mathews had sent copies and statements to all the performers. Sent him everywhere in search of Mr. Lee Morton; desired him to get the aid of the police, and offered five guineas to discover him. Note from Farren, acknowledging all.

February 18th.—Lunn came from his quest of Mr. Lee Morton; sent him again to ask Mr. Brougham his address from myself. Looked at the newspaper. My mind was in all the restlessness of expectation, and my body in the uneasy nervousness resulting from it. Disappointed; sent Lunn again to the address gained—45, Leicester Square. Tried to read a paper on education, but could do nothing. Lunn at last returned with news that he had traced him to his earth—that he was at 45, Leicester Square. The carriage returned, and I set off in it, much improved in spirits, to call at White and Whitmore's; found White—not the best man, but still a solicitor—told my tale, and suggested another witness, which I saw necessary. We called on Forster and found him at work, made him put on his clothes, and we drove to Leicester Square; alighted at some distance from the house, and, walking to it, we inquired for Mr. Lee Morton, and following the woman up-stairs, met Mr. L. M—— at the drawing-room door. A Mr. Perrott came in and was going out, but I requested him to remain as "Mr. L. M.'s friend." I explained to him—as agreed on amongst us—my object in calling on him. He said he was just coming to call on me, appealing to Mr. Perrott. I told him that Mr. Mathews had made certain statements which compromised him, and I wished to hear his own statement before I accepted another's assertions. He said that he had received letters from a friend of his, a Mr. Roynon Jones, saying he had presented the play of *Woman* to me, and that I had chosen a part in it, with the obnoxious additions, not distinctly attributed to me. I asked him if he would object to give up the letters; he said no, and I took them—they were priceless to me. Forster asked

122

him to repeat exactly what he had said to Mr. C. Mathews, as it was probable much more had been said than his words authorized. *He told his tale*, which he said he had only given to Mr. and Mrs. C. Mathews, and expressly denied the different points we put to him, *viz.* whether he had said I wished to take " the best speeches " from the woman's part, and whether he had withdrawn the play in consequence, leaving part of the falsehood with Mr. C. Mathews. Forster then observed that of course he would not object to write down what he had stated; he consented, sat down to write; he read what he had set down, which was sufficient; he signed it, and his friend Mr. Perrott and my solicitor Mr. White witnessed it. Mr. Perrott said that he had been certain I had not seen the play from the first. Left him, and gratefully returned home, parting from White and Forster. Came home, languid, weary, yet at peace, thank God! Lunched, and found a letter from Clarke, subscribing to my terms; another from Landor, crabbedly, I think, declining to be on the Siddons Committee. Went with Nina to Westminster Abbey; showed her the monuments of several poets, the choir, etc. Chantrey arrived, and we examined every part of it, marking several places as available for a monument. He stood in the places to show me the effect of the light, and made me stand for him. I am greatly pleased in listening to the ponderous sense of his remarks. He observed, as we parted, that now I might call my committee, and that it would be better to see what we could get before we decided on anything. He was very tenacious of being *forced on* the committee, and laid strict injunctions on me to beware of such a course. After the play, asked Misses H. Faucit, P. Horton, Mr. Wrench and Willmott, and read them the *proofs*, "undated and envenomed," with Mr. Lee Morton's attested retractation and confession.

February 19th.—Brydone called; held a long conversation. I saw a picture of human nature; he now sees the opportunity of being important to Mr. C. Mathews, etc., and is disposed to extenuate what before he thought so strong against them. He is not false, but is not strong-minded. I said Mr. C. M—— was altogether wrong. I had done with him. But if I were told that he wished to withdraw his letters, and I saw that written by him, I should not refuse to write to Brydone, saying I dismissed all feeling of irritation on the subject. Walked out with Dickens, left cards at Rogers's. Went into several auction-rooms, looking at curious and pretty things. Walked home; was very much tired. Wrote to Bulwer, trying to dissuade him from dining at the Shakspearian Club Festival, of which that *scoundrel* Gregory, editor of the *Satirist*, is the head. Wrote to the postmaster of Gloucester, enclosing a letter to *Mr. Roynon Jones*. Acted Evelyn very fairly. Received a note, wishing an interview with Mr. Lee Morton.

February 20th. —Mr. Lee Morton called—for what I could scarcely understand, except to seek for pity somewhere; the whole Covent Garden tribe turn like curs upon him and yelp and bark in one cry, one note against him, bearing down by clamour all he may say. *They have exaggerated his statements*, and what he told without feeling they have repeated with malignant exultation. I dealt kindly by him, and gave him some salutary advice. Paid Lunn his wages and gave him what I had promised, if he succeeded—£5 5s. for finding Mr. Lee Moreton. Acted Evelyn very well. It seems now to me, if age is not too observable in me, an artificial performance. Helen Faucit brought me some letters of Mr. Webster to ask my counsel on. Willmotti came to ask me about the plays for next season from Mr. Webster. I would give him no answer until next season. I will write to him as much. Note from White, enclosing one from Gloucester, with an account of *Roynon Jones.*

February 26th.—Lunn called, and his news was that the Queen was to visit the Haymarket to-night. Mr. Faraday had called. Acted Evelyn unequally—pretty well. I saw that Lord Normanby had placed himself in one of the boxes opposite to the Queen's side of the House.

February 27th.—Went to Lord Northampton's; thought his reception of me rather cold; saw array of Bulwer, Wheatstone, Chantrey, Cartwright, Brockedon, Babbage, Elliotson, Talfourd, who introduced me to Lord Monteagle, and to Pierce Butler, with whom I had some conversation, and one or two others—Peel, Ternan, M. Milnes, Bishop of Norwich, and a large crowd were there. Did not enjoy my evening.

February 28th.—Brydone called and gave me an account of Mr. C. Mathews—which did not quite satisfy me as direct and clear; he wished me, which I did not, to see his letter to Brydone. I looked at it, and perceiving that it professed to be written "*in consequence of* the conciliatory tone he had heard I had used," I returned it to Brydone without reading more, declining to be recorded as one seeking to *conciliate* a person who had inflicted such an injury upon me, who had behaved so slightingly and discourteously to me, and to whom I felt perfect indifference. I was content that things should rest *in statu quo.* Daniel called—talked long. I had been hesitating the whole morning, but at length walked out with Brydone to Piccadilly.

Called on Mrs. Butler; saw C. Kemble, wasted, old, decrepit; he said he had suffered much, but that now he thought he was "landed"; he looked as if he would be soon, but he had walked down to the Garrick Club and back! and felt that it was a little too much for him. Pierce Butler seemed glad to see me; an American, General Hamilton, came in, and we talked. He and Mr. Butler went out to dine with Trelawny, after Mrs. Butler came in. I liked her frank and genuine manner very much indeed; it is rarely that I have seen a person I have been so taken with. We talked long. Found Forster at home; he dined with us. Stories of country theatres and my father's amused us through an idle evening.

March 2nd.—Brydone called and read to me Mr. C. Mathews's letter to him, which I observed to him was ridiculous; he, the offending party, wrote as if requiring retractation! At Brydone's instance I wrote the letter he *ought* to have written, which I gave him, telling him I was indifferent to any further movement in the business. I spoke to him about the state of things at the Haymarket, and the seeming *necessity* there was that I should undertake one of the winter theatres. Arranged my bills and receipts and rested. At the theatre received a note from Miss Faucit asking me to act Jaques as a second piece for her; I went up to her room and *told* her I *could not.*

March 3rd.—Going out, called "to enquire" at Lord Lansdowne's; called on Rogers, whom I found at home, and with whom I passed a most delightful half-hour; he advised me to call on old Denman.[1]

March 4th.—Began to act Evelyn very languidly, but in the first act saw Mrs. Adams in the theatre, and played my very best. A note from a Mrs. Miller. Heard that the Covent Garden comedy—Mr. Lee Morton's—had been successful to the middle of the fifth act. Heard that a deputation (!) consisting of Messrs. Sheridan Knowles, Webster, Wallack, Wrench, Vining and Strickland had gone to present their cup to Mr. T. Duncombe! Forster reached home as I did, and brought news of the comedy's success.[2]

March 5th.—Saw the paper with an eulogistic account of Mr. Lee Morton's new comedy; as I have always held, the chief among the many causes of the drama's decline is the dramatic criticism of England. Acted Evelyn but indifferently, being unwell and languid. Was not

---

[1] The Lord Chief Justice.

[2] *London Assurance.* The comedy brought the author, then barely twenty-one, into immediate repute as a playwright.

pleased with the manner in which Miss Faucit spoke of the comedy—accepting evidence that against herself she would have despised; it was not well.

March 6th.—Read the papers. Indignant and disgusted with the declaration of Lord John Russell, that if Lord Cardigan had not been a *peer*, he would not have been assailed as he was! Talked and thought over with Catherine the state and prospect of my affairs. I would wish particularly to " do nothing from strife or vain-glory "—not to let the *least particle* of either motive mingle with my incentives to act for my family's good. I do not think I have any other view than to benefit them, and *I do not see* any other way than by resuming the direction of a theatre. Forster told me to-day that Dickens would put an advertisement in the paper on Monday in reference to his father [1]—which I told him he *ought not* to do.

March 7th.—Went out to call on Dickens, who read me part of his preface to *Oliver Twist*—which I liked; on Lord Denman, who was not at home; on Mr. and Mrs. Pierce Butler (with whom I found Mr. Bartley!), and with whom I talked some time, and asked them to dine. Called on Mrs. Norton, whom I found, beautiful in the languor of returning health, reclining on a sofa. The Contessina (so calling herself) Vespucci came in and sat some time. Mr. Charles Sheridan, who talked to me much about a College of Civil Engineers, just established at Putney, in which he took interest, and Lord Augustus Fitzclarence were there. I sat long. Called on Young and sat some time with him. Going home passed that bad man Bunn, looking rather shabby. Dickens was strong for me to resume the direction of a theatre. Fox, etc., also. I resolved to do so, and saw what looked auguries of good.

March 9th.—Went out earlier than usual, enjoying the sweet spring air as I walked, to call on Beazley. I learned from him that he had communicated with Dunn—had learned distinctly and positively from him that the Committee entertained no idea of retaining Mr. Bunn in the theatre, that his re-occupation was quite *out of the question;* to Beazley's mention of myself he cordially responded, and felt sure of the Committee's acquiescence.

March 13th.—Received a note from Helen Faucit, enclosing an anonymous letter and a critique from the *Morning Herald*, wishing my opinion. In a hasty discourse with her I explained to her that

---

[1] Supposed to be the prototype of Micawber. His constant pecuniary embarrassments caused Dickens no little annoyance.

it was not I whom she " imitated "—the charge against her—but that she was languid and *untrue*.

March 14th.—Bulwer called and invited me to dine on Thursday, mentioning his wish to invite Mr. Boucicault—*alias* Lee Morton—and inquiring if I objected to meet him. I told him that in dining at *his* house, I was indifferent about the persons I met, but that I thought he ought to know all I knew of Mr. Boucicault before he made up his mind to invite him. I told him of the late occurrences and showed him the " proofs, etc.," on which he drew in, and gave up the idea of our meeting.[1] Kind Elliotson called and saw the children. Mr. and Mrs. McIan, Mr. and Mrs. Brydone, Mrs. Wightwick, Mr. Stone,[2] Greaves and George Warde and Miss P. Horton came to dinner. We passed rather a cheerful day ; Mr. Stone, who is a bore, though a very clever artist, would persist in a tedious argument. While dressing for dinner, received a letter from a Mr. Mulock whom, it seems, I had met in calling on Young—arguing a sort of case for Mr. C. Mathews. I said I would send an answer.

March 16th.—Mr. Mulock called by appointment—much gratified by my letter to him. I made it a preliminary to our conversation that it should be understood and agreed between us that Mr. C. Mathews, after what had passed, had no claim on me, that I had quite done with him, that I should receive no message from him, that he was in effect " thrown overboard " ! I then came to the necessity of agreeing upon the point of the reality or not of the injury in Mr. Mathews's repeated statements. Mr. Mulock admitted that as he now saw them they were pregnant with injury to me—most injurious. We passed a long time—too long a time—in the discussion of this worthless subject ; at last it resolved itself to the complaint that others as well as Mr. Mathews had the impression that I meant to charge him with *originating* the slander against me ; this I disavowed *on my own account ;* said I would not be content with a mere verbal disavowal, but that I would *write* to him, Mr. Mulock, my denial of any such charge. It appeared that Mr. C. Mathews had *repeated* these statements and spread the slander, which was only a difference

---

[1] The Lee Morton incident, which Macready took so seriously, seems to have originated in the desire of Mr. C. Mathews and other congenial spirits to " get a rise " out of the austere and somewhat high-handed tragedian, who was far from being popular in the profession. They undoubtedly carried the affair beyond the limits of joke, but Boucicault was evidently an unwilling agent, for whose youth and inexperience Macready might well have made greater allowance.

[2] Frank Stone (1800–1859), afterwards A.R.A.

127

in degree from the *very* first issue. He left me with many declarations of *high opinion*, etc. Colonel Gurwood [1] had in the meantime called with Mrs. Gurwood, and I did not see them! Wrote the letter to Mulock, as stated. Pierce Butler called. Note from Wheatstone. Went with dear Catherine to dine with the Brayshers. Met Mr. and Mrs. Peile, a wretched "dust" called Fletcher, Helen Faucit, and some intolerables. Liked Peile and one or two others. Was very intolerant—not with due regard to good breeding—in the conversation with that uninformed, assuming, talking "dust."

March 18th.—Dined with Bulwer and met a Mr. —— of the British Museum—an awful geological dust and bore, Sir Charles Morgan, Blanchard, Fox, Forster; passed a cheerful day. Found at home a letter from the solicitor of stamps and taxes, threatening me with levy by his sheriff if I did not pay a charge, for which I had only asked for dates.

March 20th.—Going out in the carriage with Catherine, called on Colonel Gurwood; sat some time with Mrs. Gurwood and Miss Meyer [2]—sweet girl! Went to the Exhibition of British Artists, Suffolk Street. Saw Mr. and Mrs. McIan there. Found at home a letter from Mr. Mulock enclosing me one from Mr. C. Mathews to read, which I would not read.

March 22nd.—Called on Bulwer and talked with him on the business of the Siddons committee. Went to Exeter Hall. Milman came, Gally Knight, then Lord Lansdowne. We talked and waited some time, and no one coming, proceeded to business. Rogers dropped in, as we had voted three or four resolutions, [3] which were approved.

---

[1] John Gurwood (1790-1845); Colonel, C.B., editor of the *Wellington Dispatches*.

[2] Afterwards first Viscountess Esher.

[3] THE SIDDONS MONUMENT.—At a meeting of the committee held at Exeter Hall, on March 22, 1841, the most noble the Marquis of Lansdowne in the Chair, the following resolutions were unanimously agreed to—

Resolved.—That as monuments have been erected in Westminster Abbey to the memory of many distinguished professors of the dramatic art, it is an omission on the part of those who drew delight and instruction from the sublime personations of Mrs. Siddons, that the name of that actress, who, by a singular union of the highest intellectual and physical qualifications, transcended the artists of her own, or perhaps, of any other time, should have so long remained without public record or notice.

Resolved.—That in order to render justice to her rare perfections, and convey to posterity some idea of the estimation in which her surpassing powers were held by her contemporaries, a bust or statue of Mrs. Siddons be placed in Westminster Abbey.

Resolved.—That in order to afford the opportunity of participating in this object to those who enjoyed the delight of witnessing the representations of this great actress, or who have profited, in the performances of inferior artists, by the lessons her genius taught, the expenses of the proposed monument be met by a public subscription—(*note by Sir F. Pollock*).

Then Bulwer came; an excuse from Dickens and Tom Moore. The bankers, advertisements, etc., were all arranged. Lord L—— undertook to write to Chantrey on the business. I was asked if I would be treasurer. I declined, and suggested as an idle man C. Young. On breaking up, I called on Young, met his brother George with him—asked him to be treasurer; he very kindly begged off. Lady Essex and Miss Johnston came in. She is unaltered in manner, but in beauty—alas! where are the charms that made her so often present to my sight? Eheu! fugaces! Mrs. Jameson, Mrs. Pierce Butler, Kenney, Dickens, Travers, Harness and Rogers dined with us.

March 23rd.—Beazley and Dunn called, and we talked over the feasibility of re-opening Drury Lane theatre *as a theatre.* I mentioned what must form the basis of any agreement—liberty to close at a day's notice; no compulsion to pay any rent; no rent to be paid before Christmas; my salary to be included among the working expenses of the theatre; the theatre not to be opened before Christmas; to be mine in virtue of a clear lesseeship; not for the committee to have the power of letting it during my vacation, etc. As I was preparing for dinner I received by post a letter from Mr. Mulock, in which he distorts a statement of mine, in order to give it the grossest and most direct contradiction; he does not know ' why I am to assume so much importance; that I cherish an unextinguishable hate towards Mr. C. Mathews; that he shall recommend Mr. C. Mathews to publish the whole of the correspondence, and that the public may think as he hinted (so he says—*a falsehood*) that my sternness to Mr. C. Mathews arises from my envy of his great success in Covent Garden theatre.' I sat down to answer it, but found I must *give* the lie to everything he said, and that the letter was not one which a person with any pretension to gentlemanly character could indite, and that no gentleman could receive. It was really an outrage. I at last enclosed it in an envelope and returned it by post. Babbage, Mr. and Mrs. Swinfen Jervis, Lady Jenkins, Lord Nugent, Sir E. Bulwer, Dr. Quin came to dinner. Fonblanque sent an excuse at the last moment for himself and wife from Dinan. This is not right in any one; in one who judges and canvasses the dealings of others rigidly it is very objectionable. Our table was broken up, and the day was dull; in the evening the Fonblanques came, Colonel and Mrs. Gurwood and Miss Meyer, Martin, Dickenses, Sheils and Mrs. Power, Dr. Elliotson, Professor Wheatstone, Miss Hawes and mother, Miss P. Horton, Mrs. Horace Twiss, Mrs. Kitchener, Jephsons, G. Raymond, Forster, Z. Troughton, and others whom I forget. I was tired out before we were left alone—to look at the lights in the empty room, and think how much we had endured (I at least) for perhaps censorious comment. Very late in bed.

March 24th.—Wrote out the heads of my stipulations in any agreement with Drury Lane proprietors. Lord Glengall and Dunn called; I read my stipulations, which were considered admissible. Lord Glengall was earnest to carry the proposed agreement into effect. When they were gone, I wrote notes of summons to Serle and Anderson. Forster came to dine. I told him of that old vile twaddle, Molock or Mulock.

March 25th.—Brydone called; I told him that there was every prospect of an arrangement at Drury Lane; gave him directions about the advertisements. Anderson called, and informing him of the state of affairs, I questioned him on the likelihood of Ellen Tree's adhesion. He thought she would be adverse to me; Mrs. Nisbett [1] not so; Serle called, and we entered on business—discussing various people; despatched them, Anderson to Mrs. Nisbett, Serle to Keeley,[2] Mrs. Clifford, and D. Rees.

March 26th.—Mrs. Warner called—*talked very much.* She is quick-tongued, I never felt it before; I listened, watching my opportunity, and spoke on the business of Drury Lane theatre; the old sore subject came up, Miss Faucit. I brought it to this point—either make your bargain with me *en métier*, and leave me to reduce it as I can, or come to me in the confidence of a friend as you have done before. She left me to write an answer, which I suppose I shall receive. C. J. Smith called and Serle; C. J. Smith expressed his gratification in coming and stating his salary to be £3 10s., which I gave him the liberty to sign for; signed for *£3!* All are not bad yet! Anderson called with news from Mrs. Nisbett, who was anxious to come, but wished to make certain stipulations about *business* and to demand a high salary. Serle and Anderson were to call on her together to-morrow. Serle brought a letter from Keeley with the engagement of himself and wife.[3] Gave them directions with respect to Payne, Ellen Tree, etc., and they left me. After dinner wrote notes

---

[1] Louisa Craustoun Nisbett (1812–1858), *née* Mordaunt; a popular comedy actress; she afterwards married Sir William Boothby, after whose death she returned to the stage, finally retiring in 1851.

[2] Robert Keeley (1793–1869); the well-known actor, husband of Mary Ann Keeley.

[3] Mary Ann Keeley (1805–1899), *née* Goward; one of the most gifted *comédiennes* of the nineteenth century.

to Harley and Young, the "Pantomime Poet," enclosing them to Serle, and directing him to deliver them.

April 3rd.—Found Serle at home, who informed me that the committee were most anxious that I should undertake the theatre, and appointed to meet me on Monday at half-past one; that Mrs. Nisbett and others had engaged at Covent Garden theatre. I dressed and went to the Athenæum, where I met Dickens and Cattermole; accompanied Dickens to Lord Northampton's, where the meeting was not large. Saw Elliotson, Stanfield, Pickersgill, Rogers, Auldjo, Crabbe Robinson, Goldsmid, Bishop, Gally Knight.

April 4th.—Young, the pantomimist, called, and agreed to set to work. Anderson and Serle called, and we discussed the various facts before us. I mentioned my intention of writing Miss Kelly [1] to take the *old women*. They left me. Elliotson called, and prescribed for me.

April 5th.—Went to Drury Lane and, with Serle, met the Drury Lane committee, Lord Glengall, Messrs. Allen, Durrant (Burgess, Secretary; Dunn, Treasurer), and, afterwards, Sir William Curtis. They discussed the heads of the proposals submitted to them, and were all avowedly anxious for my tenancy. They wished to put the taxes of the theatre in the current expenses.

April 6th.—Called on Miss Kelly, who showed me over her theatre.[2] which is very pretty. I stated my business to her, proposing to her the line of old characters acted by Miss Pope, Mrs. Mattocks, etc.;

---

[1] Frances Maria Kelly (1790–1882); a distinguished actress, whose youthful performances had enlisted the admiration of Fox and Sheridan. She played chiefly in Shaksperian parts, enacting Ophelia to Edmund Kean's Hamlet. Charles Lamb greatly admired her and made her an offer of marriage, he being then forty-four and she twenty-nine. " I am not so foolish," he wrote, "as not to know that I am a most unworthy match for such a one as you ; but you have for years been a principal object in my mind. In many a sweet assumed character I have learned to love you ; but simply as F. M. Kelly I love you better than them all." Miss Kelly returned an amiable and appreciative refusal, to which Lamb made the following rejoinder :—

"July 20, 1819.

" DEAR MISS KELLY,

" *Your injunctions shall be obeyed to a tittle.* I feel myself in a lackadaisical no-howish kind of a humour. I believe it is the rain or something. I had thought to have written seriously, but I fancy I succeed best in epistles of mere fun ; puns and *that* nonsense. You will be good friends with us, will you not ? Let what has passed ' break no bones ' between us. You will not refuse us them next time we send for them ?

" Yours very truly,
"C. L."

(The " bones " was a joking reference to the ivory free passes issued by the theatre.)
[2] The Royalty, where she conducted a dramatic school.

talked long with her and left her, promising to send her a proposal. Forster called and promised to come to dine. Letter from Ellison, applying for the office of leader under me at Drury Lane. Looked over lists of plays for Miss Kelly. Elliotson called and saw Nina; talked long. Forster dined with me. I went to call for H. Smith, and he accompanied me to the theatre. The General Committee was sitting; we met them. I explained my views; they deliberated. We met them again, and they gave me the theatre, in which undertaking may God prosper me.

Birmingham, April 13th.—Acted Macbeth with great spirit, *i. e.* began it so, and felt that my acting begins to want spirit, which I must attend to. Was marred and utterly deprived of my effects by the " support " of a Mr. —— and others in the last act. Was in a violent passion, and in that behaved very ill. Oh, my cottage, my cottage! shall I die without visiting thee, and learning, from nature and communion with my God, the blessed lesson of self-control! What I suffer from self-reproach! Oh God, assist me!

April 14th.—Sent £1 to a Miss —— whom I only just knew, but who knew acquaintances of mine. She is now apparently destitute. I remember thinking, as a boy, her father a very proud man, who kept a gig, and a person of consequence; he had a toy-shop, well and long known in this street. The changes of things and thoughts! Received a note from Phipson, who called, and in a few words rehearsed a sad catalogue of woes that had befallen him since I last saw him. He lost a child, his only daughter, in October; he lost £12,000 in December; and, as I understood him, was bankrupt in January; during two of those months his wife kept her bed! If we only looked at the sorrows and sufferings around us, how soon we should learn *that lesson of our life*—" *to bear.*" But we are too selfish, too vain, *too ungrateful!* I was deeply sorry for him. He was so very kind; and I remember my family among my earliest recollections here. Poor fellow! I am grieved at the very heart for him. He walked with me to the theatre, where we parted. I tried to act Richelieu well, and did my best with a company and a Mr. C—— that would paralyze a Hercules. The house was enormous; I went forward to a call that I could not evade, but reluctantly. I have not had time to think before of my early days here. As I returned to my hotel, I looked for the house where I passed many days of my boyhood. It was the last house in which I saw my blessed mother alive; I received her last kiss there, to return it on her marble forehead, as she lay in her coffin (the blessed

FRANCES MARIA KELLY

From an engraving of a painting by S. Drummond, A.R.A.

woman) in Norfolk Street, Sheffield. Good God! for what are we here? The years of passion, of suffering, that have passed; the unsatisfactory sum of all they have produced; the dissatisfaction that remains, urge on the question—How much of chance is there in life? Yet how much more is there in conduct than in fortune! Of that I am sure, and I only quarrel with my imperfect education, and the painful consequences of a faulty example. Two doors from where I now am is the house in which as a child, a boy of nine years old, and *I remember it well*, I first felt a preference for one of the other sex— a girl, whom I afterwards passionately, desperately loved, vain, false, and coquettish as I knew her to be; now I feel as indifferent to her as to any being in existence. How strange is all this! I should have married her if she had encouraged me in the idea; but she had no heart—at least for me—nor, it seems, for any one else; she is still single.

Rugby, April 18th.—I went with Birch to the old church and sat where, as a boy, I used to say my prayers. I looked for old faces, but saw very few; old things, but not many persons—Stanley, the old writing-master. I was shocked at the matter-of-course way in which the service was said and sung—there is no religion there. The sermon was still worse, and made me quite impatient. And by such religion as this anti-Christian Church of England and such teachers of it men are to be kept from the knowledge of the Great and Universal *Parent*—the common Author of all good, and made to worship an idol, as limited in his protection and care as any of the Chinese, Thibetan, or negro worship. I said *my own* prayers, but with no sympathy with the tradesman in the reading desk and pulpit. We talked over the school-days, and the fates of various men who were at school with me. We parted. Birch kissed me, and was affected. Nature would whisper to him, as it did to me in meeting—God knows if we may ever meet in this world again! He has been to me the friend of my life, my relation, my tutor, my benefactor. God bless him. Posted back to Birmingham with all speed, every house almost along the road familiar to me—Bilton, where I could not repress a smile at the recollection of my boyish impudence. Arrived in good time in Birmingham.

London, May 3rd.—Acted Evelyn fairly, and was called for and well received. A gentleman sent me a snuff-box, a very pretty one, from the boxes as a token of his admiration. Miss Horton spoke to me about her engagement and wished to obtain a salary from me. I would give no promise, would not compete with Mr. Webster, and left her to do what she pleased.

May 4th.—Rested, feeling particularly unwell. Acted under indisposition as well as I could. Some parts redeemed the rest, but *my Art* must stand first in my endeavours. If I raise one part of the character of the drama at the expense of my individual superiority what good do I really do? I must be industrious, and to be so *I must be abstinent.* Was called for and well received by the audience. Requested Willmott to ask Mr. Webster what nights I played next week. He "did not know." On a second application as to whether I played *next Tuesday,* he *could not tell*—as Willmott observed—he *will not.*

May 5th.—Catherine put on a half-mourning dress to-day! it made me sadder than the deepest black could have done: my heart was quite sunk in thinking that it seemed like beginning to take leave of sorrow for and association with the memory of my blessed Joan, yet in my heart of hearts that sweet, angelic child lives. I cannot feel that she is not. Obtained Mademoiselle Rachel's address and called on her after rehearsal. Saw first some male *attachés,* and afterwards herself and mother. She is a very engaging, graceful little person, anything but plain in person, delicate and most intelligent features, a frank, a French manner, synonymous to pleasing. I talked with her some little time; invited her to dine on Sunday, which she accepted; asked her if she would visit the theatre, which she wished to do. I went to Sams and purchased the card for Mr. Morriss's box, which I took to the theatre, and sent to her. Returning home made arrangements for Sunday. Wrote to her, to Rogers, Mrs. Norton, and Cockerell. I had spoken to Miss Horton at the theatre, who evidently wished to be very grateful in going with me to Drury Lane, if I could give her, with the advantages she would have there, as good a salary as she could get elsewhere. I did not choose to do that, and left her to Mr. Webster. Acted Werner in many particulars very well—taking great pains, was called for and well received. Forster called and saw Webster, who *would* not tell him my nights of performance next week.

May 6th.—Went to the theatre; received a note from Serle, informing me that Miss Kelly's friend, Mr. J. H. Reynolds, would not consent to her acceptance of an engagement for the *Old Women*—ergo; Miss Kelly does not come to Drury Lane. A piteous note from Mrs. H. Wallack—once Miss Turpin, alas!

May 8th.—Read in the newspaper the death of Barnes, editor of the *Times*. It was a sort of surprise to me, but an event that I heard of with indifference. Perhaps of the men who were never acquainted with me none ever did me so much injury, or willed to do me so much as this man, but all strife is now at rest; he and Mr. Bacon—active agents in mischief, and wanton inflicters of mental torture—are gone where we all must soon follow.

May 9th.—Walked out and called on Lord Beaumont, on Mrs. Pierce Butler; sat and chatted for some time. Returning, overtook Hayward, with whom I walked some way. Coming in, dressed and read in *Courier*, Balzac, and Sévigné—laughing at whiles—to accustom myself to thoughts in French. Madame and Mademoiselle Rachel, Colonel and Mrs. Gurwood, Mrs. Norton, Eastlake, Young, T. Campbell, Kenney, Dr. Elliotson, and Quin came to dinner. A very pleasant and cheerful day we had. Campbell [1] was inclining to grow tiresome and intolerable; it seems he said to Letitia: "I think your brother might have placed me next to Mademoiselle Rachel. Who is that?" "Dr. Quin." "And who is Dr. Quin—what is he?" etc. This, though loud, was unheard, or unmarked by those at table. What a sad sight for the author of *Gertrude of Wyoming*! He will soon *go* altogether! I was—indeed, all were—delighted with Rachel; her extreme simplicity, her ingenuousness, earnestness, and the intellectual variation of her sweet and classic features. There was but one feeling of admiration and delight through the whole party at and after dinner. Mrs. Jameson, Mr. and Mrs. Swinfen Jervis, the Sheils, Wyse, Mr. Curran, Troughton, Babbage, Fitzgerald, Boxall, Miss Faucit, Hetta, Horace Twisses, Lovers, Forster, Fred White, Mrs. Procter, Edward Kater, Travers, came in the evening. All was cheerful and animated. Dear Rachel seemed very happy and very loth to go away. She left with Mrs. Procter. Bless her! I wish her *all* success.

May 12th.—Rogers called and told us of the pleasant day he had heard of here on Sunday. I consulted him about the Drury Lane prices; he recommended me to obey the dictates of my feelings, observing that he found generally one grain of feeling was worth a pound of reason. He was very agreeable. Thought of what I ought to say at the Literary Fund dinner. My thoughts were not obedient to my summons. I could arrange nothing. I was in despair. Dickens called for me; he told me of the wonder of this boy, under the effect of

---

[1] The poet.

magnetism, producing such wonderful effects. Dined at the Freemasons' Tavern, Lord Ripon [1] in the Chair. Lord Colborne, Sir C. Napier,[2] Sir S. Canning,[3] M. Milnes, Amyot, K. Macaulay, Barham, Brockedon, etc., were there. The speeches were mostly good, excepting Croly's [4]—oh! and mine—oh! I alluded to Government giving our theatre to persons like Morris, Forbes, etc., without mentioning names, and related the anecdote of *Gisippus.*

May 15th.—Miss Faucit came in. I told her not on any account to give up her engagement with Mr. Webster. She said she would not, if she could help it! She asked me if I would not " give " her " the same terms " she has at the Haymarket, which she was " obliged to ask." I was obliged to say *yes.*

Dublin, May 20th.—Our houses are indifferent. After an absence of four years—during which crowded houses have attended the performances of Mr. C. Kean—it is rather hard to hear persons place my performance of Othello above Kean's—(which I do *not*)—and act it to £60! Calcraft came into my room. I saw a newspaper this morning, and one was sent to me this evening—the stupid fools! to call themselves critics! It is something to account for the houses!

May 27th.—Went to the Fortescues' [5] at the Castle, and lunched with them. Saw the state-rooms, as they are called, and St. Patrick's Hall, also the Castle Chapel, and these are the externals of the Majesty of this country, a jest indeed, and, as Byron says, " a melancholy jest "! The rooms do not strike me as comparable to those in the Exchange at Liverpool.

June 7th.—Mr. James Martineau [6] called, and I talked with him apart for a few minutes; he told me that dear Miss Martineau was worse, and from his account I fear she is sinking. Her spirits are

---

[1] Frederick John Robinson (1782–1859); first Earl of Ripon, better known as "Prosperity" Robinson, a sobriquet occasioned by his optimism when Chancellor of the Exchequer during a period of great commercial stress. As Viscount Goderich he succeeded Canning in the Premiership, which he resigned after a few months without meeting Parliament. He afterwards held office under the Whigs, then returned to the Tories, under Sir Robert Peel, in whose Ministry he filled more than one unimportant post.

[2] Probably Sir Charles James Napier (1782–1853), the conqueror of Scinde.

[3] Stratford Canning (1786–1880); afterwards Viscount Stratford de Redcliffe, the famous diplomatist, known as the "Great Elchi."

[4] George Croly (1780–1860); preacher, author, and critic.

[5] Lord Ebrington, afterwards Earl Fortescue, was then Lord Lieutenant.

[6] James Martineau (1805–1900); the distinguished philosopher and Unitarian pastor; his apprehensions as to his sister were happily not realized, her life being prolonged for another thirty-five years.

low, and she is losing her appetite. God bless her. She will not leave many so good behind her.

June 30th.—Walked out with Willie and heard the news that Lord John Russell was thrown out for the City![1] This, I think, is the virtual ejection of the Ministry; I felt more than half sorry in hearing it. I regret the retardation of those measures which to be of any real service should be promptly effected, though I cannot think they ever would have been propounded by the Whigs except to keep their places. *A base motive for an act of justice!*

July 2nd.—The news of Bulwer's being unseated for Lincoln— where that foolish man, Colonel Sibthorp (!) is elected as a legislator —grieved me very much. Captain Polhill (!!!) is also re-elected by the town of Bedford—these are agricultural towns!

London, July 5th.—After dinner went to the Opera House. Read in Corneille's *Cinna* the scenes of Emilie. Watched with intense eagerness the performance of the part by Rachel. I must confess I was disappointed; she has undoubtedly genius; grace in a high degree, and perfect self-possession. But she disappointed me; she has no tenderness, nor has she grandeur. She did not dilate with passion; the appeal to the gods was not that grand swell of passion that lifts her up above the things (too little for its communion) of earth to the only powers capable of sympathizing with her. She did not seem to commune with the *Manes* of her father. Her apostrophe to the liberty of Rome was not "up to the height of the great argument." She was stinging, scornful, passionate, but *little* in her familiar descents, and wanting in the terrible struggle, the life and death conflict, between her love and her revenge. The "sharp convulsive pangs of agonizing pride" and fondness were not felt. She is not equal to Mars or Miss O'Neill, but she is the first actress of her day.

July 11th.—Walked down to H. Smith's to dinner. Forster was there. After dinner he told me of a *nasty* paragraph in the *Observer*, in which allusion was distinctly made to differences between myself and Mr. Webster—that he had sent me a message by a military man, and that I had withdrawn the expressions objected to. I was, as usual, annoyed at this, and we discussed the propriety of contradicting it. When we went up-stairs Forster and H. Smith drew out contradictions for the daily papers or the *Observer*. In other respects I passed a very pleasant day.

[1] A mistake; he was returned last on the poll. The Whig Government did not resign till August 28.

July 12th.—Looked with some anxiety to the papers as they were brought in, to see if the obnoxious paragraph in the *Observer* had been copied into any of them; it had not, which was a satisfaction to me. I altered the note of contradiction again, removing the expression " false " (*which does not prove anything more*) and confining myself to a simple contradiction, which ought to be enough for any gentleman.

July 13th.—On this day my blessed Joan would have been four years old. My heart blesses her, and yearns towards her, and feels as if it was to renew its communion with the sweet child. Oh, that I could see her in all her lovely cheerfulness! But my birthday greeting to her sweet spirit is, " Beloved, hail and farewell! Sweet sorrow of my heart! Dearest child, farewell! " Gave dear Catherine a locket with our sweet child's hair.

July 16th.—We went to the Opera House, to see Rachel in *Horace*. My opinion of her was very greatly raised. If I might apply a term of distinction to the French acting, I should say it is sculpturesque in its effect; it resembles figures in relief, no background, and almost all in single figures, scarcely any grouping, no grand composition: this sort of individual effect may be good for the artist, but not for the illusion of a play. With the drawback consequent on this national peculiarity, Rachel in Camille was generally admirable. She stood alone, her back turned to her lover or brother, as it might happen, but her feeling was almost always true. In a grand opportunity, " Courage! ils s'amollissent "—I thought her deficient. But in the last scene she was all that a representation of the part could be. It was a splendid picture of frenzied despair.

July 17th.—Willmott came into my room. He talked of the state of the theatre, told me that it was not an uncommon thing for Mr. C. Kean to be hissed, that in Shylock the disapprobation was very loud and unmingled with any applause. I did not suppose this.

July 18th.—Reading the *Examiner*, was affected by Lord Morpeth's [1] speech to the electors of West Riding. I honour, respect, and esteem that man, although, as I believe, he would do a little, if in his power, to give advantages over me; but he is not less amiable

---

[1] George William Frederick Howard (1802–1864) ; Viscount Morpeth, afterwards sixth Earl of Carlisle ; at that time Chief Secretary for Ireland and a member of Lord Melbourne's Cabinet. High-minded, enlightened, and humane, if less able than some of his colleagues, he was probably the more popular and respected of the Whig statesmen of that period.

for that.   Walked out, and called at Rogers's; found that Rachel had gone this morning.

July 21st.—I thought my poor watchmaker seemed very much confused, and I attributed it to two prints of Mr. C. Kean hung up in his parlour.   I was amused in thinking so.

July 22nd.—Looked at paper; read Lord John Russell's letter to citizens of London—too late—too late! Called at Fonblanque's, I was let in, but he was afterwards denied to me.   These things would have offended me once, but now——.   Acted Evelyn very well.   Lady Essex was in the stage-box, and I had the feeling of old times over me, that she should not see me to disadvantage.   Spoke to Willmott about Saturday's play.   He brought me a *list* from Mr. Webster, out of which I said I should not object to *Venice Preserved*, *Fatal Dowry*, *Measure for Measure*, and *Gaveston*.   He told me that Mr. C. Kean wanted him to try to make out my adaptation of *King Lear* for him—that Willmott told him he could not, and if he could he did not think he should be justified in doing it.

July 25th.—Read the newspaper; thought Fonblanque's tone and language on Sir Robert Peel not that of a high-minded adversary or dissentient—not of a man *strong in the consciousness of truth*, but splenetic and malicious.   I was sorry to see it.

July 30th.—Prepared for our long-promised expedition; Stanfields came to accompany us; we set out together, calling for Mrs. Dickens. Went to Belvedere.   Arrived there, found the other carriage with Dickens, Forster, Maclise, and Cattermole.   Viewed the house and grounds of Belvedere; the thought of my blessed child came across me when alone.   Blessings on her sweet spirit!   Leaving Belvedere, we lunched at the small inn and returned to Greenwich, where we saw the hospital, and meeting Drs. Elliotson and Quin, and Mr. Roberts, we dined at the Trafalgar.   Amused at the sight of the Nassau balloon, which came very near us—with the boys putting their heads in the mud for sixpence!!

August 6th.—Finished the play of *Plighted Troth*—a play written in a quaint style, but possessing the rare qualities of intense passion and happy imagination.   Forster called and dined; I read to him several scenes from *Plighted Troth*, with which he was greatly struck. He took away the MS. to read.   A note and MS. from C. J. M——. Wrote to Rev. C. F. Darley, author of *Plighted Troth*.   Occupied in looking into *History of England* for Bulwer's subject. . . . A suspicion has arisen in my mind from some data that the subject of

139

Gisippus has been suggested to and used by Mr. Knowles for his forthcoming play.

August 8th.—Considered for more than an hour the subject of Sir Robert Walpole as one for Bulwer's pen. Rev. C. F. Darley called; we talked over the play of *Plighted Troth.* He expressed himself happy and obliged by my opinion, and declared himself the brother of *the* Darley! [1] He left me *carte-blanche* with regard to the play. Wrote to Younge about the copyist. Resumed my search in *History of England* for matter for Bulwer. Forster came to dinner and was very agreeable, sensible, cheerful, and truly pleasing. We walked after dinner in the Park—Botanic Gardens and Park Square Gardens.

August 10th.—We walked with Nina in the Botanic Gardens. Calcraft followed us there, and came to inform me that all his views had failed—as had Mr. Webster's—that Knowles had not finished his play! that Miss E. Tree had refused her part! and that it was not certain Mr. C. Kean would accept his; the only certain thing was that Knowles had received money!

August 13th.—Letter from Darley, and from the lady who calls herself Mrs. St. Aubyn, wishing to see me this evening; I might gratify my curiosity if without trouble, but *voilà tout!* I answered her—in the hope that I may shake her off.

August 14th.—Acted Evelyn fairly; called for, but not in time to go on. Met a very beautiful woman in Portman Square, who had written to me as Mrs. St. Aubyn. I found it was an assumed name and that she was the mistress of a Lord ——. I had thought she had been connected with the St. Aubyns. *Addio, mia bella!*

August 17th.—Dr. Kuenzel, Z. Troughton, Maurice Power, and Forster with T. Landseer came to dinner. A cheerful day; in the evening a long discussion with T. Landseer on his plan of the *Animal Diorama.* Notes from Ransom and Mrs. St. Aubyn, which I answered to see her to-morrow for the last time.

August 18th.—Heard that Knowles's play was withdrawn and the workmen put off! Forster, who came into my room, mentioned a report that C. Kean had refused his part! This is very probable. A man without information or imagination (a man who could reject *Gisippus*—*par exemple!*) would not see the scope of a character—it is quite in reason. Went to keep my appointment with Mrs. St. Aubyn, to tell her that I could not see her again. She begged *very hard* that

---

[1] George Darley (1795–1846); author and mathematician.

I would, told me part of her story—of course a sad one—that she had been promised marriage and seduced by a Mr. ——, a barrister; that she was not the particular mistress of Lord ——; in fact, that her mysterious carriage with me was to keep her partiality from the knowledge of Mr. C. Kean, who was "very kind" to her. I was amused. She wished to make me promise to see her again—I avoided it.

August 23rd.—Mrs. St. Aubyn, with a gentleman, occupied the stage private-box. She is very beautiful. I inquired who she was, and it seems she had been noticed as constant in her attendance on C. Kean's performances.

August 26th.—Saw the announcement of the death of Theodore Hook—a man I did not like, always hostilely placed to my interests, and one who, by a most insidious and malignant falsehood, dealt me an injury the effects of which I have scarcely yet recovered. As I found him, so I speak of him. I thought him very vulgar in his manner, and a man whom I *could* not admire, esteem, like—scarcely tolerate. He may have had good qualities, only what was ill in him was known to me; I did not lament him. He had become indifferent to me.

August 28th.—Proceeded to the Thatched House for the meeting to show respect to Wilkie, where I was a stranger to the committee assembled and assembling until the arrival of Jerdan, Dickens, etc. Sir James McGregor[1] spoke to me about Edward, but I did not know who he was. Lord Mahon,[2] very like a little terrier pup, was fussing about the uncertainty and hope of Sir R. Peel's attendance, his presence at the House of Commons, the "division," etc. All was *fuss*. I looked on, and was amused. In the larger committee-room, to which we adjourned for the business, we mustered largely; the resolutions were discussed. Dickens objected to some—I to one, which was altered without opposition; it amused me to see the lick-spittle character of the whole proceedings, but I was disgusted with the *servile*, crouching attitude which the leading artists took, and I *broke out*, complimentarily *rebuking* Sir A. Callcott[3] for so undervaluing the position of his art—declining to move a resolution on the ground that it might have been *presuming* in him *as an artist* to stand forward. I told him, rather excited, that I thought the leading artists were the proper movers of such resolutions, and that the name of one

[1] Probably Sir James McGregor, Bart. (1771–1858); chief of the Army Medical Staff in the Peninsular campaign, and afterwards Director-General of the Army Medical Department for nearly forty years.

[2] Afterwards fifth Earl Stanhope (1805–1875); the eminent historian.

[3] Sir Augustus Wall Callcott, R.A. (1779–1844); originally a chorister-boy.

like himself or Mr. Phillips would influence me far more than any consideration of rank, as I should be certain in following such an authority I could not err in judgment nor be committed on a point of taste. D'Orsay came in and chatted a good deal. I was introduced to Leslie, introduced myself to Collins, R.A., but was *shocked* at the submissive *menial*-like tone he assumed—not supposing ' I should (I think) *condescend* to recollect him ' ! The fuss with the Duke of Sutherland, Peel, etc., while little Lord J. Russell was hardly noticed in the committee-room. We proceeded to the great room, which was very full, and after some interruption from an ambitious speaker, who opposed Peel's occupation of the Chair, but was soon set aside, the business of the day proceeded. Peel spoke in a most humdrum-ti-tum *artificial* manner without a single approach to an idea in all the words he spoke. The Duke of Sutherland much about the same. There was *great applause* when Lord John Russell stood forward, which evidently very much disconcerted Peel; but he did not speak well. Chantrey was with us, Maclise, Dickens, Forster, and self. We went out after Lord John's speech, and he followed us and passed us on the stair. Dickens asked me, " Did you ever hear such miserable commonplace—such a mere set of words without one idea? " I certainly never did.

September 9th.—Miss P. Horton called, and I went over part of Virginia with her. She *shocked* me by repeating an expression of Webster, which she said he applied to me. Acted Virginius *very unevenly*, some passages—a few, *very grandly*—others very poorly. Called for and well received. Mrs. St. Aubyn was in the stage-box— very attentive! Spoke to Miss Horton about what she repeated to me to-day, told her never to do so again. I was *very angry* during the play, and vainly tried to recover myself. *Bad!*

September 12th.—I cannot help remarking upon the apparently *indomitable* bad taste which Forster continually exhibits in laying down his opinions (and upon subjects of which he, clever as he is, knows nothing) as if it were law. Among his violent declamatory effusions was one to-night, that Cicero never touched anything that he did not depreciate!

September 13th.—Acted Virginius fairly; was called for and well received. The same audience called for Mr. Wallack!! Poole called, and in the course of conversation alluded to some persons talking of myself and Mr. C. Kean as actors!!! Now really, it is almost an excuse for expatriation, for anything in the shape of *escape*

CHARLES KEAN

From an engraving

short of suicide, to think that one has lived and *had a mind* and *used* it for so many years to be *mentioned* at last in the same breath with Mr. C. Kean! Particularly offensive!

September 14th.—Went to Covent Garden theatre to see *London Assurance*—a pert, smart trifle in five acts—beautifully set upon the stage, and in the parts of Mathews and Mrs. Nisbett extremely well acted; in other respects the acting was of equal pretension with the writing—which is of a low mark.

September 17th.—Anderson met me at the Liverpool station, and accompanied me to the theatre, where I got some tea and dressed. I acted Lord Townley—particularly the last scene—very well; was called for and well received. I led on Miss E. Tree, who disappointed me *very much* in her performance; instead of an exuberance of spirits to account for and in some respects to excuse her follies and wayward-ness, she was cool, sarcastic, and insolent, and not in a high tone of breeding; it was very bad.

September 18th.—Acted Luke, I thought, fairly; Mrs. Stirling in Lady Traffic decidedly *bad.* Clarke came into my room. Several letters of application, and one from Miss Faucit, apprising me of her recovery, of which I am delighted to hear.

September 22nd.—Received a letter from Dickens mentioning to me his purpose of going to the United States, and asking my opinion as to the best course to be pursued with regard to his children— whether to take them or leave them. I answered him on the instant, recommending him not to take them with him.

September 23rd.—As I was going to bed Dickens called in, having sent a note first, and sat with me some time canvassing his con-templated voyage to the United States. He spoke of Mrs. Dickens's reluctance and regret, and wished me to write to her and state my views, putting them strongly before her. When he was gone, I wrote to her, enclosing the note to him.

September 25th.—Read the *Acis and Galatea* to Serle, which he thought would succeed if Stanfield painted the scenery!

September 26th.—Engaged earnestly on my address on entering upon Drury Lane theatre. The Smiths, Serles, Stanfield, Maclise, and Forster came to dinner. Forster importuned me after dinner to read Browning's tragedy, which I did. He had taken *enough* wine, and was rather exaggerating in his sensibility and praise. I was not prepared, and could not do justice to it in reading. Went very late to bed.

143

September 27th.—A very fervent and grateful letter from Mrs. Dickens, in reply to mine, acquiescing in all I urged upon her. Letter, with a *triste* report of herself from Helen Faucit; one from Bulwer. Spoke to Miss P. Horton about taking lessons in singing, which she had been thinking of doing; invited her to dine on Sunday week. Notes from Serle and Forster, enclosing one he had received from Dickens, in great delight at the effect of my letter to his wife.

September 28th.—Miss Fortescue called and rehearsed. I proposed to her to believe that I was about to offer her some outrage to excite the last violence of passion in her. Catherine was in the inner drawing-room. I could only call up gleams, no continuance, but I think it will blaze forth.

September 29th.—Miss Fortescue called to her appointment, and I gave three hours to her, but could not awaken the proper rush of passion.

September 30th.—Letter, full of heart, with the returned address, from Dickens. Went to Drury Lane theatre. Went into various parts of the house. Met in the committee-room Talfourd, Fox, H. Smith, Kenney, Forster, Maclise, Stanfield, Brydone, and Serle. Canvassed the address, which I read to them—it was approved by all, but upon scrutiny considerably altered. Forster was most especially and conspicuously disagreeable—raising objections out of mere humour and caprice and not to serve the cause or his friend. I was not pleased with him. We were full two hours in arranging it. Kenney rode with me from Oxford Street, and volunteered the observation that Forster seemed to object to passages from mere caprice—he evidently did not like him. Talked with Willmott on Drury Lane theatre, etc. He told me that last night Mr. Webster had come down in a furious state from his box and pointed out Forster from the side of the curtain, calling him a butcher's boy and other expressions which were abusive. The provocation was Forster's loud laughter at some serious parts of the play.

October 1st.—Brydone informed me that Sloman objected to the carpenters being paid by any one but himself. I sent for him and told him that he had full power over his men, but that I would govern the theatre in my own way, and that every man in the theatre should be paid from the treasury. He went away—" *satisfied.*"

October 4th.—On this day I enter upon the lease and management of Drury Lane theatre. I humbly implore the blessing of Almighty God upon my efforts, praying His gracious Spirit may influence me in adopting and carrying through all wise and good measures in a discreet, equable, and honourable course, and only pursuing such a line of conduct as may benefit my blessed children, may be of service to the cause of good, and benevolent to those dependent on me.

October 6th.—A Captain —— called, a *ci-devant jeune homme*—a battered, broken-down beau, to state that his wife, a young woman, not more than twenty years old, was ambitious, etc., to go on the stage; most *strictly virtuous*, etc., but would go first in the chorus!!! I referred him to T. Cooke.

October 8th.—Coming home—having ordered the driver to pass on when I stopped at Dickens's—found Forster had been there, and that Dickens, who had been very ill, wished to see me after dinner. I immediately went to him, and to my great concern and distress found him in bed, having this morning undergone an operation. I suffered *agonies*, as they related all to me, and did violence to myself in keeping myself to my seat. I could scarcely bear it. My nerves are threads, or wires, that tremble when touched. I sat with him above an hour. Poor fellow! Thank God all is so well!

October 11th.—Browning called and went with me to call on Dickens, who is going on very comfortably; I parted with Browning in Oxford Street. Note from Bourne declining to be my executor and trustee. I am not at all displeased, though I would have done as much for him. But friends have a right to choose their own means of proving their affection. Went to Drury Lane theatre. A note from Mrs. St. Aubyn, giving me to understand that she still loves me! Note with presentation copies of *Patrician's Daughter* from Mr. Marston. Read in bed the tragedy of the *Patrician's Daughter*, which seemed to me most powerful.

October 16th.—T. Cooke and Mr. Thomas, the Drury Lane leader, Serle and Miss P. Horton called to try over the songs of *Acis*. Expecting a failure, I was most agreeably surprised and excited by a very powerful and expressive performance; all were alike struck by it, and I called up Catherine and Letitia to hear it, who were equally moved. It promises admirably. Went with Serle to Drury Lane, talking over matters in hand. Miss Fortescue came, and I sent Serle and Brydone into the upper circles to judge of her power of voice. She rehearsed the garden and banishment scenes of *Juliet*, and seemed quite to satisfy them. I went up afterwards and heard the first part of the garden scene, which was perfectly audible and clear in tone.

Another excellent promise. God speed us! Amen! I gave her directions and dismissed her. Gave Brydone his cheque and to Serle and himself their official seals.

October 19th.—Mr. King, Maclise, Macmahon Hughes, Stone, George Ward, and Forster came to dine. Forster made himself especially disagreeable by a *senseless* and furious attack upon the *Times*, to which Mr. M. Hughes had belonged—perhaps does belong. He was in his worst taste, and peculiarly rude and offensive. It is too bad. It is a subject of deep and sincere regret that with so many excellent points of character he will neutralize those that might be useful to his friends, and so often obscure those that are agreeable by a display of manners and temper which is painful and offensive.

October 25th.—Miss P. Horton gave me a note to read, as she believed, from Lord Augustus Fitzclarence—the Reverend; it was a declaration of love.[1] She supposed the bracelet she had received to come from the same person. I counselled her, if she could discover it, to return it.

November 6th.—Acted Spinola [2] *well* and with great care. Was told that I was called for, but Mr. Wallack and Miss H. Faucit went on! This was not exactly *comme il faut*. Mrs. St. Aubyn was in the stage-box.

November 7th.—Gave my whole day to the preparation of *Romeo and Juliet*, of which I finished three acts. It is a work of more labour than I had calculated upon. Mr. and Miss Emily Spicer, Dr. Quin, Knox, Maclise, Stanfield, Z. Troughton, came to dine, with whom we had a very pleasant day. Was held a long time in conversation with Stanfield and Maclise on the subject of the illustration of *Acis and Galatea*.

November 8th.—Miss Fortescue called. I gave her three hours' lesson, and called in Letitia to see her go through the garden scene, with which she was very much pleased and moved.

---

[1] A natural son of William IV by Mrs. Jordan. He held the living of Mapledurham. Fanny Kemble, in her *Records of a Girlhood*, relates a singular conversation with him during a dance. In accepting her reproof of his decidedly unclerical language, he remarked: "But you see some people have a natural turn for religion ; you have, for instance, I am sure; but you see I have not." He then proceeded to ask her to write a sermon for him, and on her telling him that he ought to write his own sermons, he replied : "Yes, but you see I can't—not good ones at least. I'm sure you could, and I wish you would write one for me. Mrs. N—— has." This Rev. Mr. Foker was far more familiar with the stage than the pulpit, and made up for the poverty of his sermons by the eloquence of his *billets doux*.

[2] In Troughton's drama of *Nina Sforza*.

November 11th.—Acted Spinola very fairly, with much care, but Mr. Wallack tasked his ingenuity to defeat my effects! Forster came into my room in his high tide of disagreeableness!

November 13th.—Anderson came. I gave him his seal, and he with Serle and Brydone saw Miss Fortescue rehearse. She was quite below herself—*nervous*, hurried, and comparatively ineffective. I regretted it, but it was well to undergo the discipline.

November 14th.—Mrs. and Miss Fortescue, Serle and Troughton came to dinner. Miss Fortescue is a very sweet little girl. Mrs. Fortescue is a counterpart of Mrs. Nickleby.

November 21st.—The darling children were with me in the course of the day. Daniel, Dickenses, Spicer, Greaves, and a most intolerable, most offensive, disgusting bore, a Dr. —— called on me. I told him I was very much occupied, but he remained an hour, and bawled so in my ears that he gave me a headache—the brute!

November 24th.—Mrs. Reynolds called. She repeated an observation which some one had made on seeing me act Spinola—"That he was sure I should end my days on a scaffold!" I cannot say I think it indicates much taste or feeling in the critic. On my way home from the theatre my mind was tortured by a rush of vindictive and furious thoughts that quite distressed me with painful sensations in the head. I fear I have much more revenge in my nature than I had believed. I have forgiven many injuries; that wretched knave Bunn I feel only scorn or indifference for; this Webster is merely contemptible; but the insult of that cowardly bully Thesiger I cannot pass over, perhaps because he is out of my reach.

November 25th.—My blessed Joan died. Rose earlier than usual in order to visit the sad place that contains the mouldering body of my sweet infant, my beautiful and blessed Joan. My thoughts were upon her, which I did not wish to communicate or betray, as I was unwilling to shed any gloom about me. But she was present to me— in her laughing joy and beauty, in the angelic sweetness that she wore when lying dead before me. O God, Thy will be done. She seems dearer to me even than these so dear around me. That wound of my heart will never be healed. But I shall meet her again, or I shall be of the element with her. What shall I be? And for what are we taught these sad and bitter lessons? I went to the cemetery, and saw the cold and narrow bed where she lies; my heart poured out its prayer by her body for the welfare and happiness of those spared to me. I had to wait the performance of a funeral service before I could go down into the vault. It brought all back to me; but what words are those to offer to the heart of grief, or to the reasoning mind? God, the true God, is all. His love to us, and circulated amongst us, is our only consolation. Bless thee, my beloved babe; often, often, when it could be little thought, your image is with me.

November 26th.—Acted Sir Oswin Mortland as well as I could under the heavy press of business. Read the two concluding numbers of *Humphrey's Clock,* which ends very sadly and very sweetly. Wonderful Dickens.

November 28th.—Looked at the newspaper—a newspaper—one of the means of strengthening and extending fraud and injustice through this wretched world—a world that few can have known long without questioning the purpose of their mission here; to *endure* without any act of their own will—and to what end? I am *sick* of it—of its injustice, and of the accursed tyranny which in one form or other rakes at our hearts, or acts upon one's brain, till one fears for its sanity. Walked out with children for air to call on Dickens. Wrote a few lines to him to thank him for *Barnaby Rudge.* Began to make out the dresses of *Merchant of Venice.* Proved the *incorrectness* of Mr. Planché's costume of Pictorial Shakspeare. Shameful! Proved by Vecchio. Heard as a truth that the Lord Chamberlain, Lord Delawarr, had given Mr. Webster an extension of two months' licence! This is *really* too bad!!! It is an attack upon one's means that would justify the last punishment that could be inflicted on a wretch who takes an office in which justice is to be administered, and sports in idle and ignorant wantonness with the fortunes, labour, and lives of his fellow-men. Oh Humanity! when will thy day come? When shall retribution pour down upon the heads of these accursed aristocrats? Be it soon!!! [1]

December 4th.—Bulwer looked in, but would not wait. Went to Dickens's, where I saw Landor, Elliotson, Quin, Stanfield, Maclise. The Talfourds *extremely disagreeable.*

December 5th.—Decided on drawing a large sum from the three per cents, and doing the utmost in reason to *perfect* the theatre. Received a kind note from Horace Twiss, proposing our dining with him on Saturday, 18th, to meet the Delanes of the *Times.* Mr. Graham called—talked with him. Considered much the matter of

---

[1] The extension of the Haymarket licence would possibly affect Macready's opening campaign at Drury Lane, but it hardly justifies so intemperate an outburst. His relations, however, with Webster had become greatly strained, which largely accounts for it.

the announce-bill, and with much thought made it out. Dined with Talfourds—met Barron Field,[1] Stanfield, Maclise, Forster, Ainsworth, Browning, Dr. Lee, etc. A more agreeable day than I had anticipated. Returning, marked the prompt book of the *Merchant of Venice*.

December 7th.—As the last day of my Haymarket engagement, I begin it with some feeling of uncertainty as to the future, invoking and imploring the blessing of God upon my endeavours, and that my course of prosperity may be continued. Miss Fortescue came and continued her lessons. I am greatly interested in her success. Went to Drury Lane theatre, taking her part of the way. Had prepared notes of the dresses to be done, and was all day *doing* even till past six o'clock, but did not accomplish nearly what I desired. I had ordered, among many others, a note to be sent to Willmott requesting him to call. He answered, and soon after my arrival came. I told him that his confident expression of the certainty of our success last night had made me think of asking him what he could suggest as a remuneration—that I had been reluctant to invite him from a good certainty to a doubtful concern. He said he was sure of the success, and if only I said to him "Come," he should not ask a question, but leave all to me—that he had got as much before with me as he had with Webster. After some talk I said, "*Then come*," and he agreed to see Webster immediately. He returned some time after to report that after a long and unmeaning conversation Webster had promised to give him an answer to-night. I had a long business in casting the plays—disarranged by the treachery of several actors! *Alas! Actors!* Made out the announcement-bill and advertisement. Spoke to Smithers. Went into painting-room; only finished the bill by six o'clock. Went to the Haymarket theatre. Acted Claude Melnotte with vigour, gaiety and energy, inspired and animated by the good house and the feeling they displayed towards me—perhaps I never acted it better; it was the *last time*. Was called for and very enthusiastically received. I bowed my adieux. Quitted the Haymarket theatre, praying God to bless my labours where I am going.

December 10th.—Reconsidered the question of acting the unimportant parts of Harmony and Valentine, and came to the decision

---

[1] Presumably Barron Field (1786–1846), a friend of Lamb and his circle ; a judge in New South Wales, and afterwards Chief Justice of Gibraltar ; at one time theatrical critic to the *Times ;* he also edited various plays for the Shaksperian Society.

that everything should be done to raise and sustain the character of the theatre; that my reputation could scarcely be affected in any way by the assumption of these parts, or, at least, not injuriously; and that it would be a sad calculation to think of propping my reputation by the ruins of the theatre. I saw that it was right to do them. Read Valentine. Read Harmony.

December 14th.—Went to Drury Lane theatre; attended to business. I have neither head nor spirits to enter into the detail of my day's labour, which began with difficulties and impediment, and ended with them and my efforts to extricate myself from the perplexing strait in which the Committee, by their want of *strict faith* and their supineness, have placed me. Mr. Beazley came, and took very coolly the condition into which his want of correctness and attention has helped to place us. The curtain was not ready; the trial of it postponed till twelve, subsequently to three, and afterwards to six— which turned out to be eight. Business with Willmott. Rehearsed the play of *Every One has his Fault.* Business with Serle, who has not *energy* for the occasion. Saw dear little Miss Fortescue. It is pleasant to see anything gentle and amiable in the midst of this feverish turmoil. Went over the whole house—on business. *I have no seconds*—Willmott is the only active officer in his place. Went over with Brydone the business that *ought to have been done.* Read some part of Harmony. Letters. Wrote to Burgess for the lease. The question of this curtain again agitated; and we are left at this last moment to do *what we can* for curtain and proscenium engaged for by the proprietors!

December 18th.—Dined with Horace Twiss to meet the Delanes. Sir G. Clerk, Emerson Tennent, Fitzgeralds, Hayward, Mr. Atkinson were there.

December 20th.—Rehearsed *Two Gentlemen of Verona.* Much dissatisfied with Miss Fortescue's rehearsal—which will not be up to my original expectation. Note from Mr. Delane wishing to see me. Occupied earnestly and painfully with business. By the want of energy in my officers affairs are in a dangerous predicament. Spoke to Miss Fortescue and rehearsed a little with her. Attended to the business of the free list. Business with the wardrobe. Much time in the ladies' wardrobe, where I find the superintendent utterly incompetent. Left the theatre in much dejection and very unwell at nearly twelve o'clock.

December 24th.—Rehearsed the *Merchant of Venice,* with which

150

I was very much pleased. Dickens and Forster came to the rehearsal. I was not very much pleased to see them there. Miss Fortescue came —I wished to speak to her about her preparation for Wednesday next. Attended to business of many kinds—went round the theatre and overlooked the various departments. Saw the rehearsal of the comic scenes of the pantomime, which were very ineffective from the incomplete state of the scenery. After it was over, spent above two hours in devising with Messrs. Willmott and Younge the best means of making it secure. They at last entered into my views, and we made an arrangement which I trust and hope will prove satisfactory.

December 27th.—Saw my darling babes, and, imploring the blessing of God upon my undertaking, went to Drury Lane theatre. Rehearsed the *Merchant of Venice*. Went round the various places. Gave direction on direction. My mind was over every part of the house. My room very uncomfortable. Lay down, but got little rest. Was much disturbed by being called for as the play began; resisted for a long while, but was at last obliged to go forward. My reception was most enthusiastic. I acted Shylock very nervously—not to please myself. I saw the pantomime afterwards.[1]

December 28th.—Rehearsed *Every One has his Fault.*[2] Incessant business until nearly half-past four o'clock. I was fearful I should not have a command of the words of my part. Note from Sir H. Wheatley, wishing to see me about the Queen's box. Read over Harmony. Acted it tolerably well. Was not known by the audience at first. Called for and well received. The play seemed to have made an agreeable impression, about which I was very anxious, as being a comedy. Mrs. Carlyle was in Catherine's box, and very glad to see me.

December 29th.—Rehearsed the play of *The Two Gentlemen of Verona*, which occupied us a very long while; it was not finished until five o'clock. Acted Valentine imperfectly, and not well. Was called for on account of the play, and warmly received. Miss Fortescue did

[1] Drury Lane theatre opened under Macready's management with the *Merchant of Venice*, and the pantomime of *Harlequin and Duke Humphry's Dinner; or Jack Cade, the Lord of London Stone*. The cast of the play included Mr. G. Bennett, Mr. Phelps, Mr. Anderson, Mr. Hudson, Mr. H. Hill, Mr. Marston, Mr. Selby, Mr. Compton; with Mrs. Warner and Mrs. Keeley, Miss Poole and Miss Gould. The prices were the same as at Covent Garden when under Macready's management. The playbill contained the announcement that the room for promenading and refreshment attached to the boxes would be strictly protected from all improper intrusion.—(*note by Sir F. Pollock.*)

[2] By Mrs. Inchbald.—(*note by Sir F. Pollock.*)

not equal, in the impression she seemed to make, my expectations. I felt very much on her account. Let us hope. Took counsel with my officers on what should be done with her. All and Catherine were of opinion that *Romeo and Juliet* should not be hazarded.

December 30th.—Looked at the newspapers, which were very cordial in their notice of *The Two Gentlemen of Verona*, and kind in their mention of Miss Fortescue. Sent for and spoke to Miss Fortescue about last night; she acknowledged that she had not done justice either to herself or me. She promised to be more attentive. Held a long consultation with Messrs. Serle, Anderson, Willmott, Stanfield upon the question of whether to produce *Romeo and Juliet* or *Gisippus*; the vote was again for *Gisippus*. Came home and read two acts of *Gisippus*, with which I was still pleased.

December 31st.—Went to Drury Lane theatre. Entered on business immediately, though no one had arrived! Acted Valentine indifferently. Called for and well received. Spoke with Miss Fortescue after the play. She was very languid in her acting. Spoke with Serle and Willmott. Detained by the bill. Read the first act of *Prisoner of War*. With the ending of this year I offer up my humble and grateful thanks to Almighty God for the blessings vouch-safed to me and mine—beseeching the continuance of His mercy upon our house, and imploring His protection and blessing upon my labours for the sake of my blessed family. God bless them.

1842

London, January 1st.—Dear Dickens called to shake hands with me.[1] My heart was quite full; it is much to me to lose the presence of a friend who really loves me. He said there was no one whom he felt such pain in saying good-bye to. God bless him.

January 2nd.—In conversation with Messrs. Serle and Brydone, it came out on the part of Mr. Brydone, when speaking of the accounts, that no bills, no material had been paid for!! It was a thunderbolt to me! I did not know what position I was in—I might be ruined! I was very angry. He had the cool impudence, when I said it was possible I might be burthened with a debt of £1000 or £1500, to observe, "I dare say." He said that I had said, "Damn the expense." I have thought upon it, and *it is a falsehood*.

January 3rd.—Sir —— and Sir —— called to see the Queen's box, and the important trifling of these two men was as tediously disgusting as mindless sycophancy could make it. Calcraft called and sat with me some time. I promised him that if I acted anywhere I would act with him, and that I would make no engagement without apprising him. Acted Shylock better than I have yet done. Was called for and well received.

January 4th.—Saw my darling little children. Went to Drury Lane theatre. Gave directions to C. Jones, from whom I learned that my liabilities would amount to at least £2500!!! This is very cruel. Gave him directions to write out a circular, refusing to pay any bills unaccompanied by my written order, previously given. Listened to the music of *Acis and Galatea* on the stage, which is much too long for dramatic purposes; all agreed in the propriety of very much reducing it. There was much debate, but it soon spoke for itself. Read a little, but could not fix my mind on business—the sum of £2500 was a spectre to me.

January 5th.—Received a letter from that unprincipled villain ——, the editor of *John Bull*, wishing to know from me if "the women of the town" were really admitted or altogether excluded, as he supposed them to be, his "duty to the public" requiring his notice, etc. The ingrained villain! It is not easy to suppress one's indignation at

[1] On going to America.—(*note by Sir F. Pollock.*)

153

such monstrous malignity, but my course is to do right, and not to give heed to these wicked attempts to slander me. Serle proposed, after some debate upon the letter, that he should reply to it, telling the editor that, as he had two nightly admissions on the theatre, he had the power to come and observe himself, which was the more necessary as a prosecution for a groundless libel had already been commenced against a paper on the same subject. Went round the promenade lobbies and third tier entrance; anything more miserable or uninviting to the profligate cannot be well conceived!

January 6th.—I called down Stanfield, with whom I arranged the whole business of the opera of *Acis and Galatea*. It occupied the whole morning.

January 7th.—Listened to the rehearsal of *Acis and Galatea*, with which I was really pleased. I liked the music, and think it must be a beautiful musical entertainment. God send us success!

January 10th.—Went to Drury Lane theatre. Received a note from Mr. Delane about some misunderstanding with respect to Mr. T. Delane's card on Saturday evening. The facts appeared to be that he, Mr. T. Delane, was impatient of not discovering the right office, and that when refused entrance and offered to be conducted to the free list office by the check-taker, he tore the card in two, and went away in dudgeon. *This was not well.* But I must not see it, for I must not arm the *Times* against Drury Lane theatre. I wrote very civilly to Mr. D——, not choosing to know the exact state of the case. Listened to some of the music of *Acis and Galatea*, which wins upon me.

January 17th.—Spoke with Serle, who told me of an insidious and false attack on the theatre by *John Bull*. Went with Willmott to see the evolutions of the ballet under Mr. Noble, which were exactly what they have always been. It would not do. We twisted them a little, but it was not good. A letter in verse from Mrs. St. Aubyn. I am vain enough, God knows, but might be much more so!

January 19th.—Business with Serle, who read to me the article in *John Bull*, a most malignant, insidious, false, and wicked article; decided on sending the letter and taking off the freedom. Ordered that, after this evening, the money of women of the town should be refused altogether at the doors.

January 20th.—Letter from Sir J. Paul [1] complaining of two women

---

[1] A well-known banker; his son, though also austerely puritanical, proved a sadly remiss custodian of his clients' securities, and was in consequence some years later consigned for a considerable period to the treadmill.

of the town, as he said, being admitted into the dress circle. Acted
Shylock very well. Forster came into my room, and wished to bring
Emerson Tennent round. After the play Forster came round with
E. Tennent, who expressed himself very anxious to establish himself
as a friend of mine; civilities passed.

January 21st.—Sir John Paul and a friend called, to complain of
the two women, said to be *of the town*, in the dress circle last night.
It is denied; he was positive, and—not a gentleman. I sickened at the
impertinent assumption of the fellow, but listened to his story, and
promised to do justice.

January 24th.—Acted Shylock well. Forster and Mr. and Mrs.
Carlyle came into my room, much pleased with the play—I was
pleased that they were.

January 26th.—A letter from Carlyle informing me that Gay was
the author of the words of *Acis and Galatea.*

January 30th.—Looked at the *John Bull* newspaper, and saw that
the editor had suppressed my letter, and published his own observations on such parts of it as he chose to allude to. The villain! Wrote
to Forster, wishing to see him. Forster called, without receiving my
letter, to speak to me about the knavery of *John Bull.* We discussed
the subject, and I cordially assented to his advice to write to the editor
of the *Times,* and request him to insert the letter to *John Bull.* I
asked him to write it for me, as I was occupied with a letter to Dickens.
Sir W. Martin called to say the King of Prussia would visit Drury
Lane theatre to-morrow night, and wished to hear the play of *Macbeth.*
I explained to him the impossibility of that or any other play but those
now acting. He recommended Serle's journey to Windsor to settle
the matter with the parties there, and it was so arranged. Serle called
soon after, and I despatched him with instructions. Returned and
copied out the letter which Forster had written for me, copied out also
the letter to the proprietors of *John Bull,* and, with a letter to Delane,
closed the affair. Serle returned with the information that the King
of Prussia had selected *The Two Gentlemen of Verona.* I could have
wished he had stayed at Windsor or gone to any other theatre, rather
than have fixed on such a play; it seems he wanted *Hamlet* or *Macbeth.*
Much annoyed about the play to-morrow night.

January 31st.—I see with great satisfaction my letter in *The Times*
newspaper. Felt most grateful for this vindication, which sets me at
ease in regard to these false and malicious attacks upon me. Thank
God. Superintended the rehearsal of *Acis and Galatea,* which looks

extremely beautiful. A Mr. Grenfell, a General Committee man, wished me to let him and his party through the stage to the pit. I declined, telling him I would not do it for £10,000. He said that was a large sum. I listened to him, but would not give way to him. Gave directions about the Queen's box. Acted Valentine very fairly. The King of Prussia was very well received. The house was not good—a complete disappointment.

February 1st.—Not at all well. Looked at the paper, and was pleased to see my letters to the *Times* inserted with a notice in the *Chronicle*. Letter from Mr. J. Delane. A noble article, the third leader, in the *Times* on the attack of *John Bull*.

February 2nd.—Wrote to Mr. Delane, thanking him for the article in yesterday's *Times*. Went to Drury Lane theatre. Attended to the rehearsal of the *Prisoner of War*. Mr. Jerrold came in during part of it. Business with Mr. Faraday (brother of the great philosopher) about the concentric burner, which he brought. Allason brought draperies. Superintended the rehearsal of the choruses of *Acis and Galatea*. Business with various people. Acted Beverley tolerably well. Called for and well received. Letter from Mr. Coakley, extracting a passage from one of Mr. C. Mathews's, in which *he said* that Mr. E. Morton *had said* that *I said* that Mr. Andrews *had said* that Covent Garden theatre was a bankrupt concern, and wishing to know if I had said so. Answered Mr. Coakley to the effect that he himself had told me Covent Garden would have stopped several times but for the pecuniary aid of his late uncle, *et voilà tout* that I had said to Mr. E. Morton.

February 3rd.—Wrote to Mr. Oscar Byrne, declining to go to the funeral of Mr. Ducrow [1] on Saturday, being compelled to attend the rehearsal of *Acis and Galatea*. Under any circumstances I should not have gone—to have met the company invited there.

February 5th.—Gave my whole attention during the day to the various matters connected with the opera. Directed the rehearsal of *Acis and Galatea*.[2] The curtain was let down, and the stage swept five

---

[1] Andrew Ducrow (1793-1842), the well-known equestrian. Macready, not without reason, declined to rank him as a brother artist.

[2] The play bill announced the opera (not divided into acts) of *Acis and Galatea*, adapted and arranged for representation from the serenata of Handel. The orchestral arrangements by Mr. T. Cooke. The scenic illustrations by Mr. Stanfield, R.A. The principal parts were: Cupid, Miss Gould; Acis, Miss P. Horton; Damon, Mr. Allen; Polyphemus, Mr. H. Phillips; Galatea, Miss Romer. The dances under the direction of Mr. Noble.—(*note by Sir F. Pollock.*)

minutes before the half-hour past six. Stanfield and the assistants painting to the last minute. Saw the performance of the opera, which was beautiful; have never seen anything of the kind in my life so perfectly beautiful. Gave my whole attention to it. At the conclusion was called for and most enthusiastically received; I gave it out for repetition. Mrs. Jameson was in Catherine's box. Went into Miss H. Faucit's box and spoke to her, the Brayshers, etc. 'Gratulations were passing everywhere. Forster, Serle, Anderson, Willmott, C. Jones came into my room, all highly excited. Gave Serle a note authorizing him and C. Jones to receive and audit Mr. Brydone's accounts. I feel very grateful for this success. Too much excited to think of sleeping.

February 6th.—Rejoiced in my absence from Mr. Ducrow's funeral, which was attended by a fearful set—Messrs. Bunn, etc. When will my funeral come? Let it be as simple as the return of dust to dust should be, and somewhere where those that love me may come to think of me.

February 7th.—Was raised to a more cheering and happier state of hope and confidence by the enthusiastic tone of the newspapers. Felt relieved and grateful. Went to Drury Lane theatre. Directed the rehearsal of the *Prisoner of War*,[1] and bestowed much pains on it. Read several letters, attended to business of wardrobes, etc. Note from Delane for a private box, which I sent to him. The *Times* was more encomiastic than the other papers, but the tone of all was in " sweet accord," and the opinions that reached me unanimously enthusiastic. Acted Shylock well. I wished the Delanes to see me to advantage, though the house was bad. *The Merchant* has broken at last! Stanfield came in and would not tell me his charge, until he saw what the piece did for me. Received a very abusive paper from a Sir J. Philipart, the *Northern and Metropolitan Gazette*, which I returned to him, saying I was " honoured by his abuse." Forster and Serle came from Covent Garden theatre, and reported the comedy of Mr. Boucicault as a failure. We shall see.

February 8th.—Went to Drury Lane theatre and saw again *Acis and Galatea*. It is beautiful. Was called for after Mesdames Horton and Romer had been on, and very warmly received. Went into Catherine's box to see the *Prisoner of War*, when I was sent for to Bulwer, who went with me into our private box to see the piece, which he liked very much.

[1] By Douglas Jerrold.—(*note by Sir F. Pollock.*)

February 10th.—Jerrold called, and, signing an agreement to write a farce, received an advance of £50. Forster called, and, after him, F. Dickens,[1] whom we examined and expostulated with, and whom I lectured. I sent him home to conduct himself more temperately with the servants, which he seemed to promise he would do. Began to mark the play of *Gisippus.* Forster brought me the slip from the *Examiner* with Mr. H. Berkeley's notice of *Acis and Galatea,* which is the notice of a badly-natured, ignorant man, with a slight knowledge and no feeling of music; it is written with great vulgarity and violent spleen. I think Fonblanque ought to be ashamed of himself for permitting such a notice to appear.

February 11th.—Forster called, and told me that Fonblanque had behaved with great consideration and kindness—also in his mention of me—concerning Mr. H. Berkeley's notice of *Acis and Galatea.*

February 12th.—Miss Romer[2] has thrown our business back by refusing the part she had accepted in *The Poor Soldier.* She is jealous of Miss Horton. The editor of *Punch* sent me a volume of the work, containing copious abuse of myself. Note of grateful acknowledgment from Miss P. Horton for her advanced salary. Letter from Mr. Dickens senior, asking me for the loan of £20. I must consult Forster upon it. Was called for and very well received. Spoke to the vocalists in the green-room, and read there Mr. H. Phillips's letter. Thanked him and those who had offered to play in *The Poor Soldier,* but was obliged to decline acting it, in consequence of the refusal of one of the ladies—Miss Romer—to play the part she had promised to do.

February 15th.—Went to Drury Lane theatre, where I attended to business, and directed a rehearsal of *Gisippus* that, with four acts, occupied me the whole day.

February 18th.—Note from Miss Faucit absurdly complaining of being cast Catherine for Monday night. She last complained of Mr. Webster for not putting her in it. Answered her.

February 21st.—Wrote to Mr. J. Dickens. Sent him £20, desiring him not to mention it to his son. Forster had advised £10—but he is Dickens's father, though——

February 22nd.—Saw Mr. Webster's letter to the newspapers about myself. I could not have dictated one to him that could, if I wished

---

[1] A brother of Charles Dickens, who was in charge of the novelist's establishment during his absence in America.

[2] Emma Romer (1814–1868); afterwards Mrs. Almond; a singer of considerable reputation.

it, have more effectually proved him *what he is*—worse cannot be said.

February 23rd.—Acted Gisippus, I must admit, not well, not finished; not like a great actor. The actor was lost in the manager. The effect of the play was success; but I am not satisfied. I hope I shall be able, if I escape severe handling in this instance, to be more careful in future. Was called for, and very warmly received.

February 24th.—Did not rise early—could not; my strength, physical and mental, was quite prostrated. I could not rally. Looked at the papers, one only of which, the *Herald*, noticed the play of last night. Walked out with Catherine in the Park, and in the Botanical Gardens, enjoying—oh, how I enjoyed—the fresh air! I seemed to drink in spirits and temporary re-invigoration with every breath I drew. I have not known such a luxurious sensation for many a day. I thank God for the comfort. Returning, received my letters; one from Miss Faucit, unable, as she said, to act in *two* parts in one night—not well—not well!

February 27th.—Rose late; saw the *Examiner*, in which was a notice, which we all thought *very cold*, of *Gisippus*. Catherine and Letitia very angry and much hurt. I did not feel it much. Looked at *King Arthur*. Arranged my accounts. Wrote a note to Betty,[1] giving him the freedom of Drury Lane theatre. Looked out for after-pieces. Elliotson called, talked with and prescribed for me. Forster called—saw that there was sore feeling and questioned me; I told him what he asked, *viz.* my impression of the effect of his article, at which he was much distressed. He, Browning, Anderson, and Jonathan Bucknill dined with us; a very pleasant, quiet day.

March 4th.—Note from Browning; looked at the paper. Went to Drury Lane, reading *Athelwold*, a printed play sent to me yesterday—another instance of the extraordinary growth of dramatic power in our time. Attended to the rehearsal of *No Song, no Supper*, which will be very well performed. Lay down, ill and fatigued, to rest; read more of *Athelwold*, and still more pleased.

March 6th.—I dined with Liston, the surgeon;[2] met Barham, Liston the actor, T. Cooke, C. Taylor, Cartwright, who came late, Stanfield. Looked at bill. Saw the *Observer*, and some dirty work in it.

---

[1] William Henry West Betty (1791–1874); the "Young Roscius." He and Macready had acted together in their younger days.

[2] Robert Liston (1794–1847); one of the most successful operators of his day. He was a relative of John Liston (1776–1846), the famous actor.

March 7th.—Acted Gisippus in the lowest state of spirits—struck down *to the earth* by the sight of the house, which was unexpectedly *awful*—and racked with rheumatism. My spirits could not rally under the blow. I could only try to say those things well that alluded to the desperate condition of my own affairs. *I could be content—content to die,* for I do not see how my life can benefit my blessed children further —and what else have I to live for—as a duty. I dearly and deeply love my blessed wife, but it will only double and prolong misery to live on beside her in the misery that I seem to foresee. Note from Stanfield, naming £200 as his payment; very kind. In very depressed spirits. We had decided in our afternoon's consultation to bring out *Macbeth* on Easter Monday, and Serle had brought back Mrs. Nisbett's promise to call on me at ten o'clock on Thursday. Spoke to Miss Fortescue about Emmeline.

March 10th.—Mrs. Nisbett called. Spoke to her on the subject of an engagement. She seemed at first rather disposed to use my overture to her as a means of raising her price at other theatres, but when I explained to her the views I had respecting her, she seemed impressed with the prospect they opened to her, and finally left me to consult with her family, under a promise of seeing me again at the same hour—one o'clock—on Saturday.

March 11th.—Acted Gisippus better than I have yet done. Called for and well received. The Queen and Prince Albert occupied their box.

March 12th.—Received a note from Mrs. Nisbett disappointing me. I ought not to be surprised—these are the commodities in which I have to deal! Oh, God! assist me. Note from Miss Turpin, thanking me for her addition of salary. Talked with Anderson, Serle and Willmott on the subject of Mrs. Nisbett; all rather desponding as to her engagement. Dressed. T. Cooke called and accompanied me to the Purcell Club, "Crown and Anchor." Saw Mr. Hogarth,[1] Bellamy [2]—quite a wreck of an old man!—Mr. Edward Taylor, the president, and my host; Cartwright, and, to my surprise—and disbelief at first—Mr. Bunn at the dinner-table. Mr. Macdonald sat next to me. Purcell's music was very charming, particularly his sacred music; but the day quite overcame me. Mr. Bunn walked off at a *very* early hour. Cartwright wished me to go with him to Murchison's,[3] but I had no

---

[1] George Hogarth (1783–1870); the well-known musical critic; Charles Dickens's father-in-law.

[2] Thomas Ludford Bellamy (1770–1843); singer and theatrical manager.

[3] Sir Roderick Impey Murchison, Bart. (1792–1871); the eminent geologist.

heart or head. Went to Drury Lane theatre. Heard of Mrs. Nisbett's intention *not to engage with us*—yielding to the persuasions of Mr. Farren, etc. Much fatigued and depressed. A letter from Sir W. Martin, expressing the Queen's wish for *Acis and Galatea* to be acted after *Gisippus* on Friday. Lord Delawarr sending word she was "delighted with the play and my acting."

March 16th.—Mrs. Nisbett and her mother called, and entered on the matter of her visit. Her terms were £35 per week. She waived the question of a Benefit, leaving it to circumstances and my consideration. All her other intended stipulations she waived, leaving all matters to my discretion. She signed her engagement for next season at £35 per week, the two next, if she remained on the stage, at £40. We parted apparently mutually satisfied. She agreed to all the regulations of the theatre.

March 19th.—The Gurwoods and Miss Meyer, Lord Beaumont, Charles Buller, Mr. Milnes, C. Young, Dr. Quin, Knox, dined with us. In the evening the Procters, Mrs. Kitchener, the Chisholm, Maclise, the Spicers, Miss P. Horton, Mr. Allen, came in.

March 20th.—Lord Nugent, Miss Adelaide Kemble, Mrs. Reid, Hetta Skerrett, Messrs. C. Kemble, Travers, Cartwright, Pierce Butler, Beazley, G. Raymond, Dr. Elliotson, Jerdan, came to dine with us. Hetta told me that the Queen had desired Marianne [1] to tell me that she was very much pleased with all she had seen at Drury Lane. Adelaide Kemble was very agreeable, and sang in the evening with a passion and fervour that satisfied me of her claims to distinction.[2] A cheerful and agreeable day.

March 25th.—Received an anonymous note informing me that Mr. Bunn *had* purchased Polhill's share in the *Age* for £100!—that he was now *sole editor* at six guineas per week! with other facts that leave me no room to doubt of the truth of my correspondent.

March 26th.—Received an intimation from Beazley that Mr. and Mrs. C. Mathews *would* come to Drury Lane if they could receive remuneration for their services. Took Serle, Willmott and Anderson into consultation upon it. We sifted the matter as we best could, and the conclusion was that we could not make them worth their

---

[1] Miss Marianne Skerrett held some small post in the Royal household. She and her sister were connections of Macready.

[2] Adelaide Kemble (1814–1879), besides being a gifted singer was an accomplished writer; after her marriage with Mr. Sartoris (in 1853) she withdrew into private life and became a well-known figure in the cultured society of the day.

cost. Dined with Kenyon. Met Rev. Dr. Hawtrey (Eton), Dr. Ashburner, Babbage, Browning, Dyce, Harness.

March 27th.—Looked at the newspaper, in which was a very good article on the drama and its scenic appliances by Forster. Mr. C. Darley called, and I went over with him the play, as to structure, of *Plighted Troth*, and showed him the necessity of further omission and dove-tailing—he assented to all. On invitation he stayed to lunch with us; his manners are very frank and pleasant.

March 29th.—Spoke with Beazley on the engagement of Mr. and Mrs. C. Mathews; treated the question as respected them with the utmost delicacy and with all proper feeling. Consulted my council, and upon that offered them £40 per week for next season.

March 30th.—Read *Plighted Troth* to Catherine and Letitia, who were much struck with it.[1] Beazley called and informed me of Mr. C. Mathews's refusal of £40 per week for himself and his wife. We talked for some time; he said from them that they would find their own clothes, and submit to costume, and be in all respects good subjects, but that they did not like half-past-nine-o'clock rehearsals. I offered them £50, which Beazley undertook to convey to them. Consulted with Serle, Anderson, etc., on the expediency of increasing the offer to the Mathews; all were against it.

March 31st.—At the theatre spoke to Phelps about his part and read the play of *Plighted Troth*, which produced a great effect. Gave subjects of scenes to the painters. Talked over various matters of business, particularly discussing the subject of the Mathewses' engagement.

April 2nd.—T. Cooke called and we settled the remaining points of *King Arthur*, but as we spoke of it he gave his opinion, and strongly, *against* producing it in the hurried way in which it must be done this season. His reasons had weight with me, and I saw the uncertainty of success—the certainty of not doing all that might be done with the piece. Went to Drury Lane theatre, calling in my way on Beazley, who was out. Heard the effects of distance in the music of *Macbeth*. A note from Sir W. Martin to intimate the Queen's visit on Monday. Miss Welsh, Mrs. Carlyle's niece, dined with us. Went to Drury Lane theatre. Spoke with my counsellors, but I did not find wisdom in the multitude. Went to see the burletta

---

[1] It is strange how completely this play falsified on production all the favourable opinions that it had previously enlisted. As will be seen, it proved an immediate and irremediable failure.

CHARLES JAMES MATTHEWS

From a lithograph of a painting by R. Jones

at Covent Garden, which was humorous, gorgeous, whimsical, and well adaped in such a theatre to its end.   In this species of entertainment (not properly belonging to a national theatre, but rather to a house for burletta, etc.), the Covent Garden theatre people bear away the bell.

April 3rd.—Mr. Charles Darley called, and we talked over the suggested alterations that had occurred to me.   He was perfectly satisfied with the suggestions and mentioned his wish, if I were not adverse, to inscribe the play [1] to me.   I could only say how proud I was of the compliment.   Tom Landseer called—poor fellow! [2]   Bulwer called, left me two French plays to read in order to judge of the subject.

April 4th.—Wrote notes to Mrs. Carlyle, thanking her for the gift of a brooch which was once Flora Macdonald's.   Acted Macbeth very fairly, was called for and well received.   The Queen and Prince Albert were present.

April 5th.—To Maclise, and was very much pleased to see his grand picture of Hamlet, which was splendid in colour and general effect.   With some of the details I did not quite agree, particularly the two personages, Hamlet and Ophelia.   Drove to Edwin Landseer's and saw some of his charming works.   Went on to Etty, and was delighted with his gorgeous colours and ravishing forms.   I went from thence to Drury Lane theatre, where I transacted business with Willmott, Serle, Sloman, the painters, etc.   Returned home, having read through the second act of the farce, *The Lady-Killer, The Trip to Margate,* one act and part of another of *The Water Carrier,* and part of *Intimate Friends.*   Employed the evening in looking through some folios of the *Galerie de Versailles* for subjects for rooms and costume for *Plighted Troth.*

April 8th.—Note from Beazley about the Mathewses.   Answered it expressing my belief they were coquetting.   Acted Gisippus, for the last time, pretty well.   Called for and well received.   Now here is a complete defeat of my calculations.   I thought it a material object in opening a theatre to have such a play.   It has produced nothing, and been well spoken of.   There is some weakness in it, which I have not yet exactly pointed out.

April 9th.—I agreed to give Mr. and Mrs. C. Mathews the terms for which they stood out, viz. £60 per week.   It is a very great salary, but it is paid in consideration of enfeebling an opposition as well as

---

[1] *Plighted Troth.*   [2] He was " stone " deaɪ.

163

adding to my own strength. Went on to Drury Lane theatre where I entered on business; told Willmott of what I had done; he was rejoiced at it. Called at Beazley's and found there Mr. C. Mathews and Madame Vestris. I met them very frankly and good-humouredly; heard much that was irrelevant, and some things that amused me; at last concluded an engagement with them for two years at the salary of £60 per week for Drury Lane theatre. Parted with them, they starting off in their carriage, I in my shattered old hack cab!

April 10th.—Dined with Sir Isaac Goldsmid [1]—a very rich house, and the daughters agreeable. Dr. Roget,[2] the Brazilian minister, Sir Robert Adair,[3] etc., dined there.

April 17th.—Rather later than I wished in rising. Counted the lines of the play, which I found to amount to at least 2236—a startling number; but I have a feeling like hope—perhaps akin to trust—in the massive language and fine thoughts properly spread over this play. I dare not, however, indulge in expectation. Gave the employment of the day to the thought and reading of my part of Grimwood in *Plighted Troth*. A note from Monckton Milnes, wishing me to meet the Prussian Minister (Bunsen) at his house on Thursday.

April 18th.—Mr. Roth came to ask me about the arrangement of a dress for Prince Albert for a fancy ball. Went to Drury Lane theatre and attended to the various businesses pressing on me. Went on the stage and attended the rehearsal of the new farce, which the actors do not seem to know how to *try* to act; and I must defer it, and take it in hand myself.

April 19th.—Went to Drury Lane theatre. Attended there to business of all kinds. Rehearsed the play of *Plighted Troth*, which occupied me the whole day. Mr. Darley was present. Business with all the departments. Fully and momentarily occupied. Coming home, found Forster, who had come to dine. In the evening read the part of Grimwood.

April 20th.—Went to the theatre, trying to keep my thoughts on the acting of my part. Rehearsed the play of *Plighted Troth*. Became confident in hope about it. Looked at the chance of a brilliant

[1] Sir Isaac Lyon Goldsmid, Bart. (1778–1859), the well-known financier; the first Jew to receive a baronetcy.

[2] Peter Mark Roget (1779–1869); an eminent physician and scientist; nephew of Sir Samuel Romilly, author of the *Thesaurus of English Words and Phrases*, which obtained a wide circulation.

[3] Sir Robert Adair, K.C.B. (1763–1855); Whig diplomatist and intimate friend of Charles Fox. Ridiculed by Canning in one of his Anti-Jacobin "squibs."

success. Serle spoke to me. Rested. Acted nervously; but *the play was unsuccessful*. Long consultation afterwards on what should be done. Anderson, C. Jones, Serle, Willmott, and Forster. I wished to do justice to the author, and we agreed at last to give it another trial. Chance, I fear, there is none. *Eloi!* A most unhappy failure; I have felt it deeply, deeply.

April 21st.—Came down, wretchedly low at heart, worn, done, and depressed by the issue of last night and the want of sleep. I did not sleep at all through the night. I cannot imagine how I could have been so mistaken. Surely I could not believe that to be poetry, thought, energy, imagination, and melody of rhythm which was totally devoid of all these! Wrote an answer to Miss Power. Mr. Darley called. We talked over the matter of last night. He was much depressed, and I agonized for him.[1] He deserved to succeed. The result of our conference was that he could not make the alterations suggested to his play by this day's rehearsal, and, therefore, that he would wish the play to be withdrawn.

April 22nd.—Received a note from Dr. Ashburner, informing me that Darley would call on me, and wishing me to speak encouragingly to him. God knows I need no prompter to act in kindness and sympathy towards him. A note—a most kind note—from Bulwer in relation to Mr. Darley's play. I enclosed it to Mr. Darley, with a cordial expression of sympathy and a cheque for £34. Looked out a play for Miss P. Horton's benefit.

April 23rd.—At dinner received a most affecting note from Darley that almost reconciles one to the misery that has been my lot this week.

April 24th.—Colonel Gurwood called with Lord Douro and Lord Charles Wellesley,[2] the latter wanting a knight's armour of Edward III's reign to attend, by order, Prince Albert at the fancy ball at the Palace! Cares of rulers and of legislators! I showed them all the attention in my power. Gave much attention to *Marino Faliero*, which I begin to like, but I never dare venture to hope again! Walked out with Edward and called on Bulwer, who was from home; on Milnes, who had two disagreeable aristocratical visitors with him. P. Butler came in and told me that C. Kemble was the manager of Covent Garden theatre, but that *he, P. B——*, had *nothing* to do with it.

---

[1] Macready was always most loyal to his authors, a quality that has never been too conspicuous among managers when confronted with a fiasco.

[2] The sons of the Duke of Wellington.

Called on Darley and left him a note; called on Rogers, left card. Found Kenyon at home. No word from Forster to smooth the fall of *Plighted Troth*. The whole evening to *Marino Faliero*, which improves on me.

April 25th.—Acted Macbeth with much energy, sustaining the character to the last. Was called for, and well received. Herr Schneider came to express his admiration in a state of great excitement; he said that he had observed to two elderly gentlemen in the boxes that he constantly read in English newspapers the "decline of the drama," the "great days of the drama that are gone"; but, he would ask, when was there such a drama as this? Englishmen do not think so. Stanfield and Forster came into my room. Notes from Bulwer about a dress for this fancy ball; from Jerdan; an envelope enclosing copious extracts from certain newspapers, *Spectator* and *Age*, I believe, abusive of me was sent to me. I crushed them up and threw them into the fire.

April 26th.—Lords Douro and Charles Wellesley called about the dress of the latter. Showed them the armour and gave Lord C. W—— directions what to do. Colonel Wilde came shortly after on the same errand. Bulwer called and tried on some dresses; fixed upon that of Ruthven.

April 27th.—Milnes called and I gave directions about his dress for the fancy ball.

April 28th.—Lord Charles Wellesley called about his dress. I left him with the wardrobe-keeper. Colonel Wilde came on the same errand. Attended to business with scene-painters, wardrobe, etc. Very much fatigued. After dinner wrote a letter to Marianne respecting a state visit to the theatre by Her Majesty. Note from Bulwer about his dress.

April 29th.—Rehearsed with care the play of *Hamlet*.[1] Acted Hamlet very fairly. Dined with the Royal Academy. Enjoyed the dinner very much, though suffering from cold. Spoke with the different Academicians, who were all most courteous to me, with the Bishop of Norwich a long while. Lord Longford, Lord Normanby, etc. Much pleased with the speech of the French Ambassador,[2] and not quite

[1] The cast was: King, Mr. G. Bennett; Polonius, Mr. Compton; Laertes, Mr. Elton; Horatio, Mr. Graham; Guildenstern, Mr. Lynne; Rosencrantz, Mr. Selby; Osric, Mr. Hudson; Marcellus, Mr. Marston; First Grave-digger, Mr. Keeley; Ghost, Mr. Phelps; Queen, Mrs. Warner; Ophelia, Miss P. Horton.—(*note by Sir F. Pollock.*)

[2] Le Comte d'Aulaire.—(*note by Sir F. Pollock.*)

satisfied with the general tone taken as to the relative merits of British and foreign art. Wondered at the want of idea in the old Duke's strange reply. Disgusted with Sir R. Peel, who first read his catalogue during the President's speech, and then yawned without disguise.

May 1st.—Read Mr. C. Mathews's speech on the closing of Covent Garden; it was worthy of Mr. C. Mathews and "the management of Madame Vestris." Players! *poor players!*

May 2nd.—I see the Queen will not command. She has no feeling for the theatre. Wrote a few lines to Dickens. Went to Drury Lane theatre. Milnes called about his dress. I did all I could for him. He went as a steward to my dinner. I am glad of the power of showing him civility.

May 3rd.—Babbage called about the Duke of Somerset's dress. I could not help him out. Went to Drury Lane theatre; found notes from an attorney about a theatre bill; another from a Mr. Barry, an actor of Birmingham, informing me that persons had been applying to him to become a witness on my trial *v. Dispatch* upon the grounds that he had been "very violently disposed of" by me, when killed as the King in *Hamlet* at Birmingham, and that he should thereupon be subpœna'd to give testimony to the "brutality of my conduct to actors," that the parties were going about collecting evidence, etc. I answered it, not objecting to any truth, but thinking it scarcely right that I should be answerable for the events of a scene of violence in acting, etc.

May 7th.—Note from Lord Normanby about armour, which I lent to him. Saw a Mr. Ryder [1] rehearse two scenes of Pierre, and thought he showed more promise of becoming a useful actor than any novice I had seen for a long time. Engaged him. Colonel Buckley (six feet three inches!) called about a dress. I did my best for him. Darley called and showed me his preface to *Plighted Troth*, which will come out next week.

May 8th.—Called on Sir R. Comyn [2]; very glad to see my old acquaintance again, very little altered, older, but not showing it very much. Called on Darley, and took him in the carriage with me. Left a card at Lansdowne House. Called at Lady Blessington's; sat with her some time. A white man was there, whom I did not know, but

---

[1] John Ryder (1814–1885); the well-known actor; this engagement initiated a long connection between Macready and Ryder, who accompanied the former in his visits to America in 1843 and 1848.

[2] Sir Robert Buckley Comyn (1792–1853); an Indian judge; Chief Justice of Madras from 1835 to 1842.

whom I imagine to have been Mr. Chorley[1]; he never spoke one word the whole time I stayed. Read *Marino Faliero* in the *carriage*. Went to Bulwer's—walked round the grounds.[2] A dinner-party of journalists and critics (!) assembled—Leigh Hunt, Bell of the *Atlas*, Ainsworth, Forster, Jerdan, Blanchard; there were also Quin and Villiers, M.P. for Wolverhampton. One of the dullest, most uncomfortable days I have spent for some years. I asked Quin once the time; he said, "A quarter-past nine; you thought it was eleven." I was not very well pleased with Bulwer inviting me to indifferent company and a very bad dinner, when I could so much more pleasantly and profitably have employed my time at home or elsewhere.

May 10th.—Milnes called about his dress, tried it on. Rehearsed part of *Marino Faliero*, which promises to act well, but which I fear will be too much for me in the time; consulted Serle and Jones about it, and as to the financial consequence of not doing it. Withheld the advertisement to make an effort. A letter from ―― asking the *loan* of £20. If she had had any *heart*, she might have married me at sixteen years of age, she was a coquette and utterly heartless—poor thing! I am very sorry for her. Acted Gisippus fairly. Called for and well received.

May 11th.—Woke early, and applied myself in bed to the words of *Marino Faliero*. Continued until twelve o'clock, and mastered all except part of one scene in act five. Looked at newspaper. Answered Miss ――, enclosing her £5. "Oh heaven! that we might read the book of fate!" Who would have supposed, when I was a boy, whose *desperate love* for this girl was played with by her, that our fates would ever have so placed us!

May 12th.—After the play went to the Queen's theatre to see a man of the name of Fuller do the Clown. It was a dreadful endurance. What places these minor theatres are! Surely it is the duty of a Government to have some care of the *decency*, if not the *moral influence* of places of public amusement, both of which were set at naught by the exhibitions before and behind the curtain at this disgusting place of obscene and ribald absurdities.

May 14th.—The Twisses, Goldsmids, Sir John Wilson, Sir Robert Comyn, Chilton, Delane junior, Harness, Leslie, Fanny Howarth came to dinner.

May 15th.—Lord Beaumont, Rogers, Sheil, Eastlake, and

---

[1] Henry Fothergill Chorley (1808–1872); the musical critic.
[2] Bulwer was then occupying his villa at Fulham.

MADAME VESTRIS

(MRS. CHARLES J. MATTHEWS)

From an engraving by J. C. Armytage

Mrs. Norton dined with us.   A party in the evening which went off flatly.

May 17th.—Forster called and read me part of Dickens's letter from Niagara.   He is *disgusted* with the Americans, and I must admit they leave their defenders a *very bad case!* [1]

[1] Shortly afterwards Macready received the following letter from Dickens, which discloses his impression of America, as it then was, with characteristic vigour—

> "*On board the Steamboat from Pittsburg to Cincinnatti.*
> "*Friday Night, April* 1, 1842,
> " (Which will account for tremulous writing.)

"My dear Macready,

"But that I know from constant experience that there are seasons and many seasons in a life of excitement and hard work when a man needs all the manhood he has in him not to give in, and to keep on doing the labour he has to do in this doing world, and facing the weather, whatever it be, bravely, I should quarrel with you for your despondent letter in which I do fear certain rotten sins, called Sunday newspapers and certain rotten creatures with men's forms and devils' hearts, (saving the demoniac ability) called writers, have greater part and share than they should.   I have been thinking all day, as we have been skimming down this beautiful Ohio, its wooded heights all radiant in the sunlight, how can a man like Macready, fret and fume and chafe himself for such lice of literature as these.   You may say that they are like lice for another reason besides their manners, because they live in people's heads.   I do not believe it.   I have no faith in their influence good or bad, I put no trust in them for good or evil.   Associating you with my recollections and meditations in this and all other journeys and becoming more and more mindful at such times, if that can be, of the images with which you have stored my brain and the human energies and great passions you have set before me, and remembering the stamp and substance you have expressed on unsubstantial thoughts, I have wondered a hundred times how things so mean and small, so wholly unconnected with your image and utterly separated from the exercise of your genius in its effects on all men, can for an instant disturb you.

"Fine talking, you will say, and so it is, for I know the vague desire to take somebody by the throat which is consequent upon the discharge of these pigmy arrows.   But it is not the more rational because I have felt it also.   And I vow to try and overcome it and gain the victory by being indifferent and feeling my own worth and bidding them whistle on.

"The theatre, Forster tells me, is doing well.   Everybody tells me, it is doing well. You yourself don't say that it is doing ill.   In the joint names of Hercules and the Waggoner cheer up then!   The work will not always be so hard.   You won't always take it so much to heart.   My mind misgives me that you have been living too long on chops and that you don't take enough 'Rosy' to drink and that you are altogether in what Beau Tibbs, with another meaning in his mind, would call 'a horrid low way.'   But if Elliotson be the man I take him to be, (and if he be not, the whole human race wear masks and dominoes,) he will already have administered the necessary restoratives.   He will have said that you must and shall have regular dinner times.   He will have spoken emphatically of nourishing meats, generous drinks, and healths five fathoms deep to the distant Dickens.   He will have created a new office in the theatre and appointed to it a strictly virtuous female whose function is to come upon the stage at 12 at noon bearing in her hand a tumbler glass containing the yolk of a new laid egg discreetly mixed with Golden sherry, concerning which the stage direction shall be, 'Macready drinks, smack his lips, and become refreshed.'

"Seriously, my dear Macready, no man can work in mind and body long, unless he uses

May 19*th*.—Rested and acted Lord Townley very fairly.   Miss H. Faucit was *very bad* and *no mistake*.   Called for and well received.

---

a dining-table as Christians should.   I have always thoroughly abominated and abjured those nasty Hemming chops.   Old Parr never dined off chops, or in his dressing-room. Chops and cheerfulness are impossible of connection, but joints and joy are clearly related, and port and peace go hand in hand.   Do say in your next that you have left off eating with your fingers on weekdays and have taken to knives and forks again.   Do say that you are better and heathfully disposed, but not unless you really are so.   And never acknowledge to yourself, so shall your affectionate confidence have no occasion to acknowledge to me, that in the smallest angle of your heart you ever framed that wish, or thought twice that thought which, seriously entertained for but one moment's space, would give pain in heaven to the spirit of your own child.   We received your letter and that of your dear wife and sister with all our other epistolary treasures this morning, most fortunately and opportunely just before we left Pittsburg.   We have been looking for them painfully these many days and if they had arrived but four and twenty hours later, would have gone on our way with heavy hearts.   The steamer that brought them had a terrible passage, her engine was disabled and she came on with her sails.   They carry but two, and neither is larger than a T.R.D.L. flat.   I mean one of a pair.   She staggered into Halifax and a stationary steamer brought on her mails and passengers.

"I will not tell you of our route, for I have written at some length to Forster and he will, no doubt, read my letter to you, nor will I tell you, for the same reason, of my extraordinary success in magnetizing Kate.   I hope you will be a witness of that many, many, many, happy times.   I have not changed, I cannot change, my dear Macready, my secret opinion of this country, its follies, vices, grievous disappointments.   I have said to Forster that I believe the heaviest blow ever dealt at Liberty's head will be dealt by this nation in the ultimate failure of its example to the earth.   See what is passing now !   Look at the exhausted treasury.   The paralyzed Government, the unworthy representatives of a free people, the desperate contests between the North and the South ; the iron curb and brazen muzzle fastened upon every man who speaks his mind, even in the Republican Hall to which Republican men are sent by a Republican people to speak Republican truths.   The stabbing and shootings and coarse, and brutal threatenings exchanged between Senators under the very Senate's roof— the intrusion of the most pitiful, mean, malicious, creeping, crawling, sneaking party spirit into all transactions of life—even into the appointments of physicians to pauper madhouses— the silly drivelling, slanderous, wicked, monstrous Party Press.   I say nothing of the egotism which makes of Lord Ashburton's appointment the conciliatory act of a benighted Government ; nothing of the boastful, vain-glorious spirit which dictates a million of such absurdities and which is not English.   I love and honour very many of the people here, but the 'mass' (to use our monarchial term) are miserably dependent in great things and miserably independent in small ones.   That's a truth and you will find it is so.   The nation is a body without a head, and the arms and legs are occupied in quarrelling with the trunk and each other and exchanging bruises at random.   God bless you, my dearest friend, a hundred times, God bless you !   I will not thank you, (how can I thank you !) for your care of our dear children ; but I will ever be, heart and soul,

"Your faithful friend
'CHARLES DICKENS.

"P.S.—I need not say that I have many pleasant things to say of America.   God forbid that it should be otherwise.   I speak to you as I would to myself.   I am a lover of Freedom disappointed.   That's all !   I am carrying this letter on to Cincinnatti to send to Boston from there."

May 20th.—Weary, weary! Rose with prayers in my heart for the success of the night's experiment. Rehearsed with much care (what occupied a long morning) the play of *Marino Faliero*. Rested and thought over my character. I could not sleep. Acted Marino Faliero in parts very well; the interest of the play grew upon the audience, and the curtain fell upon the death of Faliero with their strong sympathy. Was called for and very warmly received.

May 22nd.—Mr. and Mrs. Everett; Sir John and Miss Goldsmid; Mr. and Mrs. Emerson Tennent; Barry, R.A.; Sir M. A. Shee, P.R.A.; Edwin Landseer, R.A.; and Darley dined with us. We had an evening party, Staudigl, Miss Hawes, T. Cooke, etc. Grattan Cooke, Miss Williams (beautiful duet singers), Mr. and Mrs. Lover, the Fonblanques, Twisses, Lady Stepney, Elliotson, Babbage, Wheatstone, Carlyle, Miss Wild, Marstons, William Smith (Athelwold), Procters, C. Buller, E. Katers, Sir Charles and Lady Morgan, H. Skerrett, Mr. Nightingale, Dunn, Nicholson, Maclise, Forster, Kenyon, Boxall, Z. Troughton, Browning, etc. An agreeable dinner party and a very pleasant evening.

May 23rd.—Through the day gave every interval of thought to the speech I had to deliver at night. Rehearsed the play of *Othello*. Heard of some paragraphs in the papers about summonses being served upon me for *rates*—the first I had heard of it. I was very angry. Last night of the season. Laboured through the day to get the speech into my head, had overmastered it, but was so oppressed with fatigue of mind and body that I could not keep my eyes open; rested for about half-an-hour. Acted Iago very unfinishedly, very poorly. Spoke my speech falteringly and ill. I have had too much upon my head. Fox and Forster came into my room. I was so nervous, for all recollection of the words left me entirely. I had too much to do.

May 26th.—Took leave of my assembled dear ones—the blessed ones—and went to the railway station. Had one of the mail carriages to myself all the journey except from Coventry to Birmingham where my companion was a middle-aged man, dressed to a point of exactness with moustache and royale oiled to points which curled up at considerable distance from his face—a sort of Chinese exquisite, and these are men!—men, to whom God has given reason—they are soldiers, to whom the country gives bread and place, heroes (in their own estimation) to whom the world gives fame!!! I am sick of it— the whole great orbicular humbug. Read *The Recruiting Officer* of

Farquhar, which does not suit the theatrical genius of our time. Read *The Twin Rivals*, in which there is very much to admire, part of *The Plain Dealer*, in which there is much more. Arriving at Liverpool at seven o'clock (!) I went down to the packet and got a sofa for my berth. The evening was mild and calm. I remained on deck talking with Hudson till nine o'clock and then lay down. I listened, when woke out of my doze, to the politics of some neighbours, the captain, a Dublin citizen, etc., over their whisky punch, the captain's reasons for the law of primogeniture, all ending and beginning in his wish that there should be a head of the family. Thus advances reason—and with it civilization.

Dublin, May 27th.—Reached Kingstown in the clear grey morning about seven. What numberless recollections—as old as thirty-nine years ago!—alas!—and what various associations from books and traditions do the various points of view call up to my mind. How bountiful is God! This very exercise of the mind is an enjoyment, if we could but be sensible of it!

May 28th.—Heard that Mr. Yates [1] could not live a fortnight; his disorder has turned to rapid consumption. Poor man, he was dreadfully terrified at the idea of dying—he is now more composed. It is an awful thing, but being part of every life, I trust I shall meet it like a reasonable man. It is the fear of death, not death itself, that is really dreadful. Acted Virginius unequally—though striving to do well. The actors were very remiss. I was angry, but not *with them*, unbeseemingly so. Was called for and well received.

May 29th.—I called at Morrison's Hotel to inquire after and leave my name for Mr. and Mrs. Yates. I did not respect him, but I feel for her, poor suffering woman, and for him, and believe that any show of sympathy or pity is sweet and solacing to us under such affliction. I have felt it so.

May 30th.—Went to theatre, rehearsed Gisippus; very, very wearied. Wrote a short note to Catherine. Rested, felt wearied even to illness. Acted Gisippus better than I have ever yet done, so well, that I think, if I could have given the same truth and effect to it the first night in London, it must have attracted, and yet who can say? Called for and very well received.

May 31st.—Called on Miss H. Faucit, and gave her some general notions respecting Lady Macbeth, of which she rehearsed a part with me. Dined with John Twiss. Met a Mr. Hayes or Haynes, who has

---

[1] Frederick Henry Yates, the actor.

been much with the Duke of Wellington—I fancy on the Commissariat, a Mr. Booth, also with him, and a Mr. Frith, an old Dutch friend of John's. I listened with much patience and some amusement to the dogmas of these Conversative politicians, and cease to wonder at the little sense and justice among mankind, when I hear such principles of Government laid down or defended. I was *very* quiet.

June 1st.—Spoke to Miss Faucit about her habit of acting with her arms *in* to her side, and thus bringing herself so close to another person as to destroy all outline; also about her *smothering up* the last scene. She behaved very weakly upon these kind and good-natured remarks, and I thought would have had an hysteric in my room. I was distressed and annoyed.

June 2nd.—Looked at the paper, *filled* with accounts of the stated attempt on the Queen's life—a few passing words given to the loss of a boat laden with cockles, which was swamped in Menai Strait and twelve men perished. God help the poor families of these poor men, say I. I am glad no mischief happened to the Queen, but my sympathies are with *my kind*—with *humanity*. Went to rehearsal of *Lady of Lyons*. Spoke a few words with Calcraft, asking him if he thought Miss H. Faucit might accompany me to Glendalough, if her maid went with her. He thought there could then be no observation. Acted Claude Melnotte very well to a dull audience, commanded by the Lord Lieutenant.

June 3rd.—Rehearsed *Marino Faliero*—which is acted so badly that I can expect no effect from it. This company is certainly a justification for the citizens of Dublin on the score of taste in deserting the theatre—a *full and perfect justification*. Dined with Mr. and Mrs. Hulton; was delighted with the beauty of the scenery, commanding a most charming view of the Wicklow Hills. Met at dinner their family, a very charming one—a Mr. Kennedy; Colonel Jones; Captain ——; Mr. McCulloch, Trinity College, etc. I delighted to find in them warm lovers of art, and became quite at home.

June 4th.—Looked at the paper, in which I saw that Bishop,[1] the composer of some very pretty airs, glees, overtures, and operas, had been knighted especially by the Queen. This mere idealess administerer to the pleasures of a sense (as Carlyle says, what does it all *mean?*) is *honoured*, according to Court and Government diction, while men who have enriched the minds of their fellow-men with new thoughts, have quickened and elevated kind and noble feelings by the effects of their

---

[1] Sir Henry Rowley Bishop (1876–1855) ; the eminent composer.

intellect and imagination; in fact, *Poets*—like Knowles, Wordsworth, etc.—are passed by as *ignarum pecus*. Agh!!! I am sick of the whole rotten mass of stupid corruption. Letter from darling Neddy, which is sunshine to my heart, and they may bray kings and queens in mortars whilst I can have such holidays of the heart as these letters give. Heard from Calcraft of Miss Adelaide Kemble's purposed marriage; not surprised and not moved *at all* by it. Rehearsed with great pains and excessive trouble and annoyance *Marino Faliero*.

June 5th.—Went in the carriage at a quarter before eight o'clock to Calcraft's and took him up. He, Miss H. F——, her maid, and myself. We left Dublin for Glendalough by the Military Road, and till we reached the glen the clouds were so heavy on the hills that we could see nothing. We lunched very cheerfully and happily as we went along, and as we arrived at Glendalough the day cleared and we obtained a view of the full mountain forms. The air, the motion, the music of the sounds, the repose from thought and the sight of health, beauty, and happiness did me good. We followed our guide to the seven churches, the Round Tower, the Kevin's bed, the waterfall, etc., and in all we were all happy. The scenery was most sad and stern and beautiful. I was disappointed in my ride to Bray, which is a pretty place, and where we dined.

June 6th.—Languid, wearied, and country-sick, utterly indisposed to labour, I rose to my task this morning. Attended to the affairs of my room. Found letters from Serle on business; from my cousin ——. This made me still more sad, and low in spirits—recalling to me the years of my full youth, when in all the plenitude of spirits I was wont to give my evenings occasionally to her and her sisters at my uncle's house, and only discovered at my parting from them that she really loved me. Alas! for the innocent sufferings of this life! What is she now, poor girl? Saw in the paper a favourable account of *Marino Faliero*. Rehearsed Macbeth; was very much struck with Miss Faucit's rehearsal of Lady Macbeth, which surprised and gratified me very much. Acted Macbeth as well as my harassed mind and worn-down body would let me. Called for and well received. Would have taken on Miss Faucit, but she, against my directions, had undressed, so left her to Calcraft. Spoke with Calcraft and her afterwards about her Benefit—and with her about her acting, which was *remarkably* good.

June 9th.—Looked at the newspaper, and thought what a world of utter deceit, delusion, and falsehood this is. Great God! where is there truth?—where will it ever be found on earth? *It never will.* The world is one great lie. Bishops, statesmen, lawyers, soldiers, lords, chartists, all unworthy to be *men*—I *sicken* at the contemplation. Rested a very short time. Acted Werner to a *wretched* house in my very best style. Called for and well received. Spoke with Calcraft. He tells me his daughters are proud—proud!! Mighty heaven—of what? Spoke to Helen Faucit about Portia.

June 10th.—Looked at the papers. Read the suicide of Lord Congleton—Sir H. Parnell.[1] I scarcely wonder at thinking men wearying of life, but it is so short that there is little wisdom in incurring the risks attendant on ante-dating our doom. Rehearsed *The Merchant of Venice.* This company of actors is *too bad.*

June 11th.—Looked at the papers; discontented with all I saw there. Read a paragraph of Peel on his knees at prayer!! Let him do right and justice to his fellow-men and then *stand up* and *thank* God. Bought a waistcoat for Forster—gay one!—poplins for my women. Acted Gisippus as well as a disgusting, ill-bred party in the stage private box would let me by their noise. Called for and well received.

June 12th.—Rose very early for our day's journey into Wicklow. Called for Miss H. Faucit at seven. Called for Calcraft, who was not ready, and went on our way rejoicing through the pretty village of Dundrum, by the Scalp, through Enniskerry, all scenes of beauty; by Rathdrum to the Meeting of the Waters and to the Vale of Avoca, which, with its distant prospect of Arklow and the sea, is in its kind as beautiful as a scene well can be. We lunched on our route near the Sugar-loaf Hill; were very merry and very happy. Delighted with what we saw around us. Passed through Rathdrum, where we changed horses, and continued our route to the Meeting of the Waters. Ascended the hill behind the house at Ovoca, and enjoyed a most delightful view. Returned by Newtown Mount Kennedy, a continual succession of rich and lovely scenery, through the Glen of the Downs.

June 13th.—Acted to a *wretched house*—my benefit—as well as I could. Between the fourth and fifth acts received a letter that quite overturned me; it announced to me the death of Dr. Arnold [2]—the

---

[1] Henry Brook Parnell (1776–1842); fourth baronet and first Lord Congleton; an advanced Whig and holder of subordinate offices in Lord Grey's and Lord Melbourne's Administrations; an authority on finance and political economy; his suicide was the result of continued ill-health.

[2] Thomas Arnold (1795–1842); the famous Rugby head master.

great and good man, who has left few, very, very few, behind him who could at all compare with him. God will bless him. My prayers for such a man would be almost an impiety, but my heart's wishes rise towards God's throne for him.

Birmingham, June 20th.—Read the newspaper, receiving sensations of ineffable disgust at the paper itself—that most disgusting twaddle, the *Morning Herald*—and at all the *high* (very high in a *game* sense) world, the individuals of which it commemorates.

June 21st.—Lydia wrote to me chiefly about the lamented Dr. Arnold. Great God! if a miserable wretch like —— or any of these heartless traffickers in humbug were to die, whole columns of newspapers would be given to the record of their great and good qualities. This man, one of the greatest benefactors of his kind, goes from among us, and six lines relate his death, his occupation, and the family he has left behind. Does the world—or the world of *wealth*—deserve such men! Oh, when will Humanity *rise up* and assert itself? When will the holy vengeance of a world mash its canting and griping oppressors? "Make speed, O Lord, to save us; make haste, O Lord, to help us"! Rehearsed *Gisippus*, and pointed out to Mr. Anderson the actual son of Crummles among the actors—not to be mistaken. Called on Helen Faucit and spent a very pleasant hour with her. Wrote to Letitia and to Catherine. Looked at the paper, only to receive disgust again at the farce that is still kept up in the Houses of Parliament to amuse a starving population. To obtain the name of *patriot* in olden times, much sacrifice, whether of ease, of comfort, of wealth, of limb or life, was evidence or claim to the title. Who is a patriot in these days? Sir R. Peel, Lord Stanley, Sir J. Graham, Gladstone, Lord J. Russell, or who? Sick—sick of things and courts and all the vile jugglery, blasphemy, and blinding of a people. Thought how popular one might make *readings*, by good selection—Pope's works : *The Dying Christian to his Soul; Dryden's St. Cecilia's Day, From Harmony, Sir J. Moore,* etc. These things might *strike* even unpoetical minds.

June 22nd.—Note from ——. The means adopted to place her heart in a state of repose—to *satisfy* her affection, as she said and, I am sure, believed, appears now to me only to add fuel to the ardour of her passion. I now again lapse into doubt and fear, and *in youth,* I begin to imagine, there is no love without an intermingling of sexual love. It is therefore *dangerous,* and *to be avoided.*

June 23rd.—Wrote a few lines—wishing to direct her views to the danger of losing sight of her *understood relationship* with me—to ——.

176

Acted William Tell with a company that would have strangled the efforts of Roscius himself. Heard that the jury had given a verdict of £5—Macready v. *Dispatch !!!* Another evidence of English law and English justice. A profligate journal of extensive circulation strains its powers of abuse to *ruin* me, a hard-working, well-meaning man. The fine is £5. If I had horsewhipped the scoundrel, they would have given £500 against me! My philosophy is not proof against this. I do not think there is justice in this country—I have not found it. I am really sickened with the utter absence of truth throughout the social system that tyranny and priestcraft have built up. I do not wonder at the few men who act in desperation doing so ; I wonder that the down-trodden mass does not rise up. It is a world of suffering ; but why we should have no choice in being a part of it is what I cannot comprehend. My state of mind is one of *agony*. But it is all right, of course!

June 24th.—Wedding Day. Passed a sleepless night! For all the enjoyment, the comfort, the delight, the happiness this day—eighteen years ago—has brought to me, I thank God, and next I bless the dear, dear earthly cause and participator in my worldly bliss—my blessed Catherine. Sweet letters of congratulation from my four eldest children, which much delighted me.

*To London, June 26th.—*Packed up my clothes, etc., paid my bill, and set out by railway to Rugby. A very *roué* and low couple were put into my *coupé*, but I could not read, and dozed through the greater part of my journey. Walked from the station to Rugby, where almost all traces of my boyish days are obliterated in the improvements of the town. Called on Birch, and was glad to find him so well ; agreed to dine with him, and went on to call on Mary Bucknill. I saw her, Lydia, Sam, George, Mr. S. Bucknill and Georgiana. Sat with them till one o'clock. Heard from them most interesting details of Doctor Arnold's death. I was very much touched with the sad but beautiful account they gave me of his last moments, and the conduct of his wife. Dined with Birch, three of the little Winstanleys being at the table. He also related some pleasing anecdotes of Arnold. He walked with me down to the railway station, and stayed with me till the train came up. Found all well at home.

*London, June 29th.—*Willmott informed me that he had heard Mr. and Mrs. C. Mathews had been closeted for several hours each day at Covent Garden theatre with Mr. Robertson and Mr. Bunn, and that some persons engaged at the E. O. H. had said that Vestris, etc., were to resume the management at Covent Garden theatre, and that

177

they were engaged by her!! The tidings staggered me. Told Serle, who came, the news of Vestris. He evidently could not disbelieve it; we resolved that he should see them this evening. I was lying on the sofa when a person entered abruptly, whom I glanced at as Forster?— no. Jonathan Bucknill?—no. Who was it but dear Dickens holding me in his arms in a transport of joy. God bless him![1]

July 1st.—I am not well; weak and worn in body, and depressed in mind; its elasticity seems gone; I have no spirits, no ardour; hope gives me no strength; my course seems near its close. I often have sensations that make me feel indifferent to this world. Will there be a knowledge in another state of being of those we have loved in this?— if so, and if we may love them in spirit and without reserve, I could be well content to change the present. Letter from Bulwer; discontented that I cannot *afford* to do *Richelieu* at present at Drury Lane theatre. Answered him. Looked at paper; read Lord Mahon's and Gally Knight's advocacy in the House of Commons of the abolition of the patents. When they were in mere adventurers' hands these men were silent; now the art is ruined, and needs more than ever protection, they step forward to give it a *coup de grâce.* Called on Helen Faucit; talked to her of Lady Macbeth and Constance.

July 2nd.—Helen Faucit called, in very good spirits. The sight of her cheerfulness imparted its influence to me.

July 3rd.—After breakfast called on Elliotson, reading Tennyson's beautiful poems by the way. Consulted him on my indisposition; he prescribed for me, scarcely giving me any medicine, and that only conditionally.

July 4th.—Note from ——. It is written in all the confidence of unreserved affection, as if, happy in her security from evil, she enjoyed the power of pouring out her heart to me. May God bless her, and may she never feel otherwise than purely happy in all her thoughts of me. Went in cab, reading Alfred Tennyson's beautiful poem, to see ——. I was truly, truly rejoiced to leave her in so comfortable a state of mind. She said she felt so happy, now that she was secure in her understanding with me, that she could speak to me without restraint. I left her in a very cheerful and comfortable mood, thank God. I hope her own belief that her irreproachable relationship to me will conduce to her happiness may be proved just, or that she may make a happier change in her heart's affection.

Eastbourne, July 8th.—Read several poems of Tennyson. Some

---

[1] Dickens had just returned from his American tour.

I liked; some I thought puerile; some evincing a mean affectation of simplicity. Rested. Read some passages in the *Excursion*. Took a very delightful walk with dearest Catherine. The children went to meet Willie, who was expected by the coach. He arrived in very good spirits. God bless him. After tea, read some ballads from Tennyson to the children. Read passages in the *Excursion*.

July 9th.—A very amusing letter from Dickens. After dinner read Tennyson, whom I think very unequal, and rested. Was very heavy, having broken in upon my teetotal experiment. Read a little from the old poets. After tea read some short poems to the children.

July 10th.—Letter from ——, in an altered tone from that which she has lately used to me. I am uncertain of the cause, but shall be too glad to know—although my feelings towards her have undergone no change—that she has subdued all that was too painfully strong in her attachment to me. Wrote to Stanfield about *As You Like It* and *King Arthur*. Enjoyed the air, and sea, and sky; enjoyed the melancholy of my thoughts, as I watched the vessels with their freight of human care and passion; felt the beauty of all around me, and felt with it the little of life that is left me to enjoy it. This has been an idle day. Mr. Domville walked home from church with Catherine and the children. Katie went to church for the first time to-day. Read a little in the course of the afternoon, but spent the far greater part of it in the garden.

July 11th.—Went in a gig to Brighton; the morning made the drive over the downs, through Seaford and Newhaven, very pleasant. Where is beauty wanting in this world, if we do but choose to see it? Waited an hour and a quarter for the railway train at Brighton, reading *Philip Van Artevelde*, the first part of which I finished before I reached London. Went over to the Bank and received my dividends, from which the Income Tax was deducted.[1] Bear on, ye free people, enslaved to the worst cant that ever stultified mankind. Went to my own home; found several letters of little importance, one, in a very melancholy mood, from ——.

London, July 12th.—Mrs. Dickens and Miss Hogarth called; wished us to dine. Letitia and Susan [2] agreed to go. I declined, but promised to come in the evening. Read E. Morton's farce, which is droll, but, I fear, too broad. Went to Dickens; found Landor, Maclise, and Forster there. Dickens had been mesmerizing his wife and Miss

---

[1] The income-tax was at that time insignificant compared with its present rate.
[2] His wife's sister.

Hogarth, who had been in violent hysterics. He proposed to make a trial on me; I did not quite like it, but assented; was very nervous, and found the fixedness of the position—eyes, limbs and entire frame—very unpleasant, and the nervousness at first painful. Reasoned myself out of it, and then felt it could not affect me.

July 13th.—My blessed Joan's Birthday. My first thoughts were of that beloved child, who lives in my memory as something angel-like in its innocence and beauty. I think of her with a sorrow and a love that seems to me stronger than my feelings are to any of those dear ones whom God has spared me; but it is possible I may mistake the exact emotion which I cherish towards that beloved infant. May my spirit meet hers in another state of being. I hope and pray it may be so. Amen. Went to the cemetery at Kensal Green to visit the vault where she lies. Blessings on her sweet spirit. Went by railway to Brighton. Finished on my journey the beautiful dramatic poem of *Philip Van Artevelde.*

Eastbourne, July 14th.—Felt the beauty of the morning and the scene, and the delight of its tranquillity. Read a most charming letter from Miss Martineau. What a truly great and excellent-hearted woman that is! How little—how very little does one feel before her virtue and wisdom! Letters from Browning and T. Cooke. Gave the morning to the consideration of the plan and estimates of the scenery for *King John,* by Telbin. Wrote a letter to him with an offer of £250 and directions for several scenes. Lay down upon the grass after dinner to rest; the sea was very beautiful.

July 16th.—Letters from Bulwer proposing to me the story—or rather *a* story made up from the history of Richard Nevill, Earl of Warwick—for a tragedy. The departure from history is never, I think, effective in the drama, and I do not feel Bulwer's power to be in the high tragic vein. I wish he would not think of it, for he cannot succeed in it. Took a short run on the sands with the children after breakfast, then returned to the continuation of *King John,* which I applied myself strictly to and completed by the afternoon. Pleased with the beauty of the evening and the scene around us. Gave Willie his lesson in Virgil and in scanning, read his hymn to him, and heard him read. Heard Nina repeat. Went again over *King John,* and arranged cast, etc. Began the arrangement of *As You Like It.*

July 19th.—A letter from ——, that gave me the deepest concern; from a state of comparative health it struck me down into illness at once. My nerves were unstrung, my head in pain, and my spirits painfully depressed the whole day. She is fretting her heart with self-upbraidings for her affection to me; when the understanding has been established between us that this affection shall never violate any time, law or propriety, but be an attachment purely of heart and mind, and that such understanding seemed to make her so *very happy*, I am quite at a loss to divine the cause of this change. God bless and protect her. Wrote to her. Rested after dinner; very unwell, very unhappy. Read Tennyson, which has grown monotonous, and Beaumont and Fletcher for a subject for Bulwer.

July 25th.—Read the paper. Saw in it that on Lord Palmerston's observation on the possible need of Parliament's reassembling in October on account of the general distress, Sir J. Graham—the renegade!—observed, " We shall be pheasant-shooting in October! " And these men are governors and legislators of a people! Mighty Heaven! . . . Read the opening of the pantomime, which seems safe but expensive. Wrote to Lady Blessington.

London, July 27th.—Tried to understand the Income Tax paper, which perplexed and annoyed me. Oh, brave Britons!

July 29th.—Went out in good time; called on Dickens, who gave me his introductory chapter to his book on America. *I do not like it.* Went on to Stanfield; sat with him some time, talking over the scenery of *As You Like It* and *King Arthur*. Read Dickens's letter on the mines and collieries, which I like very much.

Eastbourne, July 31st.—Examined as strictly as I could the probable expenditure for Drury Lane theatre before the opening, and the means to meet it. It is very heavy to encounter, but I have no retreat; I take the precaution to know, as far as I can, the just amount of what I may be called upon for. With the aid of God's blessing on my efforts I hope to prosper; I pray God I may, more on account of my dearest children than for myself. During the afternoon I walked, played, and afterwards read with my children.

August 6th.—Went with Catherine and the children to see the castles of Hurstmonceux and Pevensey, as a sort of holiday in celebration of dear Willie's birthday, which occurs to-morrow. Was much interested by the happiness of my darling children on our ride, and pleased with the picturesque appearance of the ruins of Hurstmonceux. The fate of the unhappy young man, Lord Dacre, who was executed for the death of a gamekeeper—an imprudent frolic occasioning the tragical result—pressed on me, as I walked through the extensive remains. It was delightful to see the enjoyment of my dear children. Looked at the church, where are some monuments. Saw the old stronghold of Pevensey, its church, and returned home to dinner. Found letters from Miss Hamilton Smith, from Mr. Manvers, from Helen Faucit (who has not been well, poor girl), enclosing one from Mr. P. Farren, written in a very good spirit. Gave Nina her lesson, which she did not do well; she was penitent, and I heard her the remainder. Rested a little. Read the reign of John in Lingard's History. Played with the dear children. Read John's reign in Hume's History. Finished my letter begun last night to Colonel Hamilton Smith. Wrote to Mr. Manvers.

London, August 11th.—Read part of Dickens's *America*, the style and matter of which *I did not like.*

August 26th.—Looked over my Drury Lane expenditure, and calculating how much it has cost me, find that I am minus what I should have possessed—£8000. This is a sad contemplation—the earnings of a life of labour! I certainly never intended, never dreamed, never agreed to be made liable to such an amount. I was to risk nothing but what I chose. I have been ensnared or betrayed by the lax conduct—as bad to me as fraud—of the committee of proprietors. £1700—my ready money—was all I ever contemplated hazarding. My hope is in God alone. To Him I address my prayers—at least for my blessed wife and children. How gladly would I die at once to secure them what I could now leave them, if my death would save them from difficulty or distress.

August 29th.—On my way to London I read Marston's tragedy of the *Patrician's Daughter*, which is a most interesting and touching play; I will act it, if I am prosperous.

August 31st.—Went to Drury Lane theatre. Mr. Mark Lemon [1] came with the *Punch* pantomime. I spoke to him on Mr. Mayhew's plays, and at last gave him the two notes I had written to Mr. Mayhew upon them. He read me the pantomime. I did not fancy it. We discussed some points of agreement; he left me to bring me an answer upon them in an hour from his colleagues. I spoke with Serle and Willmott upon it, first having Serle's opinion on the propriety of admitting Willmott into the confidence. I read the pantomime to them. They both thought it *bad;* as a pantomime, I thought so too. Mr. M. Lemon returned. After some conversation I returned him the

---

[1] Mark Lemon (1809–1870); the first editor of *Punch*, from 1841 to 1870; also at one time editor of *Once a Week*, and the *Family Herald*.

book, and it was agreed if Covent Garden did not accept the opening, we should have the refusal of the harlequinade.

September 6th.—Uncomfortable thoughts; made angry by a paltry impertinence in the publication of *Punch*—a poor pleasantry by a set of low-mannered, ignorant, and ill-conditioned men, who rejoice in the miserable Jerrold as their captain; they abuse all they envy.

September 8th.—Looked at the paper in which was mentioned the rumoured death of the King of Hanover.[1] Will there be one hand in the whole world to drop a flower on his tomb? Will there be one breast to heave a sigh for him? Nero was mourned better than I think he will be. Found letters at theatre; the first I opened was from poor Anderson, most affectingly telling me of the death of his eldest child. God help him. My heart bleeds for him and his poor wife; I was very much moved. I wrote to him immediately, enclosing him £50 as he wished. I felt all he must be suffering, and all he has yet to bear before he can regain serenity. The loss, the sorrow for it is for life; at least, such is mine for thee, my blessed and beloved child. Blessed be thy angel spirit, and may I yet meet thee, dear, precious being!

September 10th.—Thought angrily on that—to me—offensive subject, the slander which Mr. Thesiger heaped upon me. As if to hold up to my own eyes the indiscretion of wasting mind or feeling on such subjects, there was a notice on lawyers in the *Literary Gazette*, in which Mr. Thesiger was especially quoted as the fee'd panegyrist of Lord Hertford and Nicholas Suisse! Adding to that his praise of Mr. Bunn, I think one cannot be too grateful for his abuse. Arranged my accounts, wrote a cheque and enclosed it in a note to Mr. C. Jones.

September 20th.—Went to see *Norma*. Miss A. Kemble played Norma. It was a very, very clever performance, entitled to the highest praise for the skill and energy with which it is done; but, oh, heavens! an Opera! That human beings can be found to disregard Shakspeare, and run after such *nonsense !* What must be the nature

---

[1] It was a false report. As Duke of Cumberland, the king's unpopularity in this country was excessive, and his death would undoubtedly have evoked a feeling the reverse of sorrow. How he was generally regarded is, perhaps, best expressed in a remark by Lord Palmerston that "to be well-abused by the Duke of Cumberland is no mean praise to any man." George IV, too, when asked the secret of the duke's unpopularity replied : "It is this—if a father stands well with his son, or a husband with his wife, or a lover with his mistress, the Duke of Cumberland is sure to come between them and make mischief." Recent publications have revealed the shocking scandal connected with his sister the Princess Sophia, his implication in which should have entailed his expulsion from all decent society. Curiously enough, he proved a satisfactory ruler in Hanover, where he earned the esteem if not the affection of his subjects.

of a medium of expression that strips every comedy of its laughter, and every tragedy of its pathos? I was wearied and *disgusted* with it.

September 24th.—General Palmer [1]—alas! poor man—called on me with a sort of pretence, but in reality to ask me if I could lend him £10. I told him that really I could not say I had not £10, but that I was not in a condition to lend it. About £500, that I procured for Mrs. McC——, he borrowed never to repay! Poor man!

September 28th.—Received a very charming letter from Adelaide Kemble, that gave me a high opinion of her intellect, as I already entertained such of her disposition. Spoke to Mrs. Nisbett of some effects I had thought of for her; she was very much obliged. Spoke to Keeley about the character of Touchstone; as he always does, he "thought he had done so"—it was not what he intended.

October 1st.—Went to Drury Lane theatre, calling at Delcroix's to purchase rouge. Attended to the business of the theatre, which was most harassing. Rehearsed the play of *As You Like It*, which kept me very late. Business, business all the day and all the evening. Was called for by the audience before the play began; was very enthusiastically received. Our play of *As You Like It* opened our season. May it be a prosperous one. I acted Jacques as well as I could. Was called for after the play, and led on Mrs. Nisbett.[2] Stanfield and my own people came into my room. Spoke to Mrs. Keeley, thanking her for acting Lucy for me. Very much wearied. I trust in God that this is an auspicious commencement.

October 2nd.—In a state of very uneasy doubt as to the effect of

---

[1] Charles Palmer (1777–1851); formerly of the 10th Light Dragoons; a member of the Carlton House set; M.P. for Bath (1808–1826 and 1830–1837). His father, proprietor of the Bath theatre, was the projector of mail-coaches, and the Government adopting the system, rewarded him with a sum of £50,000, most of which was lost by his son in a vineyard speculation, the failure of which he attributed to Lord Yarmouth (afterwards the "Steyne" Lord Hertford) who at a dinner-party given at Carlton House for the purpose of trying the product (a rather light claret) maliciously depreciated it, thereby causing the Regent, who at first praised the wine, to pronounce against it. The consequence was that Palmer sunk large sums in trying to enrich the vintage, but without result. He was eventually reduced almost to beggary, living principally on small loans levied on his former associates.

[2] The cast was: Duke, Mr. Ryder; First Lord, Mr. Elton; Second Lord, Mr. H. Phillips; Amiens, Mr. Allen; Jacques, Mr. Macready; Duke Frederick, Mr. G. Bennett; Le Beau, Mr. Hudson; Oliver, Mr. Graham; Jaques (son of Sir Rowland), Mr. Lynne; Orlando, Mr. Anderson; Adam, Mr. Phelps; Touchstone, Mr. Keeley; William, Mr. Compton; Pages, Miss P. Horton and Miss Gould; Rosalind, Mrs. Nisbett; Celia, Mrs. Stirling; Phebe, Miss Fortescue; Audrey, Mrs. Keeley. In the playbill Mrs. Nisbett and Mr. Ryder, Madame Vestris and Mr. Charles Mathews, were announced as the additional engagements of the season,—(*note by Sir F. Pollock.*)

the play last night from the circumstance of not having heard anything of Forster. Mrs. Dickens and Georgina [1] called; stayed a short time with them. Forster called. **He**, as Mrs. Dickens had done, expressed himself *delighted* with the play last night. Dickens called— in the same tone.

October 3rd.—Saw the other papers, which were cold! If I succeed I owe them nothing. Very uneasy, very low in spirit; very unhappy at the view that seemed to lie before me. Was cheered to hear that the house was looking well. Acted Hamlet, with the endeavour to do well, but not satisfying myself. Was called for and well received. Was very much gratified with the house.

October 5th.—Acted *Marino Faliero* nervously, but I am losing my art in attending to the people around me. Was called for. Forster, Maclise, and all my people came into my room. Letters from Captain Marryat, H. Ellis, Macleod, Dillon. A volume of poems from Knox, with a sonnet to myself.

October 6th.—Looked at paper, a very cold and discouraging notice of last night's piece. I begin to fear that I *ought* to have pondered more warily before I engaged in an enterprise of so little hope and such distressing labour as this, in which luck is paramount. Acted Jaques better than I have yet done. Dickens, Maclise, Forster and Mr. Long- fellow, a professor at one of the U.S. Universities, came into my room. Sent Jones to Covent Garden. Learned that their house was very good; thus we have an attraction established against us.

October 8th.—Went to Drury Lane theatre, but first looked through Mr. M. Lemon's farce, which I found to be really objection- able as to the part assigned to Mr. C. Mathews. I was run away with by the broad humour of the piece. Spoke with Helen Faucit about her acting last night. Mr. C. Mathews held a very long and *very silly* conversation with me, which I tried to receive as patiently as possible. I see he is not to be managed to any advantage. He was obliged *repeatedly* to admit in the presence of Serle that nothing could be more kind or courteous than my conduct had been to him. Wrote to Butler's, Rugby, with a cheque for £10, for Dr. Arnold's memorial; to Westland Marston, thanking him for his book and apprising him that his play is coming out.

October 13th.—Serle came from Covent Garden, reporting a great house, and puzzled to understand *why*. The understanding is not difficult. The English is a *brutish* public, affecting a taste, and

[1] Miss Hogarth,

therefore ready to be humbugged, and slow to understand good taste. Letter from Mrs. Nisbett which considerably disgusted me.

October 22nd.—The Duke of Beaufort called, and inquired of me about the deer-skin I wanted for *As You Like It.* He very courteously and kindly said he would send to Badminton, and if there was not one ready he would desire his keeper to send one *exprès.* It was extremely kind.

October 24th.—Acted King John fairly. Called for and very well received. Gave out the play.[1] Serle, Dickens, Forster, Emerson Tennent, Stanfield, Maclise, came into my room. All pleased. Helen Faucit much depressed and very unhappy at not having realized the expectations she had raised.

October 25th.—Little refreshed by last night's rest, which was attended with very little sleep, my mind being full of the evening's scenes and events. Looked at the newspapers, and read a very eulogistic description of what I had attempted to do, by Fox; a very malignant attack on me in the *Morning Post* by a Mr. Johnson, and a very ignorant, vulgar article in the *Morning Herald;* an ill-written notice in praise in the *Times.* With such *critical* appreciation of my labours, I begin to fear they will produce little harvest of good. The time is, I fancy, *past.* Helen Faucit came, in very low spirits, to speak to me of last night. *Wretched house !*

November 1st.—Mr. W. Murray of Edinburgh called. He expressed himself delighted with the *perfect* representation of King John, observing that his " master," J. Kemble, had only " made a step." Letitia told me of Mr. Cecil Forester, an M.P., observing to Miss Meyer that the people in *Acis and Galatea* stretched out their arms in one passage, and its effect was exactly like that at an election, where the *dirty* hands of the electors were thrust toward you, and took away from you all power of speaking or doing anything ! ! ! An English legislator ! ! !

November 5th.—About to begin rehearsal, having seen Stanfield, when Mr. C. Mathews wished to speak with me. Madame Vestris followed him into my room and began a *scene* which lasted two or three hours—on the lady's part much " Billingsgate " and false assertion, on his much weakness and equivocation. I sent for Anderson and Willmott, and Serle came in afterwards. Serle directly contradicted his

---

[1] In *King John* Elton was the Earl of Salisbury ; Phelps, Herbert de Burgh ; Anderson, Faulconbridge ; Ryder, Cardinal Pandulph ; Miss Helen Faucit was the Lady Constance.— *note by Sir F. Pollock.*)

assertions; his engagement was produced and was in direct contradiction of his statements. It was very offensive. I felt my own strength and was very cool. I would not relinquish their engagement, but offered to *refer* the pecuniary point. *She* threw down her part in *King Arthur* and left the room, stating that she would not act after next week if the *full* salary were not paid. We sent for Cooke to take measures about *King Arthur*. Consulted on a public refutation of her falsehoods, and after dinner drew up a notice which was placed in both green-rooms.

November 9th.—Went to Drury Lane theatre. Sent a note to Stanfield, requesting his presence. Rehearsed the chorus scene of third act of *King Arthur*. Was extremely displeased with the conduct of Mr. T. Cooke and others, and spoke *very strongly* to the whole community, actors and band, to the effect that they were wanting in proper feeling and duty, and that I was indifferent to the carrying on the theatre, but if the piece were not ready for Saturday, I would close the theatre till it should be. Thomas, the leader, told me that the band were not paid last year, when the actors were. I thanked him for correcting me, and told him that they should be paid. Consulted with Stanfield and council, and came to the resolution to postpone the performance to Thursday week; transacted business. Wrote the introduction to Elton for *General Palmer*. He, General Palmer, had called in the morning to ask for it. His object was this: he thought me a very good actor in some parts, but in others he thought I was deficient, and in such as Othello, etc., he believed himself to be the very best that could be found; he would not wish my opinion, as of course having my own particular views, but he wished to have that of Mr. Elton, who he heard was a man of talent! Poor man, *I fear he is mad!* Heard that the *Tempest* was not good at Covent Garden, and that there was a *Vestris* attack upon me in the *Morning Post*. *Pah!*

November 14th.—Acted King John tolerably well, was called for and well received. A letter enclosing a slip from the *Sunday Times*, which was said to be a gross libel on me—or, as Willmott termed it, "awful." I was going to put it in the fire, but handed it over to Serle, not choosing to read it myself.

November 21st.—Heard that Covent Garden was closed on account of Miss Kemble's illness. Read the abuse of myself from the *Sunday Times*—a quantity of low, ribald falsehood, which did not anger me at all. I believe it was written to provoke a prosecution.

November 22nd.—After dinner went to Covent Garden and saw the first scene of the *Tempest*. A ship was introduced and all the poetry cut out—worse acting or more inapplicable means to an end I never saw.

November 25th.—On this day my sweet and blessed child was taken from us; my little angel Joan was in the last pains of life—two *long years* since—at this very time. My precious blossom—my sweetest, loveliest child. My heart yearns to her even now, and 'tis something to feel that in death I shall be with her. May God bless her sweet pure spirit. Amen! Received a note from Dickens about his prologue, which I answered. Went to the cemetery to look upon the tomb where my darling Joan rests—my precious, my beloved child—never, never to be forgotten. . . . Heard very disgusting news, that the infamous wretch Bunn had been brought in as lessee of Covent Garden theatre by Messrs. Moore and Surman; that the players were succumbing to him and only anxious to make their engagements with him. The proprietors of Covent Garden had shown themselves, as usual, most *dishonourable men.*

November 29th.—Questioned Mr. Bennett, and found the call-boy a general object of suspicion in the theatre as the spy reporting to the *Sunday Times.* Questioned the call-boy. Ryan, his father, a penny-liner, called to exculpate his son. I told him if he would discover the traitor I would restore his son, but that I could not trust him, etc. Read over some scenes of *Mabel* with Helen Faucit. I wish I had not, for my spirits and hope sunk very low.

December 1st.—Acted Jacques very drowsily. Heard that the house of Covent Garden was well attended; depressed by the tidings, as it seems caprice is dominant over effort. I must learn to say God's will be done! Spoke to Anderson about speaking Dickens's prologue, which he declines doing. He *ought not* to have done so. I fear his self-opinion will prevent him ever rising to the point I wished. Tried to learn it myself. Talked long with Serle. Heard that the Covent Garden proprietors had engaged Mr. Bunn as the person most inimical to me! . . . My God, in Thee is my hope and trust! Amen!

December 5th.—Rehearsed *Patrician's Daughter.* Suggested to Marston, though without advising the step, the attractiveness to his play of making a conclusion a happy one. All felt the same. He undertook to make an ending to submit to me. Business with the different departments. Forster called and spoke on the subject of

Marston. He agreed in the advisability of the alteration. I was not at all sure whether it would be right to do it. Acted King John fairly. Dickens, with Maclise and Forster, came to speak to me in dissuasion about the alteration in Marston's play. I would not take any responsibility on myself.

December 7th.—Forster called to ask my opinion upon a *blustering* and silly letter of Spicer's. Forster was just as *blustering* and just as silly. I was much annoyed by his tone and remarks. I corrected a note he wrote in reply. Acted Jacques well. Peel [1] was in the theatre with his family.

December 10th.—Fox and Marston came in; Marston went on the stage in obedience to the call. Note from Lady Morgan, etc. First night of the *Patrician's Daughter.* Spoke the prologue (by Dickens) tolerably well. Acted uncertainly the part of Mordaunt, but the play was much applauded. I was told that I was called for, and was annoyed and disconcerted to hear calls, which I thought were for Miss Faucit, and which I believe them to be, but which they tell me were for the author. I gave out the play and left the matter to settle itself. Dickens and Forster came in (I spoke a few words to Helen Faucit)—they thought it a great success.

December 11th.—Wearied down, heart-sick, and depressed beyond the power of rising against it, I lay in bed very late. When I rose, all was the same. I had answered a note from Quin before I got up, and heard my darling children their hymns. Glanced at the newspaper. Received in the *Planet* a kind notice of last night, but I fear I am growing "past cure."

December 12th.—Something better in spirits and lightness than yesterday, but still little to boast of. Saw the *Morning Chronicle,* which was very fervent in its praise of the new tragedy. Went to Drury Lane theatre. Saw the other newspapers. The *Morning Post* contained a most scurrilous and abusive article, with many false statements. Mr. Planché called, and I paid him £100. I *cannot* like that man. Read *Athewold,* which I like, but I begin to doubt the success of any play now. The papers will not go with us. Mr. Michell, the *Morning Post* man, would *not* call here, but would see me at his office—where of course I would not go.

December 14th.—Rehearsal of pantomime. Serle came to report his interview with Mr. Michell—who *owned* to the article in the *Morning Post.* Saw Marston, who told me that Mr. ——, the writer, was

---

[1] The Prime Minister.

a taboo-ed, caned, beaten fellow. So much for this reptile. Wrote very civilly to Mr. Michell, dismissing him from the necessity of using our free list. Wrote to Bulwer.

December 16th.—Acted Mordaunt fairly; was called for and well received. After the play spoke in presence of Willmott and Serle to a Mr. Bonner, a musician, who, as Mr. Thomas had reported to me, had written a letter to the *Sunday Times* describing himself as a *sufferer* by my closing the theatre two nights. I told him he should have his two or four nights and go out of the theatre. He declined taking the money, and said he had acted so because he was irritated and disappointed, and thought I had accused him and others of being ungentlemanly (!) but that he had not done it vindictively! Signed bills—a *large deficiency*. God help me!

December 17th.—Heard from Mr. Beazley, through Serle, that the Queen had *commanded* the licence to be given to Van Amburgh![1] This is a civilized country!

December 24th.—Looked at the paper; read the account of Adelaide Kemble's retirement from the stage, which was not so attractive to the public as I had expected it to have been. Received a note and purse from a lady signing herself Catherine. Went to Drury Lane theatre. Dickens and Stanfield were there before me. Attended to business of various kinds. Saw the rehearsal of the pantomime, which Dickens and Stanfield thought in its opening very amusing. Helen Faucit, to my great surprise and satisfaction, seeing her in health, came in. Wrote a note to Willmott to be sent to him to-morrow with a silver snuff-box, in which I have enclosed him a bank-bill for £20—in recompense of his services during the summer vacation.

December 31st.—A sad, sad close to a year of labour and unrest, that has strewn snow upon my head and wrung my heart. I look back with regret. My only consolation—or rather defence—is, that I acted as far as I could see to judge, for the best. God has willed the result to be disastrous. I am His creature, and let me teach my heart to say His will be done.

[1] The lion tamer.

ADELAIDE KEMBLE

From an engraving of a painting by J. M. Wright

1843

London, January 1st.—The year begins to me with labour and difficulty, with care and deep anxiety. My enterprise thus far has only tended to reduce my means, and I have now adventured them as far as I think it prudent to go. I will not advance one farthing more than I see absolute occasion for. I am disappointed and in a pecuniary point of view *much worse* in the world than I was eighteen months ago. I will try to retrieve my shattered fortunes, and to God I pray, for my blessed wife's and children's sake, that I may labour with good success, or that I may die in time to leave them the means of comfort when I am gone. Bulwer called and we talked over the subject of a play. He is my hope among authors.

January 4th.—Mrs. Warner came to mention some distressing involvements of her husband, and to ask me if I could advance her £100. I spoke with great kindness to her and urged her to try and have the business settled without calling on me, but that to save her furniture I would accommodate her, if needful. Received the *Monthly Magazine*, containing a most impertinent article upon the *Patrician's Daughter*. Was angry for a minute.

January 6th.—Note from Forster, which I answered. In it he informed me that the Duke of Sussex had very pleasantly consented to present the testimonial to me next month. So that my martyrdom is fixed.

January 7th.—Helen Faucit came to read over the part of Imogen. She (to my great surprise!) was piqued about her forfeit. She became at last sensible of her error. She read over the part of Imogen to me and I gave her some suggestions.

January 8th.—Wrote a note to Mr. Lynne, explaining to him that I could not remit his fine, which I was sorry to inflict, but enclosing him a cheque for £5 to help him to procure comforts for the sick bed of his wife. Bulwer called with his boy,[1] a fine animated child,

---

[1] Edward Robert Bulwer (1831–1891), second Baron, and first Earl of, Lytton. The well-known diplomatist and *littérateur*.

who went up-stairs with Willie whilst we talked over the *subject* of plays. Read two acts of the French play which Bulwer had left with me—*médocre et rampant*.

January 10th.—Rehearsed *Cymbeline;* especially disgusted by the self-sufficient and ignorant conduct of Mr. Hudson, presuming to refuse to sing the duet of Guiderius—"Fear no more." These players!—oh! how well they merit all the indignity that can be heaped upon them. The greater part are miserable wretches. Went to sit with my darling children, who had come to see *King Arthur;* enjoyed their delight and their remarks. Returned home with them. Received third number of the *Foreign Quarterly Review* from Forster, and a note informing me that he is the editor and has been for some time.

January 13th.—Suffering from fatigue and depression of spirits. I fear that Fortune is about to " change her hand and check my pride." It is bitter to bear reverse at this time of life and with all my little children looking up to me, I feel almost as in reproach! Rehearsed *Werner;* Serle and Willmott both were in my room a long while; I was irritated, " and at this time most easy 'tis to do it, when my good stars, that were my former guides, have empty left their orbs——" I hope, however, not without the power of rising again, but I am no longer young, and *that I begin to feel.*

January 15th.—Sat with dearest Catherine, who was in low spirits. I spoke to her of America, of which I begin *now* to think seriously— it depressed her. God help us! Read the play of *Mary Stuart* by Laing, Carlyle's friend; wrote to him upon it; it possesses much merit.

January 16th.—Mr. Morton came to ask for more money for the pantomime—a thing which *lay upon* his hands and which was only to be paid for additionally in the event of great and unequivocal success. Our success is next door to failure! I refused him, and he was in dudgeon. I have no respect for and a very great dislike to him. Received a note from Priscilla Horton, informing me of her contemplated retirement from the stage at the end of the season.

January 20th.—Acted Mordaunt very fairly. Called for. Helen Faucit spoke with me, somewhat weakly and pettishly, about her dress. I was not pleased with her behaviour. Am wearied, sickened and disgusted with this employment, and bitterly repent that I ever lent myself to it. I thought I was doing for the best, but I must now suppose it is God's will that I should be punished in the worst way— by being my own punisher. I begin to look at the future with fear and pain.

January 22nd.—As a great indulgence and enjoyment walked out to call on Dickens. Wrote to Talfourd, explaining to him my ignorance of the indelicacy shown to him by the managing clerk of White and Eyre, in sending him a retainer, and then transferring the brief to Platt.[1] Thought much on what is to be done; I want help of head and hand—*I am alone!*

January 25th.—Considered well and read scenes of *Athelwold* to Catherine, who did not seem impressed with the part of Athelwold, but very much with that of Dunstan. I was shaken in my purpose as to its immediate production, and turned to Browning's *Blot on the Scutcheon.*

January 26th.—Continued the perusal of the *Blot on the Scutcheon.* Looked at paper. Mr. Grunisen called; after some general conversation he stated the chief object of his visit to be the difference which existed between myself and the *Morning Post*—that he had read with great regret the articles, which contained personalities that were unjustifiable and that were, as was the withdrawal of the advertisements, injurious to the paper; that he had remonstrated with Mr. Michell upon them, who had expressed himself in very respectful tenour of me, etc. He, Mr. G——, wished for all sakes to see things on a better footing, and either would bring Mr. Michell and myself together, or if I would send the advertisements and restore the privileges, he would undertake nothing of the kind should again occur. I told him my principle was always to be on good terms with all, if I could. He admired the *spirit* of defying the paper, etc., but thought it impolitic. All was agreeably accommodated. Finished *Blot,* etc. Went over *Athelwold*—will not do at present. Wrote to Serle for *Honest Man's Fortune.* Received and read it—*not do.* Searched, hunted, ruminated; could find nothing.

January 27th.—Low in spirits and worn down in body. I do not know how I am to wear through this effort, but I cannot help feeling that it is very hard with such endeavours, such objects and such means I am not more successful! But God's will be done! Acted Hamlet, with my wearied body and mind, tolerably well; was called for and very warmly received.

January 28th.—Went to Drury Lane theatre, finishing by the way

---

[1] Thomas Joshua Platt (1798–1862); afterwards a Baron of the Exchequer; an advocate who had considerable success with common juries. The proceeding complained of is certainly an unusual one, but Talfourd was a man of many pursuits, and there was probably some risk of his not doing justice to his case.

the *Blot on*, etc.   Planché called and seemed urgent about the acceptance of his opera.   Wrote a note with cheque for £100 to Bulwer. Willmott, to whom, on Anderson's declining, I had entrusted the reading *Blot on*, etc., came and reported to me that they laughed at it, and that Anderson passed his jokes on it—not very decorous for an official!   I fear—I fear this young man's head is gone.[1]

January 29th.—Browning called, told him of the reading on Saturday and the conduct of the actors.   Advised him as to the alteration of second act.   Note from Mr. Compton, declining the part of Verges. Not knowing what course to adopt; all at sea!

January 30th.—Thought of *Julius Cæsar* as a play to produce; was impressed with the effect I could produce in it.   Spoke with Willmott and Serle about the substitution of *Julius Cæsar* for *Much Ado*, etc. They were both against it.   I think they are wrong, but I yield it to them very indifferently.   Talked over again the subject of *Julius Cæsar* and *Much Ado*.

January 31st.—Went to Drury Lane theatre.   Found Browning waiting for me in a state of great excitement.   He abused the doorkeeper and was in a very great passion.   I calmly apologized for having detained him, observing that I had made a great effort to meet him at all.   He had not given his *name* to the doorkeeper, who had told him he might walk into the green-room; but his dignity was mortally wounded.   I fear he is a very conceited man.   Went over his play with him, then looked over part of it.   Read it in the room with great difficulty, being *very unwell*.

February 1st.—Received notes—one enclosing 5*s*. with a desire that I would advertise the day of my birthday in the *Times*.   Read Browning's play.   Rose, and read and cut it again.   Serle called, and I told him of my inability to meet my work—that I *could not* play this part of Browning's unless the whole work of the theatre stopped, that I thought it best to reduce it to its proper form—three acts, and let Phelps do it on all accounts.   He concurred with me. T. Cooke called; we discussed *Comus*.   I wrote a note to Browning. Read in bed *Orpheus and Eurydice* of Glück.

---

[1] According to a statement made by Browning in after years, Macready, not wishing to produce the play, had tried to discredit it by entrusting the reading to Willmott, the prompter, "a red-nosed, one-legged, elderly gentleman," whose reading, especially of the girls' parts, not unnaturally provoked laughter.   But this view is hardly borne out by Macready's own statements, as above quoted, and others of a later date ; though he was, of course, not justified in entrusting the reading of so delicate a piece of work to the theatre prompter, however intelligent, as Willmott undoubtedly was.

February 2nd.—Completed and cut the piece of *Comus*—as for representation. Sat with the darling children after dinner for a short time. Read carefully over Benedick and considered the play of *Much Ado*—in reference to the scenery, etc. Letters from theatre. Not £100 to the *last* night of *Acis and Galatea!* " Oh judgment! thou art fled to brutish beasts! " *I will give this up.*

February 4th.—Rehearsed Browning's play, the *Blot on the 'Scutcheon.*

February 5th.—Very little sleep last night, and this morning found me dejected, desponding—almost despairing. I have wished to be right—I cannot say that I have always tried to be right, or that I have tried enough—I have not. Perhaps that is the cause of my present unhappiness. I wish life could be past with me, so that I could leave my blessed children with hope and my dearest wife in worldly comfort. God forgive—forgive and aid me.

February 6th.—Mr. Phelps was too ill to play to-night. I decided on under-studying his part in Browning's play.

February 7th.—Went to Drury Lane theatre. Rehearsed Browning's play, with the idea of acting the part of Lord Tresham, if Mr. Phelps should continue ill. Browning came and in better humour than I have lately seen him. Read *Comus* in the green-room. A note from Mrs. Norton who had expected a private box, but found it was a Benefit. I was much vexed. Acted Claude Melnotte fairly; was called for and well received. Went to see Mrs. Norton and took her boys—her son and Lord Dufferin [1]—behind the scenes.

February 8th.—Went to Drury Lane theatre. Rehearsed three acts of *Much Ado About Nothing* and the *Blot on the 'Scutcheon,* of which I began to despair. Note from Delane, asking for places. I sent him a box. Spoke for a few minutes with Helen Faucit. Acted King John very well indeed. Stanfield brought me some sketches for *Comus.*

February 9th.—Keeley came, and having heard that Mr. Compton was troublesome about Dogberry, offered to give it up and act Verges. I was extremely pleased with the good little fellow, and told him so. Business with Serle and Willmott on the new play. Resolved to do the part of Tresham for Mr. Phelps. Business with Younge; began reading the part in the new play and cutting it; wearied out I lay down for twenty-five minutes. Acted Othello as *well* as *I could,* but

[1] The late Marquis of Dufferin and Ava, the distinguished statesman, then a youth of seventeen.

not effectively—at least the audience did not applaud me much. I was dissatisfied with them and myself, but I did my best.

February 10th.—Began the consideration and study of the part of Tresham, which was to occupy my single thoughts till accomplished. About a quarter past one a note came from Willmott, informing me that Mr. Phelps would do the part, if he "died for it," so that my time had been lost. Arrived I applied to business; offered to give to Browning and Mr. Phelps the benefit of my consideration and study in the cuts, etc. I had made one I thought particularly valuable, not letting Tresham die, but consigning him to a convent. Browning, however, in the worst taste, manner, and spirit, declined any further alterations, expressing himself perfectly satisfied with the manner in which Mr. Phelps executed Lord Tresham. I had no more to say. I could only think Mr. Browning a very disagreeable and offensively mannered person. *Voilà tout!*

February 11th.—Directed the rehearsal of *Blot on the 'Scutcheon*, and made many valuable improvements. Browning seemed desirous to explain or qualify the strange carriage and temper of yesterday, and laid much blame on Forster for irritating him. Saw the play of *Blot on the 'Scutcheon*, which was badly acted in Phelps's and Mrs. Stirling's parts—pretty well in Anderson's, very well in Helen Faucit's. I was *angry* after the play about the call being directed without me. Saw farce, *Thumping Legacy*, which was successful. Jerdan came into my room; did not like the play.

February 13th.—Morton came into my room to tell me that the wretch Gregory, of the *Satirist*, had been yelled off the stage at Covent Garden and that they had dropped the curtain upon him in the middle of the second act! The public have feeling, if the players have none.

February 16th.—Letter from the Lord Chamberlain demanding to know by what authority I had played *The Blot on the 'Scutcheon;* gave it to Serle to answer. T. Cooke and Thomas came to speak about the orchestra—it seems there had been squabbling between the singers and musicians—"tweedledom and tweedledee."

February 19th.—Looked at the paper. Dissatisfied with a humorous but uncalled-for article on Peel's life, name, etc., which looked mere party spleen, and still more dissatisfied with the silence of the *Examiner* (Fonblanque) upon the disgraceful wretch who was allowed to insult decency by coming from his lurking-place on Monday last and braving public indignation—the vile emulator of the wretch Bunn, Mr. Gregory.

SAMUEL PHELPS

From an engraving of a Daguerreotype

February 20th.—Read Benedict, which I had begun to lose heart about; I must *try*—the little ones must pull at my coat-tails. God bless them. Acted Macbeth particular well to a very indifferent house. Called for and well received.

February 22nd.—Heard that the Covent Garden actors had accepted *half-salaries* from Mr. Bunn—the wretches! They deserve the fate they have mainly contributed to bring on themselves.

February 24th.—Rehearsed *Much Ado About Nothing* and *Comus.* Acted Benedict very well. The audience went with the play and with *Comus.* They called for me after both pieces.[1]

February 26th.—Dickenses called and sat a short time. I went out with Catherine. We called on Mr. Rogers, on Helen Faucit, whom we found at home, and whom dearest Catherine asked to dine with us *en famille.* Called at the Carlyles, where we saw Mrs. C——, a Miss Jewsbury,[2] Mr. Commyn, Carlyle and his brother. I was amused. H. Faucit dined with us, and we had a cheerful evening.

March 1st.—Dow called; gave me some curious information respecting Mr. C. Kean's refusal to allow Mr. Phelps to act with him in Knowles's play *The Rose of Aragon,* which shows him to be what I have long considered—a most despicable person—a mere pitiful quack.

March 3rd.—I entered this morning upon my *fiftieth* birthday. How very little of self-approval attends the review of my past life— how much of self-reproach! I am now on the downward path of life, to prepare myself to die with resignation and content, and to make what remains of my life beneficial to my blessed children is all that remains for me to do. May God Almighty befriend me in my desire to do my duty well by them and preserve me from temptation, rendering my efforts available to their good, and my latter days the means of comfort and happiness to my beloved wife and my dear family. God protect, sustain, and direct me. Received the wishes and 'gratulations, with the remembrances of dear, dear family. God bless them!

---

[1] The cast of *Much Ado About Nothing*, at Drury Lane theatre, included Mr. Hudson, Mr. Lynne, Mr. Anderson, Mr. Phelps, Mr. W. Bennett, Mr. Allen, Mr. G. Bennett, Mr. Selby, Mr. Compton, Mr. Keeley, Mr. Bender, Mr. Hance, Mr. M. Barnett, Mr. Ryder, with Miss Fortescue, and Mrs. Nisbett. In *Comus*, Miss P. Horton and Miss Helen Faucit took the parts of the Attendant Spirit and the Lady. Miss Romer took that of Sabrina. The music was from Handel and Arne, with the exception of one air from the original composer, Henry Lawes.—(*note by Sir F. Pollock.*)

[2] Geraldine Endsor Jewsbury (1812–1880); novelist; best known from her intimacy with the Carlyles.

Low in spirits. I cannot forget that I am now declining in life, and that I have lived to do little good, that I have no comfort in retrospection.

March 12th.—Thought upon the state of the public mind in regard to theatres—the *aversion from* the English theatre. My heart and my spirits *sank down* within me. I have borne up long, but now I begin to lose hope and heart. I often, in my secret heart wish that I was at my long rest; there seems no good for me here. I toil, and hope on, but my good genius—oh God! Have done very little to-day. Had no heart to do anything—not even to bear the company of my blessed, blessed children. God help me! Read and corrected Knowles's play, read the part of Colonel Greene to Catherine, which she did not think enough for me. I think so too.

March 15th.—Received a very cordial note from Etty; in great delight with the *Much Ado* and *Comus* of last night. Listened to the rehearsal of the music of *Sappho.* Fonblanque says that Lord Brougham is mad. On his examination the other day on the law of libel, B—— said to him, F——: "You know, Mr. Fonblanque, all London jurors are cuckolds—you know it"!!!—afterwards turning to reporters: "You need not report that." Went to Drury Lane theatre. Cobden was speaking very strong truths to an assenting multitude.

March 17th.—Read the *Morning Herald,* a base, false, and malignant attack upon me. Called on Forster. He always recommends *submission* to the coward insolence of these papers. I think occasion should be used for at least endeavouring to reduce their power of mischief. Serle came; sent him to the *Morning Herald* to make an appointment with the editor.

March 18th.—Went out; met Browning, who was startled into accosting me, but seeming to remember that he did not intend to do so, started off in great haste. What but contempt, which one ought not to feel, can we with galled spirit feel for these wretched insects about one? Oh God! how is it all to end?

March 19th.—In conversation with my dearest Catherine, she gave her opinion that it would be necessary for me in the event of an unsuccessful termination to our season, to go alone to the United States. This looks cheerily, inasmuch as there is opportunity for exertion and prospect of reward, perhaps the means of recovering all I have lost, and adding to my gains. God grant it for the sake of my blessed children. This sweet instance of firmness and affection adds, if it be

198

possible, to the love I bear to this beloved woman. May God bless her!

March 20th.—Serle came in on business. Shortly after brought in Miss Clara Novello.[1] She is handsome but not winning—much assumption, some affectation, and evidently a *great* opinion of herself. She did not prepossess me. She gave me a shock and a fright in wishing to be announced " Clara Novello " with all her *titles* from the various foreign academies, etc. Serle and I combated it to the utmost, but not with much effect. The editor of the *Morning Herald* would not see Serle! The wretched dastard!

March 21st.—My morning was engaged with the rehearsal of *Sappho*, chiefly listening to it. Miss C. Novello and Mrs. Alfred Shaw were there. Miss C. Novello made herself conspicuously ridiculous— it was painful to see her. On being told that the first clarionet was in the Queen's band, and therefore not yet come, she answered : " Oh, then, I suppose either the Queen must wait or I." Mrs. A. Shaw pleased every one with her frankness and good humour. How cheap to ourselves and of what value in our dealings with others is civility! Found Miss C. N—— still stubborn on the point of her name being announced " Clara Novello." She agreed to refer it to Dickens and Jerrold.

March 23rd.—Helen Faucit called; I was not pleased with an evidence of pettishness in her. Acted Iago better, I think, than I ever have before done. Sent on Mr. Anderson, but did not go on myself. Altered the bill. There seems a destiny at work against me—the hand of fate is heavy on me.

March 24th.—Not well, and weary—weary—" wearied o' the world," God help me. Looked at the paper; saw the account of Southey's death. I envy him his rest; my only pang is the care for my blessed children's welfare, and my beloved wife's sorrow. I would not use the language of complaint or utter a murmur against the Divine Will, but my heart is borne down in thinking of them, and I say God help them almost without hope. Attended to the rehearsal of the second act of the opera. Miss Clara Novello was very much distressed by the incorrectness of the orchestra and the inefficiency of Mr. T. Cooke,[2] who was, with his back to the stage, fiddling out the passages,

---

[1] Clara Novello, Countess Gigliucci, the well-known singer. She had a success in Italy a couple of years before.

[2] Thomas Simpson Cooke (1752–1848) ; musical director at Drury Lane, 1821–1842. He was apparently more successful as a singing-master than as a conductor.

as if to learn the music, from the score! I saw her distress and requested her to be quiet. She told me Mr. Cooke *could not* do it; he did not understand it. This staggered me, and I spoke to Serle, Anderson and Willmott, who all seemed to feel in the same way. Note from Dow. Spoke to Miss C. Novello afterwards, who moderated her objections, but still was not satisfied. Spoke to Thomas; he admitted that Mr. Cooke had not made himself master of the opera. To-morrow I pay £600 to meet the deficiencies of the treasury, and the only hope of continuance is in the success of this opera. I took their opinions, all agreeing in the propriety of endeavouring to call in Benedict.[1] I commissioned Serle to seek him.

March 25th.—Went to Drury Lane theatre, reading *Sappho*. Saw Serle, who communicated to me his interview with T. Cooke, who was violent in refusing to concede the direction of the opera. I sent for Mapleson and learned from him that Mr. Cooke had never had the score, etc., away to read or study himself one single evening or day! Mr. Cooke came and a very long and useless discussion ensued. I explained to him that nothing unkind was contemplated or intended— that it was thought he had not made himself acquainted with the opera, and that with the quantity he had to do he might gracefully and without disparagement avail himself of the aid of Benedict. I could do nothing. Miss Novello came to speak to me on other things and renewed her complaint and dissatisfaction. Attended the rehearsal of the music of *Sappho*, at which I saw a striking instance of Mr. T. Cooke's *slovenliness* as a director. I was inquiring of Allen, who spoke in an absurd way, as if there were a plot to supplant T. Cooke—a man of whom he has greatly complained! Planché called and spoke to me of the Easter piece. He thought T. Cooke was not equal to the demand of the musical public in an Italian opera now, whatever he might have been or might be in other musical pieces. Acted Jacques very well. A note and some artificial flowers from a lady. Serle and Jones spoke again about T. Cooke. Serle was very positive. He took the score for Benedict to look over.

March 27th.—Fox called in the middle of the day. He told me that he stopped the insertion of a paragraph in Mr. Bunn's hand-writing, speaking of himself as "Like Cincinnatus called from the plough, Mr. Bunn had been summoned to resume the reins of manage-ment." I sent for Thomas, the leader, and in consequence of an anonymous letter I received, told him that I should pay the band

[1] Sir Julius Benedict (1804–1885); the eminent conductor and composer.

their full salaries. I shall have little thanks for it, but the game is nearly played out and they suffer much.

March 29th.—Went to Drury Lane theatre, where I attended to the business of the new opera. Rehearsed it, and had to draw upon my dexterity to hush the tempest raging between the two *prima donnas—interdum femineas componere lites*, is now a part of my duty. Phaugh! I am sick of it.

March 30th.—Attended to business and the rehearsal of the opera. Mr. Luigi, on the part of some Russian singers, came too late for his appointment. I saw Mme. Albertuzzi, with whom I could not agree. I am thoroughly *disgusted* with the whole concern. I am sick of the world—I hate it.

March 31st.—Went to Drury Lane theatre. Rehearsed the opera of *Sappho* from eleven to a quarter-past eight. Though so much has been done in all ways for this opera, I feel persuaded it will not attract, although I feel confident of a certain degree of success.

April 1st.—Saw the opera of Sappho,[1] which was certainly put upon the stage as no opera I have ever seen has been for truth and completeness; Miss Novello was very good. The house in amount was below even my calculations. In spirit, it was an assemblage of brutes. Dickens came round to speak to me; I saw also Planché, Beazley, etc. —the Doctors Fell of my imagination. I am heartsick of it all.

April 2nd.—Quite broken down in spirits—no power of enterprise or exertion of any kind. The world is burdensome to me. I feel a worse than useless being in it. Unwell in body and mind. Looked at the paper. A note from Dickens about dining with Miss Coutts on Friday. Letitia answered it.

April 3rd.—Called on Bulwer. Talked with him on his new play, which he is to send me on Wednesday. His son is ill. I am truly, truly sorry. He spoke in a very honourable way about the remuneration for his piece, wishing only to be paid for it by its nightly success. Note from Secretary of Literary Fund, asking me to be Steward.

April 4th.—Sent for Notter; heard his report of the box-office. My prognostications of the issue of this operatic attempt will prove true. Called on Etty and saw his beautiful pictures. Called on the Landseers, saw E. Landseer's two for the exhibition, and one domestic subject of the Queen and Prince Albert. Called on Stanfield, saw his pictures—not so good as I have seen his works. Called on Maclise, who was away from home; on McIan. His wife was at home; she

---

[1] By Pacini.—(*note by Sir F. Pollock.*)

was at work on her picture, of an interesting woman holding a child's shoe in her hand, and looking mournfully at a cradle in which the clothes were tumbled about. I looked for the child, and not thinking of what I said, uttered, "The cradle is empty?" "Yes." I could not speak, and the tears welled to my eyes; I thought of that blessed one with whom I have so often wished to be companioned.

April 5th.—Walked home; enjoyed very much the air and exercise —the first time that I have walked home from the theatre, I believe, this season! Received note and MS. from Bulwer. Read two acts of his play.

April 6th.—Went to Drury Lane theatre reading fourth act of Knowles's play. Directed a little of the rehearsal of *The Midnight Hour* and disgusted to see persons assuming so much in reputation and payment as actors so devoid of talent, so ignorant of their business, so utterly unworthy of the name of artists. Read Bulwer's four acts to Catherine and Letitia. Not good—heavy and sentimental.

April 7th.—Looked at the paper. Spoke with Serle about Miss Novello's conduct, which he condemned as much as we all do. Spoke with Helen Faucit about Lady Macbeth, which she was willing to do. I signed the bills, which are very heavy. Our season is not only irredeemable, but more loss must be incurred. The effort must be to keep it as low as possible. Read C. Buller's speech on Colonization—a good one, but one that convinces me the trade of statesmanship is not so difficult. Oh! what could *honesty* and *energy* not do!

April 8th.—Looked at the paper, which merely afforded another instance of the insane profligacy of that despicable wretch Brougham. Wrote note to Ransom's for sale of £1200 stock!!! Ah me! Rehearsed the Easter piece—*Fortunio*. Spoke to Miss Novello upon her haughty and unconciliatory conduct.

April 9th.—Wrote a note to Bulwer, declining his play.

April 10th.—Rehearsed the Easter piece of *Fortunio*. The chorus, to whom I had given the indulgence of full salary last week, were in an apparent state of rebellion this morning. They behaved ill. Notes from Bulwer, Abbott, etc. Heard of ——'s letter with an account of Major ——'s making love to her. Was in an ill-humour with the world and almost with her, as part of it, for her very fickleness and venal lightness. But what this world is! I hope she may be married to Major ——, but what a world! What a world!

April 11th.—Much out of humour, much depressed and annoyed— in short very wretched in feeling, wishing again and again for that long quiet rest which lulls passion and suffering for ever. Read the paper. Answered Bulwer and a Mr. Abbott, who pesters me about his trash of a play.

April 12th.—Helen Faucit called in at four o'clock, and I went over part of Lady Macbeth with her, and endeavoured to raise and dilate her mind to the conception of the full grandeur of the character, which she only sees from a distance at present, but which she shrinks into littleness before, as she comes near it. I took great pains with her. Dined with Dickens. Met Stanfield, Serle, Jerrold, Mark Lemon, Forster, Blanchard. A very cheerful day.

April 14th.—Talked with dearest Catherine over our prospects, and the only course (which involved our temporary separation) that lay before us. We now regard it more cheerfully than we used to do. Considered in part what I should say in proposing to the company to-morrow their subscription of a night's gratuitous performance towards the Fund for the Siddons monument. Called on Helen Faucit; went over part of Lady Macbeth with her. Resumed my consideration of my proposal to the actors to-morrow.

April 15th.—Thought, before I rose, of my arranged meeting with the company to-day; endeavoured to fix in my mind the order in which I would bring forward my various observations. Rehearsed the scenes of Lady Macbeth with Helen Faucit; she should have begun the study of this part earlier. Rehearsed the Easter piece *Fortunio*. Previous to my rehearsal of *Fortunio* I went into the green-room, where the actors were assembled, and addressed a few words to them as they clustered round the room, explaining to them that such a kind of meeting, though frequent at Covent Garden theatre, was rarely heard of here; that at Covent Garden theatre the actors had been summoned to make sacrifices repeatedly, had made them without consideration of the claim of character or conduct of the manager, etc. I called them to require something from them—their assent would be useless, if not spontaneous and unanimous. Neither Messrs. Serle, Anderson, nor Willmott were privy to my purpose, as I wished no influence to be used. I did not know the extent of their confidence in me, but I asked if there was one who, for himself or others, had generosity enough to agree to any sacrifice I might think it right to propose. Many, I believe *most*, called out—"I will—I will." I thanked them, and told them we had too little regard, paid too little honour to those who elevated our art in the distinction they won, that they would do honour to themselves by agreeing to my request, and

I asked them to give me their gratuitous services for one night in aid of the fund to place a monument to Mrs. Siddons's memory in Westminster Abbey. They *exclaimed,* "Yes," etc. I told them I was glad to see them receive the proposal so, and that I had some little recompense to offer them. I could promise them two holidays, for which they should be paid. I added that some, perhaps, had anticipated a reduction of their salaries, but desired them to understand that whatever agreement I signed should be fulfilled to the very letter.

April 16th.—Called on Helen Faucit, and went over the principal part of Lady Macbeth with her. Was very much pleased with her improvement, although I perceive she will not be able to realize her own intentions by to-morrow evening.

April 17th.—Rehearsed Lady Macbeth's scenes. Rehearsed the Easter piece of *Fortunio,* which occupied me till past four o'clock. Rested a short time. Acted Macbeth unequally; I was depressed at times by the extreme nervousness of Helen Faucit, who lost all management of herself. I recovered when alone. Was called for and well received. Saw the Easter piece of *Fortunio,* which was very successful.

April 18th.—Note from Clara Novello—answered it; one from Helen Faucit—suffering from illness, but in a very unkind and impatient spirit. Talked and—despaired!

April 21st.—Letter from Lord Chamberlain's office, closing the theatre on account of the death of the poor Duke of Sussex, a kind, good-natured man, of the most liberal opinions—I very much lament him.[1]

April 22nd.—I sent for Knowles, and told him that Willmott had pointed out that unless his play had *great success* it could not be acted more than three nights—which I had not before thought on. I now told him he might withdraw the play retaining the £100 in his hands, as he had given his time, etc. He would not hear of keeping the £100, but after some demur desired that the play might *go on.* Dined with Emerson Tennent; met the Hanoverian Minister, an Absolutist, M'Culloch, Delane, Law, and several others. Tennent talked to me much about bringing the fashion to the theatre. I doubt the possibility. Notes from Serle and Dunn, on

---

[1] Augustus Frederick, Duke of Sussex (1773–1843); sixth son of George III; the most unconventional of the Royal Dukes. He was a Progressive in politics, made two morganatic marriages, and by his own directions was buried at Kensal Green.

the part of committee, objecting to the lease of the theatre to the Anti-Corn Law League.

April 23rd.—Went with Catherine and Forster to hear Fox in his chapel lecture on Shakspeare. There was much that was brilliant, eloquent, humorous, learned, and profoundly philosophic in his discourse, but I was, upon the whole, disappointed. I had expected too much, or he had not taken the precaution to *arrange* his ideas.

April 24th.—Dunn came to say that the General Committee wished to see me—I went. Lord Glengall began a speech, which I took an opportunity of anticipating in part by recapitulating the points of my note to Dunn. He quoted the opinions of Pollock [1] and Follet, [2] which I begged to doubt as applying to Drury Lane theatre. I stated my determination not to go from my engagement with the Corn Law League, but left them to take what measures they pleased. I said I should not have let the theatre had I supposed it would have been objectionable to them. They were satisfied and mentioned to me, not the resolution, but the substance of one they had passed expressive of their objection to its recurrence. I told them it should not be let again, and that Mr. Serle should write to the League to say so. Acted Colonel Green [3] I know not how. Called for and well received. Knowles came and thanked me repeatedly and very gratefully for what I had done.

April 26th.—The darling children acted *Comus* in the drawing-room after dinner, interesting and amusing me very much ; they recited the poetry very well indeed, and only gave me a fear lest they should imbibe a liking for the wretched art which I have been wasting my life upon. God forbid. Went in the evening to Mrs. Pierce Butler's. Saw the Sartorises, Sir C. and Lady Morgan, who introduced me to Mrs. Dawson Damer, Lord Lansdowne, Mr. Hallam, whom I was so glad to meet, Milman, Babbage, Everetts, etc.

April 28th.—Acted Colonel Green very poorly ; called for and well received. Went to Mrs. Sartoris's. Saw Young, Benedict, Mr. Procter, Hayward, Butlers. Rogers and Lord Lansdowne were there.

---

[1] Sir Jonathan Frederick Pollock (1783–1870), then Attorney-General ; Lord Chief Baron of the Exchequer from 1844 to 1866 ; created a baronet in the latter year ; father of Macready's friend, Sir W. F. Pollock, and of the late Baron (C. E.) Pollock.

[2] Sir William Webb Follett (1798–1845), then Solicitor-General : succeeded Pollock as Attorney-General. One of the ablest advocates and acutest lawyers of the nineteenth century ; but for his premature death he would undoubtedly have been the next Tory Chancellor.

[3] In *The Secretary*, by Sheridan Knowles.—(*note by Sir F. Pollock.*)

I did not speak with them. Read the number of *Chuzzlewit*. It does not improve.

April 29th.—Received the news that Covent Garden theatre was closed. Without indulging in any feeling of vindictiveness or exultation, I cannot but regard with satisfaction the termination of this wretched attempt to degrade our miserable art still further and oppress its poor dependents by the obtrusion of such a wretch and such a villain as that Bunn. If I desired vengeance it is given to me. I only feel satisfied for the effect in a professional point of view.

May 1st.—Acted Brutus for the most part very well. Called for and well received.

May 4th.—Looked in the paper, in which I read the kind expressions of the Chairman of the League, which are likely to identify me in the minds of the Corn Law faction with the League. Went to Drury Lane theatre. Disgusted with the players; they are—*players!* Rehearsed Joseph Surface—afterwards *Acis and Galatea*. Stanfield looked in; gave me a note, wishing me to dine at the Athenæum to-morrow—to which I agreed. He also asked me again to dine at Greenwich on Monday, which I also assented to.

May 5th.—Looked at the paper. Went to Drury Lane theatre, reading *Comus*. Found Stanfield there refreshing the scene of *Acis and Galatea*, and afterwards *Comus*. Mr. Almond called about his refractory wife, who had sent him to say she *would not* play in *Comus* this evening. I very kindly showed to him that she would only injure herself by a step so imprudent. Spoke to Miss Fortescue, who declined to act Maria. I do not understand this. Read *Comus*. Went to the Athenæum to dine with Stanfield, E. Landseer and Eastlake; Barry, Wells, Romilly, etc., were of the party. We all went to the theatre; I acted Comus. Spoke to Miss Romer; to Helen Faucit, who seemed disposed to expect me to do an injustice. She little knows me, if it be so. Note from Lord Spencer,[1] wishing to speak with me.

May 6th.—Note from Shakspeare Society; looked at the paper. Went to Drury Lane theatre. Attended to business; Lord Spencer called respecting the hire of the theatre for an agricultural dinner in July 1844. He seems to me a used-up man, not very well-mannered, a farmer, and a twaddle. He disappointed me very much. These are the men to govern states—oh God! Rehearsed *The School for Scandal*. Met the committee and had a long conference with them. They will

---

[1] Formerly Lord Althorp, the Whig Chancellor of the Exchequer.

not be able to come to terms with me. Acted Joseph Surface very fairly.

May 7th.—Kenney called; soon after Forster, who was successful in his endeavour to make himself especially disagreeable. Mrs. Norton called. After dinner read first act of *Der Freischütz*, but previously —before dinner—gave much time towards getting my old books out of the way and arranging some minerals, etc. After dinner read over Athelwold, which I fear cannot do anything. Read over Benedict.

May 8th.—Helen Faucit was in ill-humour about not playing Lady Macbeth, upon which I spoke to her very roundly, telling her I would not do an injustice for *any* one. Catherine called for me, and we went to Greenwich to dine with Stanfield. Our party consisted of the Dickenses, Quin, Jerdan, Liston, Maclise, E. Landseer, Grant, Allan and niece, Forster, who was *stentorian*, Ainsworth, etc. Cheerful day.

May 11th.—Saw Willmott and T. Cooke on the entertainment for Mrs. Siddons's night. Spoke to Graham about a night for his Benefit; with Notter about the wish of the Covent Garden theatre proprietors to have me back; told him I could not permit him to say anything from me or with my cognizance, and that I could only go to Covent Garden theatre (if I were ever at liberty to entertain the idea) as a paid manager. Spoke with Serle. Wrote notes to Lumley, to Cattermole, Stanfield, Dickens, and Maclise for their votes at the Athenæum for Mr. Domville. Forster called and invited himself to dinner. Note from Dunn on the part of the sub-committee declining my propositions, on the plea of the Duke of Bedford's refusal to leave his ground rent on a chance of payment. Went down to Drury Lane theatre. Saw Miss Novello, and asked her to do Agatha in *Der Freischütz*, which she refused.

May 13th.—Rehearsed *Athelwold*. Dear old Sir W. Allan called. I gave him the Gloucester box, that he might see at his perfect ease. He seemed quite affected in shaking hands with me. Went down to the Opera House; waited an *hour* for Mr. Lumley, who had very earnest apologies to make—as needed—which I received very urbanely. Asked his permission for Grisi and Fornesari—for Monday 22nd, for Mrs. Siddons' monument. He objected his general rule, but that he would consider this.

May 18th.—Rose at five o'clock, weary, sick, and uncomfortable; applied briskly to this unpleasant task of learning the words of Athelwold, which I mastered. Looked at the paper. Went to Drury

Lane theatre. Rehearsed the play. Rested, being very, very tired. Acted, or rather scrambled through, Athelwold; was called for. After the play spoke with W. Smith, the author, who came in. I have acted against my own judgment in taking this part, but I did it for the author's interest, and to serve Helen Faucit. It has been a heavy task.

May 19th.—Wearied and worn out. I felt all the painful languor of overwork. Looked at the paper and saw, what I had before felt, that I had *really* made a sacrifice to the author and the play of *Athelwold* in taking the part of Athelwold upon myself. Went to Drury Lane theatre quite in a dejected and dissatisfied state. I have actually *over-tasked* myself for the last four days, and my mind is weary—sick in consequence. Spoke with Serle about the proposal to the proprietors, about which I am utterly indifferent.

May 21st.—Walked with Edward in the Botanical Gardens. Enjoyed the breath of air I obtained, but am really weary of life, and wish for peace and rest. Would that I were laid in rest with my sweetest angel child. God help me!—if indeed He cares for such an unhappy wretch as I am! God help me and forgive me.

May 22nd.—Wrote to Milman, asking him for an address for Siddons night.

May 23rd.—Went to Drury Lane theatre. Found Forster in my room. Went with him to Talfourd's chambers; dined with them and Maynard—who, with Talfourd, was very anxious for me to rejoin the Garrick Club.

May 24th.—Note from Talfourd, declining to write the Siddons address. Wrote to Milnes, asking his aid for some verses. Wrote to Marianne, asking her to get the Queen's name to the Siddons monument; to Lord Beaumont, moving him to the same.

May 25th.—Note from Dunn, couched in very confused and impertinent terms, informing me that the proprietors would not make any change. Enough. Planché called to know; I told him that my term would expire at the end of the season. Note from Dickens, from Milnes. Began to think of and to note down my speech, when a knock at the door startled us. Merrick gave the man's name, Pitcher—a fellow who had written insolent letters to me. I said I would not see him. Heard him talking in hall, rang the bell and told M—— to tell him to go away, and if he would not, to go for a policeman to remove him. Merrick went, and instantly the man walked in. I asked him what he meant—how he dared come into my room; to go out; this, indeed, he would not. I told him to go; he put something on the table and said, "'That's a subpœna," or something of that sort. I told him to go out of my house; he slowly went before me, turning back and saying he had been in better houses than mine. I told M—— to go for a policeman, and ordered him out; he said he would not go; I told Merrick to take him by the neck and drag him out; he threw him out into the street, and I made him take his paper and money (*untouched*) after him.

May 28th.—Called on Sir William Curtis; spoke to him on the subject of my continuance, told him I would not pay any more money, that I did not seek to leave the theatre, but was quite ready to go— demonstrating to the public that I did not *desert* the duty I had undertaken. He was very cordial, very courteous, very kind, engaged to call a committee, and left it to me to arrange with the actors the reduction of their salaries. Called on Stanfield, found the Dickenses at his house. Saw his distemper painting from *Comus*. Walked home, not well; rested. Dickens, Stanfield, Maclise, Dr. Quin, Forster, Helen Faucit came to dinner. Read her address, and after all was over, cut four lines out of it.

May 29th.—Spoke to Mrs. Nisbett on the subject of next season. She subscribed to the risk of one-third of her salary. Spoke to Keeley upon the reduction of one-third of salary next season; he agreed to it most heartily; to Hudson—the same; to Mrs. Stirling—the same. Acted King Henry IV. The house was very good, for which I am most thankful.[1]

May 30th.—Spoke to Mrs. Warner on the subject of her salary reduced one-third next season. She demurred—the only one who has not cheerfully accepted it. Fox called to express his gratification at last night's performance. Cobden and Wilson of the Anti-Corn Law League called to speak about taking Drury Lane theatre next year for fourteen nights! Ramsbottom called, and I talked long with him. Serle came in. The language of Ramsbottom was evidently anxiety to retain me, but holding on forms. Forster called to state his delight at last night's performance. Acted Leontes tamely. Called for and well received. Spoke to Anderson and Phelps about the reduction of salaries one-third—both agreed; Anderson, *if* not going to United States.

[1] The receipts of this evening's performance were to be given as the subscription of the Drury Lane Company to the Siddons Memorial Fund. The fourth act of *Henry IV* was performed; two acts of *Der Freischütz* (in which Staudigl was the Caspar); the farce of *Is He Jealous?* with Mrs. Warner, Mrs. Nisbett, Mrs. Keeley, and Mr. Hudson; and *Fortunio.* —(*note by Sir F. Pollock.*)

June 1st.—Talking with Catherine, I took up the thought of going to Westminster Hall; drove down there. Walked about the Hall, went into the Lord Chancellor's Court; saw Lyndhurst.[1] Walked in the Hall and in the street with Serle. Mr. Pitcher passed me—the poor, foolish, mischievous man. Heard that the cause was not to come to-day, and went to Drury Lane theatre. Having heard that the Committee had broken up, sent for Dunn to learn at least the nature of the resolution they had arrived at. He gave me to understand that my terms would be complied with, but there would be £700 required to move on with. I half suspect that there will yet be a demur to my discretionary power of sub-letting the theatre.

June 2nd.—Went down to Westminster. Saw Price, and received much civility from a barrister near me. Was much disgusted by the insulting sneers of Platt,[2] no way bearing upon the question of the truth of his case, with which he indulged himself upon me. Saw in this trial—Drury Lane proprietors *v.* Chapman—a picture of the falsehood, humbug, bullying, and knavery of this world. Mr. Dunn came with the *resolutions* of the Committee, the first of which was a *violation* of the established basis of our agreement, desiring to make me personally responsible for the minimum rent, etc., and again a paltry *evasion* of my primary stipulation for an uncontrolled right to sub-let the theatre. I peremptorily declined them. Dunn asked me if I would go up to the Committee. I said it was useless unless those two conditions were rescinded. He returned and said the Committee regretted my relinquishment, but it must be so. Immediately entered on the business of arrangements for extending the season so as to close on Monday, June 12th; gave orders; wrote advertisements; settled plays, etc. Wrote to Marianne,[3] asking her to apply to the Queen for a command.

June 3rd.—Went down to Westminster. Saw Talfourd and Serjeant Murphy. Talfourd walked with me some time, and then went with me into the Bail Court. He wished me to go into the Queen's Bench, but I heard that I should soon be called. Some counsel very obligingly accommodated me with a seat. Several witnesses, who were called and examined by Platt, swore falsely right on. I was called, and had my presence of mind given to me at once by the bullying demeanour of Platt, which I met with decided resolution and confronted him

---

[1] Then, for the third time, Lord Chancellor.
[2] See note, p. 161.
[3] Miss Marianne Skerrett (see note, p. 193).

with equal purpose. I overturned all he had tried by the preceding witnesses to establish, and received the applause of the Court, which was, of course, stopped, for one of the answers I gave him. I gave the real account of that man Pitcher's outrageous entry here, and on being cross-examined by Knowles, was asked : " Did you, when he made this entry, kick him out of doors ? " " No, I did not." " Then I wonder at your forbearance. I think you would have been justified in doing it." Knowles passed an eulogium upon me, which the Court applauded. I left with Serle after the Judge's charge.

June 5th.—Wrote to Mr. Anson,[1] asking him to lay the request for a State visit before the Prince. Saw Miss P. Horton on business. Sent to Staudigl to act Hecate, which he *refused.* I was glad to find so much to *disgust* me and reconcile me to my departure. Knowles called in to say he was sorry, and had intended to write a great part for me !

June 6th.—Mr. Planché called to explain his permission to the Sadler's Wells manager to act *my* piece, *Fortunio.* His conduct was dishonest, his attempt at excuse shuffling. He is what I suspected him. Serle looked in. Saw a very good letter in the *Times* newspaper about my retirement from Drury Lane. Continued my attention to the address. Forster called and told me the Duke of Cambridge[2] is to present the testimonial to me.

June 7th.—Received a note from W. Anson, informing me that the Queen would command on Monday, an act of kindness which I felt very much. Sir William Martin called to give me the official intimation of Her Majesty's visit. Dickens and Forster had called in the course of the day to tell me they were seeking a place for the presentation of the testimonial. Forster called in the evening to say it was to be Willis's rooms. Mrs. Warner spoke to me about her embarrassment between Drury Lane and Haymarket. A very courteous note from a Mr. Leech inviting me to the Rugby dinner.

June 8th.—Looked at the paper. A note from Mr. Anson brought by an orderly, wishing me to call on him at the Palace at six. I was obliged to write and explain that I could not, but suggested *Much*

---

[1] George Anson (1797-1867) ; equerry to Prince Albert (Prince Consort). One of the handsomest men of his day ; served in the Guards at Waterloo ; became eventually commander-in-chief in India, where he died just before the mutiny, to grapple with which his military experience and capacity would certainly have been far from equal.

[2] The father of the late Duke, chiefly noteworthy for his eccentricities, conspicuous among which was his invariable ejaculation, " By all means," in response to the clergyman's " Let us pray," during divine service.

Ado About Nothing as the play. Went to Drury Lane theatre considering address. Attended there to business with Mr. Elton, who wished to be paid to the end of the season and excused performing the *only night* that he is wanted! These are actors!

June 9th.—Note from Sir W. Martin, informing me that *As You Like It* and the *Thumping Legacy* are commanded. I was much annoyed by the selection, which does me *no good*. Suffered from annoyance about the Command, the benefit of which is gone, as far as any remote good is concerned. Called on Dickens, who told me of the Duke of Cambridge's purpose of presenting the testimonial at twelve for one on Monday 19th.

June 10th.—Mr. Bethune[1] called and sat with me some time. In a strictly private conversation he talked with me on the subject of the bill he is commissioned to prepare with regard to theatres. Appointed to see him at his office on Thursday next at three o'clock. Very kind note with the offer of her box for Monday night from Miss Coutts.

June 12th.—Went to Drury Lane theatre. A day of business, speaking to people, settling little matters, giving orders, etc. Gave the actors invitations, refused several applications for admission. Saw Lord Delawarr about the Queen's box, etc. Afterwards was bothered by Sir William Martin. Sent and took Andrew's box for Her Majesty's suite. Acted Jacques very well. Was called for and the Queen sent to order me to go on, but I was undressed. Lord G——[2] was as officious as if he had been stage manager on £2 per week. Saw Lord Charles Wellesley and Sir William Curtis, who *regretted* my relinquishment. When the Queen came from her box, she stopped Lord Delawarr and asked for me. She said she was much pleased, and thanked me. Prince Albert asked me if this was not the original play. I told him: 'Yes, that we had restored the original text.' After lighting them out, I went into the scene-room, which was filled with people, all delighted with their evening.

June 13th.—Notes from Charles Young, also one from a Captain Younge, inquiring if his brother H. Younge had really died from a nervous disorder brought on by the circumstance of my having discharged him! The man to whom I gave a situation—almost a sinecure, and added a gift of £25—this season! Leslie, from whom

---

[1] Mr. Drinkwater Bethune, then Parliamentary Draftsman to the Government.—(*note by Sir F. Pollock.*)

[2] The Earl of Glengall, one of the Drury Lane Committee.

I had received a note in the morning, called to see Miss Horton and sketch her dress. Laboured at my speech.

June 14th.—Wrote out my address in anticipation of inquiry for it this evening. Went to Drury Lane theatre. Attended to business; very low in spirits; could scarcely repress the tears that rose to my eyes when Miss Horton spoke to me. Rehearsed the two or three short scenes of *Macbeth*. Gave directions to Sloman, etc., to put the scenes and properties in good order to be rendered up to the proprietors. Saw Serle on business. Dined very early. Rested and thought over my character and my address. Was in the lowest state of depression—was actually ill from my state of mind. Spoke to Mr. Willmott upon what was needful to be done. On appearing in *Macbeth*, the whole house rose with such continued shouting and waving of hats and handkerchiefs that I was quite overcome; I was never so affected by the expression of sympathy by an audience. When wearied with shouting, they changed the applause to a stamping of feet, which sounded like thunder; it was grand and awful! I never saw such a scene! I was resolved to act my best, and I think I never played Macbeth so well. I dressed as quickly as I could, and went forward to receive another reception from that densely crowded house, that seemed to emulate the first. It was unlike anything that ever occurred before. I spoke my speech, and retired with the same mad acclaim.[1] Dickens, H. Smith, Forster and Stanfield, Serle came into my room. They did not seem struck with the speech.

June 16th.—Wrote to Mr. Anson a letter of thanks to Prince

---

[1] The playbills had announced the relinquishment of Mr. Macready's direction of the theatre, and his last appearance in London for a very considerable period. The season (1842-3) had been marked by the production of Shakspeare's *As You Like It, King John, Much Ado About Nothing*, and *Cymbeline ;* of the new plays of *The Patrician's Daughter, The Blot on the 'Scutcheon, The Secretary*, and *Athelwold ;* of Mr. Planché's *Fortunio* (as an Easter piece), and of the opera of *Sappho*, and of the operetta *The Queen of the Thames.* To these must be added Congreve's *Love for Love,* adapted for representation, and Dryden's *King Arthur,* which neither obtained nor deserved the success of *Acis and Galatea,* Planché's *Follies of a Night,* Morton's *Thumping Legacy,* and the other new farces of the *Attic Story* and *The Eton Boy.* There had also been performed, of Shakspeare's plays, *Hamlet, Macbeth, Othello, The Winter's Tale, Julius Cæsar, Henry IV*, and *Catherine and Petruchio ;* the other plays of *She Stoops to Conquer, The School for Scandal, The Rivals, The Way to Keep Him, The Provoked Husband, The Jealous Wife, The Stranger, The Road to Ruin, Jane Shore, Virginius, Werner, The Lady of Lyons, Marino Faliero ;* also *Acis and Galatea, The Prisoner of War,* and *The Midnight Hour ;* the operas of *Der Freischütz, The Duenna, Gazza Ladra,* and *Sonnambula,* and the minor pieces of *Patter v. Clatter, The Loan of a Lover, Is He Jealous? The Windmill,* together with the usual Christmas pantomime, which was founded on the story of William Tell.—(*note by Sir F. Pollock.*)

Albert and the Queen. Called at the Thatched House Tavern and put down my name for the Rugby dinner. Went on to Drury Lane theatre. Saw Serle, Anderson, Willmott, C. Jones, business with all; gave orders; saw my closets emptied—my heart was over full. At Sloman's request I passed round the scene-rooms and saw all put away in the best order. I could have wept to think of all these efforts and expenditure come to nothing! I desired Jones to give up the theatre to Dunn, I could not bear to look at it again. Came home dejected to the last degree. Dined with Everett; met the Leicester Stanhopes, Mrs. Norton, E. Landseer, Hayward, Rives.

June 19th.—Woke early to go over the speech; got up to hammer at the speech. Mr. Brewster called; still the speech. Note from Johnson; continued driving at this speech, disheartened, dismayed and despairing, till the hour arrived for me to attend at Willis's rooms. I drove down there, saw Dickens, Forster, D'Eyncourt,[1] Maclise at the door. D'Eyncourt took me into the committee room; Bourne was there and two sons of D'Eyncourt. The Duke of Cambridge came soon after, and asked many questions about the testimonial, which stood in the room, and which he very much admired. I was introduced to him, and he talked to me for some time about Drury Lane theatre very complimentarily. At one o'clock we went into the great room. The platform was crowded, but I could not look, and therefore recognized very few. The Duke spoke better than I have ever heard him. I hesitated, and could not proceed at the passage of the stage business. I was enabled only through the applause to recover myself. The Duke took his leave, and I, after a few words with Bulwer, whom I saw, left the room, sought my carriage, disgusted with myself and sick of all— except the love which I felt many of the assembled multitude to bear me, and yet to what good? Drove home, weary and disgusted. A note from Mrs. Norton.

June 28th.—Looked at paper; saw, what I had heard yesterday, the death of John Murray—Byron's publisher—at one time "*the* publisher." [2] How the people of my life are falling fast around me. A warning!

---

[1] The Right Hon. Charles Tennyson D'Eyncourt (1784–1861); formerly Tennyson, a relation of the Laureate; a "progressive" Whig; sat in Parliament for various constituencies from 1818 to 1852.

[2] John Murray (1778–1843); founder of the well-known publishing firm, and originator of the *Quarterly Review*. His relations with Byron are one of the most piquant features of the poet's *Letters and Journals*. His misgivings as to *Don Juan* procured for him perhaps the most pungent description that Byron ever penned: "Mr. John Murray of Albemarle

June 29th.—Dickens called for me, and calling for Forster, with whom was Procter; we went to the London Tavern and dined at the Sanatorium Dinner, Lord Ashley [1] in the chair. I sat next to Lord R. Grosvenor,[2] his left supporter. I liked him very much. Dickens spoke the best, Forster very fairly, Dillon very well. I returned thanks briefly for the stewards. Walked home with Dickens, Forster and Procter.

July 1st.—Went to breakfast with Milnes; met a captain from China, a Mr. Rowley, from the borders of Abyssinia, Carlyle, Chevalier Bunsen, Lord Morpeth and several other agreeable people whose names I did not catch. I spent a pleasant morning, liking Bunsen very much indeed, Lord Morpeth very much. Went down to Westminster Hall and saw the cartoons; most pleased with Caractacus led in triumph through Rome and the Trial by Jury, but also pleased with the Landing of Cæsar and the Battle for the Beacon. Saw several persons that I knew, to whom I did not speak, as I did not know how far they might think themselves lowered in their own opinion by speaking to me. Read the number of Chuzzlewit's landing in America, *which I do not like.* It will not do Dickens good, and I grieve over it.

July 17th.—Still very unwell, and kept in bed late from the state of my head. Mr. Phelps called, and I saw him; he came to speak about the debt due from him; in the course of conversation I asked if he would like to go to America—as it occurred to me. He said "of all things." We talked on, and I promised to consult the agent (Maywood) on the matter. I stated that I could guarantee nothing, but if the chance of £30 per week and his expenses to and fro offered as likely, would he be satisfied? He said he would. T. Landseer came to tea and to take sketches of the children.

July 23rd.—Went to Behnes.[3] Sat to him. D'Orsay came in and stayed about three quarters of an hour. What a delightful person he is! He took great interest in the bust. Mr. Lewis called and sat three hours!!! Messrs. Phelps and Maywood came to dinner, and we talked over the subject of his accompanying us to the United

Street, the most timid of God's publishers." Murray, by his honourable and liberal dealings undoubtedly improved the publisher's status, and in no way deserved the malignan strictures passed upon him by the late Lord Lovelace in *Astarte.*

[1] Afterwards the well-known Earl of Shaftesbury (1801–1885).

[2] Afterwards the first Lord Ebury (1801–1893); prominent as a Sabbatarian.

[3] William Behnes, a sculptor at one time in great request; he afterwards fell on evil days and ended miserably.

States. I would not urge him, nor press him for an answer; he would take some days to consider of it.

July 24th.—Went to Briggs.[1] Mrs. Opie[2] sat with us. Nina called for me; Mrs. Opie seemed pleased with her, dear child. She took leave of me—sadly, as if we might never meet again. I imagine we never shall. Went to the exhibition with them. Admired particularly Eastlake's Hagar, and Etty's, Hart's, Redgrave's, Eddis's, Stone's. Went to Home Office; waited and had a conference with Manners Sutton, to whom I complained of the injustice done to myself and the dramatic art by the Bill of Sir J. Graham as it stands. I urged the right of acting Shakspeare being given to the licensed theatres if the patent theatres were unable to act his works. He promised to take it into consideration.[3] Lord Hatherton, Rogers, Miss Rogers, Mr. and Mrs. Everett, Sir Charles Morgan, Mr. and Mrs. Fonblanque, Charles Buller and Kenyon came to dinner. A quiet and rather dull day.

August 1st.—Called with Nina and Katie on Richmond,[4] the artist; found him intelligent and agreeable. Called on Thorburn[5] and agreed with him for two miniatures.

August 3rd.—Mr. Ryder called, and I proposed to him to accompany me to the States; heard that Mr. Bunn was the lessee of Drury Lane. This is, on the part of the committee, shameful—to the art, actors, and the public. Mr. Ryder will give his answer to me on Saturday. Proceeded to Ling's Hotel to see Mr. Bennett of the *New York Herald.* I saw Mr. and Mrs. Bennett. He is an ugly and ungentlemanly likeness of John Wilkes. I was as civil as possible, gave him my card, hoped to see him on my return, etc.

August 5th.—Mr. Ryder called to say that he would be happy to accompany me to the United States.

August 8th.—Went to the opera—changed from *Don Pasquale* to *Semiramide.* What trash! what arrant nonsense this style of entertainment is! Oh, Voltaire, you had a little more sense, a great

[1] Henry Perronet Briggs, R.A. (1791–1844); a portrait-painter of some repute in his day.
[2] Mrs. Amelia Opie (1769–1853); *née* Alderson, novelist and poet; second wife of John Opie, R.A.
[3] The Licensing Act afterwards passed in 1843 extended the Lord Chamberlain's jurisdiction to the whole of the metropolis; and since its passing the monoply of the old patent theatres to perform the regular drama has ceased to exist.—(*note by Sir F. Pollock.*)
[4] George Richmond, R.A. (1809–1896); the eminent portrait-painter; nearly every Victorian celebrity of both sexes sat to him. Father of Sir W. B. Richmond, R.A.
[5] Robert Thornburn (1818–1885), A.R.A.; the fashionable miniature-painter of his day.

deal more taste, and a world more of virtue than the self-praised aristocracy of England—the gold-besotted, prurient, frivolous, and heartless wretches! The cellars and garrets of Manchester and the dens and pig-holes of Ireland are echoing the moans of agony, as the boxes of these *things* in the opera house are shaking with their applause of—what? Heard Grisi, Fornesari, who were very bad. Saw Cerito, a very agile and graceful dancer; Fanny Ellsler, an exceedingly vulgar one.

August 9th.—Went to my first sitting with Thorburn, whom I liked very much, and with whom I spent a very agreeable hour and a half. Paid him in cheque of £21, half his charge for Catherine's and my miniature. Returning home, saw paper, with Lord Glengall's observation in the House of Lords on my petition,[1] that it was more marked by "self-sufficiency, self-conceit, and vanity" than any petition ever presented to that House. My assailant is Lord Glengall. I rejoice in finding my enemies such men as he.

August 10th.—Took Willie into the banqueting-room, now Chapel Royal, of Whitehall; showed him the ceiling painted by Rubens. The attendant told us that the *public* were not allowed to come on Sundays into those carpeted places—the church—but might go into the gallery; the pews and centre of the church being reserved for the nobility and gentry, preached to by the Bishop of London; and God hears these *things* call themselves followers of Jesus Christ!

August 11th.—Went to Westminster, and called upon the Dean,[2] whom I found an agreeable and most good-natured man. I explained my business to him, viz. to ask the remission of the Dean and Chapter fees in the case of Mrs. Siddons's monument. He went with me into the Abbey, and I showed him the sites selected by Chantrey; we talked much. He wished me to return to see a portrait of Ben Jonson by Vandyke, a very charming thing. He showed me many others; some very good ones, a Rembrandt, a portrait of Wilson, etc. He then wished me to return to his study, and I sat with him some time.

August 14th.—Called on Milnes, on Rogers. Found at home letters from David Colden, in a more cheering tone of America; from Miss Martineau, angry with Dickens—and not unreasonably so.

August 21st.—Mrs. Norton has sent a note inviting us to meet

---

[1] Against the patent theatres.
[2] Dr. Turton, afterwards Bishop of Ely.—(*note by Sir F. Pollock.*)

Lord Melbourne at her house to-morrow, as he wished to speak to me about the theatre. Catherine accepted the invitation.

August 22nd.—A Mr. Tenniel [1] called to see me. Dined with Mrs. Norton; met Lady Conyngham,[2] Lord Melbourne,[3] Sidney Herbert,[4] Köhl and the Sheridans. Rogers came in in the evening.

August 25th.—Sat again to Thorburn. Lady Clanricarde [5] was either afraid (!) or too proud to pass me in the drawing-room to take her bonnet, and for her accommodation I walked into the room down-stairs!!

August 26th.—Went to Richmond, to the *Star and Garter*, where I was received by the party expecting me, Dickens, Maclise, Barham, E. Landseer, Fox, Dillon, F. Stone, Stanfield, Forster, George Raymond, Quin, H. Smith, Carew, an amateur singer. A very elegant dinner, and enjoyed by a company in the most perfect harmony of feeling and spirits. Dickens proposed the only toast of the evening, my health, etc., in a very feeling and eloquent speech. I had not had time before to ponder the circumstances of my departure, and I quite broke down under it. I could not speak for tears, or very inefficiently. Afterwards a most joyous evening, and the warmest emotions of regard and regret pervaded the party.

September 1st.—Forster told me at dinner that he had written a very strong letter to Dickens, endeavouring to dissuade him from accompanying me on board the steamship. I thought for Dickens's sake he was quite right, but did not feel the full amount of mischief to myself.

September 2nd.—Received a present from Forster of shirt-studs, very handsome, which I had rather he had not given. Wrote to him acknowledging it. Went to Kensal Green Cemetery to pay my parting tribute of love and sorrow at the tomb of my *blessed child*. God knows if I may ever be able to pay that dear and tender duty again. Read the number of *Chuzzlewit*, the most powerful of the book which Dickens is now employed upon, but as bitter as it is powerful, and against whom is this directed? " Against the Americans," is the answer. Against

[1] Now *the* Mr. Tenniel, the famous cartoonist.
[2] George IV's " enchantress."
[3] The ex-Prime Minister, defendant in the action for crim. con. by Mrs. Norton's husband.
[4] Sidney Herbert (1810–1861); the distinguished statesman, afterwards Lord Herbert of Lea. The dinner-party is noteworthy as including three persons who were prototypes of prominent characters in George Meredith's novel, *Diana of the Crossways*, namely, Mrs. Norton, Lord Melbourne, and Sidney Herbert.
[5] Harriet, Marchioness of Clanricarde, only daughter of George Canning, the statesman.

how many of them? How many answer to his description? I am grieved to read the book. Received a letter from him telling me that he had received a strong expostulary letter from Captain Marryat on the subject of his accompanying me, and that, on my account,[1] he would therefore deny himself the indulgence of shaking hands with me on board ship. His letter was generous, affectionate, and most friendly. But why did he say *Marryat* had written, when it was *Forster*? Went to London Library, where Catherine and the children, returning from their breakfast with Rogers, met me. Dickens and Forster came, and H. Smith and Rogers. We met Catherine at the door of Buckingham Palace Garden, were shown the pavilion in the garden (how beautiful the garden is!), and the frescoes of Etty, Stanfield, Maclise, Leslie, Sir W. Ross, a beginning by Edwin Landseer. Stanfield's looks best. Went through the state-rooms of the palace. The pictures are excellent. Took leave of Rogers, running after him in the garden; we parted most cordially. Took leave of H. Smith and Dickens, who were most affectionate. Sent note, with Catherine's signature and my book, to Ransom's. Called on the Bishops, Sir Isaac Goldsmid, Holford, Jonathan Birch, J. Morris, Mr. Butler, Mrs. Rolls. Packed up my little bag. Forster dined with us. Set off for Brighton; read a few lines of Madame de Staël. Notes and letters of introduction from Leslie, most kind.

September 3rd.—Rose early and left Brighton by the first train, reading by the way Madame de Staël's *Treatise on the Art of Acting*. Thought much. Arrived at home; instantly applied myself to business, packing with all speed. Captain Marryat called to shake hands with me. Thorburn, whom I paid for his miniatures, etc., C. Jones, General Alexander, kind man. Arranged my accounts; continued packing. T. Landseer called as we were in the carriage to call on him; he went with us to his brother's, who was from home. Called on King, Lady Blessington, whom I saw; Elliotson, not at home; Procter and Kenyon. Wrote to Leslie. Dined with the children. God for ever bless them. D'Orsay and Edwin Landseer called; just shook hands with them. Note from Lady Blessington. Sent Siddons's paper, with note and order on Coutts's to Stanfield. Wrote a note to Lord Hatherton. Packed up. Heard my blessed children

---

[1] Because he thought that Macready's reception in the United States might be prejudiced if it were known that he had been accompanied on his departure from England by the writer of *Chuzzlewit* and of the *American Notes*. (See Forster's *Life of Dickens* under this date.)—(*note by Sir F. Pollock.*)

their prayers, and then read prayers among us all. My God, hear Thou and grant me to find in a happy return those precious beings improved in health of mind and body, and progressing in the paths of wisdom and virtue, happy in their own belief of doing right. Amen.

To Liverpool, September 4th.—Rose at a very early hour; prepared for my departure; kissed my beloved children. Very nearly losing our train through the negligence of the cabman. Arrived, and started at the moment from railway station. A sleepy, dull journey. Reached Birmingham; amused with the passengers there. Landed and set off in the Liverpool train. Very much wearied and distressed with fatigue. Forster and Thompson were at the railway waiting for us. Went to Adelphi, from thence to the river, where we took boat to near the *Caledonia,* a very comfortable ship, in which I saw my luggage land. Forster gave me a very kind letter from Blanchard. Forster dined with us, and we passed a cheerful evening.

September 5th.—Took leave, after some fond and sad talk, cheerfully and well of my dearest wife and sister. Went with Forster to the quay. We reached the ship and came on board. What a scene! Bade dear Forster farewell; he was greatly affected. I looked at my fellow-passengers—eighty. Thought of my wife; watched the gorgeous sunset and the soft moon. Took tea; watched Liverpool, or where it was, till the lights could no more be seen.

September 6th.—My night had been tranquil, but it gave me little sleep; the sea was quite calm. My thoughts were, as they had been, of where my Catherine and my children were, what they were doing, and where I was. Were they thinking of me? Observed my fellow-passengers, amused with the conceit and assumption of many, the fantastic costumes that, with either perfect indifference or a sense of attractiveness, leaned, stood or paraded on the deck. I fell into conversation with a very intelligent American, apparently a Southerner. I liked him very much. Resolved to do my utmost to use my time, and felt thankful for this tranquil commencement of our voyage, which enables me to get my room in order. There are indications of a *roll.* How the weather may act upon my designs of employment is to be seen. Began to-day to feel a *little* motion. My thoughts were almost entirely of home, where Catherine might be, of what she might be thinking. I feel *now* in the drear monotony of this life my utter loneliness. The voyage, its chances, and the year—*its* chances too—before me! There is little to interest in my fellow-passengers, though much to remark, but I want convenience and freedom of mind to take advantage of it.

September 8th.—After coming on deck I introduced myself to Judge Haliburton, *alias* Sam Slick, and had some pleasant conversation with him. I chiefly noted in him the strong expression of humour in his countenance when he smiles; there is fun in every wrinkle.

September 12th.—Rose with returning spirits and passed many hours on deck. Walking and talking with several persons. In such a ship's company—eighty—it is not possible to know my fellow-passengers, and each day I am surprised by a face I have not seen before. Made acquaintance with Edward Gibbon Wakefield,[1] and talked some time with him.

September 13th.—Rose in good time but sank back again to bed, where I lay discomfited and wretched till about two o'clock. I was, however, able to use my mind in some degree, and thought over part of the character of Macbeth, and also of the view which I took of the country I am about to visit, contrasting or comparing it with that taken by my predecessors. Walked much on deck to-day, and chatted with several people. Enjoyed the beauty of the sea, and was much less *mal-aisé* than I have been. Talked a good deal with Gibbon Wakefield, who is amusing. Thought often during these sick days of home, and all I love there, with many wishes, many hopes and some fears. God bless them all, dear ones. Amen!

September 16th.—Came on deck to see a most beautiful morning and to feel as if I had not been at all unwell. Saw a barque on our starboard side. Talked a good deal with a German, whom I thought I had used rather coldly, and heard much from him that was very interesting respecting Germany, particularly of Hanover, Hungary and Bavaria. Talked much with Judge Haliburton, who is a very kindly, liberally disposed man, but the Tory of the *Quarterly Review* school of twenty years ago. I like him very much. Talked with Wakefield, about whom there is something *not quite right*. Read a small pamphlet, which he said was equally his and C. Buller's, on the responsibility of an Executive in Colonial Governments, which is very good. Looked over

---

[1] Edward Gibbon Wakefield (1796-1862); an authority on Colonial constitutions; accompanied Lord Durham to Canada, and largely inspired his policy there. Previously he had been imprisoned for abducting an heiress, his marriage with whom was annulled by Parliament, and this circumstance stood in the way of his career, which otherwise would have been a successful one, as his abilities were of a high order.

Byron's poems and read some passages in *Childe Harold*.   How inferior is he to Wordsworth, whom he derides!

Halifax, September 18th.—Rose before sunrise, and saw a glimpse of land through the haze.   Dressed, and went on deck as we entered the harbour of Halifax, which, with its rocky hills on either side, its smooth green island in the centre of the bay, and the lively looking town before us with its citadel, its ships and wharves crowded with eager spectators, looked as in lively welcome to us.   Our deck was equally alive with land costumes, gay with faces I had not seen during the voyage.   The bustle of welcome and farewell was amusing and exciting.   I went with one of our ship's company into the town of streets at right angles, of wooden houses, reminding one of the half active sort of character that a Scotch eastern town seems to have.   The shops seemed good, as I looked into them, and it appeared quite a place that a man might live in.   Before leaving the ship I had a few words of farewell with Mr. Haliburton, and exchanged cards with him. He breakfasted with us in one great party of about thirty from the ship, at the hotel, and certainly never was greater justice done to a breakfast.   The air, and the sense of being on land quite sent my spirits in an unusual flow back to me.   After taking leave of Mr. Haliburton, he came back to introduce Mr. Webster of the Rifles to me, who with great courtesy asked how he could be of use to me, etc.; if I would breakfast at the barracks, etc.   I declined, but accepted the offer of his escort, and walked with him up to the barracks and to the citadel, from whence the view of the harbour, its islands, forts, shipping, the lake on the opposite side, part of the inner harbour, etc., all come within the eye.   It is a beautiful scene, laid out as in a map before one.   He returned with me to the ship, and then I took leave of him.

Boston, September 20th.—The mate summoned me at early twilight with the news that we should soon approach the Boston Harbour Light. I had slept very little; there were noises all night on deck, from the time of stopping to take in the pilot, that disturbed me incessantly.   I left my bed with little reluctance to see in the cold grey light the land before me stretching away to the right, with the lighthouse ahead.   It was land, and the eye strained to it and rested on it as on security and comfort.   I desired to be called when we neared the Narrow, and attended to my luggage until time to see our entry into this beautiful harbour.   It must be a very unsightly haven that would not have beauty for eyes that have looked on sea and sky for nine or ten days, but the islands so various in form, the opening again of the view of the sea through the Northern Channel after passing the narrow entrance, the forts, the houses that spot the rising shores, and the seemingly rich and thriving villages that spread far along the circling shores on either side of the receding land, with the clustered masses of the city's buildings in the central distance, surrounded by the dome of the State House and the Obelisk of Bunker's Hill : all these lit up and illuminated by a most gorgeous sunrise that fretted with golden fire one half of the heavens, and was reflected in the dancing waves through which we made rapid way, all these effects of form and colour gave a beauty and splendour to the scene that required not any interest unborrowed from the eye to awaken delight and enjoyment. A small shoal of porpoises came leaping and bounding along in our course, and the vessels glided by or were passed by us, as the scene grew upon our sight in our rapid advance. The thought of the Pilgrim Fathers, the fervent, stern, resolute, and trusting men, who, in their faith in God, became the authors of all the glorious and happy life I saw about me, was a touching recollection ; the privations and sufferings of those men are not held in account by us. But the death of Charles Stuart, whose tyranny caused their martyrdom, and who suffered himself in expiation of his own violated faith, is made a compulsory subject of the prayers of those who call themselves followers of the Church of England, which I am not, being, or professing to be, a *Christian*. Having dressed and breakfasted, I exchanged cards with two or three of our passengers and civilities with others, and waited at the custom house for the examination of my ponderous baggage. I wish I could depict the truth as it occurred, because it would render weak my attempt to describe the natural politeness and hearty, kind feeling of the officer who had in charge to examine our luggage. He was not furnished out by Stultz or Inkson, but I longed to shake hands with the kind-hearted fellow. He looked into two bags, and upon the wrappers within a portmanteau ; on the book-box he demurred, but thought it better to see what it contained. I lifted out a shelf for him, and he exclaimed, "Oh, I see ! these are all library—all second-hand books—it is quite enough," and marked it as he had done the pile of my luggage that had passed in review before. I left Thompson to bring it on, and took a sort of cab from East Boston to the City. We halted in our course to let a train pass along a railway, over which we dashed, and after two minutes' more delay drove into a steamboat, crossed the water, drove out and through the crowded, noisy, rattling streets of Boston up to the Tremont Hotel. An American hotel is a type of the country. There is splendour, luxury, profusion and convenience for *the mass*, but the individual who wishes exclusive accommodation must be often disappointed and inconvenienced. I entered this noble building through a crowd of busy, bustling, chattering, scrutinizing, smoking, and spitting gentry, and made my way to the office. I am sure I had to wait very nearly half-an-hour, and I did so very patiently, in this place, which was a sort of collision of tides of humanity, continual flux and reflux from all the doors, some indifferent, some staring at me, some smoking.

New York, September 21st.—Attended to my bedroom affairs, arranged accounts; saw Mr. Ryder and D. Colden, to whom I submitted my letters of introduction. Went to rehearsal, with which I took much pains, and of course found a material very different from what I had lately been accustomed to; found that I had done right in bringing Mr. Ryder. Forrest came up to me as I was standing over a New York paper in the reading-room of the hotel. I was very glad to see him, and he came up to my room and sat with me some time, civil.

September 22nd.—Went to rehearsal and took considerable pains to make the play tell its own story. The actors were very attentive and behaved very well. Forrest came up to me in the reading-room and very cordially welcomed me. He came up to my room and sat with me some time, inviting me to dine on Thursday week. Many cards were left. Dined on a dinner that might challenge the Trois Frères. Mr. Longfellow called.[1]

September 24th.—Met Mr. Penn, or Pell, and Mr. Griffiths. A cheerful day. It was Mr. Penn who observed of Dickens that he must have been ungrateful and therefore a bad man. I defended and explained as I best could his morbid feeling about the States. Passed a pleasant afternoon. Went to Mr. Sedgwick's; saw Mrs. S—— and Mrs. *Butler*,[2] whom I dared not ask after her husband. An agreeable evening.

September 25th.—Went to the theatre, and acted Macbeth. What shall I say? With every disposition to throw myself into the character as I had never so completely done before, I was, as it were, beaten back by the heat, and I should certainly have sunk under it, if I had not goaded myself repeatedly to work out my thoughts and vindicate my reputation. The audience did not applaud very much, but really it would have been too much to expect successive rounds of applause

---

[1] The distinguished poet.

[2] Formerly Fanny Kemble ; she and her husband were not on good terms.

WILLIAM CHARLES MACREADY

AS MACBETH

*From the painting by John Jackson, R.A., in the collection of Major-General
C. F. N. Macready, C.B.*

under such an atmosphere. My reception was most enthusiastic, and very loudly cheered and with repeated cheers. The audience seemed *held* by the performance, though Lady Macbeth was a *ridiculous* drag-chain upon my proceedings. I am glad I have brought Mr. Ryder. I was loudly called for and very fervently received; the audience expected a speech, but I bowed under great weakness. D. Colden came into my room and sat; he seemed to think the impression good, though he was not of opinion the plays should be soon repeated, in which I agreed.

September 26th.—Called on Pierce Butler and sat some time with Mrs. Pierce B——. Pierce Butler came in as I was going away. Rehearsed Hamlet. Could not collect an exact opinion on the effect of last night's performance; did not choose to look at the newspaper. Mrs. Butler was delighted, and Simpson was in high tone; but on neither can I depend for the public voice, one having too clear a judgment, the other too dull a one. Still in the dark as to the tone these critical gentry will take. Read over *Richelieu*. D. Colden called and seemed to think that opinion would balance in favour. Looked over *Hamlet*. *Distressed* by the arrangements of this house.

September 29th.—Acted Cardinal Richelieu but indifferently. I was not in the vein, and though I tried and tried I was not up to the high mark. I was called, but the house did not seem simultaneously excited at any time, and when D. Colden came round he counselled the postponement at least of its repetition. It was therefore evident the sensation had not been very great.

September 30th.—Note from *Lardner !* Forrest called and took me out to see the reservoir of the aqueduct; afterwards to see Mrs. Forrest. Dined with Pierce Butler, Bryant, Mr. and Mrs. Longfellow. Mrs. Butler's conversation was such that, had I been her husband—— I should observe that Mrs. Butler spoke admirably well, but quite like a man. She is a woman of a most extraordinary mind; what she said on most subjects was true—the stern truth, but what in the true spirit of charity should not have been said in the presence of one who was obliged to listen to it. Alas!

October 1st.—After dinner Dr. Lardner called; talked about Mrs. Lardner and his young child. I felt for him; he has been most foolish.[1]

October 2nd.—Acted Macbeth tolerably well; took pains, but was, I think, unequal. Called for and well received. David Colden came

[1] See note, p. 6, Vol. I.

into my room. On this very day, seventeen years ago, Monday, October 2nd, 1826, I opened in New York in the character of Virginius.

October 3rd.—Dined with Forrest; met a very large party, too large for comfort, but it was most kindly intended. Bryant, with whom I talked very little; Halleck, and Inman the artist, were of the party. Our day was very cheerful; I like all I see of Forrest very much. He appears a clear-headed, honest, kind man; what can be better?

October 4th.—Received letters, which I had not looked for for some days from my blessed home, from dearest Catherine, Letitia, and my blessed children. Read them in bed, where I was resting from my labours. I shed many, many tears over them. God bless the dear writers. Acted Werner anxiously and partially with effect. The audience were interested, but are very sparing of applause. Was called for and well received. David Colden came into my room. At last I have got into my promised bedroom. My heart thanked God for the comfortable tidings brought from home.

October 5th.—Forrest called on me, and, agreeably to his wish, I underwent the operation of being *daguerreotyped*. Eheu! for the operation and heu! heu! for the product! (I thought to myself, and could I be so ugly!) I was very much amused.

October 6th.—Walked down to the Butlers'; met Longfellow. What a lovely scene the Bay of New York presents—or rather what scenes! I know of nothing superior to it, with that clear dome of blue over it. Acted Hamlet with the endeavour to make an effective performance, but I *could not*; I was very much *dispossessed*.

October 7th.—Called on Dr. Lardner. Alas! alas! I saw the *ci-devant* Mrs. Heaviside, now Mrs. Lardner, a very fine and handsome woman; and Lardner not now a *ci-devant jeune homme,* no longer dandy in his dress and appointments, but old and almost slovenly. There was a child there, the fruit of their indiscretion—that, poor thing! and poverty and neglect, the sad result of their blind, absurd infatuation! I pitied the *folly*, the weak vanity of both; "into what depth of sin from what height fallen!" It is a strange, mysterious world; we know not who are safe. *None* really so, except the steadfast, resolute, and constant in virtue, that only and sure wisdom—that single safeguard. God forgive me! Amen! Sat some time with them, as they finished their moderate and somewhat uncomfortable, certainly inelegant, dinner, and went with sad thoughts away.

October 8th.—Occupied long with affairs of wardrobe; arranged my

226

weekly accounts, and went out to call on Mrs. Colden, taking with me the sketches of the darling children and my Catherine's portrait. The family were much pleased with them, though Mrs. Colden could not fancy the little, slight creature she recollected my Catherine to have been now grown into a woman of a matronly air and figure. I went with George Wilkes to the church, and heard Dr. Hankes perform the whole service. He was suffering with a very severe cold, but I never heard the prayers read more unaffectedly and earnestly. His sermon was for the most part eloquent, but not argumentative; his text, "I knew a man in Christ." His selection of language was really choice, his images very powerful and graphic, but occasionally he stretched a figure out into an allegory, that attenuated its force by its extension. Upon the whole I was very much gratified. I could not help again observing the admirable manner in which the whole service is performed, the simplicity and complete equipment, the single colour of the lining of the pews, the absence of all signs of poverty, the order and respectful attention of all present were very pleasing; the music was good, too; I was much gratified.

October 10*th.*—Went to the theatre and rehearsed Virginius. From what I can learn the audiences of the United States have been accustomed to exaggeration in all its forms, and have applauded what has been most extravagant; it is not, therefore, surprising that they should bestow such little applause on me, not having their accustomed cues.

October 15*th.*—Longfellow called for me, and we went to dine with Mrs. L—— and D. Colden at the ladies' ordinary. Above 130 sat down. Mr. and Mrs. N. P. Willis next to Longfellow. He (N. P. W——) wished to be very civil to me. I was much amused. I looked for the eaters with knives, but detected none. The only indecorum I noticed was in a couple just opposite to me, who were too ostentatious of the dalliance they seemed so much to enjoy.

October 16*th.*—Dr. Wilkes drove me to the Coloured Orphan Asylum. It does great honour to the benevolence of those persons— chiefly women—who instituted and carried it to its present state; the cleanliness, economy, order, the entire arrangement seemed unexceptionable. I went through the whole building, school-rooms, bedrooms, play-rooms, hospitals, bath-rooms, washing-rooms, kitchen, store-room, etc. I heard a class read and answer questions very well, being taught to *reason* aloud, which was very good. But when I saw about seventy of these little human beings of a degraded caste eating their dinners together I could not bear it. The tears gushed to my eyes, and I was obliged to go out of the room. God help them—God help them. Acted Hamlet very fairly; striving to overmaster my evil tendencies. I must guard against unreal tones, etc.; I must practise to be the thing, despite the coldness of these audiences. I must.

October 18*th.*—Acted the part of Othello with every possible drawback; the actors were all *slow-coaches* (*incompetent*) around me. I fought against it and succeeded in interesting the audience, but my effort here not to lose ground must be great indeed. Called for and well received.

October 19*th.*—Spoke to Mr. Ryder about his tameness and inaccuracy; he is well-meaning but weak, and not made of the stuff to run far ahead of his fellows. Acted Werner unsatisfactorily to myself; I *cannot afford* to expend my spirits and alacrity by recreation or exercise on the days of performance. I have not—it is vain to strive against the fact—I have not the elasticity nor strength of youth, and to me my means of livelihood are now nearly all in all.

October 20*th.*—Called on Lardner, lest he might think I shirked him. But it was a painful visit. Alas! alas! Called on Mr. T. Moore, an old *bon-vivant* seventeen years ago, now struck down by disease, a very wreck; poor fellow; he was very glad to see me. He told me that the people had called the Five Points, an infamous receptacle of rogues, etc., by the name of "Dickens' Place," because he visited it. Acted Macbeth with extreme difficulty—quite *invitâ Minervâ*, but I would not give way. I fought against myself and the wretched actors around me, and played much of the part very fairly. Called for, and when on was fixed by a dead silence. I hesitated, and then said: "Ladies and gentlemen, the custom peculiar to this country of a performer addressing the audience on his Benefit night has long been strange to me, and I really do not know how to convey the impression which my very gratifying reception here has made on me without indulging in a fervency of expression that might call my taste in question. My endeavours to sustain my art in a manner worthy of your patronage shall speak the high estimation in which I hold your favour, and with this promise I take my leave of you till the month of December, when I shall have the honour of again appearing before you for a short engagement." The audience received these few words in a very cordial spirit, and D. Colden, who came into my room, seemed very much delighted with the effect they had produced.

October 21*st.*—Went to the National theatre, where I saw Forrest act King Lear. I had a very high opinion of his powers of mind when

I saw him exactly seventeen years ago; I said then, if he would cultivate those powers and really study, where, as in England, his taste could be formed, he would make one of the very first actors of this or any day. But I thought he would not do so, as his countrymen were, by their extravagant applause, possessing him with the idea and with the fact, as far as remuneration was concerned, that it was unnecessary. I reluctantly, as far as my feelings towards him are interested, record my opinion that my prophetic soul foresaw the consequence. He has great physical power. But I could discern no imagination, no original thought, no poetry at all in his acting. Occasionally in rage he is very strong and powerful, but grandeur in his passion there was *none;* pathos, *none.* The quiet portion—and much, too much, was quiet—was heavy and frequently inaudible; irascibility of *temperament* did not appear; there was no *character* laid out. The audience were very liberal, very vehement in their applause; but it was such an audience!— applauding all the disgusting trash of Tate as if it had been Shakspeare, with might and main. But an actor to speak the words of Tate— with Shakspeare's before him—I think criticizes his own performance; and of Forrest's representation I should like to say that it was like the part—false taste. In fact, I did not think it the performance of an artist. I did not like his curse—it was anything. In the storm (for which see Kent's description in the previous scene—oh, ye gods!) he walked on in perfect quietude; there was throughout nothing *on* his mind, fastened *on* and tearing and convulsing it with agony, and certainly his frenzy "was not like madness." His recognition of Cordelia the same. *He did not fully comprehend his poet.* He speaks very frequently in a voice *not his own,* reminding me of Kean and Vandenhoff. But the state of society here and the condition of the fine arts are in themselves evidences of the improbability of an artist being formed by them. It is a very pretty theatre, but filled with vulgar people. I looked in at the Chestnut Street theatre, which had a very elegant auditory, listening to and applauding a French opera, very indifferently performed. Walked home. Read over again dearest Catherine's letters, etc. There was much to praise in Forrest's execution frequently; he seems to have his person in perfect command, but he has not enriched, refined, elevated, and enlarged his *mind;* it is very much where it was, in the matter of poetry and art, when I last saw him. But his speaking through the play the trash of Tate, with not even the altered catastrophe to account for it—for he restored the death of Lear—manifests the extent of his genius. He had all the qualifications, all the material out of which to build up a great artist, an actor for all the world. He is now only an actor for the less intelligent of the Americans. But he is something better—an upright and well-intentioned man.[1]

October 22nd.—After dinner received some papers sent, kindly of course, by Mr. Povey; in one was an impertinence from that reptile Bunn, extracted from the *Age* newspaper, which made me for a few minutes very angry; but I very soon reasoned myself into perfect indifference to such a creature.

October 23rd.—Acted Macbeth equal, if not superior, as a whole, to any performance I have ever given of the character. I should say it was a noble piece of art. Called for warmly, and warmly received. The Miss Cushman[2] who acted Lady Macbeth interested me much. She has to learn her art, but she showed mind and sympathy with me; a novelty so refreshing to me on the stage. I do not say what the people on papers may say of me, but such a performance would have made any man's fortune in London.

October 25th.—Acted Hamlet, as I think, in a manner that would have obtained for me the highest praise in London. The audience in the stirring scenes seemed much excited, but they did not appreciate the performance sufficiently to call for me. This is a most detestable custom—most especially in the hands of an unrefined auditory. The *Philadelphia Gazette*—with a criticism which was very kind, but seemed more a defence than a challenge—was sent to me, and I read it after the play.

October 26th.—Acted Werner—not well, being much deranged by the people with me, particularly by Mr. G. Vandenhoff, who is too good or too bad for me. It did not seem to have a great success in the theatre. Looked at some papers sent me by P. Butler. The base *Morning Herald* speaks of Mr. Macready's "*failure* at Drury Lane." The wretched miscreant!

October 28th.—Saw some papers; one, signed Barlow, affecting to make a comparative criticism on Mr. Forrest and myself in Macbeth! it was too bad, as the ignorant creature showed in what he was obliged to state that Mr. Forrest did not understand the character; nor does Mr. Forrest understand Shakspeare. *He is not an artist.* Let him be an American actor—and a great American actor—but keep on this

---

[1] This estimate of Forrest's acting and character is especially interesting in view of subsequent occurrences.

[2] Afterwards well-known in London, where she played Romeo to her sister's Juliet.

side of the Atlantic, and no one will gainsay his comparative excellence. Much disgusted. Rested and thought on Richelieu; determined to act it well, if I could, as Mr. Forrest, not handsomely, I think, was put up for the same part on the same night. I did act Cardinal Richelieu—I think well—in such a manner as evidently to produce a great effect on the audience. They made a very *resolute* call for me.

October 30th.—In my performance of Hamlet I suffered a little from what Scott has described as the cause of Campbell's backwardness—I was, if not frightened, certainly flurried at the shadow of my own reputation; the impression of the previous evening had been so strong, I feared to disappoint expectation. It was, however, not a bad performance. The soliloquy ending the second act was very natural, passionate, and good. That on life and death was reality—as my French friends term it, *inspiration.* I never before approached the real self-communing which possessed me during its delivery. The audience fully appreciated, for they applauded until I actually stopped them. Read a leading article that interested me, remonstrating and declaiming—*most justly,* I think—against the servility and unreasonableness of the "Taste Committee" in England for excluding the statue of Cromwell from the *worthies* (God help the mark!—our English kings, etc.!) who are to decorate the halls of our Parliament House. Here is the curse. In England the spirit is servile, the institutions rotten. Here the taste is disgusting, and the laws little more than nominal! One is almost tempted to imprecate with Lear, "Strike flat the thick rotundity of the world; crack nature's moulds, all germins spill at once that make *ungrateful man.*" What is it going to? *Will it ever be better? I begin to despair.* Wallack called; declaimed against Forrest, on whose professional merits I was cautiously silent, whose personal qualities I praised.

October 31st.—Saw some papers, and was disgusted, annoyed and rather alarmed at an intimation of that scoundrel Bennett, that "forty or fifty unfriendly persons could, if they pleased, drive even Mr. Macready from the stage." I quite abandon all idea of settling in this country. The press is made up, with a few exceptions, of such unredeemed scoundrels, and the law is so inoperative that "the spurns which patient merit from the unworthy takes" in England are preferable to the state of semi-civilization here. I disagree with Dickens whilst I quite sympathize with his disgust at these wretches. Lost much time from my state of mind.

November 1st.—Have been much harassed, occupied, irritated, and annoyed by the assaults in certain newspapers. This is weakness, but one to which I think all—*all* are liable. Voltaire and Racine had the honesty to confess that one line of abuse gave them more uneasiness than pages of praise afforded them pleasure. It is true throughout human nature. I could reason myself into conviction for a moment, but what is that to *feeling* ? When I was here before, they attempted (and with really *more* reason) to set up Mr. Forrest as equal to myself, and Mr. Cooper as superior. What has been the fact? Acted Othello in a very grand and impassioned manner, never better. The audience I thought cold at first, but I would not give way to the influence; I sustained the character from the first to the last. Called for and very warmly greeted.

November 2nd.—Pierce Butler called in a state of unsubdued excitement from the play of last night; he seemed quite taken by surprise—as he described the audience to have been. Rested, being very much tired. Felt most *languid*, and unequal to exertion, and can account for many times seeming and being *under the mark* of energy and spirit. But I rallied and determined to do my very best, and I played Cardinal Richelieu uncommonly well; was called for and well received. I *will* henceforward assert myself in my acting. At New York, I fear, it was *I* and not the audience who were to blame— *we will see.*

November 3rd.—Entertained to-day for the first time the idea of remaining in the States until the beginning of October next, *if* my engagements here should turn out as advantageously as I have reason to expect. As this is quite a chance, I shall not let fall any hint of it to any one at home; if I should be successful I may act through the month of June—try to employ the months of July and August in observation and writing, and take my farewell engagements in the month of September, and sail at the beginning of October; " *but all this lies within the will of Heaven!* "

November 4th.—Reflected on my indulgence (not to any great extent, but beyond what I wish for the *prospect* of *health* and *time*) in wine during my performances. Viewing the subject as it bears on the *fine art*—of probable health—of clearness of thought—of consequent languor or heaviness—and therefore of time—and in no slight regard of money, I have resolved to endeavour so to regulate my diet as to reduce very much, if not altogether, the quantity of stimulant I sometimes take during performance. But I must be *most especially cautious* not to let the *spirit* of my acting evaporate with the diminution of alcohol! Paid my bills, which if I can subject to anything near the average of this week will, with God's blessing, enable me to profit largely by the success it may be His will I should enjoy. May I deserve it and obtain it. Paid my weekly bills, which were satisfactorily reasonable. Pierce Butler called; went with him to the Exhibition of Pennsylvanian Academy; not good—very little original; still, it is right to *begin*, but the arts do not *advance* much in the United States. Acted Werner in my best manner, being under no debt to stimulant; called for and well received; *acted very powerfully*. Read a paper in answer to the abuse, which I have not read; it is very kind.

November 6th.—Called on and met Pierce Butler, who went with me up-stairs and left me with Mrs. Butler and Miss Sedgwick. We talked a little while very pleasantly, but upon my observing that she did not do justice to the talents committed to her—that she might do much beside writing powerful plays, that she might in a country like this influence society, etc.—she burst into tears, our conversation became more restrained, and I took leave of her, she appearing anxious to see me again, as, I believe, really regarding me. Rested and thought on Macbeth. Acted Macbeth unequally, but *tried*. Called for. Spoke to Miss Cushman about going to Boston. She would be glad to go for $50—it would be worth my while to give it; I arranged with her.

November 7th.—Read in the papers the news from England— O'Connell's arrest,[1] which I fancy will be a triumph for him; closing of Covent Garden, etc. Saw in the American paper that Mr. N. P. Willis had been distinguishing himself by his abuse of me. Cannot I afford it? In Philadelphia all the Press had taken up against this Colley Cibber, who has been abusing me and every one connected with the Chestnut theatre.

November 9th.—Paid my bill and went down to the quay in a coach, etc., for which I was charged most extortionately, as also by a knavish driver in New York. Republican virtue is not below average, but certainly not above it. Mr. Ryder was on board the boat; from him I collected that the performance of Benedict last night had made a strong impression. He told me much of what he had heard in the bar-rooms, etc.—of persons giving their opinions, etc., on Mr. Forrest, and of the change that had been produced in some of his declaiming advocates. One critic in the earnestness of his advocacy of Mr.

[1] In connection with his agitation for Repeal.

Forrest said to another, who was extolling me for my intellectual qualifications : " Oh ! damn intellect ! " Mr. Forrest's engagement at New York has failed ; as it was got up *in opposition* to me and so *carried through*, I cannot affect regret at it.

Boston, November 10th.—Ryder called in the evening and gave me an account of Mr. Pelby, which seems to promise anything but an agreeable—indeed, a profitable engagement. He is a vulgar man of very indifferent character. He has advertised his daughter for Lady Macbeth—she is reported to be drunken, and Mr. Wallack says does not understand one word of what she says ! I must *do my best*, but this is a dreadful drawback. God speed me ! Amen !

November 11th.—Went to rehearsal of *Macbeth*. Mr. Hamilton, stage-manager, spoke to me of Mr. Pelby's annoyance at my desire that Miss Cushman should act with me, and that he had only just before answered an application of hers to the same effect, declining her assistance ; this I thought had taken place at the beginning of the season, and certainly it gave colour to his reasons for resentment. A few words, however, soon put all things straight, and everything proceeded on a perfect understanding. Received two letters from David Colden, informing me of Forrest's engagement having failed at New York. I wish he had had the tact, if not the chivalrous feeling, to have *made* his course away from me ; as it is, I must of course feel thankful that he is not in the ascendant. Went to Lardner's lecture on Washington, Napoleon, Wellington, etc. ! with transparent illustrations—miserable daubs of pictures and plans ! Poor Lardner ! What I listened to was amusing, but leaning very much to American prejudice, which is not right. What a refuge ! and how is it to end ? Oh God !

November 12th.—Received a *Times* newspaper ; a theatrical notice on the closing of Covent Garden theatre on account of the insubordination of the actors asserts that there is no *great* tragic actor—it may or it may not be assumed that my absence from England excepts me from this vilification of the writer ; but he, evidently to me, does not except me, and I cannot help thinking deals very unjustly by me. But *of course I* should think so. It annoyed me, and sunk my spirits and made me feel, as I was going over Macbeth, *what is the use of all I have done, or can try to do?* I tried to rally my spirits, but it dealt a heavy blow on me. It is disgusting. Note from Miss Cushman, announcing her arrival and wishing to see me. I am in a strange country, and I think it is only a duty to myself to be strictly circumspect. I have not the slightest purpose, dream, or intent of wrong or folly, and therefore I keep it at arm's length. Wrote to her, promising to see her to-morrow, which I will do in the common room.

November 13th.—Looked over Macbeth, being most anxious about my performance. Went to the theatre and rehearsed it; had sad misgivings as to the effect of Lady Macbeth, who does not understand the words she has to speak, and speaks words that no one can understand. After rehearsal saw Miss Cushman, and talked with her a short time. I discharged myself of my obligation to her, paying her $50 in notes. At dinner Longfellow called and invited me to dine tomorrow. Acted Macbeth—how, I really cannot say, but I can assert that I strove unremittingly. I had a drag-chain in Lady Macbeth, but I did all that I could to make an interest independent of her—is that possible? I certainly did much well, and all in earnest, but at the fall of the curtain when some voices called for me there were dissentients—I do not know how I am to interpret this.

November 14th.—Received a note from Miss Cushman in great delight at the performance last night; she described the audience as participating in the enjoyment she experienced. I hope it was so. Mr. Pelby would not allow Miss Cushman to act—*eh bien!* Rehearsed *Hamlet.* These are an awful set of Daggerwoods! Called on Miss Cushman in the common room, declined visiting her in her own. Made several calls. On our way we had called in at the Town House at Cambridge, and seen the process of voting by ballot—nothing could be simpler or more orderly. I went up to the ballot box, and everything was clearly explained to me. Dined with Longfellow; everything very elegant. Mrs. L—— is a very agreeable woman. Felton, Sumner, and Hillard dined with us.

November 15th.—Was nearly four hours and a half rehearsing *Hamlet,* so distressed and crippled am I by the conceit and inefficiency of the players of this company. I begin to fear that with all my anxiety and all my pains I *must* sink under the effect of the contagion of these wretched people. It makes me very wretched; *I have nothing to test myself by.* Acted Hamlet very unsatisfactorily. I cannot account for it; I had thought over several positive improvements, had *determined* to act *up* to my mark, took infinite pains at rehearsal, and at night, but the audience *seemed to escape me.* I heard that in the scenes, where I was not on, the audience applauded the actors in derision, and Heaven knows, they are *too bad;* if this be so, it partly accounts for the tameness in the play's acting, but not sufficiently to satisfy me. I fear it is in myself; God, how I shrink before the thought of becoming feeble and *usé* while obliged to earn my bread!

November 16th.—Waldo Emerson called, and sat with me a short time, expressing his wish to make me acquainted with Mr. and Mrs. Ward, whom he extolled greatly. I liked him very, very much—the simplicity and kindness of his manner charmed me. Mr. Abbott Lawrence called and sat with me some time. I liked him extremely; he invited me. Acted Werner as well as I could, but my intent, meaning, and efforts *paralyzed* by the Ulric, who was imperfect and utterly incapable. I was quite put *hors de moi* in the second act, could not recover myself—did not *know what to do;* the perspiration came out upon my forehead—I never felt myself so lost as to self-possession. Was very angry at the greater part of the performance, though I tried to do my very best. Spoke to Mr. Hamilton, who admitted all; to Mr. Ryder. Thought on what is to be done. The prospect of any future engagements here is gone! Alas!

November 17th.—Note and flowers from Miss Cushman. Read her poem on Babington's conspiracy—very powerful and clever. Acted Cardinal Richelieu in my *very best* style; I quite moved the audience *out of* themselves. I was very animated and real—very much in earnest. Had received a note from Colley Grattan,[1] praying me to come to him to meet General Bertrand and Webster. I thought he made a point of it, and I went. Was introduced to Bertrand; certainly, from appearance, one who could only obtain distinction by the greatness of another—a "growing feather plucked from Cæsar's wing" may be shown as of the eagle kind, but it is only the fidelity of an Eros to an Antony that has given reputation to the kind-hearted little General. He talked very pleasantly—asked me if I had acted at Paris; I told him I had, and reminded him of the period, which he recollected associated with *Virginius.* We talker of Talma, and of the Emperor's partiality to him. I asked him if it was true that they were friends previous to Napoleon's assuming the crown. He said, doubtingly, "No, it was not likely." [2] He told me in reply to my

---

[1] Thomas Colley Grattan (1792–1864); author and journalist, at that time British Consul at Boston.

[2] Nevertheless, Thomas Raikes, in his *Journal*, gives the following letter purporting to have been written by Napoleon to Talma, after the siege of Toulon—

"I have fought like a lion for the Republic. But, my good friend Talma, as my reward I am left to die with hunger. I am at the end of all my resources. That miserable fellow Aubry (the Minister of War) leaves me in the mire when he might do something for me.

"I feel that I have the power of doing more than Generals Santerre and Rossignol, and

inquiries, that Napoleon liked tragedy very much, but comedy little. That he judged well, was a good critic; described his home of retirement, the seat of small social parties in which he indulged and which he preferred; that at one of these a tragedy on Lady Jane Grey was read by Talma; that Napoleon appeared asleep during the reading, but that he gave a clear and critical opinion upon its merits: that if it had developed any truths as to the political state of England, the condition of parties, the influence of religion, or any great effect, it might have been something; but the mere story of Lady Jane Grey— Bah! The play was introduced some time after, but not with success. Was introduced to Cinti Damereau, to Mrs. Otis, who talked French to me for some time, to Bancroft, who seemed very glad to see me, as I was to meet him. Returning home I found a basket of flowers, and a note—in rapture at Richelieu—from Miss Otis.

November 18th.—Called on Miss Cushman and chatted with her some time. She told me of a conversation she had heard between two watchmakers—one of whom had seen Mr. Forrest and myself, the other had not seen me—to convey his idea of the two men, the one observed, "Why, you see Forrest is a watch upon a common lever, and Macready's a chronometer." The more I reflect upon Mr. Forrest's acting and the impression made by myself, the more I am disgusted with the knavery and impertinence of Messrs. Willis and Co. Called on W. Prescott; saw the old Judge, who just came in, shook hands with us, and passed on like an apparition through the room. Sat some time with W. Prescott and his wife, both of whom I liked very much. Dined with Felton, meeting C. Sumner's brother, Jared Sparks, Dr. Beck, Felton's brother, and Longfellow. Mr. Ware and his son came in after dinner.

November 20th.—Webster called and sat a short time. I felt

---

yet they cannot find a corner for me in La Vendée or elsewhere to give me employment. You are happy : your reputation depends upon yourself alone. Two hours passed on the boards brings you before the public whence all glory emanates. But for us soldiers we are forced to pay dearly for fame upon an extensive stage, and after all, we are not allowed to attain it. Therefore, do not regret the path you have chosen. Remain upon your theatre. Who knows if I shall ever appear again upon mine ? I have seen Monvel, he is a true friend. Barras, President of the Directory, makes fine promises, but will he keep them ? I doubt it. In the meantime I am reduced to my last sous. Have you a few crowns to spare me ? I will not refuse them, and promise to repay you out of the first kingdom I win by my sword. How happy were the heroes of Ariosto ; they had not to depend upon a minister of war. Adieu.

"Yours,

"BUONAPARTE."

pained to see him—he looked old, ill and embarrassed. His sun seems
fast setting; how changed from the gay and animated person I met
in Washington at Everett's and Vaughan's—alas! Went to rehearsal
of Othello, which seemed almost hopeless. Letter from Blake of
Philadelphia, one from dear Forster that made me happier. Answered
Ward's note of invitation. Acted Othello resolutely, and I think
fairly, but the support I had *without exception* was *too bad.*

November 21st.—Hillard read Sydney Smith's letter to the *Morning Chronicle*, which would have been good if not disfigured by some
bad temper and therefore some bad taste. Ticknor suggested to me
what he said was widely desired and requested—that I should give
Readings of Shakspeare. I talked over the matter and said I would
consider it. Dined with Grattan; met the Mayor, Brimner, Mr. and
Mrs. Otis, Abbott Lawrence, Commodore Kennequha, Mr. Gore, and
Mr. Sears. Passed a cheerful afternoon. Went to Lawrence's, expecting a small party, as "the death of one of his kindred prevented
him from seeing company "; found his rooms full; was introduced
to *herds.* Saw Ticknor, Gray, Prescott, Curtis, Bancroft, Sears,
Sumner, and most I knew; was introduced to Mrs. Bancroft—one of
the sweetest and prettiest women I ever saw—to Ward, Miss Ward,
Mrs. Chase, very agreeable. Mr. Webster, Mrs. Webster, Miss
Webster; in fact, it is impossible to recollect the very many. All were
very agreeable; would have been more so if I had been a little more a
free agent, but I was a lion, and in good earnest. I talked with a
great many people; in fact, was not one moment unoccupied, for I
was taken away from one to other, as if there was to be a guard against
any preference. I liked almost all the people I saw. Very many
spoke to me of the *Readings*, earnestly and with some persuasive
arguments. Grattan came to me from a body to ask me. It makes
it a subject to think upon.

November 22nd.—Acted Hamlet with resolution against weariness
and weakness, and for the most part very effectively. The daggers
about me are *dire!* One said to the Ghost, "*If thou art privy to thy
country's peace, which happily foreknowing may avoid, speak!* "

November 23rd.—Called on Charles Sumner; saw him and Hillard;
appointed to call on him after rehearsal and go to the Supreme Court
to see Judge Story. Ran through a rehearsal. Called on Sumner and
went with him to the Court. He showed me first a magistrate's court
—very superior to our magistrates' courts in England in point of comfort, cleanliness and general accommodation—*beyond the possibility*

238

of denial. In the Supreme Court Judge Story was presiding; he came off the Bench to speak to us, and most warmly greeted me. His manner is pleasing beyond that of most men—gentle, dignified, and hearty, he wins at once upon our respect and affection; he impressed me most strongly with the character of exceeding amiability. Went into the Criminal Court, where a trial was proceeding for violation of the Sabbath. In both these courts the arrangement for a double jury struck me as a great convenience. The accommodation also for the jury and for the counsel is infinitely superior to the models of excellence which English writers would persuade us are alone to be found in England. The juries I saw empanelled in three courts were *most respectable* men—certainly in dress and appearance above our average common juries, so much so that I inquired if they were not *special*, and learned they were not. There is a very comfortable arm-chair for each juryman—twelve on each side of the court, and when one jury retires to consult upon its verdict, a fresh cause is called on, and the opposite jury are proceeded with. There are no wigs on judge or counsel. Judge Story, as Chief Justice of the Supreme Court, wears a black gown, the only distinction of costume in the administration of justice; but there were no reproofs of the judge to any persons in court for indecorum, or noise—no interruption, nothing to disturb the gravity of the process. It was grave, reverend and, may I not say, potent to good. I saw the records of the causes, which are entered in books, volumed, numbered and indexed, and seem to me simpler and less expensive than our parchment rolls. Went to the Registry of *Deeds*, which enables the man of business to ascertain the perplexing—often destructive—question of *title* at once. Passed on to the Mayor's office. No business was going on, but I was pleased with the arrangement of this little Parliament of the Muncipality—all the city business under one roof, and all so well, so very commodiously, handsomely and yet economically laid out for business—quite fitting a great Republican City. Continued our walk to look at the market, which is an excellent one, a very long alley down the building, each side of which is occupied by roomy stalls of the various vendors of marketable viands. Old Faneuil Hall—the " cradle of liberty "—I did not go into. We went to the Exchange Room, a very handsome one, where all the papers are on labelled desks, that lead you to that you seek. I called on Miss Cushman, talked with her a little, and took leave of her most kindly, but without the slightest indication that our acquaintance is to become more intimate. She kissed my hand, but I was only kind. I sent her afterwards the verses she had lent me. Sumner left with a card a note from Mrs. Cary to him, inquiring about my nights of performance. I answered it. Rested, thinking a little—a very little—of Richelieu. No news of my letters from home! It begins to be very trying to my patience. I talked with Sumner very much to-day about the *Readings*. He discussed the matter quite in a business-like way—the pros and cons—which is the proper way to get at the probable results. On the score of profit, he talked of two evenings producing me *$2000, i. e.* £400, a sum, if doubled, to make one pause. The consideration of his plan of lecturing involves of course my prolonged stay in this country. . . . Acted Cardinal Richelieu with much effort, struggling and at last *battling* against the odious and disgusting contagion of these senseless drones and beetles that go *buzz*-ing about the scene. Succeeded, though not in pleasing myself, yet in exciting the audience. Spoke to Ryder about his acting. He had brought me an account from Mr. Pelby to-day of the auction for boxes, which was really shameful. Desired him to tell Mr. Hamilton that if it was a humbug, I would not be a party to it, but would expose it and give my share to some charity of the city.

November 25th.—On this day three years it was God's will that my sweet child, my darling Joan, should be taken from us. I feel as if she still had being, and look upon that heavenly face as it lay before me like a cherub's in tranquil beauty and innocence. I feel as if in becoming a tenant of the grave I should have companionship with her. Blessed be her sweet spirit!

November 26th.—C. Sumner dined with me, and we went together to Cambridge. Called on Longfellow, and sat some time with him and Mrs. L——. Went to Judge Story's; passed a most agreeable evening there; met Felton, Jared Sparks, Professors Beck and Williams, Mrs. and Miss Story, Mr. William Story and his wife, Judge Foy, etc. A most lively and pleasant evening.

November 27th.—Acted Virginius in a very superior manner. Went with Summer and Felton to the Oyster Saloon Concert Hall, where Hillard joined us. Supped on broiled oysters, with some of the ingenious and beautifully composed—I should say *constructed*— drinks that are conspicuous in this country. We had a very agreeable evening—at least, I had.

November 28th.—Acted Werner fairly; but there *never was* such an Ulrich—such a wretch—as the man in this company is. Received two papers with well-written articles; in one it was copied from a

New York paper that Miss Cushman was to accompany me in my Southern tour and then go to London and appear under my auspices. This is really too bad—without a shadow of truth.

November 29th.—Quite worn down by fatigue and want of sleep. Not well; rose late, and spoke to Ryder about attending the rehearsal for me. What should I have done without him? I could not have got through. Went on the stage to act and was taken all aback on seeing the pit not more than half full. I *tugged* against it—right nobly—recollected afterwards that it was the Eve of *Thanksgiving Day*. All was explained. I acted very vigorously; called for.

New York, December 4th.—Rehearsed *Melantius*—the play in a wretched state; Miss Cushman, who had her part when I was in Philadelphia, *reading!*—knowing nothing of what she had to do! How can there be artists when this lady, one of the most intelligent and ambitious, so entirely disregards the duties of her calling? Amintor—*reading!!*—without a remote guess at the meaning of his part! The drama is declining do people say!—*what drama?*

December 5th.—Talked with Miss Cushman about her want of energy and purpose in studying her art. She made the *usual* excuses. She told me that Mrs. Butler was literally wretched, that Butler's feeling to her was absolute aversion; I do not know her authority for saying so much—that Mrs. Butler had written to her that the only consoling reflection on her birthday was, that another year of wretchedness being gone, she was so much nearer its termination. Miss Cushman said that but for her children, she would go on the stage again. *That would not do.*

December 6th.—Acted Melantius—unequally, some parts good, in others felt a want of strength, in others was cut up by the people (particularly by the person acting Archas, the jailer; this man was conspicuously absurd and deficient) with me — Miss Cushman particularly.

December 7th.—Acted Werner very fairly—in some parts well. Was called for. Went to Astor's, a very magnificent house—spacious rooms, most richly and elegantly furnished, and a large number of persons of a really fashionable appearance, really elegantly-looking persons. I asked young Astor if there were many Europeans there; he said not. I saw Count Montalto there, who it seems has been staying at New York, Halleck, Murray, Davis, etc. I was tired, and felt that it was a place for *young* people to enjoy, and I have long ceased to mingle with them.

December 8th.—Went to the rehearsal of Benedict; was much dissatisfied with several. Saw enough of the unsteadiness of Miss Cushman to perceive that the *first* qualification of an artist is not there. She was speaking to me of Mrs. Butler, with whom she naturally sides in the question of disagreement with her husband; she ascribes the unhappiness to arise from his fickleness and infidelity; but I have seen enough to satisfy me that there has been enough at home to drive a loving heart from home. I admire her and like much in her, but she is unhappy in not being aware of the profit and the delight of conciliating. Forrest called after dinner. He told me that Catherine had written to him. Answered Sedgwick. Acted Benedict as well as I could to an indifferent house, who seemed much pleased. Was called for. David Colden came into my room. Spoke to Mr. Barry. *That idiot—imbecile—Mr. Simpson—has ruined this engagement. God grant that in this he may not have ruined that to come!*

December 9th.—Looked at some American Saturday papers, which state that Miss Cushman more than shared the applause of the audience with me in the *Bridal.* If it was so, I never heard one hand of it. She is an *intriguante,* I fear, a very double person. Dined with Griffin; met Prescott, Hall, J. Hamilton, Barclay, Pryor, Dr. Francis, Girard, etc. An American dinner: terapin soup, bass-fish, bear, wild turkey, canvas-back duck, roasted oysters, etc. Delicious wines; a very agreeable day.

December 11th.—A long letter from Mr. Marshall, the Philadelphia manager, proposing to me, and evidently thinking he had hit upon a most brilliant device: to act at Philadelphia in the spring " on alternate nights the same plays with Mr. Forrest." Monday, Hamlet, Mr. Macready; Tuesday, Hamlet, Mr. Forrest; Wednesday, Othello, Mr. Macready; Thursday, Othello, Mr. Forrest, etc. I answered him, of course declining. Felt very low and unwell. Rehearsed the greater part of *King Lear,* but saw that its performance would be discreditable and do *me* thereby injury in my last engagement. The treasurer came to tell me that the people would not take places for *Much Ado*—he affected to throw it on Miss Cushman, but I suppose they do not understand it or do not like it. I am agreeable, and changed to-morrow's play to *Werner.* Went home to devise some substitute for *King Lear.* Ryder came in and suggested *Marino Faliero.* I considered it, and found it the best thing to be done. Acted Melantius fairly; called for. They called for Miss Cushman here, who gets puffed in the papers—very absurdly.

CHARLOTTE CUSHMAN

From an engraving of a Daguerreotype

December 13th.—Ryder came in. I asked him to get a newspaper for me. He inquired if Miss Cushman had asked me to play for her Benefit on Saturday, which he had previously in the morning told me was her intention. I told him *no*. He said he had communicated to her how displeased and angry I should be at any application of the sort, but she said she should write to me and ask me. I was very angry. He had also told me that Mr. Hunt wished me to act for his wife's Benefit. My anger cooling (who ever does right in anger?), I thought of a mode of dealing with Miss Cushman. At the theatre sent for Mr. Hunt, asked him about his request, which he admitted, and I in the kindest manner explained to him that it was not possible, etc., but that if I did for any I would for him. I thus have fixed Miss Cushman. Acted Cardinal Richelieu and was cut up root and branch by the actors. I was anxious to play well and worked against successive annoyances. Was called for—and so was Miss Cushman !!! Much flattered! Pah! Wrote a letter to dear Forster.

December 17th.—Povey called and took the books of *Werner, Macbeth,* and *Richelieu* for New Orleans; he informed me of the rapacity of Mr. Ole Bull and his bear-leader. They seem drunk with their success in this country, which is evidently far beyond their expectations.

Boston, December 22nd.—Called on Pierce Butler, and on Mrs. Butler, they are separated. She talked much to me. My fingers are too sore and weary to note down to-night her conversation. Both, as is always the case, are to blame.

December 23rd.—Acted Melantius—indifferently well. Called for and made my bow. My money for the night's performance not forthcoming! This is my first experience of the scoundrel managers of the States—Pennsylvanian Repudiators! I desired that Mr. Ryder might be paid; but I did not learn if they had two-fifths of the requisite quantity of honesty. Went to a *Wistar-party* at Mr. Wharton's; it was a noisy standing-up supper with little to attract or make it agreeable. I remember Dr. Chapman used to boast of these parties. I do not think they bear out his commendations. At my hotel I found a letter from Miss Cushman, detailing all—and *much more* than was true —that I had not let drop before Mr. Ryder on the subject of her Benefit at New York. It is too bad that I am to be tormented thus. I answered her letter.

Baltimore, December 25th.—Rehearsed Macbeth, and oh! the rehearsal!—nothing, nothing like scene or property or trap, or movement on the stage—and the actors! I looked at it all with complacent despair, resolving to try and play my best for my own sake, but expecting a bad house, and feeling very low about the whole affair. Coming to my hotel I wrote to dear Forster. Old Mr. Barnum, a very well-mannered old man, came in and sat some time with me; talked very intelligently, but did not raise my hopes of success here, as he described the population quite priest-ridden—his own wife among the rest. Continued and finished my letter to Forster. Prompter came to apologize to me for "*no* supernumeraries." Acted with peculiar discrimination, feeling, and energy, and I think quite roused the intellectual among the audience. They called for me.

December 26th.—Looked at a Baltimore paper—one upon a file, saw in it an extract from the New York Herald—the grossest puff of Mr. Ole Bull; looking over the file saw several others; looked if my own name was there—not once in the file of papers. Went to the theatre. The afternoon had been and the night was very wet; the house was wretched—so Ryder came to inform me. Mr. Richings asked to speak to me—I guessed his object, it was to ask if I would play, as there probably would not be more than $100, or dismiss the audience. I said I would play if there were 100 cents. I acted Werner with every possible drawback—Stralenheim very bad, Idenstein, Ida and Ulric greatly imperfect. Oh, what a life for reasoning man to live, and yet, with these "hostages to fortune," what to do? I was very unhappy—all seemed to go against me.

December 27th.—Not feeling well and in very low spirits; quite depressed; the house last night spoke much to me—it seemed the title-page to a tragic volume. I could not rally against it. Went to rehearsal, having vainly striven against my dejection. Rehearsed Richelieu. Our house last night was $110. Ole Bull's concert, they say, had 260 people, so that perhaps one should not be very discontented in a city, proverbial through the Union for poor encouragement to art. Spoke with Ryder about our journey. Rested. Letter from Miss Cushman—oh! I do not like thee, Dr. Fell!

December 28th.—Acted Hamlet. Cut up from the beginning to the end—striving, struggling, vainly against the *wretches* that were sent on with me. I never remember anything worse. Polonius in a *bag*-wig of King Charles—not speaking three lines of the text consecutively—Horatio speaking *my* speches! and acting, as if on purpose, to annoy me; Rosencrantz and Guildenstern cutting out and making nonsense of the dialogue. Altogether disgraceful.

1844

To Charleston, January 1st.—Woke at an early hour in the steamboat, as, after a tranquil night and rapid run, we were approaching the Charleston light. Offered up my prayers to God for help and sustainment through the year which this day begins, and wishing to my beloved wife and family a happy new year, and many renewals of it. Prayed for these blessings on them. Dressed and went on deck, which was a relief to me after the disturbed night I had passed, haunted with imaginations of all kinds of dreadful possibilities. The morning was most beautiful, the first gleams of sunlight just beginning to break in upon the grey as I went upon the upper deck ; I watched the glory of the sunrise, and the growing objects as we neared the city, rejoicing and grateful for our safe arrival. Came on at once to my hotel, where Mr. Forbes soon called. The anticipated, indeed announced, arrival of Mr. Ole Bull made him doubtful as to the prudence of his course ; he wanted to make out of both of us if he could. Feeling from the puffery that Mr. Ole Bull must disturb my engagement, I gave my opinion that it would be best to defer my appearance one week. After long talking and deliberation and other counsel he decided on it.

January 2nd.—One good, I hope, if no more, will result from my visit to America—it will assure me, certify me, of what figures, face, the appearance of others, all things have failed sufficiently to impress upon me, viz. that I am far advanced in life—with Othello, "declined into the vale of years." I must endeavour to keep this before me in my words and actions, and let them bear the impress of my own consciousness ; for, at present, I am too much the creature of habit in allowing myself to be subject to a retiring and deprecatory style that only properly becomes a young man. I do not feel old in mind, however I may perceive a diminution of my bodily strength, but I must be careful not to let age overtake me. Continued my work, completing it, on my year's books. Mr. Ryder called to show me some further mendacious puffs by Mr. Bennett of Mr. Ole Bull,

245

in which he by a gross falsehood sacrifices the reputation of Cinti and Artot, and makes a darkling thrust at me. Called at Mr. Miller's, bookseller, to look for Dr. Irving, who had been anxious to see me. He met us as we were leaving the shop, and we were introduced. His frank, hearty greeting made me feel friends with him directly; he was at Rugby, a junior boy, when I was in the sixth form; boarded at Moore's; remembered me speaking the closet scene in *Hamlet* and a speech from *Livius*. The air was humid, but so mild that my spirits felt its influence. It was to me an exhilarating sight, which I stopped to enjoy, to see various kinds of roses in full bloom in a garden with the bulbous plants, and the hollyhocks, wild orange, etc., in healthy leaf, with several tropical plants.

January 3rd.—Took a long walk down Meeting Street, along the Battery, to top of Broad Street beyond the boundary, returning by King Street; was delighted with the warm sunshiny day, the fresh air, the foliage of the wild orange, the palmetto, the roses in bloom, the violets, the geraniums, etc., but was pained to see the coloured people go out of the way and show a deference to us as to superior beings. The white houses, with their green verandahs and gardens, were light and lively to me, and the frequent view of the river afforded often a picturesque termination to the street.

January 4th.—Irving called and sat some time. He told me he had written a notice of me for Saturday, which he had finished with the incident of the " child." [1] I told him " it was not true." He was surprised, but said " Never mind, it will do for our religious people," and was earnest to use it. I objected to it that as I never had practised humbug I should not like now to begin. After some demur, he relinquished it.

January 5th.—Spoke with Ryder, who gave me an account of a conversation with Ole Bull yesterday at dinner—which exhibits him as a most rapacious, avaricious, spiteful and envious man; he would deprive poor Artot (who seems to make little enough) of the little that he may glean, if he were not tied down by his engagements and would *follow him at once* (" the d—d fellow," as he calls him) to the Havannah : he will break or evade, he says, his engagement at New Orleans by a quibble—which he cannot do—and will either ruin Schubert, or he shall ruin him. In fact, he is quite as extravagant as a beggar on horseback; he is a quack, and a very evil-minded and

[1] An apocryphal account of a thrilling "rescue" exploit by Macready, which the Press was constantly publishing in spite of his emphatic disclaimers.

bad-hearted one : a fit subject for the eulogy of Mr. Bennett. Read some pages of the history of the Church—the very commencement of which is sufficient to show that "*The Church*" as calling itself the outward or visible sign, or the embodiment of Christianity, or the traditional assembly from the early Christians, is a gross imposture.

January 6th.—Received a note, a very kind one, from Dr. Irving, telling me that by an inadvertency the paragraph with the anecdote of "the child" had been kept by the compositors in the paper, and begging me not to notice it. Now I cannot like this, nor can I close my lips upon a falsehood that gives me consideration to which I am not entitled. I rehearsed Hamlet, taking pains with it. Judge King called for me, and asked me to accompany him to Ogilby's, where we both were to dine. I was much pleased to go with him. At Ogilby's I met Pettigrew, a lawyer, very clever and very humorous. Looked at the papers, and was sickened with the sentimental puffery of Mr. N. P. Willis over the catgut of Ole Bull.

January 7th.—Dined with Judge King ; was amused at dinner with a negro boy whose sole business was with a long feather brush to beat away the flies from the viands at table. After the ladies had retired, I introduced again the subject of the General who had shot deliberately a young man, said to have seduced his daughter, and whom an editor of this city had justified, saying that no judge or jury would find him guilty, and in fact extolling, not lamenting and palliating by circumstances the murder. The two judges, King and Chivers, both seemed to admit that of right it was a case beyond the law, and in short virtually *justified the act against the law*. Now this I cannot understand. Either the law is undisputed sovereign—it is supreme— or it is worse than nothing : when the sentence of the law is pronounced the arm of power may be extended in mercy to prevent its execution on account of extenuating circumstances ; but if such deeds as these and *practising for duels* are to be admitted as usage by the law, give me bondage before *such freedom*. Chivers said that the law was not duly enforced, but that the particular comfort of the people did not make it necessary among them ! ! ! Slavery, legalized duelling with due preparation, and deliberate assassination—um ! "*must give us pause.*"

January 8th.—Acted Hamlet, I scarcely know how. I strove and fought up against what I thought the immobility of the audience ; I would not be beaten cravenly, but such a performance is never satisfactory—at least to the actor. When he is contending with the

247

humour of his audience, adieu then to all happy moments; to all forgetfulness of self, to the *élan* of enthusiasm. I died game, for I tried to sustain myself to the last. Called for.

January 9th.—Ryder called in, and gave me some information respecting the audience of last night, and further that Vieuxtemps passed through (I saw his fiddle-case) this morning on his way to New Orleans.

January 10th.—Rose in very depressed spirits. My thoughts wander onward to painful possibilities in the chances of my life, that, for my blessed children's sake, bear down my energies. The main cause of all this is that *dreadful defect* in *my education*, having had no guide, no proper adviser to lead me to understand the value of money and the care of it. *I am shocked* when I think of the sums I have received for my labour, and the miserable balance that is left in my hands. What can I do? To lose my resolution in despondency and repining would be to make worse what is bad. I will endeavour in economy to repair, as far as is left me, the improvidence of the past, and labour with untiring energy to improve the prospects of the future. Went to rehearsal of *Macbeth*, with which I took pains, but in which I felt excessive weariness even to pain—is it " the coming on of time," etc.? *Dined lightly—which I will never omit to do again, when I have to act; it is due to myself, to my reputation, to my pecuniary interest, to my dear children's welfare. I will never trifle with my duty in this respect again.* Acted Macbeth with great care and great energy; before an applauding audience the perform-ance would have made a sensation. The treasurer brought me the return of the house, which was *exceedingly* good, when the very bad weather of the whole day is taken into account.

January 12th.—Dr. Irving called for me. We went to the gaol—it is a very small building—for both debtors and felons, who are, however, apart. It was very clean. I saw the negro crew of a ship locked up together until the sailing of the vessel, the law of the State not allowing them to be at liberty. I saw some prisoners for minor offences; one had been whipped for petty larceny; some negroes below who were kept in the premises of the gaol till they could be sold! Good God! is this right? They are an inferior class of man, but still they are *man*. They showed me the condemned cells; one in which a murderer had spent his last night last summer. The world is a riddle to me; I am not satisfied with this country as it at present is. I think it will, it must, work out its own purification. But at

present it is not high in its moral tone—vide *New York American* on
" *English fashions* "—referring to *repudiation*, etc.; it is very low
in taste—*vide et audi passim;* and in general refinement, of course,
it must be behind Europe—thought to be, and I think *must be* a great
country—great in arts, in literature, in its moral elevation. Irving
told me of a paper, *Patriot*, that had been writing against me—he
described it as speaking of me being deficient in muscular power, and
seemingly it was a sort of *Forrest* article. I did not care about it.

January 13th.—Read of a Mr. Rives, with a gang of negroes,
ripping up two and a half miles of the Norfolk and Roancha
Railroad ! ! ! These instances of defiance to the LAW are what stagger
those who hope well for self-government. *I pause.* Ogilby called,
and confidentially related circumstances of great atrocity occurring
in this State. An overseer, against his master's orders, flogging
a runaway negro, tying him up all night, getting up in the night to
repeat the torture, and repeating it till the wretched creature died
under the lash. The felon was acquitted. A person supposed by
another to trench upon ground which he claimed, was, in the midst
of his own labourers, shot dead by the villain in open day; the felon
was acquitted ! These are heart-sickening narratives. Judge King
called for me and took me to Chancellor Dunkin's, where the judges
of the State met to dine. I was introduced to all. Chivers I knew,
Chancellor Harper, Judge Butler; Johnson I liked best. About
eighteen or twenty dined; here was no want of character or manner,
nor of any needful gravity or grace befitting a meeting of republican
judges. I could not help feeling that these judges of a country
asserting itself free were waited on by slaves !

January 14th.—Ryder informed me that Mr. N. P. Willis, in
his Washington letter, stated that " Mr. Macready was continuing
his course southward, his attraction diminishing as he proceeded."
What a miserable reptile must this be ! Despicable for the malice
that would suggest the circulation of an injurious statement, *even
if true*, but pitiable when his malignity is driven to falsehood for its
indulgence. I should be very blameable to allow myself to be
irritated by the meanness of such a pitiful person.

January 15th.—Much depressed on rising this morning—I do not
know whether from my state of body or mind. My spirits, however,
were very low, and I was quite unequal to make any effort with the
rehearsal. I begin to *feel my labour* very much. I trust and hope
in God this is not the decay of strength, or *what am I to do ?* Acted

Othello—not well. I tried and began with great spirit—or great effort—but was thrown out of my feeling by the very *outré* people about me, and became very indifferent, and longing for the play to end long before the end of the play. It was one of my *bad nights* of Othello.

January 16th.—Another day of rain, rain, rain. "The heavens do frown upon me for some ill;" but I do not feel as if through my life they would ever smile again. The glimpse of bright hope and comfort which I received in the commencement of my career in this country is now overgloomed, and I have little prospect onward but of hard labour and indifferent payment. I am not young enough to live on hope, for the period over which my hope has to extend is very short. I try to cheer and fortify myself, but I fear it is a lost game. At all events I begin often to feel very, very weary of it. I have no pleasure here but in thinking I am making means for my family, and when that is scanted I am "poor indeed." Looked at the paper. Rehearsed Claude Melnotte. Acted Claude Melnotte in a fractional sort of manner. Cut up repeatedly by the bad taste, etc., of the actors.

January 17th.—Rehearsed *Virginius*, hopeless of producing any effect with such a Virginia and Icilius. Irving called. Saw a Rev. Mr. Case—the only clergyman in the country who has *dared* to attend my performances. Continued the reading of *My Neighbours;* was deeply affected by much of it, and greatly interested with all. Thought of home and dearest Catherine; kissed her dear picture and blessed her and all. The book did me good, if only in the desire to do right, and the resolution to try to do it. I was much impressed by many painful truths, but valuable as all truth must be, I felt how justly merited by myself was the scourge contained in this passage: "Bad humour, the demon with which little souls often tyrannize over those about them." I suffer—oh, what anguish and what shame!—from this vice of temper. I had once made progress in improving, but care and too much commerce with the world has caused me to relapse to moroseness and impatience. May God forgive me. Acted Virginius with all the effect I could make against *distressing* inattention and inefficiency.

January 19th.—Ryder came to speak on business. Ran through the rehearsal of *Hamlet*. The day was really beautiful, the air quite delightful, delicious, at once inspiriting and mild. Both the windows of my sitting-room were wide open; I do not know when I have felt more pleasure from the influence of atmosphere. Called on Irving and walked with him to slave-market, where no business was doing. Could not please myself in the performance of Hamlet with all the pains I could take. Ryder, as the Ghost, got upon the trap and could just get out the words "pale his ineffectual fire." When he had finished, the trap ran down and he disappeared, to his own consternation as much as mine. Was called for and got very well through an address of about half-a-dozen lines. If I do not keep watch upon myself I shall lose my art and power. Irving, Pringle and Ogilby came into my room and seemed very sorry to part with me; there is quite an excitement about the theatre; the house to-night overflowed. This has been a great engagement under the circumstances.

January 20th.—Began the day with packing my private wardrobe. Went on board the small boat that was crowded with the players and their luggage, even to the gong and, I think, the big drum. I was interested by the view of the bay and the vessel alongside of us with the negro women grinding off the rice husks and loading the hold by means of hand-mills. The morning was thick as if from heat, but the water was smooth as glass, and the passage out of the harbour was full of interest to me. Previous to going on board had received a present of six bottles of Madeira for my voyage from Mr. Pringle. Was amused on my way to the vessel by the observation of a sort of *conducteur*, that I had a "very clever house last night." Ryder told me that the excitement after the play was something quite extraordinary, the southern blood seemed to have been excited to fever pitch; it has been an unusual enthusiasm. One passenger, a planter, talked to me of his views, his desire to mix in political life, his treatment of his negroes, and his account of his resenting the contumacy of one and afterwards whipping him, giving him three hundred lashes. I thought to myself I would not have held property on such a tenure. I expressed to him, not offensively, my objection to the system. He explained to me the partial, and of course unjust operation of the tariff as affecting the interests of North and South, and the case of the Southern States is hard. It grew dark after we passed the lighthouses, and the merchant ships lying at anchor before the river's mouth. There were burning woods in different parts along the banks, and we went on our dark way between narrow banks till we reached the window lights of Savannah. Costas met me on the boat; he accompanied me to the Pulaski House; the landlord, Captain Wiltberger (I had a true instinct at the name), was standing at the door.

I was introduced, of course shook hands, and a stiffnecked old piece of fat importance I found him; he could not give me my meals in my room, then I could not stay; then he led to several rooms, all indifferent, and I finally took a double-bedded room.

Savannah, January 22nd.—Rested. Acted Hamlet pretty well; these are not theatres for Shakespeare's plays! Walked home in darkness, not visible; quite a journey of difficulty through deep sand, and threading a way through posts, etc. Costas came and spoke to me.

January 23rd.—Quite knocked up by the *actors* in my endeavour to play Macbeth. *Violent rain as the doors were opened.* A feeling of how little of enjoyment was left to me in life! I can do nothing more in my profession—I fear I can do nothing of any moment for my dear children. In fact, it seems to me, upon real examination, as if my death would benefit them much more than my life can. I am unhappy—I see no chance of happiness for me in this world. The causes may be in myself, but I fear they are beyond my power of removal. God help me. It is a despairing prayer—but God help me! It is not well or wise to look with despondency or gloom upon the future, but how hard it is to regard with complacency or equanimity a painful and embarrassing condition, which we are obliged to ascribe to our own want of conduct! Had I been reasonably economical, I might now be in the possession of a fortune that would make me indifferent to the accidents that now fret and depress me. In my present position the sole object of my labour and travel is money—money for my children's education and after maintenance. Every occurrence that diminishes my receipts weighs down my heart. There was a prospect of *large gains* in this country during my early engagements here. The dissipation of my hopes in this respect has taken away much of my mind's elasticity—which I must try to reason back again, but——

January 24th.—My spirits were very much depressed. I was not quite well, and suffering from the exertion and the temperature of last night. Spoke with Mr. Ryder. The treasurer called and paid me. The day was wretched; a deluge was descending the entire morning: *densissimus imber!* I could not go out; looked at the papers, and began a letter, which occupied me all day, to my dear Lydia Bucknill. Rested a short time. Acted Cardinal Richelieu very fairly.

January 25th.—Packed up as far as I could for my journey to

New Orleans. Walked down below the bluff, and saw the places of business, etc.; admired the novel appearance of the street upon the face of the bluff, planted as it is with trees and looking over an extent of lowland, river and sea. Was accosted by a rough person, who gave his name Nichols, whom I heard say—to the observation that " Crowds were hurrying down below "—" They need not be in such a hurry; the duel is not to be till twelve." I turned round and looked with amazement in his face. " How do you do, sir? " he answered to my surprised and shocked gaze. " Did you say a duel was to be fought? " " Oh yes; just over the water, but not before twelve." " And can such a thing be publicly known, and no attempt on the part of the legal authorities to interfere? " " Oh Lord, no, they dursn't; they've too many friends about them for any number of officers that could be got together to have any chance with them." " And are the crowds going down to see them fight? " " No; they go to wait for the news—it's across the river they fight." " Do they fight with pistols? " " I don't know; either pistols or rifles—but they generally fight with rifles in this part of the country." " Um! " " They are two gentlemen of the Bar here. It was a quarrel in Court: one said, ' the lie was stamped in the other's face,' so there was a challenge. . I suppose you don't do such a thing as take a glass of wine in the morning? " " Oh no, never." " Ah, well, it's our way; just come in and see the reading-room; it's the best room in all the South; come, it's just here." I complied with the importunity of my new acquaintance, who informed me all about himself, but my stomach felt sick with horror at the cold-blooded preparation for murder with which he acquainted me.

Macon, January 26th.—On going into the hall of the hotel about five o'clock met a Bostonian waiting for the omnibus; we all went to the depôt, where, in the open air, we had to pay in at a window, on a very dark cold morning, our fares—my amount, $39. I got on the car, but stopped on entering to look at a crowd of human beings, mostly wrapped in blankets, standing together near. A fellow on the opposite box, for it was of a very inferior grade even to the wretched cars provided for white travellers, called out, " Let the boys and women come first." They went one by one—a long and miserable train—the men entering last. These were slaves who had been bought on speculation and were being conveyed up the coast to be put up for sale in about a fortnight. I looked in occasionally to their box, and there they were in double rows; food was served out to them, and I saw a woman cut off a portion of the meat given to her, and with an expression of the strongest disgust throw it away. Mr. Ryder asked, it seems, one of the men where he was going; his answer was, "Oh, God knows, sir!" I cannot reconcile this outrage on every law of right; it is damnable. Our road lay through one vast stretch of pine-barren, greater or less, swamps, large pools of water stretching to great extent through the woods, beautiful foliage often intermingling with the stems of the tall pines, that presented every state of the tree from early growth to decay and rottenness—many half burned, many taken by their tops by whirlwind, many felled, uprooted, others propped or falling, reminding one of a scene of carnage after a battle. I slept some part of the way, but occupied myself chiefly with reading Brougham's remarks on the French Revolution, etc. They amused me very much; and often I concurred with him though he keeps out of sight or very imperfectly shows the great cause of that event—viz. the *necessity* there was for it in the oppression of the people and the profligacy of the Church and aristocracy. We did not reach Macon till nearly ten o'clock, when we found a large inn, with a very respectable and civil landlord. But it is curious what important persons these landlords generally are: they receive you much more like hosts that are going to give you shelter and entertainment than as innkeepers who are served and obliged by the preference of your custom. But this man was an exception. I got a bedroom with a comfortable bed, a chair, table, glass, and what made amends for many deficiencies, a capital wood fire. After a sorry supper I was very glad to get early to bed.

January 27th.—Rose early. Thompson brought me a letter from a Mr. —— to the stage-coach agent at Griffin, which I felt as a great civility: it requested attention from Mr. Jones, "for Mr. Macready and suite," which amused me not a little. This was a day of western travel. We were at least an hour behind our time of starting, and the passengers actually *crowded* the carriage; the dirty and ragged neighbourhood that one is forced to endure is very distasteful, to say the least. It is not to be asserted that civilization has reached these remote parts: it is forcing its way, it is clearing. But "the gentlemen"—the raggedest ruffian with a white skin receiving that appellation—need its enforcement very much. The town of Macon is a straggling, growing place, with some very good houses and an imposing building, that of the bank. The country, too, which is now hill and dale, is greatly improved, widely cultivated, growing cotton and corn,

254

and often presenting very agreeable landscapes. The effect of the frost, for we have had much ice yesterday and to-day, on the porous sands and sandstone, was often very beautiful in its glassy feathery appearance. Our journey was most disastrous; up to one o'clock we had progressed at the rate of four miles an hour; at one of our stoppages all hands turned out and pushed our car and engine. Our dinner, with coffee served by the *lady* of the house at the head of the table, was much the same as yesterday, Mr. Ryder observing to me, "If Mrs. Macready could see you, sir." After dinner the stoppages became so frequent, and I so chilled, that I asked to walk, and walked with Ryder and another about three miles. They stopped, as there was no supply, to chop the wood by the roadside to keep the fire of the engine alight! The man at last said that the engine would not make steam, and I was in despair of reaching Griffin to-night. At last, however, the many choppings brought us to a station where we got wood and water, and proceeded tolerably well, reaching Griffin about half-past eight, instead of eleven this morning. My amusement through the day has been Brougham's book. Arrived at Griffin, I asked for a bedroom, and I am now in it, with a wood fire before me that just reaches one strip of me, whilst all the rest of my body is sore with cold. The room, as the house is, is of new wood, the chimney brick, not even plastered, no carpet, no lock to the doors, one nailed up for the occasion, the other buttoned. One table, one chair, the wind blowing in all directions into the place. My supper, temperance supper, I could not eat; I could not cut the meat, and ate three eggs. In short, it is as uncomfortable as it well can be; but I must be thankful that I am not out all night, and so, blessing God for His mercies and invoking His blessing on my beloved wife and children, I go to my uncomfortable-looking bed.

Griffin, January 28th.—Kindled my fire, and made as comfortable a toilet as I could in this shivering room. Its walls are single boards, and through the chinks of their joinings and occasional splinters the keen frosty air whistles in; the skirting is completed, except that at the doors (there are three) are unfilled apertures, which give me views into two rooms below. The door is fastened by a button inside, and another opening to a bedroom for four or eight people, as it may happen, has been nailed up on my account, being buttonless. The unplastered brick chimney holds a good wood fire, that carries heat to one side of me, the other freezing with cold, and my writing-hand is nearly disabled with sensations of numbness. There have been knots

in the deal walls whose vacancies now admit the draft. Every word
of all my neighbours is distinctly heard, and there is a large family in
the room below : one chair, one little table, a broken jug and small
basin, no looking-glass, an old broken sash-window, a trunk of the
resident lodger and a few of his books and instruments—he is a civil
engineer—are scattered about this domestic desolation. The room,
not being ceilinged, is open at the top between the beams. I look out
on a rough sort of flat, scattered over which one might count, perhaps,
sixty or seventy houses; stumps, of course, everywhere except on the
railway that terminates opposite. At a little distance I read on a small
one-storey house, " Broadway Exchange." Bags of cotton lie profusely
scattered about the railway. A picture of one among many of these
germs, populous towns pushed by these pushing people into existence
and name. Around is the everlasting wood. Some signs are on cloth,
instead of board. Trees and stumps alternating through the city, and
cotton, cotton everywhere. After my attempt to make a breakfast
I sought out the persons who were to expedite us; we were thrown on
a chance for places, but one great difficulty was the luggage, which,
after much talking with several persons, I at last got an agreement
for, to be conveyed by two-horse waggons to Checaw in four days,
for the sum of $50, an extortion. That arranged, a person whom I
did not know took hold of my arm, and in a very familiar way told
me ex-Governor ——— was in the place, and would be happy to see me,
if I would call. I was taken by this youth to the opposition hotel, and
therein, a little better but very similar lodging, I was presented to
his *Excellency* and lady, rather a smart woman. He had two visitors
with him of the lowest, poorest, and most unpolished of the American
small farmers or yeomen. I thought he seemed to wish his constituent
visitors far enough. I sat a reasonable time listening to Mrs. ———
expatiating on the comforts of slavery, and with many courteous
expressions from the ex-Governor, left them to find the stage-coach
at the door and all in hurry for my departure. Paid bills, gave
luggage in charge of Thompson, and deposited myself in the stage. I
think the roads here are unmatched. The country was wood, beautiful
in its various fields of cotton and corn, stalks continually appearing
in the newly cleared woods as we jolted, crawled, pitched, tossed,
and tumbled along the horrible road. We were constantly under the
necessity of walking, which I enjoyed for the exercise and scenery.
Fielding's pleasant *Joseph Andrews* was my inside companion, and
the trees, the streams, the sky, the log-huts, and the ruminations on

their free tenants with their slaves, sufficiently engaged me in my rambling.

Greenville, January 29th.—Dressed with difficulty from the extreme cold, which prevented me from sleeping, whilst the injunctions of the landlord not to disturb his ladies in the next room prevented me from rising long before. We continued our tossing, tumbling journey through wood and clearings alternately, through streams and bogs, that made one wonder, not without something akin to despondency, how we were to reach our journey's end. Mr. Ryder was impatient of every jolt of the carriage, whilst I lay in my corner like a bag of cotton, and, letting it toss me as it would, escaped much soreness and fatigue. We reached La Grange in tolerable time. In this great infant country it is called a county town, but would be a goodly sized and pretty village in England. There were many houses built with their columns and porticoes, looking very neat and comfortable and pretty with their trim gardens in which flowers were blooming and the green leaf always visible, commanding views of a very picturesque country. It was on this route from hence to West Point that the driver, to avoid a piece of heavy, bad road, drove into a field through the broken fence, and passing through it came out by some means at the other end. This is nothing in this primeval part. The peach orchards here are very large and thriving; they have peach, quince, plum, grape, etc. At West Point, where we tried to dine, and beyond which we passed into Alabama, we got some hard eggs and ham for dinner. We see *la fin du commencement*: this infant settlement, wasting through disease, crime, and squalor into rapid decay; more than half the stores are closed, and the place itself looks like infant life dying of age's decrepitude. The beautiful river Chatteroockee—beautiful in American eyes for its water-power—divides it, and a covered bridge communicates between the banks. It appears that it was in a thriving state when the Indians came here to receive their presents, and the inhabitants enriched themselves by selling liquors to these unhappy creatures; its present appearance is a just retribution; it will soon sink to a few rotting sheds.

Caseta, January 30th.—I am forcibly struck with the effect that kindness of manner and encouragement has upon these poor negroes; it charms away their sullenness at once. Our old landlady quite answered W. Scott's description of a "kind old body." She was a pleasant old housewifely lady, with her preserved water-melons, peaches, etc., and her genuine hospitable spirit. Our road to-day was worse

than ever : through swamps, through wide streams; tracking our way
through woods by the *blazing* of the trees, through actual rivers, and
all this after an overturn, which detained us in the middle of the road
under a heavy rain for above an hour.   When thrown over, all were
in confusion and alarm, struggling to get out.   I called to them to
be still and quietly take their turns.   It was certainly a very bad
journey : by cotton, cornfields, cane-brakes, woods of oak, chestnut,
hickory, beech, and pine.   We passed by one bridge over a stream
of surpassing beauty, divided and narrowed into a deep downward gush
by a mass of granite; it continued its course between banks as charmingly diversified by rock and foliage as a painter's imagination could
suggest.   The ruined or deserted railway still accompanied our course.
Joseph Andrews was my companion till dark.   Scarcely hoping to
finish our journey, for our own management of our weight by ballast-
ing the coach preserved us repeatedly from an overturn, we at length
reached Checaw.   A man with a wretched slave, whom he sent upon
the top of the coach, had been our companion from La Grange.   This
poor negro told Mr. Ryder that he had lived with his master's father,
and that now he, the master, had sold his wife and children in Georgia,
and was taking him on to sell him in Montgomery, the poor wretch
crying like a child as he told his story.

   Checaw, January 31st.—Rose long before daylight to pursue our
journey by railway to Montgomery.   Saw our landlord's wife, a girl
of fourteen, who had run away with him.   Left Checaw at five ; swamp,
cane-brake, wood, our road lay along and through the high bluff that
overlooks the Tollapoosie river, which made some fine landscapes.   We
had a seven-foot colonel in a blanket coat, a major in a ragged one,
and a judge in one of frieze.   In cutting wood for the engine, some
one said, "Come, Judge, take a spell of chopping," which he very
readily did.   The ragged crew that filled this car, spitting in every
part of it, obliged me to change my seat.   I was very much disgusted ;
I wish the people would be more cleanly, self-respecting, and decent
in their general habits.   Reaching Montgomery, which we did from
the railway by a road through wood and swamp enough to engulf
a caravan or frighten one, we saw some persons just starting for
Mobile ; they had met and travelled with us before ; they advised our
proceeding, and we, taking their counsel, went on to the boat, the
Charlotte, in which we took our berths, and steamed away down the
Alabama, that like a "proud river, overpeered its banks," towards
Mobile.   I received much civility from the gentlemen who went on

board with me, they using their best efforts to procure me a good berth. I took a state-room to myself, and did not regret it. Our passage down the stream, whose windings extended the distance to 408 miles, the stage-coach road being 180, continually excited my attention. Here was enough to satisfy the traveller, whose thirst for change is to find something new, that he had left nothing behind in Europe resembling this. Its banks were ever changing their forms: now bold bluffs, with trees rising perpendicularly from their very edges; then long tracts of wood running in levels beyond the eye's ken or the thought's conjecture; then vast expanses of water from which were seen rising up tall blighted trees, log-huts, fodder-stacks, gates, and lines of cottages. Frequently we saw whole fields of cotton submerged by the flood, and whole clearings showing only their mills and gins and fences, etc., above the wide surface of the waters. The trees, some of them covered and seemingly pressed down by the heavy-looking mournful draperies of moss, that lent a character, I might say an expression, to the tree that strikes the observer; the white and leafless sycamores often stood out in advance of the sad and gloomy forest like ghosts of what they had been, stretching their ominous arms or long white fingery boughs above the wide ruin. The grape-vine was hanging its thready and twining branches like strong network about some of the failing trees, like voluptuousness and luxury pulling down strength. Long tracts of cane-brake below, houses on the heights, creeks, inlets, and widely devastating wastes of the waters were in frequent succession through our whole course. Bulwer's novel of the *Last of the Barons* divided, and only divided, my attention with this wild and grand and beautiful scenery of the Alabama. Amid thoughts of where I am, how far from home, and what they are thinking of, there came the news from England to crowd and to confuse my mind. Lord Lynedoch [1] and Catalani dead. Alas!

Alabama River, February 1st.—My employment to-day was to read Bulwer's novel, and to catch glimpses and views of the river and its banks. The live oak and the magnolia are among the richest of the evergreens that give rich and deep colours to the woods, and the palmetto, in its low shrubby state, is still graceful in its form and cool and pleasant in its colour. At a very beautiful indenting of the high bank, well wooded to the top, our crew and company got upon some bales of cotton and paddled them with sticks down the little

---

[1] Thomas Graham, Lord Lynedoch (1748–1843), the distinguished general; he began his military career as a volunteer when nearly fifty years of age.

inlet to the boat. One, of course, rolled over, to the hearty enjoyment of all who witnessed him. At another landing a person of ordinary appearance, more inclining to the vulgar in manner than even the respectable, came with his family and slaves on board. His manner of speaking to them made me long to give him a tip with my foot and send the ignorant tyrant and oppressor overboard. Went late to bed; lay down as the engine stopped; was told on my inquiry, about one o'clock, that we had arrived. At the dinner the very raffish or ragged appearance of many, and the table equipage, made me long to have one of our *exquisites* placed hungrily amongst them. But as Charles XII replied to the soldier, touching his bad bread: "It is not very good, but it is eatable." The tin bowl to wash in in my state-room was a peculiar privilege and very jealously permitted for a very short time; of course, a common comb and hair-brush in the saloon, which all used. One person was distressed on missing it, and asked if there was not a hair-brush, adding: "Can't you come across that brush?" All this, and with all, and above all, the beastly spitting, is very annoying, and disturbs very much one's taste and one's stomach. They are men here, and feel as men; to polish the exterior would not rub away any of their better qualities, and would make them much more pleasant to come in contact with.

Mobile, February 2nd.—Rose very early and went on board the New Orleans boat, *James L. Day*, to secure my berth. Packed up, and walked away after breakfast to change my day's abode. Went on to the Exchange; a sale of men and women. It is not to be talked or thought of: I have blamed the Abolitionists, and do blame them, for the effects their indiscreet zeal produces, but I should neither wonder nor blame if I saw these black and dusky men strike their knives into the brutal bosoms of those who assert the right of might over them. A Mr. Cole, an acquaintance of Ryder's, told him they "had no feeling; they did not mind being parted from wife and children; they forgot it in a week. You see a cat when one drowns her kittens, she soon forgets it—it's just the same with the coloured people." Is it—oh God!—the same? But time will tell. One man, about forty, a blacksmith, had his merits expatiated on in the true George Robins's style: "This hale man going for $550, it's throwing him away—no more bid? It's a sacrifice! Going, going, etc." Another mulatto, a field servant—the same language, the same odious blasphemy against nature and the God of nature. Read in steamboat extracts from Jeremy Taylor, Bishop Hall, etc. It is scarcely possible to imagine any boat of the kind more complete than this—cleanliness, neatness, elegance throughout; the dinner served in the best manner.

New Orleans, February 3rd.—Rose from my hard and ache-giving berth above half-past four o'clock; dressed and sauntered up and down the wooden pier thinking of home and the great distance I was from it, and all it contains. Passed into the sort of village, half French, half English, in its shops' inscriptions, and was interested and struck by the resemblance it conveyed, in the architecture of its small houses and gateway or arch, to an old French village or small town. I went to the St. Louis Hotel and got one room, a very poor affair, till others should fall. Went to rehearsal at eleven; did not like either theatre or actors. Rehearsed *Hamlet*.

February 7th.—Was early up and looked again over *Hamlet* before going to rehearsal, feeling that very much depends, as far as this country is concerned, upon my success in this city: if the audience are cold and scanty here, my profits may be summed up in the United States. Went to theatre, and rehearsed *Hamlet* with great care. Acted Hamlet, if I may trust my own feeling, in a very Shakspearian style; most courteous and gentlemanly, with high bearing, and yet with abandonment and, I think, great energy. Was called for, a compliment which I had really rather dispense with. I fancy the audience were borne along with the performance. But the *fatigue*, "the weight of my shield," is felt most onerously. God help me.

February 8th.—Looked at a paper, which seemed to record decisive success in its report of last night's performance. Called on Mr. Clay; saw him, seventeen years older than when, full of life and vivacity, he introduced himself to me at Washington at our Minister's, Sir R. A. Vaughan. He seems to me to have shrunk in size, and his manners, though most kind, urbane and cheerful, have no longer the vivacity and great animal spirits that then accompanied them. He remembered meeting me; he talked of Talma and of his engagements, asked me to dine with him to-morrow, which I was unable to do. Our visit was limited by an appointment visit of the Judges of the Supreme Court. I gave him Miss Martineau's letter, and we talked of her. He seemed surprised not to see me look older, saying he should not take me for more than forty. In him and Webster, two great minds, I see the pressure of the heavy hand of time; to descend to myself, I feel it. In speaking of slavery he deplored it and condemned it in the abstract, but thought the two races could not be altered in their respective positions without equal distress for both;

intimating that the coloured man is happier in his present state than he could be if free! What would Alexandre Dumas say to that?

February 9th.—Was up long before the hour noted for the sun's rising, and occupied myself till the time for rehearsal with writing to dear Dickens. Went to the theatre. Rehearsed *Macbeth;* had serious misgivings of the result. Rested; thought on the play. Tried to screw myself up to acting well. Acted Macbeth very unequally— was *lacerated* by the actors and *mise en scène;* it was too bad.

February 11th.—A Mr. Cronin called—a professor, I believe, of elocution—to tell me that in my scenes of passion he could not hear a single word, and that he had a very fine organ, requesting me to attend more to the improvement of *the vocality;* I do not know his object in coming; it was either silly, for some knavish purpose, or impertinent; matters little which.

February 14th.—Saw a paper—*Tropic*—in which was a reprint of Mr. N. P. Willis's letter asserting that the English papers stated that Mr. Dickens had been in the Queen's Bench Prison. Acted Werner very fairly, with the drawback of *wretched* support. I was most anxious that the performance should go off well, as Mr. Clay had come on purpose to see it. I therefore took especial pains, and, I think, was very impressive. The audience, who were well packed, seemed much excited. I was called for, and obliged to go on. Thought about Mr. Willis. The danger of meddling with such a reptile is that you give his name publicity, which, however unenviable it may be, is what he seeks. I think I shall not notice him.

February 18th.—Went out in cab to Hewlett's Hotel to look at the rooms he had prepared for me. Agreed to enter them on Tuesday. Arranged my accounts; looked at some papers. More news from England. Thought on the plays for the remainder of my engagement. Robinson called, above two hours after his appointment with Major Montfort, a good-natured American soldier. We went in his carriage through the city, and along the banks of the canal, and through wood and swamp, of cedar, cypress, out to the Lake Pontchartrain; the morning was very pleasant, and these melancholy woods with their ghostlike trees, in their mournful drapery of moss and vine, are always interesting to me. Large *lighter* kind of sloops were coming up the canal. A very decent house of entertainment is on the shore of the lake, all ground recovered from the swamp. It amused me yesterday to know that the French call the American portion of the city " Le Faubourg Américain." I dined with Robinson at the *table d'hôte* of

Hewlett, who gave an excellent table ; was much amused.   After dinner rode along the Levee, saw the shipping and warehouses of this wonderful place ; the waterworks, with their muddy contents ; the steamboats coming in ; the Mississippi winding round, and the buildings, wealth and bustle of the place.   The people seem so happy !   Mr. Bullett amused me ; particularly by his intended mode of curing scarlet-fever. Came home ; put by my assorted papers ; addressed newspapers. Revised the play of *King Lear* for American performance.   Cut the part of Edward for Mr. Ryder.

February 20th.—Went with Robinson and Andrews to call on M. Pepin, who conducted us to the graveyards.   There is nothing in their site to please the eye, nor is there anything in their language to interest or excite.   But he must be very insensible who can contemplate any depository of the dead with indifference, and many and various emotions are awakened here.   There are four or six of those squares formed by thick rampires, built of brick, in which are rows of square cavities one above the other, like the apertures of ovens (which is the term they are known by), and into these, as in the mausoleum at Trentham, the coffins are pushed and then built up ; the inclosed spaces are covered, filled with tombs of all pretensions as to cost and taste ; the pride of the Spaniard, the sentiment of the French, and the plain business-like English inscription are mingled through the grounds.   One was exclusively for people of colour !   There were fresh flowers placed near some and planted near others ; much that was tender and touching and chaste fronting or near to vulgar pride and ludicrous sentimentality.   Tears painted on the slabs of some, and pompous inscriptions upon others ; some simple, sad, and solemn-looking structures, others ostentatiously and even ludicrously ambitious.   I was interested and shall try to renew my visit.

February 22nd.—Washington's birthday.   A curious subject for reflection is offered by this day : in Europe there are certain ceremonies of compliment and expense, such as dinners, levees, drawing-rooms, illuminations of public offices, clubs, and specially appointed tradesmen's shops, which are called rejoicings (?) and are transmitted faithfully from one gracious and beloved sovereign to another.   But throughout these free and independent States the memory of the man who was born this day shall be hallowed by the gratitude and joy of millions of hearts that will hand down to their children's children the debt of reverence and love which they and mankind owe to him for the benefits his life conferred and his example has left.   The birthday of

Washington shall be an eternal festival wherever a freeman speaks the English tongue.

February 28th.—Occupied with affairs upon my late and wearied rising. This daily rehearsal, and earnest acting at night (for I cannot —there is no merit—I cannot be a party, a willing party, to a disgraceful performance), seem, under the effect of this warm climate, this summer in February, to exhaust my strength and spirits. Whether it is the coming on of age or the quantity of strength and energy I expend in my rehearsals and performances, I know not, but they are more than I can well discharge; certain it is, that I can do nothing else. I can see nothing, see no one. I might as well be incarcerated in Drury Lane or Covent Garden, and where there is so much that I am anxious to observe, this is fretting and vexatious. Acted Hamlet.

February 29th.—The joy, the comfort I have felt this day in the ability to repeat to myself that it is the last day but one of my New Orleans engagement is not to be described nor to be explained, except that the labour is so heavy and the conclusion of it brings me nearer home. Rehearsed Iago. Saw Forrest, who came on the stage. Acted Iago well.

March 1st.—Last day of my engagement here! The thought brings new animation to my spirits and comparative quiet to my nerves. My labour is incessant, monotonous, and with nothing in the character of my criticism to stimulate me; the money and the thought of home are the comforting reflections. The night has been rainy, and the morning is wet, but it is warm moisture, thick and steamy. My system is quite relaxed and oppressed; a sensation of general debility is most distressingly upon me. My clothes feel damp upon me and clinging to me as I change each posture. I am quite unequal to my work. Looked at the papers—the daily trash that is offered up. Pah! Rehearsed *King Lear*, with a perfect consciousness of my utter inability to do justice to my own conception of the character. I am weary of this atmosphere and this place. Dined early. Rested, and thought over my great part of King Lear, feeling that I could not satisfy myself in it, but wishing to do my utmost. A note from some *curiosa*—wishing to see me, but whom I could not answer— signing herself *Augusta*. Went to the theatre, very weak. The house not what it ought to have been, certainly not. I rallied against my lassitude, and made a very fair fight for poor Lear; parts of it I acted very fairly, and I think made a strong impression on the audience. Some parts I did really well. Was called for; an apology was made

264

by Smith for my change of dress, which the audience were not very patient under, and in a very short time I appeared before them and addressed them.

March 2nd.—Gave my first hours to the needful business of packing, which I completed in very good time. Met Mr. Ryder at the railway. Slept the greater part of the way to the lake, " quite wearied and o'erspent." We found a good deal of motion on the lake; the boats lay within the little harbour formed by wooden piers stretching out into the lake and leaving only a narrow entrance by which to pass in and out. The land, as we enter the narrow channel between the Lakes, is very low, marshy, duck, snipe-like looking ground; a neat little fort, with an artillery company, commands the passage.

Mobile, March 3rd.—Fifty-one years old. We were within the bay of Mobile and pressing over its smooth waters, strewn over with the stripped and shattered trees borne down by the freshet of the Alabama, and landed. I went with a porter as a guide about the town, and was forced to ask as a favour a bedroom at the top of the house, and glad to house myself here to wash and dress.

March 4th.—Acted Hamlet. I thought I never acted the first scene with the Ghost so well; the audience this night was very numerous. Persons going away in some of the steamboats had prevailed on the masters to delay their start till midnight in order to visit the theatre. Many *rowdy* people were there, women of the town—in short, it was an audience attracted by sheer curiosity. Perhaps I was not up to my mark, although I strove very resolutely.

March 9th.—Anzé proposed to take me a drive in the environs of the city. Called on Magee, whom I saw. Found Anzé at the door of my hotel—accompanied him in his buggy through the city, along the direction of the shore of the bay by pretty suburban houses, into woods in all the wild and picturesque confusion of self-creation and renewal. The boxes, as they are called, of the dwellers near the city are very neat, and the hedge of the Cherokee rose—like our common wild white rose—most luxuriantly in bloom over a fence of neat lattice work, presented a very neat out-work to a very neat residence. The woods and the views of the bay were most beautiful—the magnolia. Dined with Mr. Graciè—liked his wife—met Dr. Nott, Fisher, Ball, Castellan, Anzé, Ogden, etc. A very agreeable day. My drive to-day among some very pretty suburban villas with their many flowers and richly blossoming peach-trees, oranges in blossom, fig, and various ornamental shrubs was very lovely. The air was quite delicious; we came frequently close to the water's side, looking from a low cliff over this extensive bay, with its shoals, its masses of rude timber, its distant shores, and passing through clearings and wood of lofty pines till we reached the Magnolia Grove—so called from the trees which chiefly form its shade. The shrubs were very beautiful, and flowers. I gathered some violets for Catherine—not quite so deeply blue as our own sweet flower, and with no perfume.

March 12th.—Dickens's misjudgment is as clear to me as the noonday sun, and much is to be said in explanation and excuse, but Dickens is a man who fills such a place in the world's opinion, the people cannot think that he ought to need an excuse—alas! the greatest man is but a man!

March 13th.—I am quite debilitated by my labour. The audience do not help me *at all* by their applause or manifestation of sympathy, and the profit is not *great enough* to sustain my spirits against the drag which is upon them. Looked at papers, which seem to have adopted a studied silence—*eh bien !* Acted Othello—if I may compare myself with myself, or trust to the reality and grandeur of my own feelings—*splendidly* for the three first acts. The apathy and vulgar applause of the audience—bestowed, may I not say, on every one *except* myself—made the two last very laborious to me, and perhaps, therefore, not so grand and flowing in their effect ; but not bad.

March 15th.—Read a very absurd memoir of that wretch—that blackguard—Dr. Maginn.[1] I know of the man, that upon Lloyd & Hedges sending him an account and requiring payment for wine obtained, he told them he would *show them up in the Standard !* This is fact ; but he was the friend of Mr. Oastler—*jam satis.*

March 16th.—Started with a fresh breeze against us for New Orleans ; liked everything in Mobile except the hotel and theatre ; glad to go forward as beginning my return to dear, dear home. Walked the upper deck till wearied, looking at the woods or the shores, the drifting timber scattered over the bay, the fleet of merchantmen riding in the outer bay, the islands, and the gorgeous sunset.

March 19th.—Acted *The Stranger.* Leaving the theatre, was attracted by the blaze of a very great fire in Royal Street. I had heard the tocsin during the last scene of the play. Went to it and watched the terrific and sublime spectacle for upwards of an hour ; the flames rose in upward torrents of fire, and at times there was an atmo-

---

[1] William Maginn (1793-1842), the well-known author, and founder of *Fraser's Magazine ;* he was at one time joint-editor of the *Standard.*

sphere of sparks. I saw two houses fall in with tremendous crashes, and came away as the fire seemed to yield to the efforts of the firemen.

March 21st.—Two days' news from England: Marshal Bertrand, whom I met, as it were the other day, at Grattan's in Boston, *dead !* Duchesse de Berri, the profligate, silly voluptuary, dead! It is only to wait our turn, using the time permitted to us to the best advantage. What a mere pageant is life altogether. Rested and read Shylock. Acted Shylock very fairly. At supper took a gin mint-julep by way of experiment: the most deliciously cunning compound that ever I tasted; nectar could not stand before it; Jupiter would have hob-nobbed in it.

March 28th.—Called on Mr. R——. To my surprise and amuse-ment found that his wife, of whom he had taken leave on board ship last night embarked for France, was at home; had returned; could not bear to leave her friends; lost heart at the last minute. I think I should scarcely have welcomed back any woman who had cost me all the pain to part with her and then returned—so much good grief all thrown away!

April 2nd.—In the evening, two brightly reflected lights stretching far on the horizon, with smoke before them, were pointed out to us as the prairies on fire. The foliage yesterday and to-day had been beautifully enriched by the red or dark pink blossom, covering the tree like the peach, of the Arbor-Judas or red-bud; these, often side by side with the snowy blossom that powdered the dog-wood tree, diversified by colour and form the lofty and leafless cotton-wood. The voyage of the Mississippi most beautiful.

St. Louis, April 6th.—Rose in good time. Mr. Franciscus and the carriage were ready, and we started for the Ferry; drove into the boat, crossed the Mississippi, and drove out upon the other floating pier without alighting. Our road lay through Illinois Town, a small place through which a little creek, crossed by a good wooden bridge, runs; we went over it and along the high causeway built for winter or wet travel, when the soil of the country admits your carriage to the nave of the wheel or deeper. Our road lay along a country that was fatness itself, the ground oozing out richness, black loam that might be scratched to give a crop; we passed several of those Indian mounds and reached some lakes, where to my great delight I saw the habitations of the beaver, at distances from each other in the middle of the water. Our way for many miles was tame, till we reached some much larger mounds, and standing in great numbers on the plain. I cannot guess

267

if they were forts or tombs, one seems for one purpose, another for the other.   We passed through some low woods before, and now we reached some high and well-wooded hills, where woodpeckers, the beautiful turtle-dove, the blue bird, and others were numerous on the wing.   We met numerous families, with their wagons and oxen carrying their substance to some other State.   I cannot understand this.   We passed through Collinsville, where there are three churches, built by an old lady, to whom the place belongs, and who will not allow any one to live there who drinks or keeps fermented liquors.   Stopped at a *public*, kept by Clark, an English sailor, with a pretty wife, five children, nice house, garden farm, barns, in-house, etc.   We dined (!), then passed through Troy and Marcia Town; saw the stretch of the prairie; plovers, prairie hen-partridges in abundance.   Reached Colonel Madge's cottage; was hospitably received and entertained.   Saw the prairies on fire in three places; it was beautiful.

April 7th.—We drove out about a mile and a half on the prairie, which, in its bare winter garb, reminds me very much of Salisbury Plain.   I can fancy the sublime sort of awe that any one must feel in being twenty miles deep on such a wild, and it is in its extent that its grandeur consists; its beauty is in the flowers of all hues with which it is so gorgeously carpeted in the summer season.   The soil is rich to rankness.

April 11th.—Acted Virginius *most vilely*—never so bad; the house was bad, I was ill, the actors were incorrect, and one of them was very impertinent—impertinent in the literal sense of the word, for he was talking folly, and it was insolent.   He is a disgusting puppy, and looked very foolish when obliged to resort to a falsehood to screen himself.   These players!

April 12th.—Was gratified in my walk with the sight of the lilac in full bloom, and in some little gardens tulips, narcissus.   It is not only the sweet feeling which the beauty of flowers always imparts to me, a tranquil feeling of delight in their beauty of colour, form, and perfume, but they are associated in my mind with home, with dear England, and soothe me with their influence.

April 13th.—Rose very early, and coaxed the coloured waiter to give us breakfast, on which we set out in the carriage from Alton, bidding farewell to our very civil and good-natured host, and pursuing our way on a most lovely morning through the little town, through woods in all the variety of vernal beauty, passing the wreck of another railway, another monster monument of the headlong and precipitate

268

speculation of this reckless people. We held the river occasionally in view and then the thick woods would shut us from its sight.

April 15th.—Acted Iago, taking much pains with the part. The audience did not *notice* me on my appearance; to Mr. Ryder, Messrs. Field and Farren they gave long and loud plaudits in receiving them! Throughout the play, too, they really bestowed as much, if not *more*, applause upon the unmeaning rant and gabble of these people than they gave to me; and really I *tried* to act Iago in my old earnest, "honest" way, but the difference is not of importance to them. In my last scene, which I was acting in a very true manner, as I was taking my departure from the room, the *continued* vulgar speeches, ejaculations, and laughs of some ruffians in the second tier quite overcame my patience. I threw up the attempt and walked right off.

April 16th.—Mr. Maginnes called—a lawyer here, of Irish parents; his father, General Maginnes, led the rebels at Ballynahinch; his uncle Peeling was taken as aide-de-camp of Humbert at Killala, and hung by Lord Cornwallis. He shot a man in a duel in Kentucky, fled and settled here. He avowed some principles not to my taste—*e. g.* his having assisted in executing lynch-law on negroes, and his approval of men taking the law into their own hands to redress their injuries. Acted Shylock, I think, and the audience, few in number (Mr. Ryder's Benefit, poor man!), seemed to appreciate and understand the play better than any we have yet had. I suppose we had only the few who cared for Shakspeare, the large majority having been drafted off to Vieuxtemps's *only* concert at the planter's house. His bill is a curiosity; he is rivalling Ole Bull in quackery.

April 17th.—To my great satisfaction I received a large pair of buffalo horns, and a grand pair of elk horns from a Mr. Whatton. Rested. Acted Macbeth really well, too well for St. Louis, though the audience were much more decorous, attentive, and appreciative than I have heretofore found them. I suppose they begin to understand me. Was called for and bowed.

April 19th.—Went on board the *West Wind*. Saw on board two of the Scholefields of Birmingham, whom I was really delighted to meet. We went on our watery way, the river varying its form, the banks as constantly changing from bluff or wooded hill to low brake or wood, or wooded highland with rocks—most interesting.

April 21st.—Went up on deck in the early morning, and enjoyed the air, the river and the exercise very much. Began *Samson Agonistes*. Read some interesting passages in the *History of the*

269

Church, a book I must endeavour to read carefully through. Talked with a gentleman from Iowa, who had been giving a fearful account of the wild and lawless condition of that territory, when it was first put into a state for territorial jurisdiction.

Louisville, April 22nd.—Went into Louisville. Passed courthouse, jail, markets, etc. Very spacious streets, good shops, an appearance of wealth and comfort, well-dressed people, etc. Attracted constantly by the beauty of either shore of Kentucky or Indiana, which now showed more continuous cultivation, better farms and houses, etc., of more pretension; the leaf-clad hills wore every variety of form, and the rocks peeping out or showing large fronts from amidst them were always picturesque—it was a chain of lakes.

Cincinnati, April 23rd.—After a sleepless night, the first light showed me the buildings, etc., of Cincinnati. The bell rang at a quarter to five, when I rose, dressed, etc., and despatched Thompson to inquire about my hotel. Looked at *Hamlet,* and went to rehearsal; took pains, but the weather was very hot. Acted Hamlet, I think, very fairly. Came home to hotel, very much worn and exhausted, and almost dying for some tea, which for nearly an hour I could not get.

April 28th.—A young man whom I do not know, I think the land-lord's son came up and, throwing his arm round my neck, asked me if I knew Colonel Taylor. I said, "No." "That is he behind you, he has been looking for you, shall I introduce you?" "If you please." He did so, and I remained in conversation with Colonel Taylor till Mr. Foster came to accompany me in my drive through the city. It is on the bend of the river, built over by streets at right angles numbered and named chiefly from trees; the streets are wide, planted generally with trees along the foot-paths, with many small plots of ornamented ground.

April 29th.—Acted Iago as well as I could, being so ill; very much *disgusted* with the house, which was very bad. I am sick of American audiences; they are not fit to have the language in which Shakspeare wrote.

April 30th.—Foster called as I was dressing. I was very unwell, have suffered much. Acted Virginius very feebly to a very poor house; suffering from debility. Was called, went on, and bowed. My southern and western tour is ended; thank God for all it has given me. I feel, however, overwrought.

May 1st.—Dear memorandum of England this sweet day of spring, bringing with it thoughts of home and much that is sweet and dear! Felt much better.

Pittsburg, May 5th.—Was much amused by Mr. Ryder's report of the observation of a resident to him, that the "citizens of Pittsburg were very much dissatisfied with Mr. Macready for not staying to perform there." Ryder observed that I had an engagement, etc.

Harrisburg, May 6th.—We dined at McConnell's Town, a very well-built, happy-looking little town. Our weary journey jolted us on at four and a half miles an hour through the night up to eleven o'clock, when we reached Chambersburg batteries, bruised and rheumatic. Lived out two hours there and then embarked on the railway—oh, what a relief to Harrisburg!

To New York, May 7th.—Awoke to look upon this very pretty capital of Pennsylvania, situated on the Susquehanna. The country from Harrisburg to Philadelphia through Lancaster is one rich tract of the highest cultivation, comfort, industry, economy, and wealth in the farms and gardens and orchards that cover the country. At the Schuylkill the views are most beautiful, perfectly charming. Reached Philadelphia, took railway, travelled rapidly to New York.

New York, May 8th.—Wrote to Miss C. Cushman, as I had promised Simpson, wishing her to play here during my engagement. Received my dear letters from home; all well there. Thank God. Letter inclosed from dear Lydia to Letitia, answering their letters upon what struck down my heart, the news of poor dear Jonathan's death.[1] We talk of patience under these visitations, but none can truly investigate his feelings and say he does not repine, when those of virtue and high character, whom he loves, are for ever lost to him. "He stood by me like my youth." I should have been satisfied to have seen any one of my boys (God bless them) like him. He was a noble creature, dear, dear youth.

May 13th.—Acted Hamlet, I think, very well indeed; the audience were deeply attentive, and much more fervent than I remember them to have been; was called for and well received. Came home and no tea, "no nothing."

May 16th.—Mr. Gould, author of *Ludovico Sforza*, called and sat some time. I restored him his manuscript.

May 20th.—Acted Cardinal Richelieu in my very best manner. The impression upon the audience was evidently very powerful. I was called for and most enthusiastically received. It is natural that I should

---

[1] Jonathan Birch, a relation on his mother's side.

271

notice this practical comment upon the honesty of Mr. N. P. Willis, who in October last wrote letters to the *National Intelligencer*, stating how much better in this character Mr. Forrest is than myself. He has not been able to make the many think so.

May 27th.—We are the chief attraction, I may say the only one, in New York at present. Reproved the Birnam Wood messenger very sharply; he deserved it. Spoke to Miss ——, who, it seems, laughed in the banquet scene; my object in speaking to her, desiring her to call here, was to prevent the recurrence of such inconveniences as I had encountered; but she promised *to behave* for the future.

May 30th.—Acted Hamlet; the latter part, *i. e.* after the first act, in a really splendid style. I felt myself the man. Called for and well received. The house good. Hamlet has brought me more money than any play in America.

June 1st.—Calling for Colden, we walked up to Ruggles's, where we met Mrs. R——, his son, and daughter, a very pretty girl, Judge Kent, Sedgwick, Prescott Hall, Griffin, Hamilton, Inman, etc., at a very elegant breakfast, which passed off in most lively and pleasant conversation.

Buffalo, June 24th.—Wedding Day. Rehearsed Hamlet. Dined and had a "plum-pudding." Drank a bumper of champagne to my dear wife. Rested. Acted to a bad house. Oh, Buffalo!

Montreal, July 5th.—I walked out to try to get Mr. Horne's [1] poem of *Orion*, but did not succeed in my quest. At dinner read much of *Ion*, which thrilled and affected me again quite with the old feeling. I was very much moved. I could not help thinking how in this world we let petty feelings disturb those more charitable ones, which should cherish regard for what is amiable in man and indulgence for what is weak or worse. It is to be lamented that I have ever known Talfourd out of his literary calling; he is unequal but ——. I wrote a kind letter to him.

July 6th.—Looked at the papers for English news; saw flattering notices of myself. Read the death of Thomas Campbell. "How dumb the tuneful!" He outlived his acceptability, and was latterly intolerable in society; but what a charming poet. *Eheu !* By the papers I see the English people *cheered most enthusiastically* Nicholas, Emperor of Russia, who gave £500 per annum to the races of Ascot! A creditable display of national feeling on one side, and a discriminating act of bounty to suffering humanity on the other! I also perceive that

[1] Richard Hengist Horne (see note, p. 469); vol. I.

some persons have presented a piece of plate to—Mr. Bunn for his "uniform urbanity in the season of 1843–4." This wretch, who not only robbed almost every player he had dealings with, but constantly insulted those whom he dared with language of the most offensive and blackguard kind.

July 13th.—The day on which my beloved, my blessed Joan was born. Remembered, as I rose and in my prayers, this day, that gave to me that lovely child, whose face is left like that of an angel on my memory, as I look upon her, decked for the grave; part of my heart was buried with thee, sweetest child, and it is one thought which diminishes the fear of death that I shall again be associated with thee. Bless thee! oh! bless thy dear spirit! Amen! Called at the newsroom. Read there that a testimonial (my God! what are such things worth!) was presented to Mr. Bunn, and that he—he!—whom I have seen the audience *yell* with execration from before them—had delivered a " valedictory address " ! ! !

July 17th.—Acted Hamlet. . . . Lay on my sofa at the hotel, ruminating upon the play of *Hamlet;* upon the divine spirit which God lent to that man, Shakspeare, to create such intellectual realities, full of beauty and of power, inheriting the ordinary wickednesses of humanity, the means of attracting so strongly the affections and wonder of men! It seems to me as if only now, at fifty-one years of age, I thoroughly see and appreciate the artistic power of Shakspeare in this great human phenomenon; nor do any of the critics, Goethe, Schlegel, Coleridge, present to me in their elaborate remarks the exquisite artistical effects which I see in this work, as long meditation, like long straining after sight, gives the minutest portion of its excellence to my view. I am not well. Shall I live long? I do not feel at all confident that I shall. If my life be not likely to be beneficial to my children, I have no other wish for prolonging it. *In God is my trust.*

Boston, August 12th.—Hillard called for me and drove to Cambridge. Met at Longfellow's, Felton and Jared Sparkes; with Longfellow's charming wife, this was our party, and to me very agreeable it was.

Saratoga, August 20th.—Came to our rooms, where I finished *Coningsby,*[1] with which I have been much interested and pleased. There is occasionally a gaudiness of style and sometimes the affectation of a coxcombical mind, but there are character, pathos, humour

---

[1] This appreciation is in pleasant contrast to Macready's usual disparagement of Disraeli and his works.

and graphic power assisting the interest of a very well-arranged story.

New York, September 6th.—Called on Simpson, who gave me some account of the London theatricals. Mr. Bunn had ejected *the drama* from Drury Lane theatre. This is well. Mrs. Nisbett was losing herself rapidly, poor woman! Miss Helen Faucit has engaged for Paris next winter; also that Mr. Forrest was resolved to go there and act; I could not be concerned about it in any way.

September 7th.—Went to Walnut theatre; saw Forrest act Damon —a very dull, heavy-mannered, unpleasant performance. He is not a good actor—*not at all an artist.* He acts Hamlet on Monday *in opposition* to me, and, I hear, made this engagement to oppose me! This is not the English generosity of rivalry.

Philadelphia, September 8th.—Read in Wordsworth as reading exercise. I feel my voice growing more and more inflexible; the tones which I used to like to listen to I cannot now evoke, alas! Read in Hamlet.

September 9th.—Mr. Forrest in Hamlet at the Walnut Street theatre had not more (if he had that sum) than $200 to his Hamlet. If it be so, he is justly punished for his ungentlemanly conduct.

September 14th.—Rehearsed carefully and laboriously four acts of *Werner;* saw the impossibility of Mr. Conner delivering the words of the part or even scrambling through Ulric; he could not even *read* the text of his part. It was too serious to be angry about. I called Mr. Burton, etc., and consulted on what was to be done; he was for letting things go on (the actor's plan!), and then thinking of a remedy when the catastrophe had happened. This was not my course. The chance of Mr. Wheatley's aid being negatived, I proposed that an apology should be made for this Mr. Conner, and that he should *read* the part; it would quiet his mind, and get the play through. Miss Cushman said he would play a trick—he would have a fit; it seems he was drunk last night. Well, it was settled. We finished the play, and I went home dreadfully tired. Evening came. I went to the theatre; acted the first act of Werner excellently; went on to Josephine and Ulric in the second; had not spoken six lines before Ulric—Mr. Conner —gave a reel (*not a good one*—I have no faith in it) and fell!!!— a fit! What was to be done? Nothing appeared to me but to substi- tute *The Stranger.* An apology was made, our dresses changed, and *The Stranger* acted.

September 15th.—Saw Forrest, talked with him, and went to sit

EDWIN FORREST

From an engraving by D. Pound of a Daguerreotype

with Mrs. Forrest, whom I like as pretty and amiable. Talked with them for some time. He told me of Mr. Conner's *fits*.

New York, September 16th.—Looked at papers—the coarse, vulgar wretches that are the editors! How my inmost soul sickens with loathing at them, the vulgar brutes! An American editor is a creature *per se*—agh! Acted Hamlet, in *defiance* of the *dullest audience* I ever almost encountered. I believe I acted *really* well—utterly unaided by the audience. Was called for and went on. The heat was very great, and the shouts of the democrats at their mass meeting were heard distinctly through the play.

September 24th.—Saw a St. Louis paper, arraigning the stage as the ground of licentiousness. It certainly *is* licentious. The query is, whether there is not as much licentiousness in private houses. I do not know! There is certainly much temptation and opportunity among players for licentiousness—*i. e.* among the herd. I am sure the leading persons have not much!

September 25th.—The anniversary of my opening the Park theatre, New York, since when I find myself, with all my expenses paid, about £5,500 bettered in pecuniary circumstances, for which I gratefully, devoutly and earnestly thank God.

September 27th.—Acted King Lear, in many parts very well. Called for by the audience, but an apology was made whilst I changed my dress. I was most enthusiastically received, and spoke the speech I had prepared. The audience were evidently greatly pleased and moved, and at the end nearly, if not quite, the whole house rose, waving handkerchiefs, etc. I have certainly been very successful.

Boston, October 2nd.—Acted Hamlet in this barn-like stage with church-like audience, better, perhaps, altogether than I ever in my life before did! The performance was too good for the place! The house was good, but not overflowing; not full, which it ought to have been to have paid such suffering.

October 7th.—Dr. Lardner called and sat very long, wearying and annoying me with a most uninteresting string of flippant dogmas—this was bad enough—abusing Bulwer, and talking most disagreeably; but when he began to talk about his own affairs—Mrs. Heaviside's divorce, her property, his liability, etc., it was actually disgusting to witness the want of feeling and of common decency.

October 14th.—Note from Longfellow, from Grattan in answer to mine. George Curtis called with a note of the kindest import from Judge Story with his miscellaneous writings. Went out with Colden

275

in carriage to Steam Packet Office, and paid for my passage—to England! Went to rehearsal and passed through a *crowd of people* striving for places. Rehearsed, and disgusted with Mr. Rodney's behaviour in undertaking a part and then at the last moment refusing to do it. It would have been shameful enough with his help—as it was it was disgraceful. He is a fool and, I fear, a knave. Mr. Ayling, Mr. Ryder and Miss Cushman volunteered their opinions that he contemplates some *escapade*. I was wretchedly nervous. Came home and sent for Hillard. The kindest note from Colonel Perkins, who has sent *a chair* to the ship for my convenience. I was touched by his most kind attention—the good old man! Note from dear Felton. Hillard and Colden called, and we talked over my fears of Mr. Rodney; they could not think them well grounded—we shall see; I do not feel safe. Rested and tried, worn out as I was, to think of my speech. Acted Macbeth well, where I was not *cut up* by the men on the stage. Was *savagely angry* with Mr. Ryder and *quite forgot myself*. Oh, passion! passion! what a wretched, senseless, ruinous guide thou art! Was called for. Spoke. The audience attentive but not enthusiastic.

London, November 6th.[1]—Forster read me Miss Martineau's letters. They stagger one in one's incredulity on Mesmerism—is she in her clear senses?

November 9th.—Mitchell and Serle called, and after showing him the danger of announcing the English performance at Paris before Miss Cushman's and Mr. Ryder's arrival, I consented to open, if they arrived in time, on the 2nd of December. It was settled that my plays should be produced in the following order, which I marked at the time in pocket-book: *Othello, Hamlet, Virginius, Macbeth,*

---

[1] On his return home Macready found awaiting him the following warm-hearted letter from Dickens—

" Palazzo Peschiere, Genoa,
" October 14, 1844.

"MY VERY DEAR MACREADY,

"My whole heart is with you *At Home.* I have not yet felt so far off as I do now, when I think of you there and cannot fold you in my arms. This is only a shake of the hand. I couldn't say much to you, if I were to greet you. Nor can I write much when I think of you safe and sound and happy after all your wanderings. My dear fellow, God bless you twenty thousand times; happiness and joy be with you. I hope to see you soon. If I should be so unfortunate as to miss you in London, I will fall on you with a swoop of love in Paris. Kate says all kind things in the language, and means more than are in the dictionary capacity of all the descendants of all the stonemasons that worked at Babel. Again and again, and again, my own true friend, God bless you!

"Ever, yours affectionately,
"CHARLES DICKENS."

Werner, *King Lear*, and perhaps *Merchant of Venice*. God grant us success.

November 11th.—My beloved Catherine's Birthday, which I entered on by wishing her all happiness for years and years to come in the return of this dear day, for which I am truly grateful. My thanks and prayers are offered up to God for every blessing on her dear head now and for evermore. Called on Rogers, Horace Twiss, Everitt, Milnez Gibson, all from home; on Mrs. Carlyle, whom we saw; on the Stones, from home. Mr. and Miss Inman, Leslie, Maclise, Stanfield, Forster and William Birch dined with us.

November 12th.—Read the little story of *Grace and Clara* to my darling children. Calculated and pondered well my journey to Paris, and upon mature reflection and consideration of dear Catherine's state of health, and of Katie's constitution, resolved on going post to Paris.

November 14th.—Heard of Lord Napier (of logarithms), foretelling on calculation the destruction of the world in twenty-four years, and wishing to sell an estate for thirty years' purchase!

November 18th.—Forster called for me by appointment, and we went to Lady Blessington's; D'Orsay, Lady Canterbury, Miss Power, Maclise, Spencer Cowper, Captain Purvis, Powell, Guthrie the surgeon, Forster were the party.

November 19th.—Read what I could of a play of Chorley's [1]— among the worst I have read. And this is the critic who has diligently abused me! Began to read when the Carlyles came in and sat with us the evening.

November 20th.—Called on Campbell, the sculptor; saw the monument of Mrs. Siddons, much pleased with it. He told me Lord Titchfield [2] wished him to make it a full length with Adelaide and Fanny Kemble on either side. He is mad—at least on one subject.

December 4th.—Set out, Catherine and self, for the Dover station. Dined at Folkestone, where we were detained till four o'clock by the non-arrival of the packet; went on board a nasty, miserable little boat, called the *Water Witch*, stowed full of passengers; good deal of wind and very heavy sea made our passage, of four hours' duration, perfectly miserable.

Paris, December 11th.—Alexandre Dumas called and left a box for the Odéon. We went and saw his play of *Christine*—poor old Mlle.

---

[1] Henry Fothergill Chorley (see note, p. 168, Vol. II.).

[2] Afterwards the eccentric Duke of Portland, whose name figured so prominently in the bogus Druce case.

Georges,[1] quite an old woman, acted Christine. So dull a play I scarcely ever saw.

December 13th.—Eugène Sue called, whom I thought a particularly agreeable man. Dickens dined with us, and left us at half-past five, taking with him the last pleasant day that I expect to pass in Paris.

December 15th.—Went with Catherine and Willie to breakfast with De Fresne; met there Regnier, an intelligent actor of the Français; a M. B. Fontaine, the architect of the palace; Jules Janin, several others, and Miss H. Faucit, Miss Wilkes, and Mr. Farren. It is not easy for me to keep up with the French in conversation, but I managed pretty well; was amused and interested.

December 16th.—Acted Othello with great care, often with much reality, but I could not feel the sympathy of the audience; they were fashionable, and from the construction of the theatre,[2] not within the reach of my *electric contact*, to coin an expression; the shocking delay between the acts was another cause for a certain heaviness I felt to pervade the evening. This was Mr. Serle's fault, who is certainly with many good points a very slow coach. I was not satisfied with the issue, uneasy and restless in mind. Alexandre Dumas, Regnier, Vattel, etc., came "pour faire leurs compliments," but I was not assured.

December 18th.—Looked at the papers, and was most gratified by a very cordial notice of Othello in *Galignani*. Received a most fervent congratulation from Eugène Sue. Went to the theatre to see to some matters left unsettled in yesterday's rehearsal. Spoke very strongly to Mitchell about our future plays, insisting on the proper attention of the servants, etc. Rested and thought much of *Hamlet*. Acted Hamlet fairly, though somewhat disturbed by the inefficiency of persons and things about me. Called for. The play over a few minutes before twelve. Did not sleep two hours of the whole night, my excitement was so strong; painful dreams when I did sleep.

December 19th.—Bowes dined with us and we talked over the drama and other matters—amongst them touched on Talfourd and his imbecile and treacherous defence of my cause. Oh, fie upon him![3]

[1] The famous actress.

[2] This series of English performances took place in the Salle Ventadour, the theatre usually devoted to Italian Opera—(*note by Sir F. Pollock*).

[3] Macready's quite unreasonable indignation with Talfourd on this matter was, apparently, inextinguishable.

December 21st.—Went to theatre, rehearsed Virginius, a very troublesome rehearsal. It seems that Miss H. Faucit is not more smitten with Paris than I am—the audience are too fashionable, or too far off from the actor. We shall not act more than our twelve nights; the theatre is too large.

December 23rd.—Looked at the papers, which contain some very eulogistic articles on my performances here. Rehearsed the scenes of Virginius with supernumeraries on the stage till twelve; then finished the play in the saloon. Rested. Acted Virginius with much energy and power to a very excited audience. I was loudly called for at the end of the fourth act; but could not or would not make so absurd and empirical a sacrifice of the dignity of my poor art. Was called for and very enthusiastically received at the end of the play. De Fresne came into my room and detained Catherine and myself in long conversation.

December 27th.—Wrote a note with a box to Mr. Corkran.[1] Acted Virginius with some force; the audience were deeply interested, but not so tumultuous in their applause as on Monday. Called for and received with fervour.

December 28th.—Dined with De Fresne; met at dinner le Marquis de Pastoret, guardian of the Comte de Chambord (Henry V), Paul de la Roche, the great artist. In the evening, Regnier, Bertin[2] and family, a son of Talma, etc.

December 29th.—Received a very delightful note, inviting me to dine, from Eugène Sue. Called on Comte de Vigny[3]; saw him and Madame, who looks much older than himself and not handsome. Sat some time with him.

December 30th.—Went to rehearsal. News of Miss H. Faucit's illness, and inability to play. Spoke with Mr. Mitchell on what was to be done. The business was at last arranged for Mrs. Serle to do her best with Ophelia. Acted Hamlet as well as I could. The audience were interested, but not so tumultuous in their applause as on the previous evening. Mrs. Serle made a very fair effort. Two " artistes " from the Porte St. Martin came to my room " pour faire leurs hommages." De Fresne called, and was greatly excited by the performance. I was called for and well received.

---

[1] See note, p. 325, Vol. I.

[2] M. Bertin was editor and proprietor of the *Journal des Débats*—(*note by Sir F. Pollock*).

[3] The author of *Cinq Mars*.

December 31st.—Wound up my accounts for the year 1844, which, *I thank God*, are most satisfactory. Sat up to a very late hour, half-past two, preparing my books for the ensuing year. I close this with thanks for the past and prayers to Almighty God for the future, for the blessings of virtue, wisdom, and true piety on my beloved wife and children, my dear friends and my unworthy self.

1845

Paris, January 1st.—Received an Edinburgh paper, in which I was very much vilified and calumniated to raise the name of Miss Helen Faucit—things were said that must have come from her directly or indirectly. Acted Werner with great care and power, but to a bad and unsympathetic audience I would not give in; I think I acted well; was called for.

January 3rd.—Received a note from Eugène Sue proposing that we should go to the Théâtre Français to-morrow night, being the first representation of a new play by a friend of his. I answered, assenting to his wish. Acted Hamlet.

January 4th.—Dined with Eugène Sue, his *collaborateur,* and another friend, a very agreeable man. Went to the Théâtre Français; saw a play called *Guerrero,* a Mexican subject. Mlle. Plessis was sometimes graceful, but not quite concentrated enough in her passion. M. Beauvalet was melodramatic in his style, strong, but sometimes beyond the modesty of nature. Eugène Sue left me to make his compliments to the author.

January 5th.—Bowes called, and from him I learned that the play of last night had five acts, and that I had left at the end of the third! Oh! how I was distressed and annoyed! Eugène Sue must think me either very rude or very stupid—I hope the last. I called on De Fresne, who accompanied me to De la Roche, who received me most kindly, and in whose studio I saw two beautiful pictures, one of great power of colour, a Roman Beggar Family, like the strongest of Murillo; the other, in delicacy, sentiment, and harmony most exquisite, a Virgin and Sleeping Child, Joseph in the remote distance: it was a poem, and bought by Lord Hertford. La Roche expressed himself greatly pleased with my visit. We then called on a friend of Victor Hugo, and sat with his wife (the woman who was afterwards tried and punished for crim. con. with Victor Hugo) and family—he not at home; thence to the Ecole des Beaux-Arts, a building and institution to shame the British Government and people. Saw De la Roche's picture in oil on the circular wall of the theatre, and the copy of the Last Judgment. Thence to an old gentleman of ninety years of age, intimate with Garrick, Le Kain, etc. He was very interesting, but I do not wish for such a life.

January 6th.—Acted Macbeth, in my opinion, better than I have ever done before. The house was deeply attentive and interested, but did not give the quantity of applause which such a performance would have elicited in England. Was called for. Regnier, De Fresne, and Mitchell came into my room.

January 7th.—We called together on Scheffer and saw his pictures; the two from Faust, the Seduction Scene and the Sabbat, were full of beauty; the St. Augustine and his Mother most characteristic; a sketch of the Dead Christ and Marys, quite touching. A note from Mitchell informing me that the Minister refused us permission to act beyond Monday night.

January 8th.—Acted Macbeth with effort, not so well as Monday, but in spite of the *distressing* blunders and mismanagements, I think with power and discrimination. It is, however, certain, if that be any proof of skill or power, that the audience applauded Miss Faucit's sleeping scene much more than anything else in the whole play. Again I had to observe the small portion of applause, i. e. *battemens de mains,* that the audience gave to my performance; it would not have been so, I think—I am sure—before an English audience. I was called for, and Mr. Serle, as I thought *very impertinently,* said : " You had better take on Miss Faucit, for it was noticed." I was really *stung* by the unauthorized intrusion of his advice, and said : " When I want your advice I will ask for it ! "

January 9th.—Bowes returned, and sat long. He said that his wife was disgusted with the audience for lavishing so much applause on Miss Faucit, but they know best what they like. Lemoine said that she was *écrasée* by the part !

January 10th.—Acted my best; the audience, at first insensible, became gradually excited. M. et Mme. Garcia came into my room— *" pour faire leurs compliments,"* etc. In the banquet scene a wreath of bay was thrown to me, which the audience very much applauded. Called for at the end and well received. Acted really well. Spoke to Miss H. Faucit.

January 11th.—It is very clear that Paris will not make much money for me, but it adds greatly, to all appearance, to my reputation.

January 12th.—Corkran called with the *Morning Herald*—a very kind notice. Dined with Mr. Rowland Errington; met Lady Wellesley, Baring, Lord and Lady Kinnoul, Miss McTavish, Howard, etc. Liked very much Mr. and Mrs. Errington; a very pleasant evening. Went to Galignani's—kind-hearted man—the party the antipodes of what I had left.

January 13th.—Acted Hamlet for the most part extremely well; the audience were interested and attentive, but not so excitable as usual. Bouffé came into my room with Mitchell, "pour faire ses compliments." At the end of the play, just before the fall of the curtain, a person (Mr. Lucas?) hissed twice! The audience called for me and received me most cordially. Mitchell came into my room with a wreath, and expressed himself indignantly about the low and base endeavour of some persons, pointing to the front of the house. I quite understood him, but exactly value the cowardly indication at its worth.

January 14th.—Saw Mitchell on business, and understood from him his meaning in alluding last night to the endeavours of an envious clique to annoy me; he meant the friends of Miss H. Faucit; but *is it possible* that she could wish they should act so unworthily? I will not believe it. Chapman called on business; he told us that our receipts had exceeded those of any theatre in Paris! Called on De Fresne and M. Perrez with Catherine. What things he told and read to me of *Egalité*, and what treason on treason of Tallyerand! One most amusing and interesting anecdote of Napoleon and the Emperor of Russia. Showed me Talleyrand's letter, autograph, urging the execution of D'Enghien. In the evening cut and arranged *Hamlet* for the Palace.

January 15th.—Spoke to Mitchell, who gave me a letter from George Sand, most eloquent and elegant. He showed me another to Ledru in which it was enclosed. Called with Catherine on De Fresne. We went together to Mr. Pourtales, and saw his pictures and his gems. Bowes told me distinctly that *Miss H. Faucit's friends were my enemies,* and let me no room to doubt on the subject.

January 16th.—I drove to the Tuileries. We inquired for the *concièrge*, M. Lecomte, and having found his bureau and presented the order from Mr. Lambert (which Mitchell had brought me with a box for Catherine, admitting two persons), M. Lecomte conducted us to the second door *en face*. By this we entered, and passing through the lobbies and galleries came upon the front boxes of the theatre. It was all most elegant; much larger than I had anticipated from my recollection of Fontainebleau and some theatres in the Italian palaces; but it was such a theatre as befitted the palace of the king of a great nation. Whether great nations ought to have kings is a question for A.D. 2045 to decide. I went upon the stage, which was filled up exactly as at the Ventadour; even to the round trap for the Ghost's descent. With much difficulty, after being led where I could not follow, I obtained a room at a moderate height from the stage, and having secured the entrance of my servant and self, on which point there was great jealousy, I returned to my hotel. I thought much on what I had to go through, being quite aware that there could be little or no applause, and fixedly making up my mind to occupy my thoughts alone with Hamlet; to be Hamlet, and think neither of King, nor Court, nor anything but my personation. I went with Stent to the Palace and was met by Mitchell's officious man, who had nearly caused us some delay. We reached my room, and I was tolerably accommodated. The play began, and I adhered to my purpose; had neither eyes nor thought for anything but the feelings and thoughts and demeanour of Hamlet. In my mind I never gave such a representation of the part, and without a hand of applause; but indeed there was an attempt in the first scene by some one who, I suppose, because sensible of his offence against decorum, " and back recoiled, he knew not why, even at the sound himself had made." In the fourth act, where I have nothing to do, I did cast a glance at the royal box; saw the white fuzz of the Queen's head and the old King on the other side of the centre; the *salle* had altogether a very brilliant appearance, the pit was filled with military. Mr. Serle was very long between the acts. After the play one of the King's *suite* in court uniform waited on me, and, with expressions of his Majesty's pleasure, etc., presented me with a long packet or parcel. I hastily dressed. Mitchell just spoke to me. Miss H. Faucit, as I passed her, said: " Such a pretty bracelet." I hurried home to Catherine, told her all the news, and looked at the poniard [1] sent by the King.

January 17th.—Went to the theatre and saw Mitchell, who showed me the snuff-box sent to him by Louis Philippe, and amused me with the account of the King's conversation with him. Acted King Henry IV pretty well; it seemed to impress the audience; it is not a scene to excite enthusiasm. Saw and spoke a few words to Helen

---

[1] The poniard given by Louis Philippe to Macready was bequeathed by him to his daughter, Benvenuta—Mrs. Horsford—(*note by Sir F. Pollock*).

Faucit. She had on the bracelet which the King had sent her; was very curious to know what had been given to me, but I did not gratify her. She looked very well.

January 18*th.*—Went to the Opera Comique, and saw the stage, etc., which was arranged for the scene of *King Henry IV.* M. Henri, the *sous-régisseur*, was very civil in doing the honours of his establishment. Chapman told me that Mr. Forrest, whom Mr. Mitchell avoided, had seen him and told him that "*London was ringing* with the failure of the English theatre in Paris." Mr. Chapman answered him very properly. When on the stage and prepared to begin, a person came forward and introduced me to the manager of the theatre. The curtain drew up, and the audience were deeply attentive. One person tried at the commencement to disturb the performance by mimicking my voice, but it was put down instantly, and the act of *King Henry IV* was listened to with the deepest attention. Whilst I was undressing, the Committee of the Authors, etc., requested to see me and, entering, presented me with a letter and (as I afterwards found) a gold medal inscribed to me! I thanked them, etc. M. Halévy was the principal.[1]

January 19*th.*—O'Reilly wrote, wishing to have some account of the *scene* of the presentation of the ataghan at the Tuileries, but as I intimated to his messenger, "Story? God bless you! I have none to tell, sir!" I was required to show the ataghan, from which one of

---

[1] This performance was given at the request of the Committee of the Society for the Relief of Distressed Authors, for the benefit of their fund. The letter of thanks was as follows—

"*Paris, le* 18 *janvier,* 1845.

"MONSIEUR,

"La Commission de la Société des Auteurs Dramatiques Français a besoin, avant votre départ pour l'Angleterre, de vous renouveler ses remerciements. L'appui, tout puissant, que vous venez de prêter à sa caisse de secours n'a pu augmenter sans doute l'admiration que tout Paris professe pour votre grand talent; mais il a doublé l'estime que l'on doit à votre noble et généreux caractère.

"Permettez-nous, monsieur, de vous offrir, comme un témoignage de cette haute estime, la médaille d'or que nous venons de faire frapper à votre nom. Elle vous rappellera quelquefois ce que vous avez fait pour des infortunés honorables, la reconnaissance que nous en conservons, et les liens indissolubles qui existent désormais entre les artistes Anglais et Français.

"Agréez, monsieur, la nouvelle assurance de notre haute considération.

"(Signé) EUGÈNE SCRIBE.   VICTOR HUGO.   ÉTIENNE (*Président*).
          MÉLESVILLE   DALTON.
          (*Vice-Président*).   F. HALÉVY.   VIENNET (*Vice-Président*).

"À. M. Macready, artiste dramatique "—(*note by Sir F. Pollock*).

285

them knocked off one of the sapphires. Called on Mr. Ledru, who was in bed from an accident; he gave me a very cordial reception; told me of the unanimity of the enthusiasm of the literary men in Paris on my acting; gave me George Sand's address, quite the *entente cordiale*. Called on Mr. and Mrs. Errington; on George Sand. Went with De Fresne to call on Victor Hugo, in the Place Royale; the storm obliged our driver to drive the carriage under the colonnade. The house, old and cold, was quite a poet's mansion. The *salon*, hung round and ceilinged with tapestry, had large pictures; it had a gloomy air, though not dark, and looked like a poet's room. Victor Hugo received me very cordially, and was most earnest in his expressions of admiration and respect to me. I talked with several there, and had a circle of the young men around me. I saw his daughter, who was pretty. He accompanied me to the door when we left, and was most cordial in his *adieux* to me.

January 20th.—Called with Sumner on George Sand; saw her son and daughter, a sweet interesting girl; talked much of Shakspeare and of England; I liked her very much. She said she would come to England, if I would act in London, though she disliked the country so much. Purchased a *pendule* for my study. Went to Mrs. Austin's early in the evening. Mr. Austin was in the room when I entered but, after salutation, retired, and I saw him no more. M. Barbier was present, and he read part of his translation of *Julius Cæsar* into French prose. Left them to go to the Ambassador's. The people were so crammed in the reception-room that I could not approach Lady Cowley, but almost immediately the crowd began to move into the theatre, fitted up in the ball-room of the hotel or palace; our way was through a deliciously cool gallery lined with exotics—it might have been a conservatory, but I do not distinctly recollect. I got a very good seat; the ladies occupied the front benches. I sat near Broadwood and Errington, who introduced me to Lawrence Peel's son; Galignani was also near me, and I was weak enough to feel disconcerted by the proximity, but I subdued it and chatted with him, though under violence to myself—such miserable fools do pride and the influence of caste make us, and so imbecile and unjust are we beneath its power. The theatre was very prettily arranged, and some of the beauty and plenty of the pride of the English aristocracy was collected in it. The prologue, written by Lady Dufferin,[1] and spoken by Charles Sheridan

---

[1] Helen Selina (1807–1867), one of the "three Sheridan beauties"; married first, Lord Dufferin; secondly on his death-bed the Earl of Gifford. Mother of the distinguished

and Greville,[1] was very smart. The scandal scene, first scene of Sir Peter and Lady Teazle, and the screen scene of the *School for Scandal* was the play; *The Merry Monarch* was the farce. To me it was all amusing—to see how these persons, who so undervalue the theatrical art, expose themselves to ridicule and contempt when they essay it, was an entertainment. Lady Seymour [2] looked very mawkish as Maria, Lady Dufferin unmeaning in Mrs. Candour, Lady Essex more at home than either in Lady Sneerwell; Crabtree and Sir Benjamin Backbite, H. Howard, were both very bad; Sir Peter and Lady Teazle, Oriel and Lady Leveson very "tolerable and not to be endured"; Lord Leveson [3] not so bad as Joseph; C. Sheridan very tame and very like a tall and handsome Moses in Charles Surface. The farce was better; Lawrence Peel [4] made a respectable effort in Captain Copp; Greville was respectable in the King and Lord Leveson in Rochester; but the star of the night, and really one to shine on any stage, was Miss McTavish in Mary. I did not think her very pretty when I met her at dinner at Errington's, but her acting was naïve, sprightly, arch, simple, and beautiful. Saw Mrs. Errington after the play; saw Palgrave Simpson;[5] also Lord Cowley,[6] to whom I was presented by Mrs. Errington; talked some time with me, complimented me upon my success in Paris, etc.

January 21st.—Called on De Fresne, and, although with very great reluctance, in compliance with his particular wish, accompanied him to the Conservatoire. Heard the pupils of Sanson go through their course of theatrical instruction. It is an institution of the Government to train pupils, who are elected to the school, for the stage. I was interested, and saw the inefficacy of the system clearly; it was teaching *conventionalism*—it was perpetuating the mannerism of the French stage, which is all mannerism. Genius would be cramped, if not maimed and distorted by such a course. Saw Halévy there, but

---

statesman, the first Marquis of Dufferin and Ava; author of the *The Irish Emigrant* and other popular lyrics. Commemorated by Browning in his poem *Helen's Tower*.

[1] Henry William Greville (1801–1872), brother of the diarist; for some years attaché to the Paris embassy. A portion of his journal entitled *Leaves from a Diary* was published in 1883-4.

[2] *The Queen of Beauty* (see note, p. 46, Vol. II.).

[3] Afterwards the second Earl Granville (1815–1891), the well-known Liberal statesman.

[4] Presumably a son of Sir Lawrence Peel (1799–1884), first cousin of the Prime Minister; afterwards Chief Justice of Bengal.

[5] John Palgrave Simpson (1807–1857); the well-known dramatist.

[6] Henry Wellesley (1773–1847); first Lord Cowley, then British Ambassador at Paris.

could only exchange a few words with him, as I was in haste to return.[1]

London, January 28th.—Called on Forster with the small bronze ornament I had bought for him in Paris ; met Liston at his chambers. Went on to call on Mr. and Mrs. J. Delane, saw her and sat with her some time. Returned to Forster, and met at his door Edward Bulwer, whom I did not know till he came into the room. Sat with Forster until I went to Covent Garden theatre. Everything dingy, dirty,

---

[1] Dickens, who had left for Rome, wrote the following letter to Mrs. Macready relative to the Paris visit—

" Romè,
" Monday, March 10, 1845.

" My dear Mrs. Macready,

" More in recollection of your two welcome notes, heartily received and blushingly unanswered, than as one labouring under the delusion of having anything to say, I append my sign manual to the highly illegible letter of my worser half. I was so cold after leaving you and dear Macready in Paris that I was taken out of the coach at Marseilles (it was sixteen hours behind its time) in a perfectly torpid state, and was at first supposed to be luggage. But the porters not being able to find any direction upon me, led to a further examination, and what the newspapers called 'the vital spark' was finally discovered, twinkling under a remote corner of the travelling shawls which you were pleased to approbate—(love the word ; it belongs to our dear and enlightened friends, the great American people)—in the Hotel Brighton. After that, I passed three days of waking nightmare at Marseilles. I think it was three. It may have been two, but I crowded into the space the noisome smells of a patriarchal life. After that, I was so horribly ill on board a steamboat that I should have made my will if I had had anything to leave, but I had only the basin ; and I couldn't leave that for a moment. That suffering over, I rushed into the arms of my expectant family. Their happiness is more easily conceived than described. You know me and will paint the picture for yourself. I was greatly distressed to hear from you that you had been so unwell in Paris. What can have been the matter with you ? I laid down your note and thought of all manner of possibilities. My particular love to my godson. Sometimes I have a terrible apprehension that Macready, conscience-stricken beyond endurance by the reflection that he has never written a word to me of his triumphs and prospects (I have a great desire to know his secret mind upon the latter head) will play the Roman fool and die upon the jewelled dagger the French King gave him. Adjure him to be of good cheer. My forgiveness and blessing are enclosed. How anxiously I look forward to finding myself once again in the dining parlour at Clarence Terrace—just the old, snug, little party of *ourselves.* I should vainly try to say though I wrote a quire ! But midsummer, please God, will find us all together—well and happy—and mainly so, in our mutual friendship and attachment. In any case, as poor Power used to say, ' I'm mutual, and I'm sure you are too—though you do attack me sometimes.' When Willy has completed his complete guide to Paris and its environs, I shall be happy to edit the book and to preface it with some account of the author founded on a personal correspondence with him in that capital.

" With best regard to Miss Macready and all the pets,

" I am ever, my dear Mrs. Macready,
" Faithfully your friend,
" Charles Dickens."

vulgar, and poor.   A miserable coxcomb displaying the antics of a
tumbler or posture-master in *conducting* the orchestra and chorus.
The play, *Antigone*, wretchedly acted by Mr. and Miss Vandenhoff;
low, provincial rant and extravagant pantomime.   If this be the
representation of a Greek play the Athenians must have had a wretched
taste.

January 29th.—A Mr. ——, a barrister, called on the subject of
some dramas of about 3,600 lines each, which he had made, and put
into Longman's hands, upon the reigns of the Plantagenets, joining
with it a history of the Church; I backed out as courteously as I could.
Called at Gore House; Lady Blessington was just driving out.   I went
into the carriage with her and Miss Power for about five minutes and
then went in and sat with D'Orsay.   Called and left card at Bulwer's.
Called on Forster, Lady B.'s carriage was at his door.   Found him and
Leigh Hunt at dinner; sat with them about an hour.   Hunt is a *bore*.

February 3rd.—Sat and talked with Forster; he very strongly argued
for the restoration of Hamlet's speech when the King is praying.   It
is worth thinking of.

February 12th.—Catherine brought me the Louis Philippe poniard
from Smith's, and with it the information that the French *King's*
present—"Oh Majesty, how high thy glory towers, when the rich
blood of kings"—is silver-gilt!!!

February 15th.—Called on Forster; found Bulwer and Ainsworth
there; was accosted with the "dreadful news"—the sad intelligence
of poor Blanchard [1]—he was dead!   He had destroyed himself—last
night.   It was a dreadful shock; they were devising plans to keep
the statement of the suicide from the papers, and to concert means
for assisting his orphan children.

Newcastle, February 19th.—Acted Virginius very fairly, thanks to
my light dinner.   Called for.   Everything here makes me reflect.   I
see a life gone in an unworthy, an unrequiting pursuit.   Great energy,
great power of mind, ambition, and activity that, with direction, might
have done anything, now made into a player.

February 23rd.—Read at the rooms a confirmation of the account
of Forrest's disastrous and total failure in Macbeth.   I had only seen
him in Lear and Damon, which were very dull performances, but not
otherwise offensive, but in Macbeth he seems to have provoked the
patience of the audience.   I am truly sorry for him (without wishing
him *great* success) and deeply sorry for his wife.

[1] Samuel Laman Blanchard (see note, p. 86, Vol. I.)

February 25th.—Heard of the death of Sydney Smith [1] and Lord Mornington.[2] The last I knew nothing of, and of the first only his talent, which was not fitted for his station, and often used, I think, unbeseemingly. I felt little interest in him.

February 26th.—Made an extract of some lines upon *Richard II*, and an autograph for Margaret E——. That play lives in her mind, so does it in mine, when I, the first who ever acted it since the time of Shakspeare, produced it here. She was a girl then, and I not more than a boy, with no power to see the course before me, no hand to point it out, no mind to direct me—my talent, energy, and youthful activity a mere trading property in the hands of a sordid possessor. Alas! Alas! Acted Shylock very unsatisfactorily, sometimes feebly, but the whole play was so bad, I am not able to tell how much of the dulness is chargeable to me. Still, I was not good.

London, March 2nd.—Called on Mr. and Mrs. Forrest, with whom were several people; to me he observed that he was going to Paris, where he would be " better appreciated than he is here." I fancy *not*.

March 3rd.—On this day I enter on my fifty-third year.

Sheffield, March 5th.—Acted Hamlet pretty well, taking the company, etc., into account. Called for. What a farce has this absurd usage now become.

March 8th.—Saw a Mr. Brownell, who, under the remembered name of *Fenton*, had been a player in my father's theatres, when I first came on public life. He is now eighty, looking really more healthy than he did thirty-five years ago; he spoke of his son, now a player in Australia. I was glad to see the old man. Went to St. Paul's Church; inquiring at the sexton's house, the woman said, when I told her I wanted to go into the church, " Mr. Macready, is it not? " I told her, " Yes," and she would go with me. She told me the letters on my blessed mother's slab wanted deepening, which I expected and went to speak about. I stood over her remains, and the lines that record her age and death. My heart has ever, ever loved her; had she lived, my fate might have been different. How well do I remember her, in life, in joy, in sorrow, and in her maternal love; and

---

[1] Sydney Smith (1771–1845); the famous Canon. His wit was not always of the most reverent description, but his hatred of ecclesiastical cant and pretentiousness should have enlisted Macready's sympathy.

[2] William Wellesley Pole (1763–1845); third Earl of Mornington, better known as Lord Maryborough. At that time Postmaster-General in Sir R. Peel's Administration.

in death, so sweet and placid—how well do I recollect kissing that marble forehead as she lay in her serene, ethereal sleep. O God, bless her beloved spirit.

March 9th.—Read over some poems of Wordsworth; certainly where he is good, he is very good; but he is often obscure, often wordy to extreme weariness and often weak almost to silliness; his egoism [1] is, moreover, not very amiable; but he gives great lessons and kindles aspiring feelings.

March 10th.—Acted Macbeth with great pains, and as well as I could against such dreadful accompaniments as Lady Macbeth, Banquo, etc. Was rather out of temper with some ignorant people in the gallery *calling for* Mr. Ryder!

London, March 22nd.—Mr. B. Smith called about the stand for the testimonial. He told me, evidently with reluctance, that the jewels in the poniard given me by that *shabby dog*—Louis Philippe— are sham!

Manchester, March 26th.—Acted Othello, really striving, labouring to act it well; partially, I think, I succeeded; but the labour is very great when I turn to think that, with my rehearsals, which to me are careful, watchful, and fatiguing businesses, and dressing and acting, etc., I employ at least nine hours a day in the theatre in labour, to say nothing of my writing, reading, and thinking on my business elsewhere. My money is not got without some equivalent of toil. Thank God, that I can work for it. Called for, but the audience seemed to me cold and difficult to excite, very different from those who used to assemble in the old theatre—it may be raised prices depress their spirits.

March 27th.—Acted Werner very fairly. Called for (trash!). Spoke in gentle rebuke and kind expostulation to Mr. G. V. Brooke.[2] Read the *Times*. Criticism on Mr. Forrest's performance of Metamora, and an account of a presentation of a testimonial to Miss H. Faucit for her performance of Antigone—(read the stuff!)—by certain members of the Irish Academy! My God! when or where will the humbug of this world cease? . . . I fear I give vent to these expressions as much from a feeling of envy as an impatience of injustice— which cannot be enough condemned. In this profession we seem to

[1] This was amusingly exemplified on a visit which he paid to Lord Spencer's famous library at Althorp, when, according to the librarian, the only volumes that he looked at were his own poems !

[2] Gustavus Vaughan Brooke (1818–1866); a successful Shakspearian actor of the second rank, but failed as a manager both in America and Australia.

suppose that distinction, except to oneself, is an obscuration of oneself. This is very narrow and poor and bad. I am quite satisfied and glad upon reflection that Helen Faucit has met with so much good fortune, but in fairness I must say that it is ridiculous to call such trash as the language of Antigone the Greek poetry, and as absurd to talk about Helen Faucit's education—she being utterly un-educated. Unluckily the stage is the profession of all others for empiricism.

March 28th.—Was kept long awake last night in thinking on what the thoughts, sensations, and actions of the convict Tawell [1] must be during such a night. What a lottery is this world, and what a miser-able race of beings are crawling over it? What is our mission here? My uncertainty as to my future means will not allow me to be happy. I ought—I ought to be—a man of good fortune now, and what am I? What would illness make me, or any reverse? O God, befriend and support me.

April 3rd.—Spoke in terms of advice and *promise* to Mr. G. V. Brooke, who is one of those whom nature has gifted to a certain extent, but who will abuse her bounty—I feel sure of it.

To Carlisle, April 6th.—At a very early hour reached the railway station, and sat to await the mail train for Lancaster; found Mr. Ryder in the carriage. Breakfasted at Lancaster and just got a view of the Castle, which I always look at with a peculiarly painful interest, as the place of my unlucky father's confinement (for debt) when the cares of life were first devolved on me.[2]

Glasgow, April 15th.—Letter from Murray, Edinburgh, expressive

---

[1] The Quaker convicted of murdering one Sarah Hart, at Salt Hill.

[2] Up to this time (*see* Introduction) it had been Macready's intention, on leaving Rugby, to go to Oxford and afterwards to the Bar, but his father's misfortunes compelled him to take up the stage as a calling when still a school-boy. The following extract from a letter, written to his father in 1808, by his Rugby tutor and relative, William Birch, describes the high promise which he showed at school.

Rugby, December 8, 1808.

"DEAR Sir,

"We will with great pleasure take care of your sons as long as it is convenient to you at this time or any other. Your eldest son improves in everything and I think will make a very fine man, to whatever he may turn his abilities. I cannot omit (though I don't know whether you will thank me) expressing my admiration of his wonderful talent for acting and speaking. Such a combination of fine figure, expression, countenance, elegance and propriety of action, modulation of voice, and most complete power of repre-sentation I have formed an idea of, perhaps, but have never before met with ; and that is the sense of every one who has heard him. I know this rare talent may be turned to good account in the Church or at the Bar ; it is valuable everywhere. Whatever is your

of his wish to engage me when disposed to visit Edinburgh. I do not know that if I could afford to do without it I should ever wish to act there. The impertinence and ignorance of the Scotch *writers for the Press* on matters of literature and art, and their overweening conceit, disgust me with them. Ballantyne is gone; Bell too (not his equal, as cognizant of the *dramatic art*) does not write. Who are there now? Rested a very short time. Acted Virginius—in some parts *splendidly* —too well for such a house. I fear we have *broken down*. Alas! Alas! What satisfaction, what object have I in playing—if once the remuneration ceases? Called for. Spoke to Mr. Ryder and read paper. Weary of all.

April 16th.—Dr. Smith called and took me to the prison. Oh! how it wrung and sickened my heart to see crime—crime—in all its damning effects, with the life of misery attendant on it, marked as the destiny of youths and boys, children, whom I saw there, and of young women and young girls—alas! alas!

April 20th.—Letters from Catherine, from *Bowes*, mentioning— what I am loth to credit, but which I cannot disbelieve—statements of Miss H. Faucit's detraction and abuse of me. Read *Times*—the close of the debate on the Maynooth question, which has been so long agitated by this *Christian* legislature. Oh, Christ!—where is the *love of man* and *fear alone of God* upon this earth, which thou didst come to teach? *Answer*, Sir R. Inglis, Plumptre, Ashley, Sibthorp & Co.!

Carlisle, April 22nd.—Rose in good time, though with abated spirits, to finish what remained of packing and prepare for my departure. The result of this engagement has a "little dashed my spirits"; it is quite clear that I am never to look for the chance of great success; and whilst I see such things as Mr. and Mrs. C. Kean —mediocrity like Miss H. Faucit, etc.—receive *thousands*, I must be content to realize the prospect, that my doubtful hope presents, of securing enough to retire with comfort to America, for I cannot, that is very plain, expect to live—if I live—in England. I am, however, most thankful, truly thankful, in my individual person, for myself; but these things keep alive my fears and distrust. Obliged to stay all night in Carlisle. Read newspaper. Walked in the town,

---

intention I will second it, and if you determine to send him to Oxford next summer I will endeavour to prepare the way."

Macready never forgot his indebtedness to his old tutor, with whom he maintained the most affectionate relations in after life.

over the bridge, enjoying the heavy mass of shadow in which the old castle lay, the distant cathedral, the Eden, and the gorgeous red moon that rose in full red glory to the left, like a lamp above the dusky city. Old times and old feelings—the times and feelings of youth—came back upon me.

Whitehaven, April 23rd.—Looked at *Examiner*, in which I did *not like* the abuse of Peel; it is not argument, nor is it philosophy, nor is it what we expect of the *Examiner*. Acted Hamlet with considerable pains, but the set around me were enough to paralyse inspiration.

April 24th.—Rehearsed with these wretched players the play of to-night. It is not to be evaded: the members of this profession—I know of no exception—are either utter blackguards or most ignorant empirics. Oh God—and I have been thrown among these *things*.

April 25th.—Read the paper; was greatly delighted with Macaulay's speech on the Irish Church—it is a text-book.[1] Acted Cardinal Richelieu as well as I could with *such a company* and such appurtenances. How is it possible to prevent one's mind from wandering, when *in every theatre* there are seductions and allurements to engage your attention?

Dumfries, May 5th.—Tried to act Hamlet well to a house not sufficiently well filled, but was thwarted by the idleness and inattention of these *wretches* of actors; I think there is no excuse for such men. There are trades, why do they not take them as a means of life? but they come to this from the desire to *escape work*. They are disgusting.

May 7th.—Ryder called. I walked with him to see Burns's house; was in the room where he died. Unhappy Burns!—and there is Wordsworth, enriched by place and patronage,[2] and the guest of Queen Victoria and Queen Adelaide. But it is the world—a world with which I am utterly dissatisfied, and of which I am sick to

[1] This was one of Macaulay's most eloquent speeches particularly in the passage contrasting the colleges of Oxford and Cambridge, with Maynooth, and in the striking conclusion: "When I remember what was the faith of Edward III and of Henry VI, of Margaret of Anjou and Margaret of Richmond, of William of Wykeham and William of Waynefleet, of Archbishop Chichely and Cardinal Wolsey; when I remember what we have taken from the Roman Catholics—King's College, New College and Christchurch, my own Trinity; and when I look at the miserable Dotheboys Hall which we have given them in exchange, I feel, I must own, less proud than I could wish of being a Protestant and a Cambridge man."

[2] This was an exaggeration. Wordsworth's "place" yielded only a competence, and the "patronage" of Lord Lonsdale no more than compensated for the injustice to which the poet and his family had been subjected by that nobleman's predecessor.

disgust—I mean the conventional part of it. Continued our walk along the beautiful river banks.

London, May 12th.—Fox and Forster dined with us, and we discoursed on the most probable means of re-establishing the high drama again in London. The conclusion of many plans was to ascertain how far that of the St. James's was likely to meet the end held in view.

May 16th.—Went with Forster and Colden, Catherine and Georgy to Lyceum theatre. Oh!!!—who would not blush for the character of his country's taste and refinement who saw an audience crowded to listen to such stuff, so wretchedly acted; it is disgraceful to taste, and in the exposure made of the legs of a great number of women it is indecent and immoral. Oh—England's drama!

May 17th.—Went to Babbage's. Saw D. Colden and his friend, Miss Herries the younger, her cousin and her husband, Haworths, Mrs. M. Gibson, Harness, S. Jervis. A lady accosted me, and asked me after our mutual friend Dickens. I did not know her; returning home, it suddenly occurred to me it was Miss Coutts.[1] She hoped "our acquaintance might not terminate here." Met Sir R. Comyn below, and Bulwer on the stairs.

May 20th.—My spirits were very low; the sense of my *uncertain position* in society weighed quite heavily upon me; I could not fight it off. I had no heart to go out, nor to call on any one. I felt really miserable, wishing myself in America, or anywhere but where I was. Entered arrears of record. Went on to the House of Commons— waited for Sheil in the lobby. I stopped him as he was passing, by agreement, and he procured me an order, not, as I expected, for *under* the Gallery, but for the Speaker's Gallery—an exposed, inconvenient place, where I sat from six till twelve o'clock, listening to the vilest stuff and poorest trash of words that ever dulled or tormented the ear of man! Messrs. Barron, Godson, Gaskell, Lawson, Rawdon, Bellew, Shaw, Sir John Inglis—oh! such speakers! Sheil did not speak; weary and disgusted I returned home about one o'clock.

May 21st.—Read the paper, which made a very favourable report of the donkeys whom I heard braying out their stuff in the House of Commons last night. Mitchell called, and in talking over the subject of English drama at the St. James's, he asserted himself most anxious to make some arrangement, but must wait the return to town of Captain Harford, etc.

---

[1] Afterwards the Baroness Burdett-Coutts.

May 24th.—Went to see Roberts's drawings of Nubia and Egypt. Met Miss Rogers there, who seems wearing away "to the land of the leal"; was very much pleased with the drawings. Went on to Graves's and asked permission to see Power's statue of "The Slave," which was readily granted. We went in, and my gratification was *extreme.* I do not remember having been so much delighted with any work in marble of any living artist, and in some respects it rivals some points of excellence in the antique. The Delanes, the Chisholm, M. Regnier, Baroness Eichthal, Mrs. Jameson, Z. Troughton, Maclise and Etty dined with us.

May 25th.—Read some pages of Dr. Arnold's life. In considering the mind of this great and good man, it is a curious point for a philosopher to notice that the recommendation of his friends to him upon his uneasy doubts as to the *Trinity* should be to put it out of his head and pray—*i. e.* to induce a state of *excitement* in the mind that would mislead or cloud his reason. Oh! ye *cant*ers about truth, with place and pelf and power in your view!

May 26th.—Read the *Times*, and was shocked and grieved to consider the condition of Ireland and England, and the prospect there appears to be of a war with the United States. Wrote to Milman, requesting him to protect the interests of the Siddons Committee in regard to the site of the monument with the new Dean.[1] Mr. Rogers, Emerson Tennent, Tennyson D'Eyncourt, Sir de Lacy Evans, Sir John Wilson, Eastlake, Edwin Landseer, Monckton Milnes, Dr. Quin and D. Colden came to dinner. Conversation turned on Dickens's writings on America, which all concurred in blaming. In the evening several came: Fitzgeralds, the Chisholm, Mrs. Kitchener, Mrs. and Misses Stone, Staudigl, Miss M. Hawes, Baroness Eichthal, Babbage, Goldsmids, Procters, Troughton, Mrs. E. Tennent and Mulhollands, Haworths, Horace Twisses, Mrs. M. Gibson, Mrs. Duncan Stewart, Miss Rogers, Miss Moore, etc.

May 27th.—Rose late with uncertain head. Read the paper and wrote a note of appointment to Mitchell. Colden came and went with Catherine and self to take up Regnier on our way to Greenwich; the streets were crowded with carriages and spectators attracted by the Queen's drawing-room. Went in carriage to Greenwich. From the Trafalgar Hotel went to the hospital; showed M. Regnier the hall, chapel, wards; we then went into the park and enjoyed the view from the top of the hill. The Twisses, Fitzgeralds, Stanfield and Forster

---

[1] Samuel Wilberforce; he became in the same year Bishop of Oxford.

came to dine with us. Our day was cheerful, but Catherine and
myself were not very well, and Forster was particularly noisy.

To Birmingham, May 29th.—Arrived in Birmingham, I went to
the theatre; met Phipson on my way, who walked with me; saw Mr.
Ryder, but neither actors nor manager were there, nor were they
coming—"it was only *Hamlet,*" and they knew it quite well!! I
wish they did!

Norwich, June 3rd.—Read to-day's *Times.* Debates on Maynooth
and the Academical Grants—*oh, God!* are these men fit to taste Thy
bounties? But who shall question *Thy* will!

June 4th.—Serjeant McReady, 5th Fusiliers, called to ask to see me,
as he was of the "same name." He was a good soldier-looking fellow,
gave an account of himself, said he was very proud of me (!). I gave
him an order for to-morrow; he said he was not a discredit to me,
etc. I was amused, and received him very kindly.

To London, June 6th.—Set out on my journey to town. Read
Voltaire on the way—part of *L'Ingénu* and part of *L'Homme aux
quarante écus,* by both of which I was very much amused and edified.
Voltaire is maligned by our canting churchmen, who merit all the
vituperation that he justly casts on the pretenders to piety in the
Romish Church.

June 7th.—Nina and Willie, to my great regret, expressed their
aversion to go and live in America. I do not wish to *compel* them to
leave this country, but I cannot feel with its aristocracy—I dislike
it, "and something more."

Birmingham, June 10th.—Acted Cardinal Richelieu tolerably well
—at least I took great pains. Called for and well received. Looked
over the *Times.* More and more disgusted with the aristocracy and
the aristocratic spirit of this country. What is *man*—what is *God*
to these "tyrants through opinion and privilege"?

Rugby, June 14th.—To Rugby, reading *Punch* by the way.
Walked up from Rugby station to the town. Was obliged to stand
and examine well the street and houses to identify the scenes of my
boyhood. Saw dear old Birch, who received me most affectionately.
Talked with him for some time. I am always glad to pay my affectionate duty to dear old Birch, but Rugby loses, I fear, in its modern
improvements, *the old* love and interest with me—it is *not the same.*

London, June 21st.—Went to Babbage's, saw Rogers, Brockedon,
Lyell, Herries, Poole, E. Tennents, Procters, etc., Miss Coutts, who
did not come near me, so that I could not speak to her.

June 28th.—Went to Westminster—called on Milman,[1] whom I now first notice as a doubled-up old man; went with him to call on the Dean,[2] whom I found a very young-looking man; his address was very frank and agreeable. We went into the Abbey, and I showed them the site I wished for the Siddons Monument; it was agreed to, but the Dean could not permit the walls to be cut, *i. e.* the bust to be *let in*. I left them, and afterwards went to Lydia to show her the chosen spot. Afterwards we went to Campbell, who is rather a difficult person. He at last promised to send me a drawing of the design to be shown to the Committee, when they meet, if I can ever get them to meet.

June 30th.—Went to the British Gallery. Much pleased with the pictures—particularly the Van Dycks, Rembrandts, Ann. Caracci, Murillo, Sir Joshua, Gainsborough, Claude, Cuyp, Hobbema, Quentin Matsys, Titian, Callcott. The more I see of Lawrence's painting the more he sinks in my opinion—I mean, comparing him with the *great* names of art.

July 1st.—Called on Lord Francis Egerton—to whom I showed the list of the " Manuscrits inédits " of Talleyrand; he seemed to think much of them, and said he should be glad to hear of their actual price upon his return from the German Baths. I talked some time with him, and at parting he gave me a book of his—I have not yet looked at it. His manners are very gentlemanly. Called at the Athenæum—reading *Chuzzlewit*.

July 2nd.—Catherine and Willie both unwell. Catherine could not accompany me to the Twisses, where I dined and met Bingham Baring, Sir W.[3] and Lady Molesworth, Pemberton Leigh,[4] Lady Morgan, Lord Strangford, Lord Granville Somerset, and Baron Alderson. In the evening I saw the Misses Herries, Mrs. J. Delane, Mrs. Kitchener, the Chisholm, etc. Mrs. Abel, the Miss Balcombe of St. Helena, when Napoleon was there; Sir E. Bulwer Lytton, who again nodded to me from a distance! Disraeli, etc.

July 3rd.—Brewster called to cut my hair; he told me the tradesmen could not get paid in London, for all the money was employed

---

[1] Afterwards Dean of St. Paul's, then a Canon of Westminster.

[2] Wilberforce.

[3] Sir William Molesworth, Bart. (1810–1855); an advanced Liberal, who became Colonial Secretary in Lord Palmerston's Administration in 1855.

[4] Thomas Pemberton Leigh (1793–1867), afterwards Lord Kingsdown; a distinguished equity lawyer. He refused the Great Seal and other high judicial offices, but accepted a peerage in order to strengthen the appellate tribunal of the House of Lords.

in railroads. Went to Lady Goldsmid's; saw the Brockedons, Hart, Sir R. Westmacott, Ayrton, Elliotson, Mrs. Procter, Mr. and Mrs. Bates, etc. The rooms were magnificent.

July 22nd.—Catherine received an anonymous letter accusing Miss H. Faucit of depreciating me and reflecting upon her. Anonymous letters are not worthy of belief, and this I have no doubt exaggerates the truth—though I fear Miss Helen Faucit forgets what she owes to me. Fox and Forster gave up the scheme of the St. James's theatre, on the ground of its making me liable to such a risk.

To Eastbourne, July 24th.—Went to Brighton by railroad; saw that disgusting person, Mr. ——, a disgusting member of a disgusting family—one who belongs to "the order" of "*noble by convention*"; pah! Read on my whole journey to Eastbourne Carlyle's *Life of Schiller*—some contrast both in the character of the biographer and of the subject of his description to these elegant specimens of the man-made aristocracy. Delighted with the book—excited by the author and deeply interested in the character and fate of Schiller. Came on in a fly to Eastbourne.

July 25th.—Unpacked my clothes and books; enjoyed the air and prospect, and after breakfast gave the whole morning to the instruction of my dear children. My anxiety to give them a taste for acquiring knowledge—to be satisfied of their own *desire* to learn, and to see their voluntary efforts to improve themselves—makes me bestow all the time at my disposal upon them. After dinner whilst they went to play I read *Schiller's Life*, which delights me very much. Walked out with Catherine, met the children and walked with them. In the evening read to the children.

London, July 30th.—Called on Forster. He told me of an intimation he had received of Webster's wish to engage me—through Mr. Lemon; of his interview with Webster, who was desirous of knowing my terms (if I were disposed to meet him on a footing of business), and what assistance of performers in my plays I should require. I told Forster what I should ask—£100 per week for three nights per week for eight weeks. I required, *as a conditon*, no one; but if he asked me to suggest, I should name Miss Cushman as the person to act those parts I most required help in—Queen, Lady Macbeth, etc. These terms were the same Maddox had offered, and been willing to give me, and £20 per week less than Mitchell had offered. I told Forster that it was not my desire to *over-weight* the

299

theatre. After reaching home wrote a note for Forster, not wishing my name to be given *officially* to Mr. Webster as recommending Miss Cushman, which might seem unkind to Helen Faucit, and extending my proposition from eight weeks to sixteen weeks. Dined with Lord Lansdowne; met Mrs. Norton, Charles Buller, Mr. and Mrs. Milman, Bulwer Lytton, Sir James Kay Shuttleworth,[1] etc. The conversation turned much upon America, and I liked the people I met. I was glad that I went there. What luxury, what elegance, what wealth of art!

To Eastbourne, August 1st.—Walked and cabbed down to Forster, who showed me a correspondence with Mr. Webster on the subject of my engagement, which proves to me that nothing in the way of an engagement will result from it between us. Mr. Webster offers to give me my pecuniary demand for *eight* weeks if I will get the services of Miss Cushman. Forster declined the proposal without seeing me.

August 4th.—Walked on the beach with the boys, enjoying the fresh strong breeze and the playfulness of my dear little fellows. The morning was consumed with verses and Greek; and in lessons of Italian and French to Nina and Katie. Walked out with Catherine to Sea House; purchased book for Willie; walked on to top of hill and down to Eastbourne. In the evening read with the children Wordsworth and Thomson. Read in Bloxam's *Gothic Architecture.*

August 6th.—Wrote to Forster, suggesting the experiment of Covent Garden, for I am desperate as to Mr. Maddox. Gave lessons to Katie, to Nina, to Edward in Latin verses. Wrote to Letitia. Walked with the children and Catherine, who had donkeys, to Beachy Head; dined on the turf there—a warm boisterous day. The dear children enjoyed it. Read in Bloxam's book. Heard the children read and recite.

August 7th.—Letters arrived from Forster informing me of Maddox's acceptance of my terms, but asking me and hoping that I would concede the £5 per week—with other slight modifications which are better than the original proposition. I felt very grateful for this relief from a painful uncertainty, and I really did not expect this man's acquiescence.

St. Helier, August 13th.—Continued my reading of Pope, with the intention of preparing an edition for my dear children. Received

---

[1] Sir James Phillips Kay Shuttleworth, Bart. (1804-1877); the founder of English popular education.

300

a letter from Forster with reports of his negotiation. Two curious pieces of information he gives me; one, that Miss Cushman will not engage at all with Mr. Maddox, *if* it is to act with me. This is perfectly intelligible in the contemplation of the woman's perfect inconsistency; the other, that Miss H. Faucit's friends say that she must have whatever terms are given to me. What my terms have to do with Miss H. Faucit it is not easy to perceive. But I let them go on their own way—for me, God grant me the means of soon washing my hands of the low demoralizing set that make up this falsely-called "profession." *Amen!* Acted Othello quite as a study, but I was grievously discomposed by the miserable ass that was put on for Iago. The man was "*acting*" so outrageously all through the play, grimacing, mysticizing, and ranting, that it was with the utmost difficulty I could bring back my mind to my character. But I must give more pains, thought and *practice* to Othello. My performance wanted sustainment. In the apology I was better than usual, but not enough Othello.

August 15th.—Went to rehearsal. Was struck by the significant glances of one of the *corps dramatique*—one among thousands of evidences that this calling is not one to be recommended, as it is practised in this country. Perhaps its very conditions prevent its elevation. I think it must be so. Acted Hamlet with ease, but I think I did not begin it with the requisite earnestness and reality, and that the earlier part was deficient in energy. In the play and closet scene I thought myself very successful; I used the night as one of study and took great pains; but oh, what pains are not required to arrive at anything like a satisfactory performance of one cf Shakspeare's characters! Was called for. Read a very fervent encomium on my performances, written in the very kindest spirit. My defects are pointed out—which I will strive to remove.

August 16th.—Thought over last night's performance and the faults of manner and habit kindly pointed out in me; will strive—though it is *very* late—to correct them. Looked over *Hamlet.*

Stamford, August 22nd.—Saw in St. Martin's the monument and effigy of the Treasurer Burleigh; it is in excellent condition; his grandfather was a common citizen of this town. With his next descendant the talent of the family expired—but aristocratic breeding is not likely to nurture true greatness. Looked at subjects for a letter to Nina, and marked Pope. I never considered before how little he wrote to make so great a reputation, and how tender he was of it. Look at authors, and then revile the poor player—the insect of an hour—for his unhappiness at the obscuration of his little fame! Acted Cardinal Richelieu indifferently; baffled, plagued, and put out by the people.

To Norwich, August 24th.—Looked over the papers. I perceive that Wilson [1] of Blackwood, Professor of Moral Philosophy, has begun an attack on the writers of *Punch*—simply because they are of liberal politics, and he is—the friend of T. Hook, the abettor of George IV, etc.

August 29th.—Read the paper, in which I glanced over an account of the production of *The Fatal Dowry* at Sadler's Wells. It is an evidence to me what wretched creatures we must be, when I must in candour own that I am annoyed by it! Of course I soon—I may say immediately—saw my own littleness, and subjected the feeling. Perhaps my chief annoyance is in seeing, whilst I am bound to this calling, the ignorance of the great mass (writers included) respecting it. To prey on garbage after being sated in a celestial bed is to them native and to the manner born. Only let me, Oh God, escape in quiet and comfort from it!

To London, August 31st.—Came to London, reading by the way the Bible—Genesis and part of Exodus. It is a wicked thing—a *wicked thing* that men should be told that that which is the Word of God they are not to apply their *reason* to, but upon the assertion of others are to believe. Oh God, " *quoussque tandem* "? Does not the heart, that turns to Thee and adores Thee, faint in hope as it contemplates the wickedness committed under religion's name?

September 1st.—Went to Forster's chambers. Mr. Maddox called; after much random conversation, he promised to endeavour to see Miss Cushman and get her to see me. He told me that Mr. Forrest acted at his theatre for *nothing*. Forster informed me that Messrs. Bradbury & Evans promised to print my expurgated Pope's works for me, but added that, if I would put a preface to it they would publish it and Shakspeare, Milton, and Dryden on the same plan, at their own risk, giving me a share of the profits. I was pleased with the idea. Went to Sadler's Wells theatre and saw *Macbeth*—most creditably put upon the stage and very well done indeed *for such a locality*. As a piece of art considered positively, it has been greatly overpraised. Read in the *Connoisseur* that some

---

[1] John Wilson (1785–1854); the famous " Christopher North " of *Blackwood's Magazine*.

paper has been accusing me of being "jealous of Miss Faucit's success in Paris."

Birmingham to Liverpool, September 6th.—Rose very early to get my bath and start from the railway at six o'clock, which I did, for Liverpool. On my way I read over attentively Bowdler's version of *Othello*, with which I was, of course, having to do another, not satisfied—unnecessary omissions, and improper passages, I thought, continued; but I may be as wrong as I suppose him.

Liverpool, September 8th.—It has occurred to me, and is an idea that I am disposed to adopt as a theory, that it is sufficiently improbable to be spoken of in common parlance as an impossibility that any educated woman—or rather, I should say, any fashionably educated woman, any one brought up with an express view to figure in society —can ever become a great or good tragic actress. All they are taught for their own patricular *rôle* goes to extinguish the materials out of which an actress is formed—acquaintance with *the passions*—the feelings common to all, and indulged and expressed with comparative freedom in a poorer condition of life, but subjugated, restrained and concealed by high-bred persons.

September 9th.—Rehearsed. Saw Mr. ——, a gentleman of extravagant pretensions—a humbug!—like the present race of paper-carrying, introduction-carrying humbugs, of whom Mr. C. Kean is the "facile princeps." Mrs. Hammond gave me Kean's [1] autograph speech at the Fund Dinner. Such a tissue of egotistical absurdity could scarcely be found to match it. What a mind was that—out of his immediate calling! What a paradox is this art! Oh, the speech was so bad—such trash! I wish I could keep it.

September 13th.—Called on Mrs. ——, who surprised me with her improvement. She was very anxious that I should receive her as *my pupil*, but to that I say *no*—it is quite dangerous enough to be placed in closest intimacy with such a woman so many hours without any closer tie!

September 15th.—Went out at nine o'clock to the theatre to meet Mrs. —— for rehearsal; saw her rehearse two scenes of Lady Macbeth and Desdemona. It is not, and I fear cannot be, what I would wish to see it. She left me with her attendant in about half-an-hour, and I waited for the few scenes of *Macbeth*. Called Mrs. —— to explain to her that there must be something much more than what she has done to give her situation. She rehearsed

---

[1] Edmund Kean.

again, after I had shown her what the degree of passion is, and certainly with much more intensity; she was very earnest, importunate, indeed, that I should take her for a pupil, but that I steadily refused, and shall contrive to do. I do not know what to think of her, but perhaps all women are alike, varying only with circumstances. *I hope not.* Acted Macbeth—I thought *well*, but much distressed by the players.

September 16th.—Went out early—half-past eight—to meet Mrs. —— at the theatre, and hear her once more rehearse. She was already there with her companion. I heard her, but—to my regret— she did not realize the promise of yesterday. The wild hope that I had for an instant conceived was *proved*, as I could not but apprehend, fallacious.

September 19th.—Called on Mrs. —— to give her some directions, and mention to her that I should put Calcraft in communication with her. How difficult it is to understand women! She is highly educated —very intelligent, and of good family; but, though most respectful in our intercourse, we certainly have become in little more than half-a-dozen interviews *most intimate.* She either does, or affects to, admire my artistic powers, and seems to like my society; for herself she is intelligent and interesting. I took leave of her. Acted Hamlet, I think, well. Called for and very cordially received. No speech seemed expected, and I volunteered none. A very splendid engagement is terminated, and my heart full grateful—*grateful* to God for all His bounties to one so unworthy. May He make me better!

To London, September 20th.—Saw two Liverpool papers, one, as detracting as it could be in spirit; the other, very kind. Left Liverpool for London. Reached home about thirty-five minutes past six; found Catherine at home; dressed in greatest haste, and went in Mrs. M. Gibson's carriage to Miss Kelly's theatre. Rolls and Searles, who dined here, went with Catherine, Letitia and Mrs. M. Gibson before me. Found them in our box, saw the play of *Every Man in his Humour.*[1] Several of the actors were very fine as amateurs : Forster in Kitely; Dickens, Bobadil; Leech, Master Mathew; Lee, Cob; young Dickens, Cash were very fair; Jerrold very bad in Master Stephen. Old Knowell was also very fair. But it was a very dull business. Fitzgerald criticized Forster unintentionally in saying : " At one time he spoke in so strange a tone that he was very near making us laugh."

[1] Ben Jonson's Comedy performed by the Amateur Dramatic Company consisting of Dickens, Forster, John Leech, Douglas Jerrold, Mark Lemon, and others.

The fact was he played Kitely as a *tragic* character—the grand mistake; otherwise it was very commendable. The farce between Dickens and M. Lemon was very broad and laughable. Saw Lady Blessington, etc., Mrs. Carlyle, Quin, Mr. King, etc. With the greatest difficulty got our party out and off, and in Oxford Street, out of Searles' carriage into a cab, torrents of rain falling, and drove to 9 Powis Place, Great Ormond Street. Here I waited with Jerdan, Maclise, Stanfield, etc.—I think an hour—my cold torturing me. At length Dickens, Jerrold, Forster, etc., and Count D'Orsay (!) arrived; Talfourd also, who accosted me very cordially. I took some oysters, and consented to go up to supper, but got near the door, and before it was half over took an opportunity to escape. I was very unwell.

September 27th.—I read Jerdan's notice in the *Literary Gazette* of the performance of the amateur play. It was written in a false spirit, and will do harm to the persons engaged in the play.

September 28th.—Mr. Maddox called, again to speak to me about Miss Cushman; this woman is full of the idea of her own importance, and will not listen to any other notion. We must try to work through the engagement—without *her* would be easy enough, but without *any* actress!

To Leicester, September 30th.—Arrived at Leicester. Acted Hamlet well—I think *very well* to a *very wretched* house. These things will prey upon me; I am not proof to them; they prolong my term of servitude—of bondage, and life has very few pleasures or enjoyments for me. I do not know, but I think I should not care much to quit it. *God guide me!*

October 2nd.—Thought a good deal on what was needed to make the peculiar mind of an actress; am nearly confirmed in my opinion that a person educated for society can scarcely by possibility become one. Went to Mr. Maddox, recommending Mr. Loraine for Guildenstern, etc., and as likely to improve. Wrote to Catherine. Mr. Loraine called to try over the fight in Macbeth. Proceeded with my insertion of notes in Pope's works. Continued Pope, and read again carefully through the Essay on Man.

October 3rd.—Acted Macbeth; two first acts very fairly, but slaughtered by the wretched bunglers about me through the rest of the play.

To London, October 4th.—Left Leicester by railway. Read part of *Merry Wives of Windsor* and part of *Twelfth Night*. Oh! what reading is there like Shakspeare! What a bounty bestowed on man in this divine poet's thoughts and creations! Read the newspapers. Reached London in good time. Forster called and dined. I read to him two first acts of Mr. White's play of *Feudal Times*, with which he was very much moved.

October 6th.—Reflected much on the tendency to selfish and envious feelings in my nature. *I have no right* to be dissatisfied with any performer, male or female, whether I have helped them to obtain distinction or no, for choosing the course that seems most eligible to them, even though that course be in direct hostility to my interests. Should I hesitate in accepting an engagement from which I expected benefit, upon the surmise or belief that it would operate disadvantageously to any other persons on the stage? It is clear *I should not.* What right then have I to impugn others' actions, which are quite independent, or to murmur in my secret heart at their arrangements? Let me try to think with resolute judgment and to *feel* liberally on such points. Wrote to Bulwer on his supposition that I was offended with him.

October 9th.—Dickens looked in. We went to the Princess's, and in his, Forster's, presence we exchanged agreements.

October 12th.—Read Forster's most attractive and brilliant article on Defoe.

October 13th.—Acted Hamlet, fairly, but my strength failed me, though not, I think, to be perceived, in the closet scene. The reception which the audience gave me was something quite of itself; the only instance to which it can be at all likened, though in a smaller theatre, was my last night at Drury Lane, which was *awful*. But this, both at the entrance and upon the call, was quite a thing by itself. Maddox came and thanked me.[1] Forster came round and discoursed very coolly on the evening's effects. A splendid bouquet, with a quotation from Coriolanus from some old friend—without a name. My heart is grateful—*grateful* to God for all the mercies He has vouchsafed me.

October 14th.—Rose from a sleepless night anxious as to the report that might have gone abroad. Rehearsed King Lear, but was too, too weary to attempt to make any effort. Mr. Maddox spoke with me, and was very civil in his offers of boxes and orders, etc. Letters from dear Willie; a very kind one, in a spirit totally different from Forster's criticism, from Fox, and one from White. The dear children

---

[1] Macready was now engaged at the Princess's Theatre from this date to November 21, 1845—(*note by Sir F. Pollock*).

WILLIAM JERDAN

From a drawing by Daniel Maclise, R.A.

were with me in the evening. Read the papers, which, particularly the *Times*, were most gratifying—most comforting to me. Am I not grateful, oh God? My soul refers all my worldly blessings to Thy bounty. Kind note from John Delane.

October 15th.—Acted King Lear—unequally. Some things I did well, sometimes I was deficient, I thought, in power. Called for by the audience.

October 16th.—Saw the papers, which were eulogistic on my performance of King Lear. The *Chronicle* was written in ignorance both of the poetical feeling of the play, its character and power, and of its theatrical history. The writer, instead of being a critic, is an ignorant and pedantic coxcomb.

October 18th.—Dined with Horace Twiss; met Mrs. Milner Gibson, the Holmes, John Delanes, Fonblanque, Clayton, Mrs. Kitchener, the Chisholm. Spent a very agreeable day. John Delane told me that during the last fortnight they had received at the *Times* office an average of about a dozen letters per diem relative to my return to London.

October 19th.—Forster came in to tea, and informed us that Bradbury & Evans, with Paxton, Duke of Devonshire's agent, and another capitalist, a Birmingham man, had agreed on starting a daily paper on a very large scale, and that Dickens was to be at the head of it. Forster was to have some share in it, and it was instantly to be got into train for starting. I heard the news with a sort of dismay, not feeling myself, nor seeing in others, the want of such a thing. I fear the means and chances have not been well enough considered. I hope and pray all may go well with and for them.[1]

October 21st.—Looked at paper; read an account of the reception of Miss Helen Faucit and Mr. Anderson at the Haymarket, which seemed cordial and kind, but not verging towards enthusiasm. Fox, Dickens, Maclise, Stanfield, Douglas Jerrold, Forster, Mark Lemon, Z. Troughton, and Leech dined with us.

October 25th.—Looked at papers. It is not without satisfaction that I see the claims of Miss Helen Faucit (which have been urged in so hostile a spirit to me, and so unjustly as to facts) now distinctly and certainly most honestly adjudged by the public voice, which gives her the praise with which I have always readily heralded her name, but limiting it to its point of desert. She is a very pleasing, clever, and

---

[1] This paper was the *Daily News*, which Dickens edited for a time with indifferent success.

good actress, but she is not a great one. She is not Mrs. Siddons, not Miss O'Neill, not Mlle. Rachel. Dined with John Delane. Met Horace Twiss and his wife; Oxenford,[1] whom I liked; Liston; two Miss Delanes, and two gentlemen I did not know.

October 26th.—Forster came to dinner; he urged upon me giving permission to my family to see me act. I do not know; I have a feeling about their seeing me as a player. Perhaps I am wrong.

October 28th.—Murray called and expressed himself very anxious to make an engagement with me for Edinburgh; we made one, the first fortnight in March: terms, share nine nights after £20, divide equally the three best, twelve in all. Read over again the play of *The King of the Commons*, liked it much on second perusal. Wrote at length to White [2] upon both. Heard the children read and play. Read *Othello*, and looked over *King Lear*.

October 30th.—Rehearsed three acts of *Othello*; there was some difficulty with the cast. These little theatres hold so many great men and such very bad actors. Finished the perusal of L. L.'s *Philip Van Artevelde*—a presumptuous attempt after Henry Taylor's charming dramatic poem on that subject; it was poor, wild and unreadable. Dined with Milner Gibson,[3] met the Twisses, Gurwoods, Mrs. Shelley, Sir Percy Shelley,[4] Fonblanque, Ainsworth. In the evening saw Mrs. Abel, Mrs. Talfourd and Miss Hely, Fanny Haworth, Mrs. Gore, Mrs. Kitchener, the Chisholm. Passed an agreeable evening.

October 31st.—Acted Hamlet, I know not how. I took pains, but I was very thwarted by the bad acting about me, and the noises constantly disturbing the performance. Called for.

November 1st.—Looked at the *Connoisseur* paper; an endeavour to analyze my performance of Hamlet, etc. Some of its objections were reasonable, but the want of fervour and excitability in the critic often prevented him from *feeling* the meaning of the part, *e. g.* he did not understand that madness was *assumed* before Polonius! Still, it is well to consider all objections. Rehearsed *Othello*, which is in a very shameful state, and will be in most respects very badly acted. Mr. —— is—to me—*disgusting*. I have no qualification of the term,

---

[1] John Oxenford (1812–1877); the well-known dramatic critic.

[2] Rev. James White, of Bonchurch, Isle of Wight—*(note by Sir F. Pollock)*.

[3] The Right Hon. Thomas Milner Gibson (1806–1884); Corn Law Repealer; originally Conservative. Held office in Lord John Russell's first Administration; a strong opponent of Lord Palmerston, but became a member of his last Cabinet.

[4] Sir Percy Florence Shelley, Bart. (1819–1889), third baronet; son of the famous poet and Mary Godwin.

whether I consider him as an actor, or in his individual character. I know few men whom I think more lowly of; he is my Iago.

November 2nd.—Forster called and read me Dickens's Prospectus of the new morning paper—or rather I read it over twice attentively. It *increased* my apprehensions. I objected to several parts of it, but my objection is one and all. I feel that he is rushing headlong into an enterprise that demands the utmost foresight, skilful and secret preparation and qualities of a conductor which Dickens has not. Forster agreed in many if not all of my objections, but he did not seem to entertain much hope of moving Dickens.

November 3rd.—Went to the rehearsal of *Othello*, which gave me no hopes; it is *very* badly acted. Acted Othello with pains, but seemingly not with effect; the audience were not alive to my efforts and the play went heavily—it was acted very badly. Called. Spoke to Maddox about his wretched rascal of a property man, who behaved most shamefully. He promised to discharge him. He *ought* to be discharged. Forster came into my room. I thought of *Iago* for next Monday, but Forster dissuaded me. I am so *disgusted—disgusted* with that Mr. ——.

November 4th.—Wrote a note to Mr. Maddox requesting him to forgive the property man (though indeed he does not deserve forgiveness), which he answered promising he would. Mr. and Mrs. White and Forster came to dinner. After dinner I began to read his play—*The King of the Commons.* I could not go on with it and he finished it very well.

November 5th.—Looked over some pages of the *History of Scotland* and gave some thought to Mr. White's play. Acted King Lear in some instances very fairly, in others was distressed by the inattention and badness of the actors. Called for.

November 8th.—Called on Rogers, who was out; on Lady Holland,[1] whom I saw; Mr. Ward and Mr. G. E. Anson came in. The former I disliked; I thought him a puppy and arrogant; the latter was civil, but I thought his manner supercilious. Are we not provoked to despise these miserable wretches, who, because they are rich by unequal laws, call themselves " *great* "? " *Great!* "—the miserable reptiles, without an idea in their brainless skulls to set them on a level with their poorer fellow-men.

November 14th.—Had some little conversation with Maddox, who

---

[1] "The Chatelaine of Holland House."

told me that Vestris and Mathews's engagement at Dublin was a complete failure owing to the potato disease—a black look-out!

November 15th.—Mr. Rogers called. I went out afterwards and called on Mrs. Butler. Met Mr. H. Greville there, whom I liked much. Dressed, dined early and went to the amateur play at the St. James's theatre. As an amateur performance it is exceedingly good, but this commendation is held of no account with the actors, and they desire to be judged on positive grounds. Judged therefore by the poet and by the art, by what the one affords the opportunity of being done, and what the other enables the actor to do, the performance would not be endured from ordinary, or rather regular actors by a paying audience. They seem to me to be under a perfect delusion as to their degrees of skill and power in this art, of which they do not know what may be called the very rudiments. Saw at the play Fonblanque, Kenyon, Oxenford, Daniel, Lord Nugent, Mrs. Kitchener, Mrs. M. Gibson, and many others whom I could not speak to.

November 16th. Forster called, not in very high spirits about last night's performance, though it was very creditable. Mr. Greaves dined with us. I am always so glad to see this kind old friend, whose partiality I so prized thirty-five years ago, when a boy-actor, or scarcely more. Had the children with me and told them their promised story.

November 17th.—Acted Othello—not to my own satisfaction at all—with effort, but not effect. Called. Forster and Jerrold came into my room; Mr. Maddox also, and I told him peremptorily I would act this part no more—the *properties* were disgraceful, and literally interfered with the *meaning* of the action. Spoke to Embden about it, who was very glad I spoke to Mr. Maddox.

November 18th.—Went with White to the Haymarket theatre; saw two last acts of *Lady of Lyons;* an indifferent house. Anderson is deteriorated; Helen Faucit in some respects improved, in some fallen off.

November 21st.—Acted Hamlet as well, or better, than I ever did. Was called for and enthusiastically received; and thus ends this brilliant engagement. To God I turn my thoughts and heart, and bow down with fervent gratitude to acknowledge His many bounties to me.

Dublin, November 23rd.—Arrived at Kingstown about half-past seven, landed about eight o'clock and reached Dublin by railway about or before half-past eight. Oh! how I was certified that I was no longer in England by the decay, the squalor, the marks of idleness and *untidiness* that continually met my eye—the "potato at the end of everything." Came to my lodgings; on inquiring of the servant the fare of the car, he "supposed" 1*s.* 6*d.* I was astonished at the fellow's impudent knavery and asked the cabman, who demanded 1*s.*! A good beginning as a specimen of Irish honesty, but such spirits are fit to be the contributors to O'Connell! My lodgings are thoroughly Irish—the wind blowing about the muslin curtains by my windows; the fire smoking and discomfort everywhere.

November 24th.—Received a note from Miss Matilda Ross—a client of Lord Clanricarde's,[1] with an introduction from Bulwer. Umph! Acted Hamlet before one of the most—there is no qualification of the term to leave its fair description—the most blackguard audiences I ever encountered. They were grossly insulting in their continued noise and absurd words, breaking in upon the language of the play. They called "Order" at every burst of applause, and frequently completely stilled it. I was greatly provoked, but went through it without noticing the brutality of the ruffians, who had congregated together to prevent others from listening to Shakspeare. Mr. Barry came to ask me to go on to "*a call*," but I declined. Calcraft came to my room and expressed his surprise that I did not address them. It is not my wont. I dislike and despise them.

November 25th.—The anniversary of my blessed Joan's death! My heart yearns as towards her sweet angel spirit, and feels that there is something akin to and of itself in some other state of being. My beloved child—my sweet cherub, how I recall thy beauty, innocence, and playful brightness. A little while and I shall be lying in the same resting-place, where thy mortal relics lie. Bless thee, my darling

---

[1] The first Marquis; he married Canning's only daughter. Held office under Lord John Russell as Postmaster-General (1846), and under Lord Palmerston as Lord Privy Seal (1858). In consequence of his connection with a certain Irish *cause célèbre*, the latter appointment caused considerable dissatisfaction among the austerer members of the Liberal party, the *Daily News* commenting on it in the following terms: "Men of high honour, of elevated sentiments, of public morality, and of deep interest in the country cannot do otherwise than accept this act of Lord Palmerston as indicative of a personal recklessness and disregard of enlightened public opinion wholly unsuited to the position to which the generous feelings of the country have raised him." Lord Palmerston, however, characteristically stood by the son-in-law of his old chief. Lord Clanricarde's eldest son, Lord Dunkellin, inherited much of his illustrious grandfather's ability, and but for his premature death would have doubtless attained high political distinction. His brother, the present Marquis, is well known as an accomplished art connoisseur, and less favourably as an Irish landlord, though it is considered by some best competent to judge that his shortcomings in that capacity have been unfairly magnified,

child, my heart pours out its blessings on thy sweet spirit. Dear
Angel—again farewell! . . . Read the *Dublin Evening Post;* a long
defence, as he terms it, of himself by O'Connell against the *Times*
Commissioner, about whom he propagated a falsehood the other day,
and on its exposure observed, "if it was not so, it ought to have been,"
and this man arraigns others for falsehood!

November 26th.—Went to rehearsal; again detained till half-past
two. There is no doubt but that the taste for theatrical amusements
has declined in Dublin as elsewhere, but *nowhere* with such reason.
The company of my friend Calcraft does not contain one scintillation,
not of talent, but of promise or respectability. The acting manager
is three parts fool, and the rest knave and *stupe!* Oh, it is too bad;
I am sure, a clever active man might make this a property! Rested.
Acted Othello—oh!!! Calcraft Iago—*oh!* Mr. King, Cassio, and
a Miss Matilda Ross, Desdemona. Now, it was really *too* bad, too
bad. I did my best, but how could any one act with such drawbacks?
There was a loud call, but the manager, Mr. Barry, did not choose
to report it to me.

November 27th.—Went to rehearsal. It is not fancy or humour
that makes me assert it, but my work is heavier here than in any
other theatre in which I have been. The actors are *so bad*—so very
bad—my friend Calcraft (whom I *very much* like) so inexcusably bad,
the stage manager so utterly—utterly incompetent that I am in
despair; the time and suffering a rehearsal costs me is only equalled
or exceeded in acting! Acted Werner *well,* with dreadful people
about me; there was a call, but I do not go on here.

November 29th.—Went to rehearsal and underwent another trial
of endurance from the ignorance and utter incompetency of the man
to whom Calcraft has consigned the care and direction of his stage (!)
and from the gross inefficiency of the actors. It was most wearying and
distressing. Endeavoured to act King Lear, but with such actors—Kent,
Fool, Gloster, etc.—and with *such a prompter* and with such an audience
where is the man with any feeling for his author or for his art that could
make any way at all? I believe there was some call, but as no one reported
it to me I had not occasion to refuse going on. The audience (of
course I mean individuals among them—who knew they could be
guilty of such licence with impunity!—so far it is discreditable to the
whole body)—uttered their own senseless jests, when Lear is carried
off asleep—a situation that *never before* failed to excite the sympathy
and applause of an audience, when Cordelia kissed the cheek of her

sleeping father, when she lay dead in his arms—*the brutes!*—for is it not an evidence of sheer brutality of mind to be so wanting in decency and taste? I told Calcraft I would not play the play again; I want to get away from this place—I *detest* it. How I am to get through this engagement I do not know. It is one solacing reflection that they crowd to see Mr. and Mrs. Charles Kean and applaud Forrest. They are well suited.

December 1st.—Read some American matter in the *Freeman's Journal*, a paper fit for Dublin and Ireland; I cannot describe it more fitly, nor condensed disgust more effectually in phrase. Calcraft called, and took some directions about the play. I certainly am *very much* out of humour with this engagement. I have been *tricked* into it— in regard to the amount of prices, and the wretched, wretched company—with Calcraft at their head, *spoiling every play in which they appear*—utterly *disqualifies* me. I am nightly distressed to a degree that irritates and agitates my nerves to a point of intense suffering. Mr. Ryder *ought* to have been engaged; but I must bear this, the most loathsome and offensive engagement I ever underwent to my recollection. Looked at the *Morning Chronicle;* how I wish Dickens had that paper. Rested and tried to think. Acted Macbeth. With any other company and any other audience it would have been a very fine performance. I was tortured and *put out continually.*

December 2nd.—Acted Hamlet, tolerably well; unequally, but that *must* be so with such a company. My servant, too, distressed me by his idiotic stupidity, dreadfully. I had resolved to be gentle, lenient, and indifferent, but—oh God!

December 3rd.—Acted Virginius, in my own opinion, remarkably well. The house was not good, as I had anticipated; the audience very unlike the old fervent tumultuous Dublin audience; but they were, I think, moved. I think I never acted the part so decidedly from strong instantaneous feeling. The thought of my own dear child was often present to me, and more than once the tears streamed down my cheeks. After the play sent for Mrs. Ternan, and asked to see her little gifted girl, who, I saw, was in the theatre—a very sweet child.

December 4th.—Acted King Lear *well—yes, well*—to a bad and insensible audience, and with a wretched company. *Little applause,* of course. Ireland is called by some poet " *The base posterior of the world.*" I say ditto. I detest this part of it, at least.

December 8th.—Letter from Bulwer Lytton, proposing the translation and adaptation of Sophocles' *Œdipus Tyrannus*, and, as I understand him, offering it *to me* for purchase for £600, but would leave £300 contingent upon the run. If I understand him rightly, this is rather mingling the trader with the friend. Answered Bulwer, not accepting his offer.

December 9th.—My spirits are so weighed down in this place, my elasticity is so completely gone from me here, that I should be glad to " sleep out this dull gap of time "; my lothness to get up in the morning looks as if it were so; I have no heart to set about anything. I am thoroughly uncomfortable; I dislike the place I am in; I am altogether dissatisfied and uncomfortable. Looked at the paper. Saw O'Connell's answer to the *Times* Commissioner. Right or wrong in this particular case, how can we regard this man as anything but the incarnation of blackguardism? Saw Calcraft—this engagement is *too bad*. Rested. Acted Macbeth in my *best manner* to a very bad house, the visitors in which gave about half a round of applause at my death, and about a quarter on the fall of the curtain. The audience are disgusting, vulgar, ignorant, noisy, and unexcitable. How different in the latter respect from what they once were. I *hate* to go before them.

December 11th.—Looked at the paper, from which I can extract little. I know not what to make of the state of things. All seem for themselves, and the *general good* is like an antiquated garment—thrown by by all.[1]

December 12th.—Went to rehearsal. Had some conversation with Calcraft, during which Stapleton, the treasurer, brought in yesterday's *Morning Herald* containing the announcement of the Ministry's resignation! We have yet to see who will venture to take office: if the Whigs, they are pledged to such uncompromising measures in the advance of liberal government that they will not stay in long, for they cannot carry them; they have lost the confidence of the country by their dishonest shifting and vacillating when in office, and they have not men of talent among them to help them to recover it. England wants a new man—a man of the people, a genius to feel the wants of the time, and the cool foresight and courage to administer safely to them. But " where is he to be found "?

Belfast, December 16th.—Got into the mail—alas! an Irish mail-coach, the potato hanging to it, as to everything in Ireland; " alas! poor country! "—was squeezed up with three more inside, but got

---

[1] The allusion is to the Corn Law crisis, which caused the Queen to entrust Lord John Russell with the formation of a Ministry. In this, however, he was unsuccessful, and Sir Robert Peel for the time remained in office but finally retired in the following year.

along pretty well, reading *The Faerie Queene* on the way, which cheered it much; not very agreeable company—in one instance quite the reverse; at Newry thought of poor O'Hanlon, and my visit there twenty-one years ago—time! time!

December 18*th.*—Acted Virginius very well, to a very good house that seemed *borne along* by the acting of the play. How different in feeling, in intelligence, and in taste from the Dublin audience—it is most observable. Called for and enthusiastically received.

December 19*th.*—Called on Miss Knowles,[1] was pleased to hear such high sentiments in poverty. When I spoke of the hope of a pension for Knowles she ' *did not like it*—she had rather, however little, he should earn his bread; she had been at work thirty years, and preferred a potato and salt earned by labour than luxury upon a pension, it was *sweeter.*'

Liverpool to London, December 22*nd.*—Went on board the tender boat, which in a miserable, dark, and rainy morning took us to the pier, and we landed, thank God, in Liverpool. Went to the Adelphi; took a bath, and breakfasted, and glancing at the newspaper, went to the railway, where I got into the *coupé* with Lover, and proceeded to London. Went to my dear, dear home, and thank God, thank God, found all my dear ones well. Passed a happy evening.

London, December 23*rd.*—Walked out with Nina, and took a cab in Oxford Street to call on Forster, with whom I had some conversation about Bulwer. I took the opportunity of telling Forster that Bulwer's expression, in his letter to me at Dublin, of " desiring to *serve me* by writing a new play " was not very generous nor correct; that, understanding, as I believed I did, his position, it was certainly to " *serve himself.*" Forster said undoubtedly, and that Bulwer would not use such a term in speaking or writing to him on such a subject.

December 24*th.*—At dinner we burned the Yule log, and had the dear children round us; to the little ones I told a story, and afterwards to the four elder read parts of the first and second acts of *Macbeth.* Looked at *Punch,* and read *The Cricket on the Hearth,* with which I was much pleased.

December 25*th.*—My dear children came into our room to wish us a merry Christmas with bon-bons, etc. My heart had its wishes for Catherine and them and all. Went out with Willie. Called on Leslie,[2]

---

[1] Sister of Sheridan Knowles.

[2] Charles Robert Leslie (1794–1869); the distinguished R.A.; father of G. D. Leslie, R.A.

saw a very charming picture of the *Reading the Will* from *Roderick Random*—excellently designed and finished. Heard my four eldest children repeat Milton's Hymn on the Nativity, questioning them upon it. Fox, Forster and Walker dined with us. Children came after dinner. Cheerful day. Thank God for *all* His many mercies! Amen!

December 27th.—Read the paper, in which was a most *savage* attack on Dickens and his last book—*The Cricket*—that looks to me like the heavy and remorseless blow of an enemy, determined to disable his antagonist by striking to maim him or kill if he can, and so render his hostility powerless. I was sorry to see in a newspaper so powerful as the *Times* an attack so ungenerous, so unworthy of itself; but I suppose it takes up the argument of Stukeley in *The Gamester*—a bad text—" Who would undo me, nature says, undo." Alas! for human nature! Alas! for my poor dear friend Dickens! Called on Forster, with whom I found Dickens; gave them the best directions I could to two unskilled men, how to *manage* their encounter in the play of *The Elder Brother.* Forster spoke, when Dickens had gone, about the *Times,* and the injury it would do. He now *draws in* about the paper, and seems to feel it is a wrong step, and that Dickens is not qualified for the situation of director.[1] *His tone is quite altered now.* He told me that Dickens was so intensely fixed on his own opinions and in his admiration of his own works (who could have believed it?) that he, Forster, was useless to him as a counsel, or for an opinion on anything touching upon them, and that, as he refused to see criticisms on himself, this partial passion would grow upon him, till it became an incurable evil. I grieved to hear it.

December 28th.—Looked at the paper, and for the first time in my life put aside a leading article of Fonblanque's, because I thought it written in an ungenerous spirit of cavil against Sir R. Peel. I do not think he does justice to his motives, and I am really wearied with his unceasing vituperation of him. *It does no good*, it neither persuades nor convinces.

December 30th.—Took the boys to see the Mammoth Horse, a very fine animal; thence to Forster's, from whom we learned the appalling and sad tidings of poor Colonel Gurwood's death. He destroyed himself at Brighton on Saturday last at his lodgings, whilst his wife and daughters were gone out to walk. Good God! what a return

---

[1] Of the *Daily News;* he did not actually become editor till the following January, and resigned in February.

home! I was grieved—deeply, deeply grieved for the dead and for the living.

December 31st.—Received the MS. of *The King of the Commons* from Mr. White. Prepared the magic lanthorns for the children. Received a note from Forster about his *hat*—this amateur play is really a nuisance. Gave up my intention of going to the Haymarket, thinking myself better with my blessed children. Finished the reading of *Macbeth* to them, with which they were greatly pleased. The year ends. I am another step nearer to my grave; many friends in this year have gone before me. Many mercies of God have been vouchsafed to me; my heart bows down with gratitude for what is given, with submission for what is taken away. I bless His name for what is past, and implore His heavenly aid and mercy to make happy and holy my life to come. Amen.

1846

London, January 2nd.—Went out with Edward to call on Forster; found Dickens and his tailor at his chambers, he encased in his doublet and hose; it is quite ludicrous the fuss which the actors make about this play!—but I was sorry to hear of intemperate language between them, which should neither have been given nor received, as it was. Read with great attention *The King of the Commons*, of which I have hope.

January 3rd.—Note from Forster, *pestering* me about his cloak—to " wear it, or not "—absurd. Went to see the amateurs act *The Elder Brother;* the best-filled part in the play was Miramount by Lemon, but the play was not well acted. Miss Fortescue was pleasant, but rather wanting in *délicatesse.* Forster was quite beyond his depth—indeed, rather entirely out of his element in the part of Charles. The whole play was dull and dragging. Dyce and the two Stanfields, who soon left us, were in the box at first. Jerrold came in in the afterpiece. As Macbeth says—*No more sights !*

Exeter, January 5th.—Thought in very low spirits before I went to the theatre; feeling how easily a man like poor Colonel Gurwood, with the claims of a family upon him, which perhaps he could not answer, rushing from the pain and agony of thought from this world altogether. My sense of duty would never again allow me to contemplate such an alternative. Thought on my small means, and gradually rose into better heart and hope, and went to the theatre, resolved, however bad the house might be, to act for myself and as a study. Acted Macbeth very fairly in part.

Plymouth, January 12th.—Went to rehearsal, where I was much annoyed by the manifest indifference of these persons, who call themselves actors, in the scenes which I had several times rehearsed with them on Saturday. They made the *very same* mistakes, proving that they had never looked at their books, had made no memorandum, nor, in fact, ever thought upon the business for which they received the

318

price of their daily bread. It is not to be wondered at—I must acknowledge it—it is not to be wondered at that the drama is deserted; who could see such ignorant and such offensive beings obtruding themselves in the creations of Shakspeare?

January 13th.—Letter from Mrs. ——, full of talent and most entertaining, but giving me considerable pain, in the information it gave of Helen Faucit speaking in unkind terms of me. Acted Cardinal Richelieu, not at all to please myself; was cut up, root and branch, by these horrid players—but the audience chose to be satisfied. Was called for, etc. Wightwick came into my room, walked with me to hotel, and supped. Gave me some very salutary objective criticism.

January 15th.—Read and noted Mr. White's play of *The King of the Commons*, which I like. Acted Othello, pretty well, considering the disadvantage under which I stood with an inaccurate Iago, shocking Desdemona, bad Emilia, and wretched Cassio. Oh, such a company for Shakspeare! Was called, and well received.

January 16th.—Wightwick took tea and talked with me critically of my performances; mentioned some good objections to *the* soliloquy in Hamlet. I will attend to them.

January 20th.—Went into the old church; read the inscription over Mathews's grave—a falsehood; he was a *player*, and no more; a mere selfish player, without one feeling of the gentleman—a fit " friend " for Theodore Hook.

January 22nd.—Slept much of my journey to Exeter; a young gentleman in the coach knew and addressed me; a lunatic, in charge of his keeper was on the top. I thought little except of reaching home, though there was deep matter for reflection in the poor, wretched being aloft, and in the case of Lord Morley's gamekeeper, who was shot yesterday morning; the man who killed him is in the receipt of very good wages as a workman, but, I suppose, from the love of pursuing game, which he shares with Lords Morley and Co. and with Messrs. Grantley Berkeley [1] and his ruffian crew, he has been led to take the sacred life of a fellow-creature, and must expiate his offence by a shameful death. Accursed be the laws that, for the sake of the pleasures of a

---

[1] George Charles Grantley Fitzhardinge Berkeley (1800–1881); sixth son of the fifth Earl of Berkeley ; M.P. for West Gloucestershire, 1832–1852. Well known in sporting circles, and as a writer on sporting subjects. Owing to a violent attack on a novel of his in *Fraser's Magazine*, he publicly horsewhipped Mr. Fraser, and fought a duel with Dr. Maginn, the writer of the review. His autobiography throws a good deal of interesting light on the celebrities of his day, especially in the world of sport.

class, lead to such crime and misery. The *Daily News* also, which has nothing very striking or startling in it—nothing, I think, to stimulate curiosity or excite expectation. Dickens's letter from the road to Italy I did not fancy; it is too familiar, I think, for a letter in a newspaper detailing actual occurrences with a real signature. Sent off a few words by way of a starting cheer to Dickens on the sight of the first *Daily News*.

London, January 25th.—Glanced at paper, and again dissatisfied with Fonblanque's attack on Peel, whose conduct I think honourable and noble. Forster called and remained not more than ten minutes. "Thou hast described a hot friend cooling " occurs to me on observing him. *Let be !*

January 26th.—Looked at *Daily News*, not liking the leading article in its abuse of Peel. I cannot understand the sense of men who wish persons to think and act in a certain way, and when they do so abuse them for it.

January 30th.—Read the papers; pleased with the leading articles of the *Daily News*, but when the *Times* came its superiority was so manifest that I am *in despair* for the result of the *Daily News*.

January 31st.—Dined with Dickens; met Rogers, Jerrold, Maclise, Stanfield and Mr. and Mrs. Hutchinson. Mrs. Norton, the Twisses, Milner Gibsons, etc., came in the evening. That fellow Chorley was there. I am sure the instinct that shrinks back from him, despite myself, must be true.

February 1st.—White mentioned to me a very degrading anecdote of the Duke of Buccleuch.[1] This man was on the point of requesting the Dukedom of Monmouth, and to sit in the House of Peers as the descendant of Charles II's bastard, bearing the bar sinister on his arms, from which he was only diverted by the remonstrances of some influential friends in the neighbourhood of Edinburgh.

February 2nd.—Looked at the papers; the *Daily News* was very

---

[1] Walter Francis, fifth Duke of Buccleuch, and seventh Duke of Queensberry (1806–1884); a member of Sir Robert Peel's second Administration, one of the worthiest "great nobles" of his day. Mentioned by Sir Walter Scott in his *Journals*. His high-minded and patriotic support of Sir Robert Peel was in marked contrast with the attitude of many other of the Prime Minister's followers, notably Disraeli, from whom the Duke always held rigidly aloof, regarding him to the end with aversion and distrust. He was a direct descendant of the Duke of Monmouth, by Anne Scott, Countess of Buccleuch, and but for Monmouth's attainder would have inherited the title, in virtue of which he would have sat in the House of Lords as an English duke instead of as Earl of Doncaster. In any case it may be regarded as certain that Buccleuch would have remained his premier title. Even if rightly informed, Macready greatly distorted the incident.

dull indeed. The *Times* had an excellent article on the American legislators and their anxiety for war. White and Thackeray called, and I asked them to attend the reading of the play, and afterwards to dine with us on Thursday.

February 3rd.—Looked at paper, *Daily News;* nothing in it—this cannot do; *three columns* of citations from country papers about the Special Express; yesterday two and a half columns!! How can this interest its readers? The persons employed do not understand their business.

February 5th.—Busied with preparing play for the reading. White came, and I spoke to him on several points. Thackeray, Dickens and Fox came, Maddox and his brothers. I read to them *The King of the Commons;* White reading the scenes of Laird Small. I thought all parties seemed very much pleased, and was buoyed up in my own mind with the hope of success. White, Fox, Dickens, Thackeray, and Forster came to dinner. When gone, Fox gave me his opinion as adverse to the expectation of great success for the play. I was sorry and disappointed to hear it. I cannot judge of it in my present state myself. Forster spoke to me at dinner in so rude a manner, so grossly impertinent, telling me my opinions were " unworthy of me," etc., that Dickens expected I should reply very angrily to him, and White was surprised at his tone and language. He forgets himself.

February 6th.—Wrote a note of summons to White. Looked at the papers. Letter from Fanny Twiss. Called on Dickens and talked with him on *The King of the Commons.* He did not think it strong; he was *disappointed* in it. He conversed pleasantly and sensibly about it, advising me not to counsel White to withdraw it if Maddox accepted it. I saw his reasons. White called, and I developed to him the desponding opinion of Fox, Dickens, and my ladies; he was much cut down, but left tolerably well. Note from Thackeray, sticking up for White's play.

February 9th.—Acted Cardinal Richelieu tolerably. Called, and well received. Forster came into my room. He seemed in very low spirits about *the Paper,* and said he " had always felt as I did about it —it was precipitate; that no one could be a worse editor than Dickens," etc.! Alas!

February 12th.—Forster called; he told me that an acquaintance of his wished me to hear a young lady rehearse—I agreed to do so on Saturday; that Dickens had abdicated the editorship of the *Daily News,* and that he was editor. He seemed elated with his position and looked forward to improving the paper. I doubt his ability to do so sufficiently for success; read me a letter from Bulwer, stating that he, Bulwer, had finished a play on Œdipus Tyrannus, with choruses, which he had given to Mercadante to compose for the price of £150; that Forster was to dispose of the play for £500 at any theatre where I could act, but if I could not do it, it was to be done without me. He, Forster, then read a letter from Tennyson, and a copy of verses.

February 13th.—Wrote to Bulwer, *confidentially*, recommending him to contradict, if he could, the assertions of his having written *The New Timon.*[1] Rested, and thought. Acted King Lear better,

[1] See note, p. 2, Vol. I. *The New Timon: A Romance of London* was a compound of occasionally felicitous satire and somewhat overcharged sentiment. Early in the second part, in the course of a description of London, the following lines occur—

> " If to my verse denied the Poet's fame
> This merit, rare to verse that wins, I claim ;
> No tawdry grace shall womanize my pen !
> E'en in a love-song man should write for men !
> Not mine, not mine (O Muse forbid !) the boon
> Of borrowed notes, the mock-bird's modish tune,
> The jingled medley of purloined conceits,
> Outbabying Wordsworth and outglittering Keats,
> Where all the airs of patchwork-pastoral chime
> To drowsy ears in Tennysonian rhyme !
> Am I enthralled but by the sterile rule,
> The formal pupil of a frigid school,
> If to old laws my Spartan tastes adhere,
> If the old vigorous music charms my ear,
> Where sense with sound, and ease with weight combine
> In the pure silver of Pope's ringing line ;
> Or where the pulse of man beats loud and strong
> In the frank flow of Dryden's lusty song ?
> Let school-miss Alfred vent her chaste delight
> On ' darling little rooms so warm and bright,' *
> Chaunt, ' I'm aweary ' in infectious strain
> And catch her ' blue fly singing i' the pane,'
> Tho' praised by Critics, tho' adored by Blues,
> Tho' Peel with pudding plump the puling muse,
> Tho' Theban taste the Saxon's purse controuls
> And pensions Tennyson while starves a Knowles,
> Rather be thou, my poor Pierian maid,
> Decent at least, in Hayley's weeds arrayed,
> Than patch with frippery every tinsel line,
> And flaunt admired the Rag Fair of the Nine."

---

* "(O darling room, my heart's delight,
.   .   .   .
There is no room so exquisite,
No little room so warm and bright
Wherein to read, wherein to write !

" The whole of this *Poem* (! ! !) is worth reading, in order to see to what depth of silliness the human intellect can descend."

for the most part, than I have yet done. Called for, and warmly received. Mrs. Dickens and Georgina were in our box.

February 14th.—Miss Goddard called to declaim and receive from me an opinion of her want of qualifications for an actress. A Miss —somebody—followed her, who had not even studied a character, but thought she should like to be an actress. It was annoying to have time so wasted. Called on Lady Blessington, saw her and Count D'Orsay. Lord Auckland came in and sat. They pressed me to dine with them, to which I agreed. Mr. Buckstone called to ask for my advocacy in his project of building a new theatre. He promised me that women of the town should not be admitted *as such*, and I promised to give him any assistance in my power. Forster came, and in a very moody manner began to tell me that Maddox would not take Bulwer's play. I learned from him *now* that he required Maddox to take it on the same agreement he had proposed for the other, *viz.* that he should purchase it for £500, *without seeing* it, on Forster's and my judgment. This was not what Catherine and I had understood him to mean when he read Bulwer's letter to me, for he said twice, "Mind, this is all upon approval," and asked me who was the person that Maddox took as an adviser. I told him, his brother. Forster began to impute to me a concurrence with this plan of selling it *unread by Maddox*, which I disclaimed, and very angrily told him, "I would not be spoken to in that manner by him." He cut the matter very short; said he "should throw it all on Maddox" (I do not know what this exactly means), shook hands and went away.

February 21st.—Read the paper. No division yet, but a long tirade from Mr. Disraeli, a senator of imperial England! The Chittys, Delanes, Kenyon, Dyer, and Martin dined with us; a cheerful day.

February 25th.—Dined with Kenyon. Met the Procters, Longmans, Mrs. Jameson, Babbage, Eastlake, Panizzi; in the evening, Boxall, Scharf.

February 26th.—Looked at papers. In *Punch* read the lines of Tennyson on Bulwer Lytton, as the author of *The New Timon.*[1] It

---

[1] The verses were as follows—

THE NEW TIMON, AND THE POETS.

We know him, out of Shakspeare's art,
  And those fine curses which he spoke ;
The old Timon, with his noble heart,
  That, strongly loathing, greatly broke.

is not easy to conceive any verses more bitter, more graphic, more full of scorn, and powerful in their high and master tone.   Their bitterness the author felt after having written them, and, in his charitable spirit, in his sense of the littleness of revenge, of the nobleness of forgiveness, he desired Forster, to whom he sent them, to destroy them.   Forster,

So died the Old : here comes the New.
   Regard him : a familiar face :
I *thought* we knew him : What, it's you,
   The padded man—that wears the stays—

Who kill'd the girls and thrill'd the boys,
   With dandy pathos when you wrote,
A Lion, you, that made a noise,
   And shook a mane en papillotes.

And once you tried the Muses too ;
   You fail'd, Sir : therefore now you turn,
You fall on those who are to you,
   As Captain is to Subaltern.

But men of long-enduring hopes,
   And careless what this hour may bring,
Can pardon little would-be Popes
   And Brummels, when they try to sting.

An artist, Sir, should rest in Art,
   And waive a little of his claim ;
To have the deep Poetic heart
   Is more than all poetic fame.

But you, Sir, you are hard to please ;
   You never look but half content :
Nor like a gentleman at ease,
   With moral breadth of temperament.

And what with spites and what with fears,
   You cannot let a body be :
It's always ringing in your ears,
   ' They call this man as good as *me.*'

What profits now to understand
   The merits of a spotless shirt—
A dapper boot—a little hand—
   If half the little soul is dirt ?

You talk of tinsel ! why we see
   The old mark of rouge upon your cheeks.
You prate of Nature ! you are he
   That spilt his life about the cliques.

A Timon you ! Nay, nay, for shame :
   It looks too arrogant a jest—
The fierce old man—to take *his* name
   You bandbox. Off, and let him rest.—ALCIBIADES.

the friend and confidant of Bulwer Lytton, writes back to Tennyson, saying that though Lytton was his friend, yet justice was more dear than friendship to him; that Lytton denied the authorship of *The New Timon*, but that he, Forster, did not believe his denial, and, such was his sense of justice and of Tennyson's wrong, that if he wished it, on re-consideration, he, Forster, would publish them!! Tennyson was stung by Forster's letter to descend to retaliation, to fling away his magnanimity, and in the *Punch* of to-day, *auspice Forstero*, the lines are printed.[1]

February 27th.—Went to Westminster Abbey; met in the chapel Campbell, who had *placed* the cast of Mrs. Siddons's statue. The effect was admirable. I noticed to him what seemed to me a defect in the proportion; he admitted it, and promised to add length to the form below the bust. The Dean and Milman came. The Dean introduced himself to me, and, with a little criticism, seemed much pleased with it. Campbell afterwards had it turned more into light, which greatly improved it. Acted Cardinal Richelieu well. Was warmly greeted. Last night of engagement at Princess's theatre.

---

[1] According to Tennyson's statement in after years the lines were sent to *Punch* by Forster without his knowledge. At the same time he regretted having written them, and sent to *Punch* a few days later the following stanzas, which appeared without any signature—

AN AFTERTHOUGHT

Ah, God! the petty fools of rhyme
    That shriek and sweat in pigmy wars
Before the stony face of Time,
    And looked at by the silent stars.

Who hate each other for a song,
    And do their little best to bite
And pinch their brethren in the throng,
    And scratch the very dead for spite.

And strain to make an inch of room
    For their sweet selves and cannot hear
The sullen Lethe rolling doom
    On them and theirs and all things here.

Whom one small touch of charity
    Could lift them nearer Godlike state
Than if the crowded orb should cry
    Like those who cried Diana great.

And I, too, talk and lose the touch
    I talk of. Surely, after all,
The noblest answer unto such
    Is perfect stillness when they brawl.

Edinburgh, March 2nd.—Acted Hamlet really with particular care, energy, and discrimination; the audience gave less applause to the first soliloquy than I am in the habit of receiving, but I was bent on acting the part, and I felt, if I can feel at all, that I had strongly excited them, and that their sympathies were cordially, indeed, enthusiastically, with me. On reviewing the performance I can conscientiously pronounce it one of the very best I have given of Hamlet. At the waving of the handkerchief before the play,[1] and "I must be idle," a man on the right side of the stage—upper boxes or gallery, but said to be upper boxes—hissed! The audience took it up, and I waved the more, and bowed derisively and contemptuously to the individual. The audience carried it, though he was very staunch to his purpose. It discomposed me, and, alas! might have ruined many; but I bore it down. I thought of speaking to the audience, if called on, and spoke to Murray about it, but he very discreetly dissuaded me. Was called for, and very warmly greeted. Ryder came and spoke to me, and told me that the hisser was observed and said to be a Mr. W——, who was in company with Mr. Forrest! The man writes in the *Journal*, a paper, depreciating me and eulogizing Mr. F——, sent to me from this place.

March 3rd.—Fifty-three years have I lived, to-day. Both Mr. Murray and Mr. Ryder are possessed with the belief that Mr. Forrest was the man who hissed last night. I begin to think he was the man. Called at Lord Robertson's, Maclaren's, Mrs. Ogles's; saw Mrs. and Miss O——, whom I liked very much; on Dr. Alison; on Captain Rutherfurd, whom, as well as Mrs. Rutherfurd, I saw and liked very much; on Fletcher of Dunans; on Lord Murray; on Lord Jeffrey, whom, as well as Mrs. J——, I saw. He had called and left a card for me in the morning on Professor Wilson,[2] who wished me to come in; I liked him; on Professor Napier,[3] to all of whom I had letters.

March 4th.—Mr. Ryder told me that a Mr. Smibert, a *Mr. Aitken*, and some other, had informed him that they were in the box with Mr. Forrest on Monday night, and *saw him* hiss on the occasion alluded to. He also told me that a person, Mr. Mills, an amateur, had told Mr. Murray positively that he also saw him, and that it was

---

[1] A favourite practice of Macready at this particular point in *Hamlet*.

[2] "Christopher North."

[3] Presumably Macvey Napier (1776–1847), editor of the *Edinburgh Review*. His *Correspondence* gives interesting glimpses of many of the literary magnates of the day, Brougham appearing in a particularly unfavourable light.

Mr. Forrest ! [1] In the course of the rehearsal the police officer came to Mr. Murray and told him that it was Mr. Forrest who had hissed on Monday night, and that it was sent down in the report of the night (a practice here) to the police office by the officer on duty, regularly entered among the occurrences of the evening. It is alluded to in the *Scotsman* of to-day with a direct reference to Mr. Forrest. Indeed, it seems placed beyond all doubt. I feel glad that it is not an Englishman—but no Englishman would have done a thing so base; indeed he *dared* not have done it, and that was one argument in my mind for my belief in Mr. Forrest's guilt. I do not think that such an action has its parallel in all theatrical history! The low-minded ruffian! That man would commit a murder, *if he dare.* Acted King Lear, to a very middling house (they will not come to see me here) which was cold in the extreme; there were a few persons that seemed to understand me, but it is slaughterous work to act these characters to these audiences.

March 5th.—Went to rehearsal. Here I heard from Ryder that Mr. Forrest was again in the boxes last night, as he says, conspicuous by laughing and talking in my principal scenes. Poor creature! He, it seems, accosted a Mr. Gibson, asking if " that was not his name ? " He was told " it was." " If he was not the editor of the *Scotsman ?* " Mr. G—— " did not choose to answer the question—did not understand Mr. Forrest's right to ask it." Mr. F—— then inquired if he was not the writer of the article on the theatre in Wednesday's paper. Mr. G—— persisted in denying Mr. F.'s right to ask or his own to answer the question. Mr. F—— said, " Because, if he was, he was a blackguard, and, if he owned it, he would give him a good kicking." The allusion in the *Scotsman* would not justify any violent resentment of their noticing a " report " which they can " scarcely think credible," much less the ruffianly conduct of this brutal savage. Acted Cardinal Richelieu as well as I could, though I was in great doubt as to the effect I was producing, so very difficult to move to applause is an Edinburgh audience; but there was no mistake in the last scene, by which they appeared quite carried away. Was called for, and certainly most enthusiastically received.

March 6th.—Rehearsed. Heard from Mr. Ryder that Mr. Wyndham, one of the actors, had been told by a bystander that Mr. Forrest justified his act of *hissing* on the plea that he gave applause

---

[1] This incident opened Forrest's discreditable campaign against Macready, which culminated in the New York riots two years later.

to actors, and he had an equal right to hiss them! *Mr. Forrest!*
Heard of the *Courant* newspaper containing two criticisms, full of
objections, though asserting the "most profound respect for my
genius," and speaking of King Lear as acted to a delighted and crowded
auditory. Pah! Acted Othello with all the care and energy I could
summon up. The house, of course, was bad, but I would not give in.
The audience seemed really to yield themselves to full sympathy with
the performance from the first to the last. They called for me, and
cheered me very enthusiastically. Looked at *Tait's Magazine*—a most
contemptibly ridiculous article of Mr. De Quincey [1] on the performance
of *Antigone* at Edinburgh. God help us! These are our critics!
Read the *Times*. We shall have war, I think, with America. What
charming news to Mr. Forrest! Oh God!—these are *men!*

March 7th.—Ryder came, and told me that in the *Chronicle* of to-
day was *an admission* and *an attempt at justification* of *Mr. Forrest's
outrage!!* I am glad that all uncertainty on the question is at an
end. But what a wretch is this Mr. Forrest! Read the *Times*, and
the Edinburgh *Courant*, which has a sort of civil notice by a very
hypercritical connoisseur. These people can see genius in all the
harlequin quackeries, devoid of a glimpse of idea, of Mr. C. Kean, and
inspiration in the rant of Miss Helen Faucit, to which the houses are
crowded. But I am not one of the Edinburgh wonders.

March 8th.—Professor Napier called and sat some time with me.
He corrected a misapprehension of mine as to Sir Walter Scott's
involvements. I had thought he had been embarrassed by his partnership in Constable's house, and became responsible for the debts of the
firm, but it seems that the involvement was for his own personal debts,
incurred by the system of raising money on bills for the purchase of
land about Abbotsford.[2] He had the *weakness* to have a pride in
considering himself a cadet of the house of Buccleuch (*he!* and the
little duke!), which he was *not*, though distantly approaching it.
Pah! Napier seems a good-natured, but certainly a very dull man.
Called on Captain Rutherfurd, whom, as well as Mrs. Rutherfurd, I
like extremely; they seem people of heart. Called at Lord Jeffrey's;
sat with Mrs. Jeffrey. He came in, and talked for some time. Dined
with Professor Napier. Met Rutherford, Professor Wilson, Lord

[1] Thomas de Quincey (1785–1859); author of *The Confessions of an Opium Eater*.
He was a contributor both to *Tait's* and *Blackwood's Magazines*.
[2] Scott's financial ruin was primarily caused by his partnership with Constable; but no
doubt his committals of the firm in order to meet his extravagant expenditure had greatly
weakened it.

Robertson (Falstaff *redivivus*), etc. Passed an amusing day; like Rutherford and Wilson particularly.

March 9th.—Read Dickens's letter on "Capital Punishment," which I thought very good; but the question arises to me, is not the mischief in the publicity of the punishment and not in the punishment itself? Acted Hamlet. Read over Hamlet. Felt rather nervous and uneasy from the uncertainty whether this American ruffian may not have left some colleague or hireling here instructed to renew the insulting outrage on me. Reasoned against it, but it is scarcely possible to acquire *full confidence*—indispensable to acting—under such an apprehension of doubt. Acted Hamlet with care, but had upon me the restraining feeling of doubt and want of confidence in my audience, against which I battled as well as I could. Read the vulgar article defending Mr. Forrest. There are blackguards of all countries; Scotland, of course, has her share, though less, I believe, in proportion than other lands, but America is the hotbed of their growth.

March 11th.—Mr. Ryder, my "d——d good-natured friend," informs me that the other low papers here run me down, and talk of Mr. Glover [1] (!) sharing the applause in *Werner* ! All I know is that it was of such a peculiar kind that I could not *hear* it! But Edinburgh is lost to me as a place of income, a circumstance very much to be regretted by myself, and one I have striven against, unavailingly it seems; I have not talent, or the people have not taste to appreciate me, it is of little moment now which; my life is near its close—I will not go on.

March 12th.—Looked over the *Times*, and read that doting old ruffian's speech in the House of Representatives—Quincy Adams. No more of America for me!

March 13th.—Letter from Calcraft on Mr. Forrest's conduct. Miss Cushman said on reading the paper, "It is Forrest!" Acted Macbeth at, I think, my very best; took great pains, and anywhere else it would have been a most triumphant night. Read the *Times*, a paragraph in it mentioning the circumstance of my first night here, quoting from *The Scotsman*, and adding, "the person supposed is Mr. Forrest, an American actor!"

March 16th.—Read in the *Courant* a notice very different in its tone from any that had preceded it—a sort of *amende honorable*, or retractation of the objections it had before urged against my acting!

---

[1] Edmund Glover (1813–1860); actor and manager; a leading member of Murray's Edinburgh company, son of Mrs. Julia Glover, the distinguished comic actress.

Acted Hamlet, I should say in a very finished manner, of course I mean comparing myself with myself; but I was forcible, possessed of the full poetry of the part, and refined in manner. Perhaps the editor of the *Weekly Chronicle*—Mr. Forrest's friend—might say there was hissing at the handkerchief to-night ! ! !

March 17th.—This engagement is over, and for the same number of nights, over a more extended period, it returns me the same, or less amount, than I received here twenty-one years ago on much less favourable terms, and under the disadvantage of very bad weather. I was then abused and attractive; I am now admitted, at last, to be a great artist, yet *regardez l'épreuve*.

March 23rd.—Set out for Selkirk, stopping at Abbotsford, the most disagreeable exhibition I have almost ever seen, itself the suicidal instrument of Scott's fate, and monument of his vanity, and indiscretion. We must not, least of all must I, reproach any one for extravagance or precipitation. Everything seems as if he had died last week, and, in the worst possible taste, they show the clothes he last wore. Mrs. Purdey came out to show me her house, etc.

Ambleside, March 25th.—Saw a brown-faced looking woman watching for the coach, thought I knew the face, looked out of window, it was Miss Martineau. She came to the inn (a very, very bad one), where we stopped; a few words passed; she told me to get my dinner at the inn, as she had but one room, and then come to her. I got a very bad dinner and set out to her old lodgings, to which the servant had misdirected me; met her on my return in search of me, and walked with her to her newly-built, or building, house—a most commodious, beautifully situated, and desirable residence in all respects. I could not but look with wonder at the brown hue of health upon her face and see her firm and almost manly strides as she walked along with me to Foxhow, Dr. Arnold's place, from which the family are at present abroad; it is a very enjoyable home, and it is easy to conceive how a mind and heart like that good and great man's must have felt the enjoyment of such a retirement. We walked on to Rydal Mount to call on Wordsworth, who was ill in bed and had had his leeches this morning. I left my regards, etc., took a walk along his terraces, looking on Windermere and Rydal, and, returning to my inn, soon after rejoined Miss Martineau, at Mrs. Davy's, with whom and Mr. Greg [1] I took tea and passed a very agreeable evening. I had received a pamphlet and long letter from Professor Gregory on the subject of

[1] Mr. William Rathbone Greg—(*note by Sir F. Pollock*).

mesmerism, on which we had talked a little at Major Thom's on Saturday last; it is a translation of Reichenbach, and, with some curious facts mentioned by Miss Martineau, certainly made me pause in my utter rejection of this hitherto inscrutable and mysterious power, if power it really be.

March 26th.—Wrote a note to Wordsworth. Posted my letters, and walked down to Miss Martineau's cottage; I do enjoy the air, the hills and streams, that are keeping up their gentle noise all around me; the morning was one of the best of early spring's. I planted two oaks for Harriet Martineau, which, with her small spade, cost me some strain of the back. The more I see of her pretty house the more I am pleased with it; it has not, that I perceive, one point of objection, with an infinite number of recommendable qualities. We walked to the chapel over the Brathay, took a lovely view of Windermere, and walked home, talking hard the whole way.

March 27th.—Saw in a playbill Mr. Forrest's name in the new tragedy of *Aylmere !* I feel I cannot *stomach* the United States as a nation; the good there, I must admit, appears like the quantity of the grains of wheat to the bushel of chaff. Came by railway to York, reading the *Times* and *Punch*, thinking on the time when it was a long day's journey.

York, March 28th.—Called on Mrs. ——, and heard, among other things, much of Miss Helen Faucit's abuse of me, and representation that I had ill-treated and injured her. I make no comment on her conduct. I am grown seared to it. It does not now affect me. Dined at hotel, and afterwards went to see *The Provoked Husband* at the theatre. It certainly was very lamentably performed to a house that was at freezing-point. I saw Mrs. —— with much satisfaction; she was lively, piquante, with an air of extreme good-breeding, and both elegant and interesting throughout the comic scenes; in the last touching scene of the reconciliation, and in the previous scene, where she is jaded and *ennuyée*, she failed of effect. I called and spoke to her for about half-an-hour after the play, and promised to see her to-morrow to speak at full upon it.

March 29th.—Wrote to Murray about Mrs. ——. Posted my letters and called on Mrs. ——, whom I seemed to make very happy by telling her of the impression her performance made on me last night. She gave me a somewhat fuller account of Miss H. Faucit's conduct, which seems to be in the worst style and taste of caballing actresses—getting up cases of "injured innocence." Read through the part of Lady Townley to Mrs. ——, showing her where she was deficient, and pointing out to her *how* to study a character. She appears truly grateful to me. I think I have rendered her essential service. I am sure I hope so. Parted with her, and went to my hotel to dine. Read the newspaper. Paid my bill, and came on by the evening train to Derby. Saw at the station Braham [1]—fine old man, as regards energy and spirits, but it is sad to think on the change in his circumstances. He observed to me: " Poor Liston, he is gone! "—thinking, I presume, that his and my turn are not far off.

Derby, March 30th.—Took a small carriage and went to Repton, eight miles distant, the birthplace of my beloved mother; this little journey has been the object of my thoughts for many years, a wish of my heart ever since that blessed parent pointed out to me from the window of the chaise as we travelled from Birmingham to Sheffield the graceful slender spire about two miles distant. I have never forgotten it. That must be at least forty-four years ago. At last I have visited the church where she was baptized, and looked upon the trees, the fields, the river, and the houses that her infant eyes looked on. And she has been long since in her quiet grave; and my darling Joan too, my parent and my offspring, both in a more exalted state of being, I hope and trust. When am I to rejoin them? —a solemn question! My heart blesses their beloved spirits. I went into the church, and through the churchyard sought for some memorial of my grandfather, Charles Birch, but none is there. I extracted the following from the register: " 1765, August 9th. Christina Ann, daughter of Mr. Charles and Christina Birch, his wife, baptized." Then: " 1768, March 20th. Mr. Charles Birch, surgeon, buried." [2] I descended to the crypt, a very curious round-arched vault, with a sort of Doric or Etruscan-looking pillars, entwined with a roll, and supporting round arches, the centre space seeming loftier than those at the four angles. And she was an infant here, and here her

[1] John Braham, the celebrated singer.
[2] Macready's mother's grandfather was Jonathan Birch, vicar of Bakewell, in the county of Derby, where he died and was buried, 1735. Her mother was Christina Frye, daughter of Edward Frye, governor of Montserrat. The Rev. John Neville Birch, rector of Leasingham, in the county of Lincoln (died 1782) and the Rev. Thomas Birch, rector of South Thoresby, in the county of Lincoln (died 1806), were her paternal uncles. The family of Birch was originally settled in Lancashire, and it is said that Macready's great great-grandfather was disinherited by his father for taking the Royalist side in the civil wars of Charles I —(*note by Sir F. Pollock*).

father died in a state of derangement from the ruin of his property, through the treachery or misfortune of the agent to whom his savings were entrusted, at least thus I understood from my dear mother. Blessings on her—beloved one! Saw the school-house, where one might be very industrious and very happy; poor Macaulay,[1] my friend, who lies buried in the church, was, I fear, too indolent and luxurious to be either.

March 31st.—Started at a quarter-past eight for London. The train was very slow, and I heard much to justify the dissatisfaction that I heard expressed with Mr. Hudson,[2] whom I believe to be a quack—something of the " Mr. Bunn " order of person, without his rascality.

London, April 1st.—Mr. Ryder called, and informed me of an article in the *Sunday Times*, which denied that Mr. Forrest had been guilty of the offence imputed, and that the statement was made by the *Times* and *Examiner* to benefit me at his expense! Unluckily it was the *Scotsman's* statement, which Mr. Forrest himself has confirmed, observing he " would do the same again." I listened with the utmost complacency to Mr. Ryder, and told him I could not degrade myself to notice anything of the sort. Went to Richmond —Star and Garter—met Forster, Mr. and Mrs. Dickens, Miss Hogarth, Maclise and Stanfield; we had a very merry—I suppose I must say *jolly* day—rather more tumultuous than I quite like. Began the play of *King of the Commons*.

April 3rd.—Proceeded with the task of reading and arranging the play of *King of the Commons*, which, on and off, occupied me the whole day. Looked at the *Times*—disgusted with that fat monk, Robert Inglis,[3] calling the attention of the House to the propriety of introducing the name of God into the account of these battles,[4] so

[1] The Rev. John Heyrick Macaulay, eldest brother of Kenneth Macaulay, Q.C., and M.P. for Cambridge, and first cousin of Lord Macaulay, was for some time headmaster of Repton School. He was a good scholar, and possessed of many excellent qualities—(*note by Sir F. Pollock*).

[2] George Hudson (1800–1871); the " Railway King," originally a draper at York. He was then at the height of his prosperity, but a few years later, owing to over-speculation and mismanagement, he was obliged to retire to the Continent, and but for a small annuity purchased for him would have closed his life in actual penury.

[3] Sir Robert Harry Inglis, Bart. (1786–1855); M.P. for Oxford University, having won the seat from Sir Robert Peel in 1829. He began his political career as private secretary to Lord Sidmouth, of whose bigoted Toryism he was evidently an ardent admirer, for he doggedly opposed Catholic Emancipation, Parliamentary Reform, Jewish Relief, the Repeal of the Corn Laws, and the Maynooth Grants.

[4] In the course of the Sikh campaign.

333

well fought, and so valorously gained—as if the God of Mercy, the God of the Universe, were a party to the slaughter of His creatures!

April 4th.—Called on Forster. He spoke about Tennyson, Bulwer and *Punch*—not quite satisfactorily. I told him I had written to Bulwer on the subject of *The New Timon.* He has not done well in that business. He showed me the *Times,* in which is a letter of Mr. Edwin Forrest, admitting that he hissed me on my introduction of a " fancy dance " into *Hamlet;* that he had a right to do so ; that he was not solitary in the act ; and that he often led the applause which he regretted others did not follow. There are other falsehoods in the letter, which on examination will be found to prove themselves such in the letter itself. This seems to me (though, of course, offensive, as anything filthy in the physical or material world would be) to be the seal of his character. Many have been indisposed to believe such malignity and such folly, and many have refused to believe it. But here stands self-confessed this citizen of the United States, to whom the greatest harm that I can do, I will : which is to give him the full benefit of his noble, tasteful, and critical qualities, and " leave him alone with his glory."

April 6th.—Looked at *Times,* read in it a letter from F. L——commenting with severity but not violence on Mr. Forrest's " notable production "—as he styles his letter. Mr. Maddox called and informed me of a fracas between himself and Mr. Wallack, who told him he had uttered " a lie "—to which Mr. Maddox replied that it was he who was the liar, when Mr. Wallack lifted up a chair and struck him with it ; further outrage was prevented. Mr. Ryder informs me this is an incorrect version of the story. Mr. W—— struck with his fist, and Mr. Maddox's solicitor, coming in, sent a copy of a writ to Mr. Wallack.

April 7th.—Called at Edwin Landseer's ; saw his sketch for the fresco in the Pavilion ;[1] a noble picture of a Stag at Bay by Landseer ; a pair, Time of War and Time of Peace ; and another more rustic scene of a horse with vegetables, which he calls The Banquet—I do not think he was ever so great. One could write on for pages about these pictures, but there they are, what all great pictures are, poetry speaking plainly to the eye, and suggesting thoughts to the mind for hours and hours of after-rumination. We met Mrs. Talfourd and two of her sons there. I met also Miss Landseer and kind honest Tom Landseer, with whom I chatted. The

---

[1] At Buckingham Palace.

best taste seems to regulate all that E. Landseer does; it is particularly observable in the house he has built. Heard of dear Stanfield's illness. Called at Frank Stone's; very much pleased indeed with a sweet picture he has painted of an Italian family looking at a sunset, which would very well take a little more finish than he has time to give. Passed on to Stanfield's, heard better news of him, saw Miss Stanfield and his son. I am confirmed in my notion that he is scarcely up to his own high mark this year. Went to Etty, who is very thin, very asthmatic—will not, I fear, last very long : he is *revelling* in colour and in form, but is in some parts of his larger picture deficient in expression, though in other parts most powerful and most happy.

April 8th.—Mr. Stirling called, and I signed the agreement for five weeks at the Surrey, £1000. May God speed it for good.

April 19th.—Began the long and particular business of correcting, punctuating, reading and arranging White's new play of *The King of the Commons*, which occupied my whole day.

April 20th.—Two papers were sent me from Dublin—" Packet "— addressed Mr. Macready, which I, without opening, put into the fire ! [1]

April 21st.—Went to rehearsal. Doorkeeper gave me a note which I glanced at and, without reading, saw it was one from a Mr. Sala [2] —*alias* Wynne—taking me to task for my ejaculations during the performance last night, which certainly he had elicited, though not addressed *to* him, nor intended *for him to hear.* I put the note into my pocket without reading it; but reflecting afterwards that it might contain some unwarrantable language, I called him to me, and told him that, having glanced my eye upon the beginning and the signature, I presumed he was the writer—it was signed Sala, not the name he goes by—that he had no right to notice any language I might use, unless directly addressed to him, nor any right to conceive himself insulted unless an insult was purposely and directly conveyed to him, or spoken of him to another person; that I had a right to question his observations upon any words, whatever they might be, that I might use to my own thoughts, etc.; that I should not address reviling language *to* him—or to any one. He was very civil—and wished to withdraw his note, but I chose to retain it. Rehearsed

---

[1] Macready, who was always inclined to be over-sensitive in such matters, greatly resented the address of " Mr." on his letters instead of " Esq."

[2] A brother of George Augustus Sala, whom Macready, for some reason or other, particularly disliked.

Macbeth. Spoke to Mr. Maddox and assisted him in casting *The King of the Commons*—particularly avoiding anything to do with Mr. Wallack. Walked home, found Mary Bucknill there. Read part of the pamphlet on the character of Macbeth against the long-eared writer in the *Westminster Review*.

April 22nd.—Thought on the impropriety or impolicy of reading *The King of the Commons*. Wrote a letter to White, summoning him to come and undertake it. Continued the endeavour to arrange these parties. Looked at papers. Heard of Dickens's intention to go to Switzerland—much distressed by it.

April 26th.—White dined with us. Reported of the reading his play yesterday, and of Mr. ——'s refusal to act the part of Laird Small; the conduct of these ignorant and conceited *vermin* is intolerable! My patience is not proof to their trials of it. Note from Panizzi [1] informing me that the Austrian Ambassador had under very particular circumstances invited him to dinner on the 9th, and explaining his inability to refuse. Answered him, rejoicing in the circumstance for his sake.

April 28th.—Dined with Lady Blessington. Met Lord Robertson, Liston, Quin, Lord Chesterfield, Edwin Landseer, Grant, Forster, Jerdan, Guthrie, Dickens.

May 1st.—Sir William Allan called—told us some strange stories of Thorburn [2] and the *Court!* Thorburn is the man to manage royalty. Note from Forster, wishing me to meet A. Tennyson to-morrow.

May 2nd.—Took up Dickens, and with him went to the Royal Academy. Delighted with the exhibition, which surpasses in general effect any that I have seen. Saw Maclise, Stanfield, Leslie, E. and Charles Landseer, Knight, Allan, Danby (to whom I was introduced and to whom I introduced Dickens), Lane, Herbert, Chalon, Pickersgill, Uwins, Lee, Jones, Cockerell, Etty, Patten, Roberts, Mulready, Howard, Grant, S. Cooper (to whom I was introduced), Sir M. A. Shee, who presided and went through his hard day's work with great taste and feeling. I saw T. Cooke, whom I accosted and spoke to

---

[1] Sir Anthony Panizzi, K.C.B. (1797–1879) ; the distinguished Principal Librarian of the British Museum, originally an advocate in the Duchy of Parma ; conspired against the Government and took refuge in England, being sentenced to death in his absence. He proved of the greatest service not only to the museum but to the staff, which at his instance was made a permanent branch of the Civil Service. He actively interested himself in the liberation of Italy, using his influence with the Whigs in aid of the cause.

[2] The miniature-painter.

with great kindness; we shook hands; I have never entertained any but kindly feelings for him; Lord Lansdowne, Rogers, Lord Morpeth. *The* Duke was there and spoke, Sir R. Peel, Graham, etc. The day was very agreeable to me. Talfourd was there, and on breaking up, at Dickens's suggestion (with no relish on my part) Rogers, Edwin Landseer, Stanfield, Dickens, Talfourd and myself went to the Lyceum to see General Tom Thumb.

May 5th.—Went to Thomas's and to Gunter's, to give orders. Met Mr. B. Disraeli and Mr. K. Macaulay,[1] from both of whom I had the honour of a cut. This is rather amusing, considering that both of these men have felt my notice of some value to them!

May 6th.—Gave the whole of the morning to the endeavour to learn the words of *The King of the Commons*. Rested. Letter from a person signing herself C. E. L.—containing a violent declaration of affection!

May 7th.—Count D'Orsay, Lord Robertson, the Chisholm, the Dickenses, Procters, Sir William Allan, Liston, Swinfen Jervis, Edwin Landseer, Mrs. Kitchener came to dinner. Lord Robertson gave his after-dinner speeches, his Italian songs, and his Gaelic sermon with great effect. Edwin Landseer with his imitation of Mr. Wells, his story of Lord Douro's answer to the Inverness gentleman inquiring about the Duke of Wellington washing his hands in expectation of the Prussians, was very entertaining.

May 9th.—Read, but not with much effect, *The King of the Commons*. Mr. and Mrs. Rutherfurd, Sir De Lacy and Lady Evans, Fonblanque, Miss Twiss, Alfred Tennyson, Dyce and Kenyon came to dinner.

May 11th.—Gave the morning to *King of the Commons*, which I cannot like—it is hasty and trashy. Rested. Acted King Lear very languidly and not at all *possessed* with the character. Called for.

May 12th.—Went to rehearsal of *King of the Commons*. Saw Mr. Maddox. Heard of the swindling practices of that foul knave, Bunn, upon Madame Anna Thillon. Called on T. Cooke, and sat some time with him. Letter from a poor Birmingham mechanic, Willis, with a tragedy—MS. (oh! me!)—from Miss Davis, of Lynn, a perfect stranger, asking me to send her by post a £5 Bank Bill; from Mr. ——, late Captain Atkins—asking me 5s. for a book; from Mr. Green, asking for pecuniary assistance, leaving the amount to myself!

---

[1] A cousin of the historian.

May 14th.—Note from Forster excusing himself from dining with us to-day. It is not that I am disposed to take offence at one or two rudenesses or slights committed by a friend, but the frequency of them wearies one's patience, and, where very questionable behaviour has been added, excites at least indifference. Began to read in *King of Commons*, but was stopped by a ludicrous cause of alarm in the non-arrival of Messrs. Gunter's cooks and dinner. Sent down to them —at last to our relief they arrived. It was a ridiculous perplexity. Sir John Wilson, Babbage, Sir J. Lyon Goldsmid and Miss G——, Colonel and Mrs. Albert Goldsmid, Sir John [1] and Lady Burgoyne, Mr. and Mrs. Stone, Mr. and Mrs. Campbell, and Wheatstone dined with us.

May 15th.—Note from Jerdan, again asking me, in a confidential note, to lend him money; he has already £100 of mine. I cannot afford to—*risk* is a foolish word—to *lose* any more. I wrote very kindly, stating my inability to accommodate him. Answered Forster's note very shortly. Talfourd came into my room and asked me to dine with him at the Star and Garter, Richmond, on Thursday, 21st. I agreed. Note from Forster, complaining of my note of this morning —a little *touch of conscience* I fancy. I answered his note.

May 16th.—Mr. and Mrs. M. Gibson, Mr. and Miss Mackinnon, Lydia Bucknill, Mrs. Jameson, Panizzi, Sir R. Comyn, Thorburn, Hayward, Harness and Thackeray dined with us.

May 20th.—Acted King James, in Mr. White's play of *The King of the Commons*, very fairly, considering all things. Was called and very warmly received. Forster came into my room to speak of some *misses* in the play.

May 21st.—Mrs. Dickens and Georgina Hogarth came to dine with Catherine. Went to Richmond, reading *King of Commons;* dined with Talfourd—meeting Dickens, Maclise, Stanfield and Forster. The latter made a very —— speech(!) on Talfourd.

May 23rd.—Saw that disgusting wretch Mr. Bunn in Covent Garden!—a reflection on the world and on mankind! Bought a farewell present for my little godchild, Katie Dickens. A note from Forster with the MS. of *Œdipus* by Bulwer. What I have read I do not like—it lacks simplicity of style and picturesqueness and *reality.*

---

[1] Sir John Fox Burgoyne (1782–1871); the distinguished engineer general; served with Sir John Moore and throughout Wellington's Peninsula campaign; one of the chief military advisers in the Crimean War. Baronet and Field-Marshal. He was a natural son of the General Burgoyne who surrendered at Saratoga, and, being pensioned on his return home, was taunted by "Junius" in one of his scathing letters as "sitting down, infamous and contented."

WALTER SAVAGE LANDOR

From a drawing by Count D'Orsay

May 25th.—A very long note from Forster, addressed to *me* alone, making admissions and confessions of his feelings and wishing to re-establish a better understanding. He desires no answer, but that cannot be. I must explain to him the causes of my coolness for *his own sake;* one from Mrs. Dickens, thanking me for the present to my little god-daughter.

May 26th.—Wrote to Mrs. Dickens, enclosing at her request some hair for my little godchild's locket. Looked at papers. My whole morning was engrossed by writing a letter to Forster, in which I frankly, but with very considerable *reservation*, in tenderness to him, stated objectionable points in his conduct which led to estrangement between us.

May 28th.—Received a long letter from Forster, which, I fear, puts *reconciliation* out of the question. He tells me that Stanfield and Maclise were *offended* at not being asked to meet Sir William Allan, and that Dickens was surprised at his (Stanfield's) dining with me after what he had said. Dickens told me that Forster said himself to Stanfield, "You won't go, will you?"—*i. e.* to dine with me! I will try to have this explained.

May 29th.—Called on Stanfield—absent; on Maclise, who was quite outrageously affectionate, and out of all bounds of surprise that he should be supposed offended with me about Allan's dining with me! Dickens came in, and we shook hands once more. Maclise said there was nothing I could do that would offend him—and he spoke truth. Perplexed and annoyed—and *disgusted* with Forster's note; it has done more mischief to him in my *feeling* and opinion than all he has before done.

May 30th.—Exceedingly annoyed by the necessity of answering this letter of Forster's, which was a cloud of words to hide facts—busied with it. Wrote my answer to Forster, whose position with me is so much altered that it must depend upon himself whether our earlier understanding is ever restored. Dined with Lord Lansdowne. Met Lord Shelburne, T. Moore, Panizzi, Eastlake, Sir A. Gordon, Elliot, Jerrold, Mrs. Norton, Mrs. Elliot.

May 31st.—A note from Forster with an admission that he had been wrong, and asking me to give him back the two notes he had written to me—requesting our understanding might be restored, and asking me to go down and see Landor [1] who was to dine with him. I answered him very kindly and cordially, enclosing him the two letters.

[1] Walter Savage Landor (1775–1864), the poet ; he was then residing at Bath.

After dinner went down to Forster's and sat with him and Landor some time. Much talk on Milton, Shakspeare, Virgil, Horace, Homer, etc. Reconciled to Forster.

June 1st.—Looked at paper—a decided improvement in the *Daily News*—the first number at $2\frac{1}{2}d.$[1]—an experiment of doubtful result. Read the *Times*—that wonderful engine of power! Was grieved to see a stern and unkind notice of Dickens's book in it—"*Post equitem sedet atra cura.*"

June 4th.—Saw Thorburn's pictures, which are good pictures of very uninteresting persons. Called on Forster, who was from home and had left a note for me. Went to Hampstead; on my way called on Stanfield, who was just setting out for Cockerell's with May Stanfield. Arrived at North End, Cockerell's[2] place—a very pretty villa, very charmingly situated to command a view of Hendon, Mill Hill, etc. There was an elegant and beautiful assemblage on the lawn. Music and dancing—talking and promenading. I saw Cockerell and his wife, who were glad to see me; Eastlake, Bezzi, whom I was delighted to see. Milman and Mrs. Milman, Babbage, Chalon, Martin, Edwin Landseer, Knight, Lady Essex and Miss Johnstone, Maclise, Stanfield, Wyon, Rogers, Charles Landseer, Hart, Mulready, Campbell the sculptor, Thorburn, Blake, etc. The scene was very brilliant. I had great pleasure in talking with my old acquaintance, Lady Essex, now, alas! really old—who was so lovely when young, and who looked as if she could not be old! Alas! Went to Mrs. Procter's ball. Not very crowded, nor distingué. Saw Thackeray, E. Landseer, whom I brought there from home; Ayrton, Chorley, F. Stone, Mrs. Jameson, Campbell, Sir J. Goldsmid, etc.; Monckton Milnes, who was unusually cordial; *Browning*—who did not speak to me—the *puppy!* etc.—a dull party.

June 7th.—Bulwer Lytton called. I was sorry to see him so peculiar in his dress—most particularly extravagant in his attention to the costume of his face, which he makes unpicturesque and coxcomical. He talked about the state of the drama in general, which he thought might have been brought before Parliament successfully this session but for the absorbing question of the Corn Laws—and still was of opinion that a theatre might be sustained by

[1] A very low price for a newspaper in those days, though five times as much as that charged for the *Daily News* at the present time.

[2] Charles Robert Cockerell (1780-1863), R.A., the eminent architect.

a party of gentlemen. It is too much to speculate on. I gave him my opinion in part upon *Œdipus*, and he seemed struck with some suggestions, but I showed him that there was no chance of its being performed, and I also gave my opinion it would not be attractive if performed.

June 9th.—Kenney called. I was very glad to see him. He told me that Moore observed: " What a strange party that was on Thursday at Lansdowne House! " Query—Is it a compliment to be invited to make one of a " strange party "? Forster was there—*not agreeable*. Walked home. Notes from Mrs. Hall, M. Gibson, Pearson, etc. Bezzi, Eastlake, Maclise, Mulready, Knox, Procter, Forster, came to dinner. Forster was not agreeable—perhaps disagreeable. Kenyon looked in in the evening.

June 19th.—Acted King James better than usual, wishing my last night at the Princess's to leave a pleasing impression—as I think it did. Called for and very warmly received. Heard news of the other houses, Drury Lane with the vaunted attraction of the ballet, acting on Monday to £31! Haymarket to £10, etc. We therefore are still high in the scale. Thank God! Mr. Maddox came to my room, and took leave of me, emphatically *thanking* me. My engagement at the Princess's closed. Thank God for all His grace and mercy.

June 20th.—Read in the paper Sir R. Peel's defence of himself against the attacks of Bentinck and Disraeli, in which I think he turned to shame their venomed and virulent abuse. His *not supporting* Canning I thought wrong, and think so still; it seemed to me then a false step, and I think it has had, as I have watched him, an influence on his whole life.[1]

June 22nd.—Called on Miss Andrews, with whom I talked some time, explaining to her that I could not teach her to act—only to teach herself to act by opening her mind to her own emotions, perhaps dormant in her, and making her acquainted with her own passions—that the intercourse needful for this course of study was dangerous,

---

[1] Disraeli's malignant attacks on Peel were notoriously inspired by resentment at not receiving office, for which he had abjectly supplicated in a letter which Peel, in spite of overpowering provocation, magnanimously forbore to use. As regards Peel's refusal to support Canning he explained his decision on grounds which Canning acknowledged to be perfectly fair and reasonable, he being at the time an anti-Catholic and Canning a pro-Catholic. Yet, though well aware of this fact, Disraeli deliberately charged Peel with " hounding Canning to death " ! His attitude to Peel at this period was nothing short of despicable, and is an indelible blot on his career.

341

as begetting too close an intimacy. I heard her recite. She has intelligence and feeling. I gave her two sovereigns to make a better appearance, as to wardrobe, before Mr. Stirling, and recommended her to *ménager* some little defects in her figure. She seems a modest girl.

June 23rd.—Mr. Aubrey de Vere [1] called with an introduction, at Lord Monteagle's request, from Talfourd. He sat long, and I am delighted with him.

June 25th.—Looked at paper. Read the detailed account of Haydon's [2] suicide; it is most sad—most dreadful for the surviving relations, but it is a termination of a life that does not surprise me. Rogers called and sat long—telling me of *Hayter's* early life. He is breaking.

June 26th.—In the *Times* was interested by the leading article, and by one on Haydon—poor man!—with which I could not agree. I am sorry for his infirmities, but they could not, like Leigh Hunt's, lead to anything but embarrassment and suffering. Am *I* better? Alas! I have very much to reproach myself with.

June 29th.—Went, with Rutherfurds, to the French play—perfectly disgusted with the piece—with the acting of Déjazet and Lafont, and with the miserably cold and affected enthusiasm of the audience.

June 30th.—Read the paper, not losing one word of Sir R. Peel's interesting speech. His laying down office was a proud minute, far prouder than its assumption.[3] With Sterne, one might say, " Oh, how I envied him his feelings! "

---

[1] The well-known poet.

[2] Benjamin Robert Haydon (1786-1846). Pecuniary difficulties and disappointed ambition were responsible for his suicide. His body was found lying before his colossal picture *Alfred the Great and the First British Jury,* and his last entry in his diary was : " June 22. God forgive me. Amen. Finis B. R. Haydon. Stretch me no longer on this rough world." Less than a week before he had written in his diary : " Sat from two to five o'clock to-day staring at my picture like an idiot, my brain pressed down by anxiety and the anxious looks of my family, whom I have been compelled to inform of my condition. I have written to Sir Robert Peel, to ——, to ——, etc. Who answered first ? Tormented by Disraeli, harassed by public business, up came a letter from Sir Robert Peel." The letter enclosed £50.

[3] The speech is memorable for its generous and eloquent tribute to Cobden : its closing words are of peculiar interest at a time when a return to Protection is being so widely advocated : " I shall surrender power, severely censured, I fear, by many honourable gentlemen who from no interested motive have adhered to the principle of Protection as important to the welfare and interest of the country. I shall leave a name execrated by every monopolist who, from far less honourable motives, maintains Protection for his own individual benefit ; but it may be I shall leave a name sometimes remembered with expressions

July 2nd.—Went to breakfast with Rogers. Met Lyon, Aubrey de Vere, and, to my great delight, Henry Taylor,[1] author of *Philip Van Artevelde*. He talked much, and talked well; his knowledge of our poets is very extensive indeed; he quoted much and excellently well. Rogers was in very good spirits.

July 5th.—Looked at paper; particularly displeased—I might almost say disgusted—with the *Examiner*, converted from a high-toned republican (in the honourable interpretation of the word) journal into a splenetic, waspish, Whig party paper. Went out to Mortlake to lunch with Henry Taylor. Met there, with some one I did not know, Captain Elliot, whom I was very glad to meet. Was very much pleased with Mrs. H. Taylor, whom I thought most intelligent, pleasing, and attached, quite as a poet's wife should be, to her husband. Taylor took me into the drawing-room, where we talked on art and various things, until, on Mrs. Taylor's entrance, after a grand storm of rain and thunder had passed away, he mentioned the comedy he was upon, and wished to read his first act to me. It was in language very beautiful; I was delighted with it, but I criticized its construction, and in my observations was gratified to see that I imparted some truths he had not been aware of, with the knowledge of which he seemed very much pleased. I remained long, leaving them at a little past five. Returned, reading my delightful *Consuelo*. Went to Errington's to dinner. Met Miss Macdonald, whom I liked very much; Lords Granby, Foley, Fitzroy Somerset;[2] Miss Foley, very pretty; Lady F. Somerset, very dull; Lady Lyndhurst;[3] Miss Copley, very good natured; Maxse, a good-natured fellow; and a foreigner, whom I did not know. Mrs. Errington is very beautiful and very good-natured; he is most good-natured.

July 6th.—Note from ——, dated 5, *Eaton Square*. This man five years ago was worse than nothing, but he was manifestly deeply implicated in the Irish Western Railway, the knavery of which was only partially brought to light, and it is clear that he has contrived to get a fortune out of the miserable dupes that have been victimized for it! *Ainsi va le monde!*

---

of good-will in those places which are the abode of those men whose lot it is to labour and to earn their daily bread by the sweat of their brow—a name remembered with expressions of good-will when they shall recreate their exhausted strength with abundant and untaxed food, the sweeter because it is no longer leavened with a sense of injustice."

[1] Sir Henry Taylor (1800–1886). He held an important position in the Colonial Office.
[2] Afterwards Field-Marshal Lord Raglan.
[3] The ex-Chancellor's second wife, *née* Goldsmith.

July 8th.—Read; finished *Consuelo*. It is long since I have been so deeply penetrated by a book. I shall never, during at least the few years left to me of life (and do I wish them to be many? God guide me), forget this book. It is full of genius. My soul has been elevated by its perusal. Thoughts unworthy of me have been driven from my mind. May I keep my mind for ever free from them! Amen! The perusal of *Consuelo* has left a deep impression on me; it has drawn many tears from my eyes, and awakened thoughts in me for which, I trust, I am better. Let no one say it is useless or even weak to suffer and to grieve for fictitious distress; it humanizes, softens and purifies the soul. The looser thoughts and more corrupt imaginations that had place in my mind have sunk down into forgetfulness, and disappeared before the chastening and elevating influence of sympathy with nobler natures and the contemplation of our mortal condition and its liabilities. Oh God, make me better and wiser and more pure.

July 13th.—Went to Kensal Green Cemetery to visit the resting-place of my blessed Joan; the dear creature. My heart blessed her and prayed for our reunion. Went to St. James's theatre. Saw Rachel in the *Horaces*. Her acting in Camille was very good, but there was a deficiency of physical force, and, in consequence, her vehemence was too scolding, too cat-like in the spitting out of her reproaches. Saw Lord Beaumont, the Goldsmids, Lady Blessington.

July 19th.—Looked at the paper, which gave me little pleasure. It is a very great entertainment, which I now miss each Sunday morning; Fonblanque has "to party given up what was meant for mankind." The *Examiner* is nothing more than a Whig newspaper—a superior *Weekly Chronicle*.

St. Heliers, July 21st.—Came on shore in boat. Drove up to Fred. Reynolds's. After breakfast sent for Mr. Harvey. Arranged with him for the engagement to act five nights here and three at Guernsey.

July 22nd.—Received letter from Miss L. Addison with an advertisement by Mr. ——[1] of the most outrageous impertinence that malice and half-crazed spleen and envy could be guilty of. I cannot notice it, because I cannot afford to give publicity to it, but it is to me a convincing proof of what I have often feared and have never *really* wished to allow, that Mr. —— is in heart and mind a *scoundrel—voilà tout!* Acted Cardinal Richelieu very fairly. Called for.

To Guernsey, August 1st.—Went on board the *Ariadne* steam-

---

[1] A provincial manager with whom Macready had long been on strained terms.

344

boat. The company of Mr. Harvey was on board. Arrived in Guernsey.

London, August 20th.—Birth of a daughter.[1] [The day's entry is headed *Benvenuta.*]

Manchester, August 23rd.—Arrived at Manchester; I had my usual nervousness upon me, which is most extraordinary, most ridiculous; but so it is, the entering into a town where I am going to act, the sight of my name in the playbills on the walls affects me most unpleasantly. How strange!

August 24th.—Went to rehearsal; took pains, and tried, as courteously as I could, to impress the people on the stage with the necessity of attention; but they are English players—literally described by Shakspeare—"Rascals, runaways, whom their o'ercloyed country vomits forth to desperate adventures and assured destruction!" They are low, and low-minded persons, shirking honest industry for an indolent and precarious life. Tried my utmost to act Hamlet, but the audience were so peculiar that they surprised and in some degree distressed me; they would not allow of any ebullition of applause, but applauded at the end of the scene. I wish it were always so, but not being used to it, it disconcerted me at first. Called and well received.

August 25th.—A Rev. J. Hayes called and wished to know if I gave instructions in reading. I told him no, but that I would hear him read and give him any hints in my power, by which he was much obliged, and I made an appointment with him for Thursday. A Mrs. —— called, and wished me to hear her read Lady Macbeth. I heard her recite part of the first scene, which was indeed ridiculous; her husband, who has nothing and is living as he can, is the son of Sir ——, the police magistrate, and has taken his degree of M.A. I told her it was hopeless, and as she said her husband had not had a dinner these three days, I gave her 10s.

August 29th.—Acted Werner, with which I wished to take great pains, but was *lacerated* by the disgusting players—from the beginning to the end.

London, September 7th.—Went to Surrey theatre.[2] Rehearsed with care. Dined, rested; acted with great pains, very finely; I think I did act well. Spoke to Mr. Stirling. Returned home.

---

[1] Now Mrs. Horsford, Macready's only surviving child by his first marriage.

[2] The engagement at the Surrey Theatre continued from September 7 to October 9, and again from October 12 to November 7—(*note by Sir F. Pollock*).

September 29th.—On our return caught a glimpse of the great brass statue of Wellington—which has been paraded through the streets.[1] I am sick of this charlatanism of all sorts. The Horse Guards, too! Men—human beings—creations of the great God, and gifted with reason!!

September 30th.—Acted Macbeth *admirably*, with great force, reality and power—but that gallery to listen to Shakspeare! What does Knowles say in *Alfred* about the poets' verse that should be sung to kings, become the indifferent pastime of—Surrey audiences!

October 2nd.—Letter from Mr. ——. I *fear* I am angry, or annoyed, that a creature like that, so little and so base (who only could by his peculiar qualities have done the things he has done) should have juggled himself into a large fortune. What is it to me?— what to me the accidents, business, and knaveries of the world about me? I *could* not do what these low-minded men do, why, therefore, should I care whether the result of their roguery be gain or loss?

October 4th.—Went out in carriage with Katie to Mortlake to call on Henry Taylor. He was at home; walked in the garden with him and Mrs. H. T——, who was very kind to Katie. I like his conversation much; I like her. He read to me the ending of his first act altered to the suggestion I had submitted to him; it seemed delightful to me. He wished to hear me read Milton, but I was not well prepared—in voice or tone of mind, and begged to defer it. Spent the evening with the dear children. As I was preparing to go down to my study to write to Nina, to my surprise Carlyle and Mrs. C—— called. They remained till near eleven. His conversation is so amusing, so profound, so full of matter.

October 7th.—Acted Macbeth for the most part very well, but I act with clogs, with heavy weights upon me with such people as Mrs. —— in Lady Macbeth! C—— in Macduff! and Mr. —— (oh! Mr. ——!) the First Witch—and then the smaller characters!—oh!! Called for, etc. Mr. —— observed to me—" *What a slave you are to your profession!* " This proves that instead of being the rule I am *the exception*. What a comment is this upon the *players* of the day!—the artists!—oh——

October 9th.—Acted Hamlet very fairly. Called. Completed my first Surrey engagement.

October 10th.—Letter from Mr. Grantley Berkeley—complaining

---

[1] The bronze statue that used to surmount the arch at Constitution Hill, and is now at Aldershot.

of his brother, Lord Fitzhardinge, (sweet family!) endeavouring to turn him out of his seat for Gloucestershire; was well worth attention, and worth strong comment, if one had time to give it.

October 11th.—The Smiths, Cattermoles, Stanfields, White and Maclise came to dine. Thackeray came in in the evening. We passed a very cheerful day.

October 13th.—Looked over *Times;* a very good article on Mr. Grantley Berkeley. Dined with Forster. Met À Beckett,[1] White, Kenyon, Lord Nugent, Talfourd, and Douglas Jerrold. How strange —how preposterous are our prejudices. I remember when I detested the name of this Mr. À Beckett, whom I did not know, because he wrote, or was said to have written, disparagingly of me in the *Figaro!* I like him, knowing him, very much.

October 18th.—White, Maclise, King, and Forster came to dinner. Forster was in one of those humours in which he displays a rude and low-bred indifference to his friends, with a general churlishness of manner that is literally offensive. It was remarked, immediately that he left the room, by White, and directly we came up-stairs, by Catherine. Maclise says it is not possible to associate with him!

October 19th.—Looked at paper. Went to Surrey. Heard of the death of Mrs. Ternan's husband [2]—died in a lunatic asylum at Bethnal Green. How light are our woes when compared with such a weight of affliction! I think I ought to ascertain if I can at all assist or relieve her.

October 21st.—Letter from Mrs. Ternan accepting with much feeling my offer of ten pounds, and wishing it to be considered as a loan. I wrote to her, enclosing a cheque for the amount; but unwilling to hamper her with the sense of a *debt*, requested, if the surplus of her labours offered it, to transfer it as a gift from me to her little girl. Poor thing! Forster came into my room; all is not going well with him and the *Daily News.*

October 22nd.—Took a cab on, and called on Forster. He informed me that the *Times*, etc., had combined against the *Daily News*—to share the expense of Indian mails, etc., excluding only that paper; that being deserted by the *Morning Herald*, they, the proprietors of the *Daily News*, intended to go on without the Indian

---

[1] Gilbert Abbott À Beckett (1811–1856); a well-known journalist and playwright; on the original staff of *Punch*; appointed a Metropolitan police magistrate in 1849.

[2] Frances Eleanor Jarman (1803–1873), afterwards Mrs. Ternan; an actress of some vogue in Shaksperian parts.

mail, but not to state that fact, and to raise their price from $2\frac{1}{2}d$. to $3d$. This Forster resisted, and I think most honourably. He read me his letter of resignation and the acceptance of the proprietors, and expressed his intention of explaining his position to Baldwin—proprietor of the *Mornng Herald*—from which I dissuaded him.

October 26th.—Letter from D. Colden, whose news of Mr. Forrest's attraction in New York (the fellow having actually disgraced his country here, as an actor and as a man ! !) depressed me a little, in presenting America—or rather the United States—as a country for blackguards. The gentlemen are certainly the *very* small minority !

October 28th.—Looked at papers. The *Daily News* issues a manifesto, denouncing the combination of the other papers against it, asserting its independence, calling upon the public to pay $3d$. instead of $2\frac{1}{2}d$., and promising to have their *expresses*, etc., *alone*, which is a *premeditated lie !* Forster could not have remained in it.

November 4th.—Rehearsed. Poor Mrs. Ternan was much affected in reciting the *beautiful* speech on mercy (has the Bible anything better ?), and she made a woman of me. She brought her three little girls to see me, and her mother came after. Poor thing. She appears very grateful for a little act of duty ; such I feel it.

November 5th.—Went to railway station, reading Chaucer, which I find delightful, humorous, animated, various, graphic, and abounding in character most broadly, nicely and distinctly marked—the delightful old poet ! Saw Captain Williams, Inspector of Prisons, at the station. He came into the coupé with me, and we journeyed together, he returning by the same train as myself. He told me some interesting facts about commitments to prison by *clerical* magistrates of poor wretches, who were instantly released on his representation. My blood boiled !

November 6th.—Note from Miss Susan Cushman, wanting to separate from her sister, and ally herself professionally with me ! Appointed her, according to her wish, to call to-morrow—*not* to entertain her offer.

November 7th.—Miss Susan Cushman called, and I had a long conversation with her, endeavouring to persuade her of the mutual folly of herself and sister separating, but urging her to conciliate and succumb rather than part. Last night of Surrey engagement. Acted Virginius. Called for and most enthusiastically greeted.

Manchester, November 8th.—Left home for Manchester. At the station asked for a coupé, and was told it was engaged. Whilst arranging my seat in the carriage, a person of the station came to tell me that there was one seat in the coupé unoccupied, but that " Mathews and Vestris " had the others, and perhaps I might not like it. I laughed and said, " Certainly not," and that I was much obliged.

London, November 16th.—An American paper with an account of a dinner given to Mr. Forrest at New York, Bryant in the chair; Halleck one of the committee, Griffin another, and Theodore Sedgwick (*proh pudor*) a committee man!—" professional excellence and private worth "!! America!! Give me a crust in England. God speed me in my labours for my blessed family's sake. Amen! *No America.*

November 19th.—Two persons called, wishing a subscription for a new church. Will they give us ministers of *Christ ?* *No.* Mr. and Miss Fox, Mr. Tom Taylor,[1] Mr. À Beckett, Charles Eddy, Stanfield, Maclise, King, Thackeray, and Forster dined with us. À Beckett and Taylor are both agreeable men. Taylor a man of extensive information, I like him much.

To Plymouth, November 22nd.—Left Exeter for Plymouth. A most tedious journey, reaching Plymouth a little before five, from half-past eleven.

November 23rd.—Went to rehearsal, found the company most wretched; some not arrived, and Mr. Newcombe utterly ignorant of his business. The rehearsal was one of the most hopeless exhibitions I have almost *ever* seen. Rested and thought on Hamlet, resolving not to let the inaccuracy and incompetency of these wretches—they are no better!—disturb me. But we began with waiting twenty minutes for Marcellus, who, when on the stage, stunk of tobacco and a public-house to *sicken* the stomach—oh!—and all this I might have avoided had I been prudent in taking care of the money I have earned. Bitter, bitter reflection!! Acted Hamlet as well as I could. Called for. Mr. Newcombe came in, but he is *incapable.*

November 24th.—My mind has been much depressed from revolving of late at various times the state of my finances; I can easily account for, not easily excuse my improvidence and want of management. Last night I lay awake nearly the whole night recollecting the different years of my life since I rose into the character of an *attractive* actor, in 1820. Since then I have received a large sum of money, of which, through ill-management, ignorance, precipitancy, but chief and worst, a want of well-regulated economy, but little, alas! is left, and now my mind is ill at ease about the education and settlement of my beloved

---

[1] Tom Taylor (1817–1880) ; the well-known dramatist and editor of *Punch.*

children. If I were to die, I should leave them in tolerable circumstances—but God's will be done. Calculated on what I had saved this year. I cannot satisfy myself that I have saved more than £2300—very far below what I *ought* to have invested out of such an income. What am I to do—what *ought* I to do? I must think—and *act*.

November 25th.—*Our blessed Joan lost to us.* My thoughts and prayers were on that sweet, lovely child, who ever remains as a thing most exquisitely dear, precious, and mournful to my heart. My blessing is constantly wandering after her angel spirit—the beloved one! In dying, I shall rejoin her, sweet cherub! God has blessed her. May His blessing preserve and cherish to good those dear ones spared to me. Read a paper on Impey's reply to a severe, if not cruel, attack of Macaulay's on his father.[1] I do not like what I see of that man's character. He behaved poorly in Wallace's case.

November 26th.—Acted King Lear—trying—but such a company would " sink a navy "!

November 28th.—Wightwick called with Mrs. W—— for me, and took me in a carriage to Flete, the seat of Lady Elizabeth Bulteel.[2] I was introduced to her, admired her; really, a most engaging woman, elegant, simple, or rather simple and elegant, for the one quality must be the foundation of the other—a very sweet woman. Lady Morley was with her, and Mr. Courtenay also. We lunched. I went over the house, which is a monument of the feeling, taste, and talent of the deceased proprietor and builder.

November 30th.—Rehearsed Richelieu; disgusted with the—*actors !* Scarcely one of them better than my own servant, and several not so good!

December 1st.—Acted King Lear with much care, for I saw the old colonel [3] in the boxes, who had come on purpose to see it, and I wished to give him all the pleasure I could. The house was really *awful !* Not six people besides his party in the boxes!—the rest of the house proportionate. It is hard to know what to do against the advice of persons on the spot; but I ought to have ended last night. The old colonel came into my room, much pleased, and got upon the theme of

---

[1] The Chief Justice of Bengal, so trenchantly attacked in Macaulay's famous essay on Warren Hastings. Macaulay's invective was no doubt at times overcharged, but he wrote with an absolute honesty of conviction, and was wholly incapable of mean or dishonourable conduct. Wallace, who was a sort of hack-historian, had apparently been severely handled by Macaulay, who was certainly no friend to that species of writer.

[2] A daughter of the second Earl Grey, the Whig Premier.

[3] Colonel Hamilton Smith.

the ill-usage he has met with from the Horse Guards—the cold-blooded aristocrats!   "Cold shade of the aristocracy" indeed!   I sicken at them.   George Darley's [1] death is announced.   Another great spirit gone; with extraordinary powers of mind, achieving great conquests.

To London, December 5th.—Several letters and papers with accounts of the success of *Iphigenia* in Dublin—in terms of laudation that, if true, proclaim a miracle in the improvement of Miss H. Faucit, and, if not true, are foolish exaggeration; perhaps we may take the medium of both.

December 9th.—Dined with Kenyon, meeting Bancroft, American Minister.   Sir George Staunton,[2] the *Chinese* man, Panizzi, Forster, and others.   Went with Bancroft to the Graphic Society; saw there Edwin Landseer, Charles Landseer and Tom Landseer, Brockedon, F. Stone, Mr. Lovell, etc.

December 11th.—Charles Kemble called and told me a story about the old Duke of Queensberry,[3] who, to a person talking of "the finest woman in the world," observed, "Sir, there never was the finest woman in the world."

December 18th.—Mr. and Mrs. Bancroft (American Minister), Sir de Lacy and Lady Evans, Carlyle and Miss Welch, Fonblanque, Babbage, and Knox dined with us.

December 19th.—The Milner Gibsons, Horace Twisses, Delanes, Dillon, and Dyce dined with us.

December 21st.—Hardwick, Quin, Dickens, Troughton, Elliotson, Mark Lemon, Leech, Forster, Swinfen Jervis, Raymond, dined with us.

December 26th.—In the evening a party of *juveniles*—Mr. Stone's, Goldsmids's, Procter's, Fonblanque's children; H. Smith's, H. Twisses's, Mrs. C. Hall, Stanfield's, and, with theirs, Mrs. Gibson, Maclise, Haworth's, Spurgin's, Chitty's, Miss Dudgeon, Miss Wilson, etc., made a very pleasant evening, and to my dear children a *very happy one.*   God for ever bless them.

December 30th.—Came by the railway to Canterbury, sleeping the greater part of the journey.   Mr. Dowton [4] wished me to extend my term to three nights, but I evaded the promise to do so.   The actors,

---

[1] George Darley (1795–1846); a man of many gifts, whose reputation has not survived.

[2] Sir George Thomas Staunton (1781–1859), the well-known writer on China.   Joint-founder of the Royal Asiatic Society.

[3] The notorious "Old Q."

[4] Presumably a son of the well-known actor of that name.

Horatio and Marcellus, were beyond precedent disgraceful. Rehearsed. Looked at paper. Rested on sofa. Acted Hamlet, taking much pains. The Horatio and Marcellus were *infinitely* worse than the disgraceful promise of their rehearsal. Called. A soldier of the 30th, a rascal, called on me, as one of my brother's men, in distress. I was fool enough to give him 2s. 6d. Thank God, one night is over. The weather is dreadfully cold.

1847

London, January 2nd.—Called on Forster; read there a most savage but most malicious and, I think, innoxious attack on Dickens and his book in the *Times*. Talked with Forster about the proceedings for a theatre, and we agreed it was best to see if anything could be done. With this view he was strong in his exhortations to me to take the chair at the General Theatrical Fund. He says Bulwer Lytton will support me. I feel confident he will not.

To Exeter, January 3rd.—Rose in tolerably good time, and busily employed myself in packing up my clothes, etc., which occupied me some hours. On coming down-stairs I read prayers to my dear family. Came by railway to Exeter, reading by the way the *Examiner* and No. 4 of *Dombey and Son*, which I think most powerfully written. Reached my lodgings at Exeter, and finished No. 4 of *Dombey*, which I like extremely.

January 4th.—Mr. Latimer called and sat some little time. I felt much interest in him as the persecuted of the "most Christian" (!) Bishop of Exeter. He told me the case as it stood, and merely made out another blasphemy in the life of this *accursed* son of Moloch, Philpotts, Bishop of Exeter. The wretch! Rehearsed. Rested and tried to think on Othello, which I am anxious to act well, though my spirits were very low, as were my anticipations of the house. Acted Othello as well as I could with a most *grotesque* Iago, but to a very respectable house. Called and went on.

January 7th.—Called on Mr. Latimer. He talked much about the theatres; about Phelps and Mr. C. Kean, about whose *perseverance* (not wishing to compromise himself by praising his talent) he wrote a good-natured article that he scarcely thought would have been acceptable to C. Kean, who, to his astonishment, and to that of those who knew something of him also, sent for *eighty* papers! This is an evidence of the systematic *trade* this charlatan has carried on! It was a curious fact. Looked over—for there is no reading—the *Morning Herald*. The Queen had *Athalie* read to her on Christmas Day—the King of Prussia had got it up lately. When will she have Shakspeare read or acted?

Bristol, January 10*th.*—A letter from Lane to Catherine, informing her of Mrs. Butler's intent to return to the stage. I am not, perhaps, qualified to judge. I hope she is right, but fear she is wrong. She is a woman of unquestionable genius, and many good qualities, but in judgment, I think, she is deficient. If she succeeds, it will be so far well for her ; if she has not great success, her enemies will speak harshly of her.

To Bath, January 12*th.*—Came on to Bath reading *Examiner.* Went from White Hart to the theatre, walked the stage to make myself at home upon it—my usual practice. Thoughts of past days crowd on me here, my first agitated experiment, my success, my friends, my youthful vanities, and real and fancied loves, alas ! how many in the grave, how past are all these dreams of boyishness !

Bath, January 14*th.*—Read paper ; saw correspondence between *Fanny Butler* and Mr. Bunn, she asking £100 per night, he declining in a letter written, of course, in *bad English*, and offering £50 !

Bristol, January 18*th.*—Acted Macbeth ; really took pains to act well, but was put to rout by the people employed—the Seyton—oh !— the messenger ! it was not possible ; and the row of supernumeraries standing at the back of the stage during the whole of my last scene with Macduff ! I was half frenzied !

Bath, January 19*th.*—Came by rail (from Bristol) to Bath, reading *Examiner* by the way ; the correspondence of Mrs. Butler and Mr. Bunn comes in the pinch of Fonblanque's fingers. Saw a Liverpool playbill of 1778, for Mrs. Siddons's Benefit, in which the manager expresses his *great satisfaction* at having secured the *Dancing Dogs* for *one night more ! Who will talk of degeneracy ?* Acted Macbeth very fairly. Unluckily, cut poor Cooper's head, but not badly. Called and well received. Before the play spoke to one of the players, Mr. Swift, and apologized to him for coarse and impatient language I had used last night.

January 23*rd.*—Acted King James with *every individual* incorrect in the play, except Mr. Cooper, who came in " disguised," or rather " concealed," with his great broad face staring out as large as a full moon's ! The play was most imperfect ; very bad indeed. Read the *Times.* The fate of the opera speculation at Covent Garden is sealed by Lumley's advertisement. I should not, of course, repine if the whole entertainment were crushed to pieces. I do not approve it, thinking it *void of sense.*

Dublin, January 30*th.*—Looked through Saunders' newspaper, in which were continued instances of the disgusting spirit of these people seeking to thwart by all factious means the sincere purpose and endeavour of Government to aid and elevate them. One man complains that they may not catch salmon now in Ireland, whilst in Scotland and England the salmon fisheries are actively plied. Surely this is a falsehood! Read the 7th book of *Excursion* whilst waiting for Calcraft, in which are beautiful passages, but *the poem* never can be *popular*. Anecdote of Lord Norbury and Parsons, barrister, travelling to Dublin and passing a *gibbet*. " If that gibbet had its due, where would you be? "—" Travelling alone to Dublin, my lord."

February 1st.—Looked at paper, in which was an extract from a Belfast journal, that " Miss H. Faucit, the greatest actress of the day, had left, and was to be succeeded by Mr. Macready, the greatest actor." Now, certainly, if comparisons are odious, so are such classifications. Mr. Higgins—in playbill Bellew [1]—called; quite as an old acquaintance. I thought the rap was Calcraft's; I could not give him a very cordial reception—indeed I was ill, and not in tone of mind to do it; but I *ought* not to have done it, his calling was really *taking a liberty*. He *will do nothing* for himself. Rehearsed with care. Acted Macbeth well—yes, well—to an indifferent house. Called. Stapleton, poor old fellow, a thirty-two years' acquaintance, came in to speak to me. I never acted Macbeth better, and learned much in this night's performance. Hear this and understand it, if you can, you " great " young actors!

February 2nd.—Acted Virginius very fairly; was annoyed by the rudeness and impertinence of one of the players. It is a natural question, what is one to expect from such people, knowing them as I do?

February 3rd.—Reported with great temper the conduct of a Mr. F. Cooke last night to Calcraft, who felt it very properly. Acted King Lear to an audience—what can I say of them? They seemed by their deep attention much interested, and occasional murmurs showed an appreciation of feelings and passages; the applause, too, wrung as it was, seemed genuine, but enthusiasm there was none; but how could there be on so cold a night with only £40 in the house? The play seemed to grow into the hearts of the audience, and at the end they appeared much moved. Was called.

February 5th.—A note from Hayward!—who is here—wishing to

---

[1] John Chippendall Montesquieu Bellew (1823-1874), originally Higgins ; the well-known preacher and reciter. Macready became more intimate with him in later years, but eventually, for various reasons, the acquaintance ceased.

introduce me to "Prince George and Jem MacDonald." [1] Acted Othello. Went on the stage desponding, despairing of any power to act at all, but thinking to myself I would take time, having the clear idea of every word I uttered in my mind, and make the performance a study. I pursued the plan, kindling into energy, and acted the part most effectively, indeed well. The house was better than we could have calculated on, and the audience quite laid hold on by the acting. Called for.

February 6th.—Went to rehearsal, in the course of which the actress, Miss ——, was grossly rude, charging me with having called her some *unnameable* name, etc., which I in the most positive but courteous manner denied, and had to listen to much disgusting insolence —a vulgar, *conceited*, low-bred person, intriguing and illiterate. Spoke to Calcraft about her. Acted, taking great pains to work against the paralyzing slowness of these people, and made the play go very effectively. Called, and enthusiastically received. Calcraft brought me a message from the Lord-Lieutenant, [2] who was present, and wished to see me. I went to him ; saw Mrs. Maberly, etc. He invited me to lunch to-morrow. Read delightful *Punch*.

February 7th.—Calcraft accompanied me to the Castle. Ushered in to the lunch. Received by Lord Bessborough. Lunched ; chatted afterwards with Mrs. Maberly, and some of the young ladies ; Connellan, [3] etc., whom I liked.

February 9th.—Went to station. Left Dublin by train for Drogheda. Came on by mail to Belfast.

Belfast, February 10th.—Looked at paper ; *disgusted—intensely disgusted* with the speech of Lord George Bentinck on Irish railroads. [4] Interest and fashion will join in gaining to it supporters ; the money will be lent and *lost*, the gamblers will make their bargains and be saved. This fellow will make a false reputation, and the country will

[1] The late Duke of Cambridge, and his equerry, afterwards General MacDonald, a well-known figure in society.

[2] John William, fourth Earl of Bessborough (1781–1847). A popular Whig nobleman who, as Lord Duncannon, had been Home Secretary under Lord Melbourne. Lady Caroline Lamb was his sister, and Sir Spencer Ponsonby-Fane, the veteran Court official, is his only surviving son.

[3] Corrie Connellan, a popular private secretary to three Irish viceroys ; his sudden retirement in the early seventies caused a sensation in Dublin almost as great as that created by the Crown Jewel mystery.

[4] His scheme was for lending £16,000,000 to Irish Railway Companies at 3½ per cent., £2 to be advanced by the Government for every £1 subscribed by shareholders. The bill was thrown out by a majority of 214.

be *quacked*, juggled, and betrayed! Rested. Acted Macbeth. Never was more distressed; the murderer in the banquet scene laid his hand familiarly on my arm, and other things nearly as bad. But these are your English artists!

February 11*th*.—Rehearsed, and had misgivings of the performance from the specimen. Was talking with Mrs. Warner, who gave her opinion with some bitterness that theatrical people—players—were not lower in character, etc., than literary people. But I fear this is only the result of a mind, never very elevated, undergoing a process of vulgarization. A most charming, most delightful letter from George Sand. Miss Knowles, who had presided at the Ladies' Fund for the Relief of the Destitute Irish, and had given £50!! the surplus of her year's earnings (which she said she could not keep *and sleep*, whilst her country-people were in such distress—noble woman!), called on me with Mrs. Dr. Marshall—pretty Jane Knowles that was—and her sister. The sight of her brought back years of warm, affectionate feeling to my heart. I was so glad to see her. Heard of Knowles having suffered from partial paralysis. Wrote to Forster. Looked at paper. Acted Werner—cut up, root and branch, from first to last—oh, it was grievous.

To Glasgow, February 13*th*.—Read in the paper a letter from Dr. Traill, rector of Schull, on his starving parishioners, which will make me send him £5. I have been more than once probed, *strongly pressed*, to-day by the question suggesting itself to me, " *For what are we sent here ?* " The course of misery cannot be arrested; the lesson of virtue will not be learned. The most meritorious amongst us—who are they? Cleobis and Biton—if they ever existed—Miss Knowles, who does exist, and who gave £50, the computed surplus of her year's hard earnings, to the relief of the suffering Irish—she, old, and, as I fancy, with no relief to look to in old age! I cannot aspire to such proud virtue; it is really noble. My children make me fearful, and my habits, I believe, make me too selfish. I blame mankind, and yet I am not better than the large majority of them. My means of generosity have been cramped by indiscretion, want of management, and profusion, and I am now poor, timid, and filled with cause of self-reproach. I look at the wretched state of these poor creatures, my heart bleeds for them. I cannot relieve them, and I *hear* persons say (yesterday in the cabin of the steamboat such was the tone of their conversation), " they don't mind it!—they don't feel the cold as we do "—" they're used to it " ! And all this is going on in atomic infinity and littleness here, whilst the

357

great system, of which it is a part, is rolling through space round its central orb, which it will require above 18,000,000 of years to encircle! What, and for what, is this infinitesimally small and this incomprehensibly great moving onward to? The living souls that people it living, labouring, *playing*—oh!—breeding, killing, and never thinking a thought beyond?

Edinburgh, February 16th.—Read No. 5 of *Dombey and Son*, a most afflicting piece of story, but the growing ill is more deeply touching than the death of the child itself; in which the *hurry* introduced, and the too much vagueness militate against the full effect. But it is full of genius and beauty.

Glasgow, February 23rd.—*Bad* and *envious* thoughts, the consequence of the failure of this engagement, and my annoyance and mortification attendant on it, have occupied my mind very much—very much. Oh, this is very bad, very weak, very wicked. But I am skilled to know the right and choose the wrong. Answered Mr. Craig. Wrote to Catherine. Two women, mother and daughter, called on me about a piece—dramatic—written in *vairse*—and made quite a scene! With difficulty I got them to go away.

Greenock, March 3rd.—Acted Cardinal Richelieu, in which I was cut up " root and branch "—the Huguet—oh! most dreadful! but that was nothing—most incorrect; François not knowing two lines consecutively; Joseph wrong in every point of business, and, in short, the whole a complete *mess*.

Glasgow, March 6th.—Catherine tells me that Serjeant Talfourd has subscribed his name to the notice of Mr. Bunn's election into the Garrick Club. I do not know what to think of this world!—the baseness, the utter want of truth and honourable feeling *sickens* me to that degree that I feel as if I shall be easily reconciled to leave it. Of what consequence is it, in a worldly point of view whether a man is an abject wretch like Talfourd; a swindler, a pander, a blackguard, like Bunn; or a thief and ruffian like this —— here? They are all prosperous, have their backers and abettors, and no one to raise a finger at them! Great God!—and is there no hell?

March 7th.—A Mr. Jeffrey, who had sent last night to ask my autograph for himself, sent his little daughter, a child, with the album of some young lady, asking its insertion there also, with a line from any dramatic poet. The leaf marked for me contained Miss H. Faucit's name, with the signature of *Helena* Faucit. A feather shows the direction of the wind. The conceit and affectation attributed to her is put beyond doubt in my mind by this little instance. I am greatly mistaken in my reasoning (which very likely I am) if real talent of any very high grade can co-exist with such want of truth and genuineness.

London, March 10*th.*—Went to Elliotson, told my "tale of anguish" and received his kind directions and prescription. Called at Savory & Moore's, waiting in the carriage whilst they made up the prescription, all the while reading No. 5 of *Dombey.* When I reached Dickens', on whom I went to call, and saw him, the reference to what I had been reading brought again the tears to my eyes, and I could not speak to him for sobs. It is indeed most beautiful; it is true *genius.*

March 12*th.*—Looked over *The Old Curiosity Shop* of Dickens. He is a great genius.

March 13*th.*—Caught a glimpse of Mrs. Carlyle. Thought, talked, and consulted upon what we are to do. *America* appears our only *certain* dependence! I do not *like* it, but must make the best of it, if we cannot live here.

March 14*th.*—Thought again upon my fate and my condition, and at last saw my way to the decision of preparing, if needful, to leave the English stage, and of going to live with my dear family in America, which, if we did not like, we should still be able to leave. This decision had an immediate effect on my spirits; and I went forward with what I was occupied on with double alacrity. Wrote notes, about General Theatrical Fund, to Sheil, to M. Milnes, to G. Anson. Dickens and his wife, Mr. King [1] and Forster came to dine with us. Forster, through whose urgency and on whose representation *alone* I consented to preside at this dinner, who promised me the support of all our friends, mentioning Bulwer, etc., *now*, having done nothing, is talking of absenting himself. I have some difficulty in not being angry.

March 16*th.*—Mr. Cullenford called, from whose admissions I learned that no efforts were in course of making for this dinner; that *he* had issued 300 unsigned *notifications* of the dinner, and that was all! No committee meeting, no interest engaged, the whole affair left, like the fire which Sir Abel Handy happily conjectures, may "go out of itself," to work its own success! I showed him the false position in which the whole matter was placed, and set him to work—too late and

---

[1] Probably the proprietor of the private school at which Macready's eldest boy was being educated. Mr. Frederic Harrison was also a pupil of Mr. King of whom he writes with warm appreciation in his recently published *Reminiscences.*

with instruments too feeble! All due thanks from me to my *good friend* Forster! This might have been made an excellent occasion for the drama—a very good one for myself. But now I have neither heart nor hope. Looked at paper, in which was more theatrical intelligence to disgust me. I am weary of it. My mind is unhinged, my spirits depressed. I fear I am giving way. Oh, God! for my dear children's sake sustain and invigorate me. Forster called to take Catherine to the opera. I was very glad that an accident prevented me from seeing him.

March 17th.—Read the paper with Jenny Lind's [1] letter and offer of £2000—you lucky woman! £1000 would have been more than sufficient!—to that scoundrel Bunn! Knavery has its luck, as well as bungling! But honesty has, what thousands cannot buy, its consciousness. Wrote to Cullenford. Note from Forster, who now tells me, after urging me on Sunday night to write to Bulwer and ask him to attend the dinner, that he *had* asked him three weeks ago! I replied to his letter, but tore the answer, and gave up the intention of noticing it, which I cannot do without betraying my irritation and indignation. Very uncomfortable in mind, not well in body. Thought about the dinner. The Whites, Fox, and Troughton came to dine, and we passed a very delightful evening. White told me that he had had an interview with Maddox, who had expressed his wish to have me back at the Princess's, and commissioned him to sound me on the subject. I do not know that I wish it. I misdoubt the continuance of my attraction, and think our plan of getting our friends in committee to arrange courses of subscription nights for two seasons, the last being my farewell of the British stage, then taking two seasons in America, and settling down in Cambridge, Massachusetts, will be our surest plan.

March 18th.—White called and informed me that he had had another conversation with "the Jew," [2] who now seems—so I surmise— anxious to make a stand against Jenny Lind—the donkey might as well whistle against thunder—and desires to combine Mrs. Butler and myself. We shall be only *shown up* as powerless. He ought to leave me alone, and merely try his *chance* with her; if she fail, *give* up the

[1] Jenny Lind, who had not yet appeared in England, was under an engagement to Mr. Bunn which she declined to fulfil, owing to failure on his part to observe the terms of the contract. He threatened legal proceedings, to escape which she made the offer mentioned by Macready. She appeared at Her Majesty's on the 4th of May, as Alice in *Robert le Diable*, with the most brilliant success.

[2] Maddox, of the Princess's theatre.

remainder of the season and *wait*. Forster called, evidently feeling that he had drawn me into a false position, and, as usual, *talking* himself out of it, or out of breath in trying to do it.

March 20th.—Went to the Palace. Saw Mr. Anson, who was very courteous—*we were alone !* I explained to him the altered condition of the Funds and the claims of the General Theatrical Fund to her Majesty's notice. He seemed obliged, and promised to communicate with me on it.

March 24th.—Saw an advertisement from Drury Lane well worthy of a showman or country circus. This looks like approaching what the Drury Lane wild beasts set out from, a Terminus.

March 28th.—Dickens called and told me that Miss Coutts had sent him £10 for the General Theatrical Fund. This is curious after my letter. He also told me that she had expressed a wish to take charge entirely of Charley's education and the expense of his bringing-up. This is highly to the honour of both. I rejoice in dear Dickens's good fortune. Forster called. Letter from Mr. Anson, enclosing me a cheque for Theatrical Fund of £100 from the Queen. This is right royal. Answered it.

March 29th.—Theatrical Fund Dinner. Went to the London Tavern, thinking over what I had to do. I was received as some extraordinary person. In the Vice-President's room I found Horace Twiss, Buckstone, Brewster, and most of the committee; waited some time for Dickens, who at last arrived with Forster. Where were Stanfield and Maclise, etc.? Ate very little, drank very little port and water, was made to take wine with the two sides of the room—"a custom more honoured in the breach," etc. Gave out my toasts with perfect self-possession, and, on the announcement of the Queen's dona-tion, which started the evening, the cheering was great. My speech was heard with the deepest attention and interest, and with much applause. Buckstone followed as "a farce." Dickens was very powerful. Twiss spoke excellently and Forster too. The collection was £401. I cut the business short at about eleven, and, having sent Letitia, who was there, to the carriage before me, left the place, having toasted "the Ladies." Delighted to escape, and attended with the grateful homage of the committee and much applauded by the guests as I passed through them.

Liverpool, April 6th.—Went to rehearsal. No Lady Macbeth. Was kept a full hour waiting for Miss Montague; Mr. Roxby, it seems, asked her if he were obliged to put Mrs. Brougham into the part, would she object, and she answered she certainly *should*, having played it. On this offence (!) she absented herself. She has given me a very bad impression of her. Acted Macbeth, taking great pains, and much very well, but was beaten down at last by the shameful inaccuracy of these players—one a publican in the town, quite unfit to go upon the stage, another a most ambitious, sprawling fool that I could not attempt to do anything with. Oh, these wretched biped beasts !—for such they are, and no better.

April 8th.—Received a letter from Forster with a proposal to take the Lyceum guaranteed from loss on a *year's trial !* I am astonished at his entertaining such an idea! Rested. Acted Othello, really as well as I could, but in this part I felt my *deficient strength.* Called for.

April 11th.—Read *Punch*, and was much amused by his ridicule of that coxcomb, Disraeli. Looked at a newspaper—*Bell's Life in London,* and was much amused at the *sort of thing*—that men can make a *business* of such trash ! After dinner read in that beautiful *Van Artevelde.* Read Hamlet. Read in delightful *Terence.*

April 13th.—A Mrs. Fitzsimon came in for charity, whose husband had committed suicide. I gave her relief. A Mr. Brooke, who seemed to me mad, had accosted me at the stage door, and now sent up his card. He wished me to read a play that he had not yet written. I did all I could to induce the man to send it elsewhere, but was obliged to promise to read it ! And well I *know* what it will be ! A ruffian, evidently some common knave known to the police, was shown in by the waiter. He gave me a note, asking for assistance, and insisting that he had known me, then that I had known his relations at Glasgow, people owning a circus ! I rang the bell, and the fellow went off in double quick time.

April 14th.—Forster arrived, as I was reading the paper ; we talked over the matter of Maddox, theatres, etc., and sat up till about one o'clock, he being obliged to return to town by six o'clock train.

April 15th.—Heard Forster's foot in the passage as he was leaving for the six o'clock train ; his visit was certainly a great stretch of kindness. Looked at an American paper which made my gorge rise. I fear I *cannot* go among those ——— !

April 17th.—Came to Manchester by railway—my companion knew *me*, and getting into conversation with me, I found he knew my old schoolfellow Leigh. He told me Leigh had very lately received from the Bury Railway £154,000 for some land of his in Liverpool—that he was the richest man in Liverpool; but added, what I was surprised and sorry to hear, as being a *very great change* in his character, that he was "stingy." Thus varieties of character are made; one miser is made by the pinching of poverty, another by superabundance of wealth! I must not reflect on any. I have had the power to heap up a competency, and I have neglected it—a bitter self-reproach to last me to my dying day, and perhaps accelerate it.

Birmingham, April 20th.—Acted Macbeth, I thought, with much force and discrimination to a low-priced and low-minded audience, who were incapable of appreciating anything really good. The Macduff and the Lady Macbeth were *very bad*, but both were applauded, and, indeed, I think more than myself. On the fall of the curtain I certainly did not hear my own name, but that of my friend Macduff very plainly, and in consequence declined the honour of the ovation, as the *Daily News* terms it. There was a sort of tumult in consequence, and the acting manager went forward to say he could not intimate to me such a call. Then there were sundry explanations, ending in the statement that I was undressed. These are now the audiences to Shakspeare. To trash as bad as that written by "the poet Bunn "— for the libretti of the Italian operas are little better—an aristocracy crowd to fill two monster theatres. Like Cato—"I am weary of conjecture."

Birmingham, April 22nd.—Rehearsed; very much pleased with the acting of a little dumpy dumpling figured girl of the name of Sanders, who acts Albert. There was a truth and freshness about her that I have not seen for many a day. Acted William Tell very feebly, being much fatigued, and greatly put out by a miserably vulgar little ugly woman—like a dressed-up charwoman—whom they had put into Emma! Very much pleased with Albert. Called.

April 23rd.—Acted Hamlet—with the best intentions, but the Birmingham gallery, once so good, so discriminating and so fervent, are now stupid, phlegmatic and noisy! They paralyzed me. Called for. Thank God, it is over.

Manchester, April 26th.—Busied with affairs. Received a very poor attempt at imitating *Punch* from Liverpool. Acted Hamlet, taking especial pains, and, as I thought, really acting well; generally in the very spirit and feeling of the distracted, sensitive young man; but I did not feel that the audience responded to me; I did not on that account give way, but the inspiration is lost, the perfect *abandon*, under which one goes out of one's self, is impossible unless you enjoy the perfect sympathy of an audience; if they do not abandon themselves to the actor's powers his magic becomes ineffectual. Read in the papers. Saw that Peel had thrown open his gallery of art, etc., to a large conversazione. This is very good. He certainly is a man who *means well.*

April 27th.—Saw the *Times* and collected from the tone of its favourable notice of Mrs. Butler's appearance that she had not made any sensation by her acting. I did not expect she would. Rested a short time. Acted Cardinal Richelieu; distressed by the bad actors about me, Mr. G. V. Brooke in particular. Called for.

London, May 3rd.—Glanced at papers, which I put away, disgusted and outraged by the cowardly and rascally advertisement of that most atrocious blackguard Bunn against Jenny Lind—the miscreant! and the English people—to suffer this pestilent nuisance! Letter from King, of the Dublin theatre, informing me that the theatre is smashed and Calcraft in the Marshalsea prison for debt. I should feel deep concern for him if I had not concern for myself in the loss of £150 —he has unwarrantably detained—belonging to me! My old luck!

May 5th.—Waited for Dickens, who called in his carriage, and we went together to call on Mlle. Jenny Lind.[1] Called on Lady

---

[1] This call was the beginning of a cordial acquaintance, and the regard that Jenny Lind felt for Macready is testified by the following letter which she wrote to him on the occasion of his second marriage ; it is docketed in Macready's handwriting "Dear Jenny Lind."

" Argyle Lodge,
" Park Side,
" Wimbledon Common, S. W.
"April 18th, 1860.

"DEAR MR. MACREADY,

"It was very kind of you to have remembered me and Mr. Goldschmidt in sending me your wedding cards, and if I was unprepared for the news at first, my next thought was that I wished you from all my heart peace and happiness in your second marriage, and that the present Mrs. Macready may love you with as true a love as the first did ! You deserve to be happy, and I *can* understand how it is that a man might feel an empty place in his heart when he has had the misfortune of losing a beloved wife, and thus that place only can be filled by a successor. May this new choice prove to be all that you can desire, and give your charming daughter[2] a real friend, as I am sure she will be a comfort to the wife of the beloved father.

"I often wish I had Miss Macready nearer to me ; I feel that I could love her ; she is so uncommon, so free from vanity and nonsense, that I was quite charmed with her society. May she long be spared to you, dear Mr. Macready !

"You will wonder that I speak so open (sic) to you, although we have seen so little of each

---

[2] Catherine Frances Birch Macready, born in 183‹, died 1869. In addition to much attractiveness she possessed considerable poetical talent, and was the authoress of more than one charming volume of verse.

JENNY LIND

From an engraving by W. C. Wrankmore of a painting by P. O. Wagner

Blessington, and went to the Athenæum, where I met Lord Nugent, Charles Landseer, Travers, Kenyon, C. Kemble.

May 9th.—Called on Mrs. Butler, with whom was Horace Wilson,[1] Professor of Sanskrit, and Mrs. Wilson. When they were gone, she gave vent a little to her overburdened spirit, lamenting the state of the drama, to which necessity had compelled her to resort. Told me that Maddox had asked her, if she could renew, to act with me—(I fancy this must have been on *abated* terms)—that she could not give him an answer before Tuesday, and that he had stated his inability to wait so long, therefore it was given up. She hoped a chance might come yet for her acceptance of his offer. She wept—what I thought, alas! were bitter tears—I fear of wounded pride and disappointment; I am truly sorry for her. Dined with Forster. Met Regnier, Madame R—— and their little girl, Dickens and Georgina, Stanfield and Maclise. Dickens's children came in in the evening. Stanfield went home with me, and we talked of Maclise on our way, lamenting his want of energy in remaining here, where his style is growing and hardening into a manner, instead of starting off to Italy and studying and painting at Venice and at Rome.

May 10th.—Called on secretary of Literary Fund, and paid him £5 as my annual subscription, or rather donation. Requested him to say to Chevalier Bunsen (Chairman of Anniversary Dinner) that I would have dined there if I could.

May 13th.—White came and dined with us, and we went together to the amateur play at the St. James's theatre. Saw there Landor, Mrs. M. Gibson, Lord Ellesmere, Lady Essex and Miss Johnstone, Sheridan Knowles. The play *Hernani*, translated by Lord Ellesmere, was in truth an *amateur* performance. Greville and Craven were very good amateurs—but, tragedy by amateurs! Forster was by far the best, and with a little practice would make a very respectable actor. In Mrs. Butler I saw *the proof* that I had been *most honest* and *most*

---

other, but I feel that we must well understand each other's way of feeling, and, born with the artistical flame in our hearts, we have wandered through much of the same pains and trials, and this makes me to (sic) feel no stranger to you, dear Mr. Macready!

"May God's blessing rest on you and your beloved ones.

"With our kindest regards to Mrs. Macready, my love for (sic) your daughter, and deep sympathy for your welfare,

"Believe me, dear Mr. Macready,
"Yours sincerely,
"JENNY GOLDSCHMIDT."

[1] Horace Hayman Wilson (1786–1860); Professor of Sanskrit at Oxford; librarian to the East India Company; F.R.S.

discriminating in my original judgment of her. *She is ignorant of the very first rudiments of her art.* She is affected, monotonous, without one real impulse—never in the feeling of her character, never true in look, attitude, or tone. She can never be an actress, and this I never ventured to think before. After the play, looked into Dickens's box, which was crowded with himself, M. and Mlle. Regnier, Georgina, Stanfield, Maclise, Jerrold, Ainsworth. Was glad to get away from the theatre and return home. And our English aristocracy will go to see, and sit through, and applaud, an entertainment like this—of an inferior, a very inferior order, as a drama, and acted by novices—ignoramuses—in art (Forster was an exception). But for Shakspeare, for the illustration of his great works, for skill in representing his characters, they have not one thought nor one farthing to throw away.

May 14th.—Jenny Lind called. She is simplicity itself, and puts to shame all our actresses, or all actresses.

May 15th.—White, Savage Landor, Forster, Maclise, C. Eddy, M. and Mme. Regnier came to dinner.

May 19th.—Went to the French play. Saw Regnier, who acted very well indeed. Thackeray and Daniel, who bored me much, came into our box.

May 21st.—Note from Mr. Montesquieu Bellew, *alias* Higgins, asking for my certificate or testimonial in aid of his application for the office of Inspector of Schools, for which White is thinking of applying. I *therefore* answered him, stating as much—and declining.

May 23rd.—Made out a computation of the various results, pecuniary, of my different courses of proceeding to the end of my professional life. Dined with H. Twiss, met there Delanes, Rogers, Mr. and Mrs. German Reed, Lord De Lisle and Miss Villiers, Miss Courtenay, Lord Charleville, Colonel Sharp, etc. Rogers was out of humour with the extreme heat, and abused everything and everybody.

May 24th.—Looked at paper, saw the death of O'Connell. "There's a great spirit gone!" but not a good one, nor great in the qualities which constitute true greatness. How thick the shafts are flying! The angel of death is unusually busy with great names, leaving them only names. Acted Hamlet at Princess's theatre [1] very fairly; but I am growing old; my youthful vigour and elasticity—

[1] This engagement at the Princess's Theatre was from May 24 to June 18—(*note by Sir F. Pollock*).

alas! where are they? Called for. Maddox, Forster and Maclise came into my room; they were all much pleased.

May 25th.—Forster and Bulwer Lytton came to dine. Talked over the subjects of plays the whole evening, and at last we seemed to settle down upon that of Sir Robert Walpole as the best that could be devised for a mixed play. When Bulwer Lytton was gone, Forster gave us a description of the excessive weakness of Talfourd, characterizing it as a depth of contemptibility, supremely despicable!

May 26th.—Rehearsed, with a very bad company; looked at Mr. Creswick, who, I clearly see, has no scintillation of the *mens divina* that is wanting to make him a fine actor. He will be of the respectable class. Acted King Lear, in which I was sadly cut up and *dérangé* by the bad and careless actors about me. Called.

May 27th.—Went to the opera in low spirits. Saw *La Figlia del Reggimento* and Jenny Lind—the most charming singer and actress I have ever in my life seen. Her energy, vivacity, archness, humour, passion, and pathos are equally true. Her face is not handsome in feature, but beautiful in its expression, varied as it is. I was enchanted with her.

May 30th.—The Lord Advocate and Mrs. Rutherfurd, Mr. and Mrs. Dickens, Mr. and Mrs. Carlyle, Panizzi, Eastlake, Rogers, Miss Jewsbury, Edwin Landseer and Jenny Lind came to dinner. The day was very pleasant, and the party seemed to find it so. In the evening Mr. D'Eyncourt, C. Halls, Delanes, Horace Twisses, Baroness Eichthal, Staudigl, Maclise, Forster, White, Babbage, Wheatstone, Sir J. Rennie, Spurgins, Procters, Mulready, Leslies, Jerrold, Dyce, Wilkie, Mazzini, Bezzi, Sir E. Bulwer Lytton, Charles Buller, Misses Herries, Le Roy, etc., came. All was lively and agreeable, and there was but one expression, and that was delight with Jenny Lind.

June 1st.—Babbage, Dyce, Mulready, A'Beckett, White, Douglas Jerrold, Benedict, Hardwick came to dinner. Staudigl sent an excuse at the last moment. We had a very pleasant day. In the evening Catherine, whom I had dissuaded from coming down to dinner, received a good many of our neighbour friends with music—E. Goldsmid, Bishops, Popes, Thrupps, Miss Sturch, Thorburns, Brockedons, Baxendales, Ainsworths, Baroness Eichthal, Reeds, Miss Rainforth, Miss Morrison, Stanfields, Hills, Schwabes, etc. All went off very agreeably and cheerfully.

June 5th.—The Delanes, Hetta Skerrett, Fanny Howarth, Quin, the Chisholm, Thackeray, Lyon, Troughton, Travers, Knox, dined with us. A quiet, cheerful day.

June 8th.—Mr. and Miss D'Eyncourt, Mr. and Miss Mackinnon, Mr. and Miss Swynfen Jervis, Mr. and Mrs. H. Twiss, Mr. and Mrs. E. Goldsmid, Le Roy and Forster dined with us. Miss Strickland came up in the evening, and we had really a cheerful day. Went with Catherine and Forster to Procter's. Saw Procter, Mrs. and Miss Goldsmids, Milnes, Harness, Thackeray, Babbage, Ainsworth, etc.

June 10th.—Baron and Miss Goldsmid, Mr. and Mrs. Schwabe, Sir John Wilson, H. Smith, Professor Tom Taylor, Doctor Spurgin, dined with us.

June 12th.—Attended the Caxton meeting; saw Bancroft and Jerdan there; was not very comfortably placed. Milman sent Mr. Cole, the Hon. Sec., to me twice, very strongly urging me to propose a resolution, but I steadfastly declined. I was not prepared upon the subject, and, as Jerdan observed, something would be expected from me, and I ought not to commit myself before people who came primed for their display. Lord Morpeth presided, and very well. Buckland spoke very absurdly, Bancroft ungracefully and harshly, but not altogether ineffectively; Milman heavily, some others poorly, and a sort of skirmish was long kept up by Carter, Hall, Silk Buckingham, Jerdan, Wilks, Cole, Milman, etc. My name was omitted in the first reading of the committee list, but *added* afterwards with much applause from the assembly. Forster, in going home, acquainted me with his imbroglio with Thackeray and Tom Taylor. " Words, words, words! "

June 14th.—Acted Macbeth in very ablest manner—quite myself *in* the character; the audience were greatly excited. Called for and very warmly welcomed.

June 15th.—Looked at paper, in which I read ill news of the state of social and political feeling in the United States. Oh! what a country that might have been—ought to have been—and what it is! But what is man? and what is the purpose of sending such a wretched reptile here—par example!—Bishops of London, Exeter, Canterbury, York; Broughams, Bentincks, Disraelis, etc. I am *sick* of the contemplation of such wretched *shams*. Wrote note with German translation of *King Lear* to Mrs. Hall for Jenny Lind. Note from Forster. He called, and I accompanied him to the opera. Saw A Beckett, M. Lemon, Bradbury & Evans. Saw Jenny Lind in *Norma*—the opera by command of the Queen, who was present with

Prince Albert. The house was brilliant in its appearance. The Queen-Dowager was in the centre. Jenny Lind was very womanly, loving, passionate, and grand in her personation, but I doubt whether it will be a *popular* performance—it wants more vulgar effect to be so in my opinion.

June 16th.—Went to Brompton, reading *Scribe* by the way. Called on Jenny Lind. I saw her, and she was apparently pleased to see me. She was in costume of "La Figlia," etc., to sit for a statuette. She was hearing some one from "*la Cour*" who came for an opinion, or instruction, "*qui ne peut pas chanter du tout*," as she said. I waited till she was free, then saw her again, and made an appointment for Monday for Edwin Landseer with her. Called on Mrs. C. Hall, admired her beautiful cottage, beautifully and tastefully furnished.

June 17th.—Wrote to Lowne,[1] to General Birch. Dined with Baron Goldsmid, met Edward Goldsmids, Bates's, De Simmons, Elliotson, Sir Jephson Norreys, etc. Passed a very cheerful day. What a beautiful house!

June 18th.—Acted King Lear with much care and power, and was received by a most kind and sympathetic and enthusiastic audience. Jenny Lind was in one of the stage boxes and, after the play, there was a great excitement to see her. I was called on; the audience tried to make me come on after the first act, but of course I would not think of such a thing. The enthusiasm of the audience on my taking leave was very great.

June 19th.—Went to the opera—which had just finished. Saw the *Divertissement*—pah! "Give me an ounce of civet, good apothecary," etc.

June 21st.—Dined with Dickens. Met Sir A. and Lady Gordon, Sir W. and Miss Allan, Thackeray, Tom Taylor, Forster. In the evening Mrs. M. Gibson, Wilson and his daughters, Mr. and Mrs. Parry, Mr. and Mrs. Rundt, etc.

June 24th.—Spoke to Nina and Willie on the subject of a conversation, which was abruptly closed last night by the lateness of the hour. It was on the nature of my religious belief as touching the questions of "the Holy Ghost." I explained to them my conviction

---

[1] Mr. E. Y. Lowne, well known as the intimate friend and executor of J. L. Toole. He subsequently became a regular correspondent of Macready, and was one of the few outside the family invited to be present at his funeral. Mr. Lowne, who happily still survives, is the father of the accomplished and much esteemed actor, Mr. Charles Macready Lowne.

that where a real belief exists, that belief must have birth in and be peculiar to the individual mind itself—that as all minds differ more or less, so no two beliefs are likely in truth to be *exactly* the same, and that the subject of difference was a matter only between the creature and the Creator, that I did not attempt to teach them on points of doctrine, but that I was most anxious to impress them with a love for and a faith in the great fundamental truths of Jesus Christ's example, in His doing and suffering, and of His precepts. Anniversary of wedding day. Darling baby was christened Cecilia Benvenuta.[1] The Smiths, H. Skerrett, Mrs. Dickens, Wightwick, Troughton, Forster, Kenyon, Bezzi, Oxenford, Maclise, dined with us. We received a very kind excuse from Staudigl, who could not sing if he dined. A very cheerful dinner. Sir W. Allan and Staudigl came into the dining-room before the evening. We had a very charming concert by Staudigl, Miss M. Hawes, Miss Rainforth, Mr. and Mrs. Reed (Miss P. Horton), the Misses Williams, Mr. and Mrs. T. Cooke. The Eddys, Bishops, Goldsmid, Rundts, Revs. Reed and Sturch, Horace Twiss, Delane, Howarth, Walker, Thorburns, etc. We had a happy day.

June 26th.—Continued our course to Westminster Hall, where we saw the prize pictures and the others exhibited. Pickersgill's of the Burial of Harold touched me very much. I thought it full of truth, beauty and feeling. I only partially liked the rest. Saw Jenny Lind, Mrs. Hall, D'Orsay, Barry, Cockerell, Irwins, Chalon, Tom Taylor, Kenyon, Milman and Mrs. M——, Lady Morgan, etc. Took leave of Wightwick, and, going to the City, met Thackeray and Etty.

July 9th.—Called on Maclise, who was from home; on Campbell, whom I saw, but who has not made much advance with the statue. As I was leaving the house he came after me, and told me that "Father Prout"[2] was anxious to speak with me; I returned and found him in very small chambers, with wine (or brandy) before him, and smoking a cigar. He was full of Irish high-flown compliments, spoke of the Pope, of his favour with him, that he was going to make him a knight, etc. He appeared to me to be drunk, and a wild dissolute character, though certainly a clever man.

July 10th.—White and Forster dined with us. Forster showed me a letter from poor Knowles to Lord John Russell refusing an offered pension of £100 per annum!

---

[1] Now Mrs. Horsford—(*note by Sir F. Pollock*).
[2] Francis Sylvester Mahony (see note, p. 248, Vol. I.)

To Liverpool, July 11th.—Busy with affairs preparatory to departure. M. Jullien[1] called at half-past eight, and informed me that he had taken Drury Lane theatre for three years, and wished to perform the drama with his own entertainments. I told him I was engaged to Mr. Maddox, and after some conversation he left me with the expression of his wish to renew his application at the end of the next season. . . . Dined at Radley's at Liverpool, and on board fell into conversation with Chief Justice Doherty,[2] who seems a very agreeable man. The evening was beautiful, and the lovely hills of Wales suggested pleasures and delights, remembered and imagined, that awoke again a love and longing for this world's enjoyments! Beautiful world!

Dublin, July 13th.—The birthday of my blessed Joan, the sweet and mournful memory of a departed joy of which the fond love is left and ever will remain. My heart blessed and blesses her sweet spirit—now with her God, I trust. " Those who have lost an infant are never, as it were, without an infant child; the other children grow up to manhood and womanhood, and suffer all the changes of mortality; but this one alone is rendered an immortal child; for death has arrested it with his kindly harshness, and blessed it into an eternal image of youth and innocence."

July 14th.—Looked over paper, in which I see the "friends of Mr. Calcraft " are about to get up a "benefit" for him. The propriety of this is surely questionable, when in many cases his debts were incurred with the knowledge they never could be paid, and when many, many of his indigent performers have been wanting the bread that he has taken care not to want! *This is not right.*

London, July 19th.—Went with Edward to see Rachel in *Phèdre.* It was a very striking performance, all intensity; all in a spirit of vehemence and fury that made me feel a want of keeping; I could have fancied a more self-contained performance, more passionate fondness—not fury—in her love, and more pathos. I could imagine a performance exciting more pity for the character than she inspired, and equal effect in the scenes of rage and despair.

July 24th.—Went with Forster to Putney Heath to dine with Jerrold. He was *very glad* to see me. His family and young

---

[1] Louis Antoine Julien (1812–1860) ; the well-known conductor. His various enterprises ended in bankruptcy and he died insane.

[2] John Doherty (1783–1850) ; Lord Chief Justice of Ireland. Tory Solicitor-General for Ireland in 1827.

Blanchard, a Mr. Hills, Leigh Hunt, Maclise and the Dickenses were the party. Leigh Hunt I thought *particularly disagreeable*. Disputative and tedious—affecting great benevolence and arguing most malevolently. He is a good-tempered coxcomb—but coxcomb heart and soul—not meaning harm to any, but a coxcomb.

July 25th.—Went to church with Edward and Letitia. Very drowsy during a very drowsy sermon, and looked occasionally at the several members of the congregation and their various employments, and could not help asking myself, "*Is this religion?*"—"Is this the devotion taught by Christ?" Oh, God! how long—how long is this to last!

September 9th.—Went to dine with Forster. Met Stanfield. Forster became very quarrelsome over his wine; so much so as to call forth the expostulatory candour of Stanfield. When I *would not* let him quarrel with me, he tried to turn on Stanfield: it is a *disease of temper in him*.

Eastbourne, September 11th.—Children read their usual morning pages of Charles XII. Letters from Mary Bucknill, from Henry Smith, from Fourrier. Lessons from nine till half-past one. Lushington [1] called, whom I like very much. Walked with Catherine and Katie, a very pleasant ramble. Prepared lesson for Monday, giving Willie some Alcaic verses to do. Looked over the English verses of the children. Looked out sermon, looked out verses.

September 12th.—Called on Lushington, saw his brother, and Mrs. Lushington, Tennyson's sister.

September 14th.—Finished the arrangement of *Van Artevelde*.

September 19th.—Spoke to Willie about his profession, which, as it now appears, he wavers on. I do not object to his changing his previous purpose, but it is necessary that I should know to what calling in life I am to direct his studies. He told me that he had not fixed, though I had understood from him directly more than once before that he was fixed in his choice of a clergyman's profession. I have *no wish* that he should adopt this course of life, but I fear he has not energy for a lawyer. I am willing to assist him to my utmost in anything he may choose, but it is time he chose.

September 24th.—Forster dined with us, and I read my arrangement of *Philip Van Artevelde* to him, with which he was greatly struck and pleased.

---

[1] Professor of Greek in the University of Glasgow—(*note by Sir F. Pollock*). Born in 1812, died in 1893. Senior Classic. Lord Rector Glasgow University 1884.—(Ed.)

September 25th.—Maddox called, and I told him of a new play (*Artevelde*), and proposed that he should give £100 for the right of acting it one season. He was to take a day to consider of it.

October 4th.—Acted Macbeth as well as I could after so long a respite. Called for; led on Miss Cushman, who thanked me for the civility.

October 6th.—Acted Othello, under the great disadvantage of Mr. Cooper—an incarnation of stupidity for Iago. Called, and led on Miss Cushman. Maddox came in to bore me, and declined positively the play I spoke to him of—*Philip Van Artevelde*. I told him that I was thereby exonerated from any charge about the bad houses, which we *must have*.[1]

October 7th.—Looked at paper. I fancy that I am not acting with all my accustomed vigour from the tone of the newspapers, and indeed from the enthusiasm of the audience during the performances. I did not satisfy myself with Othello last night, and yet I tried, and I will try. God speed me well! Amen! Continued my work on *Wallenstein*, of which I cannot pretend to form a judgment till I see it as a whole; but I do not perceive any great or effective scenes for me in it. Gave the evening to *Wallenstein*, which I begin to lick into shape, but I cannot discover the great effects.

October 10th.—Forster called, very uneasy about Mr. Maddox's management. I groan under it, but *what can I do* more than I am doing?

October 11th.—Looked at paper. *Disgusted* with the unprincipled conduct of the swindling states Indiana and Illinois. The American nation is a humbug and a cheat. Gave up the whole of my time to *Wallenstein*. Completed the rough outline of it, and like it. Rested. Acted Macbeth (at Princess's Theatre)[2] with great power. Called and led on Miss Cushman. An anonymous letter telling me the *Sunday Times* and *Dispatch* said I was decreasing in vigour—my *kind, constant, and true* friends!

October 13th.—Walked to rehearsal. Rehearsed Cardinal Wolsey; spoke with Maddox about *Philip Van Artevelde*—he seems at last to be *coming*. Acted Cardinal Wolsey in many respects very fairly. Called on at the end of the third act, as I was undressing. Read in bed two acts of *Van Artevelde*.

[1] Mr. Maddox proved to be right in his judgment of the play, which was not a financial success.

[2] This engagement at the Princess's Theatre continued to December 7.—(*note by Sir F. Pollock.*)

October 14th.—Letter from Cullenford, sending me the Director's account of the General Theatrical Fund Dinner. I wash my hands of players and players' business. Such another class of wretched creatures I do not know out of a penitentiary. Looked at paper, in which I read a notice of last night's performance, that seemed to me most insulting and detracting—but *what* are my critics? Maddox called; after a long and tiresome conversation he agreed to give, for one season's performance of a new play, £100—thus £50 previous and £50 after the third night, on the announcement of the fourth. Gave what I could of the day to *Philip Van Artevelde;* was in low spirits, depressed and dejected by the rascally attacks that seem making on me in the Press.

October 16th.—Fox, Forster, and Maddox came to hear *Van Artevelde* read. Fox and Forster were greatly excited by the play; Maddox reiterated his agreement to get it up. Dickenses, Whites, T. Cookes, Forster, Fox, and Georgina came to dinner. Cheerful day.

October 17th.—Went out with Catherine to Mortlake to call on Mr. and Mrs. Henry Taylor; proposed to him to have *Philip Van Artevelde* acted. He seemed pleased with the idea, and would consider it. He appointed to come to me with Mrs. Taylor on Tuesday at seven to hear the play read. Read in *Van Artevelde*, and looked out authorities.

October 18th.—Received an American paper—low, stupid, vulgar trash, as all American papers are! Walked out and called on Dickens—mentioned to him *the reading* of to-morrow night, to which he engaged to come. He told me of the refuge for abandoned women prepared by Miss Coutts, and gave me the letter he had written to them. I tried to move him about Forster, but he was more stiff than I thought quite right. Walked on, and called on Stanfield, who promised to come to the reading and make sketches, if the play is to be done, for the scenes. Kind and excellent friend.

October 19th.—Mr. and Mrs. Taylor, Elliot, Mr. and Mrs. Spring Rice, Dickens, Stanfield, White and Forster came to the reading. Nina and Katie were present. The effect was very great. Taylor said he had no idea of such theatrical power being in the work. He assented readily to its performance. All were delighted. Mr. and Mrs. Spring Rice being—as I thought—the only *insensibles* of the party. Dickens, Forster, Stanfield, and White stayed supper. Let me believe this a good omen.

October 20th.—Read *Van Artevelde.* Note from Maddox. Made one scene plot of *Van Artevelde*, and sent it with note to Stanfield. Rested, and thought. Acted Cardinal Wolsey fairly. Called. Maddox came to speak to me—*to talk—bah!*

October 21st.—Began the day with the business, which I expected to last for two or three hours, of preparing a copy of *Philip Van Artevelde* for the theatre. I was busily, very busily, employed in it the whole day, and it is not nearly finished. H. Taylor called in the morning, and gave me some altered lines. He also read me his idea in which the second Stadt House scene should be played. Never let it be said that a poet knows best how his scenes should be acted; he knows nothing about it—at least he has no power of conveying a shadow of an idea of a meaning! I heard and——

October 23rd.—Continued at work on *Van Artevelde*. Went to Princess's theatre. Met Taylor, who left us immediately, Spedding, Moxon, Wilmott, and Forster. Real *Philip Van Artevelde* to them and the stupid and insensible company of players—these people to be artists! and to interfere with Shakspeare! Spoke with Messrs. Maddox and Embden about the cast. Refused peremptorily to say one word about the disposition of the two characters, Van Den Bosch and Occo; Mr. Maddox cast them.

October 24th.—Going up to dress for the evening, or undress, found on coming down Fonblanque in the study. He sat long. Forster came in. He told us afterwards that Fonblanque had got an office—Statistical Secretary to the Board of Trade with promise of preferment. He deserves it and much more. But alas, for the pleasure of reading his articles in the *Examiner*.

October 25th.—Acted Hamlet, I think, very fairly. Called and very warmly received. Mr. Maddox showed me a note in which Miss Cushman offered to him, if I had no objection, to act the part of Adriana in *Philip Van Artevelde*.

October 28th.—Mrs. Warner called, and related to me a very amusing story of the ignorance and malice of Messrs. Heraud and Tom Ince—*these critics!!*—who had accused her in an article in the *Athenæum* of introducing lines of Garrick's into *Hamlet*, proving thereby not only their ignorance of the text, but their utter ignorance of the *meaning* of the play—the lines were Shakspeare's.

October 29th.—Acted Othello, I think, very well. Called. Led on Miss Cushman who, according to Mr. Maddox, said, *in the presence of Mr. Forster*, "He and his whole theatre might go to hell," etc. He persisted that she repeated this! Our art!

375

October 30th.—A Mr. G. Bell called to speak to me about Mr. Maddox taking Miss Susan Cushman out of Ophelia—of which I knew nothing. He seemed desirous of working on my apprehensions that it would be supposed it was at my instigation. I told him that utterly ignorant as I was about the whole matter, it was of no consequence to me what either individuals or a multitude thought of me. Forster came to dinner. Went with him and Willie to Mrs. Warner's theatre. The acting of Hamlet was the most wearying and offensive thing I remember to have seen. The play was very nicely put on the stage. Went over the leaves of the books of *Philip Van Artevelde.*

November 4th.—Forster dined; was sorry to hear him speak as if the long and intimate friendship between himself and Dickens was likely to terminate or very much relax. They have both faults with their good qualities, but they have been *too* familiar. I hope Dickens is not capricious—not spoiled; he has, however, great excuse.

November 5th.—It is very wrong—very wrong—to suffer my temper to be thus affected, but even now I am suffering from the excitement of disgust and indignation into which this wretched Jew [1] has thrown me. But I will meet him with the most studious silence and cut short any future attempt at conversation. This fellow, among other things, admitted—" *You* wished to do things well, *I* wish to get money."

November 6th.—I have passed a very uneasy night, not being able for some hours to get to sleep. The cause of my wakefulness was the excited state of mind in which I most weakly and against all my endeavours of reason and management fell, on account of that wretched Maddox's impertinent conduct about the play of *Philip Van Artevelde.* I was also, I suspect—but that I afterwards discovered—uneasy at the agreement I had to propose to him, which I feared he would either refuse or make the subject of future trouble and even litigation. In thinking it over I devised a new form of agreement, which fairly expressed the claims of all parties, and gave him every extent of profit he could rightfully desire to have the chance of. It set my mind at rest immediately.

November 11th.—Went to rehearsal of *Philip Van Artevelde*— which occupied the whole morning. It is a sad thing to see such conceited and ignorant persons as these players!

November 12th.—Went to theatre. Rehearsed two last acts of *Philip Van Artevelde.* Told Mr. Embden I should get Mr. Willmott

[1] Mr. Maddox.

to assist me with the supernumeraries. He made an intimation that his province was invaded thereby—these people who are mere *fetch and carry* persons of my ordering!

November 17th.—Acted Cardinal Wolsey, as I thought very well, to a very insensible audience. Am I deteriorating as I grow older? Attended to the business of *Philip Van Artevelde*, and went over the whole part.

November 18th.—Rehearsed *Philip Van Artevelde*. Much annoyed and disgusted by the impertinence of Mr. ——, but in a theatre one must expect to meet merely knaves and blackguards; if a chance variety of character turns up among the people there, it is a happy accident; Heaven knows, a rare one!

November 19th.—Letter from Mrs. Hutchinson, asking me very strangely for a private box for an invalided friend. She is a perfect stranger to me, and, as she says, an old woman. Rehearsed Cardinal Richelieu. Looked at paper. Wrote to Mrs. Hutchinson, with card of private box. Acted Cardinal Richelieu very fairly, though not quite myself, having been occupied all the short afternoon with trying on the dresses that Palmer brought. Called both at the end of fourth act and end of play. Went on at the end of play and was very warmly greeted. Maddox—pah!—and Forster came into my room. The person who should have played Marion de Lorme fell down—*as they said*—in a state of intoxication after her first speech. A Mrs. Selby dressed, and read the scene after long delay.

November 20th.—Rehearsed *Philip Van Artevelde*, but was afraid to exert myself on account of my throat. I do not know what to think. There are people of absolute danger; Father John; the Pape; Van Æswyn, if not very careful; and Adriana is very bad, unmeaning, and dull. There is no disguising this, and where is there help? But I must now do my best, and hope, and trust. God speed me well.

November 22nd.—Production of *Van Artevelde*. Attended to business, did my best, worked my hardest. Went to rehearsal. Acted Philip Van Artevelde. Failed; I cannot think it my fault. Called for, of course. Forster, Dickens, Stanfield, Maclise, Spring Rice and his brother came into my room. I am very unhappy; I wish I were dead! My toil and life are thrown away. My disappointment was very severe, and I saw so much that might have grown out of its success for ever gone from me. I certainly laboured more than my due in regard to the whole play, and much of my own part of Van Artevelde

I acted well; but the play was so under-acted by the people engaged in it, that it broke down under their weight.[1]

November 23rd.—Rose very late, having passed a sleepless and uncomfortable night. Saw the papers, which—I should instance the *Times* and *Chronicle* as especially disgusting—did not raise my spirits; but I soon looked matters directly in the face. A very sweet letter from dear Dickens, which was much to compensate me for the injustice of the papers. Wrote to Dickens. Went to theatre and gave some directions to Mr. Embden. Wrote to H. Smith, to Forster. Languid and low-spirited. Went over the part of Philip Van Artevelde. Berlioz, M. Barnet, Benedict, Tom Taylor, Thomson, Thackeray, Hardwick, Mason, Jerdan, Elliotson, Mahlenfeldt came to dinner. T. Cookes, with his pupil, Procter and Misses Procter, Mrs. Dickens and Georgina came in the evening. A very cordial letter of thanks from Henry Taylor.

November 24th.—Very affectionate note from Forster. Answered it briefly. Wrote to Henry Taylor. Went over the words of Philip Van Artevelde. Rested. Acted Philip Van Artevelde ten times better than the last night. Called. Spoke to Maddox, and offered to take the other £50 on myself.

November 25th.—The anniversary of the death of that beloved child, whose memory is like a living thing to me, and for whom my love can never, never die. Lifted up my heart to God, that I might in another state of being again hold commuinon with her angel spirit. My blessed, my ever beloved Joan! Bless thee, bless thee, dearest child. Amen! . . . Maddox called, to whom I had written a note early. I offered to him, in addition to my proposal of paying £50 towards the cost of the play, to act *four nights* per week to Christmas, if the arrangement could be made to run the play combined with *Anna Thillon. I have done all I could* in all ways for it.

November 28th.—Forster dined with us, and we had a long and friendly discussion of the real cause of *Philip Van Artevelde's* disappointing issue. I ascribe it to the *bad acting.*

November 29th.—Acted as well as I could Philip Van Artevelde. Called. Knowles and Maddox came into my room. Maddox told me an extraordinary story about Miss Cushman! Letter from a Mr. Fuller, acting attorney, acquainting me with "injuries" done to a supernumerary called Richardson on Friday night last!!!—Ah!

[1] The play was acted again on November 29 and December 1—(*note by Sir F. Pollock*).

378

November 30th.—Henry Taylor called and talked about the play. I was obliged to tell him of my fears. I paid him £100—of which Mr. Maddox had paid me £50. Read Mr. ——'s letter, in which (really a theatre is a *hell!*), among other falsehoods, the man had the devilish effrontery to write that I had struck his wife so hard on the head that she was near fainting on the stage." My God, am I to herd with these vile wretches! Answered him, confining myself to an indignant denial of the falsehood. Wrote to Bradbury & Evans. Read the December No. of *Dombey and Son,* which I did not like. I thought it obscure and heavy. Maddox called, and expressed with great fairness his necessity of closing *Philip Van Artevelde's* career on Friday. Alas! Alas! Forster called, too ill to dine. Knowles dined. Letter from Mr. Fuller, asking for £5 for his client. Wrote copy of answer. Went over *Philip Van Artevelde.*

December 1st.—Wrote to Henry Taylor, with card of box, inform-ing him of the end of *Philip Van Artevelde* on Friday night. Acted Philip Van Artevelde as well as I could with this wretched company of players. Called. Maddox came into my room to prepare *Henry VIII* for Friday. I would not assent to it, but I would not also dissent from his withdrawal of *Philip Van Artevelde.* I left him to do what he would. *But I will remember him and his conduct about this Miss Cushman.*

December 2nd.—Note from Henry Taylor expressive of his pleasure in my personation of Van Artevelde, lamenting its withdrawal, but promising himself one more evening's gratification to-morrow night. I was quite grieved to think of his disappointment. Answered him, particularly enjoining him not to return to Maddox, as he proposed, the £100 I had paid him.

December 4th.—Note from White & Eyre, informing me that they had paid £3 to the man Richardson—in *compensation*—and £2 to Mr. Fuller for costs! And though I was perfectly satisfied with the pro-ceeding of White & Eyre, yet thus am I *robbed* by calumny and villainy! I am sick of life, and in disgust with the world about me. Went to Covent Garden theatre. Rehearsed *King Henry IV.* Spoke to Mr. Harris, whom I saw there. Asked him if he did not see the occurrence of Friday week at the Princess's with the man Richardson. He said "Yes." I desired him to describe it. He said, "You took the man *by the ear!*" "What?" I said, "I never touched the man but by his clothes." He observed, "I was at the other side of you and *did not see* it, but the *man said you did.*" "And," said I, "you

379

thought so, therefore, and *would have sworn it ?* " " *Yes !* " On such testimony, not meant to be dishonest, may life and fortune hang! Great God! He was satisfied of his mistake. Called on Forster. Met Dickens and Maclise. Dickens and Forster both agreed in the advisability of my leaving the stage. *I do not see how I am to remain on it*, and yet with what a pittance to leave it. And whose fault but my own! Wrote to White & Eyre denying the charge of that scoundrel Richardson.

December 5th.—Dickens and Charley came in, and sat long. I fear dear Dickens called to ascertain our feeling about the last number of *Dombey.* I could not speak as I wished, and therefore did not allude to it.

December 7th.—Went to Covent Garden theatre. Rehearsed my scene of King Henry. Willmott was talking with me about the state of theatrical affairs, and expressed his opinion that it was now *all* over, that they did not—the papers and the mass—appreciate what they had in my management; that it was too good for them, and now they were lauding miserable and servile followings and imitations of what was far beyond them. I told him I had decided on quitting the stage. He thought I was quite right in such a judgment. I saw Mrs. Warner, Miss P. Horton (Mrs. G. Reed), Miss Addison. Called on Forster; found Maclise there; talked with Forster on my affairs and views, all of which he thought well of. Acted King Henry IV not well—chilled by the audience and the vast expanse which separated me from the people. Called. Sent to inquire if Miss H. Faucit was dressed. She was not. Lady Boothby [1] wished to see me. She came into my room, and we had a little talk. She is a warm-hearted creature, whom I like very much. Ryder came to speak to me. He informed me that the fellow Richardson had gone to tell him that I had seized him by the ear and called him a " thief." I can to myself *attest* my God that these are *most groundless falsehoods.* In thinking on the differences of my own management and that of others, the critics might have seen that the difference was great, and the cause of this : that I thought for and acted to myself every character and every supernumerary figure, and taught them to act as I would have done had I been cast in their places. Thus there was the mind of a first actor moving and harmonizing the action of the mass :

" Mens agitat molem et magno se corpore miscet."

---

[1] Formerly Mrs. Nisbett.

December 12th.—Looked through *The Cenci* as a matter of form. The *idea* of acting such a monstrous crime, beautiful as the work is! Looked through a *thing* called a dramatic poem, by Archer Gurney [1]— *King Charles I*—such another farrago of folly and falsehood I never wearied my patience on, and yet these are men who dare to make books! The comfort is, it must cost them something, for no one would read them.

December 15th.—Wrote an answer to a very kind and flattering note from Mr. Liddell.[2] Read over a play on Athelstan—trash!— another, *Madeline*—trash!—one translated from the German, *The Son of the Wilderness*, a play full of beauty, interest and power. " Were I younger "—but it would not suit me now. As I was going to bed, Mr. Anderson sent in his card as from Osborne House. I did not recollect what Osborne House was; he came, and I recognized, on explanation, the husband of Mrs. Anderson, the *pianiste*. His message was (as he said) to convey her Majesty's wish, that I would read the words (translated from Sophocles into German and from German into English) of *Antigone* before her Majesty, accompanied by Mendelssohn's music, on the 1st of January. I questioned him very strictly to ascertain if his message was a direct command or no. He was evasive but very civil, and after a very long interview, in which I told him, if it was her Majesty's command, I would come from Exeter, where I should act on the Friday, read at Windsor on Saturday, and return to Bristol on Sunday ; but if not her Majesty's own wish, then I excused myself. I wrote to Marianne [3] that she might explain my position to her Majesty.

December 17th.—Letter from Marianne, informing me that the message of Mr. Anderson was a *command*.

December 18th.—Letter from Marianne giving me reason to believe that I should escape the impending penance of reading at Windsor. Mr. Robinson, a pert young man, called to ask me what he ought to do in going on the stage. I told him to go off it!

December 19th.—The more I reflect on the resolution I have taken, the more I am impressed with the conviction that, had I delayed longer, any effect derivable from *my retirement* would have been lost. When

---

[1] Archer Thompson Gurney (1820–1889) ; clergyman and miscellaneous writer.

[2] Henry George Liddell (1811–1898) ; Head Master of Westminster ; afterwards well known as Dean of Christchurch (1855–1891).

[3] Miss Skerrett, who held for many years a confidential position in attendance upon the Queen—(*note by Sir F. Pollock*).

Mr. Webster is tolerated to show himself in *Benedict* and even approved by the Press, is it not time for any man of intellect, education or talent to leave such an arena? Sat the whole afternoon and evening with the dear children, amusing them for some time, and after dear Willie had gone, giving them advice and instruction, which, if they remember and apply, will be of more value than sums of money to them. Nina, Katie, and Edward were my dear disciples.

December 20th.—Went with Catherine and Nina to breakfast with Rogers. Met Forster. Rogers was very agreeable, told me some amusing anecdotes, and repeated some very sweet lines. Went to the Westminster play, *The Adelphi.* Mr. Liddell welcomed me very kindly. Met Carteret Ellis, in his drawing-room. Saw the play, which was *not* well acted. To my surprise, Talfourd came in and was placed next before me. Without a *scene* I could not avoid returning his salutation, and it was no place to excite attention in. Saw Bourne at a distance, Hawes, Mr. King, Milman, who asked us to go to tea in the evening. I went and found Lords Lansdowne and Morpeth, Dean of Westminster, Talfourd, and others. Saw Willie [1] coming out from the play.

December 22nd.—Went over *Aristodemo.* What a waste of time. Went over *Timoleon, or the Brothers*—cruel waste of time. Wrote to Mr. Patmore and packed it up for him. Read to the four eldest children the first act of *King Lear.* Read *Hannibal*, by Archer Gurney!—the most cruel waste of time of all!!!

December 23rd.—A Mr. Beaumont called, an acquaintance of the late Dr. Sleath, to impose a play upon me to read! I gave him very broad hints that it was a heavy draft upon my time, but he was insensible to any thought but his own convenience and wish, and left his play. Troughton soon after called, and told me of the meddling of Government, the Board of Trade, with the Art Union! They must do something for their salaries, and, unable to do good, must do mischief. Lent Troughton my arrangement of *Van Artevelde* to read. Looked over Mr. Beaumont's *Maccabee;* found it *trash;* folded it up and addressed it with a note to him.

December 24th.—Mr. Seeley called and took with him his translation of *Aristodemo.* How happy was I to see the last of these MSS. leave my shelves! Dined with Kenyon. Met Brockedon, Rev. Brookfield,[2]

---

[1] Macready's son, then at Westminster school—(*note by Sir F. Pollock*).

[2] William Henry Brookfield (1809-1874); well known as the friend of Thackeray and Tennyson; father of the joint-licenser of plays.

382

Thackeray, Austin. At their request read some passages of Milton; they seemed pleased. Wrote note to Kenyon.

December 25th.—Interchanged with all my dear family the wishes belonging, of usage, to this dear day. Fox and Forster came to dinner and we passed a very pleasant evening. The children repeated Milton's Ode on the Nativity. We had a game at whist. My heart is thankful. Amen!

December 27th.—A very kind and courteous note from Mr. Brookfield. In the evening a party, chiefly of young people, friends of mine, Willie and Katie, with Mr. and Mrs. Brookfield, Elliotson, Kenyon, Misses Goldsmid, Walter H. Smith, Horace Twiss, Miss Cockburn, etc. The evening was very cheerful, and many seemed very happy. I was greatly pleased with Mrs. Brookfield. Slipped off to bed about half-past twelve.

Exeter, December 30th.—Dr. J. Bucknill,[1] a name of very long memory, the son of a school-fellow of mine at Rugby, a man apparently between thirty and forty (eheu! fugaces, etc.), the head of the County Lunatic Asylum, called. He sat and talked, and I found him a very intelligent man. Looked at the *Morning Herald*, a paper that I cannot read without disgust at its bigotry and illiberality. "Oh! father Abraham! what these *Christians* are "—if *Dr. Croly*[2] is one of them! Saw a sort of "summons" to me by name in a publication of Mr. Albert Smith,[3] called *The Man in the Moon*. As usual, felt angry at the impertinence; but "Silence is the safest response for all the contradiction that arises from impertinence, vulgarity or envy."

December 31st.—The last day, and almost the last hour of the year is come, and in my hurried thoughts I can but give a sad, serious, and solemn glance at this portion of time that is rapidly fading from me; at my time of life *the irrevocable* is an awful thought. I close my year's record with thanks to Almighty God for all He has vouchsafed to me, and with prayers, deep and earnest, for His continued blessings on my beloved family, and for His mercy and forgiveness to myself.

---

[1] Sir John Charles Bucknill (1817–1897); for many years Lord Chancellor's Medical Visitor of Lunatics ; F.R.S. ; father of the present Mr. Justice Bucknill.

[2] George Croly (1780–1860) ; clergyman, author and journalist.

[3] Albert Richard Smith (1816–1860) ; the popular lecturer and entertainer.

1848

Bristol, January 3rd.—Went to rehearsal, where I occasionally was impatient, but very much moderated from what I should have been without precaution and forethought. The sight of ignorant pretension excites involuntarily disgust and impatience in me, and I have not schooled myself to restrain the manifestation of it. I fear I gave *some* evidences of ruffled temper this morning, but I tried to be passive, and was more so than usual. Acted Macbeth, thinking that I took pains, and stimulating my ardour—and with not one drop of wine! That was at least a cause of exultation, or at least of self-gratulation. Much was done to disturb and disconcert me, but I bore very much. I complained, *but gently*, to Mr. Chute of inaccuracies, and altogether I bore myself much more temperately than (I grieve to say!) has been my wont. But, after all, *what are these players?* Are they not the *veriest " shams " that ever disgraced manhood?* Have they a thought or purpose beyond the escape from labour, the indulgence of their self-conceit and sensuality? *Not one.* However, I will try and bear with them to the end, though I say with Falstaff, " An' I be not ashamed of my company, then am I," etc. I will hope and strive, for I feel the comfort of " passing by " these " offences " ; although I think it a question whether an actor can preserve his *artistic ardour* and reduce his spirit to indifference or passiveness under such fearful shocks to his taste, and ruin to his effects and meaning, as he is forced to undergo. Lady Macbeth pulled me off the stage to-night by a tag of my dress!

Bath, January 4th.—Looked at the *Times.* Read a most encomiastic notice of Mr. Brooke's performance of Othello. I have seen this actor, and can most *purely* and truly say his acting warrants no such praise ; he has no pretensions to genius, judgment, taste, or any artistic quality. He has physical advantages, but a most common mind, and no real passion. Such was my impression. Rested. Went to theatre, and had *the instinct—the old sure instinct* that there was *no house.* My spirits sunk so low that I feared my power to rally them. I thought on all my precepts, on all that religion and philosophy suggested, and

I resolved *non cedere malis sed contra audentior ire*, etc., and I acted Cardinal Richelieu as well as the wretched company would let me. Called—to a *miserable house !*

Wolverhampton, January 21st.—Got my letter from dear Catherine, in which I learn the success of Mr. Lovell's play acted by Mr. and Mrs. C. Kean. I must admit the unpleasant emotion of dissatisfaction at this result; of the littleness of which a minute's thought—or less—convinced me. I, said to myself in explanation—*not excuse*—that I did not like Mr. Lovell—he is vulgar and is a coxcomb—and that Mr. C. Kean was a charlatan. But all this did not justify me, nor lift up the unworthy feeling, which I directly dismissed.

Manchester, January 22nd.—A Miss ——, the person who rehearsed Regan, called here in a cab about ten o'clock, and detained me until I quite lost my patience and had the greatest difficulty not to show it. She came about a statement made, as she said, by Mr. Beverly, that she was put out of Mrs. Oakley because I thought her so detestable in Regan ! I directly and emphatically contradicted the assertion about ten times. The fact was, I was contented with her in Regan, and understood she was to rehearse Mrs. Oakley to see if she could do it. Afterwards Mr. Beverly said she had relinquished it, and Mrs. Weston was to do it. The woman appeared to me *excited*, and went on with such unconnected rigmarole that I really could not bear it. I certainly do not think her "better than she should be," as they say.

January 24th.—Received a letter from Forster, giving me the opinion of several of my friends about Mr. Brooke. Fox is the only one mentioned who "sees merit " in him. There is certainly more mark and likelihood in him than in any of the actors now in London—even including the stale melodrama of Mr. Wallack, and the monotonous respectability of Phelps. But if he is a man of real talent, I am greatly mistaken.

January 26th.—Read the paper. In it I perceived the advertisement of the Olympic theatre, in which the lessee, Mr. Davidson, announces Mr. G. V. Brooke as "the greatest living tragedian." This is another evidence of the puppet-show condition to which the London theatres have descended ! It is time indeed to turn the back on such a state of things. *Once* this would have made me very angry; I can now almost laugh at it.

London, February 19th.—Rehearsed Macbeth, Mrs. Butler [1] the Lady Macbeth. I have never seen any one so bad, so unnatural, so

---

[1] Fanny Kemble.

affected, so conceited. She alters the stage arrangements without the slightest ceremony, and, in fact, proceeds not only *en grande artiste*, but *en grande reine*. She is *disagreeable*, but her pride will have a yet deeper fall, I feel confident. I must strive, and be careful, and hope in God for myself.

February 21st.—Looked at the paper. Saw the announcement of "Mr. Macready and Mrs. Butler's first night"; was for a moment annoyed, but immediately resolved to do my utmost to prevent the least ruffle of temper with this man during this engagement. Acted Macbeth, *I think*, with peculiar strength, care, and effect; was occasionally disconcerted by this monstrous pretender to theatrical art, who to me is most unnatural and bad. I do not know her effect on the audience, but cannot think it good.

February 22nd.— Went to rehearsal of *King Henry VIII*. Mrs. Butler was weeping at the scene of Wolsey. She is living in an atmosphere of self-delusion. There is nothing genuine in her, poor woman! Sent away several copies of the *Times*, the notice in which of the Princess's was an assertion of the most decided character respecting my own supremacy in my art.

February 23rd.—Acted Cardinal Wolsey with great care. Called. Mrs. Butler was the Queen Catherine, and C. Kemble in the stalls knocked so loud and so often with his stick—often almost *alone*—that the people called "*Turn him out !* "

February 24th.—Mrs. Butler's rehearsal of Desdemona struck me as a very correct and forcible conception of that beautiful character, and, if she would give herself up to the study of execution, she might yet become a very fine actress. Her *intention*, which is admirable, is seen in her acting the part; but her affected voice, her leaning her head, her walk, etc., so many affectations prevent *her* from *being* Desdemona.

February 25th.—Acted Othello with all the strength I had, and, I think, *well*. Called and led on Mrs. Butler. News of the abdication of *Fagin*—Louis Phillippe. A man that, as the sovereign of the Triumphs of Peace, might have had the greatest glory of any monarch, now a beaten, cowardly, despotic intriguer *chassé'd* by his subjects and despised by all.

March 3rd.—Birthday, æt. fifty-five. Acted King Lear in my best manner, which was appreciated by the audience. Called for, led on Mrs. Butler, warmly received.

March 11th.—Disgusted with that most offensive Jack-Pudding of

386

FANNY KEMBLE

From an engraving by C. Picart of a painting by Sir Thomas Lawrence, P.R.A.

the House of Commons, Mr. B. Disraeli, in his speech, termed by the *Times* (oh, *Times!*) "a flood of ridicule" against Ministers and Cobden and Peel.

March 14th.—Read the paper. Disgusted with Lord J. Russell's speech and his vacillation, or rather tergiversation, on the question of the Income Tax. I have no sympathy with these Whigs—*they are not equal to the occasion.*

March 17th.—Acted King Lear very fairly. Called. Spoke to Mrs. Butler, *who is a very indifferent actress to be placed in a prominent position.*

March 25th.—Looked over the paper, and *delighted* to see that disgusting wretch, the King of Hanover, compelled to *undo* much of his tyranny and give their demands to the Hanoverians. A letter in the paper from that most odious and disgusting beast Mr. J. O'Connell.

April 5th.—Acted Brutus in a very masterly manner. I do not think I ever acted it with the same feeling, force, and reality. Called.

April 8th.—Received a letter from *soi-disant* Miss Hamilton (really Miss ———), appointing to see me at Portsea Place. Read the paper. Called on Miss ———, saw her, and was really and deeply touched by the profound feelings of attachment she seemed to have cherished for me. I spoke to her with great kindness, inquiring much about her history, and showed the most tender consideration for her unhappy attachment with the most respectful sympathy. I wished to know if she had anything to ask of me before she left England for America; but no, she had not. I said all that I could to comfort and give her a happy recollection of the interview. Alas, for our human condition!

April 9th.—Read the paper. My activity was stopped, my whole power of business suspended by the anxious thought which suggested itself to me as to my future. England did not appear to hold out to me the means of subsistence on my hoped-for capital. I deliberated, measured, calculated, but my investigation only served to strengthen the belief that to live and educate my children I must go to the United States. Forster came to dine; he combated very earnestly my arguments, but I am not convinced that he is right, though "in my heart something battles on his side."

April 10th.—Wrote to Miss ———, with the present, as a remembrance, of the illustrated Thomson's *Seasons*. I thought it would be a solace to her to have a record of my kindly feelings towards her. I pity her very sincerely, and can only think with sorrow and respect upon such a surrender of her affections. The day has passed without any news of disturbance from the Chartist meeting, and I believe the thing will turn out a very ridiculous affair.[1] Spent the whole evening ruminating on my means, and on the best disposal of them. Several things came to light. One thing is certain, I am too poor, and it has been my own fault, or the fault of my education. God help and befriend me!

April 11th.—Thought in rising on the subject of last night's meditations. Dined with Dickens to celebrate the conclusion of *Dombey.* Met D'Orsay, Jerdan, Forster, M. Lemon, Thackeray, H. Browne, Ainsworth, Evans, F. Stone, Beard, Burnett, Hogarth. A day interesting in its occasion and progress, but strangely assorted. Still, dear Dickens was happy, and I was very, very happy to see him so. God bless him!

April 12th.—Letter from Miss ——; very pathetic.

April 22nd.—Waited till seven o'clock, and went with Catherine and Letitia into the drawing-room to see the children *act.* A humorous playbill was placed on the table, announcing Andromaque, Racine, Achilles and Agamemnon, Ilias, and Horace's satire, *Ibam forte via sacra,* dramatically arranged. The acting was very clever; there was an excellent understanding and an ardent feeling of their respective parts. If I had not the means of educating and of leaving some little means to them, I should be apprehensive that the possession of this talent, which seems like an inheritance, might lead them to this worst exercise of a man's intellect. Their dresses were ingeniously made up, and the whole proceeding was most interesting. Dear, blessed beings! May their hearts ever be as light and pure and as happy, at least, as now. God bless them.

April 24th.—Went to Marylebone theatre. Rehearsed. Looked at papers. Received an insinuation that Miss Cushman was endeavouring to do me mischief in America! Received at the theatre a note and very handsome purse from Miss ——. How very, very sorry I am for her! Rested. Letter from Mrs. Ratcliffe, quite destroying my hopes of Tonbridge. Acted Hamlet in my best style. Called. Mrs. Warner came into my room and gave me from the managers a cheque for £300!

April 26th.—Letter from Mrs. P. Butler, acquainting me with her inability to act on the Siddons Monument night, in consequence of a summons to appear on the 5th of June to answer a suit of divorce brought against her by Pierce Butler on the ground of " desertion."

[1] This proved to be the case, though there were widespread fears of a serious rising.

388

I was truly sorry to read it. Faults on both sides would have made mutual forgiveness "wisest, discreetest, best." Walked to theatre. Rehearsed *Macbeth*. Mr. Ryder called, and expressed his unqualified readiness and willingness to accompany me to the United States on the understanding that it was a "speculation" on his part, etc.

April 29th.—Went with Dickens to Royal Academy dinner. Much pleased with works of Herbert, Danby, Webster, E. Landseer, Creswick, Stanfield, Lee and Cooper, Cope, Hughes. Saw many friends—Bishop of Norwich had forgotten me; so had Denman. The day was not so lively as usual; there was a want of management, and the music was bad. Brougham was making himself absurdly conspicuous. The Duke spoke as unmeaningly as usual, and Lord Lansdowne, whom I had never heard speak in public before, greatly disappointed me.

Bath, May 9th.—Went to station. Bought paper and read it on my rapid journey. Caught some little part of a conversation between two of the pasengers—turfmen—on the amounts they had upon certain horses. Is their pursuit much less useful than my own? What is life? For what are we sent into this world? It is a mystery that saddens and bewilders me. More especially when I consider how differently we are furnished, both by nature and the accidents of birth and education, for our toilsome passage through it. Rehearsed at Bath, with a most wretched set. May not any one accurse his lot that "has fallen among" players? Very much tired; stimulated myself with some strong coffee, and wrote to Forster about this Benefit, which, I see, will very probably tumble to the ground. Forster is not a *man of business;* he does not take fast hold of the necessities of a case, and either pursue or relinquish it as reason and calculation suggest, but with a half hope, half belief, goes on and trusts to chance, on the impulse of the affair to carry him through. Wrote a very hasty note to Catherine, dear woman! Acted King Henry and Oakley. I had upon me such a presentiment—so painful a one—of a wretched house, that the hollow sound returned from the orchestra, as the overture was played, quite sunk down my spirits, looking forward, as I was doing, to a performance with such *cruel* players. I was weak enough to have recourse to brandy, and made the best fight I could of it; but such a company, and so *attired !*—such a country squire, and such a Major! Monmouth Street had contributed its refuse for them! Oh! why was—but let me not be so ungrateful as to complain. Thank God for all! *Landor* came to shake hands with me.

389

To Bristol, May 10th.—Found letters from Catherine, from a Mr. Youl, an author, who had quitted tuition for literature, and now, in destitution, applies to me. I felt very much for him, though at the same time I was sensible of his imprudence; but he was young and confident—alas!—"*J'étois jeune et superbe!*" Wrote to Youl with a cheque for five guineas.

London, May 12th.—Came to London. Met with a very good-natured *Conservative*, whom I found so entirely agreeing with every political view I had, that, without knowing it, the man was, I found, a thorough Liberal! He told me a fact about a relation or friend of his, a *beautiful* girl, a Miss Bingham, daughter of General Bingham, who, on one of the Queen's infant children stretching out its arms to her, kissed it, and, in consequence of this almost *treasonable* act, there were reprimands and a terrible commotion.

Chester, May 18th.—How beautiful England is! Read in Thomson—sweet philanthropic, philosophic spirit—he always soothes. Fretted at heart by the servile tone of the *Times*, pandering to our Court and aristocracy—utterly insensible to the sublimely heroic conduct of the French people, and seeing only excellence in our over-gorged church and the state of things that leave the rich to grow richer and the poor to become poorer. It is difficult to repress the imprecation of indignation that rises to one's lips in thinking of this. America must be my refuge, I believe; and yet, what it is to leave England! Came to Chester—the city where at sixteen I took charge of a theatre with a company nearly all three weeks in arrear—an almost unprecedented state of things then. How many and what strange memories are here!

May 20th.—Went with Catherine, Willie and Katie to Vernon's Gallery. Saw the magnificent gift that he has made to the nation. What a pity the aristocracy, that does so much honour—(?)—to the country, never does anything of the nature of this horse-jobber's noble-ness.[1] Honour for ever to him!

May 21st.—Arranged my week's accounts. Looked at *Examiner*, which, I lament to say, was very dull, and evidently wanting in deter-mined purpose. It will very soon lose its extent of circulation, if Forster does not apply himself more earnestly to the task of sustaining its character. Called on poor Dow. Saw his wife, her brother, and three of Dow's children—tenanting a second floor

[1] Robert Vernon (1774–1849). He made a fortune in contracting for Army horses; presented one hundred and fifty-seven pictures to the nation in 1847.

in Norfolk Street. He keeps his bed. He was very glad to see me—was much changed, his face swollen, his eyes and mouth swollen—alas! a stranded vessel! He wished to die in peace and to have a perfect understanding with all men, particularly his old friends. I assured him that no feeling had ever existed in my mind at variance with him—explained to him how *he had* estranged himself from us, etc. Shadwell called in and sat; Elliotson (*kind soul!*) came to see him; examined him—stomach, legs, mouth, eyes— case of dropsy—was very grave; Dow was in good spirits, laughing and bantering, but Elliotson had no response to his mirth. Dow insisted that he was better, and Elliotson seemed to acquiesce—not to believe. Dow talked of George Bucknill's kindness, of Forster's, of Knowles's, who really has been *most unjust* to me. I write this without the least emotion of anger. Dow was affected in speaking of his friends' kindness—of his readiness to die, and of his desire to live chiefly for his children's sakes. He became very merry, and I thought looked better; talked of dining with me if I would invite him again, and of the Raven of Barnaby Rudge—"Never say die." But it appeared his stomach rejected solid food, and he was too weak to rise! He was very grateful for my visit. I asked him, on his mentioning his pecuniary embarrassments—everything was lost!— whether he required aid at present. He said ' No, he should get on, and when he could get to his chambers (alas!) all would be right again.' Going out, I spoke to Mrs. Dow, who told me Elliotson had said she must not encourage any hope! I inquired of her about their pecuniary circumstances, and her tears answered me. God help them! Amen! It rained as I came out, and I took a cab home. Wrote a note to Mrs. Dow, expressive of my concern for her, and enclosing her a cheque for £20, begging her to accept it, as most agreeably to her—as a loan, or a gift to the children. Sent it by Lester. The dear children read from Cowper's *Task* to me. Note of warm acknowledgment from Mrs. Dow. God help her!

May 24th.—Whilst dressing for dinner a note from Jenny Lind to say that she could not come. We were put out, but still I sympathized with her, and admitted, in my mind, her excuse. Mr. and Mrs. Bates, Baron and Baroness Goldsmid, Mrs. Procter, Knox, Kenyon, Brookfield, Eastlake, Lumley dined with us. Quin, for whom we waited, did not come. We received no apology from him! The Dickenses, the Herrieses, Ainsworths, Twisses, Haworth,

Campbell, Denvilles, Rogers, Babbage, Wheatstone, etc., came in the evening.

May 28th.—Forster called. He did not seem in the best humour, and *I think* he came to dine, though I plainly intimated it would not be in my power to see him after Friday last. He did not stay long, and though I was studiously cordial in manner (although *unable* from my brother's presence to ask him to dine), yet I think he went away in dudgeon. If so, *how am I to help* such variations of temper and feeling?

May 30th.—Walked out with Willie; called on Lord Lansdowne; he was just going out, and walked with us to St. James's Street; we then turned back to Lansdowne House, he having forgotten some papers, and walked on again to Carlton Gardens, Pall Mall. I asked him to preside at the meeting of committee for Siddons Monument, and he promised me he would, if his business did not interfere. I introduced Willie to him. We went into the Athenæum, which I showed to Willie; but as usual the servants did not know me.

June 2nd.—Wrote to Delane about his father's election. Dined with Procters—met Brookfield, Milnes, Thackeray, the Campbells, etc.

June 3rd.—Letitia read me some verses of dear Katie—addressed to one of the younger Goldsmids, whom she had met at the baron's, and with whom she had held some interesting conversation. They talked on religion, and Katie did not wish to pursue the conversation, because, as she told the interesting little Jewess, "I might convert you, and your parents might not be pleased." The dear child! The lines and her sweet conduct made me weep most copiously, but they were tears of gratitude to God. Went with Catherine and Willie to the opera, Mr. Lumley having obligingly sent us a box. Jenny Lind sang and acted Lucia with wonderful power and sweetness, but the *thing*—the opera, as an amusement, is such a revolting absurdity that I cannot reconcile myself to it.

June 4th.—Dined with Horace Twiss. Met Pemberton Leigh, Sir Fitzroy and Lady Kelly,[1] Lady Webster, Arthur Webster, Delafield, Lord Canterbury,[2] Mrs. Fitzgerald, and unknown; in the evening were Mrs. Gurwood and Miss Meyer, Miss Woolgar, Miss

---

[1] Fitzroy Kelly (1796–1880); afterwards Lord Chief Baron of the Exchequer; Solicitor-General 1845–6 and 1852. Attorney-General 1858–9.

[2] The second Viscount; son of the well-known Speaker, Manners-Sutton, created on retirement Viscount Canterbury.

L. Addison, Mrs. C. Kean, Mr. C. Kean, Miss P. Horton, Planché, Benedict, Manby, Campbells, and many whom I did not know. Spoke with Miss Woolgar, Miss Horton; spoke to Mrs. C. Kean. Looked to Mr. C. Kean as if to speak to him, but seeing no sign or indication of any design or intention to do so, I left him alone in his glory.

June 5th.—Mrs. Rutherfurd, who brought an excuse from the Lord Advocate, detained in the House of Commons, Sir J. Wilson, Sir R. Comyn, Panizzi, Thackeray, E. Landseer, Lyon, Mrs. Murray came to dinner; a pleasant day, but a little gloomed by the empty chair of the Lord Advocate. The Bancrofts, Mrs. Thomas and her daughters, Mrs. Procter and Adelaide,[1] Mr. and Mrs. Campbell, Schwabe, Otto Goldschmidt, Carlyle and Mrs. Carlyle, Mrs. and Miss Nicholson, Madame D'Eichthal came in the evening.

June 7th.—Dined with Brookfield. Mrs. Brookfield not well enough to come down from the drawing-room. Met Hallam, Sir C. Elton, Sir A. and Lady Gordon, Hallam junior, Mr. Greave, Miss Elton. In the evening saw the Procters, Miss Wynne, Miss Thompson, etc.; an agreeable evening; met Thackeray going out.

June 8th.—C. Jones cames as secretary to the (Siddons monument) committee; dear Stanfield came, and, very kindly, Lord Lansdowne. After waiting as long as we could, I read the Report, and we concluded, without the formalities of a meeting, that it would be best to print the Report and enclose it with a letter from the secretary to such persons as would be likely to take an interest in such a measure, or who ought to do so. Jones and myself, when Lord Lansdowne had gone, made out the letter, and he took it to get the paper printed.

June 9th.—Note from Forster, who I fear is not in the best temper with me; if at all in an ill one it is *most unreasonably* that he is so. Went with Edward and Patty to Sir John Soane's house or museum, a quaint piece of coxcombry and gimcrackery, absurd I think to be left as it is, alone, for it is scarcely worth the trouble of *going* to see. Lord Aberdeen has not answered the courteous note I addressed to him. Mr. and Mrs. Jay mentioned their purpose of being presented at Court by Bancroft. *This is not permitted to me.*

June 11th.—C. Jones called, and I corrected the Report to be printed for circulation, looked out list of names, etc. Adelaide and Agnes Procter called. Catherine set us down in Hyde Park. Willie

---

[1] Adelaide Ann Procter (1825–1864); the distinguished poetess, who was then beginning to make a reputation.

and myself called on Lady Blessington, who kept us talking long; on Sheil, from home; on Hallams, from home; Mr. Murray, same; Elliotson, same; Hillard, whom we found within, and where Bancroft called. In Grosvenor Place we met Richard Jones, who must be seventy, but whom Willie thought not more than fifty. We talked of the old actors, our contemporaries, of whom so few are left. Edward and Patty and Ellen came to dinner.

June 12th.—Thought upon the constant subject, my change of home. The consideration of the purpose of life, as given by God, and the comparative power of discharging our duty in it, pressed strongly upon me. My own degraded position as being proscribed from the privileges common to my many associates, viz., that of going to court—a matter worthless in itself, but made a brand and an insult by being denied to me, as one of a class. Edward, Patty, and Ellen dined. Talked with Edward, and pushed him home upon the question of America. His opinion was that it would be his choice with my large family, to live in England upon however contracted a scale, relinquishing all but mere living, of course giving up society, and getting on in some country town as well as I could till I saw what chances my sons had, and how things might turn up. As to my daughters losing all the advantages of society, he thought nothing of that; in fact, the amount of reasoning was this: "I would stay in England under whatever circumstances, though I cannot deny the advantages which appear in the United States." This, I may say, determines me for America. God prosper us.

June 13th.—Looked at the paper; sorry and ashamed to read the account of the outrage offered to the French actors last night at Drury Lane theatre.[1] Asked for the manager and was shown to his room, the first time I have entered the stage door since I quitted it. The manager seemed alarmed at my presence. I told him in French I had called to express my concern and indignation at the outrage offered them last night, etc. They were very grateful, and asked if I had not been content with my reception at Paris. I told them how gratefully I remembered it, and ever should. They asked if I would write a line to that effect. I sat down, and in the midst of their hurried conversation wrote a note to M. Hostein, the director. They were profuse in their acknowledgments, Jullien observing two

---

[1] On Jullien attempting to introduce the *Théâtre Historique*. The piece was *Monte Cristo*, but its reception was so uproarious that not a word could be heard. Some of the more prominent disturbers were taken into custody.

or three times, "C'est digne de votre caractère." M. Hostein in great joy introduced me to two actors, as I passed, who were very grateful and respectful. Called on Henry Taylor, Mrs. H. T—— very unwell. Coming home wrote a corrected note to M. Hostein, requesting him in French to substitute it for that which I had left with him. The Dickenses and Hillard dined with us. Answer from M. Hostein.

June 14th.—We went to Drury Lane theatre, and anything more offensive, brutal, stupid and disgusting I have not seen. A number of persons, players and fellows connected with the theatres kept up a disgraceful tumult the whole night—at least till ten o'clock, when after suffering much from impatience, disgust, and indignation, we went away. The actors seemed good as far as it was possible to judge. There was a considerable crowd outside the doors.

To Hereford, June 15th.—Read the *Times,* in which my letter[1] to M. Hostein appeared, and a further condemnation of the " dull brutality " of the wretched ruffians who so disgraced themselves in last night's disturbance at the theatre. At Swindon saw Wilson, the Scotch melodist; he was open-mouthed about those vile rascals. Talked with dear Katie, who is a most engaging child. God bless her. At Gloucester I took her to see the cathedral; we could only take a hasty glance at it; saw another church; showed her the view from the terrace at Ross. Reached Hereford at five, and came to our excellent friends the Twisses; found them in good spirits; found Arthur and Godfrey here. Spent a very cheerful evening.

June 16th.—Letter from Catherine, enclosing one from Forster to her, sending her his Goldsmith bound, etc.—declining to dine on the 24th, and never noticing his invitation on Tuesday last. A civil rudeness, but in fact a conclusive demonstration that he wishes a quarrel to be either understood or got up. I need only look back to similar events to convince myself of the inutility of attempting to maintain a sensible and true understanding of affection and friendship with him. His caprice is beyond all management. I have done my utmost to show him my regard and desire to be a friend to him. I can do no more.

Leeds, June 17th.—Found at my lodgings letters from Catherine,

---

[1] The letter referred gratefully to the kind reception he had three times enjoyed when acting in Paris, and regretted that similar courtesy was not shown to the French company in London (*note by Sir F. Pollock*).

from Forster with the account that the Queen will command a night for me—(Thank God!)—from Mrs. Warner, from Wilbraham Taylor, informing me that Prince Albert gives £25 to the Siddons monument; from Gillman that the Queen-Dowager, out of her £100,000 per annum, gives—0; from Messrs. Hodgson and Burton, I presume solicitors, ' inquiring of me in the names of Messrs. Webster, C. Kean, C. Mathews, Farren, Harley, Buckstone, Wright, Meadows, Granby, P. Bedford, F. Mathews, Leigh Murray, R. Roxley, Hughes, O. Smith, Lambert, Worrett, Creswick, Howe, and numerous other members of the profession who do not concur in the course I have adopted, etc., whether the words I used to M. Hostein were actually uttered by me, and the names of the members of the profession who authorized me to protest,' etc. Occupied during the evening in making a copy of a reply to these persons. Letters from Poole about the English players. Read in paper of poor Tom Steele's [1] death. I wish I had seen him as I intended. His fate was unhappy, but not altogether attributable to the causes assigned by the papers. He had spent his fortune before he joined O'Connell.

Leeds, June 21st.—Letter from Forster, acquainting me with the circumstances of the Queen's command, communicated to Dickens by Mr. Phipps, Lord Normanby's brother, with a direction to him to make the formal application through the Lord Chamberlain. This is very gratifying. Rehearsed. Mr. Pritchard showed me a letter from some acquaintance in London, in which were these words—I took them down from the letter—" The Drury Lane affair was well managed; Webster and C. Mathews pay all expenses—*have* paid, I should say: the first time C. Mathews was ever guilty of such an indiscretion as to *pay*." The letter authorized by the men of the Haymarket, Adelphi and Lyceum companies, Delafield's reported support of the Lyceum, and A. Webster's cognizance of the proceedings seem in corroboration of this piece of villainy. Wrote a letter of summons to Ryder—to come to me on Sunday. I will see if he can lend any further clue to the authorship of this atrocity. Mr. A. Fairbairn called at the theatre, but I could not see him. Acted Macbeth and was *murdered*; Banquo was a ——, poor Lady Macbeth very, very inadequate. To complete the wretched affair, Mr. Pritchard played Macduff, and between his vapouring flourish in the morning and missing a parry at night, he got a cut in his face—not

---

[1] O'Connell's " Head Pacificator " (see note, p. 341 Vol. I.).   He committed suicide.

much, but he made the most of it. I was much distressed by it. Called.

June 22nd.—Letters from Catherine, from Mrs. Rutherfurd, who really hurt, almost offended me by a supposition of my beloved Katie becoming an *actress.* God knows how I love her, and that love makes me feel that I had rather she were early taken to God's own rest than exposed to such a fate.

June 23rd.—Acted Cardinal Richelieu; the house was the worst we have yet played to. I cannot understand this. The audience *appear* most fervent in their expressions of satisfaction, and the population is 170,000! Is it an additional evidence that the knell of theatres is sounded! I suppose so. Called and most enthusiastically received.

London, June 25th.—Ryder called. He told me that Webster had paid the fine for the rioter Attwood, and that Mr. C. Kean had rushed to tender bail for Cowell, the ringleader of the Drury Lane rioters, but had been anticipated by Carlisle, a son of the blasphemous and atheistical publisher!

June 28th.—Carlyle and Mrs. Carlyle, Sir A. and Lady Gordon, Sheil, Charles Buller, Mr. and Mrs. Jay, Lady Morgan, Hillard, Comte D'Orsay, and Brookfield dined with us; Procters and Haworths came in the evening. Sheil questioned me about my boys, their age, etc., and in the kindest manner informed me that in his office—Master of the Mint—was the nomination—by power of veto—to a place of *Moneyer*, which rose from a small salary to three or four thousand per annum. That, if one of these should fall, he had had intended, and told Mrs. Sheil he should give it to one of my sons; if it did not, I must take the will for the deed.

June 29th.—Dined with Dickens—meeting Mrs. Crowe, Mr. and Mrs. Muspratt (late Miss S. Cushman), Hillard, Mr. and Mrs. Stanfield and Forster, whose insolent coldness and supercilious bearing were too much for my patience. I returned his behaviour by not noticing him through the whole evening. I had put one letter into his hand, as I placed another in Dickens's. I would not take a paper from a servant as he took mine from me! He spoke to me at the end of the evening, because he saw that he had carried his impertinence too far. I answered very coldly. I had a note from Dickens in the course of the day with one from Miss Cushman, very cavalierly *consenting* to act Queen Catherine, if *her expenses* were paid. I answered that I would willingly dispense with such aid.

July 2nd.—Hillard came to breakfast. Mr. Addison called; I proposed to him to act Lord Sands, etc., but he regretted very much not to be able. We talked with Hillard over the subject of our retirement to Cambridge, Massachusetts. Read Felton's letters, and discussed each point of inquiry as it arose.

July 3rd.—On leaving the theatre, I passed that superannuated coxcomb, Mr. W. Farren—one of the signers of the letter to me. He called after me, wishing to speak to me, and on coming up with me protested his ignorance of everything about the letter. I told him his petition, etc., was nothing to me; that his name had been given to me as one instructing the solicitors to write to me, and if they had falsely used it, it was his business to call them to account. I left him as he was saying he should do so. He has maligned and abused me on every occasion behind my back, and I was not sorry for the opportunity of cutting for good and all his acquaintance. Note from Dickens, informing me that Forster had gone to ask Bulwer to receive the Queen with D'Eyncourt, and that if he refused, as he expected, Mitchell(! !) and "*some one about the theatre* "(! ! !) must do it, because he had an aversion to the kind of thing, etc. *This is too bad.* I could have had a committee who would have done all this. Forster, with Dickens, has taken the matter *into his own hands*, and very badly and imperfectly conducted it, marring as much as he has made, and now *creates* an embarrassment from his own vulgar officiousness and importance that I fear will be very serious. Mr. and Miss Stone, Mr. and Mrs. Campbell, Mr. and Mrs. Starr Miller, N.Y., Hillard, Mrs. Procter, Babbage, Thackeray, Berlioz, Mr. and Mrs. Benedict, Dr. Quin, Mr. Marshall, Professor Tom Taylor dined.

To Birmingham, July 5th.—Note from D'Eyncourt, accepting the offer of receiving Her Majesty. Received a note from Milnes, agreeing to receive Her Majesty. Mr. Crace called on me a little later than his appointment (three o'clock) and agreed to fit up the box, etc., for the Queen for £50 or thereabouts.

July 6th.—Read the paper. In the list of the Queen's State Ball I see numbers of my own acquaintance, and certainly several who have not the respect in society that I and mine enjoy; but I cannot be permitted to appear at Court—I am not fit to be presented where such masses of vulgarity and offensive manners and morals as the —— family have the *entrée*. Well—"*There is a world elsewhere!* " Rested. Acted Cardinal Wolsey and Mr. Oakley—not quite as I wished. Called. Led on Mrs. Warner.

398

July 7th.—Read the paper. Uneasy at an article on that detestable heap of filth, the *New York Herald*, in bitter hostility to this country—hinting at war, etc. It annoyed me much, until I reflected that this paper is spoken of as a sort of loathsome vermin by the better class in the States; and the exultation at New York on the news of the tranquillity of England was a demonstration of existing feeling which these scoundrels will not be able to disturb. Disgusted with M. Milnes's declaration in the House that the English loved the aristocracy—"They loved a lord." Disgusted, too, with Talfourd's apostate speech—which is a desperate attempt at a judgeship. Acted Hamlet—I know not how—with very little applause—and to myself very unsatisfactorily. I cannot account for it. I tried. *Am I growing old?* Called. Very much fatigued.

London, July 9th.—Reached home at five o'clock. Dickens came, and we spoke of the various points of business requiring note and attention. I spoke to him of Forster's conduct, not wishing him to think that I could be harsh or unjust to any one. He knew well Forster's temper and disposition, and was satisfied that he had shown temper (at least I judged so) to me. Looked over the book for the Queen—*one mistake in it!* Elliotson called. He told us of what Dickens had mentioned, that bills had been posted up against the walls with these words—"*Who acts for Mr. Macready?*" Does any one wonder that I hold players as a body in aversion and contempt? After—but no matter.

July 10th.—Special performance at Drury Lane. Occupied with affairs for the evening and taking my dresses. Called for Dickens, with whom I went down in the carriage to Drury Lane theatre. Saw Miss Cushman, with whom was Miss McHays. I talked with them some time. Dickens was very active all day, answered letters for me, and took on himself various arrangements. He was the acting manager; the play was very respectably set upon the stage. I lent Mr. Phelps my dress for King Henry VIII. Rehearsed two pieces; saw Braham, Knowles, Forster—who asked me "in what he had offended me"; I told him that the stage was no place for such a subject. He was very active through the day. Rested. Requested Forster to apply at Bow Street for seven or eight policemen in plain clothes to be placed in the pit, which he fortunately did. On going on the stage, indeed, as it appeared from the beginning of the anthem, an organized disturbance, similar to that got up for the expulsion of the French actors, was violently persisted in by a few persons in the pit and the galleries. My reception was very great, and the house, with Her Majesty and the Prince in state, was most brilliant. The noise continued through the scene, and in the next, wishing to ascertain the nature of the disturbance, I sent to ask leave to address the audience. The Queen granted it, and I told the galleries that, understanding they were incommoded for want of room, I had to assure them that, happy as I had been in receiving favours from them for many years, they would now add to my obligations by receiving their money and leaving the theatre. Applause, but not tranquillity, ensued, and it was only in the banquet scene that the play began to be heard. I took great pains, both in Cardinal Wolsey and in Mr. Oakley. The Queen left at the end of *The Jealous Wife*, and I was called on and most warmly greeted.[1]

July 11th.—Wrote a letter of acknowledgment to Prince Albert and the Queen through Colonel Phipps. Received a printed letter addressed to the members of the theatrical profession inciting them against me—another evidence of the unprincipled character of this rascally class!

July 12th.—Hetta told us of the kindness of the Queen, wishing her to see the baby and the Princess Helena,[2] saying that she would show the Princess to her herself. Hetta went into the room, and the Queen held the child to her; but, *restrained by etiquette*, neither spoke to Hetta, nor of course Hetta to her, though she looked and smiled and talked to the child about Hetta as " Miss Skerret's sister." What a sad condition of life! Alas!

July 13th.—My blessed Joan's birthday. Invoked blessings on the spirit of my angel child, who, I hope, has still some perception of and sympathy with the affection and yearning thoughts of her parents. God bless her, beloved one!

This night's performance at Drury Lane theatre was given by the special command of the Queen, and for Macready's benefit, on the occasion of his approaching departure for America. The Queen-Dowager, the Duchesses of Kent and Cambridge, and other members of the royal family were present, together with many representatives of political life, of art, and of literature. He was supported by the friendly services of Mrs. Nisbett, Mrs. Warner, Miss Rainforth, Miss P. Horton, Mrs. Stirling, of Mr. Phelps, Mr. Hudson, Mr. Ryder, Mr. Mellon, and Miss Forster. He was also, for assistance, or offers of assistance, indebted to Mr. Braham, who came from his retirement for this purpose, to Miss Cushman, to the Misses Williams, Mrs. Jane Mordaunt, and Mrs. Whitworth, to Mr. Leigh Murray, Mr. A. Wigan, to Mrs. Brougham, Mr. A. Younge, and Mr. Norton, to Mr. Benedict (now Sir Julius), and Mr. Willmott, to all of whom he expressed his thanks in print by a " card," dated from 5, Clarence Terrace, Regent's Park, July 12, 1848 (*note by Sir F. Pollock*).

[2] Now the Princess Christian of Schleswig-Holstein.

July 15th.—Note from Ransom, informing me that £489 3*s.* 6*d.* had been paid to my account by my committee. No account of the house yet sent me!

July 18th.—Dined with Thackeray; met the Gordons, Kenyons, Procters, Reeve, Villiers, Evans, Stanfield, and saw Mrs. Sartoris and S——, C. Dance, White, H. Goldsmid in the evening.

July 22nd.—Letter from Thackeray, sending me the copy of *Vanity Fair* he had promised me, with the inscription on the leaf—presented "to Mrs. Macready." I am not satisfied of his sincerity towards *me.*

July 23rd.—Displeased with Thackeray's behaviour, which may have no purpose in it, though I think it has. Dickens called; he told me the receipts at Drury Lane, before the people took back their money, was above £1200—above £90 was returned.

July 24th.—Stanfield, Maclise, Mr. and Mrs. Horace Twiss arrived; then Mr. and Mrs. Dickens, Miss Hogarth and Catherine and Troughton, and we sat down to one of those peculiar English banquets, a whitebait dinner. We were all very cheerful—very gay; all unbent, and without ever forgetting the respect due to each other; all was mirth unrestrained and delighted gaiety. Songs were sung in rapid succession, and jests flung about from each part of the table. Choruses broke out, and the reins were flung over the necks of the merry set. After "Auld Lang Syne" sung by all, Catherine giving the solos, we returned home in our hired carriage and an omnibus, hired for the nonce, Kenyon and I on the box of the carriage. A very happy day.

July 29th.—Mr. Evans called, and I showed him the edition of Pope which I had prepared, inquiring the feasibility of the plan to make it a students' edition, the price, etc. He seemed to enter into my views, viz., of printing it for private circulation, and, if demanded, to publish it at a price which would pay its own costs—with which I was extremely well satisfied.[1]

Hull, August 13th.—Read on my journey ninety pages of *The Princess.*[2] I cannot say that I hold a very high opinion of it—it seems in its language such *determined* poetry that peculiarity of phrase seems sought for or excogitated.

---

[1] *The Poetical Works of Alexander Pope, revised and arranged expressly for Young People,* by William Charles Macready, in one vol. small 8vo, was published by Bradbury & Evans in 1849 (*note by Sir F. Pollock*).

[2] Tennyson's poem, then newly published.

August 26th.—Wrote to Forster, offering to shake hands with him before I go. Mr. *Jerdan* junior called with a note from his father, who has been taken in execution, asking my assistance. I told him my means would not allow me to advance money. I read his note and asked the amount of his liability; he told me £50 odd, of which he had part, and wanted only £15. I therefore wrote him a cheque for the money.

August 27th.—Note from Forster saying he would come up, but that he was "unconscious of the cause" of my displeasure. I wish he would be more ingenuous—for his own sake; because if there was no cause, I had done him an *unpardonable* wrong; but however—— Forster called—we were friends—and we sat. I told him of the *Pope*, and he read the Dedication, which he approved.

August 31st.—Wrote to the Master of Balliol College, Oxford, to enter Willie. Went to Equitable Insurance Office. I saw Mr. Morgan, and he agreed to my taking the whole range of the United States, etc., per licence for £105, for which I gave him a cheque and received a receipt.

September 1st.—Looked over paper, the tone of which (*Times*) I begin, or have begun, not to like; it holds up our Government as an "aristocratic" one to the people, and speaks with scorn of what is more popular. I abhor *class* rule, be it of what grade it may. The country is *for* all, *of* all, and ought to be governed *from* all; wherever its talent may exist, it ought to be within reach. Went with Catherine and four eldest children to Elstree; enjoyed the ride with them, the beauty of the country, the recollection of every house and tree, the wandering over and through our old house, Elm Place, where so many of our children were born; walked through the neglected grounds and marked the shrubs and trees, now grown very high, that I had planted. How many happy hours have I spent there, and it is consecrated by its sorrows too. I have suffered as well as enjoyed. Walked down to the reservoir; every step was a memory. Went to Mr. Haworth's; dined there.

To Rugby, September 4th.—Letter from Jenkyns,[1] Head of Balliol College, informing me that there was no vacancy before 1852, so that Willie must either gain the scholarship or try some other college.

To Liverpool, September 6th.—Our dinner was a very silent, very

---

[1] Richard Jenkyns (1782–1854); afterwards Dean of Wells; under his mastership Balliol, theretofore a college of no particular mark, acquired the high reputation it still enjoys.

mournful one ; no one seemed disposed or able to talk, and tears stole down the cheeks of several of us. God help them all! Continued my affairs. Packed up papers. Busy with all the pressing things to be done. Went into every room in the house to look at them all—if for the last time—which God grant may not be ; it was a sad satisfaction. My dear home! Dillon and his son *most kindly* called to shake hands with me. Spoke with dearest Nina and Katie, enjoining them to live in love with their brothers and sisters and repay to them the love they had so largely received. Took leave, a very painful one, of my dear Letitia. May God grant that we may meet again in peace and joy. Amen! Went to station with Catherine, Willie and Edward. Deceived by the railway guide, were *an hour* before the time. Dickens [1] and Forster came and remained with us. Dickens gave me a note from Mrs. Dickens. Mr. Auldjo came up and

---

[1] Dickens had intended to accompany him on board, but changed his mind for the reasons stated in the following generous and affectionate letter—

> "*Broadstairs,*
> "*September* 1, 1848.

"MY DEAR MACREADY,

"I have lately had grave doubts of the propriety of my seeing you on board the steamer. It will be crowded with Americans at this season of the year and, believe me, they are not the people you suppose them to be. So strongly have I felt that my accompanying you on board would be, after the last *Chuzzlewit*, fatal to your success and certain to bring down upon you every species of insult and outrage, that I have all along determined within myself to remain in the hotel and charge the landlord to keep my being there a secret. But this morning I have heard from Marryat to whom Stanfield had chanced to mention our Liverpool design, and he so emphatically and urgently implores me for your sake not even to go to Liverpool, that I instantly renounced the delight of being among the last to say 'God bless you!' For when a man who knows the country confirms me in my fears, I am as morally certain of their foundation in truth and freedom from exaggeration as I am that I live.

"If you but knew one hundredth part of the malignity, the monstrous falsehood, the beastly attacks even upon Catherine, which were published all over America, even while I was there, on my mere confession that the country had disappointed me—confessions wrung from me in private society before I had written a word upon the people—you would question all this as little as I do. Soon after you receive this, I hope to come to Clarence Terrace to shake you by the hand. And now, my dear Macready, I have one request to make to you, the indisputable expediency of which is as clearly presented before my eyes as if it were written in fire upon the wall. Whatever you see or hear stated of me, whatever is addressed to you or to anybody else in your presence, never contradict it, never take offence at it, never claim me for your friend or champion me in any way. I not only absolve you from any such office but I distinctly entreat you to consider silence upon all such topics your duty to those who are nearest and dearest to you. It is enough for me that while you are away you hold me in your heart ; I have no desire to be upon your lips, nor have I the faintest glimmering of a wish that you should say any monstrous assertions to my disparagement are false, because you know them, knowing me, to be so. Every anxiety of my breast points in

403

talked with us. The Brazilian Minister and his wife we also saw. Reached Liverpool late. This day I parted from my blessed children and my dear home. I leave my blessings with them. God Almighty bless and protect them! Amen!

September 7th.—Acted Cardinal Wolsey and Mr. Oakley tolerably well to a very good house, which was surprising to me when I heard that Jenny Lind was singing in St. George's Hall! Addressed the audience when called on, and very agreeably received. Took leave of Mrs. Warner, saw Mr. Simpson. Heard the news of my poor dear friend Birch's death—my tutor, relation, and friend. He died yesterday morning at half-past seven o'clock. Peace to his beloved spirit, and may God receive it.

September 9th.—Set sail for America.

Boston, September 26th.—I have been much annoyed and disgusted with the vulgarity and low, coarse character of the newspapers even during these two days that I have been in the United States. I come here with a most affectionate feeling towards many friends, with a preference for the form of government established, and with a *wish,* a strong wish to make a home here for myself and my beloved children. *But* the low standard of taste, the ruffianly tone of the class immediately below *the best,* the ignorance of all appertaining to art, and may I not say of literature? shock and in truth disgust me. The complacency, indeed the *approbation* with which a paper speaks of the "*independence*" of Mr. Forrest (an ignorant, uneducated man, burning with envy and rancour at my success) hissing me in the Edinburgh Theatre, makes me feel that I seek in vain to accommodate myself to such utterly uncongenial natures. I fear it is not *possible* to live here, but that a cottage and seclusion—(alas! alas! for my dear, dear girls!)—is the prospect of my declining years; to me *alone* sufficient for happiness, but for *them,* with life before them, how *triste* and gloomy!

---

an exactly opposite direction. Further, do not write to me through the post but enclose any letter to me in some other one and let it come that way and do not be shaken out of this by your own prepossessions or by anything else, for I know that such precaution is necessary, though I do not know that I should have had the courage to tell you so but for the indescribable earnestness of Marryat who gives expression, in a perfect agony of language, to every misgiving that has haunted me for months past.

> "Ever, my dear Macready,
> "Your affectionate friend,
> "CHARLES DICKENS.

"I wish to heaven I could undedicate *Nickleby,* until you come home again."

JOHN VANDENHOFF

From an engraving of a Daguerreotype

September 27th.—Letters from Gould, treating with perfect slight the threat of Forrest disturbances.

October 8th.—Read a very scurrilous attack on myself, so very abusive and full of falsehood that it did not in the least annoy or disconcert me, in a Boston penny paper. There was a good deal of vulgar humour in it, and it was not unentertaining.

October 10th.—Bryant called, whom I was delighted to see. I took occasion to tell him and explain to him that there were " no passages between Mr. Forrest and myself " ; that I had been passive throughout all that had occurred in which his name was mentioned, and had shown him all due attention.

October 12th.—Acted Hamlet, not without some uncertainty as to whether some friends of Forrest might not be in the theatre on purpose to give colour by their disapprobation to the "justice " of his outrageous conduct in hissing me for my illustration of the " idle " [1] assumption of Hamlet on the King's approach, but there was spontaneous applause, and after a short interval, as if it were remembered that this must have been the point of Mr. Forrest's exception, another confirmatory round. I was very much cut up in the play, but made the best fight I could. Called at the end.

October 16th.—Acted Brutus with great care and energy, but I fancy the " *gentle* " Brutus was utterly misunderstood or fell flat upon the audience, who were ravished with the bawling and rant of Mr. G. Vandenhoff, whom they called on at the end of the *third* Act ! ! ! They allowed the play to finish, and I really would not let disgust have any influence upon me, but played my best to the end, and took no notice whatever of myself. I turn to April 15th of this year, and find that a London audience called me, and *I know* with enthusiasm. Ryder came to tell me that Othello was not called to-morrow. I desired Mr. Sefton to have it called. . . . *This evening has decided me.* It may be a small thing, but it shows to *such an extent* what is partially *admitted* by those who desire me to settle in this country, that I cannot reason against it. The masses, rich and poor, are essentially ignorant and vulgar—utterly deficient in taste and without the modesty to distrust themselves. A crust in England is better than pampering tables here. "*I am for England—God!* "

Boston, October 29th.—Charles Summer [2] called and sat my whole

---

[1] " They are coming to the play ; I must be idle."—*Hamlet*, Act iii. Scene 2 (*note by Sir F. Pollock*).

[2] The distinguished American statesman.

night away—not leaving till twelve o'clock. Our conversation was very interesting—on American politics, the Free Soil movement, the Presidential Election, etc. I gave him to understand distinctly that I did not see the reasonableness of his course. We then came to England, and he told much and many things of the aristocratic society of England that merely proves them the heartless, one-sided, one-idea'd, cold-blooded race they are. *Let me not forget* the anecdote of William Marshall of Leeds (talking with him as we left the Athenæum Club), of Lady Wharncliffe admitting Mrs. Norton to be "the first of plebeian beauties!"

November 2nd.—Note from G. Curtis, enclosing one of Ticknor's, *dissuading* notice of Mr. Forrest's slanders. I think the advice perfectly good as to an American of an American in England; if any person were to thus assail me in a low print, *e. g. Sunday Times*, I certainly should not notice it; but I believe George Curtis's feeling to be the *right one*, and am sorry there is so much sang-froid upon the question. Acted Othello as well as I could with my indisposition on me, and a Desdemona of 50, patched up to 45.

November 4th.—On this day, henceforward marked as one of my most sad anniversaries, my beloved brother, the playfellow of my boyhood, the cherished *protégé* and pupil of my youth, the friend of my life, Edward Neville Macready, died. Blessed, blessed, be his spirit. Amen.

November 8th.—*Look to date October 16th.* Before beginning the entry of this day I make that reference, because it is in direct accordance with the feelings forced on me by this day's events, simply stating that whilst my reason inclines to consider this the best government under which a man can live, his *momentary* feelings and perceptions of what is right and graceful between man and man are so shocked and outraged that the solid does not compensate for the misery inflicted by the superficial! *I will not live in America*—rather, *if I live to leave it, I will not return to die here—I will not.* Looked at paper. Rehearsed. The principals imperfect! Rested in rocking-chair. Hillard looked in. Acted King Lear, with a Goneril—perhaps sober, but acting the distressful!—with a Cordelia talking nonsense, haggard and old as Tisiphone, and affecting the timid; a Fool singing *horribly out of tune*, but by far the best of the bunch; that great lout, Mr. Ryder, as bad as the worst of them. I acted *against* it all, striving to keep my self-possession, and I acted *well*. The curtain fell, and the audience, who would have cheered on a thick-headed, thick-legged *brute* like Mr. Forrest, took no notice of this, my best performance. This is the civilization—the growing *taste* of the United States ! ! !

November 10th.—Rehearsed with care, but I have *brutes* to deal with—not *intelligences*—"*ignorance made drunk*" will well describe American actors from Mr. Forrest downwards! Acted Cardinal Wolsey and Oakley—with a Catherine and a Mrs. Oakley to make a dog *vomit!* Agh! Did my best.

November 11th.—Dined with Prescott—*very elegant dinner.* Ticknor, Hillard, Felton, Amorys, Warren, etc., dined. Ticknor spoke of a conversation *at breakfast* between Hallam and Sidney Smith, in which they both cordially agreed upon the *oppressive* influence of the aristocracy in England on literature and literary men, denouncing it as most odious.

November 12th.—After dinner, walked to the Nortons—the whole family were at home. How very much I like them, him, Mrs. Norton, a very elegant and well-bred woman—sister to my friend, when living, William Eliot, the sweet girls, and good-natured Charles.[1]

November 18th.—Met Mr. Forrest walking with some person. He bowed to Gould, who saluted him ; I did not look towards him. I had been telling Gould before that I should not speak to him if I saw him, and that I should decline any offer to meet him, as that would be to acquit him of the unworthy and ungentlemanlike conduct he has displayed to me.

November 20th.—Acted Macbeth. Before the play Mr. Ryder came to inform me there would be a disturbance. I would take no stimulant ; had fortunately eaten a light dinner, conscious of having done nothing even questionable. I was prepared. I heard great shouting at Mr. Ryder, who was evidently mistaken by the deputed rioters for myself. Went on, and applause, with the hissing, coarse noises, etc., of the ruffians there, attended my entry. I received it unmoved, and went on braving it. It continued growing more and more faint through the scenes, the rioters, sometimes well informed, trying to interrupt the more effective parts of the performance, but becoming gradually subdued until applause aroused them again. They were sufficiently quiet before the end of the first act. They heard the dagger soliloquy, manifestly enrapt, and the applause was a genuine burst, but of course again a signal for the ruffian blackguards assembled. The murder went triumphantly, and the second act ended as having

---

[1] Charles Eliot Norton, the distinguished Dantist ; his charm and culture were as much appreciated in this country as in his own.

407

stilled them. I went through cheerily and defyingly, pointing at the scoundrels such passages as "I dare do all," etc. The third act also had evidently a strong hold upon them; in the early part a copper cent was thrown at me, missing me, which particularly excited the indignation of the audience, and when I went on a bouquet was thrown to me. I mention all I can recollect. The fourth act passed smoothly after my entrance. In the fifth act, as if the scoundrels were aware that it was a strong point for me, they began with more than their primary violence of noise and outrage. A rotten egg was thrown on the stage. I went in active and cheerful defiance through it, though injured in the more touching and delicate effects, and in the last scene threw all my heart into the contest, and wound up with great effect. The majority—the large majority—of the audience were enthusiastic in their demonstrations of sympathy with me, and of indignation against these ruffians. I was called, and I went on—of course the tumult of applause, and of the attempts of those wretches was very great—I stood to be heard, and that for a long time, touched and moved at first by the genial and generous warmth of the bulk of the audience. Obtaining at last silence, I observed that at New York and at Boston I had been warned of an organized opposition to be in force against me, but there, as here, I had expressed my perfect confidence in the good-feeling of an American public, and I was happy and grateful to find I was not disappointed. I had had long acquaintance with, and I might say I had studied, the American character, and was convinced it was incapable of sanctioning such gross injustice. There was much difficulty in proceeding, and I had to wait long for intervals of silence, during which they gave "Nine cheers for Macready," which were carried out, and three or four feeble "cheers for Forrest." I observed that, in my country, it was an invariable principle of justice not to condemn a man unheard, and that their laws were similar to our own. There had been an impression widely and most industriously disseminated that I had shown hostility in my own country to an American actor. I declare upon my "sacred honour" that, not only were the assertions so made false in the aggregate, but that in all the circumstances carefully compiled there was not for a single one the smallest shadow of foundation. That I had been hissed in a public theatre by an American actor, an act which I believed no other American would have committed, and which I was certain no European actor would have been guilty of. That up to that period I had shown none but kindly feelings towards that person, and had never since then publicly expressed an unkind one. I begged to observe that, in my own country, some players had organized a similar outrage to the present against some French performers, and that the leading European journal had designated them as "ruffians and blockheads disgracing their country in the eyes of Europe"; that these people I was sure in the opinion of the audience would be considered as disgracing themselves in the eyes of Americans as well as Europeans. Under such unheard-of outrages as these, so unworthy of a civilized community (pointing to the filthy remains of the egg which lay upon the stage) I could not but feel grateful for the sense of the indignation which they had shown; that I should always remember the spirit in which they had resisted such proceedings, and in speaking of them should testify my gratitude for their generous sympathy; that I was perfectly ready if they desired to relinquish my engagement from that night (*No, No, No!*); and that, under any circumstances, I should recollect with satisfaction and pride the support they had so cordially rendered. Again and again I thanked them and retired.[1] The applause was most fervent. An English gentleman, a Manchester man, wished to see me. He came to express his sympathy, and to notice some evidences that he had witnessed of the cabal. Colonel Lee, the Recorder, wished to be introduced to me, and was most ardent in the same spirit. He did not wish me to go home alone. I had told Burton and Ryder that one of them must walk home with me in case of assault to be witness for me, as alone my testimony would be comparatively valueless. Colonel Lee said he would go, and that they would not dare attempt anything, knowing him. I went with him to his house to get his overcoat. He gave me a cigar, and together we went, but not the slightest indication of out-of-door hostility. He accompanied me to my hotel, and took his whisky toddy, whilst I took my tea; afterwards we smoked cigars, talking on the

---

[1] A "card" or letter, signed Edwin Forrest, appeared in print, dated Philadelphia, November 21, 1848, which contained the following passages: "Mr. Macready, in his speech last night to the audience at the Arch Street theatre, made allusion, I understand, to 'an American actor' who had the temerity on one occasion, '*openly* to hiss him.' This is true, and, by the way, the *only* truth which I have been enabled to gather from the whole scope of his address. But why say 'an American actor?' Why not openly charge me with the act? for I did it, and publicly avowed it in the *Times* newspaper of London, and at the same time have asserted my right to do so." The rest of the letter accused Macready of suborning the English Press against him, instigated by feelings of envy and jealousy of his rivalry as an actor, and that he had, in consequence, been himself hissed upon the stage in London before the occurrence of his own hissing of Macready in *Hamlet* at Edinburgh. He went on to deny having assisted in getting up "an organized opposition" to Macready in America, and to state that, on the contrary, his advice had been to do nothing and "let the superannuated driveller alone (*note by Sir F. Pollock*).

democratic policy, which, as he described it, approached very nearly to my own; he mentioned to me, in reference to my objection to the territorial extension of the democrats, Calhoun's expression of "masterly inactivity," as the means, the best means, of letting the race extend itself over this continent. I quite agree with it, and think it must be successful if acted on. We parted late.

November 21st.—I did not sleep much last night and did not rise quite so early as I wished. Wrote note to Ryder on business; to Peter, the Consul, returning him his note from Heywood sent to me. Note from W. B. Reed on the disgraceful tumult of last night, which grows worse as it is reviewed and reflected on, and when the two principal *papers* do not *notice* it—another merely as a sort of common thing, not altogether disagreeable, not at all improper or out of the way, and only one journal, the *Ledger and Transcript*, bestows space for a description and condemnation of the transaction, it makes one seriously deliberate on the question whether, although there may be, *and are*, many, many *gentlemen* in this country, whether it is a country of gentlemen or for gentlemen. I begin to think it is a land of blackguards and ruffians with a certain proportion of gentlemen obliged to live among them. I do not think it possible that I could live here—a dungeon with urbanity and decency in one's keeper would be preferable to the range (not the liberty) allowed by consorting with these ruffians. *If I live to reach England, a crust there in preference to splendour here.*

November 22nd.—A day for peculiar gratitude to God—if one is more than another—which it is not. Looked at papers—no notice in the *Gazette*, which, of course, disgusted me. The *leading* article of the *Inquirer* was a denouncement of the disgraceful conduct of the rioters. Wrote hastily to Colden. Received a kind note from Mr. Duffie, which I answered. Went to rehearsal. Mr. Ryder told me that there was in the *Ledger* a *Card* of *Mr. Forrest's*, which I ought to see, asserting the truth of all the statements that had been put forth against me, saying that I had suborned the Press, that I had got people to hiss him, etc. I was staggered and a little alarmed. Having heard so much of the violence of the low rowdies of this place, and seeing clearly that this was a reckless attempt to incite an infuriated spirit against me, I did not feel that *my personal safety* was to be relied on. I reflected—saw that I had a duty to perform, and made up my mind to do it, but thought of nothing less than an outrage on my person, with maiming, if my life were safe! Mr. Ryder was *croaking* as usual, and apprehensive that I should be attacked. I silenced him, for I did not want depressing counsellors. Sent for the *Treasurer*, and ordered him to have at least ten police behind the scenes; I thought *then* we might make fight—at least for retreat! Hurried on the rehearsal, and called on the Recorder—Colonel Lee— on my way home. He was out. Sent my card to W. B. Reed, asking him to come and see me. He was from home! The Treasurer told me that many places had been given up *in consequence of Mr. Forrest's Card*, under the expectation of a disturbance. He gave me a note from Mr. Godey, surrendering his places, which I kept as evidence of the effect of Mr. Forrest's conduct. Letters from my beloved Catherine, Letitia, dearest Nina, in the best spirit, Willie, Katie, Edward. Mr. Ryder came to my hotel, and I read *Mr. Forrest's Card* in the *Public Ledger* he gave me. *Oh! Mr. Forrest!!!* I felt the blow he had struck upon his own head, but yet was uncertain how far the low class under his influence might be affected by it. *Sent for three dozen of the papers instantly!* Wrote out a notice to be delivered at the doors, and meet the positive assertions of this most mendacious and wicked man. Mr. Duffie with Mr. Chester called, and I read them the *Notice*, which they thought "*very judicious.*" Mr. Duffie had written to me in the morning that he and his friend "apprehended some difficulty at the theatre this evening"—evidently now to me the consequence of Mr. *Forrest's Card*. *Oh! that card!!!* Rested. Prepared to go to theatre. Emptied my purse of some of its gold, in case I should have been assaulted. Determined to do my duty to the best of my power, hoping I should do it well. Commended myself to God, for I expected violence and outrage; went to the theatre. There whilst dressing I heard from Ryder that a reaction had taken place in the city, and that there would be no tumult, and that the printer thought the notice might as well not have been issued. How are men to steer in such cross seas? Colonel Lee came into my room, and sitting some time, regretted that the notice was issued, observing, however, that it was very mild and forbearing. How was I to act without counsel, and with the menaced visit of some of these Fire-Company men to the theatre? If Mr. Forrest could have induced my assassination, he would have rejoiced in doing it, and if he dare take my life, I am confident he would gladly do it. He is a ruffian, and a very unprincipled one. Went on the stage to the most hearty reception—cheers on cheers; *one* miserable *Forrester* "tried *it on*" in the middle of the pit with some call about Forrest, but he was *submerged*, actually drowned and never came up again. I acted Othello under great disadvantages—uneasy—off my balance—abroad; but I tried to do my best, and got through tolerably. Was called, and most enthusiastically greeted.

November 23rd.—Letters from Gould and from an anonymous American, expressive of sympathy. There are these occasional intimations of good-will, but look at the Press, upon which I had a right to rely to protect me against these ruffianly assaults and libellous accusations—it is conducted by *a gang of blackguards*, who either abet the villain that has incited all this tumult, or offer a cool observation on me, and when they condemn *him*, take care to mix me up with the censure! Give me a crust in England—a pot of herbs—rather than luxury with this populace, this nation of ——. I am full even to bursting with disgust and loathing.

November 24th.—Rose depressed by uneasy thoughts, disgusted with the Press, and with the ungentlemanly apathy and indifference of those persons whom I have known here, Drs. Chapman and Rush, Messrs. Wharton, Messrs. Ingersoll, etc. Not one to call upon me! Rehearsed—very low spirits. More and more disgusted with this Philadelphia Press, as I reflect on their base siding and shuffling on these slanders of Mr. Forrest. Is it not clear to any one who, *without evidence*, chooses to *reason on his conduct*, that if I had been guilty of these base and dishonourable actions, with which he " on *his own* belief " *now* publicly charges me, it was his business to *call me to account for them in England.* He was there more than a year after the dates at which the occurrences must have taken place, if they ever did. He was not only silent there, but he returned mine and my wife's several visits, and met me on friendly terms *outwardly.* He had a right, had I behaved as he says, to have sent a friend to me, and to have demanded explanation or satisfaction. He had nerve to hiss me in a public theatre (I do not call this courage), and would not have hesitated, could he have found grounds to do so, to make me personally responsible for such unworthy and unmanly proceedings. But he chose his battle-ground in the American Press and from thence he flung his aspersions on me, and there he gave me the lie and attempted insults on my years, which number ten more than his own. The ground he has taken he shall keep. I am not going to alter the relative position in which he has placed us. The proofs of my truth and honour I shall receive from England, and having put them on record I leave Mr. Forrest, his friends, and abettors to their own reflections.

November 25th.—My blessed Joan lost! Thought in my prayers and felt at my heart the dear precious angel, who was called away from us in her sweet infant beauty on this day! It comforts my heart to think of her spirit in a higher, happier state, and that in another sphere of Being we may meet again. God grant it and bless her ever! Amen! Gould called at the *Courier* and *Enquirer* office, wishing them to notice properly this transaction of Mr. Forrest's—he found them *disinclined* to do so. The *New York Herald* mentions the crowded houses to Mr. Forrest—this is the premium of his conduct—that on his appearance nine cheers were given and three groans for Macready. The language of the whole Press is as low in a moral point of view as it can well be. I am sick of it and of America. Let me once get *from* this country and give me a dungeon or a hovel in any other, so I be free from this. Mr. Read called and took the *Boston Mail* to read for his opinion on the advisability of writing to Mr. Forrest to know whether the statements were his, which he seemed *not* to approve. He spoke of the Press of this city being most low and demoralized, but " *of course* " in an undertone " *in confidence* " ! *Look here, ye free men!*

November 26th.—Busy with affairs of wardrobe. Letter from Gould, which made me rather uneasy; most kindly distressed at hearing I had replied to Forrest's Card. Was I to suffer myself to be torn in pieces by these ruffians upon his assertions? It seemed to me folly, and so I think all would have said afterwards. Answered Gould.

November 27th.—Letter from Bass, giving confirming evidence of my kindly treatment of this Mr. Forrest in London, and of *his acknowledgment of it.* Saw papers—another notice in the *Ledger*, speaking of "these actors depreciating one another." Ryder called about tickets. Rehearsed; saw Povey, a dreadful little donkey, who, however (as it should not have been), almost made me angry by hoping I had not put that "Notice " out, and thinking I should have treated Mr. Forrest's attempt to excite the mob against me with silent contempt! Yes! and I might have been silent from that time forth. Colden called and talked. Paid my hotel bill. Wrote a note to Reed; afterwards another. Rested a little, worn down in mind and body; rested in the rocking-chair. Acted King Lear pretty well; one person made an ebullition, as I thought, of laughter, at the end of the second act, whom I supposed to be that ignorant coxcomb that writes as " Colley Cibber." I was very angry, and looked at him in the next scene with some ironical exclamation, which was very wrong! and I believe it was a *friend* I sneered at. So much for the intemperance of anger. I am *baited* into a *petty frenzy!* Called. Colden came into my room, and Colonel Lee, who luckily did not stay. Colden read a paper very strong against Mr. Forrest's Card, but very lenient to his hissing me and his charges against me, and admitting my possible ill-treatment of him, and speaking of me as the second living actor—Mr. Forrest being the first! "Give me an ounce of civet, good apothecary, to sweeten my imagination," poisoned with the fœtor of this disgusting country! Colden walked home with me. Read the *Boston Atlas,* which in the expected great defence it was to make of me (pocketing up dear George Curtis's manly assertion of my claims and character), "is of opinion that Mr. Forrest has been hasty in his accusation of me!!! and entertaining the belief that my forthcoming evidence will show that Mr. Forrest has been *in error* (in error!!) and Mr. Macready unjustly assailed!!!" And *this* is high moral tone—the lofty indignation of the refined Massachusetts on a scheme of villainy as atrocious in its means as it is paltry and mercenary in its object! This is a powerful country, but its standard of morality is as low as that of its taste—and can thought descend deeper?

November 29th.—My thoughts distressed and kept still on this disgusting affair, in which my friends appear to *exult,* because a ruffian and unprincipled wretch has *by a blunder* brought himself within the contempt of the intelligent, and into general odium. I do not care for the unscrupulous miscreant. But I do care that I should be supposed to have had *squabbles* with such a low and vulgar wretch. Mr. Reed called. Thought *the Card* a libel, was glad to take Meredith as his associate and would see him on the subject. Rehearsed, and was very unwell. I find the bile has been accumulating. Received slip from the *Literary World*—most gentlemanly and satisfactory comment on the disgusting affair. Read two articles in the *Pennsylvanian* —one by that stupid coxcomb, the brush-maker, who signs himself "Colley Cibber," the other said to be by Judge—(oh! America, your Judges!)—Conrad, both most unprincipled in their attempt to excite the national feeling of the low caste, and stupid and illogical as base and false.

December 1st.—Papers, with a most offensive notice in the *Ledger,* mixing up that ruffian and myself, and suggesting "the street, the field, the town-court or the newspapers" as the best arenas for our squabblings or fights! And Curtis and Felton wish me to live in a country with such blackguards—Judge Conrad—this fellow, Bradley of the *Mail,* Gordon Bennett, N. P. Willis, etc. No.

December 2nd.—Acted Hamlet with care and energy; took especial pains to make the meaning of "*I must be idle*" clear, which was followed by cheers on cheers after the first applause, when it was understood by the house that this was Mr. Forrest's "*fancy dance.*" Oh, fie, fie! The play went off triumphantly. Was called, and enthusiastically received. I said, "Ladies and Gentlemen. My words to you shall be very few, for to whatever length I might extend them, they would fail to satisfy me in conveying to you the deeply grateful sense I entertain of the liberal support you have afforded me. The remembrance of my visit here will always be accompanied with the ready testimony of my gratitude for the truly noble and generous earnestness with which you have defended me, a stranger, from the grossest outrage, the grossest injustice. I have spoken and written of it as I shall ever do, with admiration and fervent thankfulness. I regret I cannot embody in more expressive language all I feel, but the attempt is vain; I must therefore only again and again thank you, in taking my respectful leave of you." The reception of this short address was all I could desire, and the impression left on the Philadelphian audience seems what I could most have wished.

To Baltimore, December 9th.—Set out on my journey to Baltimore. At James's Hotel, where I dined, the landlord introduced me to *Professor* (!) *Risley*—the balancer and posture-master; *of course* I shook hands with him, etc.!

December 12th.—A Mr. Bristow, a most impertinent fellow, a writing-master, English, came in, and introduced himself, as if he had been a person of importance; a vulgar, impertinent fellow.

December 21st.—Charles Buller is dead. I held him in great regard, and had a very high opinion of his talent and of his political honesty. He liked me, I am sure. Another friend, for such I am sure he would have proved himself to me, is struck away—the lesson of dying is being taught to me very earnestly. "The friends of my youth, where are they?"

Washington, December 31st.—A year of awful, stirring, fearful and afflicting events is this day brought to a close. Many friends, some most dear, and one among the very dearest, have been taken from earth, and I have been taught to feel the truth of my own mortality. The income granted to me has been very great, but the expense of the year has been great in proportion, and I have not added so large an amount to my capital as I could have wished. For all, however, I am most thankful, most grateful, O God, and bow down my heart in earnest and devout acknowledgment of Thy mercy to me.

Richmond, January 4th.—Left Richmond with a most delightful recollection of all attaching to it. *Vivent !* Thought much through the day and night on life, the dream it is. For the first time I saw in the glass to-day that I really am an old man. My mind does not feel old; and it is with a sort of wonder mixed with melancholy heart-regret that I see almost all those endeared to me by boyish affection and associated with the memories of my youth, lost to me. But I do not mistake the warning; I am fully aware of my mortality, and though I would not wish to die here, nor without seeing my beloved ones again, nor, indeed, until I had done all I really should have the power of doing to actually advance them, yet still I am not disposed to murmur whenever God may send the dark angel for my spirit; the violent deaths of this land I would avoid, but to die as my dear brother did, or dear and revered Jonathan Birch, either would be a happy quittance, after beholding my blessed ones on a promising course of active life.

> "Life ! we've been long together
> Through pleasant and through cloudy weather ;
> 'Tis hard to part when friends are dear ;
> Perhaps 'twill cost a sigh, a tear ;
> Then steal away, give little warning,
> Choose thine own time ;
> Say not 'Good-night,' but in some brighter clime
> Bid me 'Good-morning.' " [1]

January 15th.—Looked at paper, in which it is observed that " some people think the Hamlet of Vandenhoff senior superior to Macready's." What ignorant and what conceited dunces in literature and art these people are ! It is the fact ! Rehearsed. Oh, the company !

January 17th.—Read, to my astonishment—*i. e.* from not having before seen it—about ten lines of Mr. N. P. Willis in absolute *applause*

---

[1] These beautiful lines of Mrs. Barbauld's were spoken by the Rev. James Fleming (his friend, and one of his executors), who officiated at Macready's interment at Kensal Green, in the course of the touching and eloquent address he delivered at the conclusion of the funeral service over the coffin, as it descended from the chapel to the vaults below. He well knew Macready's fondness for them (*note by Sir F. Pollock*).

of *Mr. Forrest and his Card,*[1] in the *Home Journal.*   No mistake about
it.   Rested, assailed by the flies.   Acted Werner, taking all the pains
I could *against* a set of incapables enough to drown a navy.

January 31st.—Read, whilst waiting for Mr. Ryder, more of

[1] Dickens reters to the "Card" in the following letter—

"*Devonshire Terrace,*
"*Friday, February* 2, *1849.*

"MY DEAR MACREADY,

"Is it true that you gave our illustrious countryman, Mr. Forrest, £5000 to per-
petrate his published card?   I think it was very little, do you know?   It certainly was worth
£10,000 to you and I question whether £20,000 would have compensated him for eating
such a wagonload of dirt.   And so you begin to think there is something a leetle rotten in the
state of Denmark?   Ha!   I say no more.   I dined the other day with Ainsworth at the
Garrick, where I was talking before dinner with Fladgate, Dance, Wallack, etc.   It really was
wholesome and good to hear the genuine disgust and indignation that prevail in respect
of our distinguished feller-citizen.   There was nothing feigned or got up in it.   It was a comfortable, palatable, plain outpouring of divers full vessels of wrath that quite refreshed my
ears.   I have been reading the Queen's Speech this morning and the debate thereupon, and,
as a similar refreshment to myself after that awful and most frightful humbug, sit down to
write to you.   Oh! that I had the wings of a dove, and could flee (with a select circle)
to some pleasant climate where there are no royal speeches and no professed politicians.
Heavens and earth! to read the circumcized dog, Disraeli, a-propos of War and Cobden!

"You have heard perhaps how that I now stand seised and possessed of six sons and two
daughters, You! old Parr! *You!!!* Sir I am the original.   There was never was such an
old man as I consider myself to be.   You will find me very grey; my hat a world too wide
for my shrunk locks; I am quite a heavy father and think of going in, in future, for the blessing business—not the 'damme, you dog, you shall marry her!' line—that's too light—but
the 'bless thee, my child!' to slow music.

"Kate is wonderfully well eating mutton chops in the drawing-room and sends you her
dear love.   The boy is what the Persian princes might have called a moon-faced monster.

"A very curious pamphlet has been published by Barber, the solicitor who was transported
for life in the famous Miss Slack case.   You remember a whole party of men and women
being elaborately got up to represent an executrix and her friends at the Bank of England
and drawing out three or four thousand pounds of unclaimed stock.   There has since arisen
a strong presumption—one may almost say, certain proof, of Barber's innocence, and after two
years of Norfolk Island, he has been pardoned.   He now republishes his case with all the
documents that have since come into existence.   It is a tremendous illustration of the inefficiency of lords and gentlemen as Home Secretaries: of the manner in which they may receive
memorials from innocent men in the agony of supposed guilt and endurance of frightful
punishment, put them away in drawers and never so much as read them, and of the
indispensable necessity there is for a public and solemn Court of Appeal in all criminal cases.
I was going to tell you, but I should want a sheet for it, how Mrs. Macready and I *did*
dance on Twelfth Night.   We had no party here but we had a cosy little knot of us old
patriarchs to look at the children, and then we supped together (we old ones) and talked of
the days of our youth and the fashions of that remote period.   We then dashed into Sir Roger
de Coverley—then into a reel, for two mortal hours, false Parr, your great original and your
wife danced without ceasing—breathing Willy, prostrating Nina, reducing to 'tarnel smash'
(as we say in our country) all the other couples, one by one.   With shame and grief, I own,
that at last I—*I* gave in, when she was fresh and active still.

Vanity Fair, which is, I must confess, an extremely clever book, and, as far as style goes, I think, rather to be preferred to my friend Dickens's. There is more mark of the educated man in the freedom of the language. I do not think it painful; it is sometimes pathetic, but in that respect how far below dear Dickens!

February 1st.—I had a very absorbing subject—*Vanity Fair*—a very extraordinary and wise book; most entertaining; to me, who will think, and feel, and look truth in the face, most instructive. I had not given Thackeray credit for so much power. I had not done him justice, but I think this book places him in the very first rank of English novelists.

Griffin, February 2nd.—Resumed the reading of that delightful book, *Vanity Fair*. It has surprised and *conquered me*.

Montgomery, February 3rd.—Finished, with great reluctance, *Vanity Fair*. The story hangs a little after the death of Osborne; and the tour on the Continent, I think, might have been spared with advantage. Dobbin's return to Ostend is very good, as is his going away; but Becky is, to say the least, quite enough on the scene, and Jos is rather a bore; the Pumpernickel set are stupid. But the book is an extraordinarily clever one, and, differing in its kind, is second to none of the present day, which is an admission I make almost grudgingly for Dickens's sake; but the truth is the truth.

February 19th.—Acted Virginius; miserably cut up by almost all parties, but an old, ugly, and very affected Virginia is in itself such utter damnation of the play that I need not enumerate the attendant imps on this monstrous piece of diabolism.

"The little deformed child of my poor sister is (happily) just dead, and Burnett brings the little coffin up to-day to lay it in her grave at Highgate. God knows that it is good and kind it should be so, but it is difficult to fill him with that knowledge yet, poor fellow! I meant to have written you such a letter, so amusing, so pathetic, so full of news, I must try again. Better luck next time. You will like to know how our friends are: Forster, Whiggish, of necessity, but writhing under the writer's Radical onslaught; Rogers sour; H. Smith, quite white all over for want of a little wine; Kenyon smooth, oily, beaming and slippery (he is my particular friend and I dine with him to-day!); Mrs. Brockedon dining out in immense black velvet hats which servants crush in putting dishes on and blind themselves behind; Bancroft, ditto, as to dining, with his head like a blacking brush outside but good stuff within; Lord Lansdowne gouty and solemn; D'Orsay looking, as I take it, towards France; Maclise invisible; Stanfield rubicund and jovial, but extremely papal; Mrs. Stanfield cold and fishy; Dickens revolving new books in his mind and walking perpetually; Georgy and all the children sending loves innumerable; all wishing you back, and getting ready to greet you with open arms. None more so, my dearest Macready, than your

"Ever Affectionate

"C. D."

February 24th.—Ryder came to inform me of the receipts. He told me of the fulsome praises of the English papers of Mr. C. Kean's Shylock, which was greeted with the universal hiss of the audience a few years since—but acting it at Windsor—oh, Art!

March 3rd.—Kept my birthday (*æt.* fifty-six) in sympathy with the dear ones at home, and drank their healths in a small glass of hock, full to "the highest top-sparkle." God bless them. Acted Henry IV, Joseph Surface, very fairly.

March 6th.—Wrote a few lines to my beloved Catherine, an occupation that takes me out of this *odious country*—let me speak the truth! —where taste, and high feeling, and the spirit of a gentleman are understood and appreciated only by the *very, very few*—the helpless minority. Let me die in a *ditch* in England, rather than in the Fifth Avenue of New York here—and *no mistake!* But let me not in this be ungrateful to *those few* whom I affectionately regard, and whose memory will be ever, ever dear to me; but *they are not the country—they are the exceptions to it.* Rehearsed—oh, what a fatiguing, wearing business! *knowing* well that certain *brutes* would not make any alteration, *except for the worse,* in their stupidity; *and so it proved!*

March 7th.—Acted Cardinal Richelieu; not to my satisfaction, being greatly disconcerted by—what?—Ha! upon how small a thing the success of an actor's perfect identification depends—upon my beard being loose, and torturing me for four acts with the fear of its dropping off!!

March 9th.—Received three *Examiners* from England. I see it has become a *Whig paper.* I see, besides, that my friend Forster has allowed six or eight weeks to pass over without keeping my name before the public. "Is that the act of a friend, Mortimer?" as the fellow asked when another kicked him *a tergo.*

March 10th.—Acted Hamlet (with an out-wearied body, but a mind and heart determined to *win or die*) in a most superior manner, in one of my *happiest* moods, though sorely tried by physical debility, but the *spirit* was *indomitable.* Called. Went forward, and addressed the crowded audience, who had purchased their seats by *their own suggestion at auction.*

March 11th.—Arranged my week's account. Now if I die, I leave my family £20,000, besides my furniture, plate, prints, etc. Thank God! thank God! thank God!

Cincinnati, April 2nd.—Went to rehearsal. Found a most disgracefully imperfect Horatio, who had rehearsed on Saturday and now knew nothing of words or business, one of those wretches who take to the stage as an escape from labour, and for whom the treadmill would be a fitting punishment. Rested. Acted Hamlet to a rather rickety audience, but I tried my utmost, and engaged the attention of at least the greater part of the auditory. In the scene after the play with Rosencrantz and Guildenstern an occurrence took place that, for disgusting brutality, indecent outrage, and malevolent barbarism, must be without parallel in the theatre of any civilized community. Whilst speaking to them about " the pipe," a ruffian from the left side gallery threw into the middle of the stage the half of the raw carcase of a sheep! Of course, there is no commenting on such sheer brutality. The audience were, of course, indignant, and when I came on in the closet scene, quite stopped the play with their prolonged and vehement applause. I felt for them; and I feel for humanity in the degrading circumstance. Was called and went on and, bowing, came off.

April 5th.—Acted Macbeth in very good style—acted for myself, not to please these barbarians, several of whom were laughing at certain passages of the dagger and murder scenes, but at last became " hushed in grim repose." The *canaille*—the brutes! Was called and very fervently, but would not go on. I really despise my audience, and dislike them too.

April 7th.—Acted Werner as well as a very imperfect Josephine, still more imperfect Idenstein, and general inattention would let me. After the play I sent for the stage-manager, who was not in the theatre! At length he came, and I told him I would not repeat this play, as it was so very imperfect. He said that he was perfect to the letter except in one speech, and that I put him out by giving him the word! I looked at him with astonishment and indignation, and said, " Sir, I will not contradict you, but do you mean to say you were perfect in the part?" "Yes, sir, I do, except in one speech"!!! I observed, the prompter must know. He wished the prompter to be called, who came, and, as usual, shuffled; but at last said he was " imperfect." The man then became very insolent; he was evidently drunk, from his appearance, and grew quite blackguard. He left my room and went about outside, talking about what he would not do and do. He then put his head in and said, " Mr. Macready, if you ever give me the word on the stage again I will take a club to you." I said, " Get out, you ——." He was storming a little to himself, and went off.

April 9th.—Letter from Gould, expatiating upon the *Humbug*, as I knew it to be, of Mrs. Butler's reading. Oh, this most gullible of all publics! He tells me, as I read in the New Orleans papers' correspondence, it was *very bad*, and no mistake. Yet the fools "of *fashion*,"—as they called themselves—went to the amount of $8000. *So much the better for her!* She is one of the *lucky ones!* I say— *poor Pierce!!!*

April 11th.—Especially disgusted by a reference to a New York paper, which discusses the *possibility* of certain friends of mine and this blackguard Forrest making the occasion of my appearance a signal for conflict! Are not the vulgar wretches, the stupid, unprincipled dolts of this country, enough to drive a wise man mad? I am sure my patience has been tried—at least, so far that I can no longer attempt to carry on the work of reasoning *for them* and extending charity to their foolish doings. There are gentlemen—high-minded, high-hearted, cultivated gentlemen—in the country, but it is a *land of blackguards*. I cannot wonder at Dickens's *aversion*—with me it becomes *loathing !* Anonymous letter (signed *Thespis*) from one of the players in the theatre, asking for my autograph, and very respectfully and in a kind spirit expostulating with me on what he evidently conceives my harshness to the players in general. I was pleased with the feeling and tone of the letter. Rehearsed. Walked in the streets with Mr. Ryder, looking for James's shop. We went into three or four book-shops, and I was struck with the coarse, rude manner in which, in all of them, the persons there answered our civil questions. *They are a coarse people and no mistake*—a disagreeable people. Purchased some little prints of Cincinnati, and the shopkeeper gave them and took my money almost as if I was affronting him. The underbred curs!

April 12th.—Ryder told me of the *New York Herald* having my whole *speech*—with the observation, editorial, that it was given to do justice to both parties (!!!), having given Mr. Forrest's letter the other day; that Mr. Forrest's friends were to hiss me, and my friends to hiss Mr. Forrest. "*Go it, my chickens*," was the end of the article!

April 13th.—Telegraph from Gould, informing me of Mr. Forrest being engaged at the Broadway, opening on 23rd. So that it is now apparent all this villainous proceeding on his part has been to get up an excitement in the hope it will draw money to him!!! *My God !*

April 14th.—An envelope enclosing a most blackguard attack on me for my speech from the *Nation* newspaper—full of falsehood. I rejoice in having these rascally Irishmen opposed to me—the produce of the "base posterior of the world."

421

Louisville, April 21st.—Looked at papers. Saw a rumour from England of Stanley [1] being Premier!!! Oh, humanity! Oh, Englishmen!

New York, April 28th.—Dined with the Coldens. Went with them afterwards to Mrs. Butler's Reading of *King Henry VIII*, which was *too bad—I could not stay.* So D'Orsay, the kind-hearted, the elegant, the refined, "the glass of fashion and the mould of form," has left England! Alas! alas! *Another friendship lost!* [2]

April 30th.—Read paper in which Mr. Forrest's "repudiation" of his wife without cause assigned, and with the admission of her unimpeached character, and having borne him four children, is stated merely in its naked fact, and in terms much more complimentary to him than otherwise. The tenderness of the American Press towards that scoundrel is an uncontradictable evidence of its rascality and baseness.

May 1st.—Gould called, then Ryder. An anonymous note in disguised hand, recommending me to send a challenge to Mr. Forrest for his letter No. 1—to go and fight in Canada, assuring me he would not have the courage to go!!! Oh, clever gentleman! Colden called; said all agreed how bad Mrs. Butler was on Saturday. She was indeed.

May 2nd.—Looked at paper—*New York Herald. One is as good as another!* An article headed with that disgusting beginning, *Forrest and Macready.* It is really too bad. In it this Bennett turns his dislike to Forrest and his vulgar aversion to me into a concentrated spite against *Wikoff*, charging on him all this Forrest's villainy, and strongly recommending the intermediation of friends to make up this "difference" (!!!) between us! Is it thus these wretches contemplate such open violation of truth, honesty, and every bond that claims respect!

May 7th.—Rehearsed with much care. Looked at some papers (N.Y.) sent to me. Received note from Silliman, which I answered. Rested. Went to theatre, dressed. My hairdresser told me there

---

[1] Lord Stanley did not become Premier till 1852, when (as the Earl of Derby) he formed his first administration.

[2] D'Orsay's financial embarrassments, which had long been accumulating, made further residence in England impossible, and he was soon joined in Paris by Lady Blessington, who had also become hopelessly involved. Considering Macready's austere morality, his feeling for D'Orsay was singularly lenient, for, whatever the Count's fascinations, he had very little principle, while his treatment of his beautiful wife, Lady Blessington's step-daughter, was heartless in the extreme. To Lady Blessington, too, Macready displayed an exceptional degree of charity, considering her notorious relations with D'Orsay.

would be a good house, for there was—an unusual sight—a great crowd outside. My call came; I had heard immense applause and three cheers for Mr. Clarke in Macduff. I smiled and said to myself, "They mistake him for me." I went on—the greatest applause, as it seemed, from the whole house. I bowed respectfully, repeatedly. It still kept on. I bowed as it were emphatically (to coin an expression for a bow), rather significantly that I was touched by such a demonstration; it continued. I thought, "This is becoming too much." It did not cease, and I began to distinguish howlings from the right corner of the parquette. Still, I thought, it is only like the Western shriek—a climax of their applause. At length I became sensible there was opposition, and that the prolongation of the applause was the struggle against it; I then waited for its subsidence, but no cessation; I at last walked forward to address them, intending to say—"I felt pain and shame, which the intelligent and respectable must feel for their country's reputation, and that I would instantly resign my engagement rather than encounter such disgraceful conduct." They would not let me speak. They hung out placards—"You have been proved a liar," etc.; flung a rotten egg close to me. I pointed it to the audience and smiled with contempt, persisting in my endeavour to be heard. I could not have been less than a quarter of an hour on the stage altogether, with perfect sang-froid and good-humour, reposing in the consciousness of my own truth. At last there was nothing for it, and I said "Go on," and the play, *Macbeth*, proceeded in dumb show, I hurrying the players on. Copper cents were thrown, some struck me, four or five eggs, a great many apples, nearly—if not quite—a peck of potatoes, lemons, pieces of wood, a bottle of asafœtida which splashed my own dress, smelling, of course, most horribly. The first act, at least in my scenes, with these accompaniments, passed in dumb show; I looking directly at these men as they committed these outrages, and no way moved by them. Behind the scenes some attempted to exhibit sympathy, which I received very loftily, observing, "My concern was for the disgrace such people inflicted on the character of the country." The second act closed exactly in the same way. I dressed for the third and went on; the tumult the same, the missiles growing thicker. At last a chair was thrown from the gallery on the stage, something heavy was thrown into the orchestra (a chair) which made the remaining musicians move out. Another chair was hurled by the same man, whom I saw deliberately throw it, then wrench up another, and throw it too—I bowed to the audience, and going up to Mr. Chippendale, observed

423

that I thought "I had quite fulfilled my obligation to Messrs. Niblo and Hackett, and that I should now remain no longer." I accordingly went down and undressed; Colden was there and seemed to apprehend danger out of doors; I did not. However, I took my dirk, but thinking it unworthy to carry it, threw it down again. Colden (who made too much of it), Tallmadge, and Emmett walked home with me; there was no sign of any attempt in the back street, but there was a crowd at the front door, which Colden had not been able to penetrate, and which, the Chief of the Police informed me afterwards, made the strongest efforts to break into the house. Colden was with me and Ruggleston came and joined us. I was in the best spirits, and we talked over what was to be done. Several things proposed, rejected, and certain things decided on, but so hastily that when they were gone I perceived the course was yet to be fixed on. A Mr. Bennett— stranger—came, as he said, from young Astor and other names of the first, he said, to say that this should be resisted, and to convey to me the expression of their regret, etc. I was not quite sure of my man. Gould came, when they were gone, in great distress, having heard all from Duyckirck. Our conversation overturned the decision with Ruggles and Colden. He gone, Mr. Monnitt, my landlord, and one of the heads of the police called, to show me a deposition taken from one of the rioters who had been captured, and who, because he cried very much, was set at liberty. I asked leave to copy the deposition and I am about to do it, and I suppose shall have a long night's writing. And this is my treatment! Being left alone, I begin to feel more seriously the indignities put on me, and entertain ideas of not going on the stage again. Pray God I may do what is right. I will try to do so. I thank His goodness that I am safe and unharmed. Wrote to dearest Catherine.

May 10th.—I went, gaily, I may say, to the theatre, and on my way, looking down Astor Place, saw one of the Harlem cars on the railroad stop and discharge a full load of policemen; there seemed to be others at the door of the theatre. I observed to myself, "This is good precaution." I went to my dressing-room, and proceeded with the evening's business. The hairdresser was very late and my equanimity was disturbed. I was ruffled and nervous from fear of being late, but soon composed myself. The managers were delaying the beginning, and I was unwilling to be behind the exact hour. The play began; there was some applause to Mr. Clarke (I write of what I could hear in my room below). I was called, and at my cue went on

424

with full assurance, confidence, and cheerfulness. My reception was very enthusiastic, but I soon discovered that there was opposition, though less numerously manned than on Monday. I went right on when I found that it would not instantly be quelled, looking at the wretched creatures in the parquette, who shook their fists violently at me, and called out to me in savage fury. I laughed at them, pointing them out with my truncheon to the police, who, I feared, were about to repeat the inertness of the previous evening. A black board with white letters was leaned against the side of the proscenium: "*The friends of order will remain silent.*" This had some effect in making the rioters more conspicuous. My first, second, third scenes passed over rapidly and unheard; at the end of the fourth one of the officers gave a signal, the police rushed in at the two sides of the parquette, closed in upon the scoundrels occupying the centre seats and furiously vociferating and gesticulating, and seemed to lift them or bundle them in a body out of the centre of the house, amid the cheers of the audience. I was in the act of making my exit with Lady Macbeth, and stopped to witness this clever manœuvre, which, like a *coup de main*, swept the place clear at once. As well as I can remember the bombardment outside now began. Stones were hurled against the windows in Eighth Street, smashing many; the work of destruction became then more systematic; the volleys of stones flew without inter-mission, battering and smashing all before them; the Gallery and Upper Gallery still kept up the din within, aided by the crashing of glass and boarding without. The second act passed, the noise and violence without increasing, the contest within becoming feebler. Mr. Povey, as I was going to my raised seat in the banquet scene, came up to me and, in an undertone and much frightened, urged me to cut out some part of the play and bring it to a close. I turned round upon him very sharply, and said that "I had consented to do this thing—to place myself here, and whatever the consequence I must go through with it—it must be done; that I could not cut out. The audience had paid for so much, and the law compelled me to give it; they would have cause for riot if all were not properly done." I was angry, and spoke very sharply to the above effect. The banquet scene was partially heard and applauded. I went down to change my dress, the battering at the building, doors, and windows growing, like the fiends at the Old Woman of Berkely's burial, louder and louder. Water was running down fast from the ceiling to the floor of my room and making a pool there. I inquired; the stones hurled in had broken some of the pipes.

425

The fourth act passed; louder and more fierce waxed the furious noises against the building and from without; for whenever a missile did effectual mischief in its discharge it was hailed with shouts outside; stones came in through the windows, and one struck the chandelier; the audience removed for protection behind the walls; the house was considerably thinned, gaps of unoccupied seats appearing in the audience part.   The fifth act was heard, and in the very spirit of resistance I flung my whole soul into every word I uttered, acting my very best and exciting the audience to a sympathy even with the glowing words of fiction, whilst these dreadful deeds of real crime and outrage were roaring at intervals in our ears and rising to madness all round us. The death of Macbeth was loudly cheered, and on being lifted up and told that I was called, I went on, and, with action earnestly and most emphatically expressive of my sympathy with them and my feelings of gratefulness to them, I quitted the New York stage amid the acclamations of those before me.   Going to my room I began without loss of time to undress, but with no feeling of fear or apprehension.   When washed and half dressed, persons came into my room—consternation on the faces of some; fear, anxiety, and distress on those of others. "The mob were getting stronger; why were not the military sent for?"   "They were here."   "Where?   Why did they not act?"   "They were not here; they were drawn up in the Bowery."   "Of what use were they there?"   Other arrivals.   "The military had come upon the ground."   "Why did they not disperse the mob then?"   These questions and answers, with many others, were passed to and fro among the persons round me whilst I was finishing my hasty toilet, I occasionally putting in a question or remark.   Suddenly we heard a volley of musketry: "Hark! what's that?" I asked.   "The soldiers have fired."   "My God!" I exclaimed.   Another volley, and another!   The question among those surrounding me (there were, that I remember, Ruggles, Judge Kent, D. Colden, R. Emmett, a friend of his in some official station, Fry, Sefton, Chippendale, and I think the performer who played Malcolm, etc.) was, which way was I to go out?   News came that several were killed; I was really insensible to the degree of danger in which I stood, and saw at once—there being no avoidance—there was nothing for it but to meet the worst with dignity, and so I stood prepared.   They sent some one to reconnoitre, and urged the necessity of a change in my appearance.   I was confident that people did not know my person, and repeated this belief.   They overbore all objections, and took the drab surtout of the performer of

Malcolm, he taking my black one; they insisted, too, that I must not wear my hat; I said, "Very well; lend me a cap." Mr. Sefton gave me his, which was cut all up the back to go upon my head. Thus equipped I went out, following Robert Emmett to the stage door; here we were stopped, not being allowed to pass. The "friend" was to follow us as a sort of *aide*, but we soon lost him. We crossed the stage, descended into the orchestra, got over into the parquette, and passing into the centre passage went along with the thin stream of the audience moving out. We went right on, down the flight of stairs and out of the door into Eighth Street. All was clear in front—kept so by two cordons or lines of police at either end of the building stretched right across. We passed the line near Broadway, and went on threading the excited crowd, twice or three times muttering in Emmett's ear, "You are walking too fast." We crossed Broadway, still through a scattered crowd, and walked on along Clinton Place till we passed the street leading down to the New York Hotel. I then said, "Are you going to your own house?" "Yes." We reached it, and having opened the door with a latch-key, closing it after us, he said, "You are safe here; no one will know anything about you; you shall have a bed in ten minutes or a quarter of an hour, and you may depend upon all in this house." I sat down in the drawing-room, talking of the facts about us, and wondering at myself and my condition, secretly preparing myself for the worst result, viz., falling into the hands of those sanguinary ruffians. A son of Emmett's was there, Robert; in about a quarter of an hour Colden came in. Several men had been killed, how many not certainly known yet. "You must leave the city at once; you must not stay here!" It was then a consultation between these excellent friends, I putting in an occasional opinion objecting or suggesting upon the safest course to pursue. At length it was decided, and Robert was sent out to find Richard, another son, probably at the Racket Club, to put the plan in execution. He was met by Robert in the street, and both returned with additional reports; the crowd was still there, the excitement still active. Richard was sent to the livery stable to order a carriage and good pair of horses to be at Emmett's door at four o'clock in the morning, "to take a doctor to some gentleman's house near New Rochelle." This was done and well done by him; Colden and Emmett went out to reconnoitre, and they had, as I learned from Emmett, gone to the New York hotel, at the door of which was still a knot of watchers, and to Emmett's inquiries told him, if any threats were made, to allow a committee of the crowd to enter

427

and search the house for me. Emmett returned with my own hat, one from the hotel, and I had got Colden's coat. An omnibus drove furiously down the street, followed by a shouting crowd. We asked Richard, when he came in, what it was; he said, "Merely an omnibus," but next morning he told me that he asked the men pursuing, "What was the matter?" and one answered, "Macready's in that omnibus; they've killed twenty of us, and by G—— we'll kill him!" Well, all was settled; it was believed that twenty had perished. Robert went to bed to his wife. Emmett went up-stairs to lie down, which I declined to do, and with Richard went down into the comfortable office below before a good fire and, by the help of a cigar, to count the slow hours till four o'clock. We talked and he dozed, and I listened to the sounds of the night, and thought of home, and what would be the anguish of hearts there if I fell in this brutal outbreak; but I resolved to do what was right and becoming. The clock struck four; we were on the move; Emmett came down; sent Richard to look after the carriage. All was still in the dawn of morning, but we waited some ten minutes—an age of suspense—the carriage arrived. I shook the hand of my preserver and friend—my heart responded to my parting prayer of "God bless him"—and stepping into the carriage, a covered phæton, we turned up Fifth Avenue, and were on our way to safety. Thank God. During some of the time of waiting I had felt depressed and rather low, but I believe I showed no fear, and felt determined to do my duty, whatever it might be, acting or suffering. We met only market carts, butchers' or gardeners', and labourers going to their early work; the morning was clear and fresh, and the air was cooling to my forehead, hot and aching with want of sleep. The scenery through which we passed, crossing the Manhattan, giving views of the various inlets of the sound, diversified with gentlemen's seats, at any other time would have excited an interest in me, now one's thought or series of thoughts, with wanderings to home and my beloved ones, gave me no time for passing objects. I thought as we passed Harlem Station, it would never have done to have ventured there. Some of the places on the road were familiar to my recollection, having been known under happier circumstances.[1]

May 15th.—Read the telegraphic verdict on the killed: "*That the deceased persons came to their deaths by gun-shot wounds, the*

[1] In the following month of September ten of the Astor Place rioters were tried at the Court of General Sessions, New York, before Judge Daly and a jury, and after a trial of fifteen days were all convicted. The sentences varied from one month's imprisonment to imprisonment for one year and payment of a fine of $250—(*note by Sir F. Pollock*).

guns being fired by the military, by order of the civil authorities of New York, and that the authorities were justified, under the existing circumstances, in ordering the military to fire upon the mob; and we further believe that if a larger number of policemen had been ordered out, the necessity of a resort to the use of the military might have been avoided."

London, June 9th.—Letters from Miss Martineau, who wishes to consider the recent occurrences in America as "all nonsense." She was under the delusion, when there, that the people in the Slave States would have lynched her if they could have caught her, and people laughed at her very much for her credulity on the subject. She did not think *that* nonsense, but this touches another, and reflects upon the conduct of the American people! Ergo—nonsense!

June 19th.—Received a note from Colonel Phipps—I presume on some business from the Queen, to which I must submit. Answered him, saying I was just going out of town, but would attend him on the morrow, or Friday.

June 22nd.—Proceeded to Palace. Colonel Phipps came to the room to which I was shown, apologizing that the Prince was then in his own. Told me that he was instructed to inform me that the Queen wished to have theatrical performances at Windsor this Christmas as before, and wished me to act Brutus and Hotspur. I stated my readiness to show my duty to Her Majesty, and that her wishes were commands to me; that I was in the habit of acting Brutus, but that I had long discontinued the performance of Hotspur, not intending to resume it; that I should have to restudy the character—unfitted by years to personate it, etc., intimating that, if I played two nights, it must be in some other character. All most courteously. I urged the necessity of knowing the time as soon as possible, on account of my engagements, etc. He was to write to me, and we parted with the best understanding.

June 23rd.—Wrote an answer to Colonel Phipps, fixing Thursday, December 27th, as the night for my performance at the Castle—eheu!!

Birmingham, June 26th.—Delighted—constantly did the thought, the sense of *delight* recur to me—to find myself in *England*, to find myself under the security of law and order, and free from the brutal and beastly savages who sought my life in the United States. Thank God! Rested. Thought much of my character of the night. Acted Macbeth—yes, *well*. The audience, the Birmingham audience, gave me a reception such as I have never witnessed out of London, and

429

very, very rarely even there. They stood up all through the house, waving hats and handkerchiefs, till I was anxious to proceed. I thought to myself : " Will I not act for you ! " The stillness—the rigid stillness that followed—every word ringing on the ear—was really awful, but I felt it was my last night of Macbeth in Birmingham, and I resolved to *do my best. I did.* The applause was fervent, the attention deep, and the reception, when I was called on, equal to the first appearance. And the conceited prigs of America talk of the education of their *masses*—the dancing of bears ! They are *brutes and savages* compared with the galleries of our manufacturing towns.

June 28th.—Looked at papers. Saw at a grand dinner given by the Mayor to Sir R. Peel, Bancroft's health was drunk, and in reply he assured them that all Englishmen would be heartily welcomed in visiting America. Query—with asafœtida, or raw mutton ?

Liverpool, July 3rd.—Letter from Gould, with an extract from a paper containing a *circular* from some friends of Forrest (query— Forrest himself ?) to the players of America, asking of them evidence of my ill-usage of them and my *falsehood* (!), intending to publish a pamphlet against me ! What miserably stolid wretches, and what a country, where such things can be done ! ! !

July 4th.—Read *Times.* Very much pleased with a speech of Fox's on Reform ; equally disgusted with that wretched creature—Lord John Russell's—in answer !

July 5th.—Looked at paper ; especially disgusted with the coxcomb, Lord John Manners,[1] the candidate for the City of London ! ! !

July 7th.—Looked at the *Times.* More and more disgusted with that Disraeli and the aristocrats, who take up with such a miserable creature for *interest' sake*—the chivalrous nobility ! !

July 10th.—Several New York papers sent to me by Radley, I suppose. There is no concealing the fact—it may be a great country, but it is a blackguard nation ! *The gentlemen are the exceptions;* thank God, I know many of them.

July 13th.—My blessed Joan's birthday. I did not remember, as I awoke, this sweet and painful anniversary, but when it was recalled to me, my heart blessed the cherub spirit, that now inhabits some other sphere, and let me hope—oh God, with truth !—to meet me there in another state of being !

Leeds, July 16th.—Acted Othello—taking great pains, and excit-

---

[1] The late Duke of Rutland, one of the " Young England Party," and an ardent follower of Disraeli, who depicted him in *Coningsby* as Lord Henry Sydney.

ing great spirit. The house was great and *the feeling enthusiastically English*. Oh, that those American scoundrels (I mean *only* "*the faction*" by that expression) could see the effect they have produced! Called for with great enthusiasm.

Derby to Birmingham, July 22nd.—Looked over the *Times*, which, pointing the finger at the roguery of Hudson,[1] notices also in general terms his aristocratic sycophants and abettors; but why among them does he not particularize that great Bude Light of Religion : the late Archbishop of York?[2]

Eastbourne, August 9th.—Letters. One from poor Regnier, merely informing me of the sad, sad event of his only child's death, a daughter, aged fourteen years. Most deeply did I feel for them. Wrote to Regnier. Read *Copperfield;* not quite so full of interest as the preceding numbers, but very good. Called on Cobden[3] and sat with him. In the evening read to the girls from Dryden.

August 10th.—Went with the Cobdens and our children to see the cricket-match ; I was interested in the old game. Walked with Cobden and his brother, by Paradise, home ; talked chiefly on politics.

London, August 11th.—Messrs. Webster and Manby came, shook hands with them. The matter of nights, terms, characters, etc., was talked over and settled. The eight plays for the first period given in —*Macbeth, Hamlet, King Lear, Othello, Shylock, Richelieu, Werner, Virginius.* The terms £40 per night, three nights per week, £30 every extra night ; the first period for 1st of October (if possible) to the 8th of December, if Mr. Knowles would not alter his time, for the 15th of October to 8th of December, and the second period from the 15th April to June 30th inclusive. I to take my benefit in such large theatre as I may be able to procure, having the aid of such of the Haymarket performers as I may need, I paying the nightly salary of same : the privilege of writing an order for two each night of my performance.

Eastbourne, August 12th.—Letter and bankers' book of Siddons monument. I see that neither Lord Aberdeen, Lord Ellesmere, Lord Northampton, nor Monckton Milnes, has subscribed. They are valu-

---

[1] George Hudson, the "Railway King" (see note, p. 333, Vol. II) ; in spite of the vulgarity of himself and his wife, their receptions at Albert Gate were thronged with the aristocracy from the Duke of Wellington downwards.

[2] Edward Harcourt (1757-1847), formerly Vernon ; for sixteen years Bishop of Carlisle, and for forty years Archbishop of York. A worldly prelate of the eighteenth-century school ; there are amusing glimpses of him in Harriet Lady Granville's *Correspondence*.

[3] Richard Cobden, the famous "Free Trade" advocate.

able committee-men to advance a work of art! Heard the children's hymns.

August 13th.—Wrote to Lord Lansdowne about the inscription for Siddons monument. Mrs. Cobden looked in, saying they were going away; I shall not be here when they return. Wrote to dear Letitia. Cobden called and sat for a short time; his conversation is very pleasing to me, such simple good sense. Went out with Catherine and Walter; called at the library and subscribed; posted my letters; walked with them to the seat across the cricket-field and by Paradise Lane. I enjoyed the air; the wind was very high.

August 18th.—Wrote the agreement letter to Webster, made copy of it for self and copied it out to send to him; wrote him another note to let him understand my willingness not to oppose him if he wished me to play six nights, supposing myself able to do so. Gave Walter his lesson, assisted Willie. Letter from J. Delane with a letter from a gentleman about the edition of Pope, which kind Delane had noticed in Wednesday's *Times* in the most considerate and advantageous manner. From Procter, a most delightful humorous letter; from Henry Taylor, a most wise and kind one.

Brighton, September 11th.—Looked at the *Examiner*. A long article on Browning's poetry, which, except his *Paracelsus*, I cannot think any one would read twice who had choice of any other poet.

September 12th.—This morning in the rain two elderly, coarse and lusty women passed by me, coming out of a shop. They had quite gone by, when I remembered—through the *fat* and *red* and *age*—one with whom I had once been in love, Miss Stephens, now Dowager Lady Essex, and her niece Miss Johnstone. *"So fades, so languishes."* I have been made very angry—very angry indeed this evening. The actors were extremely annoying by their incorrectness. A puppy sat in the stage box in the very corner near the stage with his back to the performance; it was all I could do to restrain myself from retorting upon his insolence.

Manchester, October 6th.—Acted Hamlet as well as I could, not well, so dreadfully put out by King, Horatio, Ghost, Polonius, etc. Called and delivered my farewell address.

London, October 8th.—Acted Macbeth. Mr. Webster staggered me about the house just before I went on, implying that it was not full; there was, however, no appearance of room anywhere. The cheering on my entrance was very great from the whole house, but it did not seem to me that wild abandonment to a delighted feeling that the audience at the Princess's showed five years ago.   It may be, and I think *is*, the difference of a *Haymarket audience*—the *stock* part is false in its habits.   I never acted better, in many parts never so well, so feelingly and so true.   I said to Mrs. Warner once, "I never played that scene so well, and yet they do not seem to feel it."   She observed, "They are not educated to it;" meaning, they have been accustomed to things so different they cannot quite appreciate it.   The play ended most enthusiastically.   Was called and greatly cheered.

October 10th.—Acted Hamlet, taking all the pains in my power. The house was good, but *not great*—not what it *was* and *would have been* at the Princess's.   I am not announced as *the* attraction of the theatre, and the public do not respond to the invitation to see me as *one of the company.*   The audience was as *flat* as the people accustomed to attend Mr. C. Kean's performances can be expected to be. I took pains—played much of Hamlet, I am sure, in my best way, but the frigidity of the house was really offensive.   I almost regret that this engagement has been made.

October 16th.—Rehearsed *King Lear* with several characters absent and several not cast!   Planché calls the Haymarket "*The Patent Self-Acting Theatre.*"

October 31st.—Received a *New York Herald* from Povey; an account of the Philadelphia riots, the proceedings of the killers, the comments of the editor of the *New York Herald.*   Thank God—thank God, I am not in that country, and that I have no longer any connection with it; it is a barbarous—yes, it is a *blackguard* country!

November 1st.—Went to the rehearsal of *Othello.*   Oh! the waste of time by these *stage-managers* as they are called!   A life frittered away in self-important displays of vacuity of mind.

November 6th.—Letter from Burn with the "lot" of papers and letters of and from myself in the Winston collection.   The collection itself is a picture of the miserable weazel creature who could give his time to such little work—scraps of calumnious anecdote, false assertions in paragraphs, adverse criticisms, and notices from Messrs. Theodore Hook—as *unprincipled* a villain as ever lived—Westmacott, Bunn, *Despatch, Sunday Times,* etc.   Letters of my own, of no importance, one from my wife (!!!) with *false statements* of her and myself by the wretched compiler, make up the stock, for which I shall give no price.

November 8th.—Looked at paper; again delighted with the speech

433

of Roebuck [1] at the Sheffield Mechanics' Institute—where good-natured Lord Carlisle, Cabinet Minister, looks almost as small by his side as Lord Mahon did at Leeds on a similar occasion a few days since.

Canterbury, November 11th.—Dearest Catherine's birthday. Left Canterbury by train at a little after six o'clock, and slept almost the whole way to London. A very rude and coarse person, a Jew, addressed me in the refreshment-room at Ashford to ask whether I " was well patronized last night." I was quite at a loss to answer the man's impertinence, but, like others, he supposes players may be spoken to by any one !

London, November 13th.—Dined with Brookfield. Met Kinglake, Hallam junior, Bentinck, Spring Rice, Lushington, Forster, Mansfield. A very agreeable day.

November 15th.—The *Times* communicated news to me this morning that was quite a shock to me. Dear, kind, splendid Etty is no more. Another gone, another and another ! What is our life's dependence ? I mourn his loss, for I had a most affectionate regard for him, and he appreciated the little that I have done with even an enthusiastic spirit of admiration. *Requiescat.* Read *Othello;* passed the early evening with the children, my dearest companions. Poor dear Etty. God bless him.

Birmingham to London, November 18th.—The carriage was in waiting for me, and took me down to Westminster. I called on the Dean,[2] met Milman again for a minute; saw Professor Wilson (Oriental—no great display), an Irishman whom I did not fancy, and a naturalist, whose name I do not recollect. We went, after slight lunch, into the Abbey with the Dean, and he actually took us over it—making an excellent Cicerone, telling many things I had not before heard, and but for *the pressure on my time* would have thoroughly gratified me. He consented to the name of Sarah Siddons being placed on the statue, I to procure an inscription in the course of five or six months, or to surrender to him the office. Met Milman in the nave, and he stated that he quite agreed with me about it.

November 20th.—Letters from those two *wretched creatures,*

---

[1] John Arthur Roebuck (1801–1879), the well-known politician, then a Radical ; in his old age a supporter of Lord Beaconsfield, by whom he was made a Privy Councillor.

[2] William Buckland (1784–1856) ; Dean of Westminster from 1845, when he succeeded Wilberforce, till his death. Eminent as a geologist ; father of Frank Buckland, the well-known naturalist.

Messrs. Samuel Warren and Charles Phillips, on his (C. P.'s) conduct in the Courvoisier case.[1]

November 22nd.—Returning from rehearsal to-day I saw a poor-looking man with four children of different ages, one in his arms, straggling after him. "Need and oppression stared within their eyes," they were on the other side of the way and I *did not like*, i. e. was ashamed to cross over to them. I said to myself, if I had met them and no one saw me, I would give them something. I went on with active combatings in my mind and was going *right on*, or rather wrongly on, with the conclusion that they had passed and that perhaps they might not be legitimate objects of charity, when the principle of *right before all* came to my aid, and forced me back. I followed them and gave the poor man something.

November 23rd.—Acted Macbeth but moderately the two first acts, but hearing that Peel was in the theatre, I played my very best in the three last. I am not sure that the audience fully appreciated me; it is the most difficult criticism to criticize acting well. Called.

November 25th.—The anniversary of the death of that sweet angel child, my darling Joan. Time brings fresh griefs and heavy cares to blunt the sharpness of the anguish with which I first felt her loss, but in my heart of heart her blessed memory is enshrined, and my prayer to God is that I may re-greet her angel spirit in another world.

November 27th.—Dined with Forster, having called and taken up Brookfield; met Rintoul, Kenyon, Procter, Kinglake, Alfred Tennyson, Thackeray. Passed a cheerful evening; brought dear old Kenyon home.

November 28th.—Acted King Lear very fairly. Called. Sent to speak to Mr. —— ; he was loth to come—at last came. I told him that I had only desired to see him to say that I had no intention of saying anything offensive or disagreeable to him on Monday night; that he came on me in a moment of business and great excitement, and that had he been the King of England I should have repelled him in like manner; had he spoken to me afterwards quietly on the subject, I should have explained to him *then* how it occurred. He is an ass, and, being a player, of course a low-bred person. Mr. Wallack, whom I addressed very civilly, was really *impertinent*, not in a way that I find I can notice now, but I shall not allow it to pass.

[1] See note, p. 65, Vol. II. Allusions to his conduct of the case had been made in connection with the Manning murder trial.

November 30th.—Acted Macbeth. Called. Mr. Wallack came, without invitation, to try over the fight, and, though he had *again* been *rude* this evening, sought occasion to clear it up. I took him upon his own words, and, having listened to him with the most profound patience, and upon that rebuked him for *interrupting me,* showed him that he had no right to take offence with me for what was not *my* fault. He made many protestations, and—humbug! Forster came in and told me that Mr. Frank Talfourd, being allowed £300 per ann. at Oxford, had run into debt—as might be judged from one article—"*Cigars £100 and odd.*" He had been plucked and in consequence the Rightful Judge had made him his Marshal at £200 per ann. *Is this disgraceful, or is it not?* [1] Is the country robbed, or is it not? Note from Westminster scholars very politely inviting me to their play. Answered. Read in bed the number of *Copperfield,* which does not interest or move me much.

London, December 2nd.—Forster called and brought the news of the Queen-Dowager's death—a person of no character—latterly harmless, except in the annual prodigious sum she received from us who labour for what we get. Johnson brought me a letter from Webster, repeating the news, and very civilly leaving to me the adjustment of my own nights. I answered him very civilly, arranging them to the best of my judgment. Occupied with affairs. In the evening, with the children. Read the *Examiner*—the judgments of the papers on Mr. Commissioner Phillips. [2]

December 3rd.—Looked at paper. Notice of the Queen-Dowager's death; praised for great amiability, but no reference to a person, who, not having probably £500 per ann. before she came here, has taken during her term of widowhood close upon one million and a quarter from the country, whilst the cries of misery and even famine have been rising up to Heaven on every side of her. She built a church or two! Queen Caroline—poor, guilty, injured wretch!— received £50,000 per annum from the country and gave back £20,000 of it! [3]

---

[1] Talfourd had been made a judge earlier in the year. As the functions of a judge's marshal are mainly social, Talfourd did nothing "disgraceful" in giving his son the post, for which undergraduate extravagance and the lack of a degree are no disqualifications. But Macready was evidently still nursing his grudge against Talfourd for his ineffectual advocacy in the Bunn case.

[2] Courvoisier's counsel. He was then a commissioner of the Insolvent Debtors' Court.

[3] This statement is hardly accurate ; she declined an increase of £20,000 a year at the instance of her advisers.

December 4th.—The Dickenses, Stanfields, Dr. Elliotson, Jerrold, Oxenford, and Forster dined with us; a cheerful day. Jerrold is delightful. Gave dear Stanfield his stick.

December 5th.—Gave certificates of their stock (purchased for £32) in the South Western Railway belonging to my sister Letitia, two shares in the South Western Railway (purchased at £32 each) belonging to my daughter Catherine F. B. Macready, to the several owners. I like money transactions to be clear and exact. My father did not act thus, and the consequence was very serious. Acted King Lear at the beginning very fairly, but not so well in the late scenes, I think; disconcerted by the very bad actors, and oh! my Cordelia *is* a—well! Called and very warmly received.

December 8th.—Acted Macbeth—the last night of my first series of performances previous to my retirement. I cannot express the gratitude of heart I feel to God for all His goodness, manifested to me in so many ways, and among others in the worldly good thus accorded to me. To Him be all praise and gratitude. Amen! Forster came into my room; spoke to him about *Cheltenham reading.* He approved. *Webster* came in to say *adieu!!!* They reported Kossuth to be in the theatre to-night—it could not be.

December 9th.—Was late in rising, and detained long and late in my room by the various matters I had to attend to there. Read very attentively Forster's *demolishing* reply to Phillips's pamphlet; a more complete exposure of a —— (one of the firm of Fitzroy Kelly,[1] Wilkins,[2] Thesiger, etc.) was never made; a very pleasant handling of that most simple-minded, high-souled creature, Mr. Samuel Warren by Fonblanque in an article headed "Warren's Whiting." Read dear Fox's speech at Oldham—very good. Forster came to dinner. Afterwards we talked about the readings—or lectures. He appears sanguine. I *feel* the change from "the well-graced actor" to the frigid lecturer!

Southampton, December 10th.—Rose very early from a night which had given me very, very little sleep. Nina's cough was very bad through the night. What may be that beloved child's fate I know not, but in my inmost heart I begin to *fear*—I fear the *wearing down* of this continual nightly cough. She has been prominent in the pictures of my future years; it is a sad and dreary thing to imagine even dimly the *possibility* of any part of my life being without

---

[1] See note, p. 392, Vol. II.

[2] A prominent advocate of the "Buzfuz" type.

her; but God is all in all. That beautiful young man, Philip Brockedon, seemed a blessing on earth that parents could not survive the loss of. He is gone! I can but pray to Almighty God to spare my children to me, and to incline me to submission to His will in whatever He wills should be my lot.

December 11th.—Letter from Wightwick, wishing me much to act again at Plymouth. I wish it *very much*—it would be pleasant to me, and, I am sure, very profitable; but I shrink from paltering with my given word: I have directed the announcement of my "last night" there, and if I tamper with the *word said*, what reliance can be placed on what I may hereafter say? I feel that I could not look back on such a doing without a sense of self-degradation. No—quod dixi, *dixi.*

Shrewsbury, December 13th.—Read my letters from Catherine, from Webster, from Colonel Phipps, and from Bulwer one of the most delightful letters I have ever received—full of *bonhomie*, humour and wit, and what, of course, gives a zest to all, an offer of a house of his close to his park either to live in or to use as a place of occasional resort. Now whether this is only the generous and friendly impulse of the moment, or whether it is a pondered thing, it is most amiable, and I cannot but feel most affectionately and gratefully to the heart that could entertain such a thought. Its practicability is another question—I mean the practicability of the acceptance of the offer. Wrote to Colonel Phipps, with copy, asserting my earnest desire to do the possible to meet her Majesty's wishes. Acted Cardinal Richelieu to a bad house—partly, but only partly, caused by the Queen-Dowager's funeral. She never did me any good—nor the country either. Read again Bulwer's letter.

December 14th.—Rehearsed—the company so bad that it was utterly useless to attempt to direct them, or to have the usual business arrangements. I must do the best I can *individually.* Henry Bloxam and Mrs. Bloxam called after rehearsal, bringing a *Simnel* cake for the children. They are most kind people. He is "*the beautiful boy*" I remember, and who still lives in Lawrence's drawing of him; time—time makes *the* revolutions. Read paper—nauseated with the hypocritical cant about the Dowager; dear woman, with her million and a quarter!

Chester, December 18th.—Acted Macbeth under slaughterous obstruction. Never was worse dealt with. The Lady, oh!—Banquo —Lennox. In fact it was wholesale murder. B——, who was complaining to me of being "a pauper" yesterday, was drunk in the Witch to-night. The cause of his being rejected at theatres is too easily accounted for. Farewell to Chester; it has always used me well, but I have known, as a boy of sixteen years of age, some bitter trials here—left in charge of a theatre, distressed for rent, and a company mutinous for long arrears of salary.

To Sherborne, December 19th.—In the course of the day looked again at the *Examiner*, read the *Chester Courant*, and yielded to the extravagance of purchasing the *Times*. Read a little in *La Princesse de Babylone* of Voltaire—worth hundreds of the writers of the present time in wit, truth, and rectitude of feeling. Hear that, Christian Bishops of London and Exeter!

December 20th.—Byron remarks upon the utter *absence of idea* in the conversation of London society. He says *Hamlet is not nature*, but that Richard (Cibber's Richard!!!) is *a man!* Oh, this fellow!

December 21st.—Looked at Moore's *Life of Byron;* it is difficult to say which is the greater coxcomb, which inspires the greatest disgust of the two—the subject or the author of the biography.

London, December 25th.—Henry Taylor called. Talked over and read me the scenes in his play, which is much improved. To my extreme astonishment he showed me, after our discussion of the several passages, the first page, in which was a dedication [1] to myself. I felt quite overcome, so grateful, so proud, I could hardly keep the tears from my eyes. Have I merited such honour from such men as Bulwer Lytton, Dickens, Henry Taylor?

December 26th.—The ball of dear Nina came on. Many of our friends were with us. My darling girl was obliged to leave the room before the company assembled. She came down late in the evening and sat for about an hour by the door. My heart was wrung to see her—beloved child. The evening passed off very cheerfully, Katie exerting herself very successfully.

December 27th.—Rose late; looked at paper. Received a note from Webster, in which he mentioned that Mr. C. Kean had stated any person to be "impertinent" who suggested the cast of any character in *Julius Cæsar*, and desired him to tell me so. My usual indignation rose to my throat, but almost *immediately* subsided. I felt the miserable creature's folly disclosing his envy: decided on

---

[1] Sir Henry Taylor's drama *A Sicilian Summer*, is thus dedicated: To W. C. Macready, to whose excellent judgment in matters of art this work is largely indebted, it is with sincere respect and regard very gratefully inscribed "—(*note by Sir F. Pollock*).

temper, temper. Went to Maclise and gave him a long sitting. Thought of the terms of the note I should return to Webster. Came home and wrote to him, retaining copy of same. Note from Webster, endeavouring to extenuate the character of the expression used by Mr. C. Kean.[1] Read the dear children the two last acts of *King*

---

[1] Charles Kean had been entrusted with the direction of the "command" performances at Windsor, which were to take place in February. Macready, to whom the appointment must have been far from pleasing, sent to Kean through Webster a request that a certain actor should be cast in *Julius Cæsar*. In addition to the message complained of by Macready, Kean sent him the following letter—

"SIR,

"I am induced to believe there must be some mistake in a communication I almost accidentally received from Mr. Webster to the effect that you had requested him to ask his brother, Mr. Frederick Webster, whether he would allow his son to act Lucius with you at the Windsor Castle performance, on February 1. As the entire management and direction of these performances are entrusted to my care, it follows as a matter of course that the casting of each play devolves on *me*. Be assured I would very willingly have endeavoured to make any arrangement that could have added to your personal convenience and comfort, had you applied to me in time, but I have now engaged the younger Mr. Cathcart to perform the part, which I understand he has done frequently. Having seen him act Silvius in *As You Like It* with more than ordinary feeling, I thought him well fitted for the boy Lucius, and took some pains to secure his services. He is engaged to come from Glasgow for the express purpose. I can only add it is a pity you did not inform me of your wishes at an earlier period.

"I am, Sir,
"Yours very obediently,
"CHARLES KEAN.

"No. 3, *Torrington Square*,
"*December* 28, 1849."

This very reasonable and temperate letter was much resented by Macready (see December 28th), who replied in terms which elicited from Kean the following dignified rejoinder—

"SIR,

"In reply to your note I beg to acquaint you that I addressed you *solely* in my ministerial capacity, as Director of the representations commanded by her Majesty at Windsor, and in discharge of the duties deputed to me by her Majesty. I will therefore venture to suggest that we should not mix up any *private* difference with this transaction. When these duties are at an end I shall be always ready to account to you for any slight which you may suppose, however erroneously, that I have passed upon you, and equally ready to guard against disrespect to myself.

"I am, Sir,
"Yours obediently,
"CHARLES KEAN.

"3, *Torrington Square*,
"*Saturday, December* 29, 1849."

This rejoinder Macready chose to interpret as "most inane and senseless bluster," but it is evident that owing to his restless jealousy of Kean he had put himself entirely in the wrong.

440

MRS. SIDDONS

From an engraving by C. Turner of a painting by Sir Thomas Lawrence, P.R.A.

Lear. Katie and Edward were very much affected by it. Nina seemed agitated in her nerves.

December 28th.—Went by Great Western Railway to Windsor. The day bitterly cold, with drifting snow and sharp frost. Proceeded to the castle; after some time, cooling my heels in the basement lobbies, saw Mr. Roberts, to whom I carried a letter from Colonel Phipps. He showed me the Rubens Gallery, the theatre of the castle, explaining to me the position of the stage, etc., the dressing-rooms, and all that was needful. He then took me round the state-rooms, displaying the furniture to me, about which I was indifferent, but was charmed with the pictures of the old masters I saw there; West and Lawrence made me turn very sick. Colonel Phipps was out shooting with the Prince. Saw Marianne Skerrett, who came to me in a small basement receiving or business room. I talked with her till time to go; she threaded the passages for me, and I took leave. I had rather live in Clarence Terrace or in Sherborne than in Windsor Castle. Returned home by Slough. Note from Mr. C. Kean, apparently wishing to supersede the message sent by Mr. Webster, but in very bad taste—half-civil, half-supercilious tone; from Mrs. Wallack; from Watts. Wrote with a copy to Mr. C. Kean declining a direct correspondence with him, as he had before addressed me through his solicitor, and acknowledging his note *and his message.*

December 29th.—Went in carriage to Maclise, sat to him; from him to Mr. Wallack, with whom I arranged all my business of Brutus and rehearsed with him. He told me that there had been words between Messrs. Webster and C. Kean, and that Mr. Webster had very sharply put down this conceited and silly fellow. Returned to Maclise and sat or stood in the dress of Werner for him. He showed me his study—most beautiful—of the *Great Picture* he designs, "The Marriage of Strongbow and Eva." Forster stopped me going away, and after returning to see the study went with me home. He wished to have the correspondence of Messrs. Webster, Kean, etc. Letters from Troughton, Webster, Mr. Marshall, Mr. C. Kean—of most inane and senseless *bluster*—an intimation of readiness to attack or defend himself!!! George Webster called and rehearsed. My heart is not at ease about my beloved Nina. In God alone is my hope, to Him is my prayer—for mercy in her restored health, and strength and comfort to us all. Read Mrs. Browning's poem in the *Athenæum;* thought it overrated.

December 31st.—Left my dear home in good time for the express train to Exeter. Read the newspaper—of course the *Times*—which, containing in its leading article a political review of the past year on this its last day, makes a confession of principles most adverse, I think, to the interest and advancement of mankind. Instead of referring the ignorances, extravagances, crimes and follies of the various nations who struck for liberty to the conduct of those despots who have hitherto prevented them from learning the art of self-government, they denounce all attempt in subjugated man to liberate himself, and because they (the writer—the " we ") are wealthy, think the world ought to be perfectly satisfied and contented with the present state of things. Alas! for the improvement of mankind! Reached Exeter in good time. Went to the theatre; found a company —even *worse than my fears!*—unable to perform any music—in all respects *disgusting*—the manager superlatively and pre-eminently so. Rehearsed! to impress myself with the conviction of its inutility and to try to prepare myself for the night. Acted Macbeth—oh! such a night—I striving for patience—the Lady Macbeth the *very worst* I ever saw in all my life; Macduff very little better; Witches execrable; no music; dresses and properties shabbiness itself. The Macduff, I firmly believe, desired to cut me in the fight. I thought he had drugged himself, Malay-like, with brandy or something to do it! My sword broke, which I had *apprehended*, and was very angry with Michell. He was very rude, and increased my wrath. Oh, this temper—this wretched temper, the cause of so much misery to me. I fear I shall die with little improvement in my endeavour to subject it to reason and wisdom. How unhappy has it often made me! I must still try. Arranged my accounts—looking at the amount of investment I have been able to make out of the produce of this year. I could have wished my expenses had been less, but there have been draughts upon me—in the making good the deficit of the Siddons monument—not much less than £200;[1] the expenses thrown on me

---

[1] This is the last entry in Macready's diaries relating to the Siddons monument, and it indicates the conclusion of the matter to which he had given so much thought, time, and money in order to do honour to the memory of one of the greatest of his predecessors on the English stage. When Dean Stanley was preparing his Memorials of Westminster Abbey, the present editor was requested to obtain from Macready some account of the history of the erection of the Siddons statue, and in reply to his inquiries Macready wrote : " With the exception of, I think, about £50, the whole expense was defrayed by myself in one way or other. The site, after much deliberation, was decided on, as the best to be obtained, by Chantrey, and the subject came under the cognizance of Deans Turton, Buckland, and Wilberforce. I consulted the late Lord Lansdowne, Rogers, and some others, whom I cannot immediately recollect ; but the opinion was unanimous in regard to the inscription that ' Sarah Siddons ' should be

by that unprincipled wretch Mr. Forrest, more than £100; Mr. Ryder's heavily paid services and my travelling expenses. All these have swelled up my expenditure, and made it seem more than it really is for my family and myself. May we learn and carefully and wisely practise economy. I close this year with humble and hearty thanks to Almighty God for all His many mercies vouchsafed to me, undeserving as I am, and I humbly and devoutly implore His grace on mine and me for the remainder of our lives and for the existence which we hope beyond this transitory life.

the only words engraved on the pedestal or plinth." The place and date of birth and death were added by Dean Stanley, in 1865, when the statue of John Kemble was removed from another part of the Abbey, and placed near that of his sister—(*note by Sir F. Pollock*).

1850

Bath, January 9th.—Read paper. Grieved—if not something shocked—at the tone of the *Times* about the Game Laws. *Disgusted*, and no mistake, with that empiric Disraeli, again in Buckinghamshire! Oh! he is too much for gravity or patience! Rested. Acted Macbeth in my best, most *identifying* manner. I had not an audience to appreciate me, but I acted to *myself*. *I was Macbeth.* The audience did not, could not, feel my deep thought.

Bristol, January 14th.—Acted Iago as well as I could with a most *atrocious* Othello, one of the " free and easy "—oh! such an Othello! a miserable Cassio, and as bad a Roderigo; Brabantio was by far the best. Called, but the audience did not *understand* me; they were really dull.

January 16th.—Went to rehearsal, was kept there, vainly striving to drive some sense into those clods of *indolence*—for their ignorance is chiefly ascribable to the fact that they do not care and do not try to *know* what is placed before them. A *player* is the lowest human animal!—I think so. From ten till close on three—I was using all expedition—detained by those fellows, and *at night* what will they do? Will they remember anything they practised? Acted King Lear as well as I could with all imaginable drawbacks of inattention, bungling and neglect.

Leeds, January 22nd.—Found letter from Lord John Russell, enclosing one from Sir J. Hobhouse—offering him the promise, conditional on his retaining office, of a nomination for Mr. Macready's son, as he was interested for him. This has been a real act of kindness on the part of Lord John Russell.

January 23rd.—Wrote my letter to Lord John Russell, who has certainly shown *great kindness to me* in this affair of the writership. I can never forget it, or cease to be grateful to him.

January 25th.—Wrote to London Marble Company with a cheque on Coutts for the expense of pedestal, etc., which, to satisfy the Dean's taste, costs *me* £10 beyond the estimate—all out of my

444

pocket ! ! Too bad. I shall have the tale to tell of my aristocratic supporters and my clerical auxiliaries. Acted Cardinal Richelieu— the house so crowded that Mr. Saville came to ask me, as hundreds were turned away, if I would consent to some being behind the scenes. I refused. Called, and returned to say : " Ladies and gentlemen, I would not willingly appear to trespass upon your patience with the ceremony of a formal leave-taking, but, where I have been favoured so frequently during the course of my theatrical career with most liberal patronage, and where there will always exist for me associations of the deepest interest, I may perhaps be excused for the desire to offer at least my parting acknowledgments and to embody my sincerest good wishes in the word as I bid you in my professional capacity most gratefully and respectfully a last farewell."

January 26th.—Letter from dear Catherine with accounts of Nina, blessed child, that rather increase my apprehensions, and depress and fret me with the uncertainty of her true condition. I feel I can but pray and hope, but my fear is growing on me. In God alone I trust. Read paper. What blundering selfish boobies these Protectionists are !

Liverpool, January 29th.—Spoke to Mrs. Warner about what she supposed, *herself*, would be the course pursued at the Palace in regard to any offer of remuneration ; she had told me that the sums paid were of three classes—£10, £5, £3. That of course no attempt would be made to "*pay*" me. I was glad to hear this opinion, as it shows me I have not gone on any false pride in thinking upon this question. I do not think that there will be any disposition to subject me to annoyance. I certainly have not merited it from the Q—— or P——.

January 30th.—Rehearsed, and with a set of actual *curs*, ignorant and rude, as men can well me. Well, well, each day brings us nearer to the end of it. Acted Shylock. I do not know how ; I only know I tried to act it well. Came away before the fifth act began. Note from a Mrs. or Miss Chatterton wanting an *interview!* They all want interviews !

January 31st.—Busy with affairs for this Palace performance. I now find the trouble, the labour, and the expense so great, that I am almost angry with my own quixotism in giving way to the proposition. I surely have every reason to plead my inability ; however, I have committed myself through a strict feeling of duty, and I must go through it. Inquired of Mrs. Warner about the mode of return-

445

ing; learned that *the* train—the players' train—will not be likely to start before one, or half-past one o'clock, and on the previous occasion *she* reached home at *three*. I must therefore either take a special engine, or sleep at Windsor. If the special be too expensive, I must encounter the less expense and greater derangement. Looked at paper; begin to feel disgust at the *aristocratic* tone of the *Times*. I am sorry to see it. Saw, too, a criticism (!!) on the Othello at Drury Lane, really affronting common sense—the commonest notions of what acting is! Oh! is it not to be wished to be free from these ——? Acted Iago, taking much pains. The Othello, Mr. Barry Sullivan, was really indifferent, and vociferously applauded. The Roderigo, Mr. Brown, was *drunk!*

London, February 1st.—Found my beloved Nina beyond all evasion of even hope, ill; seriously, alarmingly ill. My blessed first-born, my own beloved Nina. She looked at first better, but when afterwards I looked at her—oh God, how painful was the sight! My beloved one! Almost bewildered with perplexity in regard to what I had to do! Note from Colonel Phipps. Attended, as well as I could, to affairs. Dressed; went to Windsor by railway, taking at the Paddington Station a special engine to return at night, for which I paid seven guineas. Dined at Castle Inn. Went in cab to the Castle; passed with my ticket into my room, a very handsome one, partitioned off from a passage; pictures of Moretto, Tintoretto, Parmegiano, exquisite, etc. Dressed; was kept in a state of irritable expectation. Mr. Wallack came to speak to me. Acted Brutus in a style of reality and earnest naturalness that I think did, and I felt ought to, produce an effect on my auditors. I cannot describe the scene; my Nina agitates my heart and shakes my nerves; I cannot write. Colonel Phipps came to me from the Queen and Prince Albert to express how much they had been pleased. I requested him to offer my duty, and that I was most happy in the opportunity of offering any testimony of my respectful homage. Came away by special train. Carriage was waiting for me. Reached home about half-past twelve o'clock.

February 2nd.—My darling child seemed something stronger and better this morning. She is my all-engrossing thought. God bless and restore her. Called on Elliotson—expressed my gratitude to him; asked him if he objected to meet Dr. Bright and Sir James Clarke in consultation. Most eagerly he said no, and readily entered into arrangements for the meeting. He gave me the history of my dearest child's disorder. I called on Dr. Bright, saw him, and appointed to-morrow three o'clock. Went on to Sir James Claike, saw him, but he could not get back from Windsor by daylight to-morrow, and proposed that Elliotson and Bright should see dear Nina to-morrow, and he and Elliotson see her on Monday. I called on Elliotson, who assented to this; then on Bright, to leave word of the hour. Elliotson called. His language was *desponding*. In God alone we can trust.

February 3rd.—Carried my dear sick child down-stairs. Sat with her. Dickens called and sat. He went up to see dear Nina, suggested his servant Anne going down to Hastings for lodgings, and *said* he "did not think she looked worse than when he last saw her." Procter and Adelaide called. Kind, dear, sympathizing Procter. Dr. Bright and Elliotson came. After seeing my beloved child they came to me in my study, where I was waiting for them. They spoke to me, and from their language I collected that the case was desperate. I felt that hope was gone. My blessed, my beloved firstborn! Went up and sat with my child—my dying child! Looked in her dear face, and saw signs which made my very heart sink down. In God alone—in God alone can we look for hope or for strength! Forster—kind Forster called and sat. Took leave of my dear, dear child, my Nina, with the feeling I should probably never see her alive again. My heart felt crushed. Took leave of my other darling children—of my dear sister, of my poor, dear, blessed wife. Went to the station as desolate, as agonized at heart as any wretch could be. My journey through the night was one long thought of my dear, dear child.

February 4th.—After this night of agony I reached the station in a state of mind indifferent to everything in this world but my Nina's state. After a time got to bed, but not for a long time to sleep. Rose with unabated feelings of wretchedness. Sent a telegraphic message home, desiring Catherine, if the consultation to-day announced *immediate* danger (as I fear the days of my darling child are *not many more* in this world), to inform me instantly that I might go up. Wrote to Glover of Glasgow and to Cunningham to relinquish my Glasgow engagement—on this view, if my dear child be dangerously ill, be near her dissolution (which God—oh! God forbid!) I may be near to comfort and pray with her; if she be able to receive consolation and amusement, I may be of use to her in that respect. Rehearsed in the lowest possible state of spirits. Acted Brutus.

447

Most especially disgusted with a *scoundrel* (*really*) *actor*. He was imperfect, atrociously bad, and impertinent. I was called. Spoke to Mrs. Warner, who told me of Mrs. Saville telling Mr. C. Kean that she acted in *Hamlet* with "the old gentleman."

Liverpool, February 5th.—Letter from my beloved wife in more comfortable spirits from the ease and cheerfulness of our precious child—though Sir James Clarke's opinion *gave no more* hope than those of the previous day. Indeed, *I feel*, as I reflect, that there is *no hope—no ground for hope*. Without accusation or unkind thoughts (which, God knows, I have neither the right nor the wish to entertain) Elliotson ought to have let her go to a more genial climate when it was *first* proposed, when dearest Edward was ready to accompany her. I *then* told him my views, that money was no consideration, that I wished the influence to be used as a *preventive*, not as a hopeless means of prolongation of a diseased life. He chose to *think for* me, in judging for himself, and my blessed child is lost to me. His motive was kind and friendly, but a physician should consult his clients' disposition. A telegraph arrived with the blessed words, "*Much better this morning.*" They gave new life to my heart, and diffused cheerfulness through me for a little time, but reflection told me, in contradiction to Elliotson's observation that "she *may* rally," *she cannot rally*. The beloved creature is death-stricken, and my heart is reft of one most precious to it. But it is the will of *God, who gave her to me*. Blessed be His name. Amen! Wrote to my Nina—to try to amuse her. Reached Holyhead an hour behind our time—I fancy from the impediment of the gale that was blowing. It was so bad that two or three parties, one of foreigners seemingly wealthy, decided on *not crossing*. I with two young officers and another traveller in one omnibus, and other parties in another, were driven on to the pier-head. I had much repugnance to go; the gale was blowing fearfully, but I did not like to show a white feather, and it was my duty. Was much perplexed to get my small quantity of luggage on board. At last, the other parties having changed their minds at the last moment, their courage having failed them, we were on board—the two officers, the Yorkshire traveller, and myself—and we let go. The night was awful. The gale was in our teeth, and the sea literally raging. To make things worse, we had a most inattentive and cowardly steward—could gain neither attendance nor information through the night. We were to be *in* Kingstown in four and a half hours! We were tossed unmercifully. I was twice flung off my sofa, and yet I stuck well, but once was clean rolled upon the floor. The seas broke over us to that degree that it was fearful to hear the lashing of the waters rolling on the deck above us. I feared the fires being extinguished, or the hold filling. The captain, it seemed, was in apprehension of the funnels not holding! Had they gone, we were gone. He came down to look at the glass, to draw some comfort from what he saw or thought he saw—the rising of the glass—that the gale was breaking. He said in all his life he had never encountered "*such a terrific night.*" He did not know where we were—could see nothing. Thus we were beating about; once catching a light, which he thought Balbriggan light— but not daring and not knowing how to take any decisive course till daylight. He then got view of points—Howth, etc., and made south for Kingstown, which we reached at half-past ten o'clock! I believed once or twice in the course of the night that my time was come—thought of my home, my dear ones, commended myself to my God, and felt it *was my duty.*

Dublin, February 6th.—With deep and devout thanks to Almighty God for my deliverance from the dangers of the night, I came on shore. Went to the station and took my seat in the railway carriage at Kingstown. Heard that nothing like the gale of the night had been known there since January 6th, 1839. I could walk with difficulty for the wind up to the station. Came to Dublin to Morrison's Hotel. We had been fifteen hours instead of four on our passage. I had more than once expected death. The captain was certainly much alarmed; indeed, so, I believe, were all at heart.

February 7th.—Letters from dear kind Forster, with a few lines from Catherine—from dear Letitia, giving an account of our precious fragile charge. They all cherish hope. I cannot, dare not, encourage any. I feel—I feel—the disease, whatever it be, has gone too far to be overcome. She is for God—no more for us. Blessed spirit! Wrote to my dear Catherine, to Letitia, and a few lines to our sweet, sweet sufferer. Acted Macbeth—in my *very finest style*— despite several drawbacks. I was determined that the last Macbeth here should be remembered by those who saw it. Called and enthusiastically received.

February 8th.—Felt upon me the exertion of last night's perform- ance, as if I had strained some muscles of the chest; much wearied. Letters, full of comfort in their love and sweet spirit, from my beloved wife and from dear Letitia. Both of them, dear creatures,

449

wish to hope, and, as I think, unconsciously persuade themselves to do so. Changes, like miracles, have occurred. My hope, alas, does not extend beyond that remote possibility! I must prepare to lose sight of my beloved child in this world. At my time of life the distance of separation cannot be very long, but I cannot help murmuring over her departure from an existence which was so full of enjoyment to her. Blessed child. But God's will is first and last.

February 9th.—Letters from my dearest Catherine, one from darling Katie, and one from dear Letitia to Catherine with the account of our blessed Nina. The physician talks of one or two "favourable symptoms"—one, the *fever lessening;* that has some gleam of promise, but it is not of substance enough to grasp. The dear child's cough is still "troublesome," and she is still so fanciful, and so apparently impatient, which are signs of deep disease. With prayer to God, submitting my heart to His decree, I fear—I fear. Thought and wrote out a few words to speak, if needed. Acted Cardinal Richelieu in my best style. The *support*(!) was—*disgusting.* Julie, François, Huguet—oh! Called. Spoke part of what I had tried to put together, but did not do it well.

Belfast, February 12th.—Acted Othello—if I have any right to judge in such cases—I should say more finely, more passionately, more nobly than I have *ever* done before; I care not where the exception may be made. The house was bad, and the audience *called on* Mr. E. Glover, Iago, after me. I merely instance the fact that I gave one of the most splendid exhibitions of passion and character in my power to give, and the audience paid the same compliment to a *provincial, tame, prosaic reading* (*not acting*) of the part of Iago. *I am right to go away.* I am not *at all* dissatisfied. Letters from dear Catherine and Letitia. The gleam of life from Sir James Clarke's words to dear Marianne—"not *quite* hopeless," etc., receives no corroborating effect from the letters from Hastings. The fever *still* holds on its fang-like grasp.

February 13th.—Letter from Catherine with Letitia's to her, the account of dear Nina not so late as those already received. Looked at paper. Perceived that Isaac Rynders, the ruffian who, haranguing the populace in the park at New York, told them he had raised $50 on his note to purchase tickets to send persons into the theatre to drive me from the stage (*notoriously* illegal and *punishable!*), and who on both nights, Monday and Thursday, led a band of ruffians down from the opera house to the Broadway and passed them *in* to the amount of forty to cheer Mr. Forrest—this man was acquitted as an instigator of the riot by the New York jury! Now, one desires to be philosophic, and in justice one is ready to enumerate many, many *gentlemen* and good men in various cities of the Union, but these men, Rynders, Theodore Sedgwick—*Boston Post, Boston Mail, etc.*—what are *they* and what are the millions of their party, the democrats, but aiders and abettors, *more or less,* of such a miscreant as Mr. Forrest? Letter from Letitia—with the gleam of a hope for our dear child—"pulse not so quick and stronger." My heart thanks God for those words.

February 14th.—Wrote to my Catherine, enclosing the letter to dear Edward, which I wrote last night. Catherine told me that the scoundrel Bunn was advertised to appear "on the stage." I sent for the *Times,* and there is the announcement—"*Mr. Bunn on the stage!*" "*Due notice, etc.*" The very mode of announcing speaks some piece of empiricism—the opportunity to see such a notorious rascal *actually* upon the stage! It is not as if Mr. Bunn had anything *to do* there, but *Mr. Bunn is to be seen upon the stage!* If the announcement does not mean that, what does it mean? Letter from dearest Letitia, with accounts of my beloved child, which as it were *balance* my heart, and draw forth my most grateful thanks to Almighty God for even this gleam of hope.

February 15th.—Acted Hamlet with all possible care and energy, and I should say well. The house was *one pound* beyond last night. Shakspeare and my last night—the deficiency of the gallery was £10!! This I cannot account for, and read as a bad sign in regard to taste. Called—went forward. There was no indication of expectation that I should speak, and I did not make essay; of which I am *extremely glad.* So ends Belfast.

Liverpool, February 18th.—Acted Macbeth. Annoyed, and thrown off my balance in the first scene by one of those blackguards who call themselves players utterly neglecting his business, and doing directly contrary to what he was directed. I am sick—sick of them. Tried to rally, but the audience were an *old Liverpool audience,* attentive and *very cold. Called.* Two letters from Letitia—quite settled my state of mind—one was the lowest despondency, the other a little relief. But I perceive—there is *no hope—no hope*—for the life of my dear, dear child; cut down in the bloom of her youth, she will drop like a sweet flower into her grave. God bless, bless her! Very, very wretched—unable to work.

February 19*th.*—Something past one o'clock—my servant gone to seek a special engine to convey me to Hastings to catch one last living look of my dear blessed Nina.   I know not what is my state of mind; I am certain my head is strange and heavy, but I have packed up my clothes, made my arrangements as were needed—clearly; and I sit here awaiting, with anxiety to depart, the carriage that is to take me away.   I cannot, to myself, disentangle this state of mind.   This day brought me accounts teeming with promises of comfort and joy. I arranged in my bed this morning the difficult task of what I should say to my audience this evening.   I rose to receive a handful of letters, all full of good news—Catherine's and Letitia's—with an account of my Nina more promising than any I have yet received!   A sweet con-solatory one from Forster.   Acted, with great care and peculiar effect, Cardinal Wolsey and Lord Townley.   Called.   Went forward, the whole house stood up to hear me, and such a house as is rarely to be seen.   Everything to gratify the pride and vanity of a person in my position, and the telegraphic despatch was waiting me at my hotel. Here is indeed a lesson of what life is; who can say he is happy or prosperous in this world? who dares to boast or feel confidence in what he enjoys?   I have thought my Nina the strongest and healthiest of all my dear ones, and, as I write—perhaps—I feel dull and half-stupid —I do not know what to do.   To God Almighty I may pray, but if my blessed child have left this earth, it has been to go to Him.   The words which I said to the Liverpool audience in taking leave were as follows: " Ladies and Gentlemen,—It has been usual for me to attend with pleasure and alacrity the complimentary summons with which you have so often honoured me; but now, I must confess, I obey your call with reluctance and regret.   I must count back many years for the date of my first appearance before you; but time has not weakened my recollection of the event; and I treasure in my memory, with grateful pride, the cheering welcome with which you greeted my more youthful essays; and equally well do I remember the many subsequent occasions, when my humble efforts have been favoured with your liberal apprecia-tion, and in which my endeavours to realize the conceptions of our great dramatic poets have ever found a ready response in the intelligence and sympathy of my audiences.   What more have I to say?   The exercise of my art I relinquish at a somewhat earlier period of life than my more distinguished predecessors have done, and I yield the scene to younger, but scarcely less ardent, aspirants to your favour, not from any imme-diate apprehension of enfeebled powers, but because I would not

452

willingly risk the chance of lingering there to read in ' the eyes of man ' bent idly on me, the melancholy fact of my decline. Even at a considerable pecuniary sacrifice, I would prefer submitting to you a proof print of my illustration, such as it is, of Shakspeare's characters, than offer you the faded and indistinct impression of a worn-out plate. It has always been a gratification to me to appear before you, it is therefore painful to me to reflect on a pleasure I shall never again enjoy. Ladies and Gentlemen, I take my leave of you with my warmest acknowledgments of your long-continued and liberal patronage, with sentiments of grateful respect, bidding you, in my profession of an actor, regretfully and most respectfully, a last farewell."

London—Hastings, February 20th.—At six o'clock left the railway station for London, and came on to Hastings. Thought, as I passed Eastbourne, of the days I had passed there with my blithe and healthful child—alas, alas! Arrived at Hastings, came to these lodgings, saw dearest Letitia. My blessed Nina wished to see me at once. I saw her—sweet, suffering child of my heart!—pale, emaciated, weakened. Oh God! how are we to address Thee!—how to acknowledge Thy goodness to us and bend to Thy dispensations, which appear *severe*—but no doubt are mercies! I sat by her, and talked cheerfully with her, caressed her dog, and tried to see nothing strange. Let me hope that if, as I fear and believe, it is God's will she must pass away from us, it may be in peace of mind and serenity of heart. God bless my beloved child. Saw Dr. Mackness, and learned from him that there was no ground for hope.

Hastings, February 21st.—Was called up at about two o'clock by dearest Letitia in manifest fear that my blessed child was dying ; threw on some clothes and went down to her ; found her in an alarming state, Letitia and Mrs. Wagstaffe watching her in evident belief that the dear creature's hour was come ; stood long beside her in the same agonizing apprehension. What thoughts passed through my brain ; what a horrid mixture of recurrences of grave and trifling things, that passed like malicious antics through my brain, like those various faces that seem in savage fiendishness to pass before the eyes at night and will not be shut out! The sweet scenes of her birth ; her infancy, her girlhood, and spring of youth came to my heart, softening and soothing it. My prayer to God, to the all-good, all-bountiful God, is for peace, peace and tranquillity, in this world. In the next, I cannot doubt her acceptance and her home with the spirits of the pure and good. But, oh!

for remission from pain to her dear wasted frame here, I pray, oh God! She became more composed after a time and sank to sleep. I returned to my room and threw myself on the bed. At seven o'clock Letitia came again to call me. When I reached her room—my child! She was again nearly as bad as she had been in the night. We remained with her till late in the morning. She grew seemingly better. I sat with her. She had letters from Catherine and Katie, which I held for her to read; also a box of little souvenirs—(souvenirs!)—from her brothers and sisters—God bless their affectionate hearts! Letitia gave me a letter from Catherine, which she had written, but not sent to me— it was very forlorn and heart-broken. Katie's letter, too, to Letitia described her as despairing in her sorrow, which I grieved to read. Arranged in my mind the course I would adopt—all, of course, dependent on the issue of this blessed child's illness. Wrote to my dearest Catherine a letter of exhortation and consolation, which I hoped might change her way of thinking; sent it by Locke, in whose place an old and favourite nurse of Nina's (a middle-aged woman) is come. Wrote to Davis to say, if not prevented by a fatal calamity, I would certainly be at Newcastle for Monday, 25th inst.; wrote to Radley for letters. Dr. Mackness called again most kindly to assist in the preparation of the water-bed, which dear Forster had sent to us. The two nurses and myself were the doctor's assistants, and we got it well filled. My darling child's strength was much reduced, and she was now not so well as when Dr. Mackness called first this morning. Talked some time with dear, good Letitia. Wrote to Forster—excellent friend. Sat with my blessed, suffering child, whose cough quite clutches and tears at my heart. Wrote to Michell—to the post-offices at Hull and Halifax for my letters. Wrote again for the morning's post to my dear wife, endeavouring to enforce my former arguments, and again expressing my utter despair of our child's recovery. With my sweet, suffering girl, who looked the image of suffering innocence as she lay there waiting, as my sister observed, for the ministering angels to bear her away to heaven. God bless her (as I believe He will in His eternity of bliss), and make her passage there easy and tranquil! Dr. Mackness called again; he said she was still weaker, and intimated that it was true it was a mere question of *time*. Saw my dear one again, urging dear Letitia to go to bed. I have seen, read, done nothing these last two days. These rooms and our house at home have been *all the world* to me. I have thought of nothing else; the past and the blank made in the future have been the successive subjects of my brooding. Anything may have happened, and I in ignorance about all. To God—to God alone my thoughts and prayers are offered. Amen.

February 22nd.—In saying my prayers last night Mrs. Wagstaffe came to summon me. My beloved child was suffering much—her difficulty of respiration and excessive weakness are her great distresses. God help her! Amen! She slept and awoke for perhaps about half-an-hour, not more, two or three times in the night; which, if her sleep refreshed her, would have been called a good night. I left her asleep at five o'clock this morning and went to bed; at eight rose and went to see her. She slept. I was partially dressed, when Mrs. Wagstaffe came to say, "You had better come down, she does not seem to have a long time to last." I found her *very ill*—very ill. Dr. Mackness was sent for, and sent her in some ether mixture. She fell asleep after a time. I dressed and returned. Letters from Catherine, Forster, Patty, Pritchard, Ransom. Whilst reading them Mrs. Wagstaffe came to me again to say, "If you wish to see the last of her, you had better come." I went to the bedside, and stood long, expecting to see her blessed spirit depart. After a long time she fell asleep again. Sat with my Nina, happy at heart in her wish that I should rub her chest— happy to do anything to give her, dear child, relief. Wrote to Catherine;[1] to Forster about Webster, etc. Passed the day between the bedside of my sinking child (chiefly there) and my writing-desk. Received some clotted cream and note from kind, good Forster. Nina wanted some one to sing to her to lull her to sleep. None could. I asked her should I say her prayer for her. Yes; and I had the comfort of repeating prayers by her bedside.

February 23rd.—Rose in tolerably good time this morning, and had the heart-comfort (for which I *thank God*) of performing some little offices of love for my sweet child; I soothed her to patience, and dearly submissive was she! (Bless her, oh, God!—oh, God! *bless* her!) After a time I had the dear and sacred satisfaction of reading her morning prayers to her, and she became quite serene. The letter from her beloved mother sent messages of love and kisses to her, which I gave to my precious child. Dr. Mackness called; he administered some medicine, which she took with patience. My heart is *full* with sorrow, but no murmurs; no bitterness exists there. I feel how much I owe to God's goodness, and believe (though hard to assent to the sacrifice required for it) that all is under His decree for the best. But I must

---

[1] Mrs. Macready was at that time in expectation of her confinement and unable to leave London.

not—I must not now dwell on all the sweet memories that have sprung up around *her* steps, and become the records of her dear life's history; when time has healed over this wound, and its aching is abated, I may make it a melancholy pleasure to recall them. I wish I could now occupy myself, but I have such a disinclination to work! My dear, dear sister! I thank God for thy love and thy devoted and affectionate care bestowed on me and mine. He will bless thee for it. Wrote a few lines, and closed my last night's letter, and then wrote another for an order forgotten, to go by the morning's post. Wrote also by the two o'clock train, as I know it is a relief to my blessed wife to hear but a word of this beloved creature—and she has been sweetly tranquil this morning. Bless her! Watched her dear, death-like face, dreading every minute to behold her last gasp; thank God, she slept. Wrote in some arrears of record. The day passed—in and out of the blessed sufferer's room—now by her bedside, now waiting for a summons there. As the evening began to close, my darling angel-child wished me to read prayers for her, which I did—happy, so far, to do so. Coming down, as she wished to try to sleep, I made an effort to look at books, papers, etc. No, I can fix my mind on nothing; a few short snatches of conversation with my beloved sister. Went up again to my Nina— my—still *my* child! She wished for me. Dr. Mackness called—gave her some soda-water; did not say anything to me about her state—in truth, he has nothing to say. All that they know is, nothing can be known! Began my letter to my dearest wife, the only tranquillizing occupation I can employ myself upon. To God I pray for rest for my child this night. Had not been an hour in bed, in disturbed sleep, when dear Letitia came in, and, alarmed at her condition, wished me to come down to her, but not as if sent for—with some excuse for coming. I did so, asking for a candle, I having burnt mine out. She was very much oppressed with the difficulty of her breathing, but I rubbed her, dear, precious child, and she soon fell asleep. It was a comfort— the only comfort I could now receive from her condition to sit beside and see her sleep so soundly and sweetly there. Letitia wished me to go to bed, but I could not leave her. At length, when she seemed likely to sleep long, I went to lie down in my dressing-gown—a disturbed, short night.

February 24th.—My beloved Christina, my firstborn, died. My thoughts are so confused, entangled, dulled, that I feel stupidly low, and stagnant in mind and heart. What have I to record for my own future reference, or for those of my children, who may ever turn over

456

these leaves? The death of my firstborn, my dearest Nina—her sweet, familiar name among us all; and I, her father, who nineteen years ago fondly cradled her infant beauty in my arms, now go at periods of the day, and not, I fear, for more than one more day, to kiss the cold marble of her forehead, and look upon her wasted, placid corpse! And this is life! But let me not, oh God of wisdom and virtue, Creator and Parent, Almighty Power, let me not murmur at Thy decree! In the fulfilment of this, to me, *sad destiny*, I acknowledge manifold mercies, most indulgent exemptions from aggravations of my misfortune, which *apparent accident* has delivered us from. "Why art thou cast down, O my soul? and why art thou disquieted within me? *Hope thou in God: for I shall yet praise Him for the help of His countenance.*" Mrs. Allen came to call me about six o'clock; I found my blessed child breathing with extreme difficulty, quick and short. She gave me her hand, said she was very ill. I uttered what words I could of comfort. She wished Dr. Mackness to be sent for. I saw it was utterly vain, and dearest Letitia, who stood by her holding her other hand, seemed not to desire him to be sent to, but I could not resist a wish of hers, as I had not hitherto done, nor could I deceive her at such a moment. I sent Mrs. Allen for him; she lay dying before us, but fell again into sleep, breathing quick and very short. Mrs. Allen returning, rang at the bell; I went down to let her in. As I came up, I heard Letitia's voice loud in lament. She, my beloved child, had just ceased to breathe. Oh God! forgive the sinful heart that, unworthy to make such supplication, prays to Thee to *bless her pure spirit. It is blessed—blessed in Thy mercy!* and my petition is for pardon for my own offences—through the sorrows of this. May they be expiatory of my many and great offences, and may this terrible bereavement awaken my heart to true repentance and lead me to a new life beneficial to my children and dearest wife, and charitable in word and deed to my fellow-creatures. Oh God, strengthen my resolves and renew a right spirit within me, and bless my beloved family with health and grace. After a time we left the dear body of my child. I closed her dear eyes, and kissed for her blessed mother and myself her pale lips. My grief was dull and stupefying. I could not weep. I dressed myself, and, coming down, met my beloved Letitia in the drawing-room, looking again upon my dead child as I came down. It is all confusion —dull, heavy grief, or sharp agony of sorrow. My head is yet confused. God—God protect me. . . . Letters from my dearest wife, from my best friend Forster, from Webster in a very kind spirit.

Obliged to turn my thoughts to the measures needful to be taken. Thought, consulted with Letitia and planned the arrangements to be made. Went with Letitia again to look on the lifeless form that was my buoyant, graceful, intelligent child. She looked most angel-like. Wrote to my poor suffering partner—to dear Forster. Went again to see *her* while daylight lasted. Found that her dog, which I *loved* for her sake, had got out and was lost. Offered reward for him. Dearest Letitia left me, and, as I saw the carriage turn the last corner, I felt lonely at very heart. Looked at a paper. Read the "Thoughts and Feelings," a private record of my beloved Nina. Saw what surprised me—though a most pure and upright spirit, indications of the prospect of an after life not so happy as her happy childhood and youth, of which she was always conscious. God bless her. Very much agitated by it. Prayed, and tears came to my relief. Wrote to dear Catherine, which greatly composed me. Walked in the bright moonlight for about two hours.

February 25th.—This morning I rise from my bed with the knowledge that my child is lost to me in this world. I try to turn the thought to good—in my own humbleness and resolutions of amendment, and in my strong purpose to devote myself to my children. My night has been uneasy, unrefreshing; but thoughts of good purpose, with tears from various causes, have given me tranquillity. I went down and uncovered the face of my dear, dear offspring; it was peaceful and serene. I knelt beside her to pray to Almighty God for help to persevere in good, and to rejoin her in another state of being. I gave to her cold forehead her blessed mother's kisses and my own, and I left her, comforted at heart. Oh God! who knowest my desire to do right, and my weakness and vanity in feebly resisting wrong, from my soul I implore thee to strengthen me for the future and to forgive me the crimes and evil of the past. Bless my dear family, oh God! with health of mind and body and with Thy heavenly grace. . . . To be here with the consciousness that my own child, her body, is in the same house, is in the room above me, and insensible to all I do or say—I, who loved her so fondly, I, whom she so loved—this is *terrible* in its painfulness. I feel now the want of a friend's presence; but let me *bear well.*

February 26th.—Passed a night, not exactly disturbed, but engaged in dreamy thoughts of my beloved child, whose image, dead and cold as she lies, was frequently before me. But meditations of a blessed nature grew out of these; the self-delusions of my past life stared, as

458

it were, upon me; the *vanity* and *selfishness*, which had disguised themselves in masks of *rectitude*, were made visible to me; and I own—I *feel*, that even in the stroke of affliction which now has smitten me, *the love of God* is manifest—*I feel it;* I feel it in the clearing of my mind—in the detection of the fact of those weaknesses and vices of character (and of their *cause*) that have so warred against my earthly peace, obscured my sight of God, my perfect understanding of *His will* in what is required of me. The thought of *myself—myself*—has hitherto been set between my sight and God. It is *that*—that I have *served !* My advance in self-knowledge has been more in these two mournful days than in years and years of my foregone life! I *see* my vanity, my pride, where I had not suspected it, where I flattered myself I was acting from just principles—I perceive my compromise with sin. What were words before in praying against, battling against, vanity and pride and envy, are now palpable things. I see *myself*, and *through* the disguises that have covered my faults to myself. In my secret heart I have vowed to my Divine Father to root evil out of my heart, to keep a watch over my thoughts and actions, to endeavour with my feeble mind to comprehend to the utmost of my ability His goodness and His powers—to act by the standard of what may be His will, and no longer think of the *opinions of men.* The uses of adversity have been made brightly clear to me. And the Paternal Benevolence of the Almighty Ordainer of events and their consequence is distinctly revealed to me. I feel my mind regenerated; I never felt thus till now. In deep humility, in grateful tranquillity of heart, I will enter on the last stage of my mortal pilgrimage. The tears that fall are refreshing to my spirit. There is no *anguish* at my heart. I have looked upon, and kissed, for her mother and myself, the dear forehead of my dead child. She is with the blessed. Oh God! my humble prayer is that I may atone my past life and be admitted to spiritual communion in another world with her and my darling Joan.

February 27th.—My night was one of very little sleep; the image of my child, the thought of her as she had been, as her dear body is, and as her better part, *herself*, may be, was present to me constantly. Endeavoured to make account with my own follies, my transgressions, and (in the computation, as I found) of my *crimes.* I could not have believed myself so *intensely selfish* as I discover myself to be! *Vanity* —most selfish vanity—seems the spring of all my actions, or more or less mixed up with *everything I do !* My dissatisfaction with others, my impatience, my reluctant admission of others' success, all—all is *selfishness* and hateful *vanity*. *I will root it out.* I will try to be more worthy of God's regard—to merit better His indulgent forbearance to my sins—to my *crimes*, I ought to say. I have been walking in a dream of vanity, with *sinful pride* for the guide of my steps, and I am awoke by my blessed child's early death to the contemplation of my state. Father of Mercy! May the innocence of my beloved one ensure her blissful immortality, and may I so redeem the time that is passed by my future life that, forgiven and purified, I may be after death permitted to rejoin her with those I love on earth. Amen! Amen! Amen! Got over what of my packing I could—oh! I am eager to leave this place! Can it be wondered at? These four long, long days. Have they been only days? And is it but *one week* this evening *since my arrival here!* And what a history! Took cab and went to railway station. Saw superintendent and learned that all had been arranged for the morrow—the morrow! Walked back under the bright crowd of stars that led my mind to its dreary speculations on *her* place of blissful rest. The red moon as it rose, the music on the terrace—all were so many leading incidents to the thought of "how she would have enjoyed the beauty of sight and sound," and "what she would have said." But this weakness should be subdued. I sometimes think of her suffering, but I will not dwell on this; I bless her, and I love her still, *still*—the blessed one! Coming to the lodgings, I found a parcel: dear letters from Catherine and Letitia. Could I have borne this without these frequent communications with home? *I doubt it.* Another cause, and most important one, of deep *gratitude*, that, happening to me, this sad event should have happened with such aids for my relief! Thank God! I now go to *that room* once more. A week this evening I was talking with her, and trying to amuse her! Sweet and pure spirit! thy little blemishes were all most venial. Thy love of God and aspiration for heaven were most fervent; thy truth immovable, thy love unbounded. May we rejoin thee in the eternity of bliss which Christ has promised us. Amen!

To London, February 28th.—Dressed in haste. I heard the carriage drive away. I went into the vacant room where she had died, where she had lain, where last I heard her voice and saw and kissed her pale face. My beloved, my blessed child! We set out. The journey was through mist and gloom—and over. Arriving, I saw my dear son Willie waiting for me. I went with him into the waiting-room while all was prepared. We went into our coach and drove away—a long, dreary journey, fortunately with dimmed windows from the coldness of the morning. On reaching the gate of the cemetery, we stopped a little, and then entered. My poor dear son looked very wretched, and was much depressed. I tried to engage his interest in questioning him about his duties at Westminster as we went along. We reached the last earthly home; the *ceremony—ceremony indeed*—was performed. The affectation, unfeeling, *acted* part of the clergyman threw me into an *agony*. I clasped my ears and tried to bring my God, with whom her soul is now, directly to my mind. This *player* seemed to profane the holiness of the rite, and of our grief, and, as it were, to drive God from us. I tried to keep in charity and peace and fix my thoughts on God. I would not see the person, that I might not dislike him. Katie sat beside me. We saw the dear mortal casket of our Nina descend below the earth—it was gone! My beloved, beloved child. May the blessed God reunite us in a better world. Met my dearest Catherine; a sad, sad meeting, our dear firstborn gone from among us! God grant that the grief of this loss so chasten and purify our hearts that we may *certainly* perceive *His mercy* in the visitation! Amen! [1]

Newcastle, March 10th.—After dinner looked at the *Times*, and saw noticed the defalcation of a clerk in the Globe Assurance Office, connected with some theatres which had closed in consequence.[2] I looked to the advertisement for the Olympic and Marylebone. They were not there! This is a sad business, as Mrs. Mowatt sinks inevitably in the wreck.

Edinburgh, March 18th.—Acted Macbeth—*one* of the best, as among the *most complete* representations I have ever given of the character. The audience, who were disposed to be friendly, but do not seem *used to applaud much*, became warmed into something like deep interest and enthusiasm as the play proceeded. I left no weak points in it. Called and very warmly greeted. Before the play received a most kind and touching letter from a person who signs " Ketelle of Newcastle "—it did my heart good. I feel grateful to God for sensations of improved health. My heart is all gratitude to the Author of all my good.

March 19th.—Letter from dear Forster—excellent friend!—with a fancy of dear Dickens's for his forthcoming publication. Acted Hamlet, fairly; not, I think, so well as at Newcastle, but not badly.

---

[1] To those who have suffered a great bereavement every word of this heart-rending record will go home. The reality and vividness of its anguish have certainly no parallel in fiction.

[2] The delinquent was one Walter Watts, well known as lessee of the Olympic theatre. His frauds involved a sum of £70,000. He was tried and sentenced to ten years' transportation, but committed suicide in his cell on the night of his conviction.

461

It is much to act these heavy characters requiring thought to *freshen* one's exertions on consecutive nights; it is really heavy labour, and, as I now am, in an uncertain state of health. Called. Read dear Dickens's story, and shed many tears over it. *My blessed Nina !* . . . The audience to-night applauded the waving of the handkerchief in so marked a manner as to show their remembrance of the outrage and its unjustifiableness of Mr. Forrest.

March 22nd.—Acted Werner, taking all pains; was very kind, I think and hope, to Mr. Pooray. Called. The house was very bad. Surely this is an odd state of things, where they will crowd to see such rant as Miss H. Faucit, and make such moderate houses to the actor who stands first in his art, and whom they never can see again!

March 23rd.—Acted Cardinal Richelieu, taking all the pains I could. The audience were as enthusiastic at the close of the play as they well could be! Called and received most fervently. Read the *Times*. I do not know what to think of the proposed Exhibition of 1851. It seems to me too vast to be an amusement for sightseers, and too extensive and too various to permit of its being a study. Then, it must make many idle persons : to be seen it must be open some months. I am not disposed to cavil, but I fear it will derange the course of business very much in this country. There may be, however, beneficial results, which even the projectors do not themselves foresee. Let us hope it. Acted Richelieu.

March 24th.—Read over again Dickens's beautiful fancy. On this day month I parted from my blessed Nina; an *age of time* has gone by since in *the crowd* of *things, thoughts, feelings* that have been and had distinct place in my mind. My beloved child!—Oh God! how inscrutable are Thy decrees! On this day my beloved wife was delivered of a son,[1] and whilst my heart was grieving for the absence of one blessed object of love, another was presented to me, and my fears for my dearest Catherine tranquillized. Thank God! Amen!

March 27th.—Read a very angry article in the *Times* on Talfourd respecting his charge in a case of murder. I can say with perfect kindly feeling to *him* personally that I did not, and do not think, he has *moral courage* for the office of judge.

March 28th.—Looked at paper—alas! for Talfourd's want of deliberate determination; weakness is often a fault as fatal as a vice. Saw *Scotsman* and *Courant*, which are highly laudatory of me!

March 29th.—Somewhat irresolute at first, I opened the box to

[1] Jonathan Forster Christian, the late distinguished surgeon.

which I had been directed by my blessed child, and found a letter addressed to her dear mother and myself, which was her will. The grief of my heart has all been broken up again from the depths under which it lay. My morning has been one of tears and heavy suffering— approaching, I fear, to discontent in its bitterness. My thoughts are constantly with her—thinking on what she has said—how she has looked, and what her thoughts and feelings have been. It is one of the most painful thoughts I have associated with her, that she might have been spared to health, and probably length of days, if Elliotson had thought of *preventing* disease instead of *waiting to cure it*. Had she gone with dear Edward to Madeira, when I went to the United States, she might have been, with him, perhaps, happy in her earthly existence still. But God's decree is past, and let me live in the hope of that assurance she inscribes, blessed child, upon the cover of her will, " *Ci rivedremo.* " She was to have had the choice of seeing me act before I relinquished my art, which was for years an earnest wish of her heart; but latterly she had begun to doubt whether she should like to " disturb her idea of *Pearse* [1] himself, by associating him with any assumed character." How many dim dreams of future occupations and pleasures had flitted before us! I long to quit London. She is so mixed up with all my thoughts there that the want of her presence is an actual pain to me. In the quiet of Sherborne, I fancy, I can more think of her in her translated state and with even pleasing emotions arising from hope and meditations. God grant it. My thoughts have been very much all this day with the sweet spirit of my blessed Nina. May she be cognizant of how her father loved her, and may we meet again, I pray, O God!

Birmingham, April 1st.—Acted Iago, taking great pains; was most affectionately received. But the Easter Monday gallery was not an audience to appreciate the kind of performance. The Othello actually *belaboured* me in the third act; it was so bad that at last I was obliged to resist the gentleman's " corporal chastisement " and decline his shaking and pummelling! It was very ridiculous and exceedingly unpleasant. Called. Set down a rough outline of what I had thought of for my last night here.

April 2nd.—Mr. Bellew called; he seems advancing in the Church; he is good-hearted, but rather too vain for one who *takes up the cross.*

London, April 7th.—Had thought and resolved upon dear Baby's

---

[1] An adopted name by which Macready's children called him (*note by Sir F. Pollock*).

name, which, in remembrance of dear, good Jonathan Birch, and also of our dear young cousin and friend Jonathan Bucknill, of our excellent friend Forster, and as a memorial of our blessed departed Christina, I decided on as *Jonathan Forster Christian*, with which all seemed well pleased. May God bless the dear child with it, and make it in Him the name of a truly good man. Forster came to dinner. Brought me a sort of regretful message from Browning, and brought me his book, *Christmas Eve*.

To Glasgow, April 8th.—Again tried to read the extracts, with Forster's review, of Browning's poem. I am willing, quite willing, to concede a want of taste and quickness of apprehension, but I *cannot* go with it, or relish it—it does not touch me; on the contrary, I object to the juxtaposition of vulgar and coarse images and high religious thoughts.

April 13th.—Tried to read Browning's poem. I *cannot* relish it. I cannot approve it.

April 16th.—Read in that precious book of Martineau's, *The Strength of the Lonely*, which was a comfort to me. Tried once more to read Browning's poem—I *cannot* like it.

London, April 26th.—Dear kind Forster came to dine. I mentioned to him my thought about reading at Oxford and Cambridge *before* leaving the stage, which he cordially approved. When I leave the *stage*, I wish to leave public life.

Bath, April 28th.—Made computation on Income Tax. I do not allow the moral right of these aristocrats to tax the brain and sinew of the industrious to keep them in place and power, and maintain them *as a class* above their fellow-men, superior to them in all the great essentials of man.

London, May 5th.—Elliotson called. I was struck by his agitated and uneasy manner. I have great fears for him—a heart too good and mind too fine to have been so unhappily misguided as, I fear by credulity and, I must fear, vanity, it has been.

May 9th.—Received Henry Taylor's *Virgin Widow*, dedicated to myself; this is indeed a distinction.

May 10th.—Note from Henry Smith, recalling to me the fact that this is the *anniversary of that Disgraceful and Atrocious Outrage of American Citizens in the City of New York upon me, an unoffending, peaceable stranger.* Murder was attempted and slaughter was fearful in the streets, and the horrors of that night are never to be forgotten. I think of it with deep gratitude to God for my own safety, with

affectionate recollection of my friends, and with sickening loathing at
the occurrence and the people concerned in it.

May 15th.—Finished perusal of *Virgin Widow*, a pleasant, romantic
story, told in dramatic dialogue, with sweet things and passages, but
not equal to H. Taylor's former works.

May 19th.—Looked at paper. My dear friend Forster does not
take the proper tone about Lord Palmerston's conduct in regard to
France and Greece!

Sherborne, May 22nd.—Left Dorchester for Sherborne; passed
through Cerne Abbas, where all was in movement for the celebration
of the meeting of a benefit club, same also at a small village nearer to
Sherborne. My spirits were rather low, thinking of the society I
was leaving, the varied, brilliant, and powerful minds I should perhaps never meet again after parting from them; the narrow limits
within which I must, in prudence, endeavour to keep my expenditure;
and the ordinary character presented to me by the country through
which I passed. Besides, I am not now what I *was;* when I sought
and longed for the country before, "*J'étais jeune et superbe,*" or
rather, I was young and enthusiastic—but let us hope and trust.
Reached Sherborne. Called on Ffooks, signed my lease. God grant
that it may be for the good and happiness of my beloved wife and
children, and that our lives may be fruitful of good and sweet in peace
here. Called on Down, went to house, went over and about it. Made
memoranda. Ffooks came in, I agreed to stay and dine with him
according to the invitation he had before given me.

May 23rd.—Went by coach to Weymouth. Dined. My dinner
in 1815 for dear Edward and self: "Small haddock, leg of Portland
mutton, small apple tart, almonds and raisins, bottle of port, bottle of
Madeira "—came to *£2!* To-day it was 5*s*. Five and thirty years ago
I travelled, posted, all night from Bath for the mere chance of finding
the transports with the 30th Regiment (returning from France) still
lying in Portland Roads. There they were! and we met after three
years' absence. I stayed with him till next day. Rumley and Pratt were
on shore with us. Alas! for life and its vanished youth and affections!

Brighton, May 31st.—Read extracts from Burke, who certainly is
a most *factious* writer—a man who writes from passion, almost from
fury, and never seems to seek for or to question fact, or to be scrupulous
about truth. I cannot regard him as a good man—nor as a philosophic
one; he might have had, as I believe he had, the intellectual power, but
not the moral qualities to make a philosopher.

London, June 3rd.—In the evening went to Forster's; found Thackeray, Edwin Landseer, *Cockburn* [1] (whom I mistook for *Colburn* (!!!) and spoke to him as an old acquaintance, afterwards discovering my mistake; I asked Forster to explain and apologize for me, but he called Cockburn, and I did it myself; he was very cordial), Chitty, Wells (?) and Curtis, who seemed out of his element.

To Sherborne, June 4th.—Called for Maclise and went with him to the South-Western Station. Left London under a very smiling sky and talked away, pleasantly enough. He told me of a coolness between Thackeray and Dickens—that Thackeray in '49 had been invited to the R.A. dinner and Dickens not, that this year Dickens was asked and wrote a very stiff note, *declining!* How weak are the wisest of us! If the invitation were a right, what pleasure would be received, what paid in it? At Southampton we took a very moderate luncheon. Maclise pointed out the Duchess of ——, a plain and very common-looking woman, with her children, resembling her. It is enough to make the blood of truth boil to hear the sycophantic falsehoods of toadies talking about the personal beauty of our aristocracy as distinguished from our common people. Let them see the peasants' faces and the bright looks of the cottagers that we have noticed to-day! or take the shopmen and apprentices from behind the counters of the London shops! I speak of the *physical*—in all else the advantage is with us. Read paper. Disgusted with that scoundrel Brougham, who *now* (in his letter on the University Commission) proves himself a traitor even to the cause of education—the last credit that remained to him. The wretch! Came on from Dorchester to Sherborne. I was much gratified to see Maclise so pleased with the scenery as we passed along. He was quite excited by the view of the Vale, though the haze very much obscured the landscape. He liked all.

June 18th.—Looked at paper; disgusted with that madman Brougham's ungentleman-like behaviour to Bunsen, who was in the Peeresses' Gallery.

June 19th.—In the evening Curtis called, and still later we were surprised by the entrance of Carlyle and Mrs. C——. I was delighted to see them. Carlyle inveighed against railroads, Sunday restrictions, almost everything, Ireland—he was quite in one of his exceptious moods. I love, however, to hear his voice. Mrs. C—— left one of his *Latter*

---

[1] Alexander James Edmund Cockburn (1802–1880); then M.P. for Southampton; afterwards successively Solicitor and Attorney-General, Lord Chief Justice of the Common Pleas, and Lord Chief Justice of England.

DANIEL MACLISE, R.A.

From an engraving by J. Smith of the painting by E. M. Ward, A.R.A.

Day Pamphlets, with a corrected sheet, from which he had expunged an eulogistic mention of me, thinking "I might not like it." He little knows what value I set upon a word of praise from him. Mrs. Carlyle wanted Catherine's aid about a dress for a great ball at Lord Ashburton's, to which Carlyle wished to go.

June 20th.—The Dickenses, Talfourd, and Forster dined with me and seemed to pass a very happy day. I scarcely remember seeing friends more perfectly happy and enjoying in a more unrestrained spirit the pleasure of conscious interchange of regard than on this occasion. I think of it with very happy feelings.

To Weymouth, July 1st.—Received a letter from Gould with an account of another display of that ruffian Forrest, who, it seems, has assaulted Mr. N. P. Willis (an antagonist worthy of his character, though with a dastardly inequality of physical strength) and severely beaten him in the public street in Washington Square. Left home and came by railway to Dorchester; on the way read the *Times*, and was most deeply concerned and grieved to read of the sad accident that befel Sir Robert Peel, a man I honour most highly and, though I do not know him, hold in the highest regard and respect.

Lyme, July 2nd.—Read the paper. Deeply grieved at the account of Sir Robert Peel. I fear that great character will never again be able to glad his family or serve his country. I fear![1]

July 16th.—Read of the suicide of Watts, the forger, defaulter, and manager of Marylebone and Olympic theatres—a most extraordinary and fearful career! "Draw the curtain close!"

July 17th.—Read the speech of that disgusting man—if man he deserve to be called—that Brougham, wishing to keep up the enormous payments of the diplomatic body!

July 18th.—Looked at paper, read in it of Mrs. Glover's[2] death. It seems she was quite unequal to the effort of appearing last Friday night, and her son was apprehensive she could not last long. She was an actress of high talent; in private life she had no principle of honesty, was possessed of great spirits, and a very sarcastic biting style of conversation. She was not likely to make or retain friends. Poor woman! Her father worked in my grandfather's employ as an up-

---

[1] Sir Robert Peel died that night from the effects of his accident. No English statesman has been so widely and truly lamented. The close of his career had been signalized by the purest patriotism; reversing Goldsmith's description of Burke, he had placed the welfare of his fellow-countrymen above all considerations of Party, and nobly illustrated in political life the character of Wordsworth's "Happy Warrior."

[2] See note, p. 107, Vol. I.

holsterer, his name was Butterton, which on coming on the stage he changed to Betterton. Byron speaks of an interview with him. Of such are theatres made up.

To Knebworth, August 3rd.—Went to station. Waiting in the room for train, read extracts from Wordsworth's " Prelude " in *Literary Gazette,* was much interested in and pleased with them. Procter arrived. Met Mrs. Gurwood, all going to Knebworth; went in railway carriage alone to Hertford; from thence with Procters in Bulwer's carriage to Knebworth, passing through a very rich country, by several parks—Panshanger and others. Reached Knebworth, a very beautiful park, not quite so happily undulating as Sherborne Park, but the house and ground immediately around it a most finished specimen of a baronial seat. The order, the latest Gothic; the architecture, internally, in perfect harmony, though sometimes of different periods, with the outer ornaments of the building. Bulwer Lytton gave me a very cordial reception, and after some delay with our luggage, brought on by a fly, we went to the drawing-room, or rather to the upper drawing-room, from thence to the great hall, where a very elegant dinner was served. The day was very cheerful. D'Eyncourt, junior, and Forster, with some of the neighbourhood, were added to our party. We were late in going to bed, Bulwer taking his long cherry-stick pipe and Forster his cigar.

August 4th.—Bulwer sent a message to me, as I was dressing, to inquire if I would like a walk with him, which I was very happy to do. We went through the park and along the road that skirts, discoursing on religion, the immortality of the soul, youth, marriage, and much interesting matter. When we came back, we changed to persons, D'Orsay, Lord Hertford, of whom he related anecdotes, showing him possessed of more talent than I had supposed. Spoke to Forster about his son, who told me that the best understanding existed between them both. I am delighted to hear it. Arranged week's accounts. Entered arrears of record. Read in Greek Testament fifth chapter of John. Bulwer came to my room, and took me over the house, showing me the rooms, the pictures in them, and the various points of interest. Walked with me again through gardens to the house and the park and home. Dined at the luncheon. Looked over some strange books, and an account of the Knebworth Ghost. Took leave of Bulwer Lytton, after another quarter of an hour's conversation with him. I like him more and more. I wish his health gave him more enjoyment. His place is beautiful. Went in the carriage to Welwyn,

468

in fly to Hertford; thence very slowly and uncomfortably by rail to London.

London, August 26th.—Called on Forster. Heard from him a detailed account of a negotiation, of which I had heard before, between himself and Mr. C. Kean, for Bulwer's *Sea Captain*, in which, according to my view of his narration, Mr. C. Kean behaved in the same *shabby* spirit that has characterized all the proceedings of which I am cognizant. Returned to Clarence Terrace. Packed up my clothes in my old bed-room—the room I have slept in for many years, where I have known deep sorrow, felt acute suffering, and often, often in fervent gratitude thanked God for the bounty that brightened my soul with joy. Events of years, and pictures of days, and memories of feelings flitted in crowded and rapid transition before me. My Nina! my Joan!—my darling stricken Henry!—and how many of you have I first kissed, and first listened to your infant voices in that very room. I am never to sleep in it again. No language can paint the lengthened and heavy sense of pain in that thought. I took my leave of it; my heart was wrung, and is now, in recalling the minute. Alas! E'en such is life! Read paper. Heard of the death of Louis Philippe, without a sigh of regret or a token of respect. How different from Sir Robert Peel!

Sherborne, September 4th.—Read a flaming puff, apparently written by himself, on whom?—Mr. Bunn—the scholar—artist—I know not what! It made me almost sick.

To Edinburgh, September 11th.—Read the *Daily News*, which I did not dislike; *Punch*, and some papers in *Household Words*. Handed *Daily News* to the gentleman next me, evidently a foreigner, and was surprised and pleased at his introducing himself to me as Mazzini! We had some talk of mutual friends, Italy, etc.

Dundee, September 13th.—Sent to Glover, who came and sat whilst I took tea. Among the news he told me that it was believed Miss H. Faucit was married to Mr. Martin,[1] and that Mr. C. Kean had questioned him closely about my illness, " believing that I had counterfeited it in order to put off my engagement, when I heard he had taken the Princess's theatre on purpose to oppose him! " Can any one fancy a more miserably small creature than this Mr. C. Kean?

September 18th.—Busy in preparing for return. Looked at paper. Read the account of the arrival of Jenny Lind among that degraded

---

[1] Afterwards Sir Theodore Martin, K.C.B.; Parliamentary agent, but better known as an author, his most important work being the *Life of the Prince Consort*, a valuable contribution to the political history of that period.

population of New York. They *make* an excitement, if one does not come to them—Ole Bull, for instance!—and they will out-Herod Herod in the cruelty of their kindness to poor Jenny Lind, who will be long before she knows what quiet is!

Aberdeen, September 20th.—On political matters I have been thinking much, and I think I see, and with true and deep regret, reasons for apprehending the decline of English greatness. It is in our Government. I really wish now to divest myself of passion and of prejudice. The Government of *a class* must be selfish—a part for the whole must have an interest in maintaining its ascendency. The principle of our Whig and Tory rulers is as much that of Metternich—" *après moi le déluge* "—as if it were in iron type over Downing Street. They do not see that there are now alternatives for the people. A monstrous antagonist is draining power, physical and moral, from our body politic more and more each year. It must soon in its plenitude of means look out for fields of enterprise and activity. America *will* become the champion (however unfitted morally) of human freedom. Canada must be fused in its Union, and Australia will only have to signify her wish for disenthralment, when aid of the people, if not the Government of the United States, will be delightedly poured forth. How long will India rest then?

Glasgow, October 1st.—Read an account of that miserable creature Forrest, who seems not sinking but plunging still more deeply in the slough of disgrace. Looked through the *Vernon Gallery*, edited by S. C. Hall. It causes one to wonder how such a fortune could have been created by a jobmaster, as Vernon was, and excites one's admiration and delight that he should have so judiciously expended it and so nobly bequeathed it, or rather that part of it which now the Nation owns.

Paisley, October 2nd.—We reached Burns's birthplace—the cottage, bed, etc. There had God given breath to that sensitive frame and lighted up that divine genius. The other room was covered over with names, seeking immortality with pencil and penknife. We went to the inn, built by Mr. Auld, whose cottage, very trimly laid out, we also saw. I drank a draught of delicious water at the well, went into the monument, along the banks of Doon's sweet river, and over " *The Brig.*" Afterwards to Alloway Kirk, now desecrated and divided into burying-places for " some booby lords "! Mr. Bridges pulled up at the cottage of Mrs. Begg—*Burns's sister!* He had sent word to the family that he should bring me to see them. She is a very respectable old lady, and her two daughters still handsome, though touched by time. They seemed much pleased to see me, were agreeable and unaffected.

To London, October 3rd.—Read *Punch*. Amused of course. Read *Times* of yesterday, and *Times* of to-day. Purchased two last numbers of *Copperfield* and read parts of each; was very much affected and very much pleased with them. His genius is very great.

October 4th.—Called on Forster; found him in an extraordinary state of perplexity and confusion. He had written to me *too late!* Could not receive me at dinner to-day, as he was setting out at five o'clock with young Robert Bulwer Lytton [1] to Liverpool to see him to-morrow on board the Cunard steamer for America (in company with the Storys) as Bulwer Lytton himself could not go, having to receive Lord Clanricarde at Knebworth. All this was soon understood and all made smooth. Thoughts, however, arose in my mind afterwards—has Bulwer Lytton a right to complain of this young man, his son, when he defers his parental attention to him for the visit of a lord, about whom he cares chiefly for his rank?

Sherborne, October 8th.—Letters, two, from Gould with an account of Jenny Lind in New York, whose first six concerts appear to have amounted to the enormous sum of £30,000!

London, October 24th.—Read over King Lear. Rehearsed King Lear. At the rehearsal saw Mrs. Warner. The recollection that we were both mourners for losses in most respects exactly similar filled my eyes with tears. Dined with Forster. Dickens and Maclise made up our party; very pleasant.

October 27th.—Called on Kenyon, who had just gone out; on Procters, saw and sat with Adelaide,[2] and after Mrs. Procter came in and lengthened my call.

October 28th.—Acted Macbeth.[3] How? I was disappointed by the sight of the house, which was not full. I was not satisfied with the feeling of the applause; it seemed to me the effort of a minority; still, I resolved to do my very best and I " went in to win "—if I could. I thought the audience cold; yet on I strove, undeterred by the apathy with which they accompanied my still sustained endeavours. Mrs. Warner told me she thought I was playing in my best manner, but the

---

[1] Afterwards first Earl of Lytton, the statesman and diplomatist.
[2] The poetess.
[3] This was the first night of the series of farewell performances at the Haymarket theatre (*note by Sir F. Pollock*).

audience did not satisfy me on the point until the banquet scene, when they burst into unanimous and long-continued applause. The play ended triumphantly, but it was at the cost of very great labour to me. Called, and very warmly received. Talfourd and Forster came into my room, and expressed themselves very fervently about the acting. Webster too, but the House was a mystery and a gloom to us. There is *not a bite!* Thank God for all. But is it not strange that the only actor remaining of a school of art should pass away in neglect and with the indifference of the public!

October 29th.—Forster called. I had called on Hogarth, the publisher, before. This man said to my face that he knew me many years ago at Covent Garden—through King!!! "King?" "The Harlequin—he grew too fat afterwards, but remained in the theatre." I never knew anything of any such person, and of course never had acquaintance with any *Harlequin* in my life! The effrontery of such people, who, I suppose, say things in *bravade* and afterwards believe them!! Wrote to Lushington at Rugby, fixing the day of reading. Dined at Athenæum; saw Fonblanque and took the table next to his— it was very agreeable to me. Lord Nugent came in afterwards, and talked. I perceived that he and Fonblanque did not *speak!*

October 30th.—Acted Hamlet, I think for the most part in a very superior manner; the house was not like those I have lately had in London, and yet there appears to me, arguing from the past, every reason why there should be great houses; but perhaps reason has little to do with "*the crowd's*" movements. I never was acting better than I have done these two last nights, and in two or three more repetitions of these characters the public can never see the same artist in them again. It seems a reason for attraction. Called. Forster came into my room. How different my sensation of weariness now from those earlier days when I felt ready to go through the whole performance again!

November 2nd.—Acted King Lear in my best manner; I do not know that I ever played it altogether better. I was careful and self-possessed and not wanting in power; I felt the mighty character. The audience seemed impressed with it. Called. Forster came round. Manby and Webster came into my room. My whole frame feels the work I have been undergoing. Thank God one week has passed so well.

November 4th.—Acted Cardinal Richelieu. The audience called for me at the end of fourth act—of course I would not go. Called. Bulwer and Forster came into my room; Bulwer delighted.

November 6th.—Looked at paper ; saw the death of young Hallam.[1] How truly, truly sorry I was—most amiable and intelligent, and then he was very partial to me—of course a bond of liking.

November 8th.—Dined at the Athenæum. Coming away met Sheil in the hall, and had some chat with him. I told him of Lord John's behaviour to me, with which he seemed much pleased, saying it did him great honour. He was at the theatre last night, and wondering at my retirement, and wishing to persuade me not to take the step, but understanding that my mind was made up, admitted that " it was of no use " ! We talked about Italy and several matters—he spoke of feeling a decline of physical power in his speaking.

November 9th.—Looked at paper. Noticed a letter from Mr. Benjamin Disraeli ! on the subject of Protestantism and Roman Catholicism ! Does it not make one's gorge rise, and turn one absolutely sick to see this miserable, circumcized, *soi-disant* Christian dare to intrude his intrigues upon such a country as this ? Rehearsed. Paid Michell. Rested. Acted Othello *well—very well*, but no critic was there to witness it—not even my friend Forster !—which I *feel* very much. *He*, too, rails at the *Times !!!*

Rugby, November 12th.—On the way thought over the few words with which I would preface my reading to the boys, and thought on the scenes I purposed reading. Found a fly waiting for me at the station, Rugby, as ordered by Mary Bucknill, and with various feelings made up of memory and present speculations, passed through the old town with its altered face, and reached Mr. Bucknill's. Mary Bucknill received me with deep joy, I may say. I arranged my dress, and called on Dr. Goulburn ; he gave me a very gentlemanlike and very cordial reception, and was very earnest in his wish that I should be his guest now or hereafter. I then returned and looked over the leaves of my book, etc., waiting for Dr. Goulburn, who volunteered to call and accompany me to the school with Lushington. They came. Lushington,[2] a very gentlemanlike boy, tendered me the cheque of £50, which I asked him to keep till after the evening. Dr. G—— pioneered my way through the dense crowd from the bottom to the top of the school, the boys applauding, but decorously. The school-room was thronged, and I was very fearful of my audience, among whom, the boys, I thought I felt unsteadiness and disposition to inattention. But as the

---

[1] Arthur Henry Hallam (1811–1833) ; best known as Tennyson's friend immortalized by *In Memoriam.*

[2] The late Sir Godfrey Lushington, K.C.B., G.C.M.G.

reading of the play, *Hamlet*, proceeded, they became mute and enrapt in its interest. I addressed a few words to them, intimating that the project of this means of contribution to the Shakspeare House fund was the suggestion of their own præpostors, and thanking Dr. Goulburn for affording me the opportunity of helping them to realize it. The reading was to begin at half-past two, but it must have been within a quarter to three o'clock before I opened my book, and I was uneasy lest the daylight should fail me, as it began to obscure during the later scenes. I took much pains to keep up the excitement, and by the abbreviation I think I succeeded in keeping alive the interest of the audience. The boys, who knew I had obtained a half-holiday for them, applauded, of course, most lustily at the conclusion. Dr. Goulburn addressed the assembly, particularly the boys, expressing their obligation to me for thus visiting them, and for giving such illustrations to the poet. He expressed himself again very earnestly desirous that I should visit him, and we parted very pleasantly. The express train brought me back to London, which I had left about twelve hours before, and all this space traversed, and all this done within that compass of time; still and still to me it is wonderful. Thus ends my projected public visit to the scene of my boyhood. Many have been the thoughts passing through my mind, the changes in others, in myself, what I might have been, what I am, what my children may be! O God, in Thee is my hope and my trust. Blessed be Thy name.

London, November 13th.—Letter from Cunningham, showing me clearly that the Vice-Chancellor will refuse me permission to read at Oxford. I was very much excited by it, but now I suffer from the least thing—*it is terrible!* Called. Forster came into my room. I see that he anticipated this dog-in-office, the Vice-Chancellor, will throw us over, though he does not like to acknowledge it. Letter from Short, which strengthens my opinion of the same result.

November 14th.—Acted Virginius. I thought to myself, it was the last time before, as they term it in playbill trickery, the final performance, and I thought I would try to show the audience the full power of the character. Miss Reynolds was the Virginia, and by her want of *attention* and sensibility distressed me very much—the supernumeraries, male and female, were outrageously incorrect. But I kept my mind on the part, and acted it, certainly never better; the audience was extraordinarily excited. Called at the end of the third act; of course I did not respond. Was greatly received at the final call. Fox and

Forster came round in great excitement, Fox almost overcome. Manby came into my room; I said I must have some assistance, Willmott, and more, if *King Richard II* was done. He said he would speak to Webster. I spoke after to Mr. F. Webster, complaining grievously and stating the necessity of help. In the second act my thoughts so fixed upon my blessed Nina that my emotion nearly overpowered me. Bless her and my beloved Joan.

November 15th.—Peter Cunningham called and informed me that although the Vice-Chancellor of Oxford, Dr. Plumptre, University College, had promised to write to him, he had not done so. This is a man to educate gentlemen!! P. Cunningham went over to the University Club to inquire the style of the Vice-Chancellor, and I wrote a letter to him, asking myself permission to read *Hamlet* in Oxford. Read the letter to Cunningham, which he thought good, and despatched it. Went to dine with Forster and Procter at the Gray's Inn Coffee House; passed a cheerful evening.

November 16th.—Note from P. Cunningham; that blackguard— (what else *is* he?)—the Vice-Chancellor of Oxford, *although he promised*, has sent no answer but to my application through Cunningham! Acted Iago; cut up by the Roderigo; beyond my ability to fence him off; it was literally disgusting; the stupid absence of all meaning or semblance of the character! I could do nothing *against* such brutal ignorance—Mr. ——, an extravaganza buffoon of second or third rate acting the Venetian gentleman, the silly gentleman, Roderigo! Mr. Davenport, very feeble and inefficient in Othello; the house *bad!* and I disconcerted and unhappy. Sir J. C. Hobhouse, to whom Lord John had applied for me, was in the stage box, came probably to see me!! I was called. Spoke to Manby about this arrangement of the plays, which is now beginning to *show itself.* My mind is in a very unhappy state.

November 18th.—Letter from the Vice-Chancellor of Oxford— according—evidently with *great reluctance* and under compulsion, as it were, permission for a reading at Oxford. Acted Brutus, in my own opinion, in my own judgment, far beyond any performance I ever gave of the character; it was my last to many, and I wished it to be impressive. I do not think the audience, in the aggregate, were equal to the performance; they applauded warmly the salient passages, but they did not seem to watch the gentle, loving, self-subdued mind of Brutus which I tried to make manifest before them. The gentle touches were done with great care, and, I think, with skill—the remonstrances with Cassius in third act about Cæsar's funeral and, in the fourth, the quarrel, were ——! Mr. Howe, who had made a very creditable *effort* with Antony, was called on after third act. This is not *criticism*—at least *it is not taste*. He made a very meritorious *effort*. Was called!

November 19th.—Note from P. Cunningham that he would call, enclosing also the Vice-Chancellor of Cambridge's ready assent to my reading. Cunningham called, and arranged to go to Oxford this evening and make final arrangements.

November 20th.—Letter from Cunningham, by which it seems that Dr. Plumptre, the Vice-Chancellor, has behaved in a very Jesuitical and tricky manner, and prevented us by a *trick* from having a reading, which he dared not openly refuse! These are your university magnates! Acted Othello—well?—with the most energetic spirit—first, second, and half third act, and *bore up* through the remainder of the play; but I think my power and spirits were affected by the wretched bad acting and *imperfectness* of Mr. Davenport's Iago, and the awfully bad acting of Miss Reynolds in Desdemona! The house was not good! Am I to be *deserted* in my last and *best* performances? Was called. What compliment is this?

November 21st.—Had just completed my toilet to go to the theatre, when Henry Taylor was announced; sat with him some time, and engaged to go and dine with him on Sunday—quite forgetting Forster's engagement, of which he afterwards reminded me. Did not know how I should grapple with my work, but was determined to play my best. The house was great. Acted Macbeth, most nobly, never better. Called. Forster came into my room. I was quite hysterical from weakness and fatigue. He showed me some charming lines on my reading at Rugby. At his request sent a brief notice of the occurrence.

November 22nd.—Cunningham called about the readings. Dr. Plumptre, Vice-Chancellor, is anything but a gentleman. Wrote a note to Dickens about Eton.

November 23rd.—Looked at paper—filled, as each day's sheet is, with the meetings about this Catholic *nonentity*. A beautiful contest between these two Churches—two falsehoods, fighting like cat and dog about mere words, that upon the declaration of the *Truth* would join to massacre and damn (if they *could*) its asserters. Oh God! how long will this trade or these trades of religion be permitted to usurp the real gospel of the blessed Jesus! Those birds I see in

476

the window opposite to my bedroom, that so often return, speak to my fancy, and appear like visiting spirits—my heart is touched as I look at them both; and this evening that spectre-like bright shadow in the window's light was so like *her*—my blessed, my beloved one, as she lay before me! . . . My mind is much depressed and impressible. Acted Cassius, tried to carry through the burning spirit of the impatient republican, but moved with heavy weights hanging to me in the actors of the play. Called. As I passed the stage-box, the gentleman near it uttered loud in my ear, "God bless you!" That was worth' the audience. The Brutus was very bad. Forster thought that he neutralized my performance—especially in the quarrel—*to a critic*, that should not have been.

November 24th.—Arranged my week's accounts. Wrote to Catherine and sent her a parcel with the *Examiner* and *Punch*. Wrote to Dickens, relinquishing for the present my projected—or hoped-for —visit to Eton. Copied out two of dear Katie's little poems for Mrs. Henry Talor. Went to Mortlake through a most fearful storm that made me feel for the coachman. Arrived there, received a very cordial welcome from Henry Taylor. In the course of the afternoon a neighbour of theirs, Mrs. Cameron, an East Indian, and a most unreserved enthusiast, came in, and Spring Rice and his wife made our party. I enjoyed the evening. Henry Taylor read a very sweet poem to "Virginia," which I read afterwards to myself. Read Katie's lines to Mrs. H. Taylor, who seemed much interested in my Katie. Coming home through a very fine night.

November 25th.—My blessed Joan lost to us. My heart turned in thought and prayer towards that sweet angel creature, who left us on earth upon the night of this sad day. Sweet, lovely, best being, how fondly my soul yearns towards thy beloved spirit! My prayers to God were and are that in a spiritualized state I may yet once again enjoy the heavenly bliss of loving that sweet type of innocence and purity. Amen!

November 26th.—Looked at paper. These interminable polemical discussions and controversial papers on Catholicism and Protestantism. Why will they not indulge us with a little Christianity to vary the subject? At Mason's it was said to-day that the anecdote recorded at a meeting by Dr. Jelf of the Queen was actually true. "Am I Queen of England?" were her words to Lord John! [1]

[1] Queen Victoria was by no means disposed to submit to "Whig domination" as practised by Lord John Russell.

November 27th.—Acted Hamlet in my very, very best manner; it is the last time but one I shall ever appear in this wonderful character. I felt it, and that to many, to most, it would be the last time they would ever see me in it. I acted with that feeling; I never acted better. I felt my allegiance to Shakspeare, the glorious, the divine. Was called and welcomed with enthusiasm. The house—private boxes (aristocracy excepted)—was *great.*

November 28th.—Looked at paper. Saw Mr. Webster's announcement of "*Last week,*" which annoyed me, having just spoken to him of it. Oh! these *dodging managers!* Acted Cardinal Richelieu; was dreadfully put out by the incorrectness of the players, who are quite as bad as any country company, very incorrect in the text—third performance—and very much so in the business. Called. Forster came into my room; told me of—what I lamented to hear—the death of Lord Nugent, a kind, good-hearted man! How all are dropping round me! Webster came in. We spoke to him about the *announcements,* and Forster was to settle some *unmistakable statement.*

November 29th.—A Mr. Lowne, a young man, called, just as I was going out to dinner, to thank me for having saved him from going on the stage.[1] I felt grateful to God that I had been instrumental in so much service to a fellow-creature.

November 30th.—Looked at paper. This interminable un-Christian warfare between two sects, neither of whom follow the teaching of Jesus Christ, but follow *schemes* or *trades* of their own, blaspheming by their conduct His blessed name. Acted King Lear; was not *quite* in the mood, but thinking that probably Henry Taylor was in the theatre I stimulated myself to my best exertions, and did not act badly. Letter from Miss ——, who seems (ridiculous enough) wildly in love with me, old enough to be her father—nay, more than double her age, but she persists in asserting her devotion, etc.

December 1st.—Thought over King Richard II. In considering its capabilities, the degree of interest it possesses, or rather that it does *not* possess, the absence of effect—equal to the principal *second* rank of *first characters* as Wolsey, King John, Brutus, Cassius, Shylock, Virginius, etc.—the production of it in the *judging* Haymarket style, in which not even a grand historical *picture* is displayed; in considering *all this*, I am struck with the want of judgment and pertinacity of opinion which Forster has shown in urging it, and, of course, making Webster (*grasping at anything*) eager to do it. I fear

[1] See note, p. 369, Vol. II.

it will *damage* the engagement—" I do fear it." It *cannot* do it good : that is my opinion, which I note down before the event. Dined at Athenæum. Saw *John Bull*—oh! what a paper!—to be condemned to read such utter trash!! Saw also the *Spectator*, which was not very lively; in it was an article on Cassius, admitting the merit of the performance and written in the worst possible taste. Thought over King Richard II.

December 2nd.—Looked at paper. These eternal *Protestants and Catholics—Mighty God—*where are the *Christians ?* Wrote to Catherine. Rehearsed—oh! with that incompetent mass of incapacity, Mr. ——, a most overpowering task! Brewster had called in the morning about my head. Rested. Went in tolerably equable spirits to act, but was put out and flurried by the neglect and mistakes of that dolt, that imbecile, Mr. ——. Struggled against it. Acted— unequally—in what *I* call a *" first night "* fashion—not as I should have done had the things been smooth and the people in their places. *" My prophetic soul "* was but too painfully certified of its reasonings for—what I had not been led to expect—the house to-night was not only bad, but certainly the worst we had played to!! Called. Forster came into my room and admitted he was wrong—(alas!)—and that I had been right. Changed the play for next Monday. Tried to rearrange the list of plays, quite deranged by this signal failure of to-night. Pray God it may not damage beyond itself. These men know nothing of the public feeling.

December 3rd.—Called on Forster, who suggested my going to dine with Dickens. I read some conversations of Goethe till ready to go. Dined with the Dickenses—he not well. After tea we had two rubbers at whist! Dickens gave me the bound volume of *Copperfield.* Walked home part of the way with Forster.

December 4th.—My first thought was the wish of many happy returns of this day to my dear, dear sister and friend, God bless her. And in my prayers my unworthy lips muttered entreaties for her continuance (it is our instinct so to do), in happiness on earth. God bless her. Acted Wolsey. Called. Read last number of *Copperfield,* which is very, very clever—full of genius. Certainly he, dear Dickens, is a most extraordinary man!

December 5th.—Am now sunk into the habit of late rising, half- past eight, which leaves me no time for anything before a ten o'clock rehearsal. The excitement of my system I have not time to lull, and thus day after day alternates between languor and feverish endeavour.

479

What a mode of blindly, and, as it were, furiously, fretting and struggling through life! For so it is. Wilkins called. I wished to give him this one parting order to please him, poor fellow. He spoke to me of having seen all my first nights of characters, except two; talked of George Barker, of his great wealth, which made me reflect. I was in the enjoyment of a very excellent income for a bachelor, I think £1000 a year, when he could scarcely have had more than £150, if so much. He is said to be now worth £10,000 per annum, and I not more than £1,200. I am not at all dissatisfied, discontented, or repining at this disposition of things. I only pray that my income may be maintained. I am grateful for it. As I reflect, look back on my past life, the thought of being rich, the ambition to be so, never once entered into my mind. I was most anxious to be independent; and, after having purchased my brother's company, thought of retiring (1829) on what I then, without children, regarded as independence, £400 per annum. God sent us children (His blessing be on them), and all my plans were altered. Still I could not think of wealth for them, as they came fast and dear, but diminished my own means to secure them by insurances the means of education and subsistence in case of my death. Thus I am what the world would call a poor man. I trust, in reality, a contented and grateful one.

December 7th.—Miss —— called. I wrote her a letter to Mr. Simpson of Birmingham and gave it her to post; gave her also an order for Thursday night. It appears to me that she has erected an idol in her own imagination and worships it under my idea. I may be mistaken, but so it seems to me. Forster came in and took tea after the play. He brought me an invitation to dine with Judge Williams [1] previous to going to the Westminster play with Talfourd, to which I assented.

December 8th.—Dined with Dickens; sent note to Kenyon. Met Bulwer, Jerrold, Hawkins, and Forster. Bulwer was not very lively; rather dull. His deafness is rendered more distressing to himself in society, because he will not admit it, and invite a more distinct mode of address to him. He seems ashamed of what all would condole with him on, and sympathize with him for.

December 9th.—Acted King John. Part of the audience came to the play, not to see it, but to *act themselves* in a foolish demonstration of hostility to Papistry. The consequence was, they interrupted

---

[1] Edward Vaughan Williams (1797-1875); Justice of the Court of Common Pleas; father of Lord Justice Vaughan Williams.

the course of interest in the play, and, together with Mr. ——'s blundering stupidity, marred my best scene. Was called. Bulwer and Forster came into my room. Mr. F. Webster also on business. I spoke to him about a private box for my family for the *last six nights*, and he promised it should be secured, a good one.

December 10th.—Dined at the Athenæum with Cattermole. Saw Fonblanque, Stokes, and Professor Sedgwick, who came up to be introduced to me.

December 11th.—Acted King Henry IV and Mr. Oakley, taking much pains with them—they both seemed to have a strong effect upon the audience. Called, and led on Mrs. Warner. Forster came into my room, quite elated with the effect of the comedy. Sent for Manby, and proposed Joseph Surface for the last Saturday. Wrote to Forster, thinking, on reflection, Joseph Surface might be *beneath my position.*

December 12th.—Called on Forster, and spoke again about *School for Scandal*, on which he was to consult Dickens. Went to Vokins's, and saw some very charming drawings of Cattermole; was tempted to purchase one—which I fear I ought not to have done. Looked at paper, reading correspondence of the two meek ministers of Jesus Christ, the Rev. Bennett and Charles John, Lord Bishop of London!!!! Busy with affairs. Wearied very much. Rested and thought over Virginius. Acted Virginius. The company all abroad in what they had to do! Called. Forster came into my room and gave his changed opinion, *on good grounds*, against acting the *School for Scandal.*

December 13th.—I went to Kensal Green; my thoughts were all upon the past; my mind filled with the pictures of my two sweet blessed children as they looked in life and in death to me. Blessed, blessed beings! The future, too, had its share in the current of my thoughts, the past has taught me to fear; and therefore I have little of cheerfulness or confidence in anticipating what may be to come. A funeral was going to the chapel as I went up the walk, and I had to linger about, reading the senseless epitaphs of esquires (!) and Major-Generals, etc., and Mr.'s, in impatience at the vanity which seems to survive the creature. A boy was the chief mourner at the funeral—a son, I presume, following in the course of things his parent to the grave. Alas, how bitter is the grief, when that natural order is inverted! When they were gone the attendant went with me to the vault, and knowing what I came to look on, went before me to the spot. There they lay—all that is earthly of my sweet innocent children—side by side, the coffins of my beloved Nina, of my darling Joan. My heart is sad to despondency as I think upon their destinies, the bright rich bud struck off its stem in all its health and beauty, and the more ripened flower in all its healthful promise blighted and drooping rapidly into the earth. My confidence in the future is overcast with fear. I can but pray to God for good to all my dear ones in this world, and a blessed reunion in an after-life. May my bones be laid with those I have been to visit this day in our quiet home of Sherborne, and may my faults and vices be so far forgiven that our spirits may have communion and participated bliss in another state of being. Amen.

December 14th.—Read the paper. Disgusted with Bishop, Bennett, and the whole tribe of quacks and impostors, blaspheming the sacred name of Christ!

December 15th.—Forster came in to call for me—went together to dine at Dickens's. The Foxes and Paxton [1] were there. Fox is always the same, intelligent and philosophic. Paxton was new to me, a self-educated man—from a mere gardener. I was delighted with him; his account of his nurture of the Victoria lily, a water-plant (river), was one of the most interesting narratives I ever listened to; an explanation of one of Nature's miracles that more and more lifted up one's heart to God and made one ask, "And are not Thy laws miracles enough?" Who would ask for their suspension to satisfy themselves of Thy will? Passed a very pleasant evening.

December 17th.—Went out in carriage, and called to leave a note and card at Lord John Russell's; called on the Sheils—saw them. Sheil [2] showed me the Waterloo medal by Pistrucci, a splendid piece of work. He gave me the direction of the parcel in the Duke's own hand with the false spelling of "*Imediate.*" They set out for Florence on Saturday. Dressed, and Talfourd called for me and we went to Judge Vaughan Williams to dine. Met Bourne, who had called here in the morning, Lord de Ros, Judge Park, and some pleasing men. From thence went to Mr. Liddell's, [3] and with his party to the

---

[1] Sir Joseph Paxton (1801–1865); designer of the Exhibition building of 1851.

[2] The Right Hon. Richard Lalor Sheil was at this time Master of the Mint in Lord John Russell's administration. A proof of the great Waterloo medal had probably been sent to the Duke of Wellington, and returned by him to the Master of the Mint. The medal was never issued (*note by Sir F. Pollock*).

[3] Afterwards the well-known Dean of Christchurch; then Headmaster of Westminster School.

Westminster play; it was the *Andria*, well acted in some parts; Davus, Pamphilo, Chremes, good. Prologue, complimentary to the defunct Adelaide and some worthies of worth. Epilogue, a fair laugh at the Peace Convention. Saw there Milman, Lord Lansdowne, and some to whom I was introduced; went to the Liddells afterwards—introduced to Mrs. L——, very beautiful and very pleasing. From thence with the Judge to Talfourd's; saw Lady T——, as usual, Procters, Pollocks, Dickens, Kenyon, Fladgate, Maclise, Pickersgill, Roberts, C. Landseer, Chittys, Forster, Mrs. H. Twiss. Left soon.

December 20th.—A paper, that disgusting journal, the *New York Herald*, from America with the affidavit of Mr. Forrest, in which are quoted passages from the letters of Mrs. Forrest, the delicate and amiable—the " fine lady " of the Americans, proving her as vulgar and as base, and indeed brutal as himself. Oh! *The taste* of these Americans! Busy with many matters. Dined with Fox. Met young Mr. P. Taylor and his wife; Forster, Mrs. Gaskell.

December 21st.—Very complimentary letter from J. Coleridge; [1] wishes me to dine, with the Wordsworth sub-committee, with his father. Acted Cardinal Wolsey—I think with particular effect. Called. Spoke to Mrs. Warner. Inquired and sent to Mr. Webster. Note and Bulwer's play from Forster. *Read play.* Mr. F. Webster came to tell me (wonderful) that Sir John Franklin [2] was alive. The hero! the hero! Glory to him! Read the whole of the affidavits of Messrs. Forrest and his people in his divorce case. Oh! such a set!

December 22nd.—Sheil called, and sat some time. Shall I *ever* see him again? I fear never. I have ever retained a most affectionate regard for him and great admiration of his brilliant powers. Though separated by the character of our respective pursuits, he has ever been a faithful friend. God bless him.

Sherborne, December 24th.—On the journey read in *Times*. Read a very charming story of Ruskin, a kind of fairy tale, the *Black Brothers*, also the *petite* comedy by Elliot, which possesses much merit. Our journey was protracted by the length of trains and badness of the roads. Reached Sherborne at about a quarter before nine. Found all my dear ones well, thank God—Catherine not quite so, but not ill. Dined and passed a happy evening. Forster very much pleased with the house.

---

[1] John Duke Coleridge (1820–1894) ; afterwards successively Solicitor- and Attorney-General, Lord Chief Justice of the Common Pleas, and Lord Chief Justice of England.
[2] The celebrated Arctic explorer.

December 25th.—Gave up the day to " far niente " pleasures and mere enjoyment. Forster made me show him all over the house, with which he was greatly pleased. Walked out with him, Willie and Edward into the park; were checked in our way by showers of rain, which turned us home again after looking at the best part of the park. Called on the Rutherfurds; found them all well. Signor Piatti [1] was with them.

December 31st.—Acted Henry IV and Oakley. The year is closed. As I looked back upon it, it appears to me a bewildering rugged view, where many objects are confusedly seen, but as yet my mind is not equal to contemplate and regard them in this regular succession. My firstborn, my beloved Nina, faded from before me; and my sweet Jonathan was granted to my heart. Oh God, let my soul be grateful, in submission to Thy decrees and in the full belief of Thy divine goodness. Amen.

[1] The distinguished violoncellist.

1851

London, January 3rd.—Acted Virginius, one of the most brilliant and powerful performances of the character I have ever given. I did indeed "gore my own thoughts" to do it, for my own Katie was in my mind, as in one part the tears streamed down my cheeks; and in another she who is among the Blest, beloved one! Such is a player's mind and heart! Called.

January 6th.—Acted Macbeth in a first-rate manner—always speaking of my own efforts as in *comparison with myself*—no one else.

January 8th.—Began to read Bulwer's play; very much pleased with it. Read about one act and a half. Read through Bulwer's play, written for the amateur actors. It is very good, but it requires actors to perform it, and actors to *produce* it—to know how to *work up* the scenes, where to omit, heighten. I fear their power of doing justice to it. Wrote cursory remarks, which I enclosed for Bulwer in a note to Forster.

January 9th.—Forster came into my room. Spoke about Bulwer's play. Told me that he had mentioned to me that Bulwer would call on me on Sunday about it. *Most certainly* I never *heard* him say anything of the sort. But *I* may have been unobservant or inattentive, or *he* may have been forgetful. There is a misapprehension between us. I do not know where it lies. *He* is evidently urgent that Bulwer should preside at the dinner suggested to be given to me. I am strongly opposed to it. I think if Monsieur le Prince (Heaven help the mark!) declines, as I am sure he will, to preside on such an occasion, it ought to be a commoner, a *real commoner*—no baronet or titled person, and that man *not a personal friend* of mine. If it were right to have a personal friend, Dickens is the person most fit. I shall rest well contented, I think, to escape the fret and *wretched* anxiety of it. Wrote to Bulwer.

January 10th.—Mrs. Warner came into my room to tell me confirmatory tidings of what I had mentioned to her, viz. Miss Faucit's abuse of me. She had heard direct from the *Foleys*—sculptors—who said, "Miss F.'s offer to act for me showed an amiable nature, as forgiving or forgetting injuries." This elicited question, and the charges were stated, that I had stopped the run of *Nina Sforza*—that I had used her ill, from jealousy, at Paris, etc.!!! It is too pitiful to be angry with.

January 11th.—Dined with Mr. and Mrs. Pollock [1] and dear Miss Herries, whom I like so much. Met Kenneth Macaulay, the handsome boy, now a fine, lusty, middle-aged man. A pleasing, cheerful day. Saw my print in the drawing-room, a welcome in itself!

January 12th.—Forster called. Bulwer came, and we went over his play, I giving all the views and advice I *could*. But the amateurs *will never be able to do justice to it*, and the play will, I fear, be lost. Bulwer wanted me to set to work and write down my views, etc., but this I was compelled to say distinctly *I could not do until after my own business was over*. I fancied he did not seem quite so pleased as he had been. But I cannot help it. *I cannot do* it till my mere business is *done*.

January 13th.—A Mr. G. Russell called about some stuff—a monument to Shakspeare. The ass! Dear Shakspeare wants no monument. Let the old Duke of Wellington have caricatures before his house to immortalize his loss; Shakspeare is eternized in the heart of mankind.

January 14th.—Bellew—or Higgins—(this assumption of a name is not good)—called. He is too *external* to be a Christian minister after my heart. Walker called, and took him for a violent Puseyite. Acted Werner better than I have ever in my life done. Much distressed by Mr. Davenport's incorrectness in text. Called. Forster, Talfourd, and Maclise came into my room. Read Mrs. Forrest's declaration in the action of divorce. She states that Mr. Forrest gave money at Boston and New Orleans to get up the excitement against me.

January 15th.—Forster came home to tea with me. He gave me the letter of Colonel Phipps to Sir E. L. Bulwer Lytton containing the (virtual) refusal of Monsieur le Prince Albert to preside at the dinner projected to me. It is what I anticipated.[2]

---

[1] Now Sir Frederick and Lady Pollock: at No. 21, Torrington Square. The print of Macready was that engraved from Thorburn's miniature, and published by Holloway in 1844—(*note by Sir F. Pollock*).

[2] The refusal was in no way personal to Macready, to whom the Prince paid (through Colonel Phipps) a high compliment, but was in conformity with a rule made by H.R.H. not to preside at any functions in honour of individuals, however eminent, his appearance being limited to those on behalf of public institutions.

WILLIAM CHARLES MACREADY

(1843)

From an engraving of the miniature by Robert Thorburn, in the collection of Major-General C. F. N. Macready, C.B.

January 16th.—It is somewhat strange that the *Times* passes with so little notice—I should say, passes *unnoticed*—the circumstance of my retirement—now just at hand—whilst it seems so deeply to interest very many of the public! Acted Virginius, for the last time, as I have scarcely ever—no, never—acted it before; with discrimination, energy, and pathos, exceeding any former effort. The audience were greatly excited. Called. Wrote to Forster, enclosing him "the part" of Virginius and the parchment I have always used in the second act, in the performance of the character. I was deeply impressed by the reflection that in this character—which has seemed one of those exclusively my own, which has been unvaryingly powerful in its effects upon my audience since the first night, in 1820, when I carried them by storm, when Richard Jones came round from the front of the theatre, Covent Garden, into our dressing-room and, laying his hand on my shoulder, exclaimed, "Well, my dear boy, you have done it now!"—that I should never appear in this again, and now I have done it, and done with it! I was much affected during the evening, very much, something with a partial feeling of sorrow at parting with an old friend, for such this character has been to me, and, alas, no trace of it remains. The thought, the practice, the deep emotion conjured up, the pictures grouped so repeatedly throughout the work, live now only in memory. Alas, for the player who really has made his calling an art, as I can stand up before all men and say I have done!

January 17th.—Letter from Sir John Hobhouse, informing me that the appointment of writership was given to my son, and instructing me where to apply respecting it. Looked at paper; unnoticed by the *Times*, which can descend to the trash of all these theatres; my houses fill, and my sun hastes to its setting. Howe came to rehearse Hubert's scenes. He bore witness to the general dissatisfaction among those he knew about these "*last*" announcements. The conclave, with dear, kind Forster among them, made a most egregious blunder!

January 18th.—Dined with Justice Coleridge to meet the Wordsworth Memorial Sub-Committee. Before dinner, whilst looking at some Christmas books, I asked, "Have you seen Ruskin's Christmas book? It is charming." "Indeed." "Oh!" I went on, "it is a most delightful book." Mr. J. Coleridge observed, "Do not you know him? This is Mr. Ruskin." And I was introduced. I like the family very much, and passed a pleasant, cheerful day. Robertson was there. Boxall and Manby called in at lodgings.

January 19th.—Read a very good article by Forster, not quite strong enough, on the invidious and secretly malignant article on Southey by Lockhart in the *Quarterly Review*. Is there a man living who has fewer persons to love him than that man Lockhart? In Edinburgh, where he passed his youth and so many years of his life, and had the shelter and countenance of Scott, I was told he had not one friend and scarcely an acquaintance—a good test of a man's disposition. Called on Forster. Met Bulwer Lytton at his chambers, who asked me to read his play again, which I promised to do, and also to *arrange* it for him, with which he was greatly pleased.

January 22nd.—Acted Iago with a vigour and discrimination that I have never surpassed, if ever equalled. There were persons in the theatre who appreciated the performance, but it was disgustingly manifest that there were a parcel of Yankee claqueurs in the gallery, who gave applause to the most vapid and senseless inertness of the miserable Othello "without remorse or dread," and the audience, with a sort of American stolidity, endured it! I was really sickened; still I did not abate my exertions nor relinquish one jot my firm hold of the mind and purpose of the character. I do not think I ever acted it so powerfully. That last performance of Iago was, in my mind, a commentary on the text, an elucidation and opening out of the profound conception of that great creative mind, that almost divine intelligence, Shakspeare, which has not been given before in the inward feeling of the part: the selfishness, sensuality, and delight in the exercise of his own intellectual power I have never seen in Cooke or Young, nor read of in Henderson, as being so developed. I don't believe, from what I saw of them, that they penetrated beyond the surface of the part, which they displayed cleverly enough and effectively. But what is the difference to an audience? To how many among them does the deep reflection, the toil of thought, carried out into the most animated and energetic personation, speak its own necessary course of labour? By how many among them is the "poor" player, who devotes himself to his art, appreciated—where are the intelligences capable of understanding his author or himself? Is Prince Albert one? Is Queen Victoria one? Let us hope and believe that there are words for us where there are no theatres, and (a far greater blessing!) where there are no puppets set up as king, queen, princes and aristocracies to intercept the honest spirit's direct thought towards his God. Amen!

January 23rd.—Acted Benedict—as well as I could with a most unfit representative of Beatrice, and two stupid dolts in the Prince and Claudio, that almost baffled every attempt I made to be understood. It was only where I was *alone* in the garden scene that I could *assert myself* before my audience, and that they could *satisfactorily respond* to me. *Called.* The *"art declining!"* What *art?* Are these *low-bred*, uneducated *fellows* from *counters* or warehouses with the ignorance of Messrs. C. Kean and Anderson—one who has been at a school, Eton, and *learned nothing*, and the other *not*, but got an appearance of knowing something—are *these* fellows to comment on, and illustrate Shakspeare? Forster had come into my room. The performance made a strong impression on the audience despite of my drawbacks. When alone, I was clear in interpreting my own feeling of dear Shakspeare.

January 24th.—Looked at paper, in which was a slight notice of Benedict, that in ordinary course would have been well enough, but as a thing never to be seen again, and the last performance but eight of the first English actor, was neither worthy of the great journal nor of the artist. Acted Brutus as I never—no, never—acted it before, in regard to dignified familiarity of dialogue, or enthusiastic inspiration of lofty purpose. The tenderness, the reluctance to deeds of violence, the instinctive abhorrence of tyranny, the open simplicity of heart, and natural grandeur of soul, I never so perfectly, so consciously, portrayed before. I think the audience felt it. Of course there must be dunces among them and Yankees.

January 26th.—Looked at the paper, in which was a warm notice of last week by Forster, and some poems, extracted from her works, by Mrs. Browning, which impressed me as possessing great power of thought and beauty. Found at lodgings a note from Mitchell offering me the St. James's theatre free for my Benefit. I wrote to thank him very warmly for it.

January 27th.—Acted Othello. It was very curious how extremely nervous I was of acting before my children; many tears I shed in thinking of them, and of the dear one who would have been their companion. I was most anxious to act my very best. I tried to do so, but am not sure that I succeeded. The audience were cold, and, as Mr. Howe observed, "slow." But this could scarcely be otherwise with such an atrocious stick in Iago as Mr. Davenport; it was really and utterly devoid of *all meaning*. I fought up, and I think I acted well, but I cannot think the play gave satisfaction. Called.

January 28th.—Letitia and darling Katie called. She told me, through her tears, in reference to last night, that she "should be glad when I had left the stage. She had rather I was away from it, and entirely with them—all theirs; that if my art was sustained and made a noble pursuit, it might be different; but, as it was, she did not like to see me associated with such minds as those about me." It is well that with minds so trained these dear children should have seen me. I trust it may be for good. Heaven grant it. Forster came into my room, and home to tea with me. Told me about this dinner, which I wish was abandoned, various matters—Dickens's objection to the Duke of Cambridge, Lord Lansdowne's declining to preside, but giving his name as a steward, Lord Carlisle's *refusal to preside.* This man I have always held in high regard, knowing little of him privately, but forming my judgment from some speeches, etc. I do not think, as a public man, he had a fair excuse for his refusal, and have reason to believe his motive was a most unworthy one. But the fewer among the class that there are to respect, the better. They will go, it is to be hoped, and the fewer to lament among them the better.

January 29th.—Acted Hamlet; certainly in a manner equal to any former performance of the part I have ever given, if not, on the whole, exceeding in power, consistency, grace, and general truth all I have ever achieved. I was possessed with the feeling of the character. The character has been a sort of love with me. The Press has been slow to acknowledge my realization of the man, of the mind, of the nature of this beautiful conception, because they have not understood it. Bowes, a critic far beyond the many who write here, observed to me, "Yours is the only intelligible Hamlet I ever saw," and this Forster, Charles Knight, and White enthusiastically admitted to-night. I was gratified by their excitement. I have in Hamlet worked against prejudice and against stubborn ignorance, and it has been a labour of love with me. Beautiful Hamlet, farewell, farewell! There was no alloy to our last parting. Called, and most fervently received. My dear boys were greatly delighted.

January 30th.—No word in the *Times* on *that performance* of Hamlet last night; nor has there been any notice of it this season. Surely this is too bad. Played Cardinal Richelieu with all my energy. The audience were much excited. Called. Felt melancholy in bidding adieu to them. Gave Mr. Howe my Philip Van Artevelde's sword.

January 31st.—Acted Macbeth, trying to produce a powerful effect on my dear children, and the house crowded to overflow. Certainly succeeded in the display of great power. Called. Willmott and Forster came to my room. Forster told me that Charles Knight intended to dedicate his *Pictorial Shakspeare* to me!

February 2nd.—Saw the deaths of James Haynes, author of *Mary Stuart*, a man of genius, but the victim of dissipation, kind-hearted and gentle-natured; of Lady Warwick, whom I remember as the lovely Lady Monson, afterwards as Lady Warwick, a great admirer of mine in the first burst of my success as Richard, etc. These many, many deaths are so many lessons to me. Let me learn by them. Dined with Dickens. Met Howe, Speaker of the Parliament of Nova Scotia—a clever man; Lyttelton, one of the sons of my old kind friend Lord Lyttelton; Forster, Sir E. Landseer, White—good fellow. Dickens's baby was ill, and I was fearful for it; but all was well when we came away. Heard of Miss Martineau's book—alas! alas! as they at table reported it, a direct and positive declaration and avowal of atheistical opinions! Now, though I do not think any reasoning being can *really* entertain such a belief, yet there are persons who may persuade themselves they do, or reasoning they do, or reasoning *partially* may think they do. But *what right* have these persons to promulgate such opinions? Whom will they make happier or better by them?

February 3rd.—Note from Forster with the printed dedication of Charles Knight's *Shakspeare* to me! I was much affected by it. Most anxious to make my last performance *one to be remembered.* Nervous, anxious and uneasy. Went to the theatre and collected myself, preparing for a great effort. Acted King Lear, certainly in a superior style to what I ever did before. Power, passion, discrimination, tenderness, constantly kept in mind. Called at the fall of curtain and went forward, lingering to see if the audience expected me to speak; it seemed as if they did not, and I left the stage. They called again, and after some time I had to appear again. After waiting some time the noise subsided, and I said: "Ladies and Gentlemen,—The period of my theatrical engagements is reached this evening, but, as my advertisements have signified, there is yet one occasion more on which I have to appear before you, and to that, the last performance in which I shall ever hope to strive for your approbation, I reserve the expression of the few words of acknowledgment and regret that I may desire and endeavour to offer you, my true, patient, and long-approved friends." This was kindly received. White, Talfourd, Dickens, Forster, Willmott, Manby, Webster, came up to my room. I do not know how

many letters were waiting me, and almost all on the subject of places
for my Benefit. My theatrical engagement is concluded. My professional life may be said to be ended. I have only to act one night
more for my own benefit, in regard to which I am bound to no man;
I have acquitted myself of my dues—I am free! Nearly fifty-eight
years of my life are numbered : that life was begun in a very mediocre
position—mere respectability; my father maintained a good character
as an honest and a liberal man ; my mother was a woman of good family,
of superior intellect, excellent heart, and of high character, but at ten
years of age I lost her counsel and example. My heart's thanks are
constantly offered to God Almighty for the share of good He has permitted to be allotted to me in this life. I have attained the loftiest
position in the art to which my destiny directed me, have gained the
respect of the honoured and respected, and the friendship of the highly
gifted, amiable, and distinguished. My education, my habits, my turn
of mind did not suggest to me the thought of amassing wealth, or I
might have been rich; I have what I trust will prove competence, and
most grateful am I for its possession. My home is one of comfort and
of love, and I look towards it with cheerfulness and delighted security
of heart, and most gratefully and earnestly do I bless the name and
thank the bounty of Almighty God, who has vouchsafed such an
indulgence to me, undeserving as I have been, and sinner as I am.
Blessed be His name. Amen.

February 4th.—Read a long review of my professional character
in the *Times*, kind and complimentary, whilst taking the analytic
process to prove its own truth. Went out with Willie and called on
Forster; found Bulwer Lytton and Dickens there. They went into the
business of the dinner, which made me very low. Spoke with Forster
about the postponement of the Benefit. He hurries too much and
undertakes too much to be certain of his counsel. He asked me to
give him the sword which Woodward was said to have worn and Lewis
to have used. I could not, of course, refuse him. Wrote a note to
the editor of *Morning Herald*, requesting him to contradict the rumour
he says is current—that I am about to accept a re-engagement. The
statement is as malicious as false!

February 5th.—Worked at my parting address to my audience. I
fear I cannot make it the direct, simple, sensible composition that I
desire so much. Cunningham called. This Vice-Chancellor has thrown
us over, despite the acquiescence of the Curators; the theatre is *now*
refused. Mitchell called to repeat the offer of his theatre. He threw

out some hints about my reading, which probably meant nothing. Forster called. He told me of the offer of Mr. Phelps, thinking my night was postponed for want of a company, to close his theatre and place his company at my disposal. It does him great honour. Forster, on this, urged the admission of him and Mr. Webster as Vice-Presidents; it is not that I object to Phelps, whom I esteem and regard very much, but I maintain Forster and Dickens are both *wrong* in this, and in taking the dinner to the London Tavern, instead of Freemasons', because they get a better dinner and plenty of champagne—which ought not to be at a business dinner—the distance—the size of the room, not holding by more than a hundred so many as the Freemasons'!

February 6th.—Mr. Laing—keeper of wine and spirit store—sent up a very modest note, wishing to secure a place with one guinea (which he sent), or more if required. He hesitated to come up-stairs, but I sent to desire he would, and told him I would arrange with the box-keeper for him. Dined with Sir Edwin Landseer, meeting Stanfield, Lyttelton, and Forster, who called for us.

February 11th.—Webster came and offered £5 for every dress; there were twenty-five, but I withdrew the armour. The deduction of this would, of course, reduce the sum total, and therefore I said if you give me the round sum of £100 I shall be satisfied. To that he instantly agreed and, I think, has a very excellent bargain, but he met me in a very gentlemanlike tone. I am glad to be rid of the clothes, etc., and glad to have the £100 in my pocket. Dined with Mrs. Dickens. Walked home; note from Kenyon. Tried to think on the subject of my dinner speech. It seems that the tickets are in active request already, and that the room will not contain the applicants.

February 12th.—A very becoming and grateful note from Phelps, acknowledging my Richelieu's order.

February 13th.—Note from Forster, enclosing one from home, with the wish of Charles Kemble to come on the stage at my leave-taking and shake hands with me before the audience!!! What ideas of taste some persons have! Wrote very kindly on the subject to Lane. Forster is now in one of his usual scrapes; he has undertaken much more than he can at all do justice to, Dickens gives orders and goes to Paris. The result is, he gets angry, and is likely to quarrel!

February 14th.—Disgusted with that mountebank Disraeli—oh! the heartless wretches called Conservatives (!)—Conservatives of abuses —laughing at the ills of the Game Laws, the sufferings of the poor. And these are the *whimpering* wretches that howl at the small retaliation of a French Revolution for *ages* of oppression and grinding tyranny. " *How long, oh God ! how long?* "

February 18th.—Heard that the box-office door at Drury Lane theatre was besieged at eight o'clock in the morning by crowds, and that it was filled with a rush at ten! This is all very touching to me. The dinner, by advertisement, removed from London Tavern to Hall of Commerce in consequence of the great demand for tickets.

February 19th.—Found Willmott at lodgings—heard his history of the events of Monday and Tuesday at the box-office—a tale to be told! Wrote to Colonel Phipps to thank the Queen, and to Duke of Bedford to thank him too for his box, which he had very obligingly sent me.

February 21st.—The *Bill* was brought from Johnson's with the names supplied, and, in addition, the names of Messrs. J. Anderson, Vandenhoff, G. Cooper, etc., put in the list of " Singing Witches." This really is an attempt at insult on the part of Mr. Anderson, that I could not have expected that he *would have dared to do*. He distinctly *refused* Willmott (who *inquired*, without my knowledge) to act for my night. Neither Mr. Vandenhoff nor Mr. Cooper made any tender of their services, and upon his own authority this man has the impudence to put their names into my bill! It is really a piece of vulgar insolence without parallel. I struck out all but the singers' names. I afterwards wrote to Johnson desiring him to *omit all*.

February 22nd.—Looked at paper; saw that the Whigs were endangered by their own customary blundering. As Fonblanque has said, " His groom ought to take Lord John out every day for two hours' ride in various omnibuses to give him some insight into the people's opinions." Wrote to Mrs. Dickens. Went to Drury Lane theatre and rehearsed ; took no notice of Mr. Anderson's impertinence about my bill, and all passed on; Mr. Anderson came up to speak to me ; I shook hands very coldly with him, and he went away. Mrs. Warner said he coloured at it ; he was evidently doubtful of his reception and forced himself to come. Close came in with news from the Reform Club that Stanley had been sent for, and that the Protectionists were trying to form an administration—Lord Aberdeen, Prime Minister ; Mr. Disraeli willing to be anything—hangman, if vacant, I hope! [1]

February 23rd.—Thought in bed of my dinner speech, which dis-

[1] The Conservatives failed to form an administration, and Lord John Russell resumed office, but in the following February his administration was replaced by that of Lord Derby, Disraeli becoming Chancellor of the Exchequer and Leader of the House of Commons.

tresses me exceedingly. I have no faith in the present race of players; I have experience of the demoralizing effect of the art in its present condition, and unless it were *greatly* elevated, I believe it ever must remain as it is, and what then, with no future of my own in which the public have interest, what have I to say? I cannot speak or think without *faith* in what I advocate. Looked at paper, in which was a very good notice of myself by Forster.

February 24th.—Beloved Nina's death. Blessed my beloved child, dear and precious is her memory to me; in my prayers to God I trust to re-greet her and that sweet angel infant that lies beside her—the blessed ones! All the painful incidents of this dreadful day came fresh upon me. My Nina! my beloved firstborn—God knows how my heart loves thee! Bless thee! Bless thee! Went to Kensal Green; looked on the coffins that inclose the remains of my two blessed children. Bless them. Letter from Bowes, speaking of Mrs. Kemble's failure in Paris.

February 25th.—Jerdan came to ask for me, to know if I could give him a stall—poor fellow! He began his *Literary Gazette* as I began my Covent Garden engagement. Found Willie at home; returned from Mr. Liddell, who was glad to receive the stall ticket. Read over Macbeth for the last time as a player. Looked over the speeches I must try to deliver.

February 26th.—*Farewell to the Stage.* My first thought as I awoke was that this day was to be the close of my professional life. I meditated on it, and not one feeling of regret intermingled with the placid satisfaction accompanying my performance of every act, needfully preparative to the coming event, as I said to myself, " I shall never have to do this again." My audience I think of with affectionate respect; they have shown actual attachment to me, and, " loving my fellow-men," I part from them with regret and think of them with gratitude. Note from Dickens, enclosing one from Miss Coutts, wishing a box or five stalls. Arranged affairs for the business of the day, a formidable one before me. Before I rose I went over, according to my wont, what I had to say this evening, and thought over the subject-matter of my dinner address. Went to the theatre. Dressed in the room which I had fitted up for myself when manager and lessee of the theatre, and, as I heard the shouts and cries of the assembled crowds at the doors, thought, with thankfulness to God, on the time when I listened to those sounds with a nervous and fretful feeling, my fortune and my children's weal depending on the result of my undertaking.

495

Acted Macbeth as I never, never before acted it; with a reality, a vigour, a truth, a dignity that I never before threw into my delineation of this favourite character. I felt everything, everything I did, and of course the audience felt with me. I rose with the play, and the last scene was a real climax. I did not see who assisted me to my room, I believe it was Mr. Simpson of Birmingham. I dressed as rapidly as I could, and, thinking of what I had to do, gave notice of "being ready," that dear old Willmott might, according to his wish, clear the entrance for me. I thought over what I had to say and went forward. To attempt any description of the state of the house, of the wild enthusiasm of applause, every little portion of the vast assembly in motion, the prolongation, the deafening cheers, would be useless. After waiting for a time that I have never in my experience seen approached, I advanced. On my first entrance, before I began Macbeth, whilst standing to receive the enthusiastic greetings of my friends, the audience, the thought occurred to me of the presence of my children, and that for a minute overcame me; but I soon recovered myself into self-possession, and assumed Macbeth returning from his triumph. On the occasion of my address I was deeply touched by the fervent, the unbounded expression of attachment from all before me, but preserved my self-possession. I addressed them in these words: "Ladies and Gentlemen,—My last theatrical part is played, and, in accordance with long-established usage, I appear once more before you. Even if I were without precedent for the discharge of this act of duty, it is one which my own feelings would irresistibly urge upon me; for as I look back upon my long professional career, I see in it but one continuous record of indulgence and support extended to me, cheering me in my onward progress, and upholding me in mortifying emergencies. I have therefore been desirous of offering you, in my own character, my parting acknowledgments for the impartial kindness with which my humble efforts have uniformly been received, and for a life made happier by your favours. The distance of more than five and thirty years has not dimmed my recollection of the encouragement which gave fresh impulse to the inexperienced essays of my youth, and stimulated me to perseverance, when struggling hardly for equality of position against the genius and talent of those artists whose superior excellence I ungrudgingly admitted, admired, and honoured. That encouragement helped to place me, in respect of privileges and emolument, on a footing with my distinguished competitors. With the growth of time your favour seemed to grow, and, undisturbed in my hold on your opinion, from year to year I found friends more thickly clustering round me. All I can advance to testify how justly I have appreciated the patronage thus liberally awarded me, is the devotion, throughout those years, of my best energies to your service. My ambition to establish a theatre, in regard to decorum and taste, worthy of our country, and to have in it the plays of our divine Shakspeare fitly illustrated, was frustrated by those whose duty it was, in virtue of the trust committed to them, themselves to have undertaken the task. But some good seed has yet been sown; and in the zeal and creditable productions of certain of our present managers we have assurance that the corrupt editions and unworthy presentations of past days will never be restored, but that the purity of our great poet's text will from henceforward be held on our English stage in the reverence it ever shall command. I have little more to say. By some the relation of an actor to his audience is considered as slight and transient. I do not feel it so. The repeated manifestation, under circumstances personally affecting me, of your favourable sentiments towards me, will live with life among my most grateful memories; and because I would not willingly abate one jot in your esteem, I retire with the belief of yet unfailing powers rather than linger on the scene to set in contrast the feeble style of age with the more vigorous exertions of my better years. Words—at least such as I can command—are ineffectual to convey my thanks; you will believe that I feel far more than I give utterance to. With sentiments of the deepest gratitude I take my leave, bidding you, Ladies and Gentlemen, in my past professional capacity, with regret, a last farewell." This address was frequently interrupted by expressions of satisfaction and sympathy, and occasionally with the warmest applause; the picture of the theatre as I bowed repeatedly in returning my thanks to them was, in my experience, unprecedented. No actor has ever received such testimony of respect and regard in this country. My dear countryman Willmott, good old fellow, came into my room; Dickens, Jerdan, Mr. Hogarth, applying for the address; Bulwer Lytton, White, Forster, Jerrold, Mark Lemon, Oxenford, for the address; Lever and Norton from Manchester, whom I was delighted to see, and whom I welcomed most cordially when I recognized them. Manby, etc., came in, all delighted with the evening, and pleased, as they expressed themselves, with the address. I gave one copy of it to Oxenford, and another to Hogarth, on the condition he sent slips to the other papers. Mrs. Reed, Mrs. Lacy, Mrs. Warner, Mrs. Gill, and Mr. Cooper came in; the persons present were amused at my kissing each of the ladies. I

497

sent for Mr. W. West, at his request promised him my autograph, and gave him my Order of the Bath, worn in Lord Townley. When they had gone, except Forster, I sent for Katie, Willie, my sisters, and Hetta, who came in to see me, of course excited and penetrated by what they had witnessed. I gave Hetta my riband of the Bath for Marianne. There was a crowd waiting to see me get into my cab, and they cheered me, kind hearts, as I drove off. Letter from Lowne. There was a crowd at the pit door at half-past one. *Thank God !*

AT this point Macready's professional career comes to a close. His farewell was not of the kind that heralds a reappearance; he made his exit with the firm resolve that it should be final. A few days later the long-projected banquet—a splendid and impressive ceremonial—brought his name once more into brilliant prominence, but that was the last occasion on which he was seen in public. Thenceforward the sphere of his numerous triumphs was exchanged for the petty compass of a west-country market-town. But if life at Sherborne was uneventful, he characteristically declined to subside into supine ease. In addition to devoting himself with increased energy to the education and discipline of his children, he established and conducted—practically single-handed—a night-school for the poorer boys of the town, which, in spite of much prejudice and many obstacles, proved an unqualified success. In the early fifties such institutions were extremely rare in the west country, and the benefit which he thus conferred on Sherborne won the warmest appreciation from his humbler neighbours. He also organized periodical lectures and readings, for which he secured the services of such distinguished *literati* as Dickens and Thackeray, who readily came down from London (no easy journey in those days) to further their old friend's beneficent scheme. But though time never hung heavy on his hands, this new phase of life was hardly congenial to Macready. With very few exceptions, the surrounding society was of the type that had so constantly aggrieved him at Elstree. In those days a retired actor, however eminent, was looked upon askance by the oracles of Quarter Sessions, and, as will have been gathered, Macready was not the man to attract amenities from individuals whom he suspected of holding him cheap. His social relations were, accordingly, not altogether comfortable, while his impatience of clerical bigotry and ineptitude—then only too prevalent in rural parishes—was the source of continual friction with the local divines and their various supporters. In fact, the iniquities of the rectory were little less heinous than those of the green-room, and served to keep his armoury of aggressive epithets in good fighting order. Occasional visits to and from London friends (notably the ever-faithful but domineering

499

THE DIARIES OF MACREADY

Forster) somewhat tempered this monotonous existence; but, on the whole, the period of his residence at Sherborne must have been a depressing one, and he looms out of its greyness for the most part a brooding, sombre figure, much engrossed with family cares, and more than once bowed down by a fresh stroke of bitter affliction. Happier times were, however, in store for him, and the evening of his life was crossed by comparatively few clouds. After many years of mourning for his "beloved Catherine," when close upon seventy he married again,[1] and thereafter took up his residence at Cheltenham. His second wife's bright and sympathetic temperament, together with the cheerfulness of his new surroundings, contributed to create what was perhaps the serenest period of his life. His remaining years, though saddened just at the last by the loss of his gifted daughter Katie, were passed in placid and dignified contentment. The old asperities gradually faded out, and his features assumed a calmness and nobility of expression that comported well with the character, so justly his due, of *ultimus Romanorum*.

When the end came, with merciful gentleness, the world recognized that although his calling could record more than one artist of greater achievement, it could point to none whose career had been so uniformly distinguished by lofty endeavour and stainlessness of conduct.

W. T.

[1] The fifth daughter of Henry Spencer, Esquire, and grand-daughter of Sir William Beechey, R.A.

500

INDEX

INDEX

502

INDEX

503

INDEX

INDEX

INDEX

INDEX

INDEX

508

INDEX

INDEX

INDEX

INDEX

INDEX

INDEX

INDEX

515

INDEX

INDEX

517

INDEX

INDEX

INDEX

INDEX

INDEX

INDEX

523

INDEX

INDEX

525

INDEX

526

INDEX

527

INDEX

INDEX

529

INDEX

INDEX

INDEX

INDEX

533

INDEX

INDEX

535

INDEX

536

INDEX

INDEX

INDEX

540

INDEX

INDEX

INDEX